Perception and Misperception
in International Politics

*Written under the auspices of the
Center for International Affairs,
Harvard University*

Robert Jervis

Perception and Misperception in International Politics

PRINCETON UNIVERSITY PRESS
Princeton, New Jersey

LIBRARY OF CONGRESS CATALOGING-IN-PUBLICATION DATA

Jervis, Robert, 1940–
Perception and misperception in international politics.
Bibliography: p.
Includes index.
1. International relations—Research. I. Title.
JX1291.J47   327'.01'9   76-3259
ISBN 0-691-05656-0
ISBN 0-691-10049-7 (pbk.)

This book has been composed in Linotype Times Roman

Princeton University Press books are printed on acid-free paper and meet the
guidelines for permanence and durability of the Committee on Production
Guidelines for Book Longevity of the Council on Library Resources

http://pup.princeton.edu

Printed in the United States of America

16   18   20   19   17

ISBN-13: 978-0-691-10049-4 (pbk.)

ISBN-10: 0-691-10049-7 (pbk.)

To Kathe

Contents

Part I
The Setting

Part II

Processes of Perception

Part III

Common Misperceptions

Part IV

In Lieu of Conclusions

ACKNOWLEDGMENTS

I AM grateful to many friends and colleagues for assistance. Chapters of this book were commented on by Hayward Alker, Matthew Bonham, Robert Bowie, William Caspary, Paul Diesing, Harold Kelley, James Kurth, Charles Lockhart, Andrew Marshall, Ernest May, Richard Merritt, Charles Osgood, Dean Pruitt, James Richardson, and Fred Sondermann. Others with greater stamina have read and offered suggestions on the entire book: Robert Abelson, Alexander George, Ole Holsti, John Montgomery, Glenn Snyder, and Kenneth Waltz. Steven Isoardi and Glen Stassen were excellent research assistants and Gail Filion of Princeton University Press made the book more readable. Joan Krasner labored over the index without ever resorting to categories like "International incidents, obscure."

Generous financial support was given by the Harvard Center for International Affairs, the Council on Foreign Relations, the Social Science Research Council, and the UCLA Research Committee. Cathy Brest, Barbara Brennecke, and Nancy Kaplan typed the disorderly manuscript more times than they like to remember.

R.J.

Los Angeles
August 1975

Perception and Misperception
in International Politics

WHAT are the causes and consequences of misperception? What kinds of perceptual errors commonly occur in decision-making? How are beliefs about politics and images of other actors formed and altered? How do decision-makers draw inferences from information, especially information that could be seen as contradicting their own views?

These questions have not been adequately discussed by specialists in either psychology or international relations. The latter have assumed that decision-makers usually perceive the world quite accurately and that those misperceptions that do occur can only be treated as random accidents. This book seeks to demonstrate that this view is incorrect. Perceptions of the world and of other actors diverge from reality in patterns that we can detect and for reasons that we can understand. We can find both misperceptions that are common to diverse kinds of people and important differences in perceptions that can be explained without delving too deeply into individuals' psyches. This knowledge can be used not only to explain specific decisions but also to account for patterns of interaction and to improve our general understanding of international relations.

If scholars trained in international relations have paid little attention to perceptions, the same cannot be said for psychologists.[1] But while their work is extremely valuable for showing the importance of the subject it is marred by five major faults. First, more attention is paid to emotional than to cognitive factors. Wishful thinking, defense mechanisms, and other motivated distortions of reality are focused on to the relative exclusion of the problem of how even a perfectly unemotional and careful person would go about drawing inferences from highly ambiguous evidence in a confusing and confused world. As Robert Abelson has noted, "there are plenty of 'cold' cognitive factors which produce inaccurate world-views."[2]

Second, almost all the data supporting the theories are derived from laboratory experiments. Whether these settings and the manipulations

---

[1] For good introductions to this literature see Charles Osgood, *An Alternative to War or Surrender* (Urbana: University of Illinois Press, 1962); Ross Stagner, *Psychological Aspects of International Conflict* (Belmont, Cal.: Brooks/Cole, 1967); Otto Klineberg, *The Human Dimension in International Relations* (New York: Holt, Rinehart and Winston, 1965); and Joseph De Rivera, *The Psychological Dimension of Foreign Policy* (Columbus, Ohio: Merrill, 1968).

[2] "The Structure of Belief Systems," in Roger Schank and Kenneth Colby, eds., *Computer Models of Thought and Language* (San Francisco: W. H. Freeman, 1973), p. 288.

that are employed reveal processes that are at work in the real world is hard to determine. Even harder to gauge is whether the influences discovered in the laboratory are strong enough to make themselves felt, and felt in the same way, when they are intermixed with the other powerful variables that affect political decision-making. For example, very few experiments give the subjects incentives to perceive accurately, yet this is the prime concern of decision-makers.

Third, a strong policy bias pervades most of the analysis—the element of conflict of interest is played down in international relations in general and in the Cold War in particular.

Fourth, and related to the last point, the structure of the international system and the dangers and opportunities peculiar to this setting are often overlooked or misunderstood. As a result of these four weaknesses, this literature contains a great deal of "over-psychologizing"; explanations, usually highly critical of the decision-maker, involving many psychological variables are given for behavior that can be explained more convincingly by political analysis. More specifically, there is little comprehension of the consequences of the lack of a sovereign in the international realm and little analysis of the reasons why even highly rational decision-makers often conclude that they must be extremely suspicious and mistrustful. These biases also lead psychologists to analyze only the views of those statesmen with whom they have little sympathy and to refrain from using their theories to treat the policy preferences of those with whom they agree. Thus images and reasoning drawn from the "hard line" approach to foreign policy are examined to show the operation of emotional influences and cognitive processes that inhibits intelligent decision-making, but arguments and belief systems that support conciliation are never analyzed in these terms.

As grave as these defects are, they are less troubling and less hard to rectify than the fifth: most psychological theories, and especially those that have been applied to international relations, do not account for the ways that highly intelligent people think about problems that are crucial to them. And few of the experiments that provide the bulk of the empirical evidence for the theories have been directed to this question. Rather, theories about the formation and change of beliefs have been constructed around beliefs that are relatively unimportant to the person, about which he has little information, and for which the consequences of being right or wrong are only minor. One reason for this is that the desire to construct theories that are rigorous and parsimonious has meant that only simple beliefs can be analyzed. Although this may be the best way to produce theories that eventually will be able to explain complex thinking, there is little reason to expect that at their present stage of development such theories will provide much assistance in understanding the ways that competent people go about making important decisions. Thus Abelson admits that a significant criticism of the theory that he co-authored and that often has been applied to foreign policy decision-making is that "it gives too little scope to the possibilities of human thought, even as practiced by mediocre thinkers, and, on the other side of the same coin, that it imputes the drawing of certain . . . conclusions which are manifestly absurd by any standard."[3] Similarly, Peter Sperlich argues that consistency theories, which are the type most commonly used by psychologists studying international relations,

> probably can provide rather adequate explanations for behaviors of the very young, of the retarded, and of some of the ill. They are also likely to give adequate explanations for behaviors of normal adults in certain circumstances, e.g., when frightened, when in completely unfamiliar environment other than by choice, when deprived of material sustenance for some length of time, or when strong emotions have attained temporary dominance over the person. What these constructs do not seem to be able to furnish are reliable and valid accounts of complex adult behavior in non-crisis situations.[4]

A useful corrective would be the adoption of a rule of thumb that a social scientist who propounds a theory that he claims is relevant to political decision-making must be willing to admit that the theory also bears some resemblance to the way he makes up his mind, not on trivial issues, but on serious matters such as his own scientific research. Of course the context of the problem should not be ignored, but it seems reasonable to assume that statesmen reach decisions by methods that are similar to those employed by other intelligent men facing important, hard choices and armed with uncertain knowledge and ambiguous information. Until there is evidence to the contrary I see no reason to believe that political decision-makers are less rational, sophisticated, and motivated to understand their environment than are scientists. Although the statesman confronts problems that are much more difficult than those facing a scientist and he must use tools for investigation that are more limited, it is not reasonable to assume that the former usually perceive and think in ways

[3] "Psychological Implication," in Robert Abelson et al., eds., *Theories of Cognitive Consistency* (Chicago: Rand McNally, 1968), p. 119. Similarly, Neal Miller says that "S-R [stimulus-response] theories do well in predicting stupid behavior, but are much less convincing in predicting intelligent behavior." Quoted in Peter Sperlich, *Conflict and Harmony in Human Affairs* (Chicago: Rand McNally, 1971), p. 56.

[4] *Ibid.*, p. 172. For a related argument that the setting in which foreign policy decisions are made reduces the applicability of many theories from psychology, see Sidney Verba, "Assumptions of Rationality and Non-Rationality in Models of the International System," in Klaus Knorr and Sidney Verba, eds., *The International System* (Princeton, N.J.: Princeton University Press, 1961), pp. 93-117.

that a scientist would be ashamed of. If a psychologist's view of ways in which decision-makers draw inferences from evidence is wildly different from the way he handles data bearing on his professional concerns, I think we are justified in being skeptical of his theory.[5]

If these criticisms mean that we cannot take any existing psychological theories as they are and apply them to political decision-making, they definitely do not mean that we should ignore all these theories. To do so would be to overlook a large amount of invaluable work and would make it difficult to detect, and almost impossible to explain, patterns of misperception. Indeed it is partly because most international relations scholars have paid no attention to psychology that they have failed to recognize the importance of misperception, let alone deal with it adequately.

It would be possible to take a single psychological theory, try to correct the defects discussed in the previous paragraphs, and see how it explains a number of international cases. Instead, I have chosen an approach that is broader and more eclectic—too eclectic for some tastes, perhaps—and have borrowed from theories and experimental findings in diverse parts of psychology. In drawing on studies of attitude change, social psychology, cognitive psychology, and visual perception, one faces the danger of mixing incommensurable theories or incompatible assumptions and failing to do justice to the theories themselves. The former danger is outweighed by the dual advantages of gaining a wider variety of insights and greater confidence in our explanations by finding that they are supported by theories in such different realms as, for example, attitude change and visual perception. The second cost—failing to discuss in detail the psychological theories in their own right—is worth paying because my goal is to understand politics. Although some of my criticisms point out what I think are failings of the psychological theories in their own terms, I will discuss and modify them only if doing so helps to account for puzzles in political decision-making.

Complementing the problem of diverse theories that were not developed to deal with problems with which we are concerned is the difficulty of mustering solid evidence. This involves two major difficulties. First,

[5] Attribution theory also affirms this position. As Harold Kelley puts it, "The underlying assumption here is that there are only a limited number of ways of making sense out of the available data about the world and that the scientific procedures are merely refined and explicit versions of methods upon which the common man also comes to rely." *Causal Schemata and the Attribution Process* (Morristown, N.J.: General Learning Press, 1972), p. 21. Also see Kelley, *Attribution in Social Interaction* (Morristown, N.J.: General Learning Press, 1971); Kelley, "Attribution Theory in Social Psychology," in David Levine, ed., *Nebraska Symposium on Motivation, 1967* (Lincoln, Neb.: University of Nebraska Press, 1967); and Edward Jones and Keith Davis, "From Acts to Dispositions: The Attribution Process in Person Perception," in Leonard Berkowitz, ed., *Advances in Experimental Social Psychology*, vol. 2 (New York: Academic Press, 1965).

there is no easy way to determine the accuracy of perceptions. It is hard to know what a person's perceptions were and even harder to know whether they were correct. Was Churchill's image of Hitler right and Chamberlain's image wrong? Until recently few historians dissented from this conclusion. But now there is no agreement on even as seemingly clear-cut a case as this. In other important instances, the experts divide more evenly. Was Germany moving to dominate the Continent before World War I? Could skillful diplomacy by the Entente have maintained the peace without sacrificing a position of equality with Germany? I cannot solve these problems, but have adopted three strategies to mitigate them. First, I have drawn most heavily from cases about which extensive evidence has been analyzed by historians who generally agree. I have, thus, taken little from recent history because of the impossibility of being confident of our views about the Soviet perceptions and intentions. Second, I have tried to note the existence of alternative historical explanations so that the reader is at least alerted to the relevant disputes. Third, some of the cases can be treated as plausible, but perhaps hypothetical, examples. At minimum they show that certain perceptions were held and could easily have been inaccurate.

An alternative approach avoids this problem entirely but raises new ones of its own. We may ask not "Was this perception correct?" but "How was it derived from the information available?" We could then seek to explain both accurate and inaccurate perceptions by the same general theory, just as many psychologists have argued that optical illusions can best be understood in terms of a broader theory of visual perception. The work on belief systems in psychology and operational codes in political science is directly relevant here. I have used this approach at many points, although without trying to produce a tightly integrated theory. We can also compare different actors' perceptions of the same object, situation, or other actor. If we can find appropriate comparisons, we can try to locate systematic differences in perceptions traceable to differences in ways of processing incoming information, differences in preexisting images of others or general views of the world, or differences in specific experiences. I have found this approach very valuable, especially when seeking to explain the determinants of a person's perceptual predispositions.

The second major problem of evidence is that, even if we are certain about the existence of misperception in any single case, we cannot generalize and locate causation if the case is atypical. Many perceptual errors are random. We can probably find instances of any kind of misperception we can think of. But this will not tell us which are most frequent, whether one kind of error is more common than its opposite, or which errors are associated with which antecedent conditions. Thus we cannot even establish correlations, let alone seek general causes. Again there is no good solution, and I must adopt an approach that is not completely satisfactory. I have studied a large number of cases from different historical periods and analyzed only those misperceptions that occur with great frequency. I have also searched for instances of misperceptions that would be inconsistent with the explanations I was developing. For many of the propositions, there were almost no cases that were the opposite of what was expected. But even if this makeshift method of gathering evidence has not led to false conclusions, it has inhibited the testing of complex explanations and the discovery of patterns of perception that are subtle or masked by confounding variables. Thus the lack of an appropriate sample of cases is less apt to mean that my arguments are incorrect than that they are limited to the more obvious relationships.

This book is limited in two other ways. First, my central concern is with perception, and I will discuss other aspects of decision-making only when they are relevant. I hope this work will add to our understanding of decision-making, but it will not cover all aspects of this subject. My focus on perception also means that I have not attempted to treat in detail all parts of the belief systems of individuals or groups. Second, I have ignored two well-known approaches to the study of perceptions—cultural differences and ego psychology. I have instead found it fruitful to look for patterns of misperception that occur within a shared culture and that are not strongly influenced by personality characteristics. The existence such patterns shows, on the one hand, that even when two actors have a great deal in common they can easily misperceive one another, and, on the other hand, that some important causes of misperception are traceable to general cognitive processes rather than to an individual's disturbed psyche.

Finally, some readers may find this work strangely apolitical because it says little about actors' interests. The reason for this is that this concept rarely can explain the kinds of perceptions and misperceptions I am concerned with. Knowing what a person's interests are does not tell us how he will see his environment or go about selecting the best route to reach his goals. When does a statesman think that others are aggressive? How is information that is discrepant from established beliefs handled? How do images change? How are images formed? Questions such as these that deal with the processes of perception cannot be answered in terms of the actors' interests. When we look at the perceptions of agencies within the bureaucracy, interest is involved, although the causal relationships are often hard to establish. Military men seem quicker to detect threats than political leaders. But at the highest levels, where the costs of perceiving other states inaccurately are a heavy burden, this method of analysis will not take us very far. It was not in Chamberlain's interest to see Hitler as appeasable, in Acheson's interest to believe that China was not likely to enter the Korean War, or in the interests of any statesman incorrectly to see his adversary's moves as the product of a coherent, centrally controlled plan. Max Weber argued that "Not ideas but material and ideal interests, directly govern men's conduct. Yet very frequently the 'world images' that have been created by 'ideas' have, like switchmen, determined the tracks along which action has been pushed by the dynamics of interest."[6] For example, neither Marxist nor traditional liberal theorists have convincingly explained postwar American foreign policy in terms of interests alone. In neither formulation can interest explain interventions in countries such as Vietnam. These actions only make sense if the decision-makers either place a high intrinsic value on seeing insignificant states remain non-communist or believe in the domino theory. I have elaborated the former explanation elsewhere[7] and here want to note only that interest cannot tell us why some people believe that the world is tightly interconnected. Once this belief is taken as given, interest can explain our policy, but this must not blind us to the crucial role played by the belief. Similarly, while either national or elite interest may have dictated that the United States strongly oppose the Soviet Union once the latter was seen as highly aggressive, the question remains of how and why this perception was formed.

A short outline of the book may prove useful at this point. The first section presents the background. Since the study of perceptions is an aspect of the decision-making approach, Chapter 1 discusses the level of analysis question and makes explicit the kinds of alternative approaches we are ignoring. Chapter 2 discusses the concept of an actor's intentions and develops a framework of rules by which observers use others' past behavior to infer how they will behave in the future. Chapter 3 analyzes the dominant psychological approach to international relations and shows that both the theorists of this approach and those they argue against—the deterrence theorists—have failed to come to grips with the issue that most sharply divides them—the intentions of other states in the system.

The second section of the study analyzes the ways that decision-makers process information and form, maintain, and change their beliefs about international relations and their images of other actors. Chapter 4 examines theories of psychological consistency in light of the logic of scientific inquiry, distinguishes rational from irrational consistency, and analyzes in detail the tendency for people to assimilate incoming infor-

---

[6] *From Max Weber*, edited and translated by H. H. Gerth and C. Wright Mills (New York: Oxford University Press, 1946), p. 280.

[7] *The Logic of Images in International Relations* (Princeton, N.J.: Princeton University Press, 1970), pp. 244-50.

mation into their pre-existing images. The next chapter discusses the influence of what is at the front of a person's mind on his perceptions. If images of others, once established, are hard to dislodge, it is especially important to try to understand how they are formed. To this end Chapter 6 examines how international history, the decision-maker's domestic political system, and his nonpolitical training create predispositions that influence his perceptions of a wide variety of situations and other actors. The chapters in this section, and many other writings on this subject, may leave the impression that beliefs and images never change. Chapter 7 draws on the literature on attitude change to illuminate the ways that discrepant information does in fact alter established views.

The third section of the book discusses several common misperceptions. Chapter 8 analyzes the tendency for actors to see others as more centralized and calculating than they are. The next chapter deals with the conditions under which actors see others' actions as autonomous as opposed to being reactions to the actor's own behavior. The arguments about and evidence for wishful thinking are examined in Chapter 10. Both laboratory experiments and international cases must be closely analyzed because the evidence, and indeed the question of what evidence would support the proposition, is not as unambiguous as it appears at first. Chapter 11 takes up cognitive dissonance, a psychological theory similar to those used in the rest of the book but distinct enough to require separate treatment. The relevance of this theory is examined, several propositions deduced, and some cases analyzed in this light.

The final section consists of a chapter that discusses ways in which decision-makers could minimize misperception. Given the complexity and ambiguity of information about international relations, perceptual and other decision-making errors will always be common. But steps could be taken to increase the degree to which disciplined intelligence can be brought to bear and decrease the degree to which decision-makers hold images and reach conclusions without thinking carefully about what they are doing. Indeed if judgment is distinguished from perception by the criterion that the latter is automatic and not under conscious control, then these proposals are designed to increase explicit and self-conscious judgment and decrease the extent to which decision-makers perceive without being aware of the alternatives that are being rejected.

Part I
The Setting

CHAPTER ONE

Perception and the Level
of Analysis Problem

Do Perceptions Matter?

BEFORE discussing the causes and consequences of the ways in which
decision-makers draw inferences from the world, we must ask a preliminary question: do the decision-makers' perceptions matter? This
is an empirical question. Logic permits us to distinguish between the
"psychological milieu" (the world as the actor sees it) and the "operational milieu" (the world in which the policy will be carried out) and to
argue that policies and decisions must be mediated by statesmen's goals,
calculations, and perceptions.[1] But it does not follow from this that we
must deal with these intervening variables in order to understand and
predict behavior. This is not an uncommon claim:

> One may describe particular events, conditions, and interactions be-
> tween states without necessarily probing the nature and outcome of
> the processes through which state action evolves. However, and the
> qualification is crucial, if one wishes to probe the "why" questions
> underlying the events, conditions, and interaction patterns which rest
> upon state action, then decision-making analysis is certainly necessary.
> We would go so far as to say *that the "why" questions cannot be
> answered without analysis of decision-making.*[2]

[1] See especially the following works by Harold and Margaret Sprout: *Man-
Milieu Relationship Hypotheses in the Context of International Politics* (Princeton, N.J.: Center of International Studies, 1956); *The Ecological Perspective on
Human Affairs* (Princeton, N.J.: Princeton University Press, 1965); and *An Ecological Paradigm for the Study of International Politics* (Princeton, N.J.: Center
of International Studies, Princeton University, Research Monograph No. 30,
March 1968).

[2] "Decision-Making as an Approach to the Study of International Politics," in
Richard Snyder, H. W. Bruck, and Burton Sapin, eds., *Foreign Policy Decision-
Making* (New York: Free Press, 1962), p. 33. For a similar argument see Fred
Greenstein, "The Impact of Personality on Politics: An Attempt to Clear Away
Underbrush," *American Political Science Review* 61 (September 1967), 631-33.
This is related to the debate about the significance of developmental sequences.
For differing views on this question see Herbert Hyman, *Survey Design and
Analysis* (Glencoe, Ill.: Free Press, 1955), pp. 254-63, and Travis Hirschi and
Hanan Selvin, *Delinquency Research* (New York: Free Press, 1967), pp. 82-85.
(The latter book [republished in paperback as *Principles of Survey Analysis*] has
much broader relevance than its title indicates and is extremely valuable not only

But theory and explanation need not fill in all the links between cause and effect. Indeed, this is impossible. One can always ask for the links between the links. High density theories have no privileged status; they are not automatically illuminating or fruitful.[3] It is true that re-creating a decision-maker's goals, calculations, and perceptions is a satisfying method of explaining his behavior because the scholar, sharing as he does the decision-maker's characteristics of being a thinking, goal-seeking person, can easily say: "If that is the way the statesman saw the situation, it is no wonder that he acted as he did." But the comfort we feel with this form of explanation should not blind us to the fact that, unless there are significant variations in the ways people see the world that affect how they act, we need not explore decision-making in order to explain foreign policy. Most case studies assume that the details presented significantly affected the outcomes. This may not be true, however. "Pleikus are streetcars," McGeorge Bundy said in explaining that the Viet Cong attack on the American installation in February 1965 had affected only the timing of the American bombing of North Vietnam.[4] If you are waiting for one, it will come along. The specifics of the triggering event cannot explain the outcome because so many probable events could have substituted for it. To understand the American policy of bombing the North we should not examine the attack on Pleiku. Had it not occurred, something else would have happened that would have permitted the same response. Logic alone cannot tell us that a similar claim about the decision-making process is invalid: the way people perceive others and make decisions only marginally influences outcomes. So we must seek empirical evidence on the question: do the important explanatory variables in international relations involve decision-making? In terms of perceptions this can be separated into two subsidiary questions: "are important differences in policy preferences traceable to differences in decision-makers' perceptions of their environments?" and "are there important differences between reality and shared or common percep-

---

for its explanation of the use of survey research data but for its treatment of general questions of theory, causation, and evidence.)

This issue is also related to the broader debate between what Maurice Natanson has called the "Two distinctively opposed philosophic attitudes . . . underlying the social sciences: . . . [the] 'objective' and 'subjective' *Weltanschauungen*." ("Foreword" in Natanson, ed., *Philosophy of the Social Sciences* [New York: Random House, 1963], p. viii.) This reader is a good introduction to the arguments.

[3] Hirschi and Selvin, *Delinquency Research*, p. 38. As Abraham Kaplan puts it, "I would not wish to say that something has been explained only when· we have traced the microconnections with their antecedents, or even only when we can believe that such conditions exist." ("Noncausal Explanation," in Daniel Lerner, ed., *Cause and Effect* [New York: Free Press, 1965], p. 146.)

[4] Quoted in Townsend Hoopes, *The Limits of Intervention* (New York: McKay, 1969), p. 30.

tions?"[5] Detailed affirmative answers to these questions will emerge in this book, but a brief general discussion is in order here.

These questions raise the familiar level of analysis problem. Although it has been much debated, agreement is lacking not only on the substantive dispute but even on the number of levels. Arnold Wolfers proposes two, Kenneth Waltz three, and James Rosenau five.[6] To fill in the sequence, we will discuss four. One is the level of decision-making, the second is the level of the bureaucracy, the third is that of the nature of the state and the workings of domestic politics, and the fourth focuses on the international environment.[7] Which level one focuses on is not arbitrary and is not a matter of taste—it is the product of beliefs (or often hunches) about the nature of the variables that influence the phenomena that concern one. To restate the first question in terms of the level of analysis problem, we need not adopt a decision-making approach if all states behave the same way in the same objective situation, if all states of the same kind (i.e. with the same internal characteristics and politics) behave the same way in the same objective situation, or if state behavior is determined by bureaucratic routines and interests.

Although the empirical questions are central here, we should also note that the level of analysis problem has important moral implications. When all people would respond the same way to a given situation, it is hard to praise or blame the decision-maker. Thus, those accused of war crimes will argue that their behavior did not differ from others who found themselves in the same circumstances. And the prosecution will charge, as it did against Tojo and his colleagues, that, "These defendants were not automatons; they were not replaceable cogs in a machine. . . . It was theirs to choose whether their nation would lead an honored life . . . or . . . would become a symbol of evil throughout the world. They made their choice. For this choice they must bear the guilt." Similarly, if all nations follow similar courses of action, one cannot argue that some deserve to be branded as immorally aggressive. Thus in 1918 Bethmann-Hollweg rebutted those who blamed Germany for the war by pointing to the "general disposition towards war in the world . . . how else explain

---

[5] The question of the existence and nature of reality need not be treated here in its profound sense. For our purposes the consensus of later observers usually provides an adequate operational definition of reality.

[6] Arnold Wolfers, "The Actors in International Politics," in *Discord and Collaboration* (Baltimore, Md.: Johns Hopkins Press, 1962), pp. 3-24; Kenneth Waltz, *Man, the State, and War* (New York: Columbia University Press, 1959); James Rosenau, "Pre-Theories and Theories of Foreign Policy," in R. Barry Farrell, ed., *Approaches to Comparative and International Politics* (Evanston, Ill.: Northwestern University Press, 1966), pp. 29-92.

[7] We refer to the international environment rather than the international system because we are not dealing with systems theories. Our concern is with explaining specific foreign policies rather than finding general patterns of interaction.

the senseless and impassioned zeal which allowed countries like Italy, Rumania and even America, not originally involved in the war, no rest until they too had immersed themselves in the bloodbath?"[8]

The three non-decision-making levels assert the importance of various aspects of the objective situation or the actor's role.[9] They say that if we know enough about the setting—international, national, or bureaucratic —we can explain and predict the actor's behavior. An interesting sidelight is that if other actors believed that the setting is crucial they would not need to scrutinize the details of the state's recent behavior or try to understand the goals and beliefs held by the state's decision-makers.[10] It would be fruitless and pointless to ask what the state's intentions are if its behavior is determined by the situation in which it finds itself. Instead, observers would try to predict how the context will change because this will tell them what the state's response will be. Decision-makers could then freely employ their powers of vicarious identification and simply ask themselves how they would act if they were in the other's shoes. They would not have to worry about the possibility that the other might have values and beliefs that differed from theirs. It is interesting, although not decisive, to note that decision-makers rarely feel confident about using this method. They usually believe both that others may not behave as they would and that the decision-makers within the other state differ among themselves. So they generally seek a great deal of information about the views of each significant person in the other country.

Of course it is unlikely that there is a single answer to the question of which level is most important. Rather than one level containing the variables that are most significant for all problems, the importance of each level may vary from one issue area to another.[11] Furthermore, which

[8] Quoted in Robert Butow, *Tojo and the Coming of the War* (Princeton, N.J.: Princeton University Press, 1961), p. 506; quoted in Egmont Zechlin, "Cabinet versus Economic Warfare in Germany," in H. W. Koch, ed., *The Origins of the First World War* (London: Macmillan & Co., 1972), p. 165.

[9] See K. J. Holsti, "National Role Conceptions in the Study of Foreign Policy," *International Studies Quarterly* 14 (September 1970), 233-309.

[10] It is interesting to note that in interpersonal perception people tend to overestimate the degree to which the other's behavior is determined by his personality and underestimate the impact of the external situation. See, for example, Gustav Ichheiser, *Appearances and Realities* (San Francisco: Jossey-Bass, 1970), pp. 49-59. But when the person explains his own behavior, he will attribute his actions to the requirements of the situation, not to his own predispositions. See Edward Jones and Richard Nisbett, *The Actor and the Observer: Divergent Perceptions of the Causes of Behavior* (New York: General Learning Press, 1971).

[11] Two recent articles explore the utility of the concept of issue areas in foreign-policy research, but they are not concerned with the level of analysis problem. See Thomas Brewer, "Issue and Context Variations in Foreign Policy," *Journal of Conflict Resolution* 17 (March 1973), 89-114, and William Zimmerman, "Issue Area and Foreign-Policy Process," *American Political Science Review* 67 (December 1973), 1204-12.

level of analysis is the most important may be determined by how rich and detailed an answer we are seeking. The environment may influence the general outline of the state's policy but not its specific responses. Thus it can be argued that, while decision-making analysis is needed to explain why World War I broke out in August 1914, the external situation would have led the states to fight sooner or later. Or the importance of variables at each level may vary with the stages of a decision. For example, domestic politics may dictate that a given event be made the occasion for a change in policy; bargaining within the bureaucracy may explain what options are presented to the national leaders; the decision-maker's predisposition could account for the choice that was made; and the interests and routines of the bureaucracies could explain the way the decision was implemented. And the same variable may have different effects at different stages of the decision-making process—for example, conflicts among subordinates may increase the variety of information and the number of opportunities for decision that the top decision-maker gets, but may simultaneously decrease his ability to see that his decisions are faithfully implemented.

The importance of variables at one level can also vary with the state of variables at other levels. Rosenau suggests that the international environment is more important in determining the policy of small states than it is of large ones, and Stanley Hoffmann argues that nuclear weapons and bipolarity have reversed this relationship.[12] More generally, the importance of the other levels decreases if the variables in one level are in extreme states.[13] Thus, maneuvering within the bureaucracy may be more important when the top decision-makers are inexperienced or preoccupied with other matters.[14] And Wolfers argues that states tend to behave the same way when they are faced with extreme danger or extreme opportunity, but that when environmental constraints are less severe there will be differences in behavior that must be explained at the decision-making level. More complex interactions among the levels are also possible. For example, the effect of internal instability on expansionism could vary with the opportunities for success in war. Unstable states may be more prone to aggression than stable ones when the chances of victory are high but might be more cautious than others when their leaders perceive a significant probability of defeat or even of temporary setback. Or

[12] James Rosenau, "Pre-Theories and Theories of Foreign Policy," pp. 47-48; Stanley Hoffmann, "Restraints and Choices in American Foreign Policy," *Daedalus* (Fall 1962), 692-94.

[13] Most of the propositions in Greenstein, "The Impact of Personality on Politics," about the conditions under which personality is most important can be subsumed under this heading.

[14] Thus the famous remark by a cabinet officer that you only have to obey the president when he repeats an order for the third time.

the stability of the regime might influence its propensity for aggression, but the nature of the regime (e.g. whether it is democratic or dictatorial) might be more important in explaining how it makes peace.

To deal with all these questions would require another book. Here all I will try to do is to outline the kinds of evidence necessary to establish the validity of simple propositions about the importance of the various levels. In doing so, I will sketch the most extreme arguments for the importance of each level. It is obvious that the questions and arguments could be rephrased in more subtle terms but since I am concerned with the kinds of evidence that the propositions call for the gain in analytical clarity is worth the sacrifice involved in ignoring more complete explanations that combine a multitude of variables at many levels.

The International Environment

To argue that the international environment determines a state's behavior is to assert that all states react similarly to the same objective external situation. Changes in a state's domestic regime, its bureaucratic structure, and the personalities and opinions of its leaders do not lead to changes of policies. Changes in the external situation, however, do alter behavior, even when variables on the other levels remain constant. To test these claims, we would need good measures of all the variables, especially the nature of the objective situation and the state's policies.[15] Even if we had such indicators, we would have to cope with the paucity of the most desired kinds of comparisons. This is easily understood by glancing at the similar issue in the study of individual behavior—the debate over the relative importance of situation and role versus idiosyncratic variables in determining individual behavior.[16] Because so many people of

[15] An excellent discussion of the evidence on this point derived from quantitative studies is Dina Zinnes, "Some Evidence Relevant to the Man-Milieu Hypothesis," in James Rosenau, Vincent Davis, and Maurice East, eds., *The Analysis of International Politics* (New York: Free Press, 1972), pp. 209-51. But these studies have limited utility for the questions being asked here because they do not provide adequate measures of the similarity of the objective situation and the similarity of the state's responses. This is also true for the growing body of literature that examines these questions using event-scaling techniques. For a study that copes with these problems relatively well and finds that differences in perceptions among decision-makers decrease as tension increases, see Ole Holsti, "Individual Differences in 'Definition of the Situation,'" *Journal of Conflict Resolution* 14 (September 1970), 303-10.

[16] For a general discussion, see Herbert Blumer, "Society as Symbolic Interaction," in Arnold Rose, ed., *Human Behavior and Social Processes* (Boston: Houghton Mifflin, 1962), pp. 180-91. For an inventory of findings see Kenneth Terhune, "Personality in Cooperation and Conflict," in Paul Swingle, ed., *The Structure of Conflict* (New York: Academic Press, 1970), pp. 193-234. This subject has received much attention from psychologists in the past few years. For a review of the literature and an excellent argument, see Daryl Bem and Andrea Allen, "On Predicting Some of the People Some of the Time," *Psychological Review* 81 (1974), 506-20.

widely differing backgrounds, personalities, and opinions fill the same role and because the same person fills many different roles, we can try to determine the relative impact of situational and idiosyncratic variables by examining how a person's behavior varies as his role changes and how people of widely differing characteristics perform in similar situations.

It is much harder to make the analogous comparisons in international relations. In only a few international systems do we find many cases in which states play, either simultaneously or consecutively, several roles and in which each role is filled by states that are otherwise quite different. This would occur in a long-lasting system where there were frequent changes in the relations among the actors. Thus each state might at one time be a neutral, a "holder of the balance," a state with aggressive designs, a defender faced by a state whose intentions are difficult to determine, and so on. To a limited degree this test is possible in a balance-of-power system. But it is not available for most other systems, for example the one prevailing since World War II. Most nations have not changed roles, and indeed cannot do so because of such permanent factors as size and geography. The United States can never play the role of a second-ranking state caught between two blocs of greater powers. France can never be the leader of one of two dominant blocs. And while the United States and France may have played roles similar to these in the past, the extensive differences in the situation mean that any differences in response that might be found would not show that roles are unimportant.

COMPULSION IN EXTREME CIRCUMSTANCES?

It is worthwhile to look at cases of the kind that are supposed to show most strongly the influence of external conditions. If there are differences of behavior here, the argument for not ignoring the other levels of analysis will apply a fortiori to a wider domain of cases. Arnold Wolfers argues that, the greater the external compulsion, the greater the homogeneity of behavior and therefore the less the need to study decision-making. In a well-known passage he says: "Imagine a number of individuals, varying widely in their predispositions, who find themselves inside a house on fire. It would be perfectly realistic to expect that these individuals, with rare exceptions, would feel compelled to run toward the exits. . . . Surely, therefore, for an explanation of the rush for the exits, there is no need to analyze the individual decisions that produced it."[17]

But the case is not as clear as this analogy suggests. If a situation were so compelling that all people would act alike, decision-makers would not hesitate nor feel torn among several alternative policies, nor would there be significant debates within the decision-making elite. In fact, key deci-

[17] Wolfers, *Discord and Collaboration*, p. 13.

sions that are easily reached, such as those involving the Truman Doctrine and Marshall Plan, stand out because they are so rare. For despite
the implication of Wolfers' proposition that we know when we are faced
by extreme danger, just as we can tell when the house is on fire, in fact
this question is often bitterly contested. (To say that once decision-makers perceive the fire they will head for the exits leads us back to decision-
making analysis.) For Churchill, the house was burning soon after Hitler
took power in Germany; for Chamberlain, this was the case only after
March 1939; and for others there never was a fire at all. To some decision-makers, the Soviet Union is a threat to which the United States is
compelled to respond. To others the threat passed years ago. Again, to
a growing number of scholars it never existed. Similarly, American
statesmen see a much greater threat from communism in both Europe
and Southeast Asia than do the leaders of our allies. Decision-makers
may even agree that their state's existence is threatened but disagree
about the source of the threat. This was true, for example, in the United
States around the turn of the nineteenth century, when the Federalists
believed France so much a menace that they favored war with her. At
the same time, the Republicans believed England an equal menace. (It
should be noted that this disagreement was rooted as much in differences
in values and interests as in divergent empirical analyses of the
situation.)

In extreme cases we can specify with some certainty an indicator of
the "fire" that all decision-makers will recognize—for example a large
armed attack—and we can be relatively certain that the state will react.
But even then the objective situation will not determine all aspects of the
state's response. There are apt to be several exits from the burning house.
Will the state limit the extent of its involvement? What will its war aims
be? While the United States may have had no choice but to declare war
on Japan after Pearl Harbor, the major decisions that followed were less
compelled and require further explanation. For example: the United
States decided not to concentrate its energies on the country that had
attacked it but to fight Germany first; the war was to be fought with few
considerations for the shape of the postwar world; and no compromise
with the enemies would be accepted (had the Japanese realized this
would be the case, they almost certainly would not have attacked).

Even if all states and all statesmen responded similarly to similar high
threats, we have to explain how the threat arose—i.e. why the adversary
was so aggressive. In some cases we may be able to do this by reference
to the other's objective situation, for example by focusing on the anarchic
nature of the international system and the resulting security dilemma that
we will discuss in detail in Chapter 3. But when this analysis is insufficient, the state (and later scholars) must examine variables at other

levels of analysis to establish some of the most important facts about the objective situation that the state faces.

Finally, one cannot prove that the external environment determines the response by simply showing that the decision-makers believed this to be the case. It is not enough to say with Kecskemeti that "In tense war situations, the decision-maker is likely to feel that he is acting from necessity rather than from deliberate choice." Nor is it sufficient to cite Holsti's finding that the decision-makers on both sides in July 1914 felt that they had no choice but to make the decisions they did, or to show that when "Mr. Acheson was advised not to favor the production of the first thermonuclear bomb, he is reported to have declared that its production was a matter of necessity and not of choice: in other words, that he was experiencing 'compulsion.' "[18] The subjective feeling of determinacy is interesting and may lead decision-makers unnecessarily to restrict their search for alternatives, but it does not show that other decision-makers in the same situation would have felt the same compulsion and acted in the same way. Indeed the theory of cognitive dissonance (Chapter 11) and other theories of irrational cognitive consistency (Chapter 4) lead us to expect that decision-makers may avoid psychological conflict by thinking that they had no choice but to act as they did. This also means that, when scholars claim that a situation permitted no policy other than the one that was adopted, it may be that at least part of the reason why the circumstances appear overwhelming in retrospect is that they were claimed to be so by the decision-makers.

These arguments are, of course, far from conclusive. The necessary comparisons have merely been mentioned, not made. But, as we have seen, there are many points at which people can disagree about what the objective situation is or what policies will best cope with it, and there is little evidence for the existence of the homogeneity of behavior that would allow us to ignore everything except the international setting.

Domestic Determinants

Even if all states do not behave similarly in similar situations, the details of decision-making and images may not be significant. Instead, the state may be the appropriate level of analysis—i.e. variations in decision-makers' policies may be accounted for by variations in social and economic structure and domestic politics of the states they are serving. Wilsonian and Marxist theories are examples of this position. Other theories at this level of analysis argue for the importance of a state's geographical position, its traditions, its national style, or the consequences, often un-

---

[18] Paul Kecskemeti, *Strategic Surrender* (New York: Atheneum, 1964), pp. 19-20; Ole Holsti, "The 1914 Case," *The American Political Science Review* 59 (June 1965), 365-78; Wolfers, *Discord and Collaboration*, p. 14.

intended, of domestic conflicts. Extreme formulations hold that the state's internal system determines its foreign policy, while weaker versions claim that foreign policies are a product of both domestic politics and international circumstances.

The forms of the assertions correspond to those discussed in the previous section. States with the same critical internal attributes behave the same way in similar situations—and often behave the same way in the face of significant variations in the environment—and this behavior is different from that displayed by other states with different attributes even when the setting is the same. The latter claim denies the overriding importance of the international environment. Thus while Cold War revisionists stress the importance of America's domestic political and economic needs, others reply that American actions were heavily influenced by external constraints and that her behavior was not peculiarly American or peculiarly capitalist but rather was typical of any great power in such a situation.[19] Because we are concerned with examining the importance of decision-making, we will not treat this part of the argument that deals with conflicts between claims for two other levels of analysis.

If states of the same type behave in the same way, then changes in a state's leadership will not produce significant changes in foreign policy, and we need not examine the images, values, and calculations of individual decision-makers. Unfortunately, claims about continuity in a state's foreign policy are notoriously difficult to judge. We might try to see whether we could deduce changes in the identities of the state's decision-makers from the course of its foreign policy. Could we tell when Democrats replaced Republicans or Conservatives replaced Labour governments? Scholars used to agree that Stalin's death led to major foreign policy changes, but now even this is in doubt.[20] Before taking office, decision-makers often claim they will introduce new policies. But these promises are often neglected. Eisenhower's foreign policy more closely resembled that of his predecessor than it did his campaign rhetoric. Gladstone pledged himself to avoid immoral and wasteful imperialism, and, although he successfully extricated Britain from some entanglements, he was eventually drawn into commitments similar to those made

---

[19] See, for example, Charles Maier, "Revisionism and the Interpretation of Cold War Origins," *Perspectives in American History* 4 (1970), 313-47; Robert Tucker, *The Radical Left and American Foreign Policy* (Baltimore, Md.: Johns Hopkins Press, 1971); James Richardson, "Cold-War Revisionism: A Critique," *World Politics* 24 (July 1972), 579-612; and Ole Holsti, "The Study of International Politics Makes Strange Bedfellows: Theories of the Radical Right and the Radical Left," *American Political Science Review* 68 (March 1974), 217-42. Comparisons with the reactions of European statesmen would also shed light on the question of whether there was anything peculiarly American in the United States' perceptions.

[20] Marshall Shulman, *Stalin's Foreign Policy Reappraised* (Cambridge, Mass.: Harvard University Press, 1963).

by Disraeli. And while in 1937 Clement Atlee said that "the foreign policy of a Government is the reflection of its internal policy," when his party took power the foreign secretary declared that "Revolutions do not change geography, and revolutions do not change geographical needs."[21]

Many arguments about the wisdom of policies can be understood in terms of claims about the autonomy of the decision-making level. Those who praise Bismarck's diplomacy claim that, had he continued in office, he would have been able to maintain German security by avoiding the errors of severing Germany's ties to Russia, being forced to rely on Austria, and recklessly antagonizing several powerful countries. The rejoinder is that the dynamics of German domestic society and of the international system would have destroyed Bismarck's handiwork no matter who was in power. The glittering skill of Bismarck's diplomacy could not alter the underlying forces at work. Debates about the origins of the Cold War must deal with the similar question of whether Roosevelt's death changed American policy. Most traditional accounts argue that F.D.R. was coming to an anti-Soviet position and would have acted much as Truman did. This view is shared by those revisionists who look to the American political and economic system for the roots of foreign policy but is disputed by those who see the Cold War as avoidable. Similarly, those who defend President Kennedy but opposed the war in Vietnam argue that he would not have acted as Johnson did. Those who either favored the war or opposed not only it but also most recent American foreign policies argue that the policies of these—and other—presidents were consistent. While those who supported the war see the determinants as international and those who criticize the general lines of America's postwar policy see the causes as domestic, both argue that few significant differences can be traced to the identity of the president.

These questions are so difficult to resolve partly because the situation facing the new government always differs from that which confronted the old. Kennedy was never forced to choose between defeat in Vietnam and fighting a major war. F.D.R. did not live to see Russia consolidate her hold over East Europe. The questions must then be hypothetical, and the comparisons that underlie our judgments are often strained. This problem can be avoided by using alternative comparisons—by examining the views of members of the elite to see whether they favor the policy that was adopted.[22] Of course disagreement with a policy does not prove that

---

[21] Michael Gordon, *Conflict and Consensus in Labour's Foreign Policy, 1914-1965* (Stanford: Stanford University Press, 1969), p. 6; M. A. Fitzsimons, *The Foreign Policy of the British Labour Government, 1945-1951* (Notre Dame, Ind.: University of Notre Dame Press, 1953), p. 26.

[22] In this group we include potential leaders who could come to power without drastic changes in the state's internal political system. Dissent from those outside this group does not undermine the arguments for the importance of the nature of

a person would have acted on his views were he in office. His opposition might be rooted in his role in the government, lack of information, freedom from the pressures that accompany holding power, or the belief that opposition is politically expedient. But when these explanations are not satisfactory, internal elite disagreement reveals the limits of the impact of both domestic politics and the international situation.

The Bureaucracy

Even if state behavior cannot be explained by the state's internal politics and external environment, we still may not need to examine the perceptions and calculations of the top decision-makers. The workings of the bureaucracy may determine policy. It is not enough for proponents of this position to show that the state's course of action appears inconsistent and lacks value integration. Such inadequacies can be the product of individual decision-making. As we will show later, normal human behavior often does not fit even a loose definition of rationality. Individuals as well as organizations fail to coordinate their actions and to develop carefully designed strategies. The fact that people must reach decisions in the face of the burdens of multiple goals and highly ambiguous information means that policies are often contradictory, incoherent, and badly suited to the information at hand. Unless we understand this, puzzling state behavior will automatically be seen as the product of either internal bargaining or the autonomous operation of different parts of the government. Thus if we did not know better it would be tempting to argue that the contradictory and erratic behavior displayed by Richard Nixon in Watergate and related matters shows that "Nixon" is not a single individual at all, but rather a title for the set of behaviors that are produced by the interaction of conflicting entities, each pursuing its own narrow interests in ignorance of or indifference to any wider goal of the "general Nixon interest." Similarly, if we were to insist that theories of individual behavior apply only when the actor is following a coherent path guided by his self-interest, we would have to say that Spiro Agnew was an uncoordinated bureaucracy rather than a person because he simultaneously accepted kickbacks and sought the presidency.

Because incoherent policy is insufficient evidence for the importance of bureaucracies, the "pure" theories of this type must make two basic assertions. First, bureaucrats' policy preferences are determined by their positions in the government: "Where you stand is determined by where you sit." The external environment and the nature of the state and do-

---

the state, and, indeed, if such people have been rejected as possible powerholders because of their foreign policy views, this would demonstrate the importance of this level of analysis rather than showing the autonomy of the decision-making level.

mestic politics have only limited and indirect impact on these preferences. Of course if the concept of bureaucratic interest is to be more useful than the concept of national interest, we must be able to specify in advance what the bureaucratic position will be.[23] Even if we cannot do this, it would still be significant if everyone in each unit of the government had the same position on a given issue. If, on the other hand, there is a good deal of disagreement within the organization about the goals to be sought or the means that are appropriate, then we would have to apply decision-making analysis to the bureaucratic level, and so this approach would lose much of its distinctiveness. More importantly, if people in different units share the same policy preferences or if preferences are distributed at random throughout the government, then the first assertion would be undermined.

The second basic claim of theories on this level of analysis is that the state's policies are formed by bureaucratic bargains and routines. Bureaucratic actions either determine the statesman's decision or else implement it in a way that renders the decision largely irrelevant to what is actually done. This point is vital because, even if bureaucrats' policy preferences were linked to their positions within the government, this would be relatively unimportant unless these preferences explain policy outcomes.[24] But we should note at the start that even if this were true we would have to explore the sources of power of parts of the bureaucracy. If we find, for example, that the military often prevails in conflicts with the organization in charge of arms control, this may be because over a period of years the state's leaders have supported the former more than the latter. Sometimes we can go back some years to find a decisive action that set the guidelines for both the policy and the distribution of power within the bureaucracy. In less dramatic cases the relative strengths of interests represent the standing decision of the decision-makers—and often of wider publics—and their choices among competing policies and values. To the extent that this distribution of power is both important and accounted for by factors outside the bureaucracy, an explanation of specific outcomes in terms of bureaucratic maneuvering will be superficial at best.

[23] Most light is shed on this subject by the writings of Philip Selznick. See his *TVA and the Grassroots* (Berkeley and Los Angeles: University of California Press, 1947) and *Leadership in Administration* (Evanston, Ill.: Row, Peterson, 1957). Also see Morton Halperin, "Why Bureaucrats Play Games," *Foreign Policy*, No. 2 (Spring 1971), 74-88, and *Bureaucratic Politics and Foreign Policy* (Washington: Brookings Institution, 1974), pp. 26-62.

[24] During the Second World War the British set up an intelligence section to try to recreate the German perspective. They did well at predicting the positions taken by various parts of the German bureaucracy but could never adequately predict when Hitler would side with a particular faction or impose his own solution. (Donald McLachlan, *Room 39* [New York: Atheneum, 1968], pp. 252-58.)

Are policy preferences determined by one's role within the government? With the important exception of questions of military hardware and doctrine, the evidence is limited and ambiguous. It is not hard to find examples of units taking consistent and unified stands and political appointees adopting their units' views and thus expressing different opinions depending upon their positions in the government. "General Marshall, while Chief of Staff, opposed the State Department's idea of using aid to promote reforms in the Chinese government. Then, when he became Secretary of State, he defended this very idea against challenges voiced by the new chiefs of Staff." In "1910, Winston Churchill, as Home Secretary, led the attack upon the demand of McKenna, First Lord of the Admiralty, for more ships; by 1913 they had exchanged offices and each, with equal conviction, maintained the opposite view." When Samuel Hoare was secretary of state for air, he strongly fought against naval control of the Fleet Air Arm; when he later served as first lord of the Admiralty he took the opposite position. When Théophile Delcassé was the minister of colonies in France before the turn of the century, he supported an expedition to the Nile that would give France a lever to use against Britain. As foreign secretary, he sought to recall the adventure.[25]

But not all policy disagreements are traceable to roles. Organizational perspectives and loyalties are less important when issues are unusual rather than routine, necessitate relatively quick decisions, and involve important and generally shared values. Beliefs about the most important issues of foreign policy—those involving war and peace—are usually unrelated to roles. When we look at the major decisions of American foreign policy—those that set the terms for future debates and established the general framework within which policy was then conducted—it does not seem to be true, at least for the top decision-makers, that "where you sit determines where you stand."

In several important cases what is most striking is the degree of unanimity. In the spring of 1947 there was general agreement within the government that massive aid for Europe was needed. Three years later most officials felt that foreign policy considerations argued for large-scale rearmament, although there was a disagreement—which was not tightly connected with bureaucratic interests—over whether domestic political and economic constraints made such a policy feasible. Once the Korean War removed this opposition, government officials were again

[25] Ernest May, "The Development of Political-Military Consultation in the United States," in Aaron Wildavsky, ed., *The Presidency* (Boston: Little, Brown, 1969), p. 668; Patrick Gordon Walker, *The Cabinet* (New York: Basic Books, 1970), p. 67; W. J. Reader, *Architect of Airpower: The Life of the First Viscount Weir* (London: Collins, 1968), p. 270; Roger Brown, *Fashoda Reconsidered* (Baltimore, Md.: Johns Hopkins Press, 1970), pp. 24-32, 85.

in general agreement. In other important cases there are basic disputes, but the key to them is not divergent bureaucratic interests. Doves and hawks on Vietnam were to be found in all parts of the American government. Views on whether to take a hard line toward Japan before World War II, and specifically on the crucial issue of embargoing oil and other vital raw materials, were only loosely related to organizational affiliations. The advice that Truman received at the start of the Berlin blockade and the Korean War and most of the differences that emerged in the discussions during the Cuban missile crisis were not predictable by the participants' roles.

In the missile crisis none of the leading officials espoused views that were linked to his position within the government. The Republican secretary of the treasury was concerned about the effects of a "soft" response on the fortunes of the Democratic party in the coming elections; the secretary of defense at first argued that the missiles did not present a major military threat; the secretary of state did not take a strong position and did not pay special attention to the political consequences of various moves; and the attorney general opposed an air strike. (It should also be noted that his view carried great weight not because of his governmental position or independent political resources, but because he was thought to speak for the president.)

The other claim—that policies can be explained by bureaucratic maneuvering—could be supported in either of two ways. First, it could be shown that different parts of the government carry out, or fail to carry out, policies in ways that are consistent with their preferences and routines rather than with the decisions of the national leaders. But the other possible linkage in the second point—the argument that authoritative decisions can be explained by the interaction of bureaucratic stands—raises difficulties that go deeper than the temporary absence of evidence. To verify this claim we must be able to specify the expected relationship between the variety of bureaucratic positions on the one hand and policy outcomes on the other. It is not enough to show that the outcome can be seen as a compromise among views that have been advocated by various parts of the government. Almost any decision could fit this description. The theory must provide generalizations that tell us more exactly what the outcome will be. If the goals of different parts of the bureaucracy are complementary, then presumably each agency will give up its position on the part of the program it cares least about in order to gain a larger voice on those issues that are more important to it. Presumably the success of an organization in conflicts with others is related to its strength (determined independently of outcomes), although as we noted this raises further questions. Still another likely pattern is that the symbols will be given to one side in a bureaucratic conflict and the substance to the other. But much more detail is needed. Furthermore, these general-izations must not involve the values and beliefs that vary with the identity of the top decision-makers, and they must be able to explain how policies change. The latter task poses great problems since bureaucratic struc-tures and interests often remain constant over periods in which policies shift.

Although the paucity of research on this level makes conclusions espe-cially tentative, it is hard to see how any of the major decisions of Amer-ican foreign policy in recent years could meet this test. The Marshall Plan, the establishment of NATO, the crucial decisions in Korea, the rearmament that followed, the decision to integrate West Germany into West Europe, the New Look in defense, American policy in the Suez crisis, Kennedy's attempt to increase conventional forces in Europe, the major decisions to fight and later withdraw from Vietnam, and crucial choices in the Cuban missile crisis cannot be explained as the outcome of intrabureaucratic conflict. That these decisions combined major ele-ments of positions held within the bureaucracy is hardly surprising be-cause different parts of the bureaucracy serve and represent divergent values that the president seeks to further. Thus what seems to be a clash of bureaucratic interests and stands can often be more fruitfully viewed as a clash among values that are widely held in both the society and the decision-makers' own minds. What embarrasses the theories under con-sideration here is that, while the decisions listed above did embody some of the preferences that had been articulated by parts of the bureaucracy, they did not combine them in a way that can be predicted by rules of bu-reaucratic politics. Or, to put the argument more exactly, until we have a theory that specifies how policy is formed out of conflicting bureau-cratic perspectives and preferences, we cannot tell whether any given outcome can be explained by this level of analysis. As things stand now, there is no way to explore the extent to which bureaucratic factors cause the outcome because we have no grounds for claiming that a different constellation of bureaucratic interests and forces would have produced a different result or that the outcome would have been different were there no bureaucracies at all.

PERCEPTIONS, REALITY, AND A TWO-STEP MODEL

Our discussion thus far leads to the conclusion that it is often impossible to explain crucial decisions and policies without reference to the deci-sion-makers' beliefs about the world and their images of others. That is to say, these cognitions are part of the proximate cause of the relevant behavior and other levels of analysis cannot immediately tell us what they will be. And even if we found that people in the same situation—be it international, domestic, or bureaucratic—behave in the same way, it is useful to examine decision-making if there are constant differences between the decision-makers' perceptions and reality. In this case all people might react in the same way to the same situation, but this behavior would puzzle an observer because it was self-defeating, based on incorrect beliefs about the world, or generally lacking in a high degree of rationality.[26] Many of the propositions advanced in this book fit in this category: they are generalizations about how decision-makers perceive others' behavior and form judgments about their intentions. These patterns are explained by the general ways in which people draw inferences from ambiguous evidence and, in turn, help explain many seemingly incomprehensible policies. They show how, why, and when highly intelligent and conscientious statesmen misperceive their environments in specified ways and reach inappropriate decisions.

Other propositions in this book deal with cases in which an analysis of decision-making is necessary because people in the same situations behave differently. This is often the case because people differ in their perceptions of the world in general and of other actors in particular. Sometimes it will be useful to ask who, if anyone, was right; but often it will be more fruitful to ask why people differed and how they came to see the world as they did.

The exploration of the images actors hold and the development of the two kinds of propositions discussed above should be seen in the context of a mediated or two-step model.[27] Rather than trying to explain foreign

[26] The knowledge gained by studying how people view the world and process incoming information can lead to the discovery of patterns in state behavior that would not be apparent to an observer who had ignored decision-making. We may be able to say, for example, that two kinds of situations, although not seeming alike to later scholars, will appear to be similar to contemporary decision-makers and will be seen to call for similar responses. Thus, once we have examined a number of cases, detected common deviations, and isolated their causes, we could apply this knowledge to theories that do not call for intensive analysis of decision-making.

[27] See Charles Osgood, "Behavior Theory and the Social Sciences," in Roland Young, ed., *Approaches to the Study of Politics* (Evanston, Ill.: Northwestern University Press, 1958), pp. 217-44. For a recent discussion and application, see Richard Jessor and Shirley Jessor, "The Perceived Environment in Behavioral Science," *American Behavioral Scientist* 16 (July/August 1973), 801-27. In an interesting critique, Robert Gorman asks "Must we look into the perception of the decision-maker at the time the decision was being made by centering our political analysis on the decision-maker himself? Or, should we concentrate on the social organization of which the decision-maker is a part and the social environment in which both the organization and the individual function? If we accept the first choice, then social factors assume a secondary, instrumental purpose. If we choose the second framework, the perceptions of the decision-maker would seem to be *logically* dependent on external rules, and investigation into the nature of individual perception would be absurd. If we combine the two, as the decision-making theorists seem to have done, we are left with a theory in which each

policies as the direct consequence of variables at the three levels of analysis previously discussed, we will examine the actor's perceptions as one of the immediate causes of his behavior. Thus Britain and France felt that their security was endangered by Germany before both world wars. They may have been mistaken in the first case and correct in the second, but both cases can be grouped together in discussing the immediate causes of their responses.

Our understanding of the actor's images and beliefs affects the further question that we ask about that event and the behavior that we expect of the actor in other cases. For example, when it was believed that most American decision-makers had thought that escalation would bring a quick victory in Vietnam, the interesting questions concerned the reasons for this error and the ways by which successive small steps increased the stakes of the conflict. If the decision-makers believed that victory was cheap, it is not surprising that they acted as they did. But by revealing that the decision-makers had a relatively accurate view of the chances of success, the Pentagon Papers and related commentaries have shown that the crucial question is why saving Vietnam was considered important enough to justify the high expected price. This then leads us to look at this and other American actions in terms of beliefs about "domino effects" rather than directing our attention to commitments that develop inadvertently and "quagmires" that trap unwary statesmen. Similarly, the question about Russian behavior raised by the Cuban missile crisis probably is not "What Soviet calculus and risk-taking propensity could explain this bold and dangerous step?" but rather "How could they have so badly misestimated the probable American response?"[28] And previous Soviet behavior can be re-examined to see if it could be explained by

---

premise is negated by the existence of the other, and the general theory itself is left to flounder in a formalistic but meaningless syncretism." ("On the Inadequacies of Non-Philosophical Political Science: A Critical Analysis of Decision-Making Theory," *International Studies Quarterly* 14 [December 1970], 408.) The use of a two-step model avoids this contradiction.

[28] Daniel Ellsberg, "The Quagmire Myth and the Stalemate Machine," in *Papers on the War* (New York: Simon and Schuster, 1972), pp. 42-135; Leslie Gelb, "Vietnam: The System Worked," *Foreign Policy* No. 3 (Summer 1971), 140-67; Klaus Knorr, "Failures in National Intelligence Estimates: The Case of the Cuban Missiles," *World Politics* 16 (April 1967), 455-67. Theodore Draper fails to see the significance of these kinds of questions in explaining the American intervention in the Dominican Republic. ("The Dominican Intervention Reconsidered," *Political Science Quarterly* 86 [March 1971], 26-28.) To take an example from another field, the fact that young people in less politicized homes share fewer of their parents' political views than do those in more highly politicized families is not to be explained by the former group having less desire to adopt their parents' beliefs, but by their lack of knowledge about what their parents believe. (Richard Niemi, *How Family Members Perceive Each Other* [New Haven: Yale University Press, 1974], pp. 200-201.)

similar misperceptions. As we will discuss in the next chapter, actors as well as scholars must engage in these kinds of analyses.

Of course perceptions, and more specifically perceptions of other actors, are not the only decision-making variables that are important. That two actors have the same perceptions does not guarantee that they will adopt the same response. But their responses will often be the same, and, when they are not, it is usually relatively easy to find the causes of the differences. Although people with different images of an adversary may agree on the appropriate response, just as people may favor the same policy for different reasons, this agreement is apt to be short-lived. As we will see in later chapters, the roots of many important disputes about policies lie in differing perceptions. And in the frequent cases when the actors do not realize this, they will misunderstand their disagreement and engage in a debate that is unenlightening.

Images, however, are not first causes, and so we will try to find the causes both of common misperceptions and of differences in perceptions. Thus the second step in the model involves relating the images held, if not to reality, then at least to the information available to the actor. How, for example, do statesmen come to develop their images of other actors? What evidence do they pay most attention to? What makes them perceive threat? Under what conditions do they think that the other, although hostile, has only limited objectives? What differentiates legitimate inducements from bribes? What kinds of behavior are most apt to change an established image?

This is not to claim that we will be able to explain nearly all state behavior. As we will discuss in the context of learning from history, propositions about both the causes and the effects of images can only be probabilistic. There are too many variables at work to claim more. In the cases in which we are interested, decision-makers are faced with a large number of competing values, highly complex situations, and very ambiguous information. The possibilities and reasons for misperceptions and disagreements are legion. For these reasons, generalizations in this area are difficult to develop, exceptions are common, and in many instances the outcomes will be influenced by factors that, from the standpoint of most theories, must be considered accidental. Important perceptual predispositions can be discovered, but often they will not be controlling.

CHAPTER TWO

External Stimuli, Internal Processes, and Intentions

[When looking at others' acts] you ask yourself such further detailed questions as who directed that act at whom? Why? Was it an act by itself, or did it follow something that others—perhaps I, myself—did or said? Or was it merely a segment of a longer act? . . . If participants in any situation did not make such assumptions or guesses about the grounds of others' action, their own action would be stymied, or at best exploratory. The imputation of motives to others is necessary if action is to occur.

[Justice Louis Brandeis] often mentioned the impression made on him by a man who wrote: "I regret that I cannot comply with your request. So that you may know that my refusal is final, I give no reasons."[1]

INTRODUCTION

IF HE is to decide intelligently how to act, a person must predict how others will behave. If he seeks to influence them, he needs to estimate how they will react to the alternative policies he can adopt. Even if his actions do not affect theirs, he needs to know how they will act in order to tailor his actions accordingly. As we discussed in the last chapter, if the person believes that the other's behavior is determined by the situation in which the other is placed (i.e. if all actors behave the same way under the same circumstances), then he can predict what the other will do if he knows what the external stimulus will be. He need only imagine what he would do in given circumstances to know what the other will do if those conditions arise. But if he believes that any of the other three levels of analysis are important, he will need to look inside the state, to its domestic policy, its bureaucratic bargaining, or the preferences and

[1] Anselm Strauss, *Mirrors and Masks* (Glencoe, Ill.: Free Press, 1959), p. 48; Dean Acheson, *Morning and Noon* (Boston: Houghton Mifflin, 1965), pp. 57-58.

calculations of its decision-makers. To the extent that he does not believe that general attributes of the state (e.g. developed or underdeveloped, democratic or dictatorial, stable or unstable) are sufficient to predict its behavior, he must employ a rough form of the hypothetico-deductive method to ask himself what constellation of forces, beliefs, and goals could explain the state's behavior. He will then use the results of this analysis, together with estimates of the external stimuli the state is likely to face, to predict how it will behave in the future.

No bit of behavior is self-explanatory or has only one plausible implication for the actor's future conduct. We must try to understand why the other acted as he did. Modifying Ruesch and Bateson's definition to fit the international context, we can say that "understanding consists largely of perceiving a [nation's] action and deducing from it the series of [intranational] processes of which it is the end result."[2] Reconstructing these internal processes permits us to respond differently to the same bit of behavior depending on our interpretation of why it occurred. If we observe an offensive act we ask ourselves whether the act was controllable, whether the person had "the capacity and training to appreciate the meaning" of his act, whether he would have behaved differently if he had known the significance of his behavior, and whether he acted freely or under duress.[3] Our answers to these questions affect our predictions of the person's later behavior and therefore affect our behavior toward him. Thus a teacher will react one way to a student whose bad work he attributes to laziness, another way to one who he believes to have had a poor education, and still another way to one whose abilities are severely limited. Directly relevant are the experiments that have shown that people react less to the actual punishment that another person has inflicted on them than they do to what they believe the other sought to do to them. "People will become less angry (and retaliate less) when they believe that their partner intended them little harm—regardless of how much they were harmed. Conversely, people become very angry (and retaliate to a greater extent) when they believe that their partner intended them harm—regardless of how much they were harmed."[4]

This inference process is also central to the way statesmen seek to understand and predict others' behavior. During World War II, many

[2] Jurgen Ruesch and Gregory Bateson, *Communication* (New York: Norton, 1968), p. 48.

[3] Erving Goffman, *Behavior in Public Places* (New York: Free Press, 1963), pp. 217-18. As Fritz Heider has noted, "Our reaction to a disagreeable experience . . . is greatly influenced by the attribution to a source. . . . The same datum may mean aggression, misfortune, or a stupid mistake." ("Social Perception and Phenomenal Causality," *Psychological Review* 51 [1944], 367.)

[4] Ted Nickel, "The Attribution of Intention as a Critical Factor in the Relation between Frustration and Aggression," *Journal of Personality* 42 (1974), 489. Also see the other experiments cited in this study.

American officials believed that Soviet demands on East Europe grew out of the fear that when the war was over the United States would withdraw from world politics, leaving Russia without support in her efforts to contain Germany. The conclusion reached was that the United States could reduce these demands by assuring Russia that her postwar security would be guaranteed by an effective United Nations with strong American support. When the American policy failed to have the desired effect, the inference drawn was that the Russians were a threat to the West. To take a later turning point in the Cold War, one reason why the Korean War triggered a huge increase in American armaments was the belief that, in the words of Dean Acheson,

> The real significance of the North Korean aggression lies in this evidence that, even at the resultant risk of starting a third world war, communism is willing to resort to armed aggression, whenever it believes it can win. In view of the threat presented by communism at many points on its borders, the nations thus threatened must immediately increase their individual and collective military strength.[5]

What was frightening was that the Soviets had chosen to expand with the full realization that this entailed a great danger of a firm American response. Had American decision-makers believed that Russia thought that there was little chance that the United States would strongly object to their taking an area we had declared to be outside our "defense perimeter," they might have been content to make clear the American commitment to defend other areas without creating so massive and threatening a military force. And if they had believed that Russia, or China in her intervention later in the war, had been willing to pay a high price only because the alternative seemed not the foregoing of aggrandizement but rather the endangering of Soviet security, a still different reaction might have seemed appropriate.

Similarly, after President Kennedy decided to blockade Cuba in October 1962 he explained his feelings to his brother. "It looks really mean, doesn't it? But then, really there was no other choice. If they get this mean on this one in our part of the world, what will they do on the next?"[6] Kennedy assumed that the Russians were willing to run high risks to expand their influence in an area of only marginal importance to them. If their future behavior was consistent with this action, they would then be much more aggressive in places and on issues in which their concern (or, to be more exact, the excess of their concern over our

---

[5] Lynn Davis, *The Cold War Begins* (Princeton: Princeton University Press, 1974), p. 84; *Supplemental Appropriations for 1951*, Hearings before the Committee on Appropriations, U.S. Senate, 81st Congress, 2nd Session, p. 272.

[6] Quoted in Robert Kennedy, *Thirteen Days* (New York: Norton, 1971), p. 45.

concern) was greater. By contrast, if Kennedy had believed that the Russians had placed missiles in Cuba because they felt emotionally or politically committed to protect Castro, he would not have inferred that they would be more "mean" on other issues that were not "in our part of the world." Still different implications for the future would have been drawn if Kennedy had thought that the Russians did not realize how "mean" they were being.

EXTERNAL VERSUS INTERNAL SOURCES OF BEHAVIOR

The observer must first try to separate the situational, or external, factors from the internal ones that produced the other's behavior. This is sometimes a matter of attempting to tell how important each of these factors was, but often more complex interactive models will have to be developed. It is also simpler if the observers assume that the internal processes are stable. But observers must realize that they may vary both with context and over time. Like scholars, actors try to understand and predict these changes by the two closely related methods of studying the internal dynamics of the other's system and examining other actors whose internal developments parallel those of the actor under consideration.

To start with the simplest case, observers learn little about the other's internal processes from cases in which he behaves just like everyone else. When the situation totally determines the response, we cannot attribute any characteristics to the person who responds. That a weak actor, either individual or national, gives in to a strong adversary when the issue is minor to him but not to his adversary tells us almost nothing about his goals, beliefs, and willingness to run risks. His behavior in this case does not help us predict how he will act under different, less compelling, conditions. Similarly, when a defense attorney pleads that mitigating circumstances should be considered in deciding the punishment his client deserves, he is saying that anyone would have committed the crime if faced with the same situation. If this is true, much of the moral and pragmatic ground for punishment is undercut. Morally, punishment makes less sense because the fault was in the situation, not the person. While the person's conduct deserves censure, it does not show that his character is worse than that of others who did not commit the crime. And because the fact that the person committed the crime does not show that he is predisposed to act in a criminal manner—or at least no more so than others who did not commit the crime—there is no reason to expect him to break the law in the future even if he is not punished.

Better yet, the case will be thrown out of court if the defense can show that characteristics peculiar to the individual were even less relevant because the government employed entrapment and, in the words of a New York law, caused the commission of an offense by "a person not otherwise disposed to commit it." Similar reasoning underlaid President Johnson's explanation of why he decided not to retaliate against the Viet Cong attack on an unprotected American hotel in Saigon in late 1964: "I have real doubts about ordering reprisals in cases where our own security seems at first glance to be very weak." An adversary would not have to be totally committed to aggression to attack a provocatively tempting target, and so attacks might cease if the targets were adequately defended.[7]

Conversely, we learn most about internal processes when the person behaves unusually—i.e. when he does not do what the situation seems to dictate. To return to Wolfers' metaphor, we know that the person who stays in a burning house is certainly odd even if, as we will discuss below, there are many alternative explanations for his behavior. Thus the Nazi persecution of the Christian churches drew special attention from the British press in part because this behavior was sharply at variance with that expected from even a normal dictatorship. And the British ambassador to Russia in the early part of this century noted that the Russian railroads leading to Afghanistan had been built "at the cost of great sacrifices." The implication was that this cost would only be justified if the tsar was, at minimum, ready to bring troops down those railroads to exert political pressure against England. If they had been cheap or if there had been economic advantages to building them, the British would have been less upset even though their strategic value would have been the same because their construction need not have been attributed to hostility.[8]

We should also note that experiments have shown that people both reason in this way and can reverse the process to draw inferences about the objective situation from their knowledge of the person and his response. Thus if a powerful person complies with a request, observers assume that he did so because of his values and desires. When a weak person complies, on the other hand, observers infer compulsion from the environment.[9]

[7] Quoted in Tom Goldstein, "Legal Questions Raised by Staged Arrests," *New York Times*, May 17, 1974; quoted in David Halberstam, *The Best and the Brightest* (Greenwich, Conn.: Fawcett, 1973), p. 619.

[8] Franklin Gannon, *The British Press and Germany, 1936-1939* (Oxford: Clarendon Press, 1971), p. 119; Hardinge to Lansdowne, October 4, 1905 in G. P. Gooch and Harold Temperley, eds., *British Documents on the Origins of the War, 1898-1914*, vol. 4, *The Anglo-Russian Rapprochement, 1903-7* (London: His Majesty's Stationery Office, 1929), p. 206.

[9] This and other experiments are discussed in Albert Hastorf, David Schneider, Judith Polefka, *Person Perception* (Reading, Mass.: Addison-Wesley, 1970), pp. 71-83. For general treatments of the theory that lies behind this inference pat-

As a prelude to predicting another actor's behavior and setting their own policies, decision-makers thus ask themselves whether the external stimuli were so compelling as to determine the other's action. If someone hurts—or helps—us because a third person is holding a gun to his head, we will not expect the behavior to recur when the third person is not around. So when Italy supported the French occupation of the Ruhr in 1923, the Italian ambassador to Germany was relieved to be able to report:

> In . . . [official] circles it is generally understood that Italy could not have acted very differently from the way she did, in view of her multiple and complex relations with France and also in view of her clear and material need to provide for the distribution of as much coal as it is possible to obtain in the present circumstances from the areas occupied by Franco-Belgian troops. In all my conversations with persons in authority I have heard in this regard only reasonable and even benevolent understanding and consideration.[10]

Germany had grounds for believing that, if the external constraints on Italy were loosened, that country would cooperate. If she thought that Italy's dependence on France was permanent, she would not care that Italy did not freely choose the path of hostility—Italy's actions would always harm Germany just as much as they would if they were derived from goals and beliefs that directly conflicted with those of Germany.[11] But if this was not the case, Germany should work to ease the external

---

tern—a theory that parallels much of the analysis of this chapter—see Edward Jones and Keith Davis, "From Acts to Dispositions," in Leonard Berkowitz, ed., *Advances in Experimental Social Psychology,* vol. 2 (New York: Academic Press, 1965), 219-66; Harold Kelley, "Attribution Theory in Social Psychology," in David Levine, ed., *Nebraska Symposium on Motivation, 1967* (Lincoln: University of Nebraska Press, 1967), pp. 192-238; Harold Kelley, *Attribution in Social Interaction* (New York: General Learning Press, 1971) and *Causal Schemata and the Attribution Process* (New York: General Learning Press, 1972). Observers tend to overestimate the importance of personality and underestimate the impact of the situation in determining a person's behavior. For a discussion of this generalization, which does not apply to one set of politically relevant events, see Chapter 9.

[10] Quoted in Alan Cassels, *Mussolini's Early Diplomacy* (Princeton: Princeton University Press, 1970), p. 146. Although the argument here is consistent with attribution theory, experiments have shown that, in violation of the theory, individuals think that actions another is forced to take do reflect the other's own views. For the most recent study on this subject, see Melvin Snyder and Edward Jones, "Attitude Attribution when Behavior is Constrained," *Journal of Experimental Social Psychology* 10 (1974), 585-600.

[11] Here there is a difference between international and interpersonal relations. In the latter arena, emotions and moral judgments play a greater role. Our anger at someone who is hurting us will be less if we believe that he is forced to hurt us even if we expect that the external compulsion and the resulting pain he is inflicting on us will continue indefinitely.

compulsion and to build good relations with Italy to facilitate their working together later. A strongly hostile response would at best do no good —because Italy could not afford to break with France—and at worst would create a dispute with Germany that would remain even after the original reasons for Italy's anti-German actions had passed.

In a somewhat weaker case, when in signing a civil aviation agreement with Communist China Japan issued a statement saying that since 1972 she had not "considered China Air Lines (Taiwan) as a carrier representing a state," she tried to soften the Nationalists' reaction by privately explaining that Communist China had made this statement a necessary condition for concluding the bargain.[12] Although the environmental compulsion is less here than it was in the previous example, and there is a clear possibility that the pressures that produced the policy will continue into the future, the Japanese could hope that the Nationalists would calculate that their best interests lay in waiting for the environment in which Japan was situated to become more benign rather than in exerting maximum pressure on Japan. By contrast, France reacted very bitterly to the American decision to violate its treaty commitments and stay neutral in the Anglo-French wars of the 1790s because she failed to appreciate the degree to which American security rested on maintaining peace with England. France did not think that the United States was forced by overwhelming circumstances to refrain from aiding her, but rather that the United States had chosen this course as a result of values and beliefs that would create continuing conflict with France.

This kind of analysis explains the seemingly odd policy advocated by the German undersecretary of foreign affairs, Arthur Zimmermann, when the initial battles of World War I ended in deadlock. Most Germans who favored making peace with one of the enemy powers in order to concentrate on the other front advocated settling with Russia. Zimmermann, however, argued that, if peace efforts were called for, France should be the target because "France, in his view, had entered the war because of 'necessity' and not preference." Easing the external constraints—something Zimmermann thought Germany could do—might permit France to live at peace with Germany, but a compromise peace with Russia would not be possible without an alteration of Russian internal politics and values. The same argument explains why a peace treaty signed by a totally defeated country is less valuable as an index of the state's future behavior than is a treaty signed under less dire circumstances. Unless the victors are willing and able to see that the defeated state never regains its strength, there is no reason for them to expect it to abide by the settlement. Thus during the negotiations that ended the

[12] Fox Butterfield, "Japan and China Sign Air Accord; Taiwan Cuts Link," *New York Times*, April 21, 1974.

Boer War, the young Boers argued, according to Kitchener, "that if no terms are made and they are forced to unconditional surrender they will hold themselves absolutely free to begin again when they get a chance and see England in any difficulty."[13]

To predict how others are likely to behave and decide how best to influence them, actors must not only try to separate the internal from the external influences on the other's past behavior but must also analyze the internal processes themselves. Knowing only that the other is not behaving as anyone placed in that situation would does not tell the observer very much. Someone may fail to leave a burning house, for example, because of abnormalities in either his goals (he wants to die) or his perceptions (he cannot smell smoke or feel heat). Without trying to be exhaustive, we can distinguish three kinds of situations in which state A harms state B. B does not adopt an identical response in each case, even though the stimulus is identical, because of differences in its analysis of the other's internal processes and the derivative differences in predictions of how the other will act in the future.

B's response will be mildest when it believes that A did not expect, intend, or approve of the outcome that resulted. To some extent, good motives can save a bad policy. "[O]n several occasions, particularly in his relations with Mexico, [President Wilson] was able to escape the consequences of a blundering policy only because he had made his real, that is his ideal, purposes clear."[14] Of course there is no guarantee that this can be done. Observers may believe that the "ideal purposes" are a smoke screen to hide from others, and even from the actor himself, the real nature of his policy. Or they may conclude that the factors responsible for the policy's having an unfortunate effect in the one instance will recur and produce a similar outcome in later cases. But, to return to the example used above, if other states believed that the United States was trying to uphold values they shared and that there were no deeply rooted obstacles to America's acting on those values, they would conclude that America would behave differently when it became aware of the impact of its actions. Concerned states would then concentrate less on trying to restrain America than on educating her about why the policy had unintended consequences. Similarly, to take the classic international relations

---

[13] L. L. Farrar, Jr., *The Short-War Illusion* (Santa Barbara, Cal.: ABC-Clio, 1973), p. 124; quoted in G.H.L. Le May, *British Supremacy in South Africa, 1899-1907* (Oxford: Clarendon Press, 1965), p. 138. Many historians have noted that this was a major weakness of the Versailles treaty. The problem did not arise after World War II both because of continuing external constraints and because the imposed treaties were accompanied by an Allied occupation that reconstituted the internal political structures of the defeated states.

[14] Arthur Link, *Wilson the Diplomatist* (Chicago: Quadrangle, 1965), p. 17. For experimental support, see Nickel, "The Attribution of Intention as a Critical Factor in the Relation between Frustration and Aggression."

problem discussed at greater length in the next chapter, state A's reaction to increases in B's armaments depends in part on whether A thinks that B is trying to decrease A's security or is only seeking to make itself safer from perceived threats, including those emanating from state A itself. If the state does conclude that the other is arming out of fear, it is more apt to conciliate the other and try to reassure the other of its own peacefulness than it is to meet the other's arms and hostility with arms and hostility of its own.

In a second case, an identical amount of harm inflicted on the state will lead to a stronger, but still restrained, response because the state believes that although, unlike in the cases just discussed, the other did seek a goal that conflicted with the state's interest, the other does not generally seek to harm the state. The other is not seen to have a stake in weakening the state; it is not believed to value negatively the state's well-being. The conflict is over specific issues; it is not seen as contaminating all aspects of relations between the states. Thus in talks with Japan in the spring of 1941 the United States sought to convince the Japanese that America supported Great Britain for reasons of self-defense, and that, while American actions often hurt Japan, there was no cause for Japan to assume that the hostility was total and to respond by becoming more closely tied to Germany.[15]

Similarly, in the British debate over German intentions before World War I, when Eyre Crowe charged that Germany had objected to the Anglo-Congolese Agreement of 1894 "although it was not explained in what way her interests would be injuriously affected," one official replied by noting that Germany's interests were indeed involved: "The objection of Germany to . . . this Agreement was that it placed Great Britain on the Western frontier of German East Africa, in lieu of the neutral Congo Free State, Great Britain being already on the Northern and South Western frontiers. For a Government which is absorbed in strategical considerations the argument has naturally a good deal of importance."[16]

In a situation where a state has to harm the other yet wants to limit the hostility of the other's response, an appreciation of this reasoning will lead the state to try to show that its action brought values that were very important to it. It may further try to show that these gains were greater

[15] Nobutaka Ike, ed., *Japan's Decision for War* (Stanford: Stanford University Press, 1967), p. 43.

[16] Eyre Crowe, "Memorandum on the Present State of British Relations with France and Germany," January 1, 1907, printed in G. P. Gooch and Harold Temperley, eds., *British Documents on the Origins of the War, 1898-1914*, vol. 3, *The Testing of the Entente, 1904-6* (London: His Majesty's Stationery Office, 1928), p. 410; Thomas Sanderson, "Observations on Printed Memorandum on Relations with France and Germany, January 1907," February 21, 1907, printed in *ibid.*, p. 424.

than the losses suffered by the other. If the other accepts this view and believes that the pattern will continue in the future, it will expect the state to harm it only when doing so would yield disproportionate benefits. Similarly, if the harm resulted from a bargain between the state and a third party, the state will try to show the other that it did its best to limit the costs imposed on the other. So when Japan signed a civil aviation treaty with Communist China, she explained to Taiwan that she had rejected the communist demand for severing the air links to Formosa. By resisting, Japan presumably paid a price in terms of some counter-concessions that otherwise could have been exacted from China and thus demonstrated that she was not insensitive to Taiwan's well-being.[17]

The other's response will be more extreme when it believes that the state not only intended the harmful result but sought it as a positive good rather than accepting it as a necessary by-product of an issue-specific conflict. The state will then be seen not as desiring some limited goal that conflicts with the other's values, but rather as seeking to weaken or destroy the other. This is the conclusion that is likely to be drawn if the state uses inappropriate tactics, employs excessive force, or inflicts injury on the other side without due cause. So it is dangerous for an actor to pay a very high price to gain a marginal advantage, or to refuse to be conciliatory on an issue he knows to be more important to his adversary than it is to him. Because the projection into the future of the set of internal processes that is believed to have produced these acts is likely to yield strong and continued hostility, the state at which these acts are aimed is likely to react very strongly even if the immediate harm is slight. This is part of the explanation for the recent American decision to decrease foreign aid to states which voted against it in the United Nations on issues in which their interests were not directly involved. That these states did not stand to gain anything concrete from their votes was taken to mean that their hostility was gratuitous and that a strong reply was called for. An earlier case, the second Moroccan crisis, was embittered by the fact that the Germans threatened to use force after the French expressed a willingness to negotiate. The German coercion then seemed unnecessary if the goal was the professed one, and the French therefore concluded that the Germans were seeking to humiliate them. Similarly, Crowe drew dark inferences from the Anglo-German colonial dispute of 1884, not so much because Bismarck sought something England valued, but because he believed that "It seems almost certain that had Germany from the outset sought to gain by friendly overtures to England what she eventually secured after a display of unprovoked aggressiveness, there would have been no difficulty in the

---

[17] Butterfield, "Japan and China Sign Air Accord."

way of an amicable arrangement satisfactory to both parties." Statesmen who are aware of this danger are apt to share Kennedy's position in the Cuban missile crisis: "I am not going to push the Russians an inch beyond what is necessary."[18]

Because our reaction to assistance, like our reaction to harm, depends on our explanation of the other's behavior, we do not automatically assume that someone who helps us is our friend. The previous analysis of the effect of believing that the other's behavior was strongly influenced by the external situation leads us to anticipate the experimental finding that "If two people have been equally helpful, we will be more impressed by the behavior of the one who seems less under our control."[19] A person who aids us when we have power over him may be less considerate under less propitious circumstances, but someone who provides assistance when he does not need to is more likely to have been moved by friendly motives that will manifest themselves in future situations. Experiments have also shown that people are less impressed and less likely to reciprocate favors if they believe that the other had no choice in helping them or produced the result by accident than if they think that the other sought to help them.[20] Under the former conditions, there is no reason for the person to expect the other's favorable behavior to continue even if the person cooperates with him. Similarly, an actor will not be favorably impressed when another helps him if he believes that these

[18] Leslie Gelb, "U.S. Linking Aid to Votes at U.N.," *New York Times*, January 9, 1976; Charles Lockhart, *The Efficacy of Threats: International Interaction Strategies* (Beverly Hills: Sage Professional Papers in International Studies, vol. 2, no. 23, April 1974), 26; Crowe, "Memorandum," p. 409; Kennedy, *Thirteen Days*, p. 105 (Kennedy was preoccupied with the immediate danger of nuclear war, but longer-run considerations can also explain this position).

An exception to this generalization should be noted: the threat to use overwhelming force can be employed by a state to enable the other side to concede without loss of honor. For example, when Britain laid plans to force the Russian fleet to delay its trip to Japan following the Dogger Bank incident, the admiralty told the local commander that if he had to use force he would be supplied with a very large fleet so that "there could be no dishonour to the Russians in yielding to it." Gooch and Temperley, eds., *British Documents on the Origins of the War, 1898-1914*, vol. 4, p. 19. For a similar incident, see James Cable, *Gunboat Diplomacy* (London: Chatto and Windus, 1971), p. 29.

[19] Lloyd H. Strickland, "Surveillance and Trust," *Journal of Personality* 26 (1958), 200-15. For a similar finding, see S. S. Komorita and Arline Brenner, "Bargaining and Concession Making Under Bilateral Monopoly," *Journal of Personality and Social Psychology* 9 (1968), 15-20.

[20] Martin Greenberg and David Frisch, "Effect of Intentionality on Willingness to Reciprocate a Favor," *Journal of Experimental Social Psychology* 8 (1972), 99-111; Gerald Leventhal, Thomas Weiss, and Gary Long, "Equity, Reciprocity, and Reallocating Rewards in the Dyad," *Journal of Personality and Social Psychology* 13 (1969), 300-305; Richard Goranson and Leonard Berkowitz, "Reciprocity and Responsibility Reactions to Prior Help," *ibid.* 3 (1966), 227-32. The interpretations given in these articles are somewhat different from the one advanced here.

actions simultaneously aid the other. Thus if Russian leaders thought that the American economy was faced with a problem of excess production after World War II and so believed that "Moscow would be doing the Americans a favor by accepting economic assistance,"[21] they would not have concluded that offers of American aid necessarily indicated that the United States expected relations between the two countries to continue to be good. If aid benefited the United States at least as much as it did Russia, America could want to give aid even if it considered Russia its enemy. On the other hand, if the other undertakes an exchange in which he gives the actor more than he needs to and/or receives less than he has the power to exact, the actor is likely to conclude that the other has a positive stake in his well-being. He may believe that the other cares about him for intrinsic reasons—e.g. specific ties of affection or a general belief that one helps others—or that the other is guided by instrumental calculations—e.g. the belief that the two actors have important long-run interests in common. In either case, the actor will infer that the other's behavior did not depend on conditions that are likely to change quickly and so he will expect friendly behavior from the other in the future.

This analysis allows us to apply usefully the concepts of generosity and gratitude to international relations. Many "realists" would argue that only a foolish statesman would be influenced by the sentiments that usually go by those names. But if we define generosity as an instance where state A does not take advantage of the weakness of state B and define gratitude as an instance in which B later responds similarly, these terms can describe state behavior even if we exclude motives of altruism (i.e. one state positively valuing the other's welfare as an intrinsic good). State A may refrain from exploiting B's weakness in order to show B that it feels they have a high degree of common interest. And state B, which has been the beneficiary of generosity, may show gratitude by responding with similar restraint not only to show others that favors will be returned but because it does not have to fear that in aiding A it is increasing the power of a nation that is apt to turn against it.[22]

The other side of this coin is that, when a state forebears from taking advantage of the other and the other is seen to respond by continued ex-

---

[21] John Gaddis, *The United States and the Origins of the Cold War, 1941-1947* (New York: Columbia University Press, 1972), p. 175. For experimental evidence in support of this argument, see John Schopler and Vaida Thompson, "Role of Attribution Processes in Mediating Amount of Reciprocity for a Favor," *Journal of Personality and Social Psychology* 10 (1968), 243-50.

[22] For the use of the concepts of gratitude and altruism in psychology, see Abraham Tesser, Robert Gatewood, and Michael Driver, "Some Determinants of Gratitude," *Journal of Personality and Social Psychology* 9 (1968), 233-36; and Dennis Krebs, "Altruism—An Examination of the Concept and a Review of the Literature," *Psychological Bulletin* 73 (1970), 258-302.

ploitation, the state will infer either that the other does not understand that relationships can be based on mutual concessions or that the other believes that the two states have few important common interests. In either event, the state will conclude that it must be prepared to defend itself against the other's continued hostility. Thus the anti-German thesis of Crowe's memorandum was underpinned by his belief that in many instances "we made a gratuitous concession, most earnestly coveted by Germany, and got less than nothing in return."[23]

Trust and trustworthiness should be interpreted similarly. Nation A trusts B in a particular situation when it believes that B will not further its own interests at the expense of A, usually because A believes that B values the prospects of long-run cooperation between the two countries more than it values the short-run gains that would accrue by exploiting its immediate power over A. If A trusts B, it will allow situations to occur in which B could harm it, and indeed, if A wants to demonstrate its trust, it may seek such situations.[24] By doing so it can show that it realizes that the other is trustworthy—i.e. that it sees that the other knows that the two of them share dominating common interests—and so can lay the basis for a harmonious relationship in which neither side is preoccupied with the distribution of short-run benefits or worried about the danger that the other might double-cross it. A striking example is the behavior of a dolphin, which shows his trust by presenting his unprotected vitals to his trainer—this is the common response of a defeated animal—and then, to show his trustworthiness, takes the trainer's wrist in his jaws and releases it. For the same reasons a state that seeks to keep an act of violence strictly limited "will often . . . make this clear to the victim by accepting military risks that would never be run in war: allowing the victim to fire first and even suffering his fire without replying."[25]

Three questions that often face decision-makers bring out clearly the importance of correctly assessing the other side's goals and beliefs: Can an issue in dispute be treated in isolation? How will the other carry out his undertakings? What threats and promises will be most effective? To elaborate on the first point, the actor must decide whether an issue is highly situation-bound or whether it is a symptom of a disagreement that will continue to produce friction even if the initial dispute is settled. If the latter is the case, dealing with the dispute "on its merits" is not likely to be an effective strategy, and even successfully solving the specific problem will do little good. If the underlying conflict is severe and cannot be dissipated by conciliation, then concessions, even if warranted by the facts of the immediate case, may lead the other to raise further demands.

[23] Crowe, "Memorandum," p. 428.
[24] For related definitions see Morton Deutsch, "Trust and Suspicion," *Journal of Conflict Resolution* 2 (December 1958), 266-76, and Bernhardt Lieberman, "*i*-Trust," *ibid.* 7 (September 1964), 279.
[25] Cable, *Gunboat Diplomacy*, p. 31.

Even if this pitfall is avoided and an agreement is reached, the chances of avoiding future conflicts will not have been greatly reduced.[26] If, on the other hand, the actor feels that the basic issues can be ameliorated, he will usually be well advised to try to set relations on a more cooperative footing rather than to negotiate about the narrow issue that is the immediate subject of contention. In either case the specifics of the issue are secondary in determining the actor's response.

Second, during the negotiation process, actors must look beyond the other's demands and promises and consider how the other will behave under various kinds of settlements. This is true even when the agreement is legally binding. No labor and management contract can cover all situations that may arise. Much depends on the attitude each side adopts during the life of the agreement. As Sidney Garfield and William F. Whyte put it: "The skillful manager or union leader does not confine his attention in bargaining to the phraseology of contract clauses. He interprets a particular clause against his estimate of the people who sit across the table from him. Would they take advantage of a technicality? Would they be willing to make adjustments for many situations that are difficult to cover in written words?" So negotiators need to assess their opponents to try to see not only how much they can get out of them but also how much they *need* to get out of them. The greater their fear and mistrust, the more detailed they will want the contract to be and the more guarantees they will believe they must exact. In the extreme case in which the union fears for its existence, changing the management's attitudes will be more important than gaining advantageous contract provisions. As Paul Diesing notes, management "can accept all sorts of union security clauses, but if management clearly indicates that it will evade or overthrow these clauses on first opportunity, working relations cannot be established. . . . Without strong evidence of voluntary management acceptance, union suspicion can never be overcome." Similarly, most British decision-makers would not consider making peace with Hitler after September 1939 no matter what terms he offered because they thought he would renew the war when it suited him. And the breakdown of the Vietnam negotiations in November and December 1972 also seems traceable in part to each side's fears that the other's unreasonable behavior showed that it would not fulfill its undertakings.[27]

Third, if the actor's estimate of his adversary's goals and beliefs influ-

---

[26] For an example from labor-management relations, see Benjamin Selekman, *Labor Relations and Human Relations* (New York: McGraw-Hill, 1947), p. 95.

[27] Sidney Garfield and William F. Whyte, "The Collective Bargaining Process: A Human Relations Analysis," *Human Organizations* 9 (Summer 1950), 7; Paul Diesing, "Bargaining Strategy and Union-Management Relations," *Journal of Conflict Resolution* 5 (December 1961), 371. For a discussion of this phenomenon from a different perspective, see Jervis, *The Logic of Images in International Relations* (Princeton: Princeton University Press, 1970), pp. 90-102.

ences the threats and concessions he makes and the assurances he demands, the accuracy of these estimates helps determine the success of his policy. The case of Bre'r Rabbit and the briar patch is well known. Similarly, when Teddy Roosevelt reluctantly said he would intervene in Cuba if turmoil and threats to American property continued, he did not realize that both the government and the insurgents thought they would gain from an American presence. The result, of course, was that the Cubans eagerly engaged in the proscribed behavior. Assurances can be ineffective for the same reasons. In the summer and fall of 1950, the United States went to some lengths to try to convince China that it would not interfere with the Yalu river power stations, believing that the fear that her industry might be deprived of this vital resource could drive the Chinese to enter the Korean War. Because American decision-makers thought that China had little fear of invasion they did not feel the need to persuade China of the obvious. But the American assurances were misguided because China did indeed fear a direct attack and was relatively unconcerned about loss of access to the Yalu power plants.[28]

An accurate explanation of the other's behavior can often bring mutual benefits, provided that the incompatibility between the two sides' goals is limited. If a party understands the beliefs and goals that have produced the other side's unacceptable proposal, it may be able to find an arrangement that gains the other's objectives without sacrificing anything the first values highly. This opens up room for creativity and imagination in negotiations. The ideal result is what Mary Parker Follett calls "integration," which signifies "that a solution has been found in which both [sides'] desires have found a place, that neither side has had to sacrifice anything." Even when this ideal is only approximated, actors can strive for a bargain in which "each clause of the contract provides maximum benefit to one side at minimum cost to the other." In Ernst Haas's terms, this involves "upgrading the common interests of the parties" rather than merely agreeing to "the minimum common denominator" or "splitting the difference." In this process the "parties succeed . . . in redefining their conflict so as to work out a solution at a higher level."[29] Richard Walton and Robert McKersie make this point well:

[28] Allan Millet, *The Politics of Intervention* (Columbus, Ohio: Ohio State University Press, 1968); John Spanier, *The Truman-MacArthur Controversy and the Korean War* (New York: Norton, 1965), p. 97; Allen Whiting, *China Crosses the Yalu* (Stanford: Stanford University Press, 1968), p. 151.

[29] Quoted in Ernst Haas, *Beyond the Nation-State* (Stanford: Stanford University Press, 1964), p. 111; Diesing, "Bargaining Strategy and Union-Management Relations," p. 376; Haas, *Beyond the Nation-State*, p. 111. As Walton and McKersie note, "By exploring the various reasons which underlie the party's interests in the issue, new possibilities may arise." (Richard Walton and Robert McKersie, *A Behavioral Theory of Labor Negotiations* [New York: McGraw-Hill, 1965], p. 133.)

The negotiator who suffers from myopia will fix on his objective and assume that there is only one alternative for getting there. The more skilled negotiator will be able to discern the connection, complex though it may be, between some new alternative and the objective which he seeks. When the UAW demanded some form of [guaranteed annual wage], the auto industry could have seen this as directly in conflict with their objectives of maintaining managerial flexibility. Rather, they saw a chain of connections as follows: the union and workers were concerned about the inadequacy of unemployment compensation; if no changes were made in the unemployment compensation picture, then new laws would be passed; new laws would mean more obligations for the company; consequently it would be an advantage for the company to take the initiative to improve the unemployment compensation picture for its employees.[30]

The company thus looked for alternatives that would meet the main objectives of the union proposal without greatly hindering managerial flexibility, and a system of supplementary unemployment benefits was worked out as a substitute acceptable to both sides.

This approach requires that the actor understand his own means-ends chain instead of falling into the easy trap of continuing to seek goals without regard to why they were originally sought. This task, always psychologically difficult, is compounded in large organizations where most people are trying to reach small and established subgoals. Upgrading the common interest and creativity in general involve the rearrangement of goals, and this cannot be done if the person must "do what he is told" without knowing why the goals are valued and seeking new ways of reaching them. Superiors decrease organizational creativity when they communicate only specific directives without explaining their broader aims and calculations. The subordinate then cannot design policies that take full advantage of the potentialities latent in changing circumstances.[31]

---

[30] Walton and McKersie, *A Behavioral Theory of Labor Negotations*, p. 156.

[31] This problem plagued the British navy before and during World War I. For a general discussion see K.G.B. Dewar, *The Navy From Within* (London: Gollancz, 1939). For a specific incident that had important consequences for the battle of Jutland, see Arthur Marder, *From the Dreadnought to Scapa Flow*, vol. 3, *Jutland and After, May 1916-December 1916* (London: Oxford University Press, 1966), p. 41. For an analogous incident in diplomacy see P. Edward Haley, *Revolution and Intervention: The Diplomacy of Taft and Wilson with Mexico, 1910-1917* (Cambridge, Mass.: M.I.T. Press, 1970), p. 59. This problem is part of the broader question of how superiors can devise a system of incentives to best guide their subordinates' behavior. The incentive system has to consist of relatively simple rules in order to be serviceable, but the simplicity often distorts the goals the superior actually seeks. This is brilliantly revealed in Joseph Berliner's discussion of the alternatives to the free market developed to guide factory pro-

Of course, explaining to an adversary why you are acting as you are will be useless at best if this explanation involves goals and beliefs that the other thinks make no sense. Thus during World War II the United States explained its desire for frequent revisions in the lend-lease schedules in terms of technical considerations. "[B]ut the Soviet officials would assume that there was some other [non-military] motive, and they would hesitate to concede or make the arrangements required . . . to fit in with the changed plans." Decisions were delayed while the Russians searched for the real reasons for the American moves. Since an accurate account of the American concerns created rather than cleared up conflict, "it was sometimes better to express the decisions in terms which a Marxist would understand so that the Soviet official might be able to say himself that at least the American proposal was sincere and there was no concealed motive which would require time to find." Toward the end of the war, the United States had great trouble getting the Russians to return swiftly the captured American troops they had liberated. American motives were strictly humanitarian, as the Russians were informed. But the Russians probably would have acted faster had they been told that the troops were needed for action against Japan, a desire the Russians would have understood.[32]

INTENTIONS

As we have seen, the analysis of an actor's behavior involves the separation of internal from situational components. But for prediction, this separation is a prelude to a re-combination: the internal processes that have been inferred from the other's previous behavior and the situation in which the other is expected to be must be considered jointly. To do this we shall utilize the concept of intentions. An actor's intentions can be defined as the actions he will take under given circumstances (or, if the circumstances are hypothetical, the actions he would take if the circumstances were to materialize). It must be emphasized that this definition varies from a common one. Many authors use intention to refer to what the actor plans to do or what goals he hopes to reach. We are using the term to designate the collection of actions the state will or would take because that is what others are trying to predict. As we will see, this means that intention cannot be totally separated from the concepts of re-

---

duction decisions in the Soviet Union (*Factory and Manager in the U.S.S.R.* [Cambridge, Mass.: Harvard University Press, 1957]).

[32] Joseph Hazard, "Negotiating Under Lend-Lease" in Raymond Dennett and Joseph Johnson, eds., *Negotiating with the Russians* (Boston: World Peace Foundation, 1951), p. 35; also see John Deane, *The Strange Alliance* (New York: Viking, 1947), and Philip Mosely, "Some Soviet Techniques of Negotiations," in Dennett and Johnson, *Negotiating with the Russians*, p. 301.

solve and willingness to run risks. Other problems with this conceptualization will be discussed later, but it seems more useful than the alternatives.

In some cases scholars and, less frequently, decision-makers want to know what a state would do in the absence of external constraints. For example, if the United States found itself in a situation where none would oppose it, would it leave other states completely alone, take their territory, exploit their natural resources, or change their domestic political systems? The answers to these questions, which of course would be very difficult to determine, would reveal what we will call the state's "utopian intentions." Examining such intentions highlights significant characteristics of a state and an historical era. Even if it were true that "aggressiveness is always latent, and is even almost mathematically proportioned to the degree to which a state can misbehave with impunity"[33]—and the analysis below will dispute this—what states want others to do varies. In the seventeenth century, utopian intentions would have involved imposing one's religion on others. In the eighteenth century, the ability to export while simultaneously protecting one's own domestic markets would have been stressed. Today different states have different utopian intentions. Those of the underdeveloped states would include gaining wealth and perhaps territory; those of the U.S.S.R. and the United States would include the spreading of their domestic political systems; those of the Scandinavian countries might be completely blank.

There are several reasons other than complete satiation why a state might not engage in aggression even under ideal conditions. It might be morally opposed to the use of force, even—or especially—against those who cannot resist. "Instrumental pacifism"—the view that force is ineffective or even counterproductive for the goals under consideration—is also possible. A state may feel that any use of force to change the status quo would undermine the legitimacy of the international system or believe that what Wolfers terms "milieu goals"—goals involving "shaping conditions beyond their national boundaries"[34] like the growth of international law—can be furthered only by uncoerced cooperation. Instrumental pacifism is also more likely to be applied to goals that require permanent internalized changes in beliefs rather than changes in behavior. Of course it is difficult to determine if professed instrumental pacifism would really bear up under the test. It usually develops only after the use of force has become clearly impossible, and a decision-maker might change his mind if external restraints were lifted.

[33] Herbert Butterfield quoted in Inis Claude, *Power and International Relations* (New York: Random House, 1962), p. 65.

[34] Arnold Wolfers, *Discord and Collaboration* (Baltimore: Johns Hopkins Press, 1962), pp. 73-77.

Of course states almost never have a chance to act on their utopian intentions, and so actors and observers are usually more concerned with how a state will act given the constraints it is likely to face. But many definitions do not incorporate this element and therefore are misleading. For example, Wolfers says that "One can think of nations lined up between the two poles of maximum and minimum 'attack propensity,' with those unalterably committed to attack, *provided it promises success*, at one pole and those at the other, whom no amount of opportunity for successful attack could induce to undertake it."[35] The italicized phrase differentiates Wolfers' formulation from ours. In his theory, all states except those whose utopian intentions are status quo would attack if success were cheap and certain. So Wolfers would have to classify most states as extremely aggressive.

Both the problem and the solution we will adopt can be seen in Dean Acheson's discussion of the implications for the future of the war in Korea: "The very fact of this aggression . . . constitute[s] undeniable proof that the forces of international communism possess not only the willingness, but also the intention, of attacking and invading any free nation within their reach *at any time that they think they can get away with it*. The real significance of the North Korean aggression lies in this evidence that, *even at the resultant risk of starting a third world war*, communism is willing to resort to armed aggression, whenever it believes it can win."[36] The first sentence, like Wolfers' definition, would not separate the Russia Acheson perceived from many other states. But in the next breath Acheson introduces the crucial claim that Russia not only would expand but would do so even when the risk was high. It is important to note that Acheson reached this conclusion because he thought that Russia knew that the United States would respond forceably to the attack, which was not entirely reasonable in light of previous American statements and actions. The main point here, however, is that we can avoid the dilemma of classifying most states as aggressive only by focusing not on the question of whether the state would change the status quo if it were easy to do so but on the question of the costs and risks a state is willing to tolerate. The latter concept can be used to develop what we will call the state's "basic intention." Thus while both the United States and the U.S.S.R. may have the same utopian intentions—to spread their domestic political systems throughout the world—they differ in their willingness to run risks and make sacrifices to further this goal and so have different basic intentions. Similarly, states generally considered to be status quo powers differ in their willingness to pay a price to preserve

35 *Ibid.*, p. 160, emphasis added.
36 Testimony before the Senate Committee on Appropriations, *Supplemental Appropriations for 1951*, p. 272, emphasis added.

the values they possess. The United States has been willing to go to great lengths to stop the spread of communism; France would not stand firm against Germany in the 1930s.

We can place states in a fourfold table according to the prices they will pay to protect or to increase their values:

Costs willing to pay to defend values possessed

		HIGH	LOW
Costs willing to pay to change status quo	HIGH	Japan in the 1930s	Hitler's Germany
	LOW	U.S.	France in the 1930s

The only box that needs further elaboration is the upper right-hand one. States in this category believe that they currently possess little of value but are striving to alter this situation. They are willing to risk or wage war if they think there is even a small chance of making major gains. But a purely defensive war that was not a prelude to a later offensive one would be seen as an expense of valuable military resources disproportionate to the object of protecting its meager possessions. Hitler captured the outlook of such a state when he said: "Germany will be a World Power or nothing at all."[37]

In most cases, however, states are willing to pay a higher price to protect what they have than to increase their values. States usually have used their resources to get what is most valuable to them, and what they possess generally increases in subjective and objective value as time passes. Even when these factors are not present, losses usually cause pain in excess of the joy brought by an objectively comparable gain; the pain we feel on losing $5.00 is greater than the pleasure we experience in finding the same amount of money.

In a world of nation-states the price a state is willing to pay to protect its lands is apt to be much greater than the price it will pay to increase at least one major value—territory occupied by other nationalities. By contrast, when decision-makers do not value the land they hold more

[37] Quoted in John Wheeler-Bennett, *Brest-Litovsk* (New York: Norton, 1971), p. xii.

highly than the surrounding territory, as in seventeenth-century Europe or China in the warlord period, the spread will be small and actors will rapidly shift from supporting to opposing the status quo as dangers and opportunities arise.[38]

The table above portrays the prices a state is willing to pay for general goals. It is also useful to consider how much a state will risk and sacrifice to reach specific objectives. Other states may correctly estimate the level of costs that the state considers bearable but still misperceive the goals for which the state will pay the price. For example, although Britain and France overestimated Hitler's resolve in questions involving the redressing of grievances imposed by the Treaty of Versailles (e.g. they did not realize that he would have backed down if they had forceably opposed his remilitarization of the Rhineland), they simultaneously underestimated his willingness to go to war in order to dominate Europe.[39]

This conceptualization is not without its problems. A state that is not willing to run major risks may misperceive or miscalculate and undertake very dangerous actions. The state's behavior would not correspond then to its basic intentions. For example, the Russians probably grossly mis-estimated the risks they were running by putting missiles into Cuba.[40] And at many points Hitler may have been reckless not because he willingly tolerated a high probability of war but because he was certain that the other side would back down. When his generals opposed his policy on the grounds that it was too dangerous Hitler did not argue that the risks were worth running. Rather he told them that the risks were slight. Indeed it may be that states that use force to alter the status quo often differ from others less in their willingness to run perceived risks than in the fact that they perceive low risks in situations where others perceive high ones.[41]

[38] Hsi-sheng Chi, "The Chinese Warlord System as an International System," in Morton Kaplan, ed., *New Approaches to International Relations* (New York: St. Martin's, 1968), pp. 405-25.

[39] Although it is often in an actor's interest to have others believe that he will pay a high price to prevail in a specific dispute but that he will not contest wider issues, this image is difficult to project. It is hard for the actor to convince others that he will go to war over a minor issue unless he ties his stand to principles of more general applicability. Hitler succeeded partly because there was a relatively clear line between those demands for revising the Treaty of Versailles (which were felt to be legitimate) and those which did more than right earlier wrongs. By initially avoiding, and indeed disavowing, demands in the latter category Hitler convinced others that his vehemence on the former did not indicate unlimited aggressiveness.

[40] Klaus Knorr, "Failures in National Intelligence Estimates: The Case of the Cuban Missiles," *World Politics* 16 (April 1967), 455-67.

[41] This problem could be avoided by categorizing aggressive and status quo powers by their answers to the hypothetical question of whether they would choose to freeze the status quo if they could—i.e. guaranteeing each state the possessions

When analyzing another's policy, statesmen and scholars should separate the state's willingness to run risks from its perceptions of costs and dangers. The focus of our attention often shifts as we learn more about the actor's perceptions. To take an example discussed in the previous chapter, the set of explanations advanced for American involvement in Vietnam depends in part on whether or not one believes that the decision-makers expected the war to be very costly. To predict others' behavior and to design appropriate strategies, statesmen must draw similar distinctions. Thus in analyzing the implications of an objectively risky German move at the end of the nineteenth century, Eyre Crowe stressed that "The hostile character of that demonstration was thoroughly understood by the [German] government, because we know that preparations were made for safeguarding the German fleet in the contingency of a British attack."[42] Others must try to determine whether the state knew it was running high risks because, while a cautious state that has blundered into a dangerous situation will not repeat its behavior if it understands that it will meet strong opposition, a state that knew what it was doing will not be deterred by a clearer picture of its environment. Strategies that would be effective against the latter kind of state are not likely to be appropriate when dealing with states that fall in the former category and vice versa.

Furthermore, a state may not see the extent to which its actions will upset the status quo. In a highly interdependent world, limited moves may have large and unforeseen consequences. By opposing an adversary a state might inadvertently lead third parties to expect support for an armed attack against that country. Or a state's concessions to its neighbor could encourage the latter to move against a third country, causing the state to reverse its policy and attack its neighbor. Or a state seeking limited gains could find that it had undermined the status quo far more than it had sought. Thus it has been argued that the leaders of pre-World War I Germany failed to appreciate that Germany's great strength coupled with its strategic location meant that even small aggrandizements would have large effects. Of a later period, A. J. P. Taylor argues that it is quite possible that Hitler was trying to achieve "international equality" for Germany without understanding that "the inevitable consequence of fulfilling this wish was that Germany would become

---

it holds in return for making it impossible to use force to get additional ones. This allows us to call France in the 1920s a status quo state even though she tried to increase her power position vis-à-vis Germany since her motive in doing so was to preserve the basic aspects of the system. But this definition is not the best for dealing with questions involving predictions of behavior.

[42] Crowe, "Memorandum," p. 411.

the dominant state in Europe."[43] For the states that surrounded Germany this distinction was important only if they could alert Germany to the consequences of her actions and Germany would then modify her policies. If this was not possible, it mattered little whether Germany was attempting to dominate out of inadvertence or design.

Inaccurate Predictions about One's Own Behavior

Because we have defined a state's intentions as the actions it will or would take under given conditions, intentions are sometimes different from what the state's decision-makers think they will or would do. This definition is useful because observers must try to predict how the actor will behave, not how he thinks he will behave. Although one might think that the actor can always accurately predict his own behavior, this is not true. Indeed observers may know the actor's intentions better than does the actor himself.

In the first place, decision-makers may not know how they will behave in the frequent cases when world politics outruns their imaginations. Many events occur that they had not contemplated. Or they may not think about how they will behave even though they believe an event is probable because they know that their reaction will be strongly influenced by unpredictable details of the context. Thus, before World War I, the British refused to make promises to the French about their stance in a possible Franco-German war on the grounds that they could not foresee the immediate causes and exact circumstances of such a war. Indeed a Russian diplomat claimed this was always the case with Britain: "The whole art of diplomacy is to mask one's intentions. And that is where the English excel. No one ever knows what they intend to do because they never know themselves."[44] Even when an event is likely, important, and the detailed circumstances are not apt to be decisive, decision-makers may not think about how they will react because the choice is politically or intellectually too difficult. During World War I the German government could not formulate serious peace terms because the

---

[43] Klaus Epstein, "Gerhard Ritter and the First World War," in H. W. Koch, *The Origins of the First World War* (London: Macmillan & Co., 1972), p. 293 (for a related analysis see Crowe, "Memorandum," pp. 415-17); A.J.P. Taylor, "War Origins Again," in Esmonde Robertson, ed., *The Origins of the Second World War* (London: Macmillan & Co., 1971), p. 139. Taylor's admission undercuts much of the revisionism of his *The Origins of the Second World War* (New York: Atheneum, 1961). Dynamics like these are discussed at greater length in Chapter 3.

[44] Quoted in R. H. Bruce Lockhart, *British Agent* (New York: Putnam, 1933), p. 154. Sazonov is wrong on two counts. First, a state often wants to make its intentions clear—e.g. when it tries to deter another. Second, as we will discuss below, an observer may be able to predict how an actor will behave even if the actor himself cannot.

attempt to do so would have split the country. Domestic disagreements in the mid-1930s similarly made it impossible for the Belgian government to know how it would react to various hypothetical German moves. And in May 1940 the United States Chief of Naval Operations wrote the commander of the Pacific Fleet: "Suppose the Japs do go into the East [without simultaneously attacking United States territory]? What are we going to do about it? My answer is, I don't know and I think there is nobody on God's green earth who can tell you."[45]

More interestingly, a decision-maker may think he knows how he will react under given circumstances, but these predictions may prove to be incorrect. There are several reasons for this. First, people may misjudge the degree to which events will stir their emotions. Before World War I most socialists thought that they would oppose the war. A few years ago many faculty members incorrectly predicted how they would react to the use of police in campus disturbances. Can anyone confidently predict the policies he would advocate in the event that nuclear weapons were used? Decision-makers have thought about this a great deal and elaborate contingency plans exist, but the actual reactions might bear little resemblance to those calm calculations.

A second and related cause for an inaccurate self-prediction is that events may lead a decision-maker to re-think his goals and values. Ernest May explains the American decision to neglect previous plans and defend Korea in these terms:

In January it had been the clearly defined policy of the United States to commit its forces only in Japan and the Philippines. In June it was the nation's policy to fight for South Korea. . . . Why? The answer is not, I think, that American policy had changed. . . . Rather it is that the United States had two *kinds* of policies and that in this case, as in others, a distinction has to be drawn between [them]. . . . The first, that of January, was a product of calculation. . . . Weighing ends and means, [United States decision-makers] made judgments on what seemed feasible. . . . The result was a set of prudential rules, or what might be termed a *calculated policy*. In June, when the North Koreans launched their attack, the President and his advisors did not judge the event in terms of this policy. Instead, their minds flew to an axiom—

[45] Ernest May, *The World War and American Isolation* (Cambridge, Mass.: Harvard University Press, 1959); David Kieft, *Belgium's Return to Neutrality* (Oxford: Clarendon Press, 1972); quoted in Robert Butow, *Tojo and the Coming of the War* (Princeton: Princeton University Press, 1961), p. 190. Alexander George and Richard Smoke, *Deterrence in American Foreign Policy* (New York: Columbia University Press, 1974), find many examples of decision-makers failing to consider carefully the evidence that a certain event is likely to occur because to do so would force them to make a difficult choice. This book arrived too late for me to fully incorporate all of its excellent analysis.

that any armed aggression anywhere constituted a threat to all nations everywhere.[46]

In the actual moment of attack, the costs of not responding loomed much larger than they had previously. The opposite phenomenon is probably more common. Decision-makers decide that they will react strongly if the enemy provokes them but change their mind when the event occurs. In the Cuban missile crisis President Kennedy accepted his advisers' recommendation that the United States should destroy an anti-aircraft missile site if a U-2 were shot down; but, when this contingency materialized, he decided to withhold the strike. Similarly, President Johnson did not respond to the Viet Cong attack on the American facilities at Bienhoa even though two months earlier he had planned to retaliate "in the event of any attack on United States units."[47] If such re-evaluations imply that decision-makers' goals and willingness to run risks are more malleable than is often assumed, it is perhaps because people do not ordinarily examine their basic beliefs unless they are confronted with shocks and unpleasant choices.

Third, the decision-maker may not act as he thought he would if the context in which the event takes place differs from what he expected. This is another reason for the American decision to disregard previous analysis and to defend Korea. Until the outbreak of the conflict, the United States thought that any communist aggression would be part of a total war. In such a context there would be no point in wasting scarce military resources in Korea. But the actual circumstances were different: the attack was an isolated one, and so the need to conserve military forces was less and the costs of not responding were greater since a failure to rebuff this probe might lead to attacks on other areas. A different kind of failure to anticipate the circumstances that surrounded an expected event explains why Britain did not carry out her commitment to aid Denmark against Prussia and Austria in 1864. Britain had not consciously bluffed—she thought she would defend Denmark if need be. But her plans and commitments were predicated on the belief that she would receive French support. Only as the war began did British statesmen realize that previous British behavior had alienated France. This knowledge of the altered international environment led Britain to back down.

Fourth, the domestic context may differ from that expected when the plans were made, perhaps because of the impact of the event itself. Thus the decision-makers may find that options are foreclosed or opened in

---

[46] "The Nature of Foreign Policy: The Calculated vs. the Axiomatic," *Daedalus* 91 (Fall 1962), 661-62.

[47] Theodore Sorensen, *Kennedy* (New York: Harper and Row, 1965), p. 713; Kennedy, *Thirteen Days*, pp. 75-76; *The Pentagon Papers* (New York: Bantam Books, 1971), pp. 320-22.

ways they had not anticipated. For example, the Korean War made it possible for the United States to more than triple its defense budget and fulfill the desired, but previously unreachable, goals laid down in NSC 68. And unexpected domestic pressures played a major role in Chamberlain's decision to alter his appeasement policy after Germany took over Czechoslovakia in March 1939.[48]

Because decision-makers do not always know how they will act, others will disregard statements of intent if they believe that their predictions of how the decision-maker will act are more accurate than those the decision-maker himself can make. The ability to make such predictions stood Bismarck in good stead. In the example cited above, he felt free to move against Denmark because he knew that France would not support Britain and that Britain therefore would not enter the war. Similarly, Theodore Sorensen claims that the Joint Chiefs of Staff approved the plans for the Bay of Pigs in large part because they believed that, if the invasion faltered, President Kennedy would reverse his previous stand against direct United States military involvement. The chiefs probably did not believe that Kennedy was purposely misleading them, but rather that he would think differently when he was faced with defeat than he did in the calm days before the operation. And they were not totally wrong. When Castro's air force proved to be unexpectedly potent, Kennedy authorized the navy to use unmarked planes to provide air cover for the refugees' B-26's.[49]

[48] William Rock, *Appeasement on Trial* (Hamden, Conn.: Archon Books, 1966), pp. 203-16.
[49] Sorensen, *Kennedy*, pp. 297-99.

CHAPTER THREE

Deterrence, the Spiral Model, and Intentions of the Adversary

Two Views of International Relations and the Cold War

DIFFERING perceptions of the other state's intentions often underlie policy debates. In the frequent cases when the participants do not realize that they differ on this crucial point, the dispute is apt to be both vituperative and unproductive. This has been the case with much of the debate in the United States over deterrence theories and policies. Although the arguments have been couched in terms of clashing general theories of international relations, most of the dispute can be accounted for in terms of disagreements about Soviet intentions. An examination of this debate will reveal the central significance of perceptions of intentions for most decision-making and will shed light on the causes and consequences of several common misperceptions.[1]

Deterrence

For our purposes we need not be concerned with the many subtleties and complexities of deterrence theory, but only with the central argument that great dangers arise if an aggressor believes that the status quo powers are weak in capability or resolve. This belief will lead the former to test its opponents, usually starting with a small and apparently unimportant issue. If the status quo powers retreat, they will not only lose the specific value at stake but, more important in the long run, will encourage the aggressor to press harder. Even if the defenders later recognize their plight and are willing to pay a higher price to prevent further retreats, they will find it increasingly difficult to convince the aggressor of their new-found resolve. The choice will then be between continuing to retreat and thereby sacrificing basic values or fighting.

To avoid this disastrous situation, the state must display the ability and willingness to wage war. It may not be able to ignore minor conflicts or to judge disputes on their merits. Issues of little intrinsic value become highly significant as indices of resolve. Thus even though President Ken-

---

[1] For an excellent treatment of the contrasting beliefs of "hard" and "soft" liners that in several respects parallels the discussion here without, and however, stressing the importance of differing perceptions of the adversary, see Paul Diesing and Glenn Snyder, *Systems, Bargains, Decisions* (Princeton: Princeton University Press, forthcoming), chapter 4.

nedy had ordered American missiles out of Turkey before the Cuban missile crisis, he would not agree to remove them as the price for obtaining Soviet cooperation. Many conflicts resemble the game of "Chicken," and, in such a game, Thomas Schelling argues, "It may be safer in the long run to hew to the center of the road than to yield six inches on successive nights, if one is really going to stop yielding before being pushed onto the shoulder. It may save both parties a collision." To take Kenneth Boulding's suggestion that we go "off on a side road" and "refuse to play the game" is to invite costly depredations.[2]

The state must often go to extremes because moderation and conciliation are apt to be taken for weakness. Although the state may be willing to agree to a settlement that involves some concessions, it may fear that, if it admits this, the other side will respond, not by matching concessions, but by redoubled efforts to extract a further retreat. (As long as the other believes that the state will retreat still further, it will refuse to accept the state's offer even if it prefers that offer to a breakdown of negotiations.) For example, shortly before ordering an attack on the French fleet in the harbor at Oran in July 1940, the British cabinet decided not to make a proposal to the French which, if accepted, would have provided a better outcome for the British than opening fire. It reasoned that this proposal "not having been included in the alternatives first offered, we should not offer it now, as this would look like weakening."[3]

The fear that concessions may be taken by the other as indicating that the state can be beaten at the game of Chicken also inhibits the state from making overtures that might end a conflict. Thus, toward the end of the Russo-Japanese War, a Japanese statesman replied to the British suggestion that his country take the diplomatic initiative of calling for mediation: "that would be little short of madness, for the War Party in Russia would at once look upon it as a sign of weakness, and be strengthened in their resolve to continue the war." More recently, President Johnson believed that the most telling argument against halting the bombing of North Vietnam was that this action might lead the North to conclude that American resolve was weakening. Even civility is dangerous because it is often misinterpreted by aggressors. Thus two days before Germany attacked Poland, Chamberlain sent her a note that he thought made clear his country's determination to fight. But the German impression, as recorded in General Halder's notes, was very different: Chamberlain's "letter conciliatory. Endeavour to find a *modus vivendi.*

---

[2] "Uncertainty, Brinkmanship, and the Game of 'Chicken,' " in Kathleen Archibald, ed., *Strategic Interaction and Conflict* (Berkeley: Institute of International Studies, University of California, 1966), p. 87; Anthony de Reuck and Julie Knight, eds., *Conflict in Society* (Boston: Little, Brown, 1966), p. 298.

[3] Quoted in Arthur Marder, *From the Dardanelles to Oran* (London: Oxford University Press, 1974), p. 253.

... Dignified tone. ... Face must be saved. England gives assurance that Poland will come to conference. ... General impression, England 'soft' on the issue of a major war."[4]

This does not mean that the state should never change its position. At times superior power must be recognized. Legitimate grievances can be identified and rectified, although care must be taken to ensure that the other side understands the basis on which the state is acting. In other cases, fair trades can be arranged. And at times concessions will have to be made to entice the other to agree. But while carrots as well as sticks are to be employed, the other's friendship cannot be won by gratuitous concessions. As Eyre Crowe put it in his famous memorandum: "there is one road which . . . will most certainly not lead to any permanent improvement of relations with any Power, least of all Germany, and which must therefore be abandoned: that is the road paved with grateful British concessions—concessions made without any conviction either of their justice or of their being set off by equivalent counter-services."[5]

The other side of this coin is that, if the distribution of power is favorable, firmness can check aggression. The combination of the high cost of a war, the low probability that the aggressor can win it, and the value the aggressor places on retaining what he has already won will lead even a minimally rational state to refrain from an expansionist attack. And it will not strike in the mistaken belief that the first side is planning aggression because it knows that the latter is defensive. Thus once it realizes that the defender cannot be bullied, the other side will try to increase its values by peaceful and cooperative means. Complementing his argument quoted above, Crowe claimed that, in the period following the successful Anglo-French display of firmness in the first Moroccan crisis, "our relations with Germany, if not exactly cordial, have at least been practically free from all symptoms of direct friction, and there is an impression that Germany will think twice before she now gives rise to any fresh disagreement. In this attitude she will be encouraged if she meets on England's part with unvarying courtesy and consideration in all matters of common concern, but also with a prompt and firm refusal to enter into any one-sided bargains or arrangements, and the most unbending determination to uphold British rights and interests in every part of the globe."[6] With

---

[4] Quoted by the British ambassador to Russia in his dispatch printed in G. P. Gooch and Harold Temperley, eds., *British Documents on the Origins of the War, 1898-1914*, vol. 4 (London: His Majesty's Stationery Office, 1929), pp. 72-73; Lyndon Johnson, *The Vantage Point* (New York: Holt, Rinehart and Winston, 1971), pp. 136, 234, 237, 250, 368, 377, 408, 413; quoted in Ian Colvin, *The Chamberlain Cabinet* (New York: Taplinger, 1971), p. 253.

[5] Eyre Crowe, "Memorandum on the Present State of British Relations with France and Germany," January 1, 1907, printed in Gooch and Temperley, eds., *British Documents*, vol. 3, p. 419; also see p. 428.

[6] *Ibid.*, pp. 419-20.

only slight changes in wording, this analysis could be applied to the changes in Soviet behavior that followed America's firm stance in the Cuban missile crisis.

In this view, the world is tightly interconnected. What happens in one interaction influences other outcomes as each state scrutinizes the others' behavior for indications of interests, strengths, and weaknesses. As the German foreign minister said during the Moroccan crisis of 1905, "If we let others trample on our feet in Morocco without a protest, we are encouraging a repetition of the act elsewhere."[7] As we will discuss below, this view often rests on the belief that the other side's aims are unlimited. Thus Robert Butow paraphrases Tojo's argument in September 1941: "The real purpose of the United States [is] the domination of the Far East. Consequently, to yield on one matter would be to encourage other demands, until there would be no end to the concessions required of Japan." The Japanese foreign minister agreed: "Relations between Japan and the United States leave no room for improvement through comity and good will. Rather, . . . such conciliatory attitudes would aggravate the situation." This position was later colorfully put by Khrushchev: "It is quite well known that if one tries to appease a bandit by first giving him one's purse, then one's coat, and so forth, he is not going to be more charitable because of this, he is not going to stop exercising his banditry. On the contrary, he will become ever more insolent."[8]

In a less extreme version, the other side is seen as without a plan but opportunistically hoping to move where there is least resistance. Lord Palmerston urged firmness in dealing with the United States over a minor dispute: "A quarrel with the United States is . . . undesirable . . . [but] in dealing with Vulgar minded Bullies, and such unfortunately the people of the United States are, nothing is gained by submission to Insult & wrong; on the contrary the submission to an Outrage only encourages the commission of another and a greater one—such People are always trying how far they can venture to go; and they generally pull up when they

[7] Quoted in E. L. Woodward, *Great Britain and the German Navy* (Oxford: Clarendon Press, 1935), p. 84. During the Seven Years' War the French foreign minister had a similar perception of Russia although the two countries were allied. See L. Jay Oliva, *Misalliance* (New York: New York University Press, 1964), p. 98. For the argument that most deterrence theorists have overestimated the degree of interdependence among conflicts because they have overstressed the importance of resolve and paid insufficient attention to each side's interest in the issue at stake, see Robert Jervis, "Bargaining and Bargaining Tactics," in J. Roland Pennock and John Chapman, eds., *Nomos*, vol. 14: *Coercion* (Chicago: Aldine Atherton, 1972), pp. 281-83.

[8] Robert Butow, *Tojo and the Coming of the War* (Princeton: Princeton University Press, 1961), p. 280; quoted in Ryuzo Sejima, *Reminiscences* (privately printed, 1972), p. 70; quoted in Nathan Leites, *Kremlin Thoughts: Yielding, Rebuffing, Provoking, Retreating*, Rand RM-3618-ISA (May 1963), pp. 12-13.

find they can go no further without encountering resistance of a formidable Character."[9]

The Spiral Model

The critics of deterrence theory provide what seems at first to be a contrasting general theory of international influence. The roots of what can be called the spiral model reach to the anarchic setting of international relations. The underlying problem lies neither in limitations on rationality imposed by human psychology nor in a flaw in human nature, but in a correct appreciation of the consequences of living in a Hobbesian state of nature. In such a world without a sovereign, each state is protected only by its own strength. Furthermore, statesmen realize that, even if others currently harbor no aggressive designs, there is nothing to guarantee that they will not later develop them.[10]

So we find that decision-makers, and especially military leaders, worry about the most implausible threats. In 1933, although the British army was willing to assume that war with France was out of the question, the air force and navy were not. Maurice Hankey, the influential secretary of the Committee of Imperial Defence, agreed with them: his subordinate noted that "Hankey's opinion is that we cannot neglect France completely—times change and policies with them; there are plenty of examples of that in the past, and the changes can be rapid." The year before, the United States staged a war game in the Pacific Ocean in which the envisaged enemy was an Anglo-Japanese coalition. In the 1920s Canada's only war plan "held that the principal external threat to the security of Canada lay in the possibility of armed invasion by the forces of the United States," and the director of military operations and intelligence conducted reconnaissance missions around Portland and Seattle. In 1929 the United States developed "Basic War Plan Red" that envisaged war with Great Britain growing out of Anglo-American commercial rivalry. And lest we are too quick to laugh, it should be noted that for years historians confidently concluded that Frederick the Great of Prussia was paranoiac to have believed that the Seven Years' War was preceded by a foreign conspiracy aimed at his state. But the opening of the most secret archives revealed that Frederick's fears were actually justified.[11]

---

[9] Quoted in Kenneth Bourne, *Britain and the Balance of Power in North America, 1815-1908* (Berkeley and Los Angeles: University of California Press, 1967), p. 182.

[10] This point is missed by Butterfield in his argument quoted on page 69 below that it is the inability of each side to "see the inside of [the other's] mind" that drives the Hobbesian spiral.

[11] Brian Bond, ed., *Chief of Staff: the Diaries of Lieutenant-General Sir Henry Pownall*, vol. 1: *1933-1940* (London: Leo Cooper, 1972), p. 21; Christopher

The lack of a sovereign in international politics permits wars to occur and makes security expensive. More far-reaching complications are created by the fact that most means of self-protection simultaneously menace others.[12] Rousseau made the basic point well:

> It is quite true that it would be much better for all men to remain always at peace. But so long as there is no security for this, everyone, having no guarantee that he can avoid war, is anxious to begin it at the moment which suits his own interest and so forestall a neighbour, who would not fail to forestall the attack in his turn at any moment favourable to himself, so that many wars, even offensive wars, are rather in the nature of unjust precautions for the protection of the assailant's own possessions than a device for seizing those of others. However salutary it may be in theory to obey the dictates of public spirit, it is certain that, politically and even morally, those dictates are liable to prove fatal to the man who persists in observing them with all the world when no one thinks of observing them towards him.[13]

Germany

In extreme cases, states that seek security may believe that the best, if not the only, route to that goal is to attack and expand. Thus the tsars believed that "that which stops growing begins to rot," the Japanese decision-makers before World War II concluded that the alternative to increasing their dominance in Asia was to sacrifice their "very existence," and some scholars have argued that German expansionism before World War I was rooted in a desire to cope with the insecurity produced by being surrounded by powerful neighbors.[14] After World War I France held a somewhat milder version of this belief. Although she knew that the war had left her the strongest state on the Continent, she felt that she had to increase her power still further to provide protection against Germany,

---

Thorne, *The Limits of Foreign Policy* (New York: Putnam, 1973), p. 75 (also see p. 73); James Eayrs, *In Defence of Canada*, vol. 1: *From the Great War to the Great Depression* (Toronto: University of Toronto Press, 1965), pp. 70-78 (the civilians had no knowledge of these plans and activities); "1929 File Reveals War Plan on Britain," *Los Angeles Times*, December 19, 1975; Herbert Butterfield, *George III and the Historians* (revised ed., New York: Macmillan Co., 1969), pp. 27-28.

[12] For this reason, whether anarchy produces the unfortunate effects we are discussing is strongly influenced by two variables: the extent to which the weapons and strategies that are useful for defending oneself are also useful for threatening and attacking others, and the relative advantage of the offense over the defense. The effects of these variables will be explored in a later paper.

[13] *A Lasting Peace through the Federation of Europe*, translated by C. E. Vaughan (London: Constable, 1917), pp. 78-79.

[14] Quoted in Adam Ulam, *Expansion and Coexistence* (New York: Praeger, 1968), p. 5; quoted in Butow, *Tojo and the Coming of the War*, p. 203; Klaus Epstein, "Gerhard Ritter and the First World War," in H. W. Koch, ed., *The Origins of the First World War* (London: Macmillan & Co., 1972), p. 290.

whose recovery from wartime destruction might some day lead her to try to reverse the verdict of 1918. This view is especially likely to develop if the state believes that others have also concluded that both the desire for protection and the desire for increased values point to the same policy of expansionism.

The drive for security will also produce aggressive actions if the state either requires a very high sense of security or feels menaced by the very presence of other strong states. Thus Leites argues that "the Politburo . . . believes that its very life . . . remains acutely threatened as long as major enemies exist. Their utter defeat is a sheer necessity of survival." This view can be rooted in experience as well as ideology. In May 1944 Kennan wrote: "Behind Russia's stubborn expansion lies only the age-old sense of insecurity of a sedentary people reared on an exposed plain in the neighborhood of fierce nomadic peoples."[15]

Even in less extreme situations, arms procured to defend can usually be used to attack. Economic and political preparedness designed to hold what one has is apt to create the potential for taking territory from others. What one state regards as insurance, the adversary will see as encirclement. This is especially true of the great powers. Any state that has interests throughout the world cannot avoid possessing the power to menace others. For example, as Admiral Mahan noted before World War I, if Britain was to have a navy sufficient to safeguard her trading routes, she inevitably would also have the ability to cut Germany off from the sea.[16] Thus even in the absence of any specific conflicts of interest between Britain and Germany, the former's security required that the latter be denied a significant aspect of great power status.

When states seek the ability to defend themselves, they get too much and too little—too much because they gain the ability to carry out aggression; too little because others, being menaced, will increase their own arms and so reduce the first state's security. Unless the requirements for offense and defense differ in kind or amount, a status quo power will desire a military posture that resembles that of an aggressor. For this reason others cannot infer from its military forces and preparations whether the state is aggressive. States therefore tend to assume the worst. The

---

[15] Nathan Leites, *A Study of Bolshevism* (Glencoe, Ill.: Free Press, 1953), p. 31; quoted in Arthur Schlesinger, Jr., "The Origins of the Cold War," *Foreign Affairs* 46 (October 1967), 30. As Kennan later put it: "Many people in the Western governments came to hate the Soviet leaders for what they *did*. The Communists on the other hand, hated the Western governments for what they *were*, regardless of what they did." *Russia and the West Under Lenin and Stalin* (New York: Mentor, 1962), p. 181. For a general discussion of the impact of the demand for high security, see Arnold Wolfers, *Discord and Collaboration* (Baltimore: Johns Hopkins Press, 1962), pp. 92, 150-51.

[16] Cited in Bernard Brodie, *War and Politics* (New York: Macmillan Co., 1973), p. 345.

other's intentions must be considered to be co-extensive with his capabilities. What he can do to harm the state, he will do (or will do if he gets *en bloc of Hobbesian state* the chance). So to be safe, the state should buy as many weapons as it can afford.[17] *Prisoner's Dilemma*

But since both sides obey the same imperatives, attempts to increase one's security by standing firm and accumulating more arms will be self-defeating. Earlier we quoted Palmerston's belief that, when dealing with "Vulgar minded Bullies" like the Americans, "the submission to an Outrage only encourages the commission of another and a greater one." In a dispute a few years earlier, James Polk expressed the same sentiment, arguing that "if Congress faultered [sic] or hesitated in their course, John Bull would immediately become arrogant and more grasping in his demands; & that such had been the history of the Brittish [sic] Nation in all their contests with other Powers for the last two hundred years."[18] These symmetrical beliefs produce incompatible policies with results that are in neither side's interest.

With hindsight, decision-makers may recognize the undesired effects of their actions. Lord Grey, the British foreign secretary before World War I, saw this as he looked back over the diplomacy of this period:

> The increase of armaments, that is intended in each nation to produce consciousness of strength, and a sense of security, does not produce these effects. On the contrary, it produces a consciousness of the strength of other nations and a sense of fear. Fear begets suspicion and distrust and evil imaginings of all sorts, till each Government feels it would be criminal and a betrayal of its own country not to take every precaution, while every Government regards every precaution of every other Government as evidence of hostile intent.[19]

[17] It is reported that the dispute between First Lord of the Admiralty Winston Churchill and Chancellor of the Exchequer David Lloyd George over the 1914 naval budget was resolved when the latter told the former: "Oddly enough, my wife spoke to me last night about this Dreadnought business. She said, 'You know, my dear, I never interfere in politics; but they say you are having an argument with that nice Mr. Churchill about building Dreadnoughts. Of course I don't understand these things, but I should have thought it would be better to have too many rather than too few.' So I have decided to let you build them." Randolph Churchill, *Winston S. Churchill*, vol. 2, *The Young Statesman, 1901-1914* (London: Heinemann, 1967), p. 681.

Of course weapons and security are not free goods and nations have to balance them against other values. See Wolfers, *Discord and Collaboration*, pp. 147-66. This is also recognized by theorists who have developed mathematical models of arms races.

[18] Quoted in Bourne, *Britain and the Balance of Power in North America*, p. 182; quoted in Charles McCoy, *Polk and the Presidency* (Austin: University of Texas Press, 1960), p. 91.

[19] Edward Grey, *Twenty-five Years*, vol. 1 (London: Hodder and Staughton, 1925), p. 92. This was not Grey's position at the time. He did not believe "that one nation can put a stop to the rivalry by dropping out of the race. . . . On the

The German chancellor's retrospective view was similar: "Ignoring the fact that in the existing power constellation any major shift among the Great Powers of Europe was bound to involve the whole world, those Powers had their eyes fixed only on the growth of their own power." At the time, states may warn others about the dangerous implications of their security policies. Thus Ramsay MacDonald told the Japanese ambassador that "Japan would have to be very careful that in seeking her own security she did not upset the sense of security of other nations." But this perspective rarely enlightens the state's own posture.[20]

These unintended and undesired consequences of actions meant to be defensive constitute the "security dilemma" that Herbert Butterfield sees as that "absolute predicament" that "lies in the very geometry of human conflict. . . . [H]ere is the basic pattern for all narratives of human conflict, whatever other patterns may be superimposed upon it later." From this perspective, the central theme of international relations is not evil but tragedy. States often share a common interest, but the structure of the situation prevents them from bringing about the mutually desired situation. This view contrasts with the school of realism represented by Hans Morgenthau and Reinhold Niebuhr, which sees the drive for power as a product of man's instinctive will to dominate others. As John Herz puts it, "It is a mistake to draw from the universal phenomenon of competition for power the conclusion that there is actually such a thing as an innate 'power instinct.' Basically it is the mere instinct of self-preservation which, in the vicious circle [of the security dilemma], leads to competition for ever more power."[21]

Arms races are only the most obvious manifestation of this spiral. The competition for colonies at the end of the nineteenth century was fueled by the security dilemma. Even if all states preferred the status quo to a division of the unclaimed areas, each also preferred expansion to running the risk of being excluded. The desire for security may also lead states to weaken potential rivals, a move that can create the menace it was designed to ward off. For example, because French statesmen feared what they thought to be the inevitable German attempt to regain the position she lost in World War I, they concluded that Germany had to be

---

contrary, it might very well be that if one nation dropped out of the competition it might momentarily give a spurt in expenditure in some other." Quoted in A. J. Anthony Morris, *Radicalism Against War, 1906-1914* (London: Longmans, 1972), p. 228.

[20] Quoted in Egmont Zechlin, "Cabinet versus Economic Warfare in Germany," in Koch, ed., *The Origins of the First World War*, p. 167; quoted in Gerald Wheeler, *Prelude to Pearl Harbor* (Columbia, Mo.: University of Missouri Press, 1963), p. 167. For examples of self-restraint, see below, pp. 88-89.

[21] Herbert Butterfield, *History and Human Relations* (London: Collins, 1951), pp. 19-20; Wolfers, *Discord and Collaboration*, p. 84; John Herz, *Political Realism and Political Idealism* (Chicago: University of Chicago Press, 1959), p. 4.

kept weak. The effect of such an unyielding policy, however, was to make the Germans less willing to accept their new position and therefore to decrease France's long-run security.[22] Finally, the security dilemma can not only create conflicts and tensions but also provide the dynamics triggering war. If technology and strategy are such that each side believes that the state that strikes first will have a decisive advantage, even a state that is fully satisfied with the status quo may start a war out of fear that the alternative to doing so is not peace, but an attack by its adversary. And, of course, if each side knows that the other side is aware of the advantages of striking first, even mild crises are likely to end in war. This was one of the immediate causes of World War I, and contemporary military experts have devoted much thought and money to avoiding the recurrence of such destabilizing incentives.

If much of deterrence theory can be seen in terms of the game of Chicken, the spiral theorists are more impressed with the relevance of the Prisoner's Dilemma. Although they realize that the current situation is not exactly like the Prisoner's Dilemma because of the unacceptable costs of war, they believe that the central characteristic of current world politics is that, if each state pursues its narrow self-interest with a narrow conception of rationality, all states will be worse off than they would be if they cooperated. Not only would cooperation lead to a higher level of total benefits—and this is of no concern to a self-interested actor—but it would lead to each individual actor's being better off than he would be if the relations were more conflictful. States are then seen as interdependent in a different way than is stressed by the theorists of deterrence; either they cooperate with each other, in which case they all make significant gains, or they enter into a conflict and all suffer losses. A second point highlighted by the Prisoner's Dilemma is that cooperative arrangements are not likely to be reached through coercion. Threats and an adversary posture are likely to lead to counteractions with the ultimate result that both sides will be worse off than they were before. As we will discuss below, states must employ and develop ingenuity, trust, and institutions if they are to develop their common interests without undue risks to their security.

PSYCHOLOGICAL DYNAMICS

The argument sketched so far rests on the implications of anarchy, not on the limitations on rationality imposed by the way people reach decisions in a complex world. Lewis Richardson's path-breaking treatment of arms races describes "what people would do if they did not stop to

[22] Similar dynamics fueled the war between France and the Second Coalition before Napoleon's seizure of power. See Steven Ross, *European Diplomatic History, 1789-1815* (Garden City, N.Y.: Doubleday, 1969), p. 194.

think." Richardson argues that this is not an unrealistic perspective. The common analogy between international politics and chess is misleading because "the acts of a leader are in part controlled by the great instinctive and traditional tendencies which are formulated in my description. It is somewhat as if the chessmen were connected by horizontal springs to heavy weights beyond the chessboard."[23]

Contemporary spiral theorists argue that psychological pressures explain why arms and tensions cycles proceed as if people were not thinking. Once a person develops an image of the other—especially a hostile image of the other[24]—ambiguous and even discrepant information will be assimilated to that image. As we will discuss in greater detail in the next chapter, people perceive what they expect to be present. If they think that a state is hostile, behavior that others might see as neutral or friendly will be ignored, distorted, or seen as attempted duplicity. This cognitive rigidity reinforces the consequences of international anarchy.

Although we noted earlier that it is usually hard to draw inferences about a state's intentions from its military posture, decision-makers in fact often draw such inferences when they are unwarranted. They frequently assume, partly for reasons to be discussed shortly, that the arms of others indicate aggressive intentions. So an increase in the other's military forces makes the state doubly insecure—first, because the other has an increased capability to do harm, and, second, because this behavior is taken to show that the other is not only a potential threat but is actively contemplating hostile actions.

But the state does not apply this reasoning to its own behavior. A peaceful state knows that it will use its arms only to protect itself, not to harm others. It further assumes that others are fully aware of this. As John Foster Dulles put it: "Khrushchev does not need to be convinced of our good intentions. He knows we are not aggressors and do not threaten the security of the Soviet Union." Similarly, in arguing that "England seeks no quarrels, and will never give Germany cause for legitimate offence," Crowe assumed not only that Britain was benevolent but that this was readily apparent to others. To take an earlier case, skirmishing between France and England in North America developed into the Seven Years' War partly because each side incorrectly thought the other knew

[23] Lewis Richardson, *Statistics of Deadly Quarrels* (Pittsburgh: Boxwood Press, Chicago: Quadrangle, 1960), p. xxiv; Lewis Richardson, *Arms and Insecurity* (Pittsburgh: Boxwood Press, Chicago: Quadrangle, 1960), p. 227.

[24] Any number of incidents and conflicts can establish such an image of the other as hostile. The theory does not discuss what initially sets the spiral in motion. Thus Kenneth Terhune and Joseph Firestone hypothesize that "hostility and mistrust . . . are important not as initial causes of conflict, but as contributing factors in the feedback cycle by which conflict escalates." "Global War, Limited War, and Peace: Hypotheses From Three Experimental Worlds," *International Studies Quarterly* 4 (June 1970), 218.

that its aims were sharply limited.[25] Because the state believes that its adversary understands that the state is arming because it sees the adversary as aggressive, the states does not think that strengthening its arms can be harmful. If the other is aggressive, it will be disappointed because the state's strengthened position means that it is less vulnerable. Provided that the state is already fairly strong, however, there is no danger that the other will be provoked into attacking. If the other is not aggressive, it will not react to the state's effort to protect itself. This means that the state need not exercise restraint in policies designed to increase its security. To procure weapons in excess of the minimum required for defense may be wasteful, but will not cause unwarranted alarm by convincing the other that the state is planning aggression.

In fact, others are not so easily reassured. As Lord Grey realized—after he was out of power:

> The distinction between preparations made with the intention of going to war and precautions against attack is a true distinction, clear and definite in the minds of those who build up armaments. But it is a distinction that is not obvious or certain to others. . . . Each Government, therefore, while resenting any suggestion that its own measures are anything more than for defense, regards similar measures of another Government as preparation to attack.

Herbert Butterfield catches the way these beliefs drive the spiral of arms and hostility:

> It is the peculiar characteristic of the . . . Hobbesian fear . . . that you yourself may vividly feel the terrible fear that you have of the other party, but you cannot enter into the other man's counter-fear, or even understand why he should be particularly nervous. For you know that you yourself mean him no harm, and that you want nothing from him save guarantees for your own safety; and it is never possible for you to realize or remember properly that since he cannot see the inside of your mind, he can never have the same assurance of your intentions that you have. As this operates on both sides the Chinese puzzle is complete in all its interlockings and neither party can see the nature of the predicament he is in, for each only imagines that the other party is being hostile and unreasonable.[26]

Because statesmen believe that others will interpret their behavior as they intend it and will share their view of their own state's policy, they

---

[25] Quoted in Richard Nixon, *Six Crises* (Garden City, N.Y.: Doubleday, 1962), p. 62; Crowe, "Memorandum," p. 407; Patrice Higonnet, "The Origins of the Seven Years' War," *Journal of Modern History* 40 (March 1968), 57-90.

[26] Grey, *Twenty-five Years*, p. 91; Butterfield, *History and Human Relations*, pp. 19-20.

are led astray in two reinforcing ways. First, their understanding of the impact of their own state's policy is often inadequate—i.e. differs from the views of disinterested observers—and, second, they fail to realize that other states' perceptions are also skewed. Although actors are aware of the difficulty of making their threats and warnings credible, they rarely believe that others will misinterpret behavior that is meant to be more compatible with the other's interests. Because we cannot easily establish an objective analysis of the state's policy, these two effects are difficult to disentangle. But for many purposes this does not matter because both pressures push in the same direction and increase the differences between the way the state views its behavior and the perceptions of others.

The degree to which a state can fail to see that its own policy is harming others is illustrated by the note that the British foreign secretary sent to the Soviet government in March 1918 trying to persuade it to welcome a Japanese army that would fight the Germans: "The British Government have clearly and constantly repeated that they have no wish to take any part in Russia's domestic affairs, but that the prosecution of the war is the only point with which they are concerned." When reading Bruce Lockhart's reply that the Bolsheviks did not accept this view, Balfour noted in the margin of the dispatch: "I have constantly impressed on Mr. Lockhart that it is *not* our desire to interfere in Russian affairs. He appears to be very unsuccessful in conveying this view to the Bolshevik Government." The start of World War I witnessed a manifestation of the same phenomenon when the tsar ordered mobilization of the Baltic fleet without any consideration of the threat this would pose even to a Germany that wanted to remain at peace.[27]

Similarly, when at the start of the Korean War Truman and his advisers decided to "neutralize" Formosa, they had little idea that by doing so they were depriving Communist China of a central national value. And later in the war the United States failed to realize the degree to which its advance to the Yalu objectively menaced Chinese security. Looking back on this incident, Dean Acheson argued that "no possible shred of evidence could have existed in the minds of the Chinese Communist authorities about the [peaceful] intentions of the forces of the United Nations." That China probably overestimated the danger should not obscure the American failure to realize that conquering North Korea would have given it a greater ability to threaten China. Because Ameri-

[27] Quoted in John Wheeler-Bennett, *Brest-Litovsk* (New York: Norton, 1971), pp. 295-96; Ole Holsti, *Crisis Escalation War* (Montreal and London: McGill-Queen's University Press, 1972), p. 132. During the Vietnam war, Walt Rostow tried to stop the State Department from circulating memoranda that attempted to show that North Vietnam probably saw the United States as more aggressive than the United States thought it was. (David Halberstam, *The Best and the Brightest* [Greenwich, Conn.: Fawcett, 1973], p. 775.)

can leaders thought they would never utilize this resource, they failed to understand that their actions in fact decreased China's ability to protect herself. Four years later, President Eisenhower similarly failed to see the extent to which American signals of readiness to "unleash" Chiang Kai-shek were arousing Communist Chinese insecurity.[28]

The same inability to see the implications of its specific actions limits the state's appreciation of the degree to which its position and general power make it a potential menace. As Klaus Epstein points out in describing the background to World War I, "Wilhelmine Germany—because of its size, population, geographical location, economic dynamism, cocky militarism, and autocracy under a neurotic Kaiser—was feared by all other Powers as a threat to the European equilibrium; this was an objective fact which Germans should have recognized."[29] Indeed even had Germany changed her behavior, she still would have been the object of constant suspicion and apprehension by virtue of being the strongest power in Europe. And before we attribute this insensitivity to the German national character, we should note that United States statesmen in the postwar era have displayed a similar inability to see that their country's huge power, even if used for others' good, represents a standing threat to much of the rest of the world. Instead the United States, like most other nations, has believed that others will see that the desire for security underlies its actions.

The psychological dynamics do not, however, stop here. If the state believes that others know that it is not a threat, it will conclude that they will arm or pursue hostile policies only if they are aggressive. For if they sought only security they would welcome, or at least not object to, the state's policy. Thus an American senator who advocated intervening in Russia in the summer of 1918 declared that if the Russians resisted this move it would prove that "Russia is already Germanized." This inference structure is revealed in an exchange about NATO between Tom Connally, the chairman of the Senate Foreign Relations Committee, and Secretary of State Acheson:

> Now, Mr. Secretary, you brought out rather clearly . . . that this treaty is not aimed at any nation particularly. It is aimed only at any nation or any country that contemplates or undertakes armed aggression against the members of the signatory powers. Is that true?

[28] John Spanier, *The Truman-MacArthur Controversy and the Korean War* (New York: Norton, 1965), p. 97; Alexander George and Richard Smoke, *Deterrence in American Foreign Policy* (New York: Columbia University Press, 1974), p. 279. Similarly, it is often argued that the American protests against the Soviet takeover of East Europe threatened the Russians more than the United States thought or intended. But for a contrary view, see Raymond Aron, *The Imperial Republic* (Cambridge, Mass.: Winthrop, 1974), pp. 20, 25-35.

[29] "Gerhard Ritter and the First World War," p. 293.

Secretary Acheson. That is correct, Senator Connally. It is not aimed at any country; it is aimed solely at armed aggression.

The Chairman. In other words, unless a nation other than the signatories contemplates, meditates or makes plans looking toward, aggression or armed attack on another nation, it has no cause to fear this treaty.

Secretary Acheson. That is correct, Senator Connally, and it seems to me that any nation which claims that this treaty is directed against it should be reminded of the Biblical admonition that "The guilty flee when no man pursueth."

The Chairman. That is a very apt illustration.

What I had in mind was, when a State or Nation passes a criminal act, for instance, against burglary, nobody but those who are burglars or getting ready to be burglars need have any fear of the Burglary Act. Is that not true?

Secretary Acheson. Very true.

The Chairman. And so it is with one who might meditate and get ready and arm himself to commit a murder. If he is not going to indulge in that kind of enterprise, the law on murder would not have any effect on him, would it?

Secretary Acheson. The only effect it would have would be for his protection, perhaps, by deterring someone else. He wouldn't worry about the imposition of the penalties on himself, but he might feel that the statute added to his protection.[30]

To return to a case discussed earlier, the United States thought that China's intervention in Korea showed that she was aggressive, not that she had legitimate concerns about her security.

When the state believes that the other knows that it is not threatening the other's legitimate interests, disputes are likely to produce antagonism out of all proportion to the intrinsic importance of the issue at stake. Because the state does not think that there is any obvious reason why the other should oppose it, it will draw inferences of unprovoked hostility from even minor conflicts. Thus the belief that the Open Door policy was in China's interest as well as in America's made the United States react strongly to a Chinese regime that disagreed. If, on the other hand, each side recognizes that its policies threaten some of the other's values, it will not interpret the other's reaction as indicating aggressive intent or total hostility and so will be better able to keep their conflict limited.

[30] Quoted in Peter Filene, *Americans and the Soviet Experiment, 1917-1933* (Cambridge, Mass.: Harvard University Press, 1967), p. 43; Senate Committee on Foreign Relations, *Hearings, North Atlantic Treaty*, 81st Congress, 1st Session, p. 17. Inexperienced policemen patrolling the streets similarly fail to understand how innocent people react with alarm when they are stopped. See Jonathan Rubinstein, *City Police* (New York: Farrar, Straus and Giroux, 1973), p. 233.

The perceptions and reactions of the other side are apt to deepen the misunderstanding and the conflict. For the other, like the state, will assume that its adversary knows that it is not a threat. So, like the state, it will do more than increase its arms—it will regard the state's explanation of its behavior as making no sense and will see the state as dangerous and hostile. When the Soviets consolidated their hold over Czechoslovakia in 1948, they knew this harmed Western values and expected some reaction. But the formation of NATO and the explanation given for this move were very alarming. Since the Russians assumed that the United States saw the situation the same way they did, the only conclusion they could draw was that the United States was even more dangerous than they had thought. As George Kennan put the Soviet analysis in a cable to Washington:

> It seemed implausible to the Soviet leaders, knowing as they did the nature of their own approach to the military problem, and assuming that the Western powers must have known it too, that defensive considerations alone could have impelled the Western governments to give the relative emphasis they actually gave to a program irrelevant in many respects to the outcome of the political struggle in Western Europe (on which Moscow was staking everything) and only partially justified, as Moscow saw it, as a response to actual Soviet intentions. . . . The Kremlin leaders were attempting in every possible way to weaken and destroy the structure of the non-Communist world. In the course of this endeavor they were up to many things which gave plenty of cause for complaint on the part of Western statesmen. They would not have been surprised if these things had been made the touchstone of Western reaction. But why, they might ask, were they being accused precisely of the one thing they had *not* done, which was to plan, as yet, to conduct an overt and unprovoked invasion of Western Europe? Why was the imputation to them of this intention being put forward as the rationale for Western rearmament? Did this not imply some ulterior purpose . . . ?[31]

The Russians may have been even more alarmed if, as Nathan Leites has argued, they thought that we behaved according to the sensible proverb of "whoever says A, says Z" and had knowingly assigned Czechoslovakia to the Russian sphere of influence during the wartime negotiations. "How could, they must ask themselves, the elevation of an already dominant Czechoslovak Communist Party to full power in 1948 change the policies of Washington which had agreed to the presence of the Soviet Army in Czechoslovakia in 1945? Washington, after all, could

[31] *Memoirs*, vol. 2: *1950-1963* (Boston: Little, Brown, 1972), pp. 335-36. Kennan also stresses the ideologically rooted Soviet predispositions to see Western aggressiveness.

hardly imagine that Moscow would indefinitely tolerate the presence of enemies . . . within its domain!" The American protests over the take-over must then be hypocrisy, and the claim that this event was alarming and called for Western rearmament could only be a cover for plans of aggression.[32]

This perspective leads to speculation about possible Soviet perceptions of the American alert at the end of the 1973 Arab-Israeli war. The alert was justified by the claim that the Russians were threatening to send troops to Egypt. If this was a real danger, the American response may have been appropriate. But if Russia was not seriously contemplating this measure, an unfortunate misunderstanding would have been produced.[33] For in this case Russia probably would have assumed that the United States knew that there was no danger. Why, then, she would ask herself, did the United States mobilize? Either because she had militant plans of her own or because she wanted to humiliate Russia by later claiming that her vigorous actions had made Russia retreat. This inference could be avoided only if Russia realized that the United States had overestimated the challenge she was posing.

With a disinterested perspective and access to documents from both sides, historians have seen a number of cases that fit the spiral model. Sometimes contemporary third parties also detect them. In 1904 President Roosevelt noted that the kaiser "sincerely believes that the English are planning to attack him and smash his fleet, and perhaps join with France in a war to the death against him. As a matter of fact, the English harbour no such intentions, but are themselves in a condition of panic terror lest the Kaiser secretly intend to form an alliance against them with France or Russia, or both, to destroy their fleet and blot out the British Empire from the map! It is as funny a case as I have ever seen of mutual distrust and fear bringing two peoples to the verge of war." The humor was lost on the powers concerned. Each side's claim that it was peaceful and afraid of the other only deepened the dilemma. Since each knew that there were no grounds for the other's supposed anxiety and believed that the other had enough of a grasp on reality to see this, each sought a darker meaning for the assertion. Thus the British foreign secretary wrote to his ambassador in Berlin: "They cannot seriously believe that we are meditating a coup against them. Are they perchance meditating one against us and are they seeking to justify it in advance?" Similarly, a few years earlier when Salisbury heard that the kaiser

[32] Leites, *A Study of Bolshevism*, pp. 42, 34.

[33] Ray Cline, who was Director of Intelligence and Research in the State Department when these events occurred, argues that the evidence available to him did not indicate that the Soviets were going to intervene. "Policy Without Intelligence," *Foreign Policy* 17 (Winter 1974-75), 132-33.

thought that he was the kaiser's enemy, he wrote: "So groundless is the charge that I cannot help fearing that it indicates a consciousness on the part of His Majesty that he cherishes some design which is bound to make me his enemy—and that he looks forward to the satisfaction of saying . . . 'I told you so.' "[34]

The explication of these psychological dynamics adds to our understanding of international conflict, but incurs a cost. The benefit is in seeing how the basic security dilemma becomes overlaid by reinforcing misunderstandings as each side comes to believe that not only is the other a potential menace, as it must be in a setting of anarchy, but that the other's behavior has shown that it is an active enemy. The inability to recognize that one's own actions could be seen as menacing and the concomitant belief that the other's hostility can only be explained by its aggressiveness help explain how conflicts can easily expand beyond that which an analysis of the objective situation would indicate is necessary. But the cost of these insights is the slighting of the role of the system in inducing conflict and a tendency to assume that the desire for security, rather than expansion, is the prime goal of most states. As we will discuss at greater length below, spiral theorists, like earlier students of prejudice, stereotypes, and intergoup relations, have given a psychological explanation for perceptions of threat without adequate discussion of whether these perceptions are warranted.[35]

Both the advantages and pitfalls of this elaboration of the security dilemma are revealed in Kenneth Boulding's distinction between

> two very different kinds of incompatibility. . . . The first might be called "real" incompatibility, where we have two images of the future in which realization of one would prevent the realization of the other.
> . . . The other form of incompatibility might be called "illusory" incompatibility, in which there exists a condition of compatibility which

[34] Quoted in R. B. Mowat, *The Diplomatic Relations of Great Britain and the United States* (London: Edward Arnold and Co., 1925), p. 296; quoted in Eugene Anderson, *The First Moroccan Crisis, 1904-1906* (Hamden, Conn.: Archon Books, 1966), p. 115; quoted in J.A.S. Grenville, *Lord Salisbury and Foreign Policy* (London: Athlone, 1964), p. 277 (another example is p. 260).

[35] See, for example, John Burton, *Controlled Communication* (New York: Free Press, 1970) and Leonard Doob, ed., *Resolving Conflict in Africa* (New Haven: Yale University Press, 1970). A parallel criticism of many theories of race relations is made in Jessie Bernard, "The Conceptualization of Inter-Group Relations," *Social Forces* 29 (March 1951), p. 244.

Scholars sometimes talk of "paranoia" or "misunderstandings" without adequately exploring the vital question of whether the actors' perceptions are accurate. For a discussion of this question in the context of the origins of World War I, see Robert Jervis, "Reply to Professor North," *International Studies Quarterly* 12 (June 1968), 225-27. For a similar argument about the origins of the American Civil War see the letters by David Brion Davis and William Freehling, *New York Review of Books* 17 (December 2, 1971).

would satisfy the "real" interests of the two parties but in which the dynamics of the situation or illusions of the parties create a situation of perverse dynamics and misunderstandings, with increasing hostility simply as a result of the reactions of the parties to each other, not as a result of any basic differences of interest.[36]

This distinction can be very useful, and we shall employ it in much of this chapter. But it takes attention away from the vital kind of system-induced incompatibility that cannot be easily classified as either real or illusory. If both sides primarily desire security, then the two images of the future do not clash, and any incompatibility must, according to one reading of the definition, be illusory. But the heart of the security dilemma argument is that an increase in one state's security can make others less secure not because of misperception or imagined hostility, but because of the anarchic context of international relations.

Under some circumstances, several states can simultaneously increase their security. But often this is not the case. For a variety of reasons, many of which have been discussed earlier, nations' security requirements can clash. While an understanding of the security dilemma and psychological dynamics will dampen some arms-hostility spirals, it will not change the fact that some policies aimed at security will threaten others. To call the incompatibility that results from such policies "illusory" is to misunderstand the nature of the problem and to encourage the illusion that if the states only saw themselves and others more objectively they could attain their common interest.[37]

SELF-FULFILLING PROPHECIES AND PROBLEMS WITH INCREMENTALISM

As this analysis suggests, the spiral model stresses the prevalence of self-fulfilling prophecies, defined by Merton as "a *false* definition of the situa-

[36] Kenneth Boulding, "National Images and International Systems," *Journal of Conflict Resolution* 3 (June 1959), 130. But how do we determine the "real" interests of the parties? A more detailed treatment of the concept of illusory incompatibility would draw distinctions on the basis of what beliefs and values would have to change to bring about agreement. The more that the necessary changes are in the lower parts of the actors' means-ends chains, the more we can consider the incompatibility to be illusory.

[37] Another problem with Boulding's distinction arises in those cases in which actors' "bargaining ranges" overlap—i.e. there are solutions that both sides prefer to a breakdown of negotiations—and yet they fail to reach agreement because each is trying to exact as many concessions as possible. Potential settlements exist that are minimally satisfactory to both parties, but the incompatibility is still real since within the bargaining range one side's gains are the other's losses. To say that the failure to reach agreement shows the existence of illusory incompatibility is misleading because the threat of not agreeing is one of each side's most powerful bargaining weapons. The breakdown of negotiations may neither produce nor be the product of a spiral of hostility.

tion which makes the originally false conception come true." As examples, he cites bank runs and racial prejudice. But there are differences between these situations that have implications for the strategies one could use to cope with them. While the bank would become solvent if the people believed it was and therefore stopped making panic withdrawals, the mere belief that all men are equal would not erase the characteristics of the minority group that are both caused by, and used to justify, discrimination.[38]

This distinction reminds us that for our purposes the crucial question is the degree to which a state's actions that are based on an initially false image have transformed the other state's intentions. If the prophecy of hostility is thoroughly self-fulfilling, the belief that there is a high degree of real conflict will create a conflict that is no longer illusory. Overtures that earlier would have decreased tensions and cleared up misunderstandings will now be taken as signs of weakness. If the prophecy that Russia is like Nazi Germany has been truly self-fulfilling, a policy appropriate for dealing with an aggressor would be called for.

Even if a prophecy can be so self-fulfilling that the origins of the conflict are irrelevant to its treatment, the spiral perspective is valuable for revealing a major drawback with policy-making by incrementalism. Charles Lindblom and James March and Herbert Simon have shown that, because most problems are too complex to be amenable to total or synoptic rationality, decision-makers must start from the existing policy and take small, remedial steps to cope with problems as they arise. These alterations may not only cure specific ills but also provide valuable information about the environment.[39]

The spiral model reveals two difficulties with this approach. First, as we have seen, the state's policy not only probes the environment but can alter it. Second, as long as the basic beliefs about the other side's intentions are wrong, policy will lead down a blind alley. Not only are minor changes insufficient but the information produced by them will be of slight value and will exact a high price.[40] Marginal adjustments in a con-

---

[38] Robert Merton, *Social Theory and Social Structure* (revised ed., Glencoe, Ill.: Free Press, 1957), p. 423.

[39] Charles Lindblom, "The Science of Muddling Through," *Public Administrative Review* 19 (Spring 1959), 74-88; David Braybrooke and Charles Lindblom, *A Strategy of Decision* (New York: Free Press, 1963); Charles Lindblom, *The Intelligence of Democracy* (New York: Free Press, 1965); Herbert Simon, *Administrative Behavior* (2nd ed., New York: Free Press, 1965); James March and Herbert Simon, *Organizations* (New York: Wiley, 1958).

[40] This case presents even more of a problem than do those noted by Hirschman and Lindblom in which "we cannot afford to do our learning about the imperfections and imbalances of a system through the failures, irritations, and discomforts that are the natural concomitants and signals of the imbalance. Such situations present us with a well-nigh insoluble task, similar to the one which would face a child who had to learn to walk without being permitted to fall."

ciliatory policy toward a state that is incorrectly believed to support the status quo will eventually provide self-correcting information, but only after a number of values have been sacrificed. When the error is in treating a status quo power as though it were aggressive, the necessary information may never appear even if the prophecy is not completely self-fulfilling. Unless the other side goes to unusual lengths to demonstrate its peacefulness, the state, in good incrementalist fashion, is apt to tinker with its policy only within the accepted assumptions. For the decision-maker to use the information derived from the effects of his behavior in order to determine what alterations are called for, he will have to discern exactly what the other country is doing, estimate whether and how it is responding to him rather than following internal imperatives, and use the immediate impact of his policy to estimate its long-term effects. Under these conditions, the feedback will be highly ambiguous and, for reasons given in Chapters 4 and 7, will be seen as calling for only minimum changes in the current policy.

Self-Defeating Power

When we compare deterrence and spiral theories, what is most striking is that they give opposite answers to the central question of the effect of negative sanctions. Deterrence theory, while elaborating a sophisticated logic of bargaining that often runs counter to common sense, generally endorses the conventional view that power must be met by power. The only way to contain aggression and cope with hostility is to build up and intelligently manipulate sanctions, threats, and force. The greater the aggressor's relative strength, the more valuable the concessions that will have to be made to him. Even Neville Chamberlain recognized this. In defending the Munich agreement, he told the cabinet: "I hope . . . that my colleagues will not think that I am making any attempts to disguise the fact that, if we now possessed a superior force to Germany, we should probably be considering these proposals in a very different spirit. But we must look facts in the face." In the current context this sentiment was expressed by Senator Henry Jackson when he argued that the increases in Soviet nuclear force would lead to political outcomes unfavorable to the United States:

> You see, this is what really disturbs me. The Russians have taken enormous risks when they have been in a totally inferior position; they took Czechoslovakia when they didn't even have a nuclear bomb; they tried to move into Cuba with missiles when they were at a 7 to 1 stra-

Albert Hirschman and Charles Lindblom, "Economic Development, Research and Development, Policy Making: Some Converging Views," in Bruce Russett, ed., *Economic Theories of International Politics* (Chicago: Markham, 1968), p. 482.

tegic disadvantage, I think it was, 5 or 7 to 1, but it is way up there, was it not, in October of 1962? Look at the risks they took. I wonder what kind of risk they are going to take in the mid-1970's and late 1970's and the 1980's when they have a situation that is totally reversed with this enormous power and a more confident Soviet Union, in my judgment, that will be a more dangerous Soviet Union?[41]

Since, for a variety of reasons, it is easier to defend than to alter the status quo,[42] as long as the aggressor does not possess a preponderance of power even hasty and biased calculations should convince him not to press his challenges to the point of war. Of course, as we mentioned above, deterrence does not prevent all changes. Because the other's legitimate interests should be respected and reasonable compromises made, an expansionist's skill, resources, and interest will allow him to prevail in some conflicts. But careful diplomacy will see to it that these incidents occur without leading dissatisfied states to expect more general concessions. Furthermore, the long-run effects of the successful application of power to halt disruptions are often beneficial. Once it learns that the defender is strong, the aggressor may become reconciled to the status quo.

Although deterrence theory denies that threats set off self-fulfilling spirals of fear and hostility, it does not claim that threats always work. First, deterrence may fail because the threat is not believed. Deterrence theory stresses both the importance and the difficulty of establishing credibility and acknowledges that, for reasons that are often beyond the scope of the theory, these attempts may fail. Thus after years of appeasement, Britain and France were unable to make clear to Hitler that they would not only go to war over Poland but also fight to the end. Second, the theory does not hold that even credible threats will always be successful. No issue could be worth an all-out nuclear war, and a state that convinces the other that it will fight such a war rather than retreat will prevail in a confrontation. In cases where the costs of war are less, however, the adversary may prefer war to retreat. Thus the problem with the United States' strategy of putting pressure on North Vietnam was not that the threats were not believed, but rather that the North preferred to take the punishment rather than stop supporting the war in the South. Third, threats can fail if they are applied in a case where the other side has situational advantages and can "design around" them to reach its

[41] Roger Parkinson, *Peace for Our Time* (London: Rupert Hart-Davis, 1971), p. 41; Senate Committee on Armed Services, *Hearings on the Military Implications of the Treaty on the Limitations of Anti-Ballistic Missile Systems and the Interim Agreement on Limitation of Strategic Offensive Arms*, 92nd Congress, 2nd Session, p. 273.

[42] Thomas Schelling, *Arms and Influence* (New Haven: Yale University Press, 1966), pp. 69-91.

goal without having to resort to any of the proscribed actions.[43] To take a recent example, Israeli threats were probably sufficient to deter Syria from sending her army to the aid of the Lebanese Moslems in the 1975-1976 civil strife, but they did not inhibit her from allowing the Palestine Liberation Army, based in Syria, to intervene.

Fourth, threats can not only fail but also increase the other side's hostility by revealing the existence of great conflicts of interest. But when this spiral proceeds through the intervening variable of increasing the accuracy of each side's perception of the other, the deterrence model is not damaged (although it says little about the process), and the spiral model is not confirmed. The aggressor, of course, is hostile because its expansion is blocked, but it does not develop the unfounded fear that the status quo power is menacing its existence. It may increase its arms because it sees that its foreign policy aims have outrun its military strength, and the increases of arms and tensions can continue for several cycles as each side matches the other's belligerence. But this process resembles that explained by the spiral model only superficially. It is completely rational. Each side is willing to pay a high price to gain its objectives and, having failed in its initial attempt to win a cheap victory, is merely acting on its unchanged beliefs about the value of the issues at stake. The heightening of the conflict does not represent, as it does in the spiral theory, the creation of illusory incompatibility, but only the real incompatibility that was there from the beginning. Thus the spiral explanation of the process is not correct, and an attempt to apply the spiral prescriptions (see below) would not have the intended effects.

The spiral model, in contrast to deterrence, argues that it is often not to the state's advantage to seek a wide margin of superiority over its adversary. In situations that resemble the Prisoner's Dilemma rather than Chicken, coercion is not likely to produce the desired results. There are two general reasons for this. First, an increase in the adversary's military strength may lead, not to greater assertiveness, but to a more conciliatory stance. The explanation for this is the other side of the dynamics that drive the security dilemma. If the adversary is mainly seeking security, increased arms may give it the confidence to be reasonable. Thus some students of Soviet behavior take the opposite position to the one of Senator Jackson quoted earlier in this section: they argue that the U.S.S.R. is more tractable when it has enough strength to feel secure. A similar argument was made in 1894 when the German ambassador to France told the French minister of war that the Franco-Russian alliance will make it "very difficult for you to remain quiet." The French leader replied that the Germans did not understand the roots of French policy:

[43] George and Smoke, *Deterrence in American Foreign Policy*, pp. 561-65.

What makes us sensitive and touchy as you say, is mainly the idea that we are thought to be weak and that insufficient account is taken of us. The stronger we shall be the less distrustful we shall be. Rest assured that our relations with you will become easier when we shall feel on a footing of equality. So long as we were facing the Triple Alliance our pride was constantly on the alert. We shall now be much less easily impressed. As you can see, our understanding with Russia is a token of peace.[44]

The second branch of this position is the argument that threats and negative sanctions, far from leading to the beneficial results predicted by deterrence theory, are often self-defeating as a costly and unstable cycle is set in motion. Short-run victories are possible, but will prove Pyrrhic if they convince the other that the victorious state is a threat that must be met by force.

Thus, if the spiral theory is correct, it is so partly because the actors do not understand it or follow its prescriptions. By acting according to a crude version of deterrence theory, states bring about results predicted and explained by the spiral theory. The former then provides an understanding of the world as seen by decision-makers and thus an explanation for their specific actions, but the latter provides an explanation for the dynamics of the interaction.[45] Acting on the premises of deterrence theory creates a self-denying prophecy, and if statesmen understood the validity of the spiral theory they could behave in ways that would similarly undermine its validity.[46] Thus it is interesting to note that people

[44] Lincoln Bloomfield, Walter Clemens, Jr., and Franklyn Griffiths, *Khrushchev and the Arms Race* (Cambridge, Mass.: M.I.T. Press, 1966); quoted in René Albrecht-Carrié, *Britain and France* (Garden City, N.Y.: Doubleday, 1970), pp. 254-55. Even though an official in the British Foreign Office believed there was a high degree to real incompatibility between his country and Japan, he argued that a hard line policy was not wise because Japan's "recklessness is apt to grow the more when she is threatened." Quoted in Wm. Roger Louis, *British Strategy in the Far East, 1919-1939* (Oxford: Clarendon Press, 1971), p. 243. Also see below, pp. 88-89.

[45] Although Rapoport is correct to call the spiral model a systemic perspective, his claim that deterrence theory, as a subset of "strategic" theories, deals only with the calculations of individual actors is misleading. ("Systemic and Strategic Conflict," in Richard Falk and Saul Mendlovitz, *The Strategy of World Order*, vol. 1: *Toward a Theory of War Prevention* [New York: World Law Fund, 1966], pp. 251-82.) Deterrence theory also attempts to explain and predict the complex interactions of national decision-making, for example the way unnecessary wars can result from appeasement. Rapoport has recently recognized this in *Conflict in Man-Made Environment* (Baltimore: Penguin, 1974), pp. 161-65.

[46] This type of paradox is not limited to international relations. Arend Lijphart argues that the commonly held theory that overlapping social cleavages produce strong and often violent political tensions does not apply to Austria and the Netherlands because the political elites in these countries understand the dangers of the situation and consciously moderate their policies to counteract the forces

who understand the nature of the Prisoner's Dilemma play the game more cooperatively than do those who do not.[47]

Prescriptions

The ideal solution for a status quo power would be to escape from the state of nature. But escape is impossible. The security dilemma cannot be abolished, it can only be ameliorated. Bonds of shared values and interests can be developed. If actors care about what happens to others and believe that others care about them, they will develop trust and can cooperate for mutual benefit. When two countries are locked in a spiral of arms and hostility, such bonds obviously are hard to establish. The first step must be the realization, by at least one side but preferably by both, that they are, or at least may be, caught in a dilemma that neither desires.

On the basis of this understanding, one side must take an initiative that increases the other side's security. Reciprocation is invited and is likely to be forthcoming because the initiative not only reduces the state's capability to harm the other but also provides evidence of its friendly intentions.[48] For these measures to be most effective, the state should place them in the proper setting; i.e. they should not be isolated gestures but must be part of a general strategy to convince the other side that the first state respects the legitimate interests of the other. Indeed the initiatives may not be effective unless the state first clearly explains that it feels that much of the incompatibility is illusory and thus provides the other with an alternative to the conflict framework in which specific moves can be seen.[49]

The central argument is that properly executed concessions lead the other side to reciprocate rather than, as in the deterrence model, leading it to expect further retreats from the first state. The first state does not, and does not appear to, retreat under pressure. Indeed "concedes" is not the best term for what the first state does. It makes a move to break the arms-hostility cycle. The end result is not that the state has given something up, or even that it has proposed a trade, but that a step is taken toward a mutually beneficial relationship. The states must learn to approach issues from a problem-solving perspective rather than from a competitive one. Instead of seeking to gain an advantage over each other, both sides should work together to further and develop their common

---

that, if allowed to take their natural course, would shatter their fragile systems. ("Consociational Democracy," *World Politics* 21 [January 1969], 207-25.)

[47] David Kanouse and William Wiest, "Some Factors Affecting Choice in the Prisoner's Dilemma," *Journal of Conflict Resolution* 11 (June 1967), 206-13.

[48] For a detailed discussion of this strategy see Charles Osgood, *An Alternative to War or Surrender* (Urbana: University of Illinois Press, 1962), pp. 85-134, and Amitai Etzioni, *The Hard Way to Peace* (New York: Collier Books, 1962), pp. 83-110, 141-72.

[49] Osgood, *An Alternative to War or Surrender*, pp. 6-9.

interests.[50] Such a new and better relationship can be created, Boulding argues, because perceptions of friendships can be made into self-fulfilling prophecies:

> George F. Kennan once said: "It is an undeniable privilege of every man to prove himself in the right in the thesis that the world is his enemy; for if he reiterates it frequently enough and makes it the background of his conduct, he is bound eventually to be right." ("The Roots of Soviet Conduct," *Foreign Affairs*, July 1947.) If for "enemy" we read "friend" in this statement, the proposition seems to be equally true but much less believed.

The British ambassador to Germany, Nevile Henderson, expressed the same sentiment in February 1939, when he cabled London: "My instinctive feeling is that this year will be the decisive one, as to whether Hitler comes down on the side of peaceful development and closer cooperation with the West or decides in favour of further adventures eastward. . . . If we handle him right, my belief is that he will become gradually more pacific. But if we treat him as a pariah or mad dog we shall turn him finally and irrevocably into one."[51]

Implicit in these prescriptions is the belief that, once each side loses its unwarranted fear of the other, some level of arms can be maintained that provides both sides with a reasonable measure of security. Here the spiral theorists' stress on understanding the position of the other side makes them more optimistic than the earlier proponents of the security dilemma. First, the latter's concentration on the degree to which the dilemma is inherent in the anarchic nature of the international system leads them to doubt that an understanding of the situation is sufficient for a solution. Even if the state does not fear immediate attack, it will still have to design policies that will provide safety if this trust is misplaced or if peaceful rivals later develop aggressive intentions. So even if both sides believe that the other desires only protection, they may find that there is no policy and level of arms that is mutually satisfactory. Second, those who stress the impact of the security dilemma usually are keenly aware that states often seek expansion as well as security and that conciliation, no matter how skillfully undertaken, will sometimes lead to greater demands.

---

[50] For discussion of the problem-solving approach, see Richard Walton and Robert McKersie, *A Behavioral Theory of Labor Negotiations* (New York: McGraw-Hill, 1965), pp. 126-83, and Dean Pruitt and Steven Lewis, "Development of Integrative Solutions in Bilateral Negotiations," *Journal of Personality and Social Psychology* 31 (1975), 621-33.

[51] Boulding, "National Images and International Systems," p. 127; quoted in Parkinson, *Peace for Our Time*, p. 103. Osgood argues similarly when he states that GRIT "is a learning process" and if applied "we might expect [an aggressive state] to be modified in course." (*An Alternative to War or Surrender*, p. 147.)

UNIVERSAL GENERALIZATIONS?

In summary, both the spiral and the deterrence theorists are deeply concerned with the danger of misunderstandings and the consequent importance of states' making their intentions clear. But the deterrers worry that aggressors will underestimate the resolve of the defenders, while the spiral theorists believe that each side will overestimate the hostility of the other. Policies that flow from deterrence theory (e.g. development of potent and flexible armed forces; a willingness to fight for issues of low intrinsic value; avoidance of any appearances of weakness) are just those that, according to the spiral model, are most apt to heighten tensions and create illusory incompatibility. And the behavior advocated by the spiral theorists (attempts to reassure the other side of one's nonaggressiveness, the avoidance of provocations, the undertaking of unilateral initiatives) would, according to deterrence theory, be likely to lead an aggressor to doubt the state's willingness to resist.[52]

Spiral and deterrence theories thus contradict each other at every point. They seem to be totally different conceptions of international relations claiming to be unconditionally applicable. If this were true, it would be important to gather evidence that would disconfirm at least one of them.[53] A look at the basic question of the effects of the application of negative sanctions makes it clear that neither theory is confirmed all the time. There are lots of cases in which arms have been increased, aggressors deterred, significant gains made, without setting off spirals. And there are also many instances in which the use of power and force has not only failed or even left the state worse off than it was originally (both of these outcomes can be explained by deterrence theory), but has led to mutual insecurity and misunderstandings that harmed both sides.

Evidence against the Spiral Model

The most obvious embarrassment to the spiral model is posed when an aggressive power will not respond in kind to conciliation. Minor conces-

[52] It is possible for a state to combine the undesired images stressed by both theories. Bradford Perkins points out that the American embargo on trade with Britain in the early nineteenth century "was worse than useless." The British did not think it could possibly achieve the declared objectives. "This posture of feeble defiance strengthened the hands of those in Great Britain who insisted that America was malignantly but ineffectively anti-British." *Prologue to War* (Berkeley and Los Angeles: University of California Press, 1961), p. 113.

[53] First, of course, the theories would have to be made more specific and operational than they are now. There is, however, the danger of making theories easily testable at the price of rendering them so crude as to be caricatures. This is the problem with William Gamson and André Modigliani, *Untangling the Cold War* (Boston: Little, Brown, 1971). For a critique of this book see Stanley Michalak, "Will the Methodology of Science Resolve the Continuing Debate Over Soviet External Conduct?" paper presented to the 1972 meeting of the American Political Science Association.

sions, the willingness to treat individual issues as separate from the basic conflict, and even an offer to negotiate can convince an aggressor that the status quo power is weak. Thus in 1903 Russia responded to British expressions of interest in negotiating the range of issues that divided them by stiffening her position in the Far East, thus increasing the friction that soon led to the Russo-Japanese War.[54] Whatever the underlying causes of Anglo-German differences before World War I, once the naval race was under way the kaiser interpreted any hesitancy in the British building as indicating that, as he had predicted, the British economy could not stand the strain. As he read a dispatch describing a debate on naval estimates in Parliament in which more attention was paid to the costs of the program than to the two-power standard, the kaiser scribbled in the margin: "They respect our firm will, and must bow before the accomplished fact [of the German naval program]! Now further quiet building."[55] And, as events of the 1930s show, once an aggressor thinks the defenders are weak, it may be impossible to change this image short of war. Unambiguous indicators of resolve are infrequent, and the aggressor is apt to think that the defender will back down at the last minute.

Concessions made in the incorrect belief that the other is a status quo power are especially apt to be misinterpreted if the other does not understand that the state's policy is based on a false image. The spiral theorists have made an important contribution by stressing the serious consequences that flow from the common situation when a status quo power does not realize that others see it as aggressive, but they have ignored the other side of this coin. Aggressors often think that their intentions are obvious to others and therefore conclude that any concessions made to them must be the result of fear and weakness. Thus, by the time of Munich, Hitler seems to have believed that the British realized his ambitions were not limited to areas inhabited by Germans and concluded that Chamberlain was conciliatory not because he felt Germany would be sated but because he lacked the resolve to wage a war to oppose German domination of the Continent. Since Hitler did not see that British policy rested on an analysis of German intentions that was altered by the seizure of the non-German parts of Czechoslovakia, he could not under-

[54] George Monger, *The End of Isolation* (London: Nelson, 1963), pp. 50-56. Similarly, the stiffening of the French position in negotiations with Italy over a variety of colonial issues in 1925 is partially explained by the fact that the Italian foreign minister "in a grandiose attempt to heal the rift between Italy and France, had proposed a broad colonial entente covering a variety of issues and places. . . . Paris may well have perceived an opportunity to win from Italy desiderata in Tunisia in return for spectacular but general promises which probably could never be realized, in which case there was no need to make immediate and precise payment to Italy in Tangier." Alan Cassels, *Mussolini's Early Diplomacy* (Princeton: Princeton University Press, 1970), p. 358.

[55] Quoted in Raymond Sontag, *European Diplomatic History, 1871-1932* (New York: Appleton-Century-Crofts, 1933), p. 143.

stand why British policy would be different in September 1939 than it had been a year earlier.[56]

Even when the adversary aims for less than domination, concessions granted in the context of high conflict will lead to new demands if the adversary concludes that the state's desire for better relations can be exploited. Thus Germany increased her pressure on France in the first Moroccan crisis after the latter assumed a more conciliatory posture and fired the strongly anti-German foreign minister. Similar dynamics preceded the outbreak of the Franco-Prussian war. More recently, the United States responded to Japanese concessions in the fall of 1941 not by making counter-concessions, but by issuing more extreme demands.

Less frequently, even a status quo power may interpret conciliation as indicating that the other side is so weak that expansion is possible at little risk. As Herman Kahn notes, prophecies can be self-denying. To trust a person and place him in a position where he can make gains at your expense can awaken his acquisitiveness and lead him to behave in an untrustworthy manner.[57] Similarly, a state's lowered level of arms can tempt the other to raise, rather than lower, its forces. For example, the United States probably would not have tried to increase NATO's conventional forces in the 1960s were it not for the discovery that the Soviet Union had fewer troops than had been previously believed, thereby bringing within grasp the possibility of defending West Europe without a resort to nuclear weapons. It is also possible that the Soviets drastically increased their missile forces in the late 1960s and early 1970s not only because of the costs of remaining in an inferior position but also because they thought the United States would allow them to attain parity.

Hostile moves can also produce effects different from those predicted by the spiral model. If statesmen possess even a modicum of rationality, returning conciliation for hostility may seem the best policy under some circumstances. The state may be in no position to pay the price of high arms and hostility. As long as its central values are not directly threatened, a small state is apt to retreat in the face of hostility from a great

[56] When an aggressor does not see that others think he is a status quo power he will not only misinterpret their concessions but also will not realize that his hostility can increase their opposition to him. Thus Leites argues the Soviets did not foresee the Western reaction to their policy in the postwar years because of their confidence that their adversaries "know for certain that the Politburo strives to annihilate them (as they strive to annihilate [capitalism]). Their estimates of basic Politburo intentions will not be changed whether it simulates friendliness or hostility." (*A Study of Bolshevism*, p. 40.) One wonders what Stalin thought when in 1946 the American ambassador told him the U.S. policy "will depend to a large extent on what our people believe to be the policies of the Soviet Union." (*Foreign Relations of the United States, 1946*, vol. 6 [Washington: Government Printing Office, 1969], p. 733.)

[57] Herman Kahn, *Thinking About the Unthinkable* (New York: Horizon Press, 1962), p. 29.

power. Larger states also often find this policy wise. States cannot afford to make too many enemies. Confronted by American resistance in 1897, Japan altered her opposition to the American annexation of Hawaii. She needed her military and diplomatic strength "to deal with a gathering crisis in her own home waters as the fleets of Europe maneuvered for a possible showdown over China." Emotional reactions often give way to calculation. For example, when the British refused to help France stop the Russo-Japanese War, the French foreign minister was "incensed" because he saw his whole policy crumbling. "His better judgment soon calmed him, however, for with France's ally eliminated from European affairs, he needed British cooperation more than ever."[58]

Without arguing that the deterrence model is always appropriate, there are many cases in which hostility checks an aggressor without producing unintended and undesired consequences. For example, two aspects of Bismarck's diplomacy in the Balkan crisis of 1885-1887 show the effectiveness of hostility. First, under German guidance the British-Austrian-Italian coalition succeeded in deterring Russian moves against Bulgaria. A year later, the Triple Alliance of Germany, Austria, and Italy, supplemented by ties to Britain, dampened French belligerence.[59]

Policies consistent with deterrence theory were followed by Britain in the Fashoda crisis with France and had the desired effect. Indeed, in this case, British hostility not only met the French threat but paved the way for a reconciliation between the two countries by showing France that she could not afford to be enemies of both Britain and Germany. The resulting willingness to make concessions to the former was a necessary condition for reaching an entente in 1904. In this case the British had not contemplated such long-run consequences in 1898; in another important case a state increased the level of hostility with the conscious aim of convincing the other not only to retreat but to be more friendly. After Germany's support for Austria in the Balkan crisis of 1877 had alienated Russia, Bismarck sought to bring her back into the alliance. To do this, he did not make overtures to the tsar, but instead made a pact with Austria to show Russia that the path of hostility toward Germany was not

[58] William Braisted, *The United States Navy in the Pacific, 1897-1907* (Austin: University of Texas Press, 1958), pp. 13-14 (similarly, Secretary of State Hay met Russian charges of lack of neutrality during the Russo-Japanese War by replying that Russia was "not so rich in friends" that she could afford reckless accusations [*ibid.*, p. 158]); Anderson, *The First Moroccan Crisis*, p. 101.

[59] William Langer, *European Alliances and Alignments, 1871-1890* (2nd ed., New York: Vintage, 1964), pp. 464-68. The coalition that blocked Russia was created by Bismarck when he successfully threatened the British that if they did not cooperate, he would turn the contending states against them. In a similar case of skillful coalition management, Castlereagh isolated Tsar Alexander in 1821-1822 and discouraged him from meddling in the Greek rebellion without alienating him. See Christopher J. Bartlett, *Castlereagh* (New York: Charles Scribners' Sons, 1966), pp. 225-29.

an easy one. Bismarck made Russia choose between friendship on German terms and a high level of hostility by foreclosing the course that
Russia preferred. This policy was successful (i.e. Russia returned friendship for German hostility) because Russia saw how much harm would
come to her if Bismarck turned sharply against her. Similarly, when King
Louis XI of France learned that King Edward IV of England was aiding
his enemies, Louis replied with hostility, halting the payments he had
been making to Edward and aiding the Scots in their attacks along the
border. Louis' "hard line" succeeded as Edward decided that the costs
of French enmity were too high.[60] In all of these cases, threats not only
accomplished the desired immediate result but also did not produce an
unintended worsening of each side's image of the other.[61] There was a
high level of real incompatibility to begin with, and the exercise of power, far from creating additional illusory incompatibility, either left the
underlying conflict untouched or lowered the incompatibility by showing
one side that its interests would be better served by abandoning
its hostility.

Hostility may also succeed if the other believes that the state can be
satisfied with small concessions. This is part of the reason why Britain
and France gave in to Hitler. Similarly, a decision-maker will not feel
that he needs to match the other's arms and hostility if he believes that
the other's behavior is caused by insecurity. As we noted earlier, if a state
believes that it and its adversary are in a security dilemma, the adversary's use of threats and power will not be self-defeating. It is significant
that there are not many cases where statesmen, correctly or not, perceive
that others are unduly afraid of them, but we should not ignore those
instances that have occurred. British policies in the 1930s again come to
mind. And when in 1907 the British military attaché in St. Petersburg
reported that, although Russia had a "magnificent [military] position"
in Central Asia, she still seemed to fear British moves in this area, the
foreign secretary noted: "I am convinced that the apprehension of the
Russians that we might adopt an aggressive policy against them in Central Asia is a real one on their part."[62]

Some American perceptions of the Soviet Union in the Cold War years
showed similar insight. One of the reasons why Secretary of State Mar-

---

[60] Paul Murray Kendal, *Louis XI* (New York: Norton, 1971), pp. 324-30. A
similar case in domestic politics occurred in England in 1915 when the Conservatives threatened to increase their hostility toward the Liberal government. In
response, the prime minister quickly invited them to join in a coalition government.

[61] To use Morton Deutsch's terms, one side's prevailing in the "manifest" conflict did not increase the "underlying" conflict. ("Conflict: Productive and Destruc-
tive," *Journal of Social Issues* 25 [January 1969], 7-42.)

[62] Edward Grey in Gooch and Temperley, eds., *British Documents on the Origins of the War*, vol. 4, p. 532.

shall opposed Secretary of Defense Forrestal's appeals for an increased military budget was his worry "that American rearmament might exercise an adverse effect on Russian intentions." Similarly, when Secretary of Defense Wilson was asked to explain the Russian bomber build-up in 1954 he said: "My analysis would indicate that the Russians have been much more afraid of us than we are of them, and their build-up has been a defensive buildup." The Russians "were afraid of our monopoly [of atomic weapons]; they were afraid we would use it on them, I suppose. They shouldn't have been, but I think they probably were." These sentiments were echoed almost twenty years later by Gerald Smith, the head of the Arms Control and Disarmament Agency, when he testified that "I think sometimes we tend to minimize the . . . potential threat that our accurate ICBMs offer to the Soviets." But the spiral model is supported by the fact that these perceptions rarely dominate policy. More often they represent a minority position (see, for example, Henry Wallace's testimony on the ratification of the proposed NATO treaty) that is not taken seriously by most decision-makers. So although Kennan's brilliant presentation of the way in which the Russians may have been puzzled and frightened by the moves by which the United States sought to ensure its security through the establishment of NATO reminds us that statesmen can recommend policies based on an understanding of the security dilemma, the fact that his cable was ignored shows us how hard it is to convince most people that they may be inadvertently threatening others.[63]

In summary, the spiral model holds that statesmen see hostility as indicating that the other is out to get them and believe that the best, if not the only way to cope with this threat is with negative sanctions. But the examples cited here show that neither link is universal. Decision-makers sometimes believe that the other is acting out of insecurity or that real incompatibility, although significant, is limited. Even if they see the other as extremely hostile, decision-makers usually weigh, however roughly and inadequately, the costs of responding with hostility, the gains of conciliation, and the possibility of compromise. The spiral theorists are right to argue that the level of tensions and arms is not under the complete control of any one country. Unintended and undesired consequences fre-

---

[63] Warner Schilling, "The Politics of National Defense: Fiscal 1950," in Schilling, Paul Hammond, and Glenn Snyder, *Strategy, Politics, and Defense Budgets* (New York: Columbia University Press, 1962), p. 147; quoted in *Study of Air Power*, Hearings Before the Subcommittee on the Air Force of the Committee on Armed Services, U.S. Senate, 84th Congress, 2nd Session, 1956, pp. 1757-60 (I wish to thank George Quester for calling these fascinating statements to my attention); Senate Armed Services Committee, *Hearings on the Military Implications of the Treaty on the Limitations of Anti-Ballistic Missile Systems and the Interim Agreement and Limitation of Strategic Offensive Arms*, p. 416, Kennan, *Memoirs*, vol. 2, pp. 137-39, 143-44, 327-51. Also see above, pp. 80-81.

quently follow from a state's actions. But this is not always the case. We should not overlook the extent to which statesmen look to the future, seek to manipulate the levels of tension and hostility in order to reach their goals, and frequently succeed.

Evidence against Deterrence

It is thus easy to find many cases that do not fit the spiral model and in which not only the outcomes but also the actors' perceptions and calculations are consistent with deterrence theory. Unfortunately from the standpoint of theory building, it is equally easy to find cases of the reverse. Hostility can be self-defeating, and conciliation does not always lead to further demands. Appeasement often works, even when there are major conflicts between the countries. By making many concessions to the United States around the turn of the century Britain succeeded in cementing American friendship. The number of conflicts settled by one side's retreating is unknown because these cases have little drama and often pass unnoticed. And it is at least plausible that many major disputes could have been avoided by small concessions that were withheld not because the state valued what was asked for but because it feared that conciliation would be mistaken for weakness. For example, had France followed a more flexible policy toward Germany before 1933, she might have drained much of the discontent that produced Hitler.

Our memories of Hitler have tended to obscure the fact that most statesmen are unwilling to pay an exorbitant price for a chance at expansion. More moderate leaders are apt to become defenders of the status quo when they receive significant concessions. Of course the value of these concessions to the status quo power may be high enough to justify resistance and even war, but the demands are not always the tip of an iceberg. To use the more common metaphor, the appetite does not always grow with the eating. It partly depends on how one gains the meal and what suits one's taste. Concessions that are wrenched from the state by dire threats are more apt to lead to an image of it as weak than are concessions that appear to be freely given. And concessions on issues that are understood to be important to the side receiving them but not to the side making them are especially likely to be self-limiting.[64]

Threats, which have been more closely studied than concessions, often do not have the effect predicted by deterrence theory. Before discussing examples, we should remember that this theory is not embarrassed by threats that fail because they are not believed or can be "designed around," because the punishment is insufficient to outweigh the aggres-

[64] For a further discussion of how to minimize the costs of making concessions, see Robert Jervis, *The Logic of Images in International Relations* (Princeton: Princeton University Press, 1970), pp. 139-224.

sor's expected gains, or because they set off responses based on accurate assessment of the real incompatibility. What does count against the theory are cases where threats not only fail and hostility not only increases, but where conflict develops in a way and to a degree that cannot be explained by the original conflict of interest. Here hostility, far from containing the enemy, creates him. Thus judgments as to whether the spiral theory explains a case often involve difficult analysis about the degree of real incompatibility present at the start. For example, the relevance of the theory to Japanese-American relations before World War II largely turns on whether Japan preferred war to foregoing domination of Asia and gaining proper, if not cordial, relations with the United States and whether the United States preferred war to permitting such Japanese expansion. It is true that American economic pressures accelerated rather than restrained Japanese expansion, and the Japanese alliance with Germany, rather than having the intended deterring effect, led America to see that a firm stand was even more important since Japan was now closely linked to America's primary enemy. But a necessary condition for the possible success of a conciliatory policy was the existence of solutions that both sides preferred to war.[65]

Limited spiral effects can occur that, while not completely fitting the spiral model, are not easily reconciled with deterrence. In 1887, Bismarck tried to show Russia that she needed German friendship by cutting off the sale of Russian bonds on the Berlin money market. But Russia was able to sell the bonds in France, thereby not only gaining the desired funds but creating a link to France that reduced Russian dependence on Germany. The next year Germany tried to push Britain into a closer association with the Triple Alliance by playing on British fears of an invasion by France. The rumors were convincing enough to be taken seriously; the problem was that Britain reacted differently from Germany's prediction. The cabinet resolved to be especially careful to avoid war in the immediate future and embarked upon a program of naval expansion. Thus Britain not only refused to draw closer to Germany but equipped herself with the means of later establishing even greater independence. Similarly, in an effort to draw the United States into a Far Eastern entente in 1907, Germany spread rumors that a Japanese-American war was likely and that, if it occurred, Japan would probably win. But like England in the 1880s, the United States responded not by in-

---

[65] For balanced treatments of this vital question, see Chihiro Hosoya, "Miscalculations in Deterrence Policy: Japanese–U.S. Relations, 1938-41," *Journal of Peace Research*, No. 2 (1968), pp. 97-115; Akira Iriye. "Japanese Imperialism and Aggression," in Esmonde M. Robertson, ed., *The Origins of the Second World War* (New York: St. Martin's, 1971), pp. 257-59, and Iriye, "Japan's Foreign Policy Between the Wars," in *ibid.*, pp. 268-71.

creasing foreign ties, but by strengthening its navy.[66] In none of these cases was either side's image of the other significantly changed, and the effects were not as far-reaching as they are in pure spiral cases. But there were undesired consequences that outran the initial interaction. In the first case, a bridge, weak as it was, was thrown between France and Russia. Each now had a larger stake in the other's well-being. In the other two cases, the target state decreased its vulnerability and thus became better able to resist German threats and blandishments. In all three cases, German hostility had backfired.

When threats lead the recipient to believe that the sender is highly aggressive, the classic spiral of arms and hostility is apt to be set in motion. The best-known examples are provided by Anglo-German relations in the pre-World War I era. Around the turn of the century the Germans tried to improve relations with England by using the tactic that Bismarck had successfully employed against Russia in the late 1870s. Believing that England was isolated from France and Russia and that she therefore had no choice but to turn to Germany, the German leaders refused British offers of informal cooperation. They wanted a closer and more binding arrangement and, seeing Britain as vulnerable, believed that increasing German hostility would force Britain to agree. But Germany overestimated the gaps that separated England from France and Russia and failed to realize that German behavior might convince England that Germany was an irresponsible and dangerous power. Thus the kaiser vigorously opposed British policy in South Africa before the Boer War, most notably with the famous Kruger Telegram. But this attempt "to frighten England into joining the Triple Alliance" produced the opposite effect as both elite and public opinion concluded that a state that would gratuitously interfere with another's vital interest was unprincipled, reckless, or unreasonably hostile. Germany tried a similar policy in 1905 when she continued the first Moroccan crisis in order to break the newly formed Anglo-French entente by showing France that Britain was an unreliable partner. But the foreign secretary and one of his key subordinates regarded the German demands "a great piece of effrontery," the king believed that the Germans were "politically blackmailing," and the entente not only held, but was solidified.[67]

Interestingly enough, Germany had tried a similar policy toward the United States in 1898. It produced the same unintended results. During the Spanish-American War, Germany sent a fleet to Manila to impress

[66] Langer, *European Alliances and Alignments*, pp. 491-92; C. J. Lowe, *The Reluctant Imperialists* (New York: Macmillan Co., 1969), pp. 151-52; Braisted, *The United States Navy in the Pacific*, p. 209.

[67] Lowe, *The Reluctant Imperialists*, p. 205 (also see p. 216); quoted in Monger, *The End of Isolation*, p. 161.

the Americans with Germany's interests and power in the area. But what the Americans perceived was Germany's "evident hostility," and, by contrast, they appreciated Britain's friendship to a greater extent than before. At the same time Germany demanded the Samoan and Caroline islands in return for the gains the United States was making at the expense of Spain. The American decision-makers reacted just as the British were to do several years later. The Germans were considered to be unusually greedy and presumptuous in demanding payment for refraining from meddling in an area where the United States had won the right to do as it pleased. Their behavior seemed to go beyond the accepted pattern of advancing one's self-interest and to show a willingness to interfere at any point on the globe at the slightest excuse.[68]

The German attempt to separate England from France was not completely unwise since the entente was far from firm and the consequences of hostility could not be foreseen. Indeed had the initial effort been conducted with more skill and moderation, it probably would have succeeded. But later German policy was equally counterproductive and is more difficult to understand. In the absence of intrinsic issues dividing Germany from England and in the face of increasing evidence of the incorrectness of the German assumption that England could never find alternative allies, Germany persisted in believing that hostility would bring Britain around. Under this pressure, British policy did indeed alter —but not in the desired direction. Initially Britain wanted only to curb German excesses. Then German behavior convinced her that Germany was a menace to France. Finally as German hostility—and her navy— increased, Britain came to see Germany as a direct threat to her own security. Germany, the British believed, had chosen to make an enemy of England. Why else should Germany develop a navy that rivaled England's? Germany had no long sea-lanes to protect. The British navy was no danger to Germany, because Britain had no army with which to invade. A German naval victory, on the other hand, would leave the island defenseless against a German attack.

From the German perspective, the relationship looked entirely different. Britain had aligned herself with Germany's avowed enemy. Protestations that Britain was not pursuing an anti-German policy were beside the point if not hypocritical. England's stance in fact harmed Germany since it buttressed France. Therefore German hostility was morally and pragmatically justified. At best, firmness would convince Britain that she could not afford to menace Germany. Even if increasing arms did not make Britain more conciliatory, at least it would prepare Germany for the coming war. The British claims that German naval construction was

[68] Braisted, *The United States Navy in the Pacific*, pp. 36, 39-40.

unnecessary and menacing could hardly be taken seriously. Germany was a world power, and as such needed a large navy. The fleet would be used against Britain only if the latter joined an anti-German war. Indeed Germany had promised to halt the naval race if Britain would agree to remain neutral in the event of a war between France and Germany. Britain's refusal of this bargain revealed the anti-German nature of her policy.

A version of spiral dynamics was also an immediate cause of the outbreak of war in 1914. Each of the continental powers believed that the side that struck first would gain a major military advantage. Since to wait for the other side to clarify its intentions could mean defeat, even a country that preferred the status quo to a war would feel great pressures to attack.[69] There was no way for a country to increase its ability to defend itself without simultaneously increasing its ability to destroy others. Under these conditions it would have required unusual empathy and statesmanship—and unusual willingness to risk receiving the first blow— to halt the final rush toward war.

DETERRENCE AND WORLD WAR II; SPIRAL MODEL
AND WORLD WAR I

These examples are sufficient to show that neither the deterrence nor the spiral theories can account for all the evidence. Indeed, the previous discussion indicates that each theory has roots deep in an individual case. The sketch of one of the main versions of the origins of World War I that we have just given not only fits the spiral model very well, it is this case that has provided much of the inspiration for the model.[70] Lewis Richardson applied his equations to this era, and later scholars have used

[69] If the conflict is structured as a Prisoner's Dilemma (i.e. if each side is better off attacking than waiting no matter whether the other side is about to launch a strike or not), neither side has to make predictions about the other's short-run behavior in order to decide immediately to go to war. For a re-examination of the conventional wisdom about the 1914 mobilizations, see L.C.F. Turner, *Origins of the First World War* (New York: Norton, 1970), pp. 60-115.

[70] Historians differ on the degree of real incompatibility dividing the alliances, and especially that dividing Britain and Germany. British statesmen believed that Germany sought to dominate the Continent, and it is not clear that they were wrong. The immediate causes of the war have also been re-analyzed, and scholars have argued that Germany was not dragged into the war by giving a "blank check" to Austria—she played a far more active role. Indeed Germany may have seen the crisis as an opportunity to launch a preventive war in the belief that the military balance would shortly turn against her. The book that re-opened these debates is Fritz Fischer, *Germany's Aims in the First World War* (New York: Norton, 1967). He replies to his critics in *World Power or Decline* (New York: Norton, 1974). For excellent reviews, see Koch, ed., *The Origins of the First World War*, Turner, *Origins of the First World War*, and V. R. Berghahn, *Germany and the Approach of War in 1914* (New York: St. Martin's, 1973). It should also be noted that, even if the conflict between Germany and Britain was largely illusory, the war might have been prevented had Britain made clear her commitment to fight.

both the Anglo-German interaction and the frantic maneuvering of the last weeks of peace to drive home their arguments. The deterrence theorists, on the other hand, often hark back to, and derive much of their analysis from, the failure of appeasement in the 1930s. Given the histories of these two conflicts, it is not surprising that deterrence theories have little to say about World War I and that the spiral theorists rarely discuss the 1930s.[71]

Although both sets of theorists fail to discuss the conditions under which their theories will not apply, and so imply that they are universal, what they say on the infrequent occasions when they discuss the war that does not fit their model shows that they actually do not apply their model to all cases. When the deterrence theorists discuss World War I, they do not concentrate on how either side could have made their threats more credible. Instead they talk about the mobilization races in terms that are consistent with the spiral theory.[72] Indeed one of the major policy contributions of the deterrence theorists was to stress that mutual first strike capability, by creating a "reciprocal fear of surprise attack," is highly destabilizing.[73]

Deterrence theorists thus understand the workings of spiral dynamics and see them operating in some conflicts; they merely deny that the Cold War fits this model. Two possible exceptions: Dean Acheson appears not merely to deny that the exercise of American power has led to Soviet hostility, he seems not to understand how such a reaction could be possible. David McLellan argues that "Acheson discounts the counterproductive effects of situations of strength . . . by contending that weakness is a cardinal sin. . . . This insufficient sensitivity to the interactive quality of international relations may have been the Achilles' heel of Acheson's diplomacy. It dulled him to the likelihood that a Japanese Peace Treaty would have repercussions in Peking and in Moscow, in the same way it dulled him to the implications for China of MacArthur's advance to the Yalu." More recently, Senator Henry Jackson has denied the possibility of spirals. In describing how the senator reaches decisions, his assistant for national security policy said he "goes back to that formula: if we go ahead with a system, and it's not needed, then we've just wasted some money. But if we don't go ahead, and it turns out that we were wrong, then we're running extreme risks, like losing our independence."[74]

[71] See Aaron Wildavsky, "Practical Consequences of the Theoretical Study of Defense Policy," *Public Administration Review* 25 (March 1965), 90-103.

[72] Herman Kahn, *On Thermonuclear War* (2nd ed., New York: Free Press, 1969), pp. 357-72.

[73] Thomas Schelling, *Strategy of Conflict* (New York: Oxford University Press, 1963), pp. 207-29.

[74] David McLellan, "Comparative 'Operational Codes' of Recent U.S. Secretaries of State: Dean Acheson," paper presented to 1969 meeting of the American Political Science Association, p. 34 (also see Acheson's reply to Gaddis Smith's questions ["Mr. Acheson Answers Some Questions," *New York Times Book*

Similarly, spiral theorists do not claim that deterrence is never possible or necessary. Even Neville Chamberlain argued that "we must not by showing weakness encourage Mussolini to be more intransigent," and noted that "it would be a tragic blunder to mistake our love of peace, and our faculty for compromise, for weakness." He finally realized that "it is perfectly evident . . . that force is the only argument Germany understands." Were the spiral theorists to argue that their model always applies, they would have to claim that events of the 1930s fit their analysis of the Cold War—"the arms race is a tension-inducing system," "both sides are caught in the same blind alley of trying to achieve 'peace through military strength,' " and "mutual insecurity rather than the struggle for power has become the major source of international tensions." Churchill would have to be, to use the term Osgood applies to those who seek security through arms, a "Neanderthal," and Chamberlain, in Fromm's words, a "sane" thinker. In fact, there are only occasional hints of this universalistic position, as when Singer argues that the Anglo-German negotiations for arms limitations in the mid-1930s "to some extent . . . resulted in a temporary reduction of mutually perceived threat and consequently of international tensions." More frequently the spiral theorists, like the deterrers, see Hitler as someone who could not have been conciliated. Thus when Albert Wohlstetter asked Anatol Rapoport whether he considered the spiral prescriptions to be "a sort of general rule" that could be applied to all cases including Hitler, Rapoport said that, while it could be applied to the Russians because they were "reasonable," it would not have worked with the Nazis.[75]

When Will Force and Threats Work? The Decision-Maker's Choice

If neither theory covers all cases, if force is sometimes effective and sometimes self-defeating, we are faced with two questions. First, what explains the differences between the spiral and deterrence theorists? What are they arguing about? Second, more important but much harder to answer, what are the conditions under which one model rather than the other is appropriate? When will force work and when will it create

---

Review, October 12, 1969, p. 31] following the publication of his memoirs); quoted in Daniel Yergin, " 'Scoop' Jackson Goes for Broke," *Atlantic Monthly* (June 1974), 81.

[75] Keith Feiling, *The Life of Neville Chamberlain* (London: Macmillan & Co., 1970), pp. 272, 392, 341 (also see pp. 265, 268, and 300); Osgood, *An Alternative to War or Surrender*, pp. 8, 49, 142; Erich Fromm, *May Man Prevail?* (Garden City, N.Y.: Doubleday, 1961); "Threat-Perception and the Armament-Tension Dilemma," *Journal of Conflict Resolution* 2 (March 1958), 101; Archibald, ed., *Strategic Interaction and Conflict*, p. 224.

a spiral of hostility? When will concessions lead to reciprocations, and when will they lead the other side to expect further retreats?[76]

Decision-makers face these vital questions all the time. Israel has had to grapple with them from the beginning. Could the Arabs be conciliated? Would reprisals and punishments stop guerrilla raids? Similarly, one common facet of the Berlin conflict from 1958 to 1962 was the need for Western decision-makers to predict whether the Russians believed that "if the Western powers could accept the free city proposal as a model of change they would be psychologically prepared to accept the other 'realities,' as Moscow called them, of two Germanys and . . . a nuclear-free zone,"[77] or whether, by contrast, Western concessions over Berlin would call forth Soviet concessions on German security. In disputes between a large and a small power the former must calculate the reaction not only of the latter but of third parties. Thus to make concessions to Panama in the conflict over the canal President Johnson had to believe that not only that country but others as well would not infer that pressure and riots were a generally effective tool. Even if he thought that he could convince Panama that flexibility was not produced by weakness and that after our initial retreats our resistance would grow, not diminish, he would have to satisfy himself that others would not take our willingness to concede to a small state on a question previously considered vital as showing that we would give up much more to stronger states on other issues.

To return to the cases of World Wars I and II, the British had to predict the effects of firmness and conciliation. Would a commitment to outdo the Germans in the building of Dreadnoughts curb the naval race? Could the conflict be ameliorated by meeting German grievances? Similar questions arose in the last days of peace. Asquith, the prime minister, and Grey, the foreign secretary, considered sending an ultimatum but decided that to do so would only antagonize Germany and destroy the possibility of a peaceful settlement. Similarly, in March 1938 Foreign Minister Halifax told the cabinet that moves to protect Czechoslovakia would lead to unintended consequences: "The more closely we associate ourselves with France and Russia, the more we produce on German minds the impression that we are plotting to encircle Germany." At the time of the Nuremberg rally six months later, two leading foreign office officials wanted to send Germany a stiff warning "to prevent Hitler com-

---

[76] For a similar attempt to answer the last question, see S. S. Komorita and Marc Barnes, "Effects of Pressures to Reach Agreement in Bargaining," *Journal of Personality and Social Psychology* 13 (1969), 245-52.

[77] Jack Schick, *The Berlin Crisis* (Philadelphia: University of Pennsylvania Press, 1971), p. 19.

mitting himself irretrievably." But the view prevailed that such a measure would infuriate, not deter, Hitler and reduce the chances of British mediation in the conflict. In March 1939 the permament undersecretary of the foreign office, Alexander Cadogan, summed up his disagreement with the ambassador in Berlin, Nevile Henderson, when he wrote the latter: "you express the wish that we could rearm a little more quietly, as you say that the noise we make about it leads Germans to believe that we want after all to attack them. . . . What seems to me to be a far greater danger is that they might believe they could attack and smash us. . . . For that reason, I had always hoped that, when the time came . . . we should advertise our strength as much as possible."[78]

Similar questions were central to the formation of British policy in the Far East. One reason why Ramsay MacDonald halted the building of a naval base at Singapore in 1924 was that he believed, contrary to the views of his military advisers, that the show of force was more likely to increase than to decrease Japanese pressure on China. More than ten years later, the British and American ambassadors to Japan disagreed about the advisability of a program of strong warnings and sanctions. To the former, "a private threat of this sort would encourage the civil government to extend its control over the actions of the military; to [the latter], on the other hand, such a step would only encourage the military to increase their independence."[79]

Even before the German demands were strongly raised, Britain and France had to decide the relative merits of firmness and conciliation. At Versailles they debated how punitive the peace settlement should be, and over the next two decades they quarreled over whether they should relax their harsh verdict or forceably resist German attempts to re-establish her position. The British, partly because they accepted the spiral explanation of the origins of war, favored making concessions in the expectation that Germany would become a defender of the new status quo. France opposed leniency on the grounds that German hostility was implacable. Concessions, she argued, would increase Germany's strength and lead her to doubt her adversaries' resolve. Prussia made the same choice in 1871. French bellicosity was ineradicable: hundreds of years of history had shown that she would never be peaceful or trustworthy. So she must be kept weak. As the minister of war put it: "We can, for the sake of our people and our security, conclude no peace that does not dismember France." Another decision-maker argued that Prussia

[78] Roy Jenkins, *Asquith* (London: Collins, 1964), p. 326; Cameron Hazlehurst. *Politicians at War* (London: Jonathan Cape, 1971), p. 84; quoted in Colvin, *The Chamberlain Cabinet*, pp. 109, 148; David Dilks, ed., *The Diaries of Sir Alexander Cadogan, 1938-1945* (New York: Putnam, 1972), pp. 155-56.

[79] B. B. Schofield, *British Sea Power* (London: Batsford, 1967), p. 111; Nicholas Clifford, *Retreat From China* (London: Longmans, 1967), p. 51.

"should treat the French as a conquered army and demoralize them to the utmost of our ability. We ought to crush them so that they will not be able to breathe for a hundred years." Bismarck agreed: France was "irritable, envious, jealous and proud to excess." Because she could never be trusted not to try to avenge the defeat, "We must have land, fortresses and frontiers which will shelter us for good from the enemy attack."[80]

The French position after World War I posed a second choice for Britain. Would conciliation or firmness be more likely to lead France to adopt a more reasonable view? Would security guarantees assuage France's fears, or would the resulting lack of restraint only embolden her to pursue an even more anti-German policy? Would threats make France abandon her harsh policy rather than risk losing British support? Or would they, by increasing French insecurity, lead her to hold even more strongly to her plan of keeping Germany down? When the tsar criticized Britain for having violated her proclaimed neutrality during the Russo-Japanese War by signing a new treaty with Japan that gave "encouragement and moral support to the Japanese," the British ambassador replied that in fact the treaty worked to the benefit of the Russians because it "enabled the Japanese to make peace on terms that were acceptable to Russia while without the safety assured to them by the Agreement they would probably have preferred to continue the war."[81]

Similar questions had to be answered by the United States government in 1971–1972 in deciding whether sending jet planes to Israel would make that country more or less flexible in negotiations with the Arabs. Some American officials "said that to the extent that Tel Aviv became independent of American supplies, Washington's diplomatic leverage would be reduced. Others argued . . . that a friendlier atmosphere between the two countries might increase American influence." After the United States decided to sell the planes, an American official said that

[80] Quoted in Michael Howard, *The Franco-Prussian War* (New York: Collier, 1969), pp. 228, 221. Napoleon made a similar choice after defeating Austria in 1805. "Napoleon then had to choose between imposing mild or harsh terms on Vienna. Talleyrand favored a 'soft' peace in order to influence Austria to turn her attentions toward the Balkans, which would bring on a clash between the Hapsburgs and the Romanovs and leave the French a free hand in Germany. The Emperor, however, believed that the Hapsburgs would never give up the desire to regain their influence in Italy and Germany and decided to rob them of the means of resuming hostilities in the near future. . . . The Continent lay at [Napoleon's] feet. No power east of the Channel dared openly defy him. Despite these triumphs, however, Napoleon had failed to establish the basis for a lasting peace. He forced his victims into submission by the imposition of peace terms so rigorous that the treaties invariably were little more than truces under which the defeated powers thirsted for revenge and constantly sought a favorable opportunity to resume their contest of arms." (Ross, *European Diplomatic History, 1789-1815*, pp. 253, 381.)

[81] Gooch and Temperley, eds., *British Documents on the Origins of the War,* vol. 4, p. 216.

withholding them "never proved very effective anyway. Perhaps we can influence them more if there is a feeling of mutual respect and confidence." In early 1973, when the United States decided to sell more airplanes, it was explained that "As the Israelis become increasingly confident that their relative military strength will be preserved, they should be willing to take a few more risks in negotiating a peace settlement."[82] Russia also has had to decide whether aid and commitments are more likely to restrain or to encourage allies. By signing an agreement with India in 1971, for example, did Russia increase the chances that India would attack Pakistan because India would expect Russian support to deter other great powers from interfering? Or did the pact increase the chances of peace by reassuring India that she was not isolated and did not have to act rashly? These calculations are difficult to make and therefore often yield bad policies. When Britain signed a defensive alliance with Japan in 1902, she thought that the increased security would make Japan less likely to go to war with Russia. In fact, the agreement removed the remaining Japanese doubts about the safety of fighting.[83] (Ironically, the outcome of the war ended the Russian threat to India, a problem that had preoccupied British diplomacy for decades.)

When Will Force and Threats Work? Hypotheses

Unfortunately no well-structured or verified theory exists that tells us when force and threats work. Several fairly obvious propositions can be advanced, however, and one simple but important conclusion drawn. Threats are more apt to work and the deterrence model is more apt to apply when: 1) The other side sees the costs of standing firm as very high. More specifically, this will be the case when: 1a) The other side is relatively weak or vulnerable; 1b) the other places an especially high subjective value on preserving the lives and property of its citizens;

---

[82] Articles in the *New York Times* by William Beecher, "U.S. Said to Plan to Help Israelites Make Own Arms," January 14, 1972; "U.S. Said to Agree to Supply Israel with 42 Phantoms," February 6, 1972; "Israelis Will Buy More Jets in U.S.: Total Is Put at 48," March 14, 1973.

The discussion here deals with concessions rather than rewards—i.e. side-payments for "good behavior." It is often argued that rewards are more likely to be effective than are punishments, especially in changing attitudes and images as well as behavior, and that rewards produce fewer unintended and undesired consequences. (See John Raser, "Learning and Affect in International Politics," *Journal of Peace Research*, No. 3 [1965], 216-26, James Tedeschi, "Threats and Promises," in Paul Swingle, ed., *The Structure of Conflict* [New York: Academic Press, 1970], pp. 155-91, and David Baldwin, "The Power of Positive Sanctions," *World Politics* 24 [October 1971], pp. 19-38.) But many questions need to be explored: are there many possible rewards that do not involve prohibitive costs to the state giving them? Are rewards only useful when the incompatibility is largely illusory? When will rewards be seen as bribes, encouraging the recipient to repeatedly show that he will make mischief unless he is continually paid? Should one reward the other for altering undesired behavior but not for continuing a friendly policy?

[83] Monger, *The End of Isolation*, pp. 419-20.

1c) the other is highly risk-averse; and 1d) the other has a short-run perspective.[84] 2) The other side believes that the state making the threats sees its costs of standing firm as low. The specifics of this proposition are the reverse of those we have just given. 3) The other side sees the costs of retreating as relatively low. More specifically, this will be the case when: 3a) the other's central values are not involved in the issue at stake; 3b) the issue does not involve principles that apply to other important cases; 3c) the other can retreat without breaking important commitments; 3d) the goals of the side making the threat are seen as limited; 3e) the other believes that the demands derive from the state's desire for security and thinks that the state may see the other as a menace; 3f) neither the goals sought nor the means employed violate common standards of proper relations between juridically equal actors; and, related to the last proposition, 3g) the actor making the threat refrains from humiliating the other, inflicting gratuitous punishment, raising demands that lack any legitimacy, or asking for something that is of significantly greater value to the other than it is to him. All these kinds of behavior limit the costs of retreating to the other side by decreasing the other's fear that a retreat will be followed by further demands. They involve avoiding those traits that observers associate with extreme ambitions and taking care to observe lines of salience that differentiate present demands from many others that could be raised in the future.

To turn from the question of whether an actor will back down in the face of a threat to the question of the effects of retreats, concessions are more apt to encourage new demands, as the deterrence theory holds, when: 4) a retreat takes the state past a salient point; 5) the adversaries do not have a common conception of fair play and reciprocation; 6) the concession is made in a way that indicates that the state would sacrifice a great deal in order to avoid a war; and 7) the state retreats even though the costs of doing so are very high (i.e. the conditions specified in proposition 3 are not met).

To discuss these hypotheses in detail would take us away from the theme of this book. We should, however, note one thread that runs through them. A major determinant of the effect of threats is the intention of the other side. When faced with an aggressor, threats and force are necessary. Concessions may serve important tactical needs,[85] but they will not meet the underlying sources of dissatisfaction. When con-

[84] For empirical support for these propositions, see Komorita and Barnes, "Effects of Pressures to Reach Agreement in Bargaining," and James Tedeschi et al., "Social Power and the Credibility of Promises," *Journal of Personality and Social Psychology* 13 (1969), 253-61.

[85] Alexander George, David Hall, and William Simons, *The Limits of Coercive Diplomacy* (Boston: Little, Brown, 1971) have found that concessions are important even in those cases, like the Cuban missile crisis, that are usually thought of as being settled by a complete retreat by one side.

cessions are made under pressure or when the aggressor thinks that the status quo power is under no illusions about the nature of the conflict between them, the concessions are likely to quicken the pace of future demands. (We should briefly note the other side of this coin, which is important for other parts of this book: when a state believes that the other has responded to conciliation by claiming that the state retreated only because of the other's superior force and by raising new demands, it will be likely to infer that the other is an aggressor who must be dealt with firmly.) And when the status quo state stands firm and the aggressor responds in kind, the spiral model will not apply because the parties are correctly perceiving real incompatibility. On the other hand, when conflict erupts between two status quo powers, the spiral model will probably provide the correct explanation and policy prescription. Threats will tend to be self-defeating because neither side realizes that the other is afraid of it. Initiatives and concessions, carefully undertaken, can help the states out of the dilemma.

This does not mean, of course, that the states' basic intentions are the only variables that determine how they will react to threats and concessions. The details and context of the moves, each side's operational code, and the specific goals held and attributed to others need to be examined. Not all status quo or aggressive powers behave alike or interpret others' actions in the same way. Thus we are not claiming that conciliatory moves will be seen as an indication of weakness only by a state that seeks to overthrow the status quo. This interpretation can spring from a much more contingent analysis of alternatives available to the other state. Similarly, the attempt to increase power can increase illusory incompatibility even if there is a high degree of real incompatibility between the parties. But these qualifications should not obscure the importance of each side's intentions in determining which model is likely to provide the best fit.

If this conclusion is correct, then the argument between the spiral and deterrence theorists is not over a general model of international relations, but over which model applies to the Cold War and, as a main determinant of the answer to this question, what Soviet intentions are. This is why Rapoport asks: "Why is the power game being played at all? Is the game worth the candle?"[86]

PERCEPTIONS OF INTENTION AND ANALYSES OF WHAT IS AT STAKE

Differences in perceptions of Soviet intentions also explain why spiral and deterrence theorists have such different attitudes toward the handling of minor issues. The former see them as opportunities for reducing ten-

---

[86] In de Reuck and Knight, eds., *Conflict in Society*, p. 293.

sions. The outcomes are less important than the learning that can take place. Each side can show that it is no menace and respects the other's legitimate interests. This view was presented by Neville Chamberlain when he briefed his advisers after returning from Godesberg: "Herr Hitler had said that if we got this question [of the Sudetenland] out of the way without conflict, it would be a turning point in Anglo-German relations. That, to the Prime Minister, was the big thing of the present issue."[87]

Deterrence theorists agree that the way the conflict is handled is usually more important than the intrinsic value of what is at stake. But they fear positive feedback of a different kind. As Schelling has explained, "what is in dispute [in the game of Chicken] is usually not the issue of the moment, but everyone's expectations about how a participant will behave in the future." Khrushchev agrees: "Think what would have happened if we had sat down to negotiate [in the Paris Summit Conference of 1960] without having received an apology from the United States. . . . The aggressors would have wanted to bend us. But if we had bent our back, they would immediately have thrown a saddle on us, and then they would have sat themselves on top of us and begun to drive on us."[88]

For the same reasons, both sides in a labor-management conflict may expend resources on an issue out of all proportion to the money immediately at stake. In one plant the union fiercely opposed the effort of the new manager to deny a small group of workers overtime pay. Even though only a few people and small sums were involved, "the union officers . . . felt that this was a crucial issue; if [the new manager] got away with this particular move, there was no telling how far he would go." In another case the union strenuously fought a management effort to change the piecework rates on a relatively insignificant machine because "it seemed possible that management might take an inch here and an inch there until the whole rate structure was in jeopardy."[89]

---

[87] Quoted in Colvin, *The Chamberlain Cabinet*, p. 162.

[88] *Arms and Influence*, p. 118; quoted in Leites, *Kremlin Thoughts*, pp. 11-12. At another point, Khrushchev said, "It is clear to everybody that this is only the beginning. Those who entered upon the path . . . are not going to stop at the half-way mark." (*Ibid.*, p. 11.) As these quotations indicate, several aspects of what Leites sees as the Soviet operational code—e.g. the requirements to "push to the limit" and "resist from the start" (*A Study of Bolshevism*, pp. 30-34, 50-57)— can be seen not as a uniquely Bolshevik outlook, but rather as the common view of a state that believes that it is confronted by an implacably hostile adversary. The frequently noted Russian refusal to reciprocate minor concessions and adjustments (Raymond Dennett and Joseph Johnson, eds., *Negotiating with the Russians* [Boston: World Peace Foundation, 1951], pp. 295-96; Fred Iklé, *How Nations Negotiate* [New York: Harper and Row, 1964], pp. 105-106; John Deane, *The Strange Alliance* [New York: Viking, 1947]) can also be partly explained by this image.

[89] William F. Whyte, *Pattern for Industrial Peace* (New York: Harper and Brothers, 1951), pp. 42, 68.

When one state sees another as extremely hostile, it is apt to find most compromises on specific issues unattractive. Since the other's demands are considered illegitimate, having to give in even slightly will be seen as unreasonable. And since the other will be expected to accept the compromise only as a temporary solution, at best a little breathing space will have been gained. At worst, the state will have lost a clear and tenable position by sacrificing a defensible principle and placing itself in an unstable middle ground from which it can be more easily forced back. If the other is aggressive, what is at stake is not an issue of little intrinsic importance, but each side's image of the other's values, strength, and resolve. Firmness can help set relations right; retreats incur a high, long-run cost because they lead the adversary to expect further retreats. Thus in 1885 a British cabinet minister argued for a strong response to Russian expansion in Afghanistan: "It is now not a mere question about a few miles more or less of Afghan territory but of our whole relations with Russia in Asia." In the Agadir crisis the anti-German faction in Britain argued "the point that it is not merely Morocco which is at stake. Germany is playing for the highest stakes. If her demands are acceded to . . . , it will mean definitely the subjection of France. . . . The details of the terms are not so very important now. . . . Concession means not loss of interest or loss of prestige. It means defeat with all its inevitable consequences." In July 1914 Eyre Crowe made the same kind of argument: "France and Russia consider that these charges are the pretext and the bigger cause of the Triple Alliance versus the Triple Entente is definitely engaged. . . . [T]his struggle . . . is not for the possession of Serbia, but . . . [is] between Germany aiming at political dictatorship in Europe and the Powers who desire to retain individual freedom."[90]

The belief that the other side is highly aggressive and the resulting analysis of the issues at stake will also lead the state to refrain from reciprocating if the other modifies its demands. Thus, those Finns who favored standing firm in the negotiations with Russia in 1939 were not swayed when the Soviets eased their position. If Russia were out to dominate Finland, true compromise was impossible.[91]

Debates over policies often center on whether what is at stake is a specific matter or the wider question of security. This was true, for example, of the arguments over the Munich settlement. Chamberlain's opponents argued, in the words of Duff Cooper, that "It was not for Serbia that we

---

[90] Quoted in Lowe, *The Reluctant Imperialists*, p. 88; quoted in Hazlehurst, *Politicians at War*, p. 62; quoted in Berghahn, *Germany and the Approach of War in 1914*, pp. 95-96; quoted in Zara Steiner, *The Foreign Office and Foreign Policy, 1898-1914* (Cambridge: Cambridge University Press, 1969), p. 156.

[91] Max Jakobson, *The Diplomacy of the Winter War* (Cambridge, Mass.: Harvard University Press, 1961), pp. 133-39.

fought in 1914. It was not even for Belgium. . . . We were fighting then, as we should have been fighting last week, in order that one Great Power should not be allowed . . . to dominate by brutal force the continent of Europe." Chamberlain did not disagree with this principle—he only argued that it did not apply to the case at hand. Calling the dispute "a quarrel in a far-away country between people of whom we know nothing," he said:

> However much we may sympathize with a small nation confronted by a big and powerful neighbour, we cannot in all circumstances undertake to involve the whole British Empire in a war simply on her account. If we have to fight it must be on larger issues than that. I am myself a man of peace to the very depths of my soul. Armed conflict between nations is a nightmare to me; but, if I were convinced that any nation had made up its mind to dominate the world by fear of force, I should feel that it must be resisted. Under such a domination life for people who believe in liberty would not be worth living; but war is a fearful thing, and we must be very clear, before we embark on it, that it is really the great issues that are at stake.[92]

The anti-appeasers did not disagree with this position; they advocated a different policy because they were sure that "the great issues" were at stake.

Major difficulties will arise if one side thinks that an issue can be treated in isolation when its adversary believes that all matters are closely interrelated. Attempts to treat individual issues on their merits may appear to the latter as indications of general weakness. In the midst of Franco-British conflict over the Near East in 1840, Palmerston accepted French mediation of a dispute involving Britain and Sicily. "Moreover, Palmerston showed admirable feeling in facilitating the transfer of Napoleon's remains from St. Helena to France. . . . But Thiers was quite wrong in thinking that this meant any relaxation of Palmerston's standpoint in the Eastern Question." When one side regards an agreement as

[92] Quoted in John Wheeler-Bennett, *Munich* (New York: Viking, 1964), pp. 186, 158. Also see the minutes of the cabinet meetings during the crisis in Colvin, *The Chamberlain Cabinet*, pp. 156-59. One bit of evidence counts against this view, however. When Chamberlain went to Godesberg to tell Hitler that the Czechs had agreed to the original German ultimatum, Hitler added new demands. Chamberlain insisted on certain minor modifications, and when Hitler stood firm, declared that Britain was ready to go to war. The fact that the British were willing to fight over an issue much smaller than the future of the whole Sudetenland even though they did not believe German aims were unlimited seems to undermine the argument that the image of the adversary largely determines the view of what issues are at stake. But the appeasers took this stand only with great reluctance. Furthermore, between the time the declaration was issued and the crisis resolved Chamberlain, rather than displaying firmness, took even the slightest retractions by Hitler as an excuse to revert to appeasement.

limited to the specific issue at hand and the other side views it as indicating that a general settlement will be forthcoming, charges of deception and bad faith will be raised as soon as either side acts on its beliefs. The conflict over the basic issues will not only have been postponed but exacerbated. This is illustrated by the consequences of the resolution of the Stamp Act dispute between England and the American colonies. In developing a compromise, the British prime minister

> had been able to hide from Parliament the full extent of the Americans' objections to its authority and from the Americans the full extent of Parliament's assertion of it, [but] he had actually heightened the incompatibility of the two positions. When this incompatibility became evident, as it soon did, the happy misunderstanding he had fostered served only to exaggerate the difference. The English were encouraged to believe that the Americans were seeking independence in easy stages and the Americans to think that the English were trying to enslave them by slow and insensible degrees.[93]

Before closing this section we should acknowledge that one's image of the adversary and the resulting beliefs about what is at stake do not totally determine the way in which one handles small issues. First, even if the other is seen as aggressive, tactical considerations—e.g. the need to buy time, the belief that your side will be more united if you retreat and make the other show his aggressiveness clearly—may dictate treating small issues as though they were isolated. Second, there are other reasons why small issues develop into large conflicts. If the issue involves moral values, retreat or compromise may be prohibitively costly. Or if the two sides are coalitions and the issue is important to one member of the coalition, the others may feel obliged to lend support lest the alliance break up. This was part of the explanation for the outbreak of World War I. Small issues can also lead to large conflicts if both sides believe that only a little more effort is required to achieve victory. The model for this is an auction in which each bidder must pay his highest bid whether he wins the object or not. The bidding can easily go much higher than the value of the object at stake because previous bids are sunk costs that are not relevant to the question of whether to bid higher. The "quagmire" explanation of American policy in Vietnam is of this type. But the Pentagon Papers and the articles based on them show that the decision-makers actually were pessimistic about the chances that each step would bring

[93] Robert William Seton-Watson, *Britain in Europe, 1789-1914* (New York: Macmillan Co., 1937), p. 204; Edmund and Helen Morgan, *The Stamp Act Crisis* (New York: Collier, 1963), p. 365. These difficulties are not considered in Roger Fisher's "Fractionating Conflict," in Fisher, ed., *International Conflict and Behavioral Science* (New York: Basic Books, 1964), pp. 91-109.

the conflict to a successful conclusion. And when cases do fit this model, one of the intervening variables is likely to be the development of an image of the other as hostile and the accompanying belief that what is at stake is the state's ability to contain its adversary.

Finally, astute strategy and tactics can permit an actor to treat one issue as separate from others, refuse to take up challenges, and limit the damage to his image when he has to back down after he has been engaged. Positions can be re-interpreted, definitions of the situation defined and re-defined, retreats justified by the special circumstances of the case, and the failure to contest an issue explained by temporary disabilities. In these ways the actor can increase the chance that his behavior on one issue will be seen as highly context-bound rather than as reflecting traits that will influence what he does in later cases. Retreats will then cast less of a shadow on the actor's ability to preserve other values, and concessions will be less likely to call up future demands.[94]

Other Explanations for the Differences between the Spiral and Deterrence Theories

The differences in images of the Russians are sufficient to account for the dispute between the deterrence and spiral theorists. There may be, however, other sources of disagreement. First, people differ in their propensity to perceive aggressiveness. Second, there may be residual differences in general views on the effect of threats. Even if the theorists agree on how to cope with the extreme cases, they could disagree on those toward the middle of the continuum. These two sources of disagreement often spring from differences in people's predispositions to see politics in general and international politics in particular as characterized by conflict or cooperation. Whether because of differences in personality, previous experiences, or ideology, people differ in their beliefs about the degree to which cooperation among nations is possible and in their readiness to perceive relations as conflictful. The result is that given the same situation some observers will see high threats and conflict of interest which they believe can only be coped with by firmness and strength, while others will see less threat and believe that conciliation can lead to a mutually beneficial solution.

A third argument, put most strongly by Anatol Rapoport, is that because deterrence theory concentrates on conflict it leads those who use it to become preoccupied with discordant as opposed to common interests. Deterrence theorists may have misperceived Russia and the Cold War, but it is more convincing to reverse the causation in Rapoport's argument. The theorists have applied their model to the Cold War be-

---

[94] For a further discussion of this topic, see Jervis, *The Logic of Images in International Relations*, pp. 174-224.

cause they believe the Soviets are aggressive. The approach was selected because its assumptions were believed to fit the problem to which it was being applied. Deterrers do not see a predominance of conflicting interests in other contexts, for example among allies. The famous Law of the Instrument (give a man a hammer and he will find that everything needs pounding) cannot be ignored, but to concentrate on it is to obscure the more important differences of opinion about Soviet behavior.[95]

DIFFERENCES IN VALUES

A final claim is that spiral and deterrence theorists arrive at their differing positions because they have different values and codes of morality. But because their empirical analyses differ so much, it is hard to tell whether there are any significant differences on these dimensions. Philip Green is certainly correct to say that deterrence theorists "are not 'anti-war' in the ethical sense of being themselves committed to some kind of non-warlike stance."[96] But this can also be said of the spiral theorists. They are not pacifists or nuclear pacifists. As we have shown, they do not deny that force is appropriate when confronted with an aggressor. Rather they claim that, faced with the Soviet Union, our threats have created a dangerous situation. We can afford to adopt a "non-warlike stance" because the Soviets are not a menace.

Because defenders and critics of deterrence policies disagree about the probable outcomes if deterrence is continued or dropped (e.g. war, communist expansion), disagreement about policies is not evidence of differences in the values accorded these outcomes. Such inferences could be drawn only by obtaining their answers to questions about what policy they would favor with a large number of empirical factors assumed as givens. In the absence of such information there is no reason to accept Robert Levine's claim that the key difference between the two groups of theorists lies in their different relative fears of war and of communism, leading them to give different answers to questions such as: "How much risk of war are you willing to take in order to increase your chances for freedom?" Similarly, J. David Singer's claim that "Apparently Mr. Kahn dislikes the possibility of an occasional Soviet diplomatic victory more

[95] Abraham Kaplan, *The Conduct of Inquiry* (San Francisco: Chandler, 1964), pp. 28-29. For Rapoport's arguments see his *Strategy and Conscience* (New York: Harper and Row, 1964), "The Sources of Anguish," *Bulletin of the Atomic Scientists* 21 (December 1965), 34, and "Strategic and Nonstrategic Approaches to the Problems of Security and Peace," in Archibald, ed., *Strategic Interactions and Conflict*. For arguments similar to those expressed here, see Donald Brennan, "Strategy and Conscience," *Bulletin of the Atomic Scientists* 21 (December 1965), 30, and Schelling's review of Rapoport's book in the *American Economic Review* 54 (December 1964).

[96] Green, *Deadly Logic* (New York: Schocken, 1968), p. 250, italics omitted.

than he dislikes the possibility of nuclear war while I would—given these two alternatives—opt for the other," is misleading because Singer and Kahn differ in their estimates of the probability that various policies will in fact lead to war.[97]

It may well be true that security policies actually involve trade-offs of this kind. We may be able to gain a larger chance of physical survival only by decreasing the probability that we, and our NATO allies, can have the government we desire. But the theorists have not argued in this way. Both sides justify their recommendations on the grounds that their policies will increase the chances for both peace *and* freedom. Not only Amitai Etzioni and Charles Osgood but their opponents, too, claim to be offering "the hard way to peace" and "an alternative to war or surrender." The spiral theorists do not admit that their policy would involve any significant risk to American national security. And the proponents of deterrence argue that their policies are more likely to prevent war than are unilateral initiatives.

Claims for a Dominant Strategy

Because they do not recognize the trade-offs implicit in their analyses, both sets of theorists imply that the strategy they advocate is, to borrow a term from game theory, a dominant one—i.e. one that is better than the alternative no matter what the Soviets are like.[98] Deterrence theorists assume that, in the unlikely event that the United States has been wrong to see Russia as a threat, its policy would cost little except money because the Russians would understand that American arms would never be used for aggression. Our discussion of arms-hostility spirals is sufficient to indicate that this confidence is misplaced.

Lacking political power, the spiral theorists have had to provide a fuller defense of their views. But their treatments of the dangers of applying their prescriptions to an aggressive U.S.S.R. are both brief and inadequate. The worst outcome they envisage is that Russia would not cooperate and tensions would not be lowered. If this happens, gradualism can be considered to have been a test that has indicated, at low cost, that the U.S.S.R. is aggressive or that the screen of misunderstanding is too great to be penetrated by this strategy. No dangers are foreseen. As Osgood puts it: "Even if [the Russians] proved to be inherently and unalterably evil, the very gradualness of [the program] and the fact that we retain our ultimate capacity to retaliate means that we could make sure

[97] "Facts and Morals in the Arms Debate," *World Politics* 14 (January 1962), 257-58 (Levine places more stress on differences in theorists' analysis in *The Arms Debate* [Cambridge, Mass.: Harvard University Press, 1963]); "The Strategic Dilemma," *Journal of Conflict Resolution* 5 (June 1961), 203.

[98] The tendency to avoid value trade-offs appears in many other contexts, as we will discuss in the next chapter.

that this was their nature without shifting the present balance of power to any significant degree." Similarly, Etzioni claims that "since the initial concessions are only symbolic or limited, such generosity [which gradualism calls for] would not imperil national security. . . . Should [gradualism] fail, the more hazardous extreme strategies [of deterrence or unilateral disarmament] are still available. It is a 'maximum gain,' 'minimum regret' strategy."[99]

DANGERS OF APPLYING GRADUALISM TO AN AGGRESSIVE ADVERSARY

If the arguments summarized above were true, it would be hard to see why anyone would oppose the policy. This fact should be enough to make us suspicious of these claims, and indeed this position ignores three dangers in gradualism. Initiatives might be understood by the state's allies as evidence that it was willing to settle problems with the adversary regardless of the interests of others. This might be fine so long as such agreements were possible. But if the spiral assumptions were wrong, the state would have to face a hostile opponent with a weakened alliance system. A second, and related, danger is that the two major powers would be able to cooperate once or twice at the expense of their allies but would feel they must support them strongly in the next crisis lest the allies permanently defect. In 1912–1913 Germany and Britain worked together to dampen one of the perennial Balkan crises, but further cooperation did not follow; the reaction of their allies led them to refuse to play similar roles the next year. The danger is compounded if one or both of the major powers expects the other to continue its cooperative behavior. Thus it has been argued that the 1913 Anglo-German attempt "to lessen antagonism [by opening] negotiations . . . on specific colonial questions. . . . [may have done] more harm than good by encouraging each government to hope that the other might desert its allies in a crisis."[100]

The third and most important problem should have been obvious to those concerned with psychological variables. The adversary could develop an image of the state that would lead the adversary to take more

[99] Osgood, *An Alternative to War or Surrender*, p. 147; Etzioni, *The Hard Way to Peace*, pp. 105, 110.

[100] C. J. Lowe and M. L. Dockrill, *The Mirage of Power*, vol. 1: *British Foreign Policy, 1902-1914* (London: Routledge and Kegan Paul, 1972), pp. 107-18; Sontag, *European Diplomatic History*, p. 171. This also indicates that the common claim that the rigidity of the alliances was an important cause of World War I is only a half-truth and that the claim that 1914 shows that bipolar systems are unstable cannot be sustained. Cohesive intrablock relations might have led to flexible interblock relations. See Kenneth Waltz, "The Stability of a Bipolar World," *Daedalus* 93 (Summer 1964), 900-902. (This is not to deny that a total absence of stable coalitions could also have contributed to system stability.)

aggressive actions. The very separability between military capability and psychological gestures that the spiral theorists see as permitting a state to "design initiatives that will reduce tensions significantly without also endangering [its] vital interests"[101] means that a state can decrease its security without changing the military balance. In a situation in which outcomes are heavily influenced by interests and resolve, perceptions of others' interests and resolve, and perceptions of others' perceptions of one's interest and resolve,[102] policies designed to show that the state is not a menace can lead others to think that the state can be bullied. A statement that no issues worthy of a war divide the two blocs may imply to a country that wishes to exploit this belief that the state will back down rather than risk a war. Gestures designed to reduce the adversary's presumed sense of insecurity may make it believe that the state has given up all pretense of being able to protect others against attacks. Concessions in small matters could lead the adversary to believe that it had overestimated the value the state placed on a wide range of goals and that it therefore could prevail in disputes it had previously shunned.

Ironically, the spiral theorists commit the same errors that they attribute to deterrence theorists. They underestimate the difficulty of projecting a desired (and accurate) image and forget that the adversary draws inferences from the state's behavior in light of what it thinks the state knows of its intentions. If the deterrers' beliefs about the adversary are correct, initiatives are especially likely to be misperceived because the adversary not only does not fear the state's aggressiveness but also believes that the state knows this. The adversary would then see only one possible explanation for the state's behavior—the state is indicating in a face-saving way that the adversary is free to expand. The history of the 1930s again comes to mind.

SUGGESTIONS

Instead of incorrectly believing that he is calling for a dominant strategy, the policy advocate should try to reach the more modest goal of developing policies that have high payoffs if the assumptions about the adversary that underlie them are correct, yet have tolerable costs if these premises are wrong. One way to do this would be to procure the kinds and numbers of weapons that are useful for deterrence without simultaneously being as effective for aggression. Such a posture would break out of the security dilemma. Given the logic of nuclear weapons, this would mean avoiding systems that are useful only for a counterforce first strike (e.g. large, soft missiles) and paying extra for weapons that are especially

---

[101] Osgood, *An Alternative to War or Surrender*, p. 158.
[102] Jervis, *The Logic of Images in International Relations*, pp. 225-53.

effective for retaliation (e.g. relatively invulnerable Polaris-type submarines). There are three major problems, however. First, it is hard to tell what inferences the adversary would draw from various military postures. What would appear threatening to one state's decision-makers may not be so to another's. Second, a state that is pledged to protect a third area that it cannot defend with conventional forces will need to rely for deterrence on the threat to launch a nuclear strike in response to a conventional attack. To the extent that the state cannot convince the adversary that it values the third area as much as it values its own homeland, it will need something more than a second strike capability. Third, and most important, nuclear weapons do not have to be used all at once. One side could threaten to destroy one or more of the other's cities if the other did not do as it demanded. While there are reasons why, if both sides are close to equal in general resolve, threats of this kind are more apt to be credible if they are deterrent (demanding that the other not do something) rather than compellent (demanding that it take positive action),[103] the military hardware required cannot be classified as either defensive or threatening.

A second suggestion brings us closer to the concerns of this book. Because the effect of initiatives and threats depends to a large extent on the other's intentions and its perceptions of the first state, people who are debating policy should not only realize what they are arguing about but should also ask themselves what possible behavior on the part of the adversary would they take as evidence against the interpretation that they hold. This is especially true of those who see the other as aggressive because, as we will discuss in a later chapter, it is easy to see almost any evidence as consistent with this image. This means that it is often very hard for the other to show that it has only limited ambitions, especially if it fears that the first side is aggressive. The more such an adversary adheres to the familiar view that the state is apt to interpret friendly overtures as weakness, the more hesitant it will be to take unambiguous actions and the more sensitive the state should be to evidence of the adversary's willingness to support the status quo. Decision-makers would certainly have cause to worry if the only actions that would convince them that the adversary is not aggressive are measures they believe to be too risky for their own state to undertake (e.g. drastic arms cut, abolition of spheres of influence, or even unilateral initiatives). Similarly, those who feel that the adversary is not aggressive should consider what behavior would distinguish an aggressive, but cagey, state from a peaceful one caught in the security dilemma.

These suggestions show that the well-known arguments for the importance of empathizing with one's adversary in order to predict how he will

103 Schelling, *Arms and Influence*, pp. 69-91.

react are insufficient. One must try to empathize with a variety of possible outlooks, any one of which could be a true representation of the adversary. It is not enough to calculate how the other will respond to your action if your image of him is correct. You must also try to estimate how the other will respond if he has intentions and perceptions that are different from those that you think he probably has. (In doing so you must also keep in mind that he is likely to think that you do understand him and so will view your policy as though it were designed to deal with his own policy as he, rather than you, sees it.)

If it is true that perceptions of the other's intentions are a crucial element of policy-making and that such perceptions are often incorrect, we need to explore how states perceive others and why and where they often go wrong. This is the subject of the rest of this book. Military analysts talk of the "fog of battle"—the severe limits on the ability of each side to tell what the other's army (and often what its own army) is doing. But more important is the "fog of foreign policy-making." It is terribly hard to tell what others are up to, to infer their predispositions, and to predict how they will behave. Because of the importance and difficulty of these tasks, decision-makers do and must employ short-cuts to rationality, often without being aware of the way they are doing so. But these short-cuts often produce important kinds of systematic errors, many of which increase conflict.

Part II

Processes of Perception

CHAPTER FOUR

Cognitive Consistency and the Interaction between Theory and Data

IN STRESSING that images of the other side as hostile are maintained in the face of a wide range of evidence to the contrary, the spiral model draws on balance, congruity, and consistency theories of attitude organization.[1] In this chapter we will show that distinguishing between two kinds of consistency—rational and irrational—casts a new light on these psychological theories and their application to decision-making. Consistency can largely be understood in terms of the strong tendency for people to see what they expect to see and to assimilate incoming information to pre-existing images. These important processes should be explored in detail, for scholars too often apply the labels of closed-mindedness and cognitive distortion without understanding the necessary role of pre-existing beliefs in the perception and interpretation of new information. But while a proper appreciation of this role reveals that many common arguments about decision-making pathologies are incorrect, this does not mean that people strike an optimal balance between being open to new information and retaining beliefs that have demonstrated their utility. We will therefore discuss premature and excessive cognitive closure, isolate the variables that are at work, and show the political effects of these processes.

CONSISTENCY: RATIONAL AND IRRATIONAL

Scholars have found that people's belief structures tend toward consistency or balance. A balanced structure is one in which "All relations among 'good elements' [i.e. those that are positively valued] are positive (or null), all relations among 'bad elements' [i.e. those that are negatively valued] are positive (or null), and all relations among good and bad elements are negative (or null)."[2] We tend to believe that countries we

---

[1] For the purposes of this discussion, these theories can be considered to be the same and the terms used interchangeably.

[2] Robert Abelson and Milton Rosenberg, "Symbolic Psycho-Logic," *Behavioral Science* 3 (January 1958), 5. Three points about this definition should be noted. First, consistency is not to be equated with clear, coherent thinking. Second, consistency is not an all-or-none matter, and one can talk of degrees of consistency. But for complex belief systems, this conceptualization is not easy, and there are alternative formulations of the necessary measurements. Third, consistency is an

like do things we like, support goals we favor, and oppose countries that we oppose. We tend to think that countries that are our enemies make proposals that would harm us, work against the interests of our friends, and aid our opponents.

There is little doubt that this simple principle does indeed organize an impressive array of our cognitions. We feel more comfortable when configurations are balanced; we learn them more quickly, remember them better when they are balanced, and interpret new information in such a way as to maintain or increase balance.[3] For our purposes the explanations of why people see the world this way—e.g. because balanced structures form a "good Gestalt" or because they maximize simplicity[4]—are of interest mostly as they bear on the related question of the validity of the perceptions produced and the impact of this way of thinking on the quality of decision-making. Most psychologists who address these questions argue that the reasoning processes underlying consistency would "mortify a logician" and therefore should be called "psycho-logic rather than logic."[5] But while it is true that the elements of a balanced structure do not proceed by the rules of logic, a logician would be mortified only if the person who held the attitudes believed that they did so proceed.[6] To argue, as Charles Osgood does, that the inferences produced by consistency theory are not "logically necessary"[7] is correct but unenlightening. Deduction cannot provide the answers to most of the questions of

---

internal property of the person's belief system and does not depend on an outsider's view about what is consistent. All the observer has to know is the evaluation a person places on the elements and the relationships the person sees among them.

[3] The literature on this subject is immense. Much of it is summarized in Robert Zajonc, "Cognitive Theories in Social Psychology," in Gardner Lindzey and Elliot Aronson, eds., *The Handbook of Social Psychology*, vol. 1 (2nd ed., Reading, Mass.: Addison-Wesley, 1968), pp. 345-53. The more recent literature is discussed in Steven Sherman and Robert Wolosin, "Cognitive Biases in a Recognition Task," *Journal of Personality* 41 (1973), 395-412, and Jesse Delia and Walter Crockett, "Social Schemas, Cognitive Complexity, and the Learning of Social Structures," *ibid.* 41 (1973), 411-29. Also see Edward Blanchard, Marilyn Vickers, and Katina Price, "Balance Effects in Image Formation," *Journal of Social Psychology* 87 (1972), 37-44, and Chester Insko, Elaine Songer, and William McGarvey, "Balance, Positivity, and Agreement in the Jordan Paradigm: A Defense of Balance Theory," *Journal of Experimental Social Psychology* 10 (1974), 53-83. As we will discuss on pp. 126-28 below, the tendency to perceive structures as balanced is not universal.

[4] For a good discussion of this question see Norman Feather, "A Structural Balance Approach to the Analysis of Communication Effects," in Leonard Berkowitz, ed., *Advances in Experimental Social Psychology*, vol. 3 (New York: Academic Press, 1967), pp. 155-56.

[5] Abelson and Rosenberg, "Symbolic Psycho-Logic," p. 5.

[6] For a further discussion of this, see below, pp. 181-87.

[7] "Cognitive Dynamics in the Conduct of Human Affairs," *Public Opinion Quarterly* 24 (Summer 1960), 352.

concern to decision-makers. To estimate others' intentions, to predict the consequences of one's own actions, to draw inferences from ambiguous information, one must employ less certain intellectual tools. The questions to ask of these ways of thinking are whether they yield perceptions that are as accurate as those that would be produced by other processes and, at a minimum, whether they are rational.

By *rational* I mean those ways of interpreting evidence that conform to the generally accepted rules of drawing inferences. Conversely, irrational methods and influences violate these rules of the "scientific method" and would be rejected by the person if he were aware of employing them.[8] Although irrational processes presumably are less likely to lead to accurate perceptions and effective policies than are rational ones, rationality is only a very loose constraint that cannot designate a single conclusion. Contradictory inferences can be equally rational. But in a complex world of ambiguous information it is questionable whether a useful definition could have it otherwise. By making rationality only a loose constraint, to say that a process of thought is not rational is a strong statement.

Rational Consistency

Balanced attitude structures do not reveal irrationality if the cognitive consistency can be explained by the actor's well-grounded beliefs about the consistency existing in the environment he is perceiving. The only motivation to reduce inconsistency may be the drive to understand the world. Our cognitive structure is in balance when we think that two of our friends will like each other, or will like similar objects. The expectation that this will be the case is not irrational nor does it require a psy-

---

[8] For a similar definition, see Sidney Verba, "Assumptions of Rationality and Non-Rationality in Models of the International System," in Klaus Knorr and Sidney Verba, eds., *The International System* (Princeton: Princeton University Press, 1961), p. 94. One problem with this conception is that it is not useful when people disagree about the general rules for judging evidence and making decisions, as Premier Konoe and General Tojo did in the fall of 1941. "At one of their meetings, Tojo told Konoe that at some point during a man's lifetime he might find it necessary to jump, with his eyes closed, from the veranda of [a temple located on one of the heights of Kyoto] into the ravine below. That was Tojo's way of saying that he and others in the army believed that there were occasions when success or failure depended on the risks one was prepared to take, and that, for Japan, such an occasion had now arrived. . . . It was a pronouncement in the tradition of the samurai, whose willingness to take up any challenge, regardless of the odds, was legendary." (Robert Butow, *Tojo and the Coming of the War* [Princeton: Princeton University Press, 1961], p. 267.) For another case, see Steven Roberts, "Turkey, Long Loyal to U.S. Amid Westernization, Feels Betrayed by Arms Cutoff," *New York Times*, July 7, 1975. For the argument that many people do not accept certain axioms of rational decision theory, see Paul Slovic and Amos Tversky, "Who Accepts Savage's Axiom?" *Behavioral Science* 19 (1974), 368-73.

chological explanation if most people have found that their friends in fact do tend to like each other and do share common values.[9] Similar rationality due to learning is demonstrated in the "halo effect"—the influence of judgments about some of a person's traits on beliefs about other dimensions of his personality. If the perceiver has evidence that certain traits are correlated, halo effects can make perceptions relatively accurate at low cost.[10]

In other cases, perceived consistency not only accords with experience but involves linkages that, if not strictly required by logic, are supported by it. Osgood argues that "if we like [the president] and he happens to praise some diplomat from Afghanistan, we tend to feel favorably disposed toward this otherwise unknown individual. But let [the Soviet premier] comment on this same diplomat's sound idea—a kind of association known as 'the kiss of death'—and we suddenly find ourselves distrusting the man." But this is not the substitution of "emotional consistency for rational consistency," as Osgood claims.[11] It is quite rational to believe that many of the people your enemy supports will have interests opposed to yours. If you think the Russians are aggressive, there is nothing irrational about viewing their suggestions with suspicion—not only will you know of previous attempts at deception, but the belief that the Russians are adversaries implies, by definition, that you should be skeptical of their proposals. The parallel claim that "It is cognitively inconsistent for us to think of people we dislike and distrust making conciliatory moves" should similarly be seen in light of the fact that the meaning of *trust* implies that an actor who distrusts another will think it unlikely that the other will help him.[12]

COGNITIVE-AFFECTIVE BALANCE

An examination of the meaning of affective (i.e. like–dislike) judgments in international relations similarly indicates the rationality of many cases of affective-cognitive balance. William Scott's hypothesis is typical of

[9] For a similar argument about stereotypes, see Frances Korten, "The Stereotype as a Cognitive Construct," *Journal of Social Psychology* 90 (1973), 29-39.

[10] Julius Wishner, "Reanalysis of 'Impressions of Personality,'" *Psychological Review* 67 (1960), 96-112.

[11] Charles Osgood, *An Alternative to War or Surrender* (Urbana: University of Illinois Press), pp. 26-27.

[12] Osgood, "Cognitive Dynamics in the Conduct of Human Affairs," p. 341. Reanalysis of one of Abelson and Rosenberg's examples of psycho-logic shows that these inferences can be more rational than these authors believe. They claim that the beliefs that United States policy is anti-communist and that India opposes United States policy lead by psycho-logic to the conclusion that India favors communism. ("Symbolic Psycho-Logic," pp. 4-5.) But if we make the reasonable assumption that decision-makers are able to distinguish purposes from effects, those who believe that the American policy is effective will reach the unobjectionable conclusion that India acts in a way that aids communism.

many on this subject: "Favorable characteristics tend to be attributed to liked nations, and unfavorable characteristics to disliked nations."[13] But, for decision-makers at least, can we meaningfully talk of an independent affective dimension? Partly because statesmen strive to eliminate irrelevant considerations from their images of others, whether they "like" or "dislike" another state is usually determined by their beliefs about the degree of conflict between that country and their own. American leaders "like" Russia more in the 1970s than they did in the 1950s because they think that Russian policies are now more compatible with those of the United States.[14]

To demonstrate the value of their approach, consistency theorists would have to show that when a person likes another state, he also comes to evaluate it favorably on dimensions that are not logically linked to the attributes that caused him to like it in the first place. This would be the case, for example, if people believed that allied powers produce outstanding music and art. In fact, decision-makers often recognize that states whose interests coincide with theirs have as many undesired characteristics as their enemies. In the late 1930s, while many Chinese leaders felt that the United States would eventually "intervene against Japan, . . . such an expectation did not lead the Chinese to view America as any less selfish than Japan."[15] Disliking another's internal regime need not lead to opposing its foreign policy. Because an exclusive concern with foreign policy considerations is the hallmark of political "realism," it is not surprising to find Lenin and Churchill acting in ways not predicted by cognitive-affective consistency. In 1918 when the former was asked if he favored accepting Western aid in the event of a renewed German attack, he replied with the note: "Please add my vote in favor of the receipt of support and arms from the Anglo-French imperialist

---

[13] William Scott, "Psychological and Social Correlates of International Images," in Herbert Kelman, ed., *International Behavior* (New York: Holt, Rinehart, and Winston, 1965), p. 100.

[14] For evidence that people's evaluation of objects can be largely determined from more basic personal values and beliefs about the degree to which those objects contribute to the values, see Milton Rosenberg, "Cognitive Structure and Attitudinal Affect," *Journal of Abnormal and Social Psychology* 53 (1956), 367-72; Martin Fishbein, "A Consideration of Beliefs, and Their Role in Attitude Measurement," in Fishbein, ed., *Readings in Attitude Theory and Measurement* (New York: Wiley, 1967), pp. 257-66; Fishbein and Fred Coombs, "Basis for Decision: an Attitudinal Analysis of Voting Behavior," *Journal of Applied Social Psychology* 4 (1974), 95-124; Michael Shapiro, "Rational Political Man," *American Political Science Review* 63 (December 1969), 1106-19. A change in attitude toward an object has been found to follow from an experimentally produced change in the perceived instrumentality of that object for other values. See Earl Carlson, "Attitude Change through Modification of Attitude Structure," *Journal of Abnormal and Social Psychology* 52 (1956), 256-61.

[15] Akira Iriye, *Across the Pacific* (New York: Harcourt, Brace, 1967), p. 194.

brigands."[16] And when the latter announced that Britain would aid the U.S.S.R. after Germany's attack, he said: "If Hitler invaded Hell, I would make at least a favourable reference to the Devil in the House of Commons." These cases lend support to the proposition that when political judgments display cognitive-affective consistency, the reason is that the "liking" of another state and views about its specific characteristics are linked through the third factor of the actor's beliefs about the other's interests and intentions.

SOURCE–MESSAGE INTERACTION

Consistency between attitudes toward the source of a message and attitudes toward the truth value of the message is also, under many circumstances, rational. While it is important to consider separately—as most intelligence services do—the reliability of the source, as indicated by previous record, and the inherent credibility of the message, as indicated by its compatibility with other evidence, the final judgment should rest on an evaluation of both factors. Obviously one can rely too much on authorities, blindly accepting whatever they, and only they, say. But a judicious use of those believed to be experts—and this implies source-message consistency—brings benefits in excess of the costs.

Experimental evidence indicates some of the more complex ways in which views about a source and evaluations of its message interact rationally.[17] The credibility of the source, and thus the influence of later messages it sends, is diminished if an initial message is too discrepant from our beliefs.[18] Second, when a source is shown to be wrong on one issue, he and his other views are judged more severely. Thus advisers and experts who are proved incorrect are apt to lose some of their influence. American leaders discounted the sanguine accounts of General Westmoreland and others after the Tet offensive of 1968 revealed the fallibility of their judgments. The Chinese entry into the Korean War had a similar effect. In the last stages of the Battle of Jutland, Admiral Jellicoe ignored a message from the Admiralty that provided correct intelligence on the course of the German fleet because its earlier reports had been baseless.[19] Third, the reputation of the source is less important in con-

[16] Louis Fischer, *The Soviets in World Affairs* (New York: Vintage, abridged edition, 1960), p. 38 (emphasis omitted).

[17] The specific interactions between source and message credibility is the subject of several related theories. For an excellent review, see Chester Insko, *Theories of Attitude Change* (New York: Appleton-Century-Crofts, 1967), pp. 69-85.

[18] Carolyn Sherif, Muzafer Sherif, and Roger Nebergall, *Attitude and Attitude Change* (Philadelphia: Saunders, 1965); Carolyn Sherif and Norman Jackman, "Judgments of Truth by Participants in Collective Controversy," *Public Opinion Quarterly* 30 (Summer 1966), 173-86.

[19] Arthur Marder, *From the Dreadnought to Scapa Flow*, vol. 3: *Jutland and After (May 1916-December 1916)* (London: Oxford University Press, 1966), pp.

sidering an argument whose components are easily accessible to independent analyses. Experiments have found that a message that seems to make sense will be accepted regardless of to whom it is attributed, but one with a questionable content is apt to be accepted only if it comes from a respected source.[20]

In some cases the recipient of a message need be concerned only with the competence of the source. But in examining political communications, actors also have to inquire about possible conflicting perspectives and interests between the actor and the source. What are the source's concerns and biases? Do the source and the actor have different values? Is deception likely? Such skepticism will at times discredit valid information, but is on balance beneficial. Thus the Kennedy administration's down-grading of the Republican reports that the Russians were installing offensive missiles in Cuba need not be explained by psychological pressures toward cognitive consistency because it was obviously in the Republicans' interest to make exaggerated claims. Similarly, part of the reason why U.S. decision-makers were skeptical of the report by the Indian ambassador to China that the Chinese had threatened to enter the Korean War was that the ambassador was known to oppose American policy. On other occasions a person's interest gives his message added force. Participants in labor disputes may accept from a mediator arguments that they would reject if presented by the other side. And a hostile note is more apt to be believed if the recipient feels the agent conveying it is friendly.[21]

The influence of the source on interpretations of the message is best explained by consistency theory only when the person excludes other legitimate influences or allows irrelevant beliefs about the source to con-

---

148-49. For experimental evidence, see Percy Tannenbaum, "Mediated Generalization of Attitude Change Via the Principle of Congruity," *Journal of Personality and Social Psychology* 3 (1966), 493-99.

[20] Carl Hovland, Irving Janis, and Harold Kelley, *Communication and Persuasion* (New Haven: Yale University Press, 1953), pp. 19-55. It is also common and appropriate for an actor to consider the source when he is confronted with an assertion whose validity he can establish only with great expenditures of time, energy, or money. It is therefore not surprising that "Especially when work is published in abstract form or when full details of experimental procedures or mathematical proofs cannot be given, scientists often estimate the probable validity of the work on the basis of its author's reputation or, in some fields, on that of the organization in which the author works." (Warren Hagstrom, *The Scientific Community* [New York: Basic Books, 1965], p. 24.)

[21] See the incidents reported in John Wheeler-Bennett, *Munich* (New York: Viking, 1964), p. 121; Franklin Ford and Carl Schorske, "The Voice in the Wilderness: Robert Coulondre," in Gordon Craig and Felix Gilbert, *The Diplomats* (Princeton: Princeton University Press, 1953), p. 568; and Peter Gretton, *Former Naval Person* (London: Cassell, 1968), pp. 144-45. In these cases there was consistency between valuing the source and believing the message even though the content of the message was negatively valued.

taminate his perceptions. Thus while we should be concerned about the professional reputation of a scientist or policy analyst when considering his latest experiments or recommendations, we should not be influenced by whether he beats his wife or is obnoxious. A similarly illegitimate influence on perception is "the power of authority [which] does not at all hinge upon cognitive correctness but solely on the ability of authority to mete out arbitrary rewards and punishments."[22] Although the evidence is not conclusive, most experiments have found that irrelevant characteristics of the source have little or no influence on the message's credibility.[23]

IMPLICATIONS

For our concerns, the two central questions raised by these theories are the related ones of the source of the tendency to perceive patterns of relations as consistent and the question of whether this perceptual bias is a net asset or a net liability to decision-making. Several strands of evidence indicate that the tendency is derived from people's experiences with their environments and that it is, at minimum, rational. Social structures are more likely to be balanced than they would be by chance alone. If person A likes B and B likes C, A will probably like C. And people do tend to like the enemies of their enemies. This tendency is also apparent in international relations. Patterns of alliances and hostility often approximate balance as states that share the same enemies join forces and states that form close bonds with others earn the enmity of their new friends' foes.[24]

[22] Milton Rokeach, "Authority, Authoritarianism, and Conformity," in Erwin Berg and Bernard Bass, eds., *Conformity and Deviation* (New York: Harper and Row, 1961), p. 235. Rokeach's discussion of "party-line thinking" as a manifestation of closed-mindedness does not make this point clearly. See *The Open and Closed Mind* (New York: Basic Books, 1960), pp. 225-42.

[23] Much of the large body of literature is analyzed by William McGuire, "Attitudes and Opinions," in Paul Farnsworth et al., eds., *Annual Review of Psychology* 17 (Palo Alto: Annual Reviews, 1966), 487-90. In addition, see Jean Kerrick, "The Effect of Relevant and Non-Relevant Sources on Attitude Change," *Journal of Social Psychology* 47 (1958), 15-20; Ellen Berscheid, "Opinion Change and Communicator-Communicatee Similarity and Dissimilarity," *Journal of Personality and Social Psychology* 4 (1966), 670-80; Wolfgang Stroebe et al., "Balance and Differentiation in the Evaluation of Linked Attitude Objects," *ibid.* 16 (1970), 38-47; David Landy and Harold Sigall, "Beauty is Talent: Task Evaluation as a Function of the Performer's Physical Attractiveness," *ibid.* 29 (1974), 299-304; Herbert Simons, Nancy Berkowitz, and R. John Moyer, "Similarity, Credibility, and Attitude Change," *Psychological Bulletin* 73 (1970), 1-15. Irrelevant aspects of the person were found to be unimportant in a slightly different context in Douglas Bray, "The Prediction of Behavior from Two Attitude Scales," *Journal of Abnormal and Social Psychology* 45 (1950), 64-84.

[24] Nathan Kogan and Renato Tagiuri, "Interpersonal Preference and Cognitive Organization," *Journal of Abnormal and Social Psychology* 56 (1958), 113-16; Stephen Davol, "An Empirical Test of Structural Balance in Sociometric Triads,"

Because many of the structures in the world are balanced, the tendency to perceive balance will often serve people well. It will of course lead people astray when the stimuli do not fit this pattern. This is one reason why American decision-makers were slow to recognize that two .of their enemies (i.e. Russia and China) were hostile to each other. But errors like this and the associated finding that people perceive their environment as more consistent than it is[25] do not mean that they should perceive it differently. If we have to bet on whether outcome A or outcome B will occur and we know that A will occur 60 percent of the time, we should not fall prey to the fallacy of the probability-matching strategy of betting on A only three out of every five plays. As long as the chance of A's occurring is greater than that of B, we should always bet on it. This helps explain why it is that when people judge strangers "they make inferences from their relatively gross knowledge of the subgroup to which they think the stranger belongs and . . . [when they try to utilize specific cues from the other's behavior] the effect is to reduce accuracy."[26] Furthermore, as the a priori probability that a given characteristic or object will be present increases, it is rational for the person to perceive that characteristic in the face of increasing amounts of discrepant information. Unfortunately, however, psychological theories and experiments have not been designed to deal with questions arising from this perspective. Little attention has been paid to the degree to which various environments are in fact balanced, and most experiments provide the subjects with minimal and/or extremely ambiguous information in order to bring out any preconceptions, however slight, that the subjects have, and so cannot reveal how much or what kind of information would be necessary to override the pressure to perceive consistency. Indeed, although no one has precisely measured the strength of this tendency, it is clear that it is not strong enough to make perceptions of inconsistency unusual. Especially when the amount and clarity of the evidence is high,

---

ibid. 59 (1959), 393-98; Theodore Newcomb, "An Approach to the Study of Communicative Acts," *Psychological Review* 60 (1953), 393-404; Elliot Aronson and Vernon Cope, "My Enemy's Enemy Is My Friend," *Journal of Personality and Social Psychology* 8 (1968), 8-12; Frank Harary, "A Structural Analysis of the Situation in the Middle East," *Journal of Conflict Resolution* 5 (June 1961), 167-78; Brian Healy and Arthur Stein, "The Balance of Power in International History," *ibid.* 17 (March 1973), 33-61.

[25] Kogan and Tagiuri, "Interpersonal Preference and Cognitive Organization."

[26] N. L. Gage, "Judging Interests from Expressive Behavior," *Psychological Monographs* 66, No. 18 (whole No. 350) (1952), 10. Also see W. J. Crow, "The Effect of Training Upon Accuracy and Variability in Interpersonal Perception," *Journal of Abnormal and Social Psychology* 55 (1957), 355-59; William Soskin, "Influence of Four Types of Data on Diagnostic Conceptualization in Psychological Testing," *ibid.* 58 (1959), 69-78. A different conclusion is reached in Victor Cline and James Richards, "Accuracy of Interpersonal Perception—A General Trait?" *ibid.* 60 (1960), 1-7.

people realize that some of their friends do not like each other, that people they admire sometimes behave in a reprehensible manner, and that valued objects can be associated with undesired ones. Furthermore, the tendency to perceive balance is stronger in cognitively simple people than in cognitively complex ones.[27] So, striking as the findings of balance theory are, they do not show that the rules people are following diverge from those optimally designed to produce accurate perceptions and valid inferences.

This argument applies as well to the other cognitive biases that often lead to the perceptions of relations as balanced. There seem to be reciprocity effects (if A likes B, we think B is apt to like A) generalization effects (if A likes B, we think A will like other people and that other people will like B); positivity effects (we expect A to like B); agreement effects (we expect A and B to have similar opinions).[28] Here too evidence about the actual environment is more limited than evidence about people's cognitive structures, but these biases probably correspond to reality.[29] If A likes B, the chances are greater than 50/50 that B will like A. If A likes B, this is also some indication that A tends to like other people and that B is likable. In a society in which most people are friendly, it makes sense to guess that two people will like each other. And an agreement bias could readily have been learned from society characterized by a great deal of consensus.

Finally, and most importantly, the tendency to perceive balance is not universal, but is limited to certain contexts—contexts that, furthermore, are in fact likely to be balanced. The effect shows up most clearly when people are asked about friendship relations. It does not appear with perceptions of acquaintanceship, and such relations probably do not tend to be balanced in the world. Other cases in which people do not tend to see consistency can also be explained by well-grounded beliefs about the environment. If two boys love the same girl, we do not expect them to like each other. If two people share the same views on integration, we think they will like each other, but if they share the same opinions about *Newsweek* we have no such expectation. The scholars who conducted this study argue that the explanation for this difference is that integra-

[27] For some evidence on perceived inconsistency, see Irwin Silverman, "On the Resolution and Tolerance of Cognitive Inconsistency in a Natural-Occurring Event," *Journal of Personality and Social Psychology* 17 (1971), 171-78. Data on the differences between cognitively simple and cognitive complex people are presented in Allan Press, Walter Crockett, and Paul Rosenkrantz, "Cognitive Complexity and the Learning of Balanced and Unbalanced Social Structures," *Journal of Personality* 37 (1969), 541-53; and Delia and Crockett, "Social Schemas, Cognitive Complexity, and the Learning of Social Structures."

[28] These findings are summarized in the literature cited in footnote 3.

[29] Stephen Jones, "Some Determinants of Interpersonal Evaluating Behavior," *Journal of Personality and Social Psychology* 3 (1966), 397-403.

tion is "important" to people and *Newsweek* is not. This account is incomplete and unsatisfying, however, unless we extend it to argue that people seem to believe, probably correctly, that knowing a person's views on an important issue tells us much more about him than does knowing his views on a trivial one. There is more disagreement on the merits of integration than on the merits of *Newsweek*, and opinions on the former issue are related to more aspects of the person's character and beliefs than are his views on the latter subject. For these two reasons, knowing that a person shares our opinion on an important and controversial issue gives us grounds for thinking we will like him; knowing that he reads the same newsmagazine that we do provides no such grounds. That people reason in this way and that these beliefs make sense is indicated by an analysis of friendship groups that showed that, although friends tended to share the same general values, they did not tend to share characteristics that provide less information about the person—e.g. tastes in foods. Indeed other studies have shown that a person—even if he is prejudiced —is more likely to select as a partner in a task someone who shares his views on significant topics than someone who shares his race.[30]

Not only does the balance bias appear only in certain contexts, but other biases or, to use Clinton De Soto's term, schemas are employed when people are perceiving certain other kinds of relationships. Thus when people are asked about influence or dominance relations, they expect to find a hierarchical rather than a balanced pattern. It is not the mere absence of the bias toward seeing consistency that is important, but the existence of another bias that is operating in another kind of setting, thus indicating that "balance and other complex schemas will be invoked when the individual knows he is dealing with information from an interrelated social system to which the schema is appropriate."[31] People learn both the schemas and the situations that they are likely to fit and apply them in the proper contexts. Reasoning and experiences can thus go a

[30] The evidence on acquaintanceship comes from Clinton De Soto, Nancy Henley, and Marvin London, "Balance and the Grouping Schema," *Journal of Personality and Social Psychology* 8 (1968), 1-7; the experiment dealing with integration and *Newsweek* is Robert Zajonc and Eugene Burnstein, "The Learning of Balanced and Unbalanced Social Structures," *Journal of Personality* 33 (1965), 153-63; Theodore Newcomb, "Interpersonal Balance," in Robert Abelson et al., eds., *Theories of Cognitive Consistency* (Chicago: Rand McNally, 1968), pp. 47-48; Milton Rokeach, *Beliefs, Attitudes, and Values* (San Francisco: Jossey-Bass, 1970), chapter 3.

[31] Clinton De Soto, "Learning a Social Structure," *Journal of Abnormal and Social Psychology* 60 (1960), 417-21. Also see James Kuethe, "Pervasive Influence of Social Schemata," *ibid.* 68 (1964), 248-54; Clinton De Soto and Frank Albrecht, "Conceptual Good Figures," in Abelson et al., eds., *Theories of Cognitive Consistency*, pp. 504-11, and De Soto and Albrecht, "Cognition and Social Orderings," *ibid.*, pp. 531-38. The quote is from Delia and Crockett, "Social Schemas, Cognitive Complexity, and the Learning of Social Structures," 423-24.

long way toward accounting for the cases in which people tend to perceive balance and those in which they do not.

Irrational Consistency—Avoidance of Value Trade-Offs

One type of consistency, although not treated separately by psychologists, merits special attention because it cannot be explained by rational procedures for making sense out of the world: people who favor a policy usually believe that it is supported by many logically independent reasons.[32] When a person believes that a policy contributes to one value, he is likely to believe that it also contributes to several other values, even though there is no reason why the world should be constructed in such a neat and helpful manner. This would not be irrational if in order to agree with a proposition the person had to affirm a number of necessary conditions.[33] But often the person holds a number of beliefs, each of which would be sufficient to justify his policy preference. In opposing a proposal, many people fit Dean Acheson's description of Arthur Vandenberg's characteristic stand: "He declared the end unattainable, the means harebrained, and the cost staggering."[34]

[32] This hypothesis can be viewed as an application of consistency theories to one category of cognitions (those concerning a policy and the various advantages and disadvantages believed to go with it) and is compatible with theories dealing with the avoidance of psychological conflict. For support of this hypothesis from consistency theory, see Edward Jones and Harold Gerard, *Foundations of Social Psychology* (New York: Wiley, 1967), pp. 180-81, and Herbert Kelman and Reuben Baron, "Inconsistency as a Psychological Signal," in Abelson et al., eds., *Theories of Cognitive Consistency*, pp. 331-36.

Irrational consistency has also been found in decision-making experiments (John Steinbruner, *Some Effects of Decision Procedures on Policy Outcomes* [Cambridge, Mass.: M.I.T. Center for International Studies, February 1970]) and in the systematic mapping of belief systems (Robert Axelrod, "Psycho-Algebra: A Mathematical Theory of Cognition and Choice with an Application to the British Eastern Committee in 1918," *Peace Research Society (International) Papers* 18 (1972), 113-31; and G. Matthew Bonham and Michael Shapiro, "Explanation of the Unexpected: Computer Simulation of a Foreign Policy Adviser," in Robert Axelrod, ed., *The Structure of Decision* [Princeton: Princeton University Press, forthcoming]). Also see John Steinbruner, *The Cybernetic Theory of Decision* (Princeton: Princeton University Press, 1974).

[33] Thus one scholar argues that, since most Americans traditionally opposed overseas expansion, the imperialism of the turn of the century would not have occurred had there not been several strong and independent motives supporting it. (A. E. Campbell, "Afterword" in Campbell, ed., *Expansion and Imperialism* [New York: Harper and Row, 1970], p. 179.) But in these circumstances there is no logical reason why those who oppose the new departure should disagree with the proponents on all points.

[34] Quoted in Dean Acheson, "Arthur Vandenberg and the Senate," in Nelson Polsby, ed., *Congressional Behavior* (New York: Random House, 1971), p. 95. Similarly, George Kennan points out that "Anton Chekhov, who was also a doctor, once observed that when a large variety of remedies were recommended for the same disease, it was a pretty sure sign that none of them was any good." (*American Diplomacy, 1900-1950* [Chicago: University of Chicago Press, 1951], p. 17.)

Belief systems thus often display overkill. People who favored a nuclear test-ban believed that testing created a serious medical danger, would not lead to major weapons improvements, and was a source of international tension. Those who opposed the treaty usually took the opposite position on all three issues. Yet neither logic nor experience indicates that there should be any such relationship. The health risks of testing are in no way connected with the military advantages, and a priori we should not expect any correlation between people's views on these questions. Similarly, those who favored allowing large numbers of Jewish refugees into this country before and during World War II disagreed with those who opposed this policy on a whole range of logically unrelated issues—the availability of shipping, the security risk presented by the refugees, the danger to the Jews if they remained in Nazi territory, and the efficacy of threatening Germans with war-crimes trials and bombing if they carried out mass murder.[35] To shift to another arena, it was not a personal foible of Secretary of Defense Charles Wilson that led him to believe that what was good for his company was also good for his country. What professor sees conflicts between the advancement of his career, the development of his discipline, the good of his university, and the best interests of the nation?[36] (Of course we try to arrange incentives so as to bring these values into alignment, but can we succeed so often?) Similarly, when I send my two-year-old to her room because she is interrupting my work with her demands to play with the typewriter, I tell myself that it is good for her to learn to respect the rights of others and to defer her gratification.

It is frequently argued that values and the resulting goals are treated as constraints in complex decision-making. Rather than engaging in trade-offs, an actor strives to insure that he does not fall below some minimum level on any of his goals.[37] Although this model is often appropriate, it cannot be applied to cases where the necessary information is absent or highly ambiguous. For example, even if a decision-maker formulated as constraints his goals of reducing the danger of war and minimizing the chances of costly political defeats, he would still need accurate information on whether the current policy or its alternatives

---

[35] Henry Feingold, *The Politics of Rescue* (New Brunswick, N.J.: Rutgers University Press, 1970).

[36] Erving Goffman notes a similar "prearranged harmony" in psychiatric theory: "I have found especially refreshing the discussion of the psychological importance of the patient's appreciating that the therapist has a life of his own and that it would not be good for the patient if the therapist postponed his vacation, or saw the patient in response to midnight telephone calls, or allowed himself to be physically endangered by the patient." (*Asylums* [Garden City, N.Y.: Doubleday, 1961], p. 371.)

[37] Richard Cyert and James March, *A Behavioral Theory of the Firm* (Englewood Cliffs, N.J.: Prentice-Hall, 1963).

was performing or would perform satisfactorily. When this is the very question at issue—as it often is in important foreign policy choices— then trade-offs are likely to be avoided by the more severe methods under examination here.

When cognitions are organized to produce irrational consistency, choices are easier since all considerations are seen as pointing to the same conclusion. Nothing has to be sacrified. But, since the real world is not as benign as these perceptions, values are indeed sacrificed and important choices are made, only they are made inadvertently. The unforeseen and unfortunate consequences of this process are explored below.[38]

When the goal is agreed upon, all that is logically needed to affirm a strategy is the belief that it is most likely to work at lowest cost. But people often go further than this by placing both a very high estimate on the probability of their plan's succeeding and a very low estimate on the chances that the alternative would work. In the debate on strategy that bitterly split the British throughout World War I, for example, the "Easterners" (i.e. those who opposed concentrating Allied efforts on the Western trenches and urged strengthening a variety of fronts in order to knock Germany's allies out of the war and outflank her) differed with the "Westerners" about both the prospects for a breakthrough in France and Belgium and the potential gains of offensives elsewhere. (Since the Westerners agreed that the maintenance of control over the British empire was an important war aim, they had to resort "to the unlikely argument that the tribesmen of Arabia, Persia and Afghanistan had their eyes fixed firmly on the western front and could safely be expected to hold the British in awe and cause them no trouble provided they won victories in France.") In the parallel debate between the British and Americans in early 1942, the British argued that their ally not only overestimated the ease of crossing the Channel but also underestimated the dangers in not retaking North Africa.[39]

People rarely differ about the value of an objective without also disagreeing about the probability that it can be attained and the costs this would entail. It is common, for example, for people who disapprove of the goals of a protest movement to believe that the movement's tactics are ineffective. When the debate is phrased in cost-benefit terms, those who favor a project are likely to estimate the costs as lower and the benefits as higher than do the opponents. If the dispute is less technical, one side is apt to say that the goal is vital and attainable without the sacrifice

[38] Pp. 138-41.
[39] V. H. Rothwell, *British War Aims and Peace Diplomacy, 1914-1918* (Oxford: Clarendon Press, 1971), p. 88; Maxwell Schoenfeld, *The War Ministry of Winston Churchill* (Ames: Iowa State University Press, 1972), p. 167.

of other important values, while the other side will argue that the goal is both less important and more costly.

Thus it is not surprising that the French, who favored stringent military terms but lenient naval terms for the 1918 armistice, thought that the punitive naval terms sought by Britain might lead the Germans to reject the armistice, while the British were confident the Germans would surrender their navy but doubted whether they would accept the French demands for crippling their ground forces. And the next year one of the German statesmen who opposed signing the Treaty of Versailles "Not only . . . believe[d] that the treaty was so unjust that to sign it would mean the eventual ruin of Germany, but . . . he had even managed to convince himself that Germany could force the Allies to revise it."[40]

This inverse relationship between the importance of the goal and the expected cost of reaching it has characterized many disputes over American foreign policy. During the Chinese civil war those policy-makers who believed that economic and military aid would not increase the chances of a Nationalist victory also believed that a communist government in China would have neither the desire nor the ability to menace the United States. Those who favored aid thought that a victory for Chiang was both possible and important. An identical pattern is revealed by the debate in the United States over aiding the Allies before Pearl Harbor. Many of those who favored aid believed that a German victory would endanger American national security and that Hitler would be defeated by American material aid. The isolationists thought that the United States could co-exist with Germany and that a German victory could not be prevented by American supplies and arms.[41] In a more recent debate, most of those who favored withdrawing from Vietnam believed both that the war could not be won and that the costs of defeat were relatively low. Those who thought we could win felt that the costs of losing were high (i.e. that the "domino theory" applied).[42]

Debates ranging over subjects from the broadest lines of policy to the procurement of specific weapons systems often display a similar lack of perception of trade-offs. At the most general level, many writers have joined morality and expediency by echoing the view of an eighteenth-

[40] Harry Rudin, *Armistice 1918* (Hamden, Conn.: Archon Books, 1967), pp. 288-90; Richard Watt, *The Kings Depart* (New York: Simon and Schuster, 1968), p. 461.

[41] Tang Tsou, *America's Failure in China, 1941-50* (Chicago: University of Chicago Press, 1963), p. 550; Wayne Cole, "American Entry into World War II: A Historiographical Appraisal," in Arnold Offner, ed., *America and the Origins of World War II* (Boston: Houghton Mifflin, 1971), pp. 13-14.

[42] While these cognitive elements can be linked through general beliefs about the nature of guerrilla war (one view holding that outcomes are determined mostly by indigenous factors, the other arguing for the importance of external military involvement), this does not seem to be enough to explain the degree of consistency.

century liberal that "The true interests of a nation never yet stood in opposition to the general interest of mankind; and it can never happen that philanthropy and patriotism can impose on any man inconsistent duties." Or, as *The Times* put it in 1885: "If Great Britain has turned itself into a coal-shed and blacksmith's forge, it is for the behoof of mankind as well as its own." More recently, "taking an internationalist consciousness for granted, the [British] Labour Party also took it for granted that national interests and international obligations coincided."[43] The policies to implement these lofty goals are also claimed, almost by definition, to maximize all important values. For example, both the advocates of free trade and of protection claimed that their respective polices: 1) were best on purely economic grounds, 2) led to international harmony, and 3) contributed to economic preparations for war. And "Within the Mercantilist conception of wealth, a conflict between wealth and power aims of the state is well-nigh unthinkable."[44]

On more specific questions also, morality is rarely seen to conflict with other values. Many states have echoed the claim put before the Athenian assembly by the Corinthians: by aiding us "you will be acting as you ought to act and at the same time you will be making the wisest decision in your own interests." In the debate over U.S. policy toward East Pakistan in 1971, both sides claimed that morality and national interest would be served by their proposals. So it is not surprising that the advocates of strategic bombing argued that this "doctrine was . . . humane, on the grounds that by taking the war direct to the enemy people it would be made short and quickly decisive."[45]

[43] Quoted in E. H. Carr, *The Twenty Years' Crisis* (New York: Harper and Row, 1964), pp. 45, 76; Michael Gordon, *Conflict and Consensus in Labour's Foreign Policy* (Stanford: Stanford University Press, 1969), p. 17. Dean Rusk's view was similar. See G. G. Gutierrez, "Dean Rusk and Southeast Asia: An Operational Code Analysis," p. 44, presented at the 1973 meeting of the American Political Science Association.

[44] Albert Hirschman, *National Power and Foreign Trade* (Berkeley and Los Angeles: University of California Press, 1969), pp. 5-6. As Hirschman implies, beliefs that establish the framework for a person's general political and social views often incorporate a harmony of interests at such a deep and conceptual level that a conflict among them would require the person to abandon, or at least revise drastically, much of his view of the world. This was obviously the case when, in stressing the importance of self-determination in the postwar world, Franklin Roosevelt announced: "No nation in all the world that is free to make a choice is going to set itself up under the Fascist form of government, or the Nazi form of government, or the Japanese warlord form of government." (Robert Sherwood, *Roosevelt and Hopkins* [New York: Harper and Brothers, 1948], p. 702.)

[45] Thucydides, *The Peloponnesian War*, translated by Rex Warner (Baltimore: Penguin, 1954), p. 37; Walter Millis, *Arms and Men* (New York: Capricorn, 1967), p. 259. In many cases decision-makers will deny the relevance of morality to their actions. But it is rare to find avowals like that of the French minister of defense: "morally, the arms sales [to underdeveloped countries] are condemnable,

A common way that trade-offs are avoided on national security policies is illustrated by Asquith's solution to the dilemma he faced before World War I.

On the one hand he was a Liberal Chancellor of the Exchequer, the inheritor of the retrenchment traditions of Gladstone and Harcourt. On the other, he was the leader, within the Government, of the group which believed in a strong Britain. Sometimes he sought to compromise his two responsibilities by seeing proposed expenditure as militarily unnecessary.[46]

When the British found they could not afford to station a fleet in Singapore after the war, they "reassured themselves by arguing that in the event of trouble in the Far East, the fleet could always go out there." And in the debates over the re-evaluation of British defense policy in 1933-1934, those who argued that Britain could not afford to take a strong stand against Japan also claimed that British and Japanese goals were compatible.[47] In these and similar cases the government argued that those calling for greater defense spending were overestimating the threat, but that, if the threat did materialize, their proposals would cope with it.

Similarly, when British policy-makers decided to reduce their country's conventional military forces in the late 1950s, they were able to believe that they did not need also to reduce their commitments by holding to inadequately examined assumptions about airlift capability and tactical nuclear weapons. At the start of the preparedness debate during World War I, Woodrow Wilson adopted a variant of this stance—he believed that the foreign threat was not great enough to justify a "nation trained to arms," but that the equivalent military strength could be provided by asking men to "volunteer for training."[48]

Beliefs about specific policies often display the same kind of consistency, as we can see from debates about Korea and Vietnam. In discussions that preceded the Chinese intervention, MacArthur supported his belligerent stand by several independent claims: minor concessions to China would do no good, establishing a buffer zone in northern Korea would be seen in Asia as a defeat, sending U.S. troops to the Yalu would not provoke Chinese intervention, and if China did enter, her troops

but politically they are not so condemnable as people say." (Quoted in James Clarity, "Arms Sales Stir Dispute in France," *New York Times*, January 25, 1976.)

[46] Roy Jenkins, *Asquith* (London: Collins, 1964), p. 167.

[47] Russell Grenfell, *Main Fleet to Singapore* (New York: Macmillan Co., 1952), p. 47; Stephen Endicott, *Diplomacy and Enterprise: British China Policy, 1933-1937* (Vancouver: University of British Columbia Press, 1975), pp. 71-72.

[48] Phillip Darby, *British Defence Policy East of Suez, 1947-1968* (London: Oxford University Press, 1973), pp. 118-20; Millis, *Arms and Men*, p. 216.

could be destroyed from the air. After the Chinese joined the war, Mac-Arthur argued that bombing China would be militarily effective and would not increase the risk of world war. Truman and his advisers disagreed on both points. Similarly, officials who favored bombing North Vietnam felt that this would: 1) decrease American casualties, 2) drastically increase the cost of the war to the North, 3) increase the chance of the North's entering negotiations, without increasing the danger of Soviet or Chinese intervention. Those who opposed bombing disagreed on all points. As the Pentagon Papers analysts put it: "there was no dearth of reasons for striking North. Indeed one almost has the impression that there were more reasons than were required."[49]

Multiple, independent, reinforcing arguments also appear in debates over weapons systems. During the First World War, those in the British Admiralty who opposed the introduction of convoys to thwart U-boats claimed that the necessary escorts were not available, port congestion would be intolerable, and merchant ships would not be able to maintain the required tight formation. Similarly, in the recent debate over the Anti-Ballistic Missile, those who felt that the growing Soviet missile force was a danger to America's second-strike capability also were likely to think that a thin city defense would be useful in confrontations with China. People who disagreed on one of these points not only usually disagreed on the other, but also argued that: 1) an ABM system would destabilize the arms race, 2) in the event of a war, it would not save many lives, 3) it would generate strong pressures to build a thick system, and 4) the costs were grossly underestimated.[50]

A common and important manifestation of this kind of consistency is the belief that the favored policy will minimize the danger of foreign domination and maximize the chances of maintaining peace. In the last chapter, we argued that both the spiral and deterrence analysts of the Cold War take these positions. In many previous cases, too, both those advocating concessions and those calling for firmness have argued that their policies offered "an alternative to war or surrender." These claims were made, for example, in the debate within the United States on policy toward Japan before World War II, and that between the United States and Britain on policy toward Spain and Portugal during the war. Even more striking are the cases of disputes within countries that are the direct target of demands. Thus those in Finland in 1939 who believed that con-

[49] Tsou, *America's Failure in China*, p. 584; *The Pentagon Papers* (New York: Bantam Books, 1971), p. 344.

[50] Arthur Marder, *From the Dreadnought to Scapa Flow*, vol. 4, *1917: Year of Crisis* (London: Oxford University Press, 1969), pp. 115-37. (Similar consistency exists in the debate over the utility of aircraft carriers. See Robert Smith, "Congress Panel Studies Carrier," *New York Times*, February 24, 1970, p. 9); Aaron Wildavsky, "The Politics of ABM," *Commentary* 48 (November 1969), 55-63.

cessions to Russia would only lead to greater demands also thought that the Soviets would back down in the face of Finnish firmness. And those who denied that concessions would lead to loss of major values believed that Russia would fight for what she had demanded. Similarly, at the end of the nineteenth century those British officials who believed that a Russian port on the Persian Gulf would constitute a major threat to India also thought that firmness could deter Russia, and those who believed that a Russian port would not change the political balance also believed that Russia could not be stopped without forcing her into a hostile diplomatic coalition or a war.[51] This consistency not only lacks a rational explanation, but logic would indicate that the belief that the other side would fight for its demands should be linked to the view that it had threatening long-run intentions since it is likely that the adversary would be willing to incur the high costs of a war only if it sought extensive gains.[52]

A related claim of actors to have a dominant strategy—i.e. one that is best no matter what the other state does—is common outside of the Cold War debate. Thus Austria's Schuschnigg felt that his German policy was best whether or not Hitler's intentions were friendly. And in calling for the bombing of North Vietnam, McGeorge Bundy argued that "even if it fails, the policy will be worth it. At a minimum it will damp down the charge that we did not do all that we could have done, and this charge will be important in many countries, including our own."[53] Of course it is wise to seek a strategy that is dominant, but one may wonder whether the world is arranged so benignly that these strategies can occur as often as they are claimed.

Although these pathologies are by no means unique to the United States, American leaders' views have contained irrational consistency on an alarming number of important issues, as many of the cases discussed

[51] Herbert Feis, *The Road to Pearl Harbor* (Princeton: Princeton University Press, 1950); Feis, *The Spanish Story* (New York: Knopf, 1948); Max Jakobson, *The Diplomacy of the Winter War* (Cambridge, Mass.: Harvard University Press, 1961), pp. 136-39; Briton Cooper Busch, *Britain and the Persian Gulf, 1894-1914* (Berkeley and Los Angeles: University of California Press, 1967), pp. 212-29. The consistency in the common tendency for actors to argue that an adversary will not enter a conflict, and that if he does the actor can easily defeat him, is not necessarily irrational. Assuming that the actor believes the adversary shares this perception of their relative strengths, the belief that he would win is one of the causes of the actor's low estimate of the probability that the enemy will undertake hostile actions.

[52] This was the argument used by some anti-appeasers. Cf. the dispatch of the French ambassador to Germany quoted in Lewis Namier, *Diplomatic Prelude, 1938-39* (London: Macmillan and Co., 1948), p. 241.

[53] Gerhard Weinberg, *The Foreign Policy of Hitler's Germany* (Chicago: University of Chicago Press, 1970), p. 268; *The Pentagon Papers* (Senator Gravel edition) (Boston: Beacon Press, 1971), vol. 3, p. 314.

above have shown. Indeed the major theme of Robert Osgood's study is that both "realists" and "idealists" refused to recognize any conflict between "ideals and self-interest in America's foreign relations." While one group favored employing a high degree of military power and the other group did not, both claimed that their policies served the values of both national interest and international well-being and morality.[54]

Three strands contribute to this American propensity. First, economic plenty has encouraged the belief that choices can be avoided by expanding the pie. Second, liberalism with its emphasis on harmony of interests is not conducive to the examination of trade-offs among important values.[55] Thus many aspects of American culture share an optimistic outlook. For example, in their brilliant study Martha Wolfenstein and Nathan Leites found that American movies, as contrasted with those of the British or French, portray situations in which one can have his cake and eat it too. Good and evil are rarely combined in one person. Death and guilt lose their sting. Instead tension is supplied by

> discrepancies between appearance and reality; the hero and heroine in melodramas frequently appear different from what they really are. We are shown how the hero appears to the police, as a criminal, how the heroine appears to the hero, as a wicked woman. The plot is less one of action than of proof or rather disproof. The incriminating false appearance must be dispelled. It must be proved that what was supposed to have happened did not happen. The potentialities of the hero and heroine for serious action are realized only in a false appearance, which indicates what they might have done if they had been carried away by dangerous impulses. . . . We can see the hero and heroine carrying out forbidden wishes and in the end see them escape penalties since these acts are shown to be merely a false appearance. Hence the character who sees things mistakenly has a special importance in American films. It is from his point of view that we can see the fulfilment of forbidden wishes, while at the same time we get the assurance that nothing has happened.[56]

A third strand has been provided by America's international experiences. As Wolfers shows, America's advantageous geographical position has permitted her great freedom of choice.[57] Enjoying a large element of "free security," the United States has not had to make the same hard

---

[54] *Ideals and Self-Interest in America's Foreign Relations* (Chicago: University of Chicago Press, 1953).

[55] Kenneth Minogue, *The Liberal Mind* (New York: Vintage, 1968). I am grateful to Paul Weaver for discussions on this point.

[56] *Movies: A Psychological Study* (Glencoe, Ill.: Free Press, 1950), pp. 243-44. A brief summary cannot do justice to this fascinating and subtle book.

[57] *Discord and Collaboration* (Baltimore: Johns Hopkins Press, 1962), pp. 233-51. This argument applies, with reduced strength, to Great Britain.

choices that others have faced.[58] American statesmen have been slower to perceive trade-offs because in their benign environment they have had to make fewer sacrifices.

Although it is difficult to speak with confidence of the processes by which this consistency develops, it seems clear that decision-makers do not simultaneously estimate how a policy will affect many values. Instead they at first look at only one or two most salient values. As they come to favor the policy that seems best on these restricted dimensions, they alter their earlier beliefs and establish new ones so that as many reasons as possible support their choice. (As we will discuss later, the operation of cognitive dissonance contributes to this process.) That policy preferences precede and determine at least some of the arguments in favor of that policy is suggested by the unlikely coincidence of so many considerations. It is hard to imagine any other mechanism that could produce this arrangement of beliefs. It seems implausible, for example, that Neville Chamberlain would have argued against the creation of a British Expeditionary Force on the grounds that any German attack on France would develop too rapidly for the British army to intervene effectively had he not already concluded that Germany could be appeased.[59]

Even stronger evidence for this explanation is provided by cases in which inconsistent premises are used to support a conclusion. Thus the U.S. navy argued that it needed a new attack airplane because its longer range would allow the aircraft carriers to remain further out at sea, but also that it needed a large number of missile ships to protect the carriers against Soviet short-range planes.[60] Similarly, contradictory beliefs are used to justify different preferences that are held simultaneously. For example, liberals argue that social change in South Africa will be speeded by ostracizing her, but that change in East Europe can be maximized by contact with the West. Conservatives make the opposite claims. Of course the situations are different enough so that isolation could have opposite effects in the two cases, but those who hold these views do not provide the detailed analysis that is called for.

That conclusions can call up supporting beliefs is also shown by the cases in which the latter change in order to preserve the former. For example, in 1917 General Haig originally claimed that the planned offen-

[58] C. Vann Woodward, "The Age of Reinterpretation," *American Historical Review* 66 (October 1960), 2-8. For criticisms of this view that, in my opinion, leave many of the basic arguments untouched, see Richard W. Van Alstyne, *The Rising American Empire* (Chicago: Quadrangle 1965), and William Goetzmann, *When the Eagle Screamed* (New York: Wiley, 1966).

[59] Peter Dennis, *Decision by Default* (Durham, N.C.: Duke University Press, 1972), pp. 61-62.

[60] Alain Enthoven and K. Wayne Smith, *How Much is Enough?* (New York: Harper and Row, 1971), pp. 109-10. For another example, see Piers Mackesy, *Statesmen at War: The Strategy of Overthrow, 1798-1799* (London: Longmans, 1974), p. 316.

sive in Flanders depended on a supporting French attack, but later asserted that "the possibility of the French army breaking up . . . compelled me to go on attacking." Similar reasoning can explain why it was that

> In the years immediately preceding the Korean War, the Truman administration led the nation through a series of dramatic and far-reaching changes in the nation's foreign policy commitments that marked the first of the two major revolutions in the American security position following World War II. Yet expenditures on the armed services for these years remained relatively uniform . . . as did the proportions in which these sums were divided among the services, an approximately even split.[61]

The same combination of constant conclusions and changing rationales appeared when President Nixon responded to the criticism that his program of subsidized school lunches for the needy was insufficient by proposing a program with a different allocation formula—but one that involved spending exactly the same amount of money as his original plan.[62] And a change in policy preferences is apt to produce reversals in supporting beliefs. For example, at those periods during the Munich crisis when Prime Minister Daladier "felt that France could not fight, then [he thought] the French air force was terrible. When he felt that France had to fight, then the French air force was not so bad, and quite without basis, he included 5,000 Russian planes on the French side."[63] Although the detailed interrelationships among the beliefs vary in these cases, they all display puzzling changes that indicate that policy preferences preceded many of the supporting views.

The effects of irrational consistency are unfortunate. One ironic consequence springs directly from our analysis of its causes. If preferences are formed on the basis of one or two values that dominate in a particular situation, then there is likely to be inconsistency over time and varying contexts. By contrast, if people weighed values against each other in all cases, their behavior in different situations would serve the same mix of values. This is not to say that their responses would be invariant—people would contour their behavior to the opportunities and dangers of the situation. But in so doing they would be furthering a coherent and in-

---

[61] Leon Wolff, *In Flanders Fields* (New York: Viking, 1958), pp. 111, 202-203, 259; Warner Schilling, "The Politics of National Defense: Fiscal 1950," in Warner Schilling, Paul Hammond, and Glenn Snyder, *Strategy, Politics, and Defense Budgets* (New York: Columbia University Press, 1962), p. 220.

[62] Jack Rosenthal, "The Script Called for Some Empty Trays," *New York Times*, October 17, 1971, Section 4, p. 30.

[63] Herbert Dinerstein, "The Impact of Air Power on the International Scene, 1933-1940," *Military Affairs* 19 (Summer 1955), 70. For another example, see Brian Bond, *France and Belgium, 1939-1940* (London: Davis-Poynter, 1975), p. 84.

tegrated value structure. But if we have accurately described the process by which irrational consistency dévelops, and if the same value does not dominate in every situation, then the person will act on the basis of one value in one context and another value in another context. Although this will have the beneficial effect of insuring that no important values will be entirely neglected, there is no reason to believe that they will be optimally combined over time. Indeed the resulting inconsistency is likely to reduce further the effectiveness of each separate policy.

Other problems are apparent when we examine any specific instance of irrational consistency. Decision-makers are purchasing psychological harmony at the price of neglecting conflicts among their own values and are establishing their priorities by default. For if the world is not arranged in a benign way mirroring this consistency, the decision-maker is unknowingly sacrificing some values to reach others. Unless the cost of balancing values is terribly high[64] or some invisible hand is operating, it will be in the decision-maker's interest to choose explicitly. Were he aware of the costs and conflicts, he might examine his own values and the evidence more carefully, extend his search to additional alternatives, and seek creative solutions. For example, the American belief that multiple goals were served by encouraging cooperation between the nationalists and communists in China inhibited the study of other policies that might have proven more successful. Similarly, had American decision-makers recognized that their policy of postponing the settlement of East European issues until after the war was not, as they incorrectly believed, without high costs, they might have more carefully weighed the alternative courses of action or sought new policies that would have preserved some of the advantages of the existing one without all of its liabilities. And had British admirals in World War I not felt that closing with the enemy was both dangerous (because of the threat posed by torpedoes) and unnecessary (because of the effectiveness of long-range gunfire), they would have had greater incentives to develop tactics that would have reduced the risks of fighting at less than extreme range and permitted greater offensive flexibility.[65]

[64] The prohibitive political costs of openly facing certain choices explains some important cases of excessive consistency. The leading members of the pre-World War I British cabinet realized that a frank discussion of the issues of politico-military policy would bring the government down, and President Johnson may have felt that the costs of his Vietnam policy could not be explored without doing irreparable damage to his domestic programs. (See Nicholas d'Ombrain, *War Machinery and High Policy: Defence Administration in Peacetime Britain, 1902-1914* [London: Oxford University Press, 1973] and David Halberstam, *The Best and the Brightest* [Greenwich, Conn.: Fawcett, 1973], pp. 723-25, 735.)

[65] Tsou, *America's Failure in China*, pp. 145-56; Lynn Davis, *The Cold War Begins* (Princeton: Princeton University Press, 1974), pp. 75-76, 87-88, 371, 386-87; Marder, *From the Dreadnought to Scapa Flow*, vol. 3: *Jutland and After*, p. 17.

Even if some of the irrational consistency follows rather than precedes the decision, it contributes to the tendency for people to maintain policies when they are no longer appropriate. For if a decision-maker believes that a policy is better than the alternatives on all relevant dimensions, he will react very slowly to evidence that it is failing to reach some of his goals because he will believe that it is still best on other dimensions. By contrast, an appreciation of the costs of the policy will make the decision-maker more sensitive to new evidence that other policies would be more effective than the one he has adopted.

Irrational consistency often leads to a policy that fails to reach any goals because it attempts to reach too many. Resources are spread too thin and contradictions go unrecognized. Thus during World War II Americans strongly supported free elections in East Europe and yet believed that, as Roosevelt put it at Yalta, the governments that would emerge "will be thoroughly friendly to the Soviet [Union] for years to come. This is essential."[66] Had the United States faced the conflicts between these two goals, it might have chosen to abandon its support for free elections and gained some concessions from Russia, or at least avoided the unnecessary hostility that it earned. And as long as the United States could not see that elected governments were likely to be hostile to Russia, the Soviet position could not be explained as an understandable demand for security that had as a byproduct unfortunate consequences for Allied values, but had to be perceived as indicating the complete unreasonableness of an ideologically driven enemy.

Seeking too many objectives often results in making too many enemies. This was a main fault of Wilhelminian diplomacy, which failed to rank its goals and choose the states with which it had the most important quarrels and the objectives that had to be given up to gain allies. Britain, France, and Russia had little in common; only a reckless Germany that tried to do everything at once could have forced them together. (The other powers were not immune from this pathology but were spared its severe consequences not only because of better leadership but because they experienced crises [e.g. Fashoda for France, the Boer War for England, and the Russo-Japanese War for Russia] that forced them to drop some of their goals and enemies.) Japan's policy in the mid-1920s was similarly faulty.

It was believed that the nation's economic interests should and could be promoted in all directions, that problems of noneconomic nature could be handled individually, and consequently that there was no need to develop a comprehensive foreign policy. Independent action

---

[66] Quoted in John Gaddis, *The United States and the Origins of the Cold War, 1941-1947* (New York: Columbia University Press, 1972), p. 161.

in China, understanding with the West outside of China, indifference to the military implications of Soviet and Chinese radicalism, unwillingness to relate the naval rivalry with the United States to the question of overall Japanese-American relations—all were expressions of this policy.[67]

Irrational cognitive consistency can thus spawn policies that create the worst of all possible worlds.

In many of these cases further unfortunate consequences follow because the decision-maker fails to recognize the trade-offs between advancing his interests and harming those of others. Since he does not believe that his policy is creating legitimate grievances, he underestimates the opposition that arises and sees resistance to his actions as unprovoked hostility that indicates aggressive intentions. The perceptions of decision-makers in Germany before World War I and Japan before World War II fit this pattern. As a result, illusory incompatibility was added to the pre-existing real incompatibility, the spiral of tensions and hostility discussed in the previous chapter was fueled, and possible compromise solutions were first unappreciated and then rendered unacceptable.

We should acknowledge four arguments against our claim for the importance of this kind of consistency. First, there may be nothing that needs to be explained. Trade-offs are infrequently perceived in the policies decision-makers choose because they seek policies that in fact serve multiple goals. They have chosen one course of action over all others for the very reason that it minimizes value conflict. Although no one would deny that this is the decision-maker's object and debates are often punctuated with the assertion that a course of action can be found that will avoid sacrificing any one of several important values, this argument can be sustained only if one believes that decision-makers are extremely creative and that the world is benign enough to permit such solutions to be found frequently. Furthermore, unless decision-makers immediately hit upon the perfect solution, one would expect their previous deliberations to show careful consideration of trade-offs. This is rarely the case.

[67] Akira Iriye, *After Imperialism* (New York: Atheneum, 1969), p. 301. (Also see Butow, *Tojo and the Coming of the War*, passim and especially pp. 103-105.) For an example of a policy's failing because the actor did not choose between competing goals in designing a military strategy, see Rothwell, *British War Aims and Peace Diplomacy, 1914-1918*, p. 50. Cognitive factors were not the only ones that inhibited Germany's choosing among her enemies. The tensions in the German social and political structure and the resulting foreign policy strategies and compromises contributed to the self-destructive behavior. For excellent treatments, see V. R. Berghahn, *Germany and the Approach of War in 1914* (New York: St. Martin's, 1973), and Jonathan Steinberg, "Germany and the Russo-Japanese War," *American Historical Review* 75 (December 1970), 1965-86.

Second, actors may consciously misrepresent their views for political purposes. To attract support, the decision-maker may claim that a policy maximizes a large number of values rather than say that it is on balance best but is worse than some alternatives on certain dimensions. But if this were a conscious political strategy, one would expect to find acknowledgments in decision-makers' diaries and other private sources. A third and related argument is that irrational consistency occurs only after a decision is made and that explicit value trade-offs are perceived earlier. As we have seen, decisions do bring supporting arguments in their train. But in many cases we cannot find a pre-decision period in which trade-offs are explicitly weighed.

Fourth, the theory of cross-pressures implies that those whose policy preferences are supported by multiple independent beliefs will be most vocal. Those whose values are in conflict are apt to take a less vehement stand and thus to attract less attention. This would mean that, while many of the active participants in a policy debate would hold a suspicious kind of consistency, they would not constitute a larger percentage of the relevant class than would be expected by chance. Although there is no firm evidence, I do not think that the number of people rendered inactive by conflicting beliefs is high enough to validate this contention. Furthermore, if this explanation were correct, the number of those active in the debate should drop sharply as the number of independent values involved increases. For the greater the number of values, the greater the number of people who should feel conflicted in the absence of irrational consistency. But there is no evidence that this drop-off occurs.

I am not saying that value trade-offs never occur—obviously they often do[68]—but only that they occur less frequently than the logic of the situation would dictate. We might speculate as to the conditions that influence this effect. It is hypothesized that trade-offs are less likely when: 1) the values involved are vague and ill-defined; 2) money, which facilitates comparisons, is not involved; 3) the effects of actions are hard to predict (e.g. the important effects are long-run, or the theory in the area is poor); 4) the values are deeply held; 5) any policy will entail major sacrifices. Thus irrational consistency is especially likely to be found when trade-offs are easy to avoid (hypotheses 1–3) or when they are especially painful (hypotheses 4–5).

[68] Peter Sperlich has shown that, contrary to the conventional wisdom about cross-pressures, people do not always seek to avoid psychological tension and value-conflicts (*Conflict and Harmony in Human Affairs* [Chicago: Rand McNally, 1971]). In rare cases, decision-makers will even acknowledge the existence of conflicts between their state's security and the good of others. For examples, see G.H.L. Le May, *British Supremacy in South Africa* (Oxford: Clarendon Press, 1965), p. 11, and Hans Schmidt, *The United States Occupation of Haiti, 1915-1934* (New Brunswick, N.J.: Rutgers University Press, 1971), p. 59.

ASSIMILATION OF INFORMATION TO PRE-EXISTING BELIEFS

The process of drawing inferences in light of logic and past experience that produces rational cognitive consistency also causes people to fit incoming information into pre-existing beliefs and to perceive what they expect to be there. In the next sections of this chapter we will argue that this phenomenon does not constitute irrational distortion of evidence by showing that these processes are necessary for understanding and that they characterize investigations in science. We will then point out the implications of our analysis for decision-making.

It is striking that people often preserve their images in the face of what seems in retrospect to have been clear evidence to the contrary. We ignore information that does not fit, twist it so that it confirms, or at least does not contradict, our beliefs, and deny its validity.[69] Confirming evidence, by contrast, is quickly and accurately noted. For example, Ole Holsti has shown that John Foster Dulles readily accepted any information about the U.S.S.R. that conformed to his image (e.g. evidence of economic failings) but required overwhelming evidence before he would take seriously information that contradicted his views.[70]

In many cases, discrepant information simply is not noticed. Intelligence analysts, not expecting the Soviets to bring large but light-weight offensive missiles into Cuba, did not pause over the arrival of ships with wide hatches that were riding high in the water. And in World War II, a British photographic reconnaissance analyst who thought the German secret rockets would be a "70-ton monster, launched only from enormous rail-served projectors," studied pictures of a German facility sev-

[69] These resistances will be reinforced if people tend to expose themselves selectively to information that supports their beliefs. Until recently it seemed well-established that such a tendency existed, but a re-analysis of the evidence casts doubt on the hypothesis. (See the citations in footnote 14, Chapter 11.) Of course, in political decision-making selective exposure can be created by organizational as well as individual variables. Subordinates have to decide what information to pass on to their superiors, and it is usually argued that they withhold a disproportionate amount of discrepant information. I am grateful to Glen Stassen for discovering that in the months after the German takeover of Czechoslovakia in March 1939, Foreign Minister Ribbentrop sent Hitler a copy of the one cable by the German ambassador in London indicating doubts about British resolve and did not send on the myriad reports that Britain would indeed fight. Similarly, one scholar found that in the 1920s British "Dispatches critical of fascist [Italy's] actions and intentions frequently were seen only by comparatively junior officials, while the more favourable and reassuring reports were passed further up the hierarchy and more commonly reached the desks of the Permanent Under-Secretary and the Secretary of State." P. G. Edwards, "The Foreign Office and Fascism, 1924-1929," *Journal of Contemporary History* 5 (1970), 154.

[70] Ole Holsti, "Cognitive Dynamics and Images of the Enemy: Dulles and Russia," in David Finlay, Ole Holsti, and Richard Fagen, *Enemies in Politics* (Chicago: Rand McNally, 1967), p. 86.

eral hundred yards from the nearest railway line and paid little attention to what he saw as "a thick vertical column about forty feet high and four feet thick." The "column" was actually an erected V-2.[71]

When actors do not spontaneously perceive evidence as conforming to their views, they often explicitly interpret it as compatible with their beliefs. Dulles interpreted a Soviet troop cut not as evidence of softening Soviet intentions, but as the response of a hostile nation to economic difficulties. More recently, Secretary of State Kissinger acknowledged that the American government missed the meaning of the evacuation of Soviet civilians from Syria a few days before the Arab attack on Israel in October 1973. Because the government was certain that the Arabs were too weak to contemplate starting a war, "the explanation we gave to this information was absurd: it was that a crisis broke out between Egypt and Syria on the one hand, and the Soviet Union on the other, and that the Soviets decided to transfer their men because of this crisis."[72]

Common also are cases of outright refusal to believe reports that contradict a firm belief. A week before the Germans launched their first poison gas attack, a deserter came over the French lines, bringing a warning and "one of the crude respirators with which the German infantry . . . had already been issued. . . . [The French] corps commander . . . dismissed the concept as 'absurd' and administered a sharp rebuke at the manner in which the usual channels had been bypassed to warn the British and French units." When Hermann Göring was informed that an Allied fighter had been shot down over Aachen, thus proving that the Allies had produced a long-range fighter that could protect bombers over Germany, he told the pilot who had commanded the German planes in the engagement: "I'm an experienced fighter pilot myself. I know what is possible. But I know what isn't, too. . . . I officially assert that American fighter planes did not reach Aachen. . . . I herewith give you an official order that they weren't there." Similarly, Yugoslavs who had not been privy to the friction with Stalin after World War II could not believe the newspaper accounts of the Cominform resolution denouncing their country. Their delegate to the U.N. said: "This must be the result of some confusion; the communiqué cannot be true." An even more extreme response was elicited by the message from a Soviet front line unit on the morning of June 22, 1941, "We are being fired on. What shall we do?" Headquarters replied, "You must be insane. And why is your signal not

---

[71] Roger Hilsman, *To Move a Nation* (Garden City, N.Y.: Doubleday, 1967), pp. 186-87 (for a different view, see Roberta Wohlstetter, "Cuba and Pearl Harbor: Hindsight and Foresight," *Foreign Affairs* [July 1965], p. 700); David Irving, *The Mare's Nest* (Boston: Little, Brown, 1964), p. 67.

[72] Holsti, "Cognitive Dynamics and Images of the Enemy"; *Al-Akhbar*, October 14, 1974 (I am grateful to Mr. Ephraim Kam for providing me with this citation and translation).

in code?" Similarly, when the secretary of the navy was told of the Japanese attack on Pearl Harbor, he said, "My God, this can't be true. This [message] must mean the Philippines." It is not without significance that the common reaction is not that the report *is* incorrect, but that it *must be* incorrect. "This *can't* be true."[73]

The Impact of Expectations on Perceptions

These reactions seem to be puzzling and misguided aberrations. But studies of psychology have shown that they are extreme cases of a pervasive phenomenon: expectations or perceptual sets represent standing estimates of what the world is like and, therefore, of what the person is likely to be confronted with. In everyday life, in the interpretation of other states' behavior, and in the scientific laboratory, expectations create predispositions that lead actors to notice certain things and to neglect others, to immediately and often unconsciously draw certain inferences from what is noticed, and to find it difficult to consider alternatives. Furthermore, as we will discuss below, this way of perceiving is rational. Intelligent decision-making in any sphere is impossible unless significant amounts of information are assimilated to pre-existing beliefs.

People are predisposed, set, or ready to see what they expected to be present.

A fruitful way of thinking of the nature of perceptual readiness is in terms of categories for use in coding or identifying environmental events. . . . Conceive of a person who is perceptually ready to encounter a certain object, an apple let us say. . . . We measure the accessibility of the category "apples" by the amount of stimulus input of a certain pattern necessary to evoke the perceptual response "there is an apple". . . . The greater the accessibility of a category, (a) the less the input necessary for categorization to occur in terms of this category, (b) the wider the range of input characteristics that will be "accepted" as fitting the category in question, (c) the more likely that categories that provide a better or equally good fit for the input will be masked. To put it in more ordinary language: apples will be more easily and swiftly recognized, a wider range of things will be identified

---

[73] Alan Clark, *The Donkeys* (New York: Morrow, 1962), p. 78; Albert Speer, *Inside the Third Reich* (New York: Macmillan Co., 1970), pp. 345-46 (on another occasion Göring told a Gauleiter that his report of damage in an air raid was incorrect. "Impossible," he claimed. "That many bombs cannot be dropped in a single night." [*Ibid.*, p. 332]); quoted in Valdimir Dedijer, *The Battle Stalin Lost* (New York: Viking, 1970), p. 140; quoted in John Erickson, *The Soviet High Command* (London: Macmillan and Co., 1962), p. 587; quoted in Harry Howe Ranson, *Central Intelligence and National Security* (Cambridge, Mass.: Harvard University Press, 1958), p. 54. For other examples, see Wolff, *In Flanders Fields*, pp. 158-61.

or misidentified as apples, and in consequence the correct or best fitting identity of those other inputs will be masked.[74]

This means not only that when a statesman has developed a certain image of another country he will maintain that view in the face of large amounts of discrepant information, but also that the general expectations and rules entertained by the statesman about the links between other states' situations and characteristics on the one hand and their foreign policy intentions on the other hand influence the images of others that he will come to hold. Thus Western statesmen will be quicker to see another state as aggressive if a dictator has just come to power in it than if it is a stable democracy. Less evidence will be required for a decision-maker to believe that another state is a potentially loyal ally if the two states have interests and other allies in common than if they do not. Only slight and ambiguous evidence is needed before American decision-makers will see a state dominated by communists as an enemy. Although we cannot discuss this topic in detail here, understanding the general predispositions held by decision-makers is an important step in explaining their specific perceptions. We therefore need to learn about both the predispositions that are frequently held by whole classes of decision-makers and about how the general predispositions held by an individual decision-maker relate to each other. Operational code studies can help accomplish the latter task, but many questions remain to be answered even for individuals who have been carefully examined.[75] We know, for example, that John Foster Dulles was predisposed to see information as indicating that the Russian people did not support the Soviet regime. But we do not know what other kinds of states were covered by this predisposition. It probably applied to Communist China, a state that was both communist and an enemy. But did it apply to all adversaries? Or to all communist states? Or to all dictatorships?

The sources of perceptual predispositions are several, but the outlines of our argument follow our earlier discussion of the propensity to see relations as consistent. Perceptual predispositions grow out of the person's experiences with his environment. Even though this learning is

[74] Jerome Bruner, "On Perceptual Readiness," *Psychological Review* 64 (1957), 129-30. For a further discussion of the masking effect, see below, pp. 193-94. For recent analyses of the arguments and evidence about perceptual set and expectancies, see Ralph Haber, "Nature of the Effect of Set on Perception," *ibid.* 73 (1966), 335-51, and Howard Egeth, "Selective Attention," *Psychological Bulletin* 67 (1967), 41-57.

[75] See, for example, Nathan Leites, *A Study of Bolshevism* (Glencoe, Ill.: Free Press, 1953); Holsti, "Cognitive Dynamics and Images of the Enemy"; Holsti, "The 'Operational Code' Approach to the Study of Political Leaders: John Foster Dulles' Philosophical and Instrumental Beliefs," *Canadian Journal of Political Science* 3 (March 1970), 123-57; Alexander George, "The 'Operational Code,'" *International Studies Quarterly* 13 (June 1969), 190-222.

often badly flawed, as we will discuss in Chapter 6, readiness is to a large extent based on what the past has led the person to expect in the future. Familiarity is therefore an important determinant of predispositions, but we should stress from the start that it is not familiarity *per se* that produces perceptual readiness, but familiarity as a factor that gives the person reason to expect the stimulus to be present in the particular situation he is in. Thus a person will become predisposed to perceive even a rare stimulus if preceding events indicate it is likely to appear. I do not often see lightning, for example, but I will be quick to detect it on hot, humid afternoons when the sky is full of dark clouds.

Numerous psychological experiments have confirmed what is obvious from daily experience—the more familiar a phenomenon is, the more quickly it will be recognized. Less evidence is needed for a person to recognize a common object than an unusual one. Rare objects are mistaken for usual ones. And expected things may be seen when actually nothing is being shown. In one experiment a person is shown two balloons, one of which is being inflated and the other deflated. But the observer sees the balloons as staying the same size, explaining the perceived change in size as being caused by motion toward or away from him. "The most reasonable explanation of [this] visual phenomen[on] seems to be that an observer unconsciously relates to the stimulus pattern some sort of weighted average" of the past correlations between the stimulus and the identity of the object. The observer sees the balloons moving because "it is rare indeed to see two stationary objects at the same distance, one growing larger and the other smaller; almost always in everyday life when we see two identical or nearly identical objects change relative size they are in motion in relation to each other."[76] By the same process, if a state has frequently attacked its neighbors, they will quickly take ambiguous evidence as indicating renewed aggressiveness even though they know that other explanations are possible.

As William James put it 70 years ago:

When we listen to a person speaking or read a page of print, much of what we think we see or hear is supplied from our memory. We overlook misprints, imagining the right letters, though we see the wrong ones; and how little we actually hear, when we listen to speech, we realize when we go to a foreign theatre; for there what troubles us is not so much that we cannot understand what the actors say as that we cannot hear their words. The fact is that we hear quite as little under

[76] Israel Goldiamond and William Hawkins, "Vexierversuch: The Log Relationship Between Word-Frequency and Recognition Obtained in the Absence of Stimulus Words," *Journal of Experimental Psychology* 56 (1958), 457-63; W. H. Ittelson and F. P. Kilpatrick, "Experiments in Perception," *Scientific American* 185 (August 1951), 54, 52.

similar conditions at home, only our mind, being fuller of English verbal associations, supplies the requisite material for comprehension upon a much slighter auditory hint.[77]

Thus it is not surprising to learn that, if a Mexican and an American look into a stereoscope arranged so that one eye sees a picture of a baseball game and the other a bullfight, the American will report seeing only the former and the Mexican only the latter. Similarly, scholars who first studied early childhood speech or the languages of newly discovered peoples "heard" most readily sounds that approximated those of their language. "German observers [of African languages] heard umlauts that evaded the British."[78]

Even more vivid demonstrations of the impact of experiences, and the resulting expectations, on what we see are provided by situations outside the laboratory. It may seem obvious that vision is a completely nontheoretical task. The light that strikes our retinas forms images that explain themselves; we see the world as we do because that is the way the world is. But this is not so. People who gain their sight after having been blind all of their lives do not immediately see the world as we see it—at first they do not see anything except William James's famous "bloomin' buzzin' confusion."[79] Seeing involves conceptualization and learning which both renders the world intelligible by making us sensitive to common configurations of stimuli and reality and leads us to misperceive these stimuli when they are linked to rare or unexpected phenomena. This is shown by the fact that some optical illusions are not universal but are perceived only by people who live in industrialized, as opposed to primitive, societies. The world the former inhabit includes certain forms rare in the latter's world, and the illusions are similar to parts of these shapes and are correct perceptions when the entire figure is present in its normal form. The illusions have been learned from certain recurring patterns and make possible the accurate perception of the world as it usually is.[80] This effect was also noted by an anthropologist who accompanied

[77] William James, *Talks to Teachers on Psychology and to Students on Some of Life's Ideals* (New York: Holt, 1899), p. 159.

[78] James Bagby, "A Cross-Cultural Study of Perceptual Predominance in Binocular Rivalry," *Journal of Abnormal and Social Psychology* 54 (1957), 331-34; Eugene Webb et al., *Unobtrusive Measures* (Chicago: Rand McNally, 1966), p. 143.

[79] R. L. Gregory and J. C. Wallace, "Recovery from Early Blindness: A Case Study," in Paul Tibbetts, ed., *Perception: Selected Readings in Science and Phenomenology* (Chicago: Quadrangle, 1969), pp. 359-88.

[80] Marshall Segall, Donald Campbell, and Melville Herskovits, *The Influence of Culture on Visual Perception* (Indianapolis: Bobbs-Merrill, 1966); Franklin Kilpatrick, ed., *Explorations in Transactional Psychology* (New York: New York University Press, 1961); R. H. Day, "Visual Spatial Illusions: A General Explanation," *Science* 175 (March 24, 1972), 1335-40.

a Pygmy on his first trip outside his native forest. His account should be quoted at length for it is as instructive as it is charming. As Kenge was driven down the road

> he saw the buffalo, still grazing lazily several miles away, far down below. He turned to me and said, "What insects are those?"
>
> At first I hardly understood; then I realized that in the forest the range of vision is so limited that there is no great need to make an automatic allowance for distance when judging size. Out here in the plains, however, Kenge was looking for the first time over apparently unending miles of unfamiliar grasslands, with not a tree worth the name to give him any basis for comparison. The same thing happened later on when I pointed out a boat in the middle of the lake. It was a large fishing boat with a number of people in it but Kenge at first refused to believe this. He thought it was a floating piece of wood.
>
> When I told Kenge that the insects were buffalo, he roared with laughter and told me not to tell such stupid lies. When Henri, who was thoroughly puzzled, told him the same thing and explained that visitors to the park have to have a guide with them at all times because there were so many dangerous animals, Kenge still did not believe, but he strained his eyes to see more clearly and asked what kind of buffalo were so small. I told him they were sometimes nearly twice the size of a forest buffalo, and he shrugged his shoulders and said we would not be standing out there in the open if they were. I tried telling him they were possibly as far away as from Epulu to the village of Kipu. . . . He began scraping the mud off his arms and legs, no longer interested in such fantasies.
>
> The road led on down to within about half a mile of where the herd was grazing, and as we got closer, the "insects" must have seemed to get bigger and bigger. Kenge, who was now sitting on the outside, kept his face glued to the window, which nothing would make him lower. I even had to raise mine to keep him happy. I was never able to discover just what he thought was happening—whether he thought that the insects were changing into buffalo, or that they were miniature buffalo growing rapidly as we approached. His only comment was that they were not real buffalo, and he was not going to get out of the car again until we left the park.[81]

When we look at less deeply-rooted predispositions we can see the influence not of overall familiarity but of cues that give the person reason to believe that he is likely to be confronted with a given stimulus in the situation he is entering. Thus once a person is given a description of an

[81] Colin Turnbull, *The Forest People* (New York: Simon and Schuster, 1961), pp. 252-53, reprinted with the permission of the publisher.

object and told it may be present, he will be quick to see it even if he has never seen it before. In one experiment playing cards were rapidly flashed on a screen. Some of the cards were normal, others a type the subjects had never seen—they had colors and suits mismatched (e.g. red spades, black diamonds). The subjects recognized the normal cards quickly but required a much longer exposure before they accurately perceived the others. Once they realized what they were being shown, however, they were able to recognize further anomalous cards much more quickly even though they were still unfamiliar.[82]

Expectations and predisposition can also be influenced by explicit instructions about what the person is about to see. Again, familiarity is not the issue. For example, the length of lines will be misestimated if they are incorrectly labeled by the experimenter as long or short. In another experiment, some subjects were shown words relating to animals, and others were told they would be shown words dealing with travel. The result was the "facilitation of correct perception of those stimulus-words which fitted the [perceptual] sets, distortion of irrelevant stimulus-words to form words related to the sets, and conversion of ambiguous items (not actually words) into words appropriate to the sets." Thus when items such as "dack" and "sael" flashed quickly on the screen, those who were set for animals perceived "duck" and "seal," and those set for travel saw "dock" and "sail." This influence has been shown to operate in a more realistic setting: people told that a speaker would be cold saw him as cold, those told he would be warm saw him as fitting this description. When people viewing a skit are given different information about what the skit will concern, they see it differently. The same effect is revealed when, in copying an ambiguous figure, the drawing a person produces is influenced by the title that he saw on the original. Similarly, there is some evidence that weapons systems have been badly employed because perceptions of their potential uses had been affected by the weapons' names.[83]

---

[82] Jerome Bruner and Leo Postman, "On the Perception of Incongruity: A Paradigm," in Jerome Bruner and David Krech, eds., *Perception and Personality* (Durham, N.C.: Duke University Press, 1950), pp. 211-12. Also see Mary Henle, "An Experimental Investigation of Past Experience as a Determinant of Visual Form of Perception," *Journal of Experimental Psychology* 30 (1942), 1-21. For an interesting discussion of another determinant of perceptual predispositions, see Amos Tversky and Daniel Kahneman, "Availability: A Heuristic for Judging Frequency and Probability," *Cognitive Psychology* 5 (1973), 207-32.

[83] Henri Tajfel, "Cognitive Aspects of Prejudice," *Journal of Social Issues* 25 (Autumn 1969), 83-85; the experiment dealing with the perception of travel and animal related words is Elsa Siipola, "A Group Study of Some Effects of Preparatory Set," *Psychological Monographs* 46, No. 6 (1935), 27-38 (the quote is from 37). For similar experiments see Hulda Rees and Harold Israel, "An Investigation of the Establishment and Operation of Mental Sets," *ibid.*, pp. 1-21, and Albert Hastorf, "The Influence of Suggestion on the Relationship between Stimulus Size

The person's background and culture can serve the same function as instructions in creating perceptual predispositions. So it is not surprising that

All the reports of U[nidentified] F[lying] O[bject] sightings describe artifacts as visualized by the technology previous to the sightings. In fact, *all* of them look like the interplanetary vehicles in science-fiction illustrations. . . . In the literature of Tibetan travels there are many reports of "sighting" materialized devils. But they do not look like "advanced technology" devils, not even like the devils in western iconography. *All* of them resemble in every detail the pictures of devils in Tibetan books.[84]

Similarly, the members of a tribe of American Indians saw the tracks and heard the sounds of creatures whose existence was indicated by their mythology. Sometimes they even saw the animals themselves. This was true even though the men "were excellent hunters and were accustomed to differentiate the tracks of the various animals that inhabit this region."[85] Everybody in the culture knows what a UFO or devil is supposed to look like, and the resulting perceptual sensitivities make it likely that ambiguous stimuli will be seen as taking the appropriate shapes. Thus the Indian mythology holds that some creatures never or rarely appear, and few people report having seen or heard them.

Predispositions can also be established by the context in which the stimulus is placed. For example, one group of subjects was shown a series of numbers and the other a series of letters. Both groups were then exposed to the ambiguous stimulus of a symbol β , or a "broken B." Those who had previously looked at numbers were set to perceive another number and so saw a 13; those who had previously seen letters saw a B. Similarly, if people are shown an ambiguous figure that could be either a cat or a bird, those who had previously been shown pictures of birds will see a bird whereas those who had been looking at cats will see another cat. Perceptions of more complex stimuli show the same

and Perceived Distance," *Journal of Psychology* 29 (1950), 195-217. Harold Kelley, "The Warm-Cold Variable in First Impressions of Persons," *Journal of Personality* 18 (1950), 431-39; the experiment about the skit is from Jerry Zadny and Harold Gerard, "Attributed Intentions and Informational Selectivity," *Journal of Experimental Social Psychology* 10 (1974), 34-52; K.R.L. Hall, "The Effect of Names and Title upon the Serial Reproduction of Pictorial and Verbal Materials," *British Journal of Psychology* 41 (1950), 109-21; G. S. Hutchison, *Machine Guns* (London: Macmillan and Co., 1938), pp. 9-10, 151-52.

[84] Carlos Garcia-Mata, "UFO Iconography," *Science* 159 (March 15, 1968), 1187.

[85] A. Irving Hallowell, "Cultural Factors in the Structuralization of Perception," in David Beardslee and Michael Wertheimer, *Readings in Perception* (Princeton: D. Van Nostrand, 1958), p. 555.

influences. In one experiment, subjects watched two people play a competitive game. The players had contrasting styles; one took his moves rapidly and decisively, the other played slowly and deliberately. When the former won, he "was seen more as a quick thinker than impulsive, more astute than careless, and more decisive than rash." The opposite was true when he lost. When the latter won, he "was perceived . . . as more deliberate than sluggish, and more attentive than uncomprehending." The opposite impressions were formed when he lost. Apparently without the subjects realizing it, their perceptions were strongly shaped not only by the players' styles, but also by the presumed effects of those styles.[86]

Outside the laboratory, too, we find the similar influence of context-induced predispositions. The three television networks covered the 1952 presidential nominating conventions quite differently. NBC stressed the behavior of key individuals in personal terms. When ABC was not doing this, it carried the speeches from the podium with minimal commentary. CBS supplied information and evaluations of the political strategies that were probably being followed. As a result, subjects saw the same pictures and events very differently depending on which network they were watching. This was true even though all subjects were politically sophisticated social science graduate students. Thus in the midst of a confusing debate on the seating of a southern delegation

> As the pool camera lingered over a "huddle" in the New York delegation, those watching NBC saw the delegates "arguing" and contributing to the general confusion. CBS monitors perceived the huddle as a "conference" of floor leaders formulating some undetermined strategy (the nature of which they tried to surmise); in other words, it was interpreted as part of the overall contest. Monitors covering ABC evidently failed to take any "cue" whatsoever from this huddle, for in their attempt to understand the fast-moving proceedings they focused almost exclusively on Rayburn and other convention officials.

A bit later:

[86] Jerome Bruner and A. Leigh Minturn, "Perceptual Identification and Perceptual Organization," *Journal of General Psychology* 53 (1955), 21-28; K.R.L. Hall, "Perceiving and Naming a Series of Figures," *Quarterly Journal of Experimental Psychology* 2 (1950), 153-62. For similar experiments, see Abraham Luchins and Edith Luchins, *The Rigidity of Behavior* (Eugene, Ore.: University of Oregon, 1959), pp. 555-63. Also see the interesting experiment in Charles Osgood, *Method and Theory in Experimental Psychology* (New York: Oxford University Press, 1953), p. 207. The experiment with players displaying different styles is Robert Jones and James Welsh, "Ability Attribution and Impression Formation in a Strategic Game," *Journal of Personality and Social Psychology* 20 (1971), 171. For a further discussion of the related subject of the "primacy effect," see below, p. 189.

. . . a rumor concerning a pending Kefauver-Harriman coalition was reported equivalently on all three networks. Yet only CBS monitors, their sensitivities sharpened to such clues, were able to connect this information with the floor proceedings. The CBS monitors—but none of the others—took the vote of Tennessee, the only Southern state solidly against seating, as a clear test for the existence of such a Kefauver-Harriman coalition, even without guidance from the CBS commentary.[87]

Context is supplied not only by the situation, but also by the concerns and information that dominate the person's thought at any particular time. This "evoked set," as it is called, is the subject of the next chapter.

Whatever creates the predisposition, the result is that, if an actor expects a phenomenon to appear, he is likely to perceive ambiguous stimuli as being that phenomenon. When one is sure that an object will be present, it takes very little information, or information that bears little resemblance to the object, to convince one that one is seeing it. Thus the lament of a naval intelligence officer: "When there was a general hunt on for a particular ship . . . it was easy to think that any warship must be *the* ship. Witness the brief attack by the Fleet Air Arm planes . . . on the British cruiser *Sheffield* in May 1941 while searching in mid-Atlantic for the *Bismarck*." The error occurred even though the *Sheffield* did not look like the *Bismarck*—she had two funnels to *Bismarck*'s one—and was very familiar to the aircrews since she had long accompanied the aircraft carrier from which they had been launched. Similarly, after British intelligence analysts were told that V-2 rockets were launched off a "steel cone surrounded by a square framework," they examined pictures of a German test area and "found no fewer than 12 large conical objects, 15 feet in diameter," which they took to be the platforms. When the objects later disappeared and the analysts calculated that they could not have been lifted over the surrounding wall or taken out through the narrow gap in it, they correctly realized the "conical objects" were standard tents, which they had often seen before, which had been folded up and removed. And it is not surprising that within 24 hours after British naval intelligence incorrectly announced that a new German ship was being deployed it received news that the ship had been sighted.[88]

As several of the preceding examples have shown, although the role

[87] Kurt Lang and Gladys Engel Lang, *Politics and Television* (Chicago: Quadrangle, 1968), pp. 119-21.

[88] Donald McLachlan, *Room 39* (New York: Atheneum, 1968), pp. 37, 38; Irving, *The Mare's Nest*, pp. 274-75. There is an obvious danger of self-fulfilling prophecies here. The analyst tells agents in the field that phenomenon X is likely to appear; the agents are more likely to report ambiguous stimuli as evidence of X; the analyst becomes more certain of his original belief and conveys this information to the field; agents are then even more apt to perceive X.

of expectations in forming predispositions and influencing perceptions aids decision-making when the environment conforms to what it is thought to be, when the regular pattern is not present—and when magicians or deceptive actors take advantages of our expectations—then this process of simplifying and filling-in misleads us. Thus in the experiment mentioned earlier people who were shown anomalous playing cards initially believed that they were seeing normal ones. Similarly, when subjects are shown an object whose color is somewhat different from that which they have come to expect it to be, they report seeing the expected rather than the actual color.[89]

The Necessary Interdependence of Facts and Theories

It seems obvious that these cases show irrational cognitive distortion. Evidence is being ignored, misremembered, or twisted to preserve old ideas. Instead of the correct perception of the facts that are clear in retrospect, we find strained interpretations and tortuous arguments. But while it is true that these processes indeed do injustice to some bits of information, we cannot quickly conclude that they constitute distortion—i.e. that they "are forces operating against accurate representation" of reality.[90] They would decrease accuracy if data were completely unambiguous or if all states of the world were equally probable. But since the evidence always permits multiple interpretations and because theories developed from previous cases must provide a guide to the explanation of new information, the influence of expectations on perception is not only consistent with rationality, but is "essential to the logic of inquiry."[91] One can be too open-minded as well as too closed to new information. Karl Deutsch puts this point in a more general context:

> Autonomy . . . requires both intake from the present and recall from memory, and selfhood can be seen in just this continuous balancing of a limited present and a limited past. . . .

[89] Bruner and Postman, "On the Perception of Incongruity," pp. 213-15; Jerome Bruner, Leo Postman, and J. S. Rodrigues, "Expectation and the Perception of Color," *American Journal of Psychology* 64 (1951), 216-27. Also see E. E. Jones and J. Bruner, "Expectancy in Apparent Visual Movement," *British Journal of Psychology* 45 (1954), 157-65.

[90] Jack Brehm, "Motivational Effects of Cognitive Dissonance," in M. R. Jones, ed., *Nebraska Symposium on Motivation, 1962* (Lincoln, Neb.: University of Nebraska Press, 1962), p. 53. See Donald Campbell, "A Phenomenology of the Other One," in Theodore Mischel, ed., *Human Action* (New York: Academic Press, 1969), pp. 54-65, for the argument that "If the model of rational decision-making is an accurate representation of a survival-relevant relationship to the environment, biological evolution is apt to have hit upon and retained approximations to such decision rules in the very structure of the brain, and from an anatomical point of view there is no reason why these processes should not be located in the pre-phenomenal parts of the brain."

[91] I have borrowed this phrase from Abraham Kaplan, who uses it in a related context in *The Conduct of Inquiry* (San Francisco: Chandler, 1964), p. 86.

No further self-determination is possible if either openness or memory is lost. . . . To the extent that [systems cease to be able to take in new information], they approach the behavior of a bullet or torpedo: their future action becomes almost completely determined by their past. On the other hand, a person without memory, an organization without values or policy . . . —all these no longer steer, but drift: their behavior depends little on their past and almost wholly on their present. Driftwood and the bullet are thus each the epitome of another kind of loss of self-control."[92]

Gardner Murphy's treatment of "human potentialities" shares this perspective. He discusses a number of human natures, one of which demands order and stability from the environment and implies some degree of cognitive rigidity, and another of which is the drive toward creativity and discovery. These inevitably clash, and it is best for the individual that they do so since both represent impulses required for full human development. Theorists concerned with the narrower question of the functions of beliefs make the parallel point that "adjustive behavior requires the stabilizing keel that strong cognitive structures such as attitudes provide. The balance between flexibility and stability that is essential for effectiveness would seem to require revision of attitudes in the light of some preponderance of evidence, rather than ready influence by the isolated fact."[93]

This conflict is also present at the level of organizations. Like individuals, they must develop standard operating procedures to deal with recurring problems, but must also try to maintain the openness necessary to recognize and handle creatively new issues.[94]

[92] *Nationalism and Social Communication* (Cambridge, Mass.: M.I.T. Press, 1954), pp. 167-68. Also see Deutsch's *The Nerves of Government* (New York: Free Press, 1963), pp. 98-109, 200-56. Thus it is not surprising that in constructing an "ultrastable system" that duplicated many of the adaptive features of intelligent behavior, Ross Ashby found that "Both extremes of delay may be fatal: too hurried a change from trial to trial may not allow time for 'success' to declare itself; and too prolonged a testing of a wrong trial may allow serious damage to occur. . . . [T]here can be little doubt that on many occasions living organisms have missed success either by abandoning a trial too quickly, or by persisting too long with a trial that was actually useless." *Design for a Brain* (2nd ed., London: Chapman and Hall, 1960), p. 120.

[93] Murphy, *Human Potentialities* (New York: Basic Books, 1958); M. Brewster Smith, Jerome Bruner, and Robert White, *Opinions and Personality* (New York: Wiley, 1956), pp. 251-52. For a discussion of the functionality of similar sets of opposed motives see T. C. Schneilea, "An Evolutionary and Developmental Theory of Biphasic Prophecies Underlying Approach and Withdrawal," in M. R. Jones, ed., *Nebraska Symposium on Motivation: 1959* (Lincoln, Neb.: University of Nebraska Press, 1959), pp. 1-42; Donald Campbell, "Egocentric and Other Altruistic Motives," David Levine, ed., *Nebraska Symposium on Motivation: 1965* (Lincoln, Neb.: University of Nebraska Press, 1965), pp. 304-306.

[94] For similar arguments applied to specific intellectual endeavors, see John Ziman, *Public Knowledge* (Cambridge: Cambridge University Press, 1968), p. 69,

THE INTERDEPENDENCE BETWEEN FACTS AND
THEORIES IN SCIENCE

To develop this argument we must examine the arena that comes closest to embodying our definition, and most definitions, of rationality—science. Both scientists and policy-makers must draw inferences from ambiguous evidence. And philosophers of science have shown that the need to fit data into a pre-existing framework of beliefs, even if doing so does not do justice to all the facts, is not, or at least is not only, a psychological drive and does not necessarily decrease the accuracy of perceptions. While evidence must be adduced to support a theory, the inferences drawn depend on our theories: "theories are built on facts, while at the same time giving significance to them and even determining what are 'facts' for us at all." Thomas Kuhn has shown that fields of science are characterized by an accepted body of concepts and theories that set the framework for research. These constitute the "paradigm" (e.g. the Ptolemaic system) that is challenged and changed only during a "scientific revolution" (e.g. the Copernican revolution). The paradigm sets limits on what explanations "make sense" and helps determine what phenomena are important and in need of further research. It similarly marks out areas to be ignored either because they can shed no light on problems defined as interesting or because the paradigm indicates that there can be nothing there. Indeed instruments built on these assumptions may not be able to detect unexpected phenomena. The bulk of science then consists of problem-solving within the paradigm and "does not aim at novelties of fact or theory and, when successful, finds none."[95]

Most important for our purposes, the paradigm leads scientists to reject flatly evidence that is fundamentally out of line with the expectations that it generates. An experiment that produces such evidence will be ignored by the scientist who carries it out. If he submits it to a journal the editors will reject it. Even if it is printed, most of his colleagues will pay no heed even if they cannot find any flaws in it.[96]

Scientists maintain cognitive consistency and retain their images and beliefs in the face of discrepant information. This is done in the belief that the basic theory is correct and that information that is not compatible with it must be either invalid or susceptible of reinterpretation. The

---

and Fred Greene, "The Intelligence Arm: The Cuban Missile Crisis," in Roger Hilsman and Robert Good, *Foreign Policy in the Sixties* (Baltimore: Johns Hopkins Press, 1965), p. 130.

[95] Stephen Toulmin, *Foresight and Understanding* (New York: Harper and Row, 1961), p. 95 (also see Kaplan, *The Conduct of Inquiry*, p. 89); Thomas Kuhn, *The Structure of Scientific Revolutions* (Chicago: University of Chicago Press, 1962; 2nd ed. 1970), p. 52.

[96] For an example, see Michael Polanyi, "Commentary," in A. C. Crombie, *Scientific Change* (New York: Basic Books, 1963), p. 376.

cost of this practice is that major discoveries will be missed and the paradigm will continue to be accepted even when enough discrepant information is available to discredit it. Thus the astronomer Lalande did not follow up observations that could have led him to discover the planet Neptune because they did not fit the prevailing theories. "He found that the position of one star relative to others . . . had shifted. Lalande was a good astronomer and knew that such a shift was unreasonable. He crossed out his first observation, put a question mark next to the second observation, and let the matter go." Fifty years later an astronomer who sought to test the prediction that there should be a planet at that particular place "sighted the planet four times . . . and once even noticed that it had a disc, but these facts made no impression on him since he doubted the hypothesis he was testing. Before its discovery as a planet . . . , Uranus had been recorded as a fixed star at least seventeen times: seventeen times its motion had gone unnoticed." Similarly, a leading physicist, Otto Hahn, did not correctly interpret one of his important experiments. Prevailing theory indicated that the bombardment of a uranium nucleus should yield a heavier element, and when Hahn found lighter elements he admitted to being "extremely reluctant to announce as a new discovery a result that did not conform to existing ideas." He could not accept an associate's claim that the only explanation could be fission because "This conclusion violated all previous experience in the field of physics."[97]

Because one's estimate of the validity of an hypothesis is determined not only by the evidence that bears directly on it but also by how well the proposition fits with well-confirmed theories, one can rationally reject one hypothesis and affirm another even if as many facts support the former as do the latter. For example, I can firmly disbelieve in the existence of Unidentified Flying Objects and tentatively believe in the existence of Big Foot (a large ape-like creature alleged to inhabit the forests of the Northwest) not because the photographs, traces, and reports of sightings are more convincing in the case of the latter than they are in the case of the former, but because Big Foot could exist without drastically altering other bits of accepted knowledge, whereas an affirmation of the presence of UFOs would require changes in many basic laws of nature. It is then rational for an individual, and the scientific community as a whole, to cease collecting information on UFOs and to dismiss out of hand most reported sightings.

[97] Jerome Bruner, Jacqueline Goodnow, and George Austin, *A Study of Thinking* (New York: Wiley, 1956), p. 105; Michael Polanyi, "The Unaccountable Element in Science," in *Knowing and Being, Essays by Michael Polanyi*, Marjorie Grene, ed. (London: Routledge and Kegan Paul, 1969), p. 114; quoted in William Gilman, "The Road to the Bomb," *New York Times Book Review*, January 8, 1967, p. 38.

Although the rejection of discrepant information may lead to incorrect conclusions, this process is a necessary part of theory-building. Scientific investigation could not be carried out if men were too open-minded. Pure empiricism is impossible: facts do not speak for themselves. It is not wise—indeed it is not possible—to follow Thomas Huxley's injunction to "sit down before fact as a mere child, be prepared to give up every preconceived notion, follow humbly wherever nature leads, or you will learn nothing." Rather it is inevitable that "Every step of the [scientific] procedure—from the initial identification of 'phenomena' requiring explanation to the final decision that our explanation is satisfactory—[be] governed and directed by the fundamental conceptions of the theory."[98]

The world is not so cleanly constructed that all the evidence supports only one theory. There are so many variables, accidents, and errors in observations that "There is no such thing as research without counter-instances."[99] No parsimonious explanation for any actor's behavior in a complex set of cases will be completely satisfying. Some aspects of the truth simply do not make sense. To take a recent example, it is hard to believe that the numerous and significant errors in the transcripts of conversations that President Nixon released in the spring of 1974 were accidental. But it is equally implausible that he would knowingly falsify the transcripts of recordings which he knew the House Judiciary Committee had true copies of and that he would invite the chairman and ranking minority member of the committee to listen to tapes whose transcripts he had altered.

Because it is rare that all the facts are consistent with the same conclusion, the closer one looks at the details of a case the greater the chance that some of them will contradict the accepted explanation. So it is not surprising that in cases that attract a lot of attention—such as political assassinations—many people are dissatisfied with the official account. The trouble with their objections is not so much that they imply the existence of conspiracies, but that they fail to appreciate that even the correct explanation will not be able to tie up neatly all the loose ends.

The rejection or "distortion" of evidence that contradicts the paradigm does not merely show that scientists are human and are attached to their

[98] Quoted in W.I.B. Beveridge, *The Art of Scientific Investigation* (3rd ed., New York: Norton, 1957), p. 50; Toulmin, *Foresight and Understanding*, p. 57 (also see Norwood Hanson, "Observation and Interpretation," in Sidney Morgenbesser, ed., *Philosophy of Science Today* [New York: Basic Books, 1967], p. 99).

[99] Kuhn, *The Structure of Scientific Revolutions*, p. 79. Also see Kaplan, *The Conduct of Inquiry*, p. 152. For an excellent related argument about the myth of the critical experiment, see Imre Lakatos, "Falsification and the Methodology of Scientific Research Programs," in Lakatos and Alan Musgrave, eds., *Criticism and the Growth of Knowledge* (Cambridge: Cambridge University Press, 1970), pp. 154-77.

theories. Science depends on this behavior. If the astronomers mentioned above "had gone on testing every new star on the possibility of its being a very slowly moving planet, they might well have wasted all their time in obtaining an immense mass of meaningless observations." This point applies to all aspects of scientific investigations:

> The process of explaining away deviations is in fact quite indispensable to the daily routine of research. In my laboratory I find the laws of nature formally contradicted at every hour, but I explain this away by the assumption of experimental error. I know that this may cause me one day to explain away a fundamentally new phenomenon and to miss a great discovery. Such things have often happened in the history of science. Yet I shall continue to explain away my odd results, for if every anomaly observed in my laboratory were taken at its face value, research would instantly degenerate into a wild-goose chase after imaginery fundamental novelties.[100]

A similar response is necessary at the institutional level. Only by refusing to accept findings or arguments that are too discrepant from prevailing theories "can contributions of cranks, frauds, and bunglers be prevented from flooding scientific publications and corrupting scientific institutions."[101]

This closed-mindedness furthers science because the paradigms and theories that mold the interpretation of data are not mere prejudices. They have gained acceptance by their ability to explain economically a wide variety of events. They are supported by a large body of evidence, have withstood the challenges of competing theories, and have pointed the way to fruitful lines of research. If the acceptance of novel data or interpretations means changing the established theories, there are good reasons for resistance.

> The most notorious cases of obstructive conservatism, the resistance of the Peripatetics to Galileo and the Copernicans, and the stubbornness of Priestley in his refusal to give up phlogiston, were by no means instances of sheer obscurantism and pigheadedness. The Aristotelian-Ptolemaic doctrine was one of the most comprehensive and consistent explanatory systems ever constructed. In terms of a single princi-

---

[100] Polanyi, "The Unaccountable Element in Science," p. 114; Polanyi, *Science, Faith, and Society* (Chicago: University of Chicago Press, 1965), p. 31. For a further discussion of this problem see *ibid.*, pp. 16, 26-41, 90-94, and Polanyi, *Personal Knowledge* (London: Routledge, 1958), pp. 8-15, 30, 143-68, 269, 310-11. Also see Martin Deutsch, "Evidence and Inference in Nuclear Research," in Daniel Lerner, ed., *Evidence and Inference* (Glencoe, Ill.: Free Press, 1959), p. 102. For a related argument, see Nicholas Rescher, *Scientific Explanation* (New York: Free Press, 1970), pp. 107-15.

[101] Polanyi, *Science, Faith, and Society*, p. 16.

ple, the relation of matter and form, with its associated and implied ideas (potentiality and actualization, the four causes, dispositionalism and the "logos" or ratio of combination) Aristotle explained the genesis of the physical elements from the basic opposites, chemical combinations, the phenomena of change and movement, generation and corruption, the motion of the heavens, the relation of body and soul, the interrelation in living forms, of nutrition, sensation and locomotion, reason and intelligence, and the principles of moral action. Aquinas, by incorporating this system into the teachings of the Christian Church, gave rational support by means of its scientific principles to religious belief. By his own innovation, Copernicus threatened the whole of this impressive structure with destruction. . . .

The phlogiston theory gave, for the first time, a general conception of chemical combination and analysis and the possibility of something like a chemical equation. . . . It also explained how air supported combustion by absorbing the emitted phlogiston, and ceased to do so when it became saturated or "phlogisticated". Here was a unifying principle that could produce order out of the chaos of alchemical "canons" and "principles".[102]

Because an established theory has so successfully explained a wide range of phenomena and has led to the development of so much new knowledge, its proponents not only see the great loss entailed in abandoning it, they also are confident that it will be able to account for the troublesome new findings. As Kuhn notes in his study of the Copernican revolution: "What to Copernicus was stretching and patching was to [the defenders of the established view] a natural process of adaptation and extension, much like the process which at an earlier date had been employed to incorporate the motion of the sun into a two-sphere universe designed initially for the earth and stars. Copernicus' predecessors had little doubt that the system would ultimately be made to work."[103]

The striking instances in which this faith was misplaced are well-known. But these cases are rare. "Experience has shown that, in almost all cases, the reiterated efforts . . . [of scientists] do at last succeed in producing within the paradigm a solution to even the most stubborn problems." And, as Polanyi notes, "There is always the possibility that, as in [the cases of the periodic system of elements and the quantum theory of light] . . . a deviation may not affect the essential correctness of a proposition." Sometimes more research will reveal that the evidence can be fitted to the theory without difficulty. In other instances the scientist

[102] Errol Harris, *Hypothesis and Perception* (London: Allen and Unwin, 1970), pp. 228-30.
[103] Kuhn, *The Structure of Scientific Revolutions*, pp. 150-51, and *The Copernican Revolution* (New York: Vintage, 1959), p. 76.

will find that a simple amendment to his theory accounts for the discrepant data. In still other cases the original experiments will be shown to be faulty. On occasion "the objections raised by a contradiction to a theory may eventually be met not by abandoning it but rather by carrying it one step further. Any exception to a rule may thus conceivably involve, not its refutation, but its elucidation and hence the confirmation of its deeper meaning."[104]

It would be unwise and even irrational for the scientist to drop or significantly modify a well-established theory to conform to a small amount of discrepant information. Instead he must follow the implications of the weight of the evidence. This will necessarily involve ignoring or twisting bits of evidence that seem to contradict the theory he thinks is correct. To a person who holds a new theory, it will seem obvious that the proponents of the established theory are ignoring crucial evidence and devising unnecessarily complex and ad hoc explanations to try to save it. But the alternative to this way of treating evidence is to abandon any attempt to understand the world.

Choosing among competing beliefs about world politics and images of other states does not involve all the problems that arise in choosing among scientific paradigms. First, foreign policy analysts usually can utilize previously developed alternative images, whereas scientists must often create a new framework. Second, the competing images usually have more in common than do competing paradigms. Different paradigms employ different concepts and vocabularies and look at different kinds of evidence. Grasping the new paradigm is very difficult for those who hold the established one, and useful tests are hard to arrange. Since the differences among competing images are less radical, the degree to which interpretations of specific bits of evidence must be influenced by pre-existing beliefs is less. Nevertheless, evidence about another state's foreign policy cannot make sense without the use of some framework of beliefs. Many of the cases in which scientists ignore or seem to twist information that contradicts their beliefs do not involve conflicts between paradigms, but rather conflicts between theories within the same paradigm, and so are similar to many foreign policy situations. Even though decision-makers usually do not have to cope with the problems created by incommensurable paradigms, it will still be the case that much of the information will not easily and immediately fit any one explanation. Thus, like the scientist, the statesman who wants to create and maintain a view that has even minimal coherence will have to refuse to give full weight to evidence that others would see as discrepant with his beliefs. Furthermore, the decision-maker, unlike the scientist, can

[104] Kuhn, "The Function of Dogma in Scientific Research," in Crombie, ed., *Scientific Change*, p. 363; Polanyi, *Science, Faith, and Society*, p. 31.

account for some seemingly discrepant information by the belief that the other is trying to deceive him.

THE IMPACT OF CATEGORIZATION

Theories also impinge indirectly on perception by influencing the way incoming information is categorized and filed in the individual's or organization's memory. Two important consequences follow. First, the label placed on an event or idea influences the way it is seen.[105] Of course labeling represents an opinion about the nature of the object. But, once made, this choice encourages the person to see further resemblances between the object and others in the same category. So, once the offense-minded British navy thought of the convoying of merchantmen in World War I as a defensive measure, "it was grouped with the arming of merchant ships, the use of smoke apparatus, . . . defence gear against mines, and other measures and devices. Convoy was contrasted, to its disadvantage, with the 'offensive' side of the [anti-submarine] war." This categorization may have rested initially on the belief that convoys at best only protected the ships in them without facilitating the destruction of submarines. But it also inhibited analysts, even those who favored the system, from seeing that the convoys, by drawing enemy submarines to the escorts, would in fact destroy more submarines than would "offensive" tactics such as patrolling.[106]

A second problem arises because the availability of a bit of information depends on whether it has been filed under the categories for which it is later seen as relevant. Thus the British navy was unable to compare the effectiveness of convoys and patrolling because the contemporary reports "analysed the destruction of submarines by types of vessels involved, not by the operational task in which the craft were engaged." Similarly, in the spring of 1950 the American ambassador to South Korea sent home an alarming report on the capability of the North Korean army. The State Department considered the report to be part of a drive to increase military aid to South Korea and placed it in a file with

---

[105] For an experimental demonstration of this effect, see Hall, "The Effect of Names and Title upon the Serial Reproduction of Pictorial and Verbal Materials." In the cases we are considering, the label is chosen by the person rather than supplied by the experimenter.

[106] Marder, *From the Dreadnought to Scapa Flow*, vol. 5, *Victory and Aftermath (January 1918-June 1919)* (London: Oxford University Press, 1970), pp. 99-100. To combat this rigidity, General J.F.C. Fuller told his colleagues to "get the present form of war out of [their] heads" and think in terms of tactical functions rather than types of weapons. Just as Wellington "did not think in terms of archers, pikemen and knights," so later generals should not merely distribute newer arms to maintain what should be temporary tactical organization, but should design new configurations that would employ the new technology to perform the classical military functions. Jay Luvaas, *The Education of an Army* (Chicago: University of Chicago Press, 1964), p. 357.

other appeals. When North Korea did attack and the U.S. government sought information about that country's army, an examination of the relevant files revealed little since the ambassador's report had not been put there.[107]

Because the actor files information in terms of the concepts and categories he holds at the time the information is received, new ideas are hard to develop and test even when they do not require a radical recasting of the most elementary facts. Since the actor's information is treated and filed under the old system he cannot be sure how adequately the new one could order it. Any student has experienced these frustrations. When he starts work on a research paper he takes notes within a framework ordered by his preliminary beliefs. As he proceeds, however, he is apt to change his ideas and conclude that other questions are important and other concepts needed. Much of his earlier work will then be wasted. He can go over his notes again, but this will not retrieve information that is solely relevant to his present concerns. The problem is apt to appear in a slightly different form as he begins to write. He will have indexed and filed his notes in accord with the topics and phenomena he plans to discuss. But as he writes he sees new problems and new ways to organize his data. A great deal of the material in his notes is relevant but there is no way to retrieve it because it cannot be located by the filing system he used.

DIFFERENT THEORIES, DIFFERENT PERCEPTIONS

The influence of theories and expectations on perceptions is apparent when we examine how different people look at the same information and how people change their minds. An example from vision provides a vivid illustration of the first question. Although the British photographic analyst who thought that any German rockets would be huge and located next to a rail line saw only a vertical column in some pictures from Peenemünde, another analyst who expected that the rockets would be smaller and more mobile recognized that the "column" was an upright rocket. Similarly, Lewis Anthony Dexter's finding is also not surprising: because of their differing predispositions "one Congressman may hear a demand for more unemployment insurance while another hears a demand for imposing quotas on foreign textiles and shoes—even though the complaints are couched in similar language by the same sort of people."[108]

[107] Marder, *From the Dreadnought to Scapa Flow*, vol. 5, *Victory and Aftermath*, p. 102; Joseph De Rivera, *The Psychological Dimension of Foreign Policy* (Columbus, Ohio: Merrill, 1968), p. 19.

[108] Irving, *The Mare's Nest*, p. 67; Dexter, *The Sociology and Politics of Congress* (Chicago: Rand McNally, 1969), p. 6 (also see p. 136).

The same effect is apparent in matters involving more conscious interpretation. Modern analyses of sixteenth-century naval warfare that utilize the Mahanian framework of control of the sea provide a very different picture of the naval leaders, battles, and strategies than does the framework employed by the actors at the time. To take the impact of more specific beliefs, when the U.S. army maneuvers of 1911 showed many weaknesses, German observers "blamed the volunteer system and the low esteem in which the military profession was held in America." By contrast, American officers who had long argued that troops should be concentrated in large units "tended to blame the archaic dispersion of the Army in frontier posts." The same pattern is apparent in the frequent cases in which different people use the same event to support different policies. In 1938 both supporters and opponents of collective security felt that the Anschlus showed the wisdom of their views. Similarly, the imposition of the American embargo against Japan in the summer of 1941 confirmed the contradictory views of both the militant and the conciliatory factions inside Japan. A decade later, the outbreak of the Korean War reinforced both the State and Defense Departments in their conflicting beliefs about the advisability of quickly concluding a peace treaty with Japan.[109] We should not be surprised by this phenomenon. In many scholarly debates the proponents of conflicting theories cite the same facts. Indeed most of us have had the frustrating experience of presenting information that seemed to provide strong evidence for our point of view only to find that someone with a different position not only failed to change his mind but refused even to acknowledge that the information counted against his position. Instead, the other person claimed that the evidence fit his theory without difficulty.

We therefore expect that the reactions of visitors to a controversial country will be better predicted by their prior views than by what they see during their visit. "Most Western travelers to China [in the nineteenth century] who reported on the subject [of infanticide] explained it as a function of poverty and therefore restricted to the lowest classes in China. The missionaries, however, related it to paganism and hence reported infanticide as a universal practice in the Celestial Empire." If President Kennedy had thought about the impressions brought back by early travelers to the Soviet Union, he might not have asked "You two

[109] John Guilmartin, *Gunpowder and Galleys* (Cambridge: Cambridge University Press, 1974), pp. 18-23, 51-53, 107; Forrest Pogue, *George C. Marshall*, vol. 1: *Education of a General* (New York: Viking, 1963), p. 114; Neville Thompson, *The Anti-Appeasers* (Oxford: Clarendon Press, 1971), p. 163; Paul Schroeder, *The Axis Alliance and Japanese-American Relations* (Ithaca: Cornell University Press, 1958), p. 146; Graham Allison and Morton Halperin, "Bureaucratic Politics," *World Politics* 24 (Supplement, Spring 1972), 63.

did visit the same country, didn't you?" when members of a fact-finding mission to Vietnam returned with incompatible reports.[110]

THE EMERGENCE OF NEW THEORIES AND IMAGES

This line of reasoning gives some hints on the vital and murky question of how and why paradigms are abandoned and adopted, a question that parallels that of how and why decision-makers adopt new images of others. Kuhn argues that old paradigms lose their hold as they are unable to solve more, and more important, problems. The paradigm itself becomes blurred as different scientists meet the growing difficulties by developing somewhat different versions of it. Uncongenial intellectual currents outside the narrow scientific field may also undermine the old paradigm. While there are many questions still unanswered about this process, the same interaction between theory and fact that operates when inferences are drawn within an accepted framework of "normal science" takes place in the development of a new paradigm. The appeal of the old view is weakened by its inability to cope with some known facts, but much of the evidence for the new paradigm seems persuasive only after people see the world within the new framework. Although many observations that in retrospect are considered sufficient to discredit the old theory are made while the old theory holds sway, they are misinterpreted until the new theory has established itself. Crucial observations are so difficult and facts so ambiguous that "the route from theory or law to measurement can almost never be travelled backwards."[111]

In both science and judgments about other actors, the mere presence

[110] Stuart Miller, *The Unwelcome Immigrant* (Berkeley and Los Angeles: University of California Press, 1969), pp. 67-68; quoted in Roger Hilsman, *To Move a Nation* (Garden City, N.Y.: Doubleday, 1967), p. 502. Similarly, those psychologists who stress the impact of "implicit personality theories" on a person's perceptions "may be tempted to say that the perceiver's inferences about another reveal more about the perceiver than about the stimulus person." (Albert Hastorf, David Schneider, and Judith Polefka, *Person Perception* [Reading, Mass.: Addison-Wesley, 1970], p. 44.)

[111] Thomas Kuhn, "The Function of Measurement in Modern Physical Science," in Harry Woolf, ed., *Quantification* (Indianapolis: Bobbs-Merrill, 1961), pp. 44-45. The argument in the rest of this section does not require delving deeply into much of the important debate that Kuhn's work has stirred up on how scientists choose among paradigms. This involves such important and intriguing questions as: can and do the same rules that apply in judging research within a paradigm be used in paradigm choice? What non-scientific factors are at work? Is the choice subjective and irrational? For a discussion of these issues see Lakatos and Musgrave, *Criticism and the Growth of Knowledge*, especially the essays by Kuhn, Lakatos, and Popper; Israel Scheffler, *Science and Subjectivity* (Indianapolis: Bobbs-Merrill, 1967); and Dudley Shapere, "Meaning and Scientific Change," in Robert Colodny, ed., *Mind and Cosmos* (Pittsburgh: University of Pittsburgh Press, 1966), pp. 41-85.

of the facts from which the correct inference could be drawn does not mean that it will—or should—be drawn. Roberta Wohlstetter's claim that "If no one is listening for signals against a highly improbable target, then it is very difficult for the signals to be heard" is paralleled by Albert Einstein's: "No collection of empirical facts, however inclusive, can ever lead to the setting up of . . . complicated equations. A theory can be tested by experience, but there is no way from experience to the setting up of a theory." Laymen exaggerate the empirical nature of science. In some cases the most convincing evidence for the validity of a theory—or even the only evidence—appears only after the new theory has indicated what experiments are to be performed, what instruments are to be designed, and how the results are to be interpreted. Thus the experiment that confirmed the existence of the neutrino "would almost certainly never have occurred if it had not first been deduced in order to preserve a law in defiance of empirical evidence." In other cases the theory may call for rearranging the data into a new form, a form that supports the theory. This was true, for example, in the case of Dalton's theory of chemical bonding. Not only was the theory not supported by evidence when it was proposed but "It was only after Dalton's view was accepted that the evidence for it became so much as recognizable." The law of multiple proportions could not be discovered inductively because it does not hold for all cases that exist in nature—e.g. for mixtures, solutions, and alloys. The regularities appeared only after the relevant cases were isolated, and the search for them was a consequence of the acceptance of Dalton's theory as at least plausible. This search also required that the data be re-ordered: because Dalton stressed the importance of the relative weights of the atomic particles that combined, "Chemists stopped writing that the two oxides of, say, carbon contained 56 per cent and 72 per cent of oxygen by weight; instead they wrote that one weight of carbon would combine either with 1.3 or 2.6 weights of oxygen. When results of the old manipulations were recorded in this way, a 2:1 ratio leaped to the eye." Similarly, much of the evidence sufficient to establish the plausibility of the continental drift theory was available fifty years ago, but no one sought to organize the information in this way because theory was rejected as beyond the realm of possibility.[112]

Acceptance of a new theory produces alterations of perceptions and interpretations on both unconscious and conscious levels. Some changes seem to be quite calculated and deliberate. Polanyi points out that observations of the transmutation of elements have always been common,

[112] Wohlstetter, *Pearl Harbor: Warning and Decision* (Stanford: Stanford University Press, 1962), p. 392; quoted in Harris, *Hypothesis and Perception*, p. 121; see also 112, 109; Kuhn, *Structure of Scientific Revolutions*, p. 133; Ziman, *Public Knowledge*, pp. 56-57.

but since the acceptance at the end of the eighteenth century of La-
voisier's views on the nature of the elements they were explained as
mere dirt-effects. Such at least was the case up to the beginning of the
twentieth century. Then, suddenly, under the stimulus of Rutherford's
and Soddy's discovery of radioactive transmutation . . . , a series of
erroneous claims were made by careful observers to have achieved in
their own way a transmutation of elements. . . . [However these claims
ceased in 1929 with the] establishment of the theory of radioactive
disintegration which showed clearly that the attempts described above
to transform elements had been futile. Since then . . . no new claims
were made in this direction although the evidence of transformation
of the kind [previously set forth] . . . is always at hand.[113]

Other changes in the viewing of evidence take place at a less conscious
level. As scientists look at the data again they immediately see things
they had completely overlooked before. Phenomena that they had not
even bothered to explain away now stand out as both important and natural. The world looks different because new beliefs are entertained. As
Kuhn asks:

Can it conceivably be an accident, for example, that Western astronomers first saw change in the previously immutable heavens during the
half-century after Copernicus' new paradigm was first proposed? The
Chinese, whose cosmological beliefs did not preclude celestial change,
had recorded the appearance of many new stars in the heavens at a
much earlier date. Also, even without the aid of a telescope, the
Chinese had systematically recorded the appearance of sunspots centuries before these were seen by Galileo and his contemporaries. Nor
were sunspots and a new star the only examples of celestial change to
emerge in the heavens of Western astronomy immediately after
Copernicus. Using traditional instruments, some as simple as a piece
of thread, late sixteenth-century astronomers repeatedly discovered
that comets wandered at will through the space previously reserved
for the immutable planets and stars. The very ease and rapidity with
which astronomers saw new things when looking at old objects with
old instruments may make us wish to say that, after Copernicus, astronomers lived in a different world. In any case, their research responded as though that were the case.[114]

---

[113] Polanyi, *Science, Faith, and Society*, pp. 91-92.
[114] *The Structure of Scientific Revolution*, pp. 115-16. Erving Goffman points
out that once a person has been judged to be mentally ill many episodes in his
life that had previously been interpreted as normal are now seen as grossly inappropriate and showing a pattern of sickness. Goffman, *Asylums*, pp. 155-58.

In the same way, once a new image of another state is established, the other's actions appear very different than they had before. New bits of behavior are noticed, some old ones are dismissed, and other bits are reinterpreted. The onset of the Cold War led Americans to an entirely different view of Russia's conduct during World War II than had prevailed previously. Similarly, the Stamp Act led the American colonialists "to redefine their situation in a way that permitted them to interpret as grievances things that had previously gone unremarked and to regard components of the earlier ad hoc imperial reform program as part of a comprehensive assault upon the existing moral order that had been in progress for some time." This process helps explain why it is that images can often be reversed only with great difficulty. A bit of behavior can crystallize an image, and that image will not return to its original state if the actor later reverses his position. This was true, for example, of crucial Japanese moves in the 18 months preceding Pearl Harbor. The image of Japan as a menace that was solidified in American minds by Japan's signing the Tripartite Pact with Germany was little affected by subsequent Japanese moves to draw back from the Pact. And while the introduction of Japanese troops into southern Indochina led the United States to take the fateful step of cutting the flow of oil to Japan, the Japanese offer to negotiate a withdrawal was dismissed as worthless.[115]

A new image brings a change in what is considered obvious and what requires special explanation.[116] If one adopts the view that Russia is essentially a status quo power, Soviet restraint in Laos and the Congo is self-explanatory and her seemingly aggressive placement of missiles in Cuba becomes puzzling. Examining the mid-1940s with a new perspective has led revisionist scholars to stress incidents that had been passed over before, such as Soviet concessions at Yalta, the desire of some American decision-makers to open Russia and East Europe to American trade and capital, and the American role in changing the status quo in Iran by seeking control of the oil. Once a person believes that Russia wanted mainly security and could easily have seen the United States as threatening, he becomes sensitive to such things as the differences in Soviet policies toward the countries of East Europe and the degree to which the Soviet treatment of Allied representatives and rights in these states conformed to the precedents the Allies had set in Italy and Japan. Not only is one apt to note such data if one sees Russia as a status quo power, but the interpretations seem natural consequences of this image.

[115] Jack Greene, "An Uneasy Connection," in Stephen Kurtz and James Hutson, eds., *Essays on the American Revolution* (Chapel Hill: University of North Carolina Press, 1973), p. 78; Schroeder, *The Axis Alliance and Japanese-American Relations*, pp. 24-25, 47-72, 80, 181.

[116] See Toulmin, *Foresight and Understanding*, pp. 41-57.

Because established theories give a coherent, interrelated view of reality, contradicting facts cannot be appreciated until the theory is displaced. It is not only that the interpretation of a mass of data that previously seemed unintelligible suddenly makes sense once a new theory is grasped, but, more radically, the facts that are later believed to be vital in supporting the theory can be seen only after the theory is accepted. A famous and perhaps apocryphal story from science makes this point well:

> After having discovered the moons of Jupiter through his telescope, Galileo is supposed to have tried to convince a group of Ptolemaist church fathers of the fact that Jupiter has moons by having them look through his telescope; the fathers looked through the telescope but denied that they saw that Jupiter had any moons. Although they saw the same light images Galileo did, their background beliefs (which, as Ptolemaic astronomers, included belief that there was a single center of rotation in the universe) made it impossible for them to see that these light images were of satellites rotating around a second center of rotation, and so they failed to see that Jupiter has moons.[117]

Similarly, Fabricius, a sixteenth-century scientist, discovered

> that the valves [in the veins] operated to check only the outward passage of blood from the heart. . . . Such being the case, one might have expected that Fabricius would have realized that the normal passage was . . . inwards, towards the heart. . . . The mind of Fabricius was so shaped [by the prevailing theory] . . . however, that he missed the whole point of his own discovery, and produced an explanation which left the large question exactly where it had stood before. . . . [Other] predecessors of Harvey had observed by cuts and ligatures the flow of blood in the veins towards the heart. . . . But they were so dominated by [the established theory] . . . that they said the blood behaved irregularly when it was tortured by such experiments—rushing off in the wrong direction like a fluttering frightened hen.[118]

And as Polanyi points out, "Both Copernicus and Vesalius discovered new facts *because* they abandoned established authority—not the other way round. . . . When Vesalius first examined the human heart and did not find the channel through the septum postulated by Galen, he assumed it was invisible to the eye; but some years later, with his faith in authority shaken, he declared dramatically that it did not exist."[119] So we

[117] Frederick Suppe, "The Search for Philosophical Understanding of Scientific Theories," in Suppe, ed., *The Structure of Scientific Theories* (Urbana, Ill.: University of Illinois Press, 1974), p. 212.

[118] Herbert Butterfield, *The Origins of Modern Science* (New York: Collier, 1962), pp. 57-59.

[119] Polanyi, *Science, Faith, and Society*, pp. 26-27.

can often reverse the well known saying and state of a phenomenon: "I'll see it when I believe it."

These arguments from philosophy of science parallel those of consistency theory discussed earlier. If a person's attitude structure is to be consistent, then incremental changes among interconnected elements cannot be made. Change will be inhibited, but once it occurs it will come in large batches. Several elements will change almost simultaneously. Hanson argues that "theories . . . constitute a 'conceptual Gestalt.' A theory is not pieced together from observed phenomena; it is rather what makes it possible to observe phenomena as being of a certain sort." Kuhn supports this view, noting the similarity between the development of a new paradigm and the change in visual gestalt that occurs when a person who has previously seen a drawing as a vase suddenly sees it as two facing profiles.

> No ordinary sense of the term "interpretation" fits these flashes of intuition through which a new paradigm is born. Though such intuitions depend upon the experience, both anomalous and congruent, gained with the old paradigm, they are not logically or piecemeal linked to particular items of that experience as an interpretation would be. Instead, they gather up large portions of that experience and transform them to the rather different bundle of experience that will thereafter be linked piecemeal to the new paradigm but not to the old.[120]

In some cases, usually involving vision, a new perception is so overwhelmingly satisfactory that the person will accept it as soon as it is pointed out to him. Arguments are not necessary. This happens when a person who has seen only a scattering of unconnected blotches in a picture is told what object it portrays. Indeed, not only does the new perception seem natural and obvious, but the person cannot understand how he failed to see it in the first place and cannot, by an act of will, return to his earlier state of visual disorganization. Thus when the rocket was pointed out to the first photo interpreter in the example above, he not only grasped the new perception, but was able to go back over previous reconnaissance photographs and easily detect additional missiles. As a biologist noted after discovering a pattern in the leaves of a certain kind of plant: "When that visual fact had at last succeeded in forcing its way into the mind, any plant that came under observation was found to show this salient feature so strikingly as to leave the observer bewildered and humiliated at having been totally blind to it year after year."[121]

[120] Hanson, *Patterns of Discovery*, p. 90; Kuhn, *The Structure of Scientific Revolutions*, p. 122.
[121] Quoted in Harris, *Hypothesis and Perception*, pp. 209-10.

But more often the interaction between theories and facts renders diffi-cult a debate on the merits of opposing paradigms and, to a lesser extent, images. What counts as an important fact in one framework may not be significant in another. Both sides can find bits of evidence that the other cannot easily or adequately explain. Furthermore, the same bit of infor-mation can often be cited in support of conflicting conclusions.

For these reasons disagreements are rarely settled by an appeal to one or two facts. James Joll's comments on the dispute between Gerhard Rit-ter and Fritz Fischer over the interpretation of one of Bethmann-Hollweg's memorandums have wide relevance:

> If one reads the report in question dispassionately, it can, it seems to me, be taken *either* way, and one's interpretation is not conditioned by the document itself, or even entirely by the circumstances in which it was drafted, but rather by one's view of Bethmann-Hollweg's char-acter and policies as a whole. A historian's view of a man's aims and motives is formed to a large extent by the documents, but it neces-sarily also influences the way he reads them; and it is unrealistic to expect Professor Fischer, who, on his reading of the evidence, has formed one opinion of Bethmann-Hollweg's political personality, to agree with Professor Ritter, who, from the same evidence, has come to a radically different conclusion. Each, when interpreting a particu-lar document, is looking for support for a view already formed through reading many other pieces of evidence.[122]

In most political questions it is then impossible to separate judgments about the validity of specific inferences from the larger question of the merits of contending theories and images that both support and are sup-ported by the inferences. This contrasts with the simpler situations, usu-ally involving physical evidence and statistical trends, in which the facts, even if not automatically leading to a conclusion, can at least be judged apart from the validity of the hypotheses to be tested. For example, one might be asked to estimate whether there are more red than blue balls in a large opaque jar. To provide evidence, balls are drawn from the jar one at a time. The color of each ball can be determined objectively, un-influenced by beliefs about the proportion of different colored balls in the jar. But the analogy cannot be extended to a judgment of another's inten-tions: a state's acts are not neatly labeled "aggressive" or "peaceful," as the balls are clearly red or blue. Rather—although the statesman often does not realize this—the interpretation of each act is unavoidably con-ditioned by the hypotheses that are held. Thus, for example, in the de-bate over Soviet intentions within Finland before the Winter War both

---

[122] James Joll, "The 1914 Debate Continues," *Past and Present* No. 34 (July 1966), 105. Emphasis in the original.

sides drew on the same facts to support their differing conclusions. The same pattern recurred a year later when Finland again had to decide whether Russia was planning an attack.[123] Neither side's interpretations were unreasonable, and the argument could not have been settled by merely discussing the most recent Russian behavior. Rather the general images of the U.S.S.R. that lay behind the specific interpretations should have been debated.

Cognitive Distortion and Implications for Decision-Making

In politics too, ignoring discrepant information or assimilating it to pre-existing beliefs will perpetuate inaccurate images and maintain unsatisfactory policies, but these processes are necessary if decision-makers are to act at all.[124] Thus actors who refuse to alter their images when some evidence does not fit cannot automatically be condemned for cognitive distortion or self-defeating blindness. Only when the assimilation of incoming information involves violations of generally agreed-upon rules for treating of evidence can we detect irrationality.

There are some ways of protecting an established belief that do fall into this category and increase the chances of error. A person may not even begin to come to grips with a large amount of information that could indicate that his views are incorrect or, in the absence of an open dispute, may fail to notice events of obvious import. For example, Douglas Haig, the general in charge of British troops in France in World War I, took no account of the implications of the withdrawal of Russia from the fighting or the American declaration of war.[125] In other cases information will be rejected because its consideration is too painful. Occasionally a decison-maker will acknowledge that he is seeking to spare himself psychological difficulty, although the presence of more legitimate reasons for this behavior usually makes it hard to establish that this is the case. Thus when Stanley Baldwin was shown a report on German rearm-

---

[123] Jakobson, *The Diplomacy of the Winter War*, pp. 134-42; H. Peter Krosby, *Finland, Germany, and the Soviet Union, 1940-1941* (Madison: University of Wisconsin Press, 1968), pp. 77-78.

[124] It is interesting to note that the necessary interaction between facts and theories in foreign policy analysis is denied not only by the spiral theorist critics of American foreign policy but also by many of those professionals concerned with intelligence. Hilsman found that policy-makers and intelligence officials alike believed that conclusions flowed directly from the facts and that theory was dangerous at the fact-collection stage and unnecessary at the fact-evaluation stage. (Roger Hilsman, *Strategic Intelligence and National Decisions* [Glencoe, Ill.: Free Press, 1956].) This outlook is not new—it can be found in the State Department in the 1930s (see William Kaufmann, "Two American Ambassadors, Bullitt and Kennedy," in Craig and Gilbert, eds., *The Diplomats*, pp. 679-80)—and has not faded. Hilsman found that it characterized many of the internal debates on Vietnam (*To Move a Nation*, chs. 28-34).

[125] Wolff, *In Flanders Fields*, p. 205.

ament, he said: "Oh, for God's sake, take that stuff away. If I read it I shan't sleep."[126] The person might refuse to discuss the arguments of those who disagreed with him[127] or be unable to understand simple but powerful considerations that indicate that he is wrong. For example, Air Marshal Dowding, who had been in charge of the Fighter Commander during the Battle of Britain, looked back over the controversy involving the proposal to employ very large fighter formations, even if this meant that the German bombers could be attacked only on their return flights, and argued: "Every effort had to be made to stop the enemy before he bombed, not afterwards. Surely that was a basic fact. I find incomprehensible the view that it would have been better to try to shoot down fifty of them after they'd done their bombing than ten before. Our job was to stop as much as we could of all the bombing before it took place, not to indulge in statistical studies."[128] Although it is impossible to know whether the increase in bombers shot down would have been high enough to justify the increased British casualties and lowered morale that the proposal would have entailed, had the number been very high the tactic would have been an effective one. Dowding certainly had the intellectual ability to see this, and his refusal, even after the fact, to acknowledge the logic of the argument indicates the working of pressures that hinder the quality of decision-making.

Since intelligent decision-making involves not only the weighing of considerations that are brought to one's attention but also the active seeking of information, the failure to look for evidence that is clearly available and significant constitutes an irrational way of processing information. For example, it was only after most of the Flanders offensive had been fought that Haig's chief of staff made his first trip to the front, observed the incredible mud that had made movement, let alone fighting,

[126] Quoted in Dennis, *Decision by Default*, p. 23. A few years earlier Neville Chamberlain noted in his diary that Baldwin "says he has got to loathe the Americans so much that he hates meeting them and he actually refused an invitation to dine with Ramsay [MacDonald] to meet the James Roosevelts . . . ; I myself am going—to look at the creature." (Stephen Pelz, *Race to Pearl Harbor* [Cambridge, Mass.: Harvard University Press, 1974], p. 117.)

[127] For an example see Krishna Menon's attitude toward nuclear weapons as reported by Michael Brecher, *India and World Politics* (New York: Oxford University Press, 1968), pp. 228-32. But there may have been political calculations behind this attitude—see the review of this book by Dina Zinnes in *American Political Science Review* 63 (December 1969), 1341. A person may refuse to receive emotion-laden information in order to ensure that he will not be influenced by it. Secretary of State Lansing noted that Wilson's "attitude toward evidence of German atrocities in Belgium and toward accounts of the horrors of submarine warfare . . . [was that] he would not read of them and showed anger if the details were called to his attention." Arthur Link, *Wilson the Diplomatist* (Chicago: Quadrangle, 1965), p. 35.

[128] Quoted in Robert Wright, *The Man Who Won the Battle of Britain* (New York: Charles Scribner's Sons, 1969), p. 215.

so difficult, and asked, "Good God, did we really send men to fight in that?" And although the cornerstone of Ambassador Hurley's policy in China was his belief that the communists were weak and would therefore have no choice but to accept Chiang's offers, he lacked a "careful evaluation of the actual strength of the Chinese Communists . . . [and] made no systematic efforts to seek the information necessary to arrive at the best possible estimate." Similarly, the British plans to force the Dardanelles in 1915 rested on the assumption "that the arrival of the fleet at the capital would finish the Turks: there would be a revolution in Constantinople." The decision-makers asked for few arguments on this vital prediction. Later in the war, intelligent British thinking about how to cope with the crisis created by the renewed U-boat offensive was rendered more difficult because the Admiralty, which insisted that traditional methods could deal with the threat, failed to collect statistics to judge whether a convoy system could be instituted. Forty years later Britain's initial response to the nationalization of the Suez Canal was to try to show that the Egyptians could not run it. Since they knew that almost all of the pilots who guided the ships through the canal were European and would quit, they concluded that the canal would have to close. But they never sought information on whether it really took much training to produce competent pilots. Any ship's captain could have told them (and did tell the Norwegians, who made enquiries) that little training was required, and Nasser had no trouble keeping the canal open, thus undermining England's plans. The failure to seek important information is even more striking when it continues over several years. For example, although the war plans developed by both the British and the American air forces in the interwar period were predicated on the effectiveness of strategic bombing, neither organization gathered much evidence—or evaluated the evidence they had—on the crucial question of whether the necessary targets could be located and hit.[129]

But in other cases in which some information is ignored or stretched to fit a prevailing view, automatic condemnation is not appropriate. Roberta Wohlstetter's study of Pearl Harbor points out that "For every signal that came into the information net in 1941 there were usually several plausible alternative explanations, and it is not surprising that our

[129] Quoted in Wolff, *In Flanders Fields*, p. 253 (also see pp. 160-61); Tsou, *America's Failure in China*, p. 194; Marder, *From the Dreadnought to Scapa Flow*, vol. 2, *The War Years*, p. 217 (interestingly enough, this vital assumption was not questioned by the expedition's opponents); the convoy example is from Marder, *From the Dreadnought to Scapa Flow*, vol. 4, *1917: Year of Crisis*, pp. 150-52; Terence Robertson, *Crisis: The Inside Story of the Suez Conspiracy* (New York: Atheneum, 1965), pp. 94-95, 109. As in the attempt to force the straits, the British appear to have believed that Nasser's government would fall as soon as the Allies made a show of force. The air forces case is discussed further below, pp. 420-22.

observers and analysts were inclined to select the explanation that fitted the popular hypotheses." But as long as the hypotheses were popular because they successfully accounted for a great deal of data, this is not only not surprising but not unwise. A theory is necessary if any pattern is to be seen in the bewildering and contradictory mass of evidence. Thus Tang Tsou's explanation of Ambassador Hurley's inability to comprehend the situation in China:

> One could have understood the complexity of Soviet policy toward China only if one had perceived that this complexity arose out of the necessity for constantly balancing national against ideological interests, immediate against long-range considerations, temporary expediency against fundamental hostility, tactical objectives against strategic aims, the apparent strength of the Nationalists against the potentiality of the Communists, and, finally, Soviet capabilities against the uncertainty about America's intention to intervene. Hurley's naiveté and optimism prevented him from even beginning to tackle this complex problem.[130]

Observers who lack a theoretical framework will be strongly influenced by the most recent bits of data they receive or the latest short-run trend. For this reason American observers of China in the 1940s who lacked "a firmly rooted intellectual orientation and a tight grasp of the essentials of foreign policy" exhibited a marked instability of opinion. An experiment provides an intriguing parallel. People who were given some training in judging others' personalities became less accurate in their perceptions because they developed views of others as very diverse. Training seems to have destroyed their confidence in their naive, but powerful, modes of perception and made them sensitive to putative individual differences which, contrary to what they believed, they could not interpret accurately.[131]

The necessary interaction between evidence and images helps explain why it is hard to find general differences between the ways in which those people who are right and those who are wrong draw inferences. Wohlstetter's studies of why the government was taken by surprise at Pearl Harbor and the Cuban missile crisis[132] could be replicated in a perverse way. We could look at an event that did not take place, and, acting as though it had occurred, find a large number of clues indicating the event's probable occurrence which the officials had ignored or explained away.

[130] *Pearl Harbor*, p. 393; Tsou, *America's Failure in China*, p. 340.

[131] *Ibid.*, p. 228; Crow, "The Effect of Training upon Accuracy and Variability in Interpersonal Perception."

[132] *Pearl Harbor*; "Cuba and Pearl Harbor."

Scholars often have been unsympathetic with people whom history has proven wrong, implying that only a person unreasonably wedded to his views could have warded off the correct information. But in most cases those who were right showed no more openness to new information nor willingness to modify their images than did those who were wrong. Robert Vansittart, the British Permanent Undersecretary in the Foreign Office who earned a reputation for courage and foresight by his opposition to appeasement, keenly noted all indication of German aggressiveness. But he was convinced that Hitler was aggressive when the latter had been in office only a few months[133] and did not open-mindedly view each Nazi action to see if the explanations provided by the appeasers accounted for the data better than did his own beliefs. Instead, like Chamberlain, he fitted each bit of ambiguous information into his own hypotheses. Similarly, Robert Coulondre, the French ambassador to Berlin in 1939 who appreciated the Nazi threat "was painfully sensitive to the threat of a Berlin-Moscow agreement. He noted with foreboding that Hitler had not attacked Russia in his *Reichstag* address of April 28. . . . So it went all spring and summer, the ambassador relaying each new evidence of an impending diplomatic revolution and adding to his admonitions his pleas for decisive counteraction."[134] His hypothesis was correct, but it is difficult to detect differences between his methods of noting and interpreting information and those used by ambassadors such as Nevile Henderson who were wrong.[135]

When evidence gradually accumulates that a view is wrong, those who hold the view often seem willfully stubborn as they refuse to recognize that, while their beliefs may have been tenable in the past, they are now clearly incorrect. But those who are wrong may seem more stubborn because they receive more discrepant information. Those who are right may appear more open-minded only because their initial views were correct.[136] If large amounts of discrepant information had later appeared,

[133] Ian Colvin, *Vansittart in Office* (London: Golancz, 1965), p. 23; Martin Gilbert and Richard Gott, *The Appeasers* (London: Weidenfield and Nicolson, 1963), p. 34.

[134] Ford and Schorske, "A Voice in the Wilderness," pp. 573-74.

[135] In an earlier article ("Hypotheses on Misperception," *World Politics* 20 [April 1968], 460-61) I applied this argument to Churchill. While it is difficult to show that he did modify his beliefs more quickly than Chamberlain, one bit of evidence does point in this direction. In the 1920s Churchill argued strongly for appeasing Germany, relaxing the economic clauses of the Treaty of Versailles, and treating her as a member in good standing of the family of nations. This is especially impressive in light of the fact that before the First World War Churchill had been quite suspicious of Germany's intentions. For the contrary argument that Churchill suffered from "an inability to envisage changed situations," see Robert Rhodes James, *Churchill: A Study in Failure* (New York: World, 1970), p. 381.

[136] Similarly, Cantril's analysis of why people believed Welles's broadcast of *War of the Worlds* is badly flawed by the failure to distinguish the person's "criti-

they too might have assimilated it to their images. In other words, instead of a person's being wrong because he is stubborn, he may be stubborn because he is wrong.[137]

For our purposes, even more significant than the proposition that those who are later shown to have been wrong are not necessarily more closed-minded than those who were right is the argument that it is difficult to specify when a person is being "too" closed-minded. There is no way to draw a neat, sharp line between that degree of holding to existing beliefs and disparaging of discrepant information that is necessary for the intelligent comprehension of the environment and that degree that leads to the maintenance of beliefs that should be rejected by all fair-minded men.[138] For example, although several authors have examined the seemingly pathological maintenance of the horse cavalry well into the twentieth century, "It is debatable which is the more extraordinary," the unwarranted faith in this weapons system, or the fact "that the lance and sword managed to hold their own as respectable weapons 450 years after the first serious use of gunpowder in war."[139] As we saw in our discussion of science, sometimes the stubborn man is vindicated.

One reason for the lack of systematic differences between those meth-

---

cal ability," one of the key variables identified, from a predisposition to accept, not information in general, but information of a particular type—that indicating catastrophe. Hadley Cantril, *The Invasion From Mars* (Princeton: Princeton University Press, 1947).

[137] If case studies do not reveal general differences between the way people who were right and those who were wrong handled information, experimental evidence is available but not totally relevant. Personality variables of dogmatism, persuasibility, and conformity have been located, and it has been found that people with low tolerance for ambiguity maintain images in the face of more contradictory information than do those who are not disturbed by ambiguity. (Else Frenkel-Brunswik, "Tolerance of Ambiguity as an Emotional and Perceptual Personality Variable," *Journal of Personality* 18 [1949], 108-83; Milton Rokeach, *The Open and Closed Mind*; Irving Janis et al., *Personality and Persuasibility* [New Haven: Yale University Press, 1959]; David Shaffer and Clyde Hendrick, "Dogmatism and Tolerance for Ambiguity as Determinants of Differential Reactions to Cognitive Inconsistency," *Journal of Personality and Social Psychology* 29 [1974], 601-608.) More directly relevant is the finding that "those individuals scoring high on the dogmatism scale perceived the broadcasts [from Radio Moscow] as they had expected them to be, while the low dogmatics found the broadcasts to be something different from what they expected." (Don Smith, "Radio Moscow's North American Broadcasts," *Public Opinion Quarterly* 34 [Winter 1970-71], 549-50.) But we do not know if these relationships would hold true within the highly selected group of decision-makers.

[138] That this is the case actually serves to advance knowledge by increasing the heterogeneity of beliefs within the decision-making community. Different people pursue different lines of inquiry and so an intellectual discipline as a whole hedges its bets. But when an actor must choose a policy, this logic applies with only reduced force.

[139] Bernard and Fawn Brodie, *From Crossbow to H-Bomb* (Bloomington: Indiana University Press, rev. ed., 1973), p. 42.

ods of drawing inferences that lead to correct conclusions and those that lead to error is that the correct explanation often is not supported by the bulk of the evidence. This point is well illustrated by a scientist's discussion of the eighteenth-century debate between the preformationists, who argued that a miniature homunculus inhabited the ovum and grew after it was fertilized, and the epigenesists, who argued that the egg began as a simple and undifferentiated cell and became more complex as it developed. That the latter view is correct should not blind us to the fact that it is highly implausible and for a long time did not render the best account of the available data. "What could be more fantastic than the claim that an egg contains thousands of instructions, written on molecules that tell the cell to turn on and off the production of certain substances that regulate the speed of chemical processes? The notion of preformed parts sounds far less contrived to me. The only thing going for coded instructions is that they seem to be there."[140] In politics it is even more frequently the case that an incorrect belief makes most sense out of the available data. Watergate is only a recent reminder that the actual facts and correct explanations may be highly implausible. Only after access to most of the behind-the-scenes dealings has permitted the reconstruction of the flow of events and decisions are we able to understand what has happened. Even then we may lack confidence in our explanations or feel that they are not totally satisfying. So when the evidence is much less complete it is not surprising that the known facts are often best accounted for by an incorrect explanation.

For this reason those who have reached the right conclusion may be less reasonable and may be treating the information in less justifiable ways than those who are wrong. Hunches, luck, and an accurate general analysis of the other and his situation often explain why a person is able to predict correctly what others would do. Those who disagree, far from being blind to the facts, are often truer to them. A piece of black cloth in the bright sun reflects more light than a white cloth at dusk, yet we see the former as darker than the latter. Because context so heavily influences the perception of each single bit of information, a correct appreciation of the general situation often leads to doing injustice to particular facts. For example, in three cases Churchill was correct, but most reasonable men would probably have said that alternative conclusions were better supported by the evidence at hand. When the attempt to force the Dardanelles faltered because of an uncharted string of mines, Churchill wanted to push ahead. We now know that a renewed attack probably would have succeeded—but, as most officials argued at the time, most of the information indicated that it would fail. To take a larger case, it

[140] Stephen Gould, "On Heroes and Fools in Science," *Natural History* 83 (August-September 1974), 32.

would be hard to argue that Churchill's view best explained the available evidence about German foreign policy in the mid- and even late 1930s. Similarly, Churchill was right to see that Hitler would launch a surprise attack against Russia in the spring of 1941, but alternative hypotheses were at least as well supported by data.

Those who are right, in politics as in science, are rarely distinguished from those who are wrong by their superior ability to judge specific bits of information. The preformationists were no less "careful and accurate in their empirical observations as the epigenesists."[141] Rather, the expectations and predispositions of those who are right have provided a closer match to the situation than did those of those who are wrong. Thus many of the people who interpreted early bits of information about Watergate as indicating that President Nixon was implicated drew correct inferences because they had previously distrusted the man. The very fact that they were so quick to consider him guilty points to the importance of their previous views and the relatively slight role played by close observation of the immediate events. Those who took the opposite position were wrong not because of their faulty reading of the direct evidence—until near the end their reading was at least as plausible as was that of those who were correct—but because of their basic misunderstanding of the president. This line of argument is supported by findings concerning children's perceptions of their parents' political activities which, because the investigator did not hold the view set forth here, were unanticipated: "it was originally hypothesized that student reports of parents' political characteristics would be more accurate among highly politicized families. In the case of turnout, the data lend no support to the hypothesis. Among parents who voted, there are practically no variations at all in the rate of student accuracy. . . . Sizable variations do occur in reporting nonvoting, but, surprisingly, the lowest rates of accuracy are among the most politicized families! Students' strong expectations that their parents will vote, or a greater sensitivity about reporting nonvoting, apparently overshadow any perceptual gain from the highly politicized environment." The same effect appears when we look at data on students' perceptions of their parents' interest in politics. As the parents' education increases, their children judged their interest in politics to be higher: "it is more befitting less-educated parents to be uninterested in public affairs, and consequently more are reported to lack interest. When parents' own reports coincide with these expectations, students' reports are correct. When they conflict with student expectations, however, students have 'guessed' wrong." Our earlier discussion of cognitive biases and schemas is relevant here. People learn and remember relatively accurately when the schema they apply fits the arrangement of the stimuli. Thus

[141] *Ibid.*, pp. 30-31.

a study showing that cognitively simple people are more prone to perceive balance notes that "complexity is not always functional nor lack of complexity always dysfunctional. Noncomplex subjects made fewer errors than complex ones when their simplifying hypotheses matched the social structure" they were facing.[142]

One implication of this analysis is that successful detection of military and diplomatic surprises is less likely to be explained by the skill of the intelligence service in piecing together arcane bits of information than by the degree to which the service's predispositions and expectations fit the actions that the other is planning to undertake. This also means that an actor who is trying to surprise another should find out what the other expects him to do and then do something else rather than to try to alter the other's predictions about what he will do. It is better to take advantage of the fact that people assimilate discrepant information to their pre-existing beliefs than it is to fight this pressure. Thus one of the most elaborate and sophisticated deception campaigns—the Allied effort to convince the Germans that they would land near Calais rather than at Normandy—probably would not have succeeded had Hitler not already believed that Calais would be the target.

This analysis of course raises the question of when will the person's expectations be likely to mirror the stimuli that he is presented with? Luck is one answer and perhaps applies in more cases than we like to think. This may be the best explanation, for example, of why the predispositions of many of the anti-appeasers were appropriate in the 1930s. Under most leaders Germany would have tried to regain a powerful position in Europe, but she would not have been willing to run very high risks in order to dominate and so she could have been appeased. Had Hitler not come to power, many of the Englishmen who now seem wise would have been dangerous warmongers. A second possibility is that the person's predispositions fit the environment in which he is acting. A statesman who is sensitive to threats to his state's security is likely to perceive correctly if his state is often menaced. A person who correctly gauges general trends will also be well served by his predispositions in many cases. Those observers who doubted that democracy could be maintained in the underdeveloped states often provided the best interpretation of the ambiguous evidence about politics in the third world. The

---

[142] Richard Niemi, *How Family Members Perceive Each Other* (New Haven: Yale University Press, 1974), pp. 68-69; Press, Crockett, and Rosenkrantz, "Cognitive Complexity and the Learning of Balanced and Unbalanced Social Structures," pp. 549-50. For related arguments from other parts of the field of person perception, see the research summarized in Mark Cook, *Interpersonal Perception* (Baltimore: Penguin, 1971), pp. 108-16, and Hastorf, Schneider, and Polefka, *Person Perception*, pp. 30-34.

creation of appropriate predispositions is the rationale for job training programs that alter perceptual thresholds, a subject we will touch on in the appendix to Chapter 6. Furthermore, people select, and are selected for, jobs in the expectations of a match between predispositions and environment, but this is no guarantee that there will be such a match. Those who are predisposed to see foreign threats, for example, may fill positions of responsibility in relatively secure as well as in relatively insecure states. A third and related cause of match comes into play when the person's previous experiences provide a good guide to the current situation. This will be treated at length in Chapter 6. An aside here is that, when self-fulfilling prophecies operate, shared predispositions make more accurate the perceptions of those who hold the dominant view.

Unless we realize that the differences between those whose perceptions have been accurate and those whose have been wrong are not likely to lie in differences in ability to examine specific facts, we will have unwarranted faith that those who were right will continue to perceive accurately under changed circumstances. We will be likely to assume quickly that superior intellectual virtues are possessed by those who perceived accurately, to promote those people to positions of greater responsibility, and to adopt their views in the future.

FAILURE TO RECOGNIZE THE INFLUENCE OF PRE-EXISTING BELIEFS

Not being aware of the inevitable influence of beliefs upon perceptions often has unfortunate consequences. If a decision-maker thinks that an event yields self-evident and unambiguous inferences when in fact these inferences are drawn because of his pre-existing views, he will grow too confident of his views and will prematurely exclude alternatives because he will conclude that the event provides independent support for his beliefs.[143] People frequently fail to realize that evidence that is consistent with their hypothesis may also be consistent with other views. When choosing between two hypotheses, the vital concern is the data that can be accounted for by only one of them. But it is common to find actors believing that strong evidence, if not proof, for their views is supplied by data that, they fail to note, also supports alternative propositions. Thus they often see evidence that conforms to their hypothesis as confirming it—i.e. as disconfirming competing hypotheses. Because people do not understand the degree to which their inferences are derived from their

---

[143] This may partially account for the finding that when people deal with consistent information, those with high cognitive complexity tend to be less confident of their judgment than do people of low complexity. See James Bieri, "Cognitive Complexity and Judgment of Inconsistent Information," in Abelson et al., eds., *Theories of Cognitive Consistency*, p. 637, and the experiments cited there.

expectations, they tend to see their interpretations of evidence as "compelling" rather than "plausible."[144] For example, one reason why the German attack on Norway took both that country and England by surprise even though they detected German ships moving toward Norway was that they were expecting the Germans to try to break out into the Atlantic. The initial path of the ships was consistent with either plan, but the British and Norwegians took this course to mean that their predictions were being borne out.[145] This is not to imply that this interpretation was foolish, but only that the decision-makers should have been aware that the evidence was also consistent with an invasion and they should have been a bit less confident.

If the person believes that his inference is based only on the event itself, he will think that a reasonable man holding a different hypothesis, even though he might not change his mind because of the event, would still admit that the event is best explained by, and counts as evidence for, the first person's view. This consequence of not understanding the inference process multiplies the problem: because people cannot understand how others can claim that the event supports a different conclusion, they become more intolerant of others' positions. "After all," it is easy to reason, "if those on the other side are incapable of seeing that this event must count against their position, why should I pay any attention to them?"

Many psychological experiments indicate that people do not understand the impact that their beliefs have on their interpretations of new information. In one case employers were asked to give their impressions of a man shown in a picture. Half were told that the person was a business leader and half were told he was a union organizer. The impressions formed by the latter subjects were far less favorable than those held by the former. Union members drew opposite inferences. Furthermore, the subjects did not realize that the accounts they gave were influenced by the person's reported profession. Rather, they seemed to believe that their judgments were based solely on physiognomy. In another experiment, subjects were asked to rate pictures of girls on such dimensions as beauty, intelligence, and character. When they were shown the pictures again two months later, only this time with Italian, Irish, or Jewish names attached, their judgments shifted in conformity with ethnic stereotypes. Here again the subjects did not seem aware that the names influ-

---

[144] These terms are used by Robert Merton, *Social Theory and Social Structure* (rev. ed., New York: Free Press, 1959), pp. 93-94. Also see John Platt, "Strong Inference," *Science* 146 (October 16, 1964), 347-53 and Fritz Heider, "Social Perception and Phenomenal Causality," *Psychological Review* 51 (1944), 366.

[145] Johan Holst, "Surprise, Signals, and Reaction: The Attack on Norway," *Cooperation and Conflict* No. 1 (1966), 34. The Germans similarly thought that the Allied ships destined for the North Africa landings were headed for Malta (see William Langer, *Our Vichy Gamble* [New York: Norton, 1966], p. 365).

enced their perceptions; indeed they had been explicitly warned about the halo effect. Similarly, subjects who reported different impressions of a person described in a sketch realized only slowly, if at all, that they disagreed because they had previously read different reports about the person. Much prodding was needed before they could see that the inferences they had drawn from the sketch were strongly influenced by the images they already held. Finally, the subjects who watched the 1952 conventions in the experiment with television discussed earlier were not aware that they were influenced by the networks' coverage—instead they thought they had "seen for themselves."[146]

If the inference process stops here, the unfortunate consequences are relatively minor. But if the person learns from his experiences his conclusions will be unwarranted. Thus if the people who looked at the pictures discussed above had reflected upon their impressions they would have held more strongly to their ethnic and economic stereotypes since they would think that these beliefs had received independent support from the pictures. Circular reasoning can similarly solidify political party identification. People often take their cues on issues from the stand taken by their party.[147] A loyal Democrat, for example, may support unions because he knows his party does. As long as the person has little interest in the issue and trusts the party, this is rational. But he will deceive himself if his trust in his party is increased by his knowledge that its position on this issue is congruent with his.[148] This means that even in the absence of the political dynamics by which the stake that an actor has in a posi-

[146] Mason Haire, "Role Perceptions in Labor-Management Relations: An Experimental Approach," *Industrial Labor Relations Review* 8 (1955), 204-12; Gregory Razran, "Ethnic Dislikes and Stereotypes: A Laboratory Study," *Journal of Abnormal and Social Psychology* 45 (1950), 7-27; the experiment with personality sketches is from Luchins and Luchins, *Rigidity of Behavior*, pp. 562-63; Lang and Lang, *Politics and Television*, p. 149. Also see Hans Toch, Albert Rabin, and Donald Wilkins, "Factors Entering in Ethnic Identifications: An Experimental Study," *Sociometry* 25 (1962), 297-312; Gustav Jahoda, "Political Attitudes and Judgments of Other People," *Journal of Abnormal and Social Psychology* 49 (1954), 330-34.

[147] For a demonstration that party identification influences the evaluation of foreign policy issues, see George Belknap and Angus Campbell, "Political Party Identification and Attitudes Toward Foreign Policy," *Public Opinion Quarterly* 15 (Winter 1951-1952), 601-23.

[148] This process may explain why psychological clinicians became too sure of their judgments. See Stuart Oskamp, "Overconfidence in Case-Study Judgments," *Journal of Consulting Psychology* 29 (1965), 261-65.

If, however, the judgment the actor is making depends in part on the judgments that others are making, then the interpretations the actor makes because of his pre-existing beliefs may legitimately reinforce these beliefs. For example, since the ability of a bank to meet its obligations depends in part upon others' beliefs about the bank's solvency, a person who sees an ambiguous event as consistent with the conclusion that the bank is insolvent will be justified in increasing his confidence in this opinion if he believes that others view the evidence the same way he does.

tion increases as he defends it, continuing involvement with an issue is likely to decrease the ease with which the person can change his mind. Changing at a later stage not only has the high cost of admitting error but is inhibited by the increased amount of apparently supporting evidence. This effect will be even greater if people's pre-existing beliefs lead them to mis-remember the facts they have been presented with.[149]

This perspective allows us to develop a useful definition of the "double standard." Because theory plays a necessary role in perception, it is not sufficient to discover that "The same item of behavior, objectively considered, has an entirely different meaning, depending on whether it is one's own or another nation which is responsible for it."[150] But an irrational double standard is constituted when a person uses the same behavior as compelling evidence for different images. Franz From provides a nice example:

> A young lady has told me the following observation, which is a nice example of how strongly the experienced behavior can be shaped according to the pattern to which it belongs. The young lady saw Professor X, whom she dislikes, walk on the pavement in front of her and in the same direction as she was walking, and she thought: "This man does walk in a very theatrical and pompous fashion; he clearly thinks very highly of himself." When she got a little closer to the man, she saw that it was not at all Professor X but her beloved teacher, Doctor Y, whom she thought was not rated according to his deserts because of his humility. And now, walking just behind Dr. Y., she thought: "this man's whole appearance shows his humility; his walk is so straight-forward and humble." Only then did she realize the curious fact that the same person had made two such different impressions on her.[151]

Although it is difficult to determine whether decision-makers realize that their inferences are influenced by their images or whether they think that any reasonable person would agree that the event under consideration provides independent evidence that their image is correct, the latter reasoning process seems common. In the debate within Finland over Soviet intentions in 1939, both sides felt that several events supported

[149] For conflicting experimental evidence on this point, see Nicholas Johnson, "Development of English Children's Concept of Germany," *Journal of Social Psychology* 90 (1973), 259-67, and Zadny and Gerard, "Attributed Intentions and Informational Selectivity."

[150] Otto Klineberg, *Social Psychology* (New York: Henry Holt, 1954), p. 556. For an experiment based on this definition, see Stuart Oskamp, "Attitudes Toward U.S. and Russian Actions: A Double Standard," *Psychological Reports* 16 (1965), 43-46.

[151] Franz From, *Perception of Other People*, translated by Erik Kvan and Brendan Maher (New York: Columbia University Press, 1971), pp. 36-37.

their views, failed to realize that their perceptions were heavily colored by their images, could not understand how others could draw different inferences from the events, and became more confident of the validity of their views. At the end of the First World War only a few Englishmen realized that in scuttling their fleet at Scapa Flow, the Germans acted as the British would have in similar circumstances. This form of illegitimate reasoning occurs even with factual questions that lack moral overtones. If it was foggy when the British or Germans launched an offensive in World War I, they believed that the fog aided the defenders; when they were attacked, they believed fog hurt the defense.[152]

Another example had major international repercussions. After Britain and France agreed that neither would oppose the other's sphere of influence in Egypt and Morocco, respectively, Germany demanded compensation. Britain reacted with anger. One high Foreign Office official saw this as "effrontery," the king called it "political blackmail," and the foreign secretary said that "the suggestion that the consent of the German government to a perfectly innocuous arrangement in Egypt can only be bought at the price of concessions elsewhere" was unpalatable. Later in the dispute the Germans used what would usually be considered more friendly tactics. A British official responded: "The damned Germans have had the audacity to offer us inducements to get us away from France!"[153] Thus the incidents were taken as evidence that Germany was hostile to England and greedy beyond the norms of the times. But while this judgment was perhaps not inconsistent with the evidence, it seems clear in retrospect that the British conclusions were largely the product of their image of Germany.

Most important for international politics are the cases in which a state takes as evidence of another's hostility actions that, if it had carried them out itself, it would have believed were consistent with its own peacefulness. At the start of the Cold War, conflict was heightened by the American reaction to the Russian rejection of the Baruch Plan. Any suspicious state, whether or not she was aggressive, would have found the plan unacceptable. But American decision-makers, not realizing that their inferences depended on what they already thought of Russia, concluded that the Soviet stand showed that she was hostile. Although records from the other side are not available, it seems likely that the Russians similarly thought that any observer would agree that the American maneuvers were consistent only with the hypothesis that America was expansionist.

[152] Jakobson, *The Diplomacy of the Winter War*; Marder, *From the Dreadnought to Scapa Flow*, vol. 5, *Victory and Aftermath*, pp. 284, 287; Barnett, *The Swordbearers*, p. 349. For another example, see Clark, *The Donkeys*, p. 24.

[153] Quoted in George Monger, *The End of Isolation* (London: Nelson and Sons, 1963), pp. 161-62; quoted in Raymond Esthus, *Theodore Roosevelt and the International Rivalries* (Waltham, Mass.: Ginn-Blaisdell, 1970), p. 93.

The other side of this coin is that a state will do many things that it believes are at least consistent with an image of itself as peaceful—if not consistent only with that image—which the other side will see as compelling evidence of aggressiveness. Thus, it was only with difficulty that George Kennan was able to prevent "a certain step of a military nature that the Pentagon proposed to take for the purpose of strengthening our military posture in a region not far from the Soviet frontiers. I paled when I read [the proposal]. It was at once apparent to me that had I been a Soviet leader, and had I learned . . . that such a step was being taken, I would have concluded that the Americans were shaping their preparations towards a target of war within six months."[154] And would the United States have doubted that Russia was planning aggression if Russia, knowing that she had more missiles than the United States, had accelerated her procurement of strategic weapons as the United States did in 1961?

As usual, Vietnam provides examples. Dean Rusk claimed that the resupplying of the North Vietnamese forces in the southern part of their country during the truce in February 1967 showed that the North was "not particularly interested in an actual cease-fire." But the North's behavior could also have been seen as prudent preparations for self-defense. Indeed during the truce the United States moved a record amount of supplies to its units. When a State Department spokesman was asked how the North's efforts differed from ours, he said the former was "clear evidence of their intent to continue their aggressive action" and that the United States was combatting aggression. Similarly, a week before the 1972 negotiations broke down, an American spokesman pointed to the alarming increase in North Vietnamese activity and said: "If you add up the men they are sending, the supplies, and the documentary evidence we've accumulated, a cease-fire is going to be nothing more than an interlude in the war." But American leaders apparently did not think that the North might draw similar inferences from the fact that the United States was pouring military supplies into the South.[155]

Of course identical actions can be taken for different reasons, and the same events can have different meanings depending on the context. But decision-makers often assume that the context is different and perceive the other's actions as inconsistent with the hypothesis that the other is non-aggressive, thereby solidifying their image of the other as hostile. When they take similar actions themselves they cannot understand how others could draw the same conclusion. This is not only a double standard, but a very dangerous one.

[154] George Kennan, *Memoirs*, vol. 2, *1950-1963* (Boston: Little, Brown, 1972), pp. 136-37.
[155] Quoted in *I.F. Stone's Bi-Weekly*, February 20, 1967, p. 3; Larry Green, "Hanoi Seen as Continuing War," *Boston Globe*, December 11, 1972, p. 1.

A final consequence of the lack of realization of the impact of beliefs and expectations on perceptions is that actors often fail to maximize their ability to communicate both specific messages and general images. It is rare for actors to realize that what matters in sending a message is not how *you* would understand it, but how *others* will understand it. An aspect of this problem will be discussed in the next chapter, and here we only need make the basic point that if an actor does not understand others' beliefs about international relations and about the actor, he is not apt to be able to see what inferences others are drawing from his behavior. And if he is incorrect in his estimates of the other's beliefs or if he thinks that perceptions are influenced only by the immediate stimulus, he will be confident that he knows how the other is seeing him, and he will be wrong. To put oneself in another's skin is terribly hard. But the costs of acting as though the meaning of one's behavior is self-evident are enormous. As many of the cases we have discussed show, decision-makers do not realize how important this task is and devote few resources to trying to determine how the other sees the world and how his perceptions of the actor's behavior differ from those of the actor.

Excessive and Premature Cognitive Closure

While we have seen that there is no way to specify exactly how open or closed-minded a person should be, actors are more apt to err on the side of being too wedded to an established view and too quick to reject discrepant information than to make the opposite error of too quickly altering their theories. People often undergo premature cognitive closure.

Before we discuss the evidence for and implications of this hypothesis, two considerations should be raised. First, the choice is often not between the prevailing image and one agreed-upon alternative. Rather there may be several competitors, and knowing that one image is wrong does not tell us which is right. So an actor may believe that while the probability that his image is correct is less than one-half, it is still higher than that attached to any single alternative. Second, political strategy could account for some of this apparent cognitive rigidity. The requirements of effective political leadership coupled with the costs of dissenting from the established view could lead decision-makers to withhold doubts about existing policies and images. These motives do not provide an adequate explanation for all the cases, however. Decision-makers maintain their private, as well as public, images even when they have become inappropriate, and the hypothesis applies not only to decision-makers but also to scholars and scientists, who have fewer reasons to conceal their doubts and to delay changes in their theories.

The starting point for our argument is that the initial organization of the stimuli strongly structures later perceptions. Some cognitive processes can be reversed only with great difficulty. Once a belief has taken hold, new information will not have the same impact it would have had at an earlier stage. Earlier, when the person is trying to make sense out of the evidence, he will experiment with different interpretations of incoming information. Later, when he thinks he understands the stimulus, he will automatically perceive new information as having a certain meaning. Psychologists and philosophers of science have made parallel arguments: "Once a dominant percept . . . is established, there is a tendency to suppress inharmonious cues and to enhance harmonious cues." The "most difficult mental act of all is to rearrange a familiar bundle of data, to look at it differently and escape from the prevailing doctrine." If increasing amounts of evidence do not fit the image, people are apt to realize that something is wrong without being able to specify the exact reasons for their unease. Indeed they may even realize that an image is clearly incorrect and still find "it hard to exclude that [perceptual] organization and see something else." This task is so difficult that many optical illusions persist even after the viewer is told what he is actually seeing. The problem is not so much that the new perception is inherently difficult to grasp, but that the established one is so hard to lose.[156]

There is a close link between being too closed to discrepant information and forming one's hypothesis too soon, before sufficient evidence is available. In the experiment in which subjects were shown incongruous playing cards, Bruner and Postman concluded that "Perhaps the greatest single barrier to the recognition of incongruous stimuli is the tendency for perceptual hypotheses to fixate after receiving a minimum of confirmation. . . . Once there had occurred in these cases a partial confirmation of the hypothesis that the card [was normal] . . . it seemed that nothing could change the subject's report."[157]

It follows that initial incorrect hypotheses will not be quickly altered in light of later evidence but will delay accurate perception for a long time. This is shown by an experiment in which subjects viewed a blurred photographic slide that was brought into sharper focus in a number of stages. Some subjects watched this progression from the start when the slide was extremely blurred and were asked to guess even if they were not sure what they were seeing. These subjects maintained their images—which were usually incorrect because they were formed when the in-

---

[156] Franklin Kilpatrick, "Perception in Critical Situations," in Kilpatrick, ed., *Explorations in Transactional Psychology*, p. 319; Beveridge, *The Art of Scientific Investigation*, p. 106 (as Butterfield puts it, this transformation "virtually means putting on a different kind of thinking-cap." [*The Origins of Modern Science*, p. 13]); see, for example, Bruner and Postman, "On the Perception of Incongruity," p. 220; Robert Leeper, "A Study of a Neglected Portion of the Field of Learning—The Development of Sensory Organization," *Journal of Genetic Psychology* 46 (1935), 59.

[157] Bruner and Postman, "On the Perception of Incongruity," p. 211.

formation was extremely ambiguous—far past the point at which others, who were exposed to the slide only in its later stages of clarity, were able to identify the object correctly.[158] Thus exposure to early and ambiguous information, far from giving subjects a head start, impaired their ability to extract information from later evidence and delayed their recognition of the slide. This effect has also been demonstrated by an experiment in which one of the subject's eyes sees face A while the other sees face B. At the start only A is exposed. Then both A and B are shown, with B very faint. In successive exposures B gradually increases in brightness and A grows dimmer. Throughout this transformation, including the last exposure, when only B is presented, the subjects see only face A.[159]

Less dramatic are the demonstrations that, under many conditions, the first parts of a description of a person have more impact than later information.[160] It is not clear whether the "primacy effect," as it is called, occurs because the later facts are given meanings that depend on the framework established by the initial ones—an explanation that strongly supports the argument of this chapter—or whether the later facts merely have less impact because they receive less attention.[161] Even the latter

[158] Dale Wyatt and Donald Campbell, "On the Liability of Stereotype or Hypothesis," *Journal of Abnormal and Social Psychology* 44 (October 1950), 496-500. Even when the subjects who saw the slide in its initial, blurred state were urged not to guess, this effect occurred. (Jerome Bruner and Mary Potter, "Interference in Visual Recognition," *Science* 144 [1964], 424-25.) For a similar experiment see Gerald Davison, "The Negative Effects of Early Exposure to Suboptimal Visual Stimuli," *Journal of Personality* 32 (June 1964), 278-95. The same results are found with auditory perception in Robert Blake and James Vanderplas, "The Effects of Prerecognition Hypothesis on Veridical Recognition Thresholds in Auditory Perception," *Journal of Personality* 19 (1950), 95-115.

[159] E. Engel, "Binocular Methods in Psychological Research," in Kilpatrick, ed., *Explorations in Transactional Psychology*, p. 303. Also see the experiments cited in footnote 86.

[160] The large body of literature on the relative impact of "primacy" versus that of "recency"—i.e. whether information received first or last has most influence—is summarized in Insko, *Theories of Attitude Change*, pp. 49-61, and Peter Warr and Christopher Knapper, *The Perception of People and Events* (London: Wiley, 1968), pp. 283-88. Here we are concerned only with the causes and consequences of initial exposure to information that leads to the relatively quick formation of an initial hypothesis, and so the fact that the primacy effect seems to be strongest on matters of low familiarity and low controversy and on impressions of objects and people rather than on opinions about issues supports our arguments and some of the findings of recency effects do not disturb it. (See, for example, Robert Lana, "Familiarity and the Order of Presentation of Persuasive Communications," *Journal of Abnormal and Social Psychology* 62 [1961], 573-77.) For an argument that is consistent with the one taken here, see Edward Jones et al., "Primacy and Assimilation in the Attribution Process: The Stable Entity Proposition," *Journal of Personality* 40 (1972), 250-74.

[161] Solomon Asch, "Forming Impressions of Personality," *Journal of Abnormal and Social Psychology* 41 (1946), 258-90; Douglas Chalmers, "Meanings, Impressions, and Attitudes: A Model of the Evaluation Process," *Psychological Review* 76 (1969), 450-60; David Hamilton and Mark Zanna, "Context Effects in Impres-

explanation is consistent with our conclusions. If initial information has disproportionate impact, then images will not reflect the totality of the evidence available.

Diverse situations more closely corresponding to those common outside the laboratory reveal the same basic phenomenon. After trying to approximate the setting in which clinical inferences are drawn, one scholar concluded that "where observers make judgments [about other people] after reading a small amount of data, their ability to develop further understanding from additional data is impaired. The premature judgment appears to make new data harder to assimilate than when the observer withholds judgment until all data are seen." Similarly, an "experimental analysis of a tactical blunder" showed that when facing a new problem a person often finds "an idea that seems to put him on the right track. Consequently, he persists in modifying and testing that hypothesis. The net effect of this partial support may be to seduce him into keeping a false or incomplete hypothesis" by giving him "a set which is difficult to break." Consistent with these arguments is the finding that a hint to a person about how to solve a problem will have little impact once he has developed an incorrect idea of how to proceed, since he will merely assimilate the new information into the approach he has adopted.[162]

Before extending this analysis to foreign policy perceptions, we should note that in most of the experiments the value of the later information is greater than that which is received first—for example, at each stage the slide becomes clearer. But the nature of the political and social phenomena do not automatically become more apparent as time passes, as though a fog were lifting. Of course perceptions are more apt to be accurate if they are based on a large amount of evidence, and images that are formed later can be based on more information than those formed

---

sion Formation," *Journal of Personality and Social Psychology* 29 (1974), 649-54; Norman Anderson, "Primacy Effects in Personality Impression Formation Using a Generalized Order Effect Paradigm," *ibid.* 2 (1965), 1-9.

[162] Charles Dailey, "The Effects of Premature Conclusion upon the Acquisition of Understanding of a Person," *Journal of Psychology* 32 (1952), 149-50; Albert Myers, "An Experimental Analysis of a Tactic.l Blunder," *Journal of Abnormal and Social Psychology* 69 (1964), 496; Ronald Burke, Norman Maier, and L. Richard Hoffman, "Functions of Hints in Individual Problem-Solving," *American Journal of Psychology* 79 (1966), 389-99 and the literature cited there. The quotation is from p. 399. The development of an incorrect hypothesis can also reduce the value of information retrieved from memory, as the following lesson from military intelligence illustrates: "Again and again [Naval Intelligence] had to stress to those at sea that preliminary interrogation . . . might do more harm than good. It was almost always true that inexpert questioning in the earliest stage could spoil witnesses for later examination. They would be pressed to be more specific than their observation justified; ideas would be put into their heads; and they would be biased in favor of those explanations that the first officer they met seemed to prefer." (McLachlan, *Room 39*, p. 49.)

earlier. But if the early bits of information are as valuable as the later ones, the images of others that are based on them will not be as misleading as are those produced in the experiments.

IMPLICATIONS FOR DECISION-MAKING

Three implications for policy-making flow from the tendency toward premature cognitive closure. First, the stability of policy is increased because perceptions are slow to change. Of course one's policies can change even though one's images of other actors do not (e.g. a statesman who perceives that another state is moderately aggressive may first try to build a blocking coalition, but if this fails he may try appeasement). But a major change in image almost always brirgs with it a change in policy. Thus in the absence of increases in other causes of policy change, image stability contributes to the incremental nature of policy-making. Furthermore, the argument that incrementalism permits decision-makers to fashion more effective policies because the information derived from probes and small alterations allows them to correct false premises and adjust to the environment assumes that there are no important systematic biases in the perception of the new information. As we have seen, however, people assimilate information to their pre-existing beliefs; so all but the most unambiguous feedback will be seen as confirming the validity of at least the main thrust of the established policy. That incrementalism governs the modification of images as well as the later stages of decision-making therefore means that actors will proceed longer down blind alleys before they realize that their basic assumptions need revision. This will of course benefit the state when its image is correct and the discrepant information either is erroneous or indicates only temporary changes in the other's behavior. And the stability of images will limit the impact of frictions within an alliance that can erode the friendly relationship. But when the other state changes or the initial image was incorrect, the costs of maintaining the established image will be very high.

Second, like Lindblom's incrementalism, Simon's concept of satisficing can be applied to perceptions as well as to the later stages of decision-making. People do not compare a large number of images to see which best explains all the evidence. Rather they adopt the first one that provides a decent fit. Only when the image fails very badly are alternatives examined. Until and unless this happens, the good (or even the adequate) inhibits the consideration of the better. For example, in science as well as public affairs once it is believed that a given independent variable is powerful, when it is present it will be seen as having caused important effects without being subjected to rigorous analysis. When the expected effect occurs, it will take little evidence to convince people that the independent variable was present and responsible. Alternative causes will not be carefully examined. Thus a student who thinks that she will be badly treated because of her sex will usually interpret all slights and discourtesies as evidence of sexual discrimination without trying to see whether the incidents could not be better explained by her status as a student. Furthermore, the argument that satisficing is identical with maximizing with due consideration for information costs does not apply to the process described here, which can be called "perceptual satisficing."[163] This process is not under conscious control and the costs of trying a new interpretation to see how well it would fit would be low were it not for the strong hold of the image that is already formed.

Perceptual satisficing means that rough estimates of the other's intentions, meant at the time to be merely tentative, exercise a powerful influence. Once Theodore Roosevelt and his secretary of state had seized on the idea of solving the problems caused by Japanese immigration with a treaty of mutual exclusion, it took a great deal of evidence indicating that Japan would not accept this approach before they would pay any heed to Japanese suggestions of alternative arrangements. If the suspicion that the other is being deceptive can partly explain the tenacious hold of initial images in this case, this is not true in other instances. At the start of World War I, the British government gave its admiral in the Mediterranean two objectives—the protection of French ships bringing troops from North Africa to France and the sinking of the German battle cruiser *Goeben*. The admiral understood this message to mean that the first objective was the overriding one. This was a reasonable, but incorrect, interpretation. What is significant here is that he maintained this belief even though subsequent messages tried to make it quite clear that the sinking of the *Goeben* had priority.[164] Similarly, once the Japanese ambassador came to believe that President Roosevelt was willing to open negotiations on Japanese terms in the spring of 1941, "nothing he was told later, on far better authority than that of [the person he had first talked to], made any lasting impression" on him. The same factor helps explain why the Czech leadership remained confident that the Soviet Union would not invade in the summer of 1968. The early Russian measures, being contradictory and ambiguous, were compatible with the Czech belief that only a war of nerves was planned. Once this image was established, it inhibited a proper appreciation of later Soviet moves.[165]

[163] I am grateful to Kenneth Waltz for discussion on this point.

[164] Charles Neu, *An Uncertain Friendship* (Cambridge, Mass.: Harvard University Press, 1967), p. 64; Marder, *From the Dreadnought to Scapa Flow*, vol. 2, *The War Years*, pp. 22-23 (see Chapter 8 for a discussion of the German interpretation of this incident).

[165] Robert Butow, *The John Doe Associates* (Stanford: Stanford University Press, 1974), p. 158; Jack Snyder, "The Cognitive Roots of a Diplomatic Tragedy: Czechoslovak Estimates of Soviet Intentions, 1968," Harvard Senior Honors Thesis, 1972. For another example, see Allen Whiting, *The Chinese Calculus of Deterrence* (Ann Arbor: University of Michigan Press, 1975), p. 48.

This points out a danger in any policy that gradually increases the pressure on an adversary. The common claim that less belligerent measures leave undamaged the options of stronger actions overlooks the danger that the first actions will set an image that cannot easily be altered.

A third implication is that two kinds of people are apt to have a relatively high proportion of accurate perceptions: those whose perceptual predispositions match the stimulus presented to them and those who avoid forming initial estimates until a lot of data are available. Van Gogh said that he would "strive in the early stages [of working on a painting] to keep vague."[166] It is often in the interest of decision-makers to make similar efforts. To this end, the slow pace of the State Department, a source of anguish for presidents and scholars, contributes.

Little more can be said about variables influencing the accuracy of people's initial hunches,[167] but we can advance some propositions about when an image or hypothesis will be formed on the basis of relatively little information. First, the amount of evidence received before an hypothesis is formed will vary inversely with the compatibility of this evidence with any well-known pattern. Thus images were formed quickly in the card-recognition experiment because the incongruous stimuli closely resembled normal playing cards.[168] Second, the amount of conforming evidence necessary for cognitive closure varies inversely with the degree to which the person expects to be presented with the object he thinks he sees. Thus an actor is apt to quickly think that he understands another actor when the other's behavior resembles an expected model. And an early and incorrect perceptual set will be formed if the other has unusual intentions whose behavioral manifestations are similar to those produced by actors harboring more common aims. For example, the widespread misperception of Hitler's intentions is largely explained by the fact that others believed that any defeated, proud, and powerful state would try to alter the enforced peace settlement to regain a legitimate, but not commanding, place in the world. Indeed, Nazi behavior was designed to conform closely to the policies that such a state would follow.

These two propositions elaborate the "masking effect" of pre-existing beliefs. Because information that is highly compatible with an established belief will be quickly assimilated to it, that belief will inhibit the development of alternatives that are similar to it. For example, Admiral Kimmel, the naval commander at Pearl Harbor, explained that he did not consider the report that the Japanese had ordered their missions in Allied territories to burn their codes "of any vital importance" because it was consistent with all the information "we had received about a Japanese

---

[166] Quoted in John Haefele, *Creativity and Innovation* (New York: Reinhold, 1962), p. 43.

[167] See above, pp. 180-81.

[168] Bruner and Postman, "On the Perception of Incongruity."

movement in Southeast Asia." Although the congressional committee investigating the disaster thought that Kimmel's lack of response to this bit of data showed a "strange contrast with the view of the code burning intelligence taken by . . . virtually all witnesses who agreed that this was the most significant information received between November 27 and December 6 with respect to the imminence of war," the contrast is less surprising once it is realized that Kimmel already expected a Japanese attack on British and Dutch territory.[169] This prediction could explain the code burning, and so there was no reason for Kimmel to conclude that the Japanese target list was longer than he had thought. To take a general example, the belief that the other side is bluffing is likely to mask the perception that it will actually fight because the behaviors that follow from these two intentions closely resemble each other.

A third hypothesis is that an image will be formed on the basis of little information if there are pressures to reach a quick conclusion. From a rational decision perspective this is not surprising. As the costs of with-holding judgment increase, it will be in the actor's interest to reach a conclusion more quickly even if he realizes that he may be incorrect.[170] A corollary is that the pressures on a statesman to quickly form an image of another actor varies directly with the importance of the other to the statesman. When the interaction between the statesman's country and another is slight, little is sacrificed by postponing the formulation of policy. This would lead us to expect that even though a country studies those states that are more important to it more carefully than those that are less important, its perceptions of the former may be no more accurate than those of the latter.

Finally, the probability of the early formation of an image varies inversely with the costs the actor believes this entails. If the actor believes that his first, tentative guesses will soon be corrected if they are wrong and can be of aid if they are right, he will not hesitate to make them. In experiments, warnings to wait until all the evidence is in rather than make snap judgments are effective.[171] In policy-making, actors of course

[169] Quoted in T. B. Kittredge, "United States Defense Policy and Strategy; 1941," *U.S. News and World Report*, December 3, 1954, p. 120.

[170] Indeed an actor may be quick to reach a conclusion if doing so removes him from an unpleasant situation. One experiment found that "bitingly disruptive criticisms from the experimenters" led the subject to develop "premature and often nonsensical interpretations of the stimuli." Leo Postman and Jerome Bruner, "Perception under Stress," *Psychological Review* 55 (1948), 322. The reverse of this argument is also true: images will be developed less quickly if the decision-maker believes that waiting has significant payoffs, for example if he believes that valuable information about the other is expected in the near future.

[171] Abraham Luchins, "Experimental Attempts to Minimize the Impact of First Impressions," in Carl Hovland, ed., *The Order of Presentation in Persuasion* (New Haven: Yale University Press, 1956), pp. 62-75.

know that an incorrect image that leads to an incorrect policy is apt to have high costs, but they do not realize that an incorrect image will delay the development of accurate perceptions. Thus statesmen underestimate the costs of forming preliminary hypotheses and so form images more quickly than they would if they understood the processes at work.

Confidence, Commitment, and Ambiguity

Three corollaries flow from the hypothesis that incoming information tends to be assimilated to pre-existing images: this tendency is greater the more ambiguous the information, the more confident the actor is of validity of his image, and the greater his commitment to the established view.[172] The first corollary needs little comment. Since ambiguity is defined in terms of the ease with which the evidence can be interpreted in a number of ways, the greater the ambiguity the less likely that the evidence will embarrass the established image.

The second corollary also follows closely from the hypothesis. To say that an actor is confident of his image implies that he believes that it is supported by a large amount of data. If this is true he will and should be slow to modify it to accommodate bits of discrepant information.[173] The impact of confidence is shown by an experiment in which subjects are shown a photographic slide that becomes increasingly out of focus. The subjects can maintain their image until the slide becomes blurred far past the point at which they could have recognized it initially.[174] Of course the people know what they are seeing, but apparently they are not merely acknowledging this fact. Rather their certainty permits them to perceive a pattern in what would otherwise have been a meaningless blur.

The effect of confidence sheds light on Dean Pruitt's argument that "The flexibility of an image seems to be an inverse function of the extremity of its level. The higher the level of trust or distrust, the lower its flexibility."[175] But there are two meanings of "extreme"—the degree to which a person is sure of his belief and the distance of the belief from the midpoint of a continuum. We have explained why the first kind of extremeness should yield a relatively resistant image. To the extent that there is a correlation between the two, we would expect images of other actors as very aggressive or very peaceful to be strongly entrenched. This

[172] For experimental evidence, see, for example, Bruner, Postman, and Rodrigues, "Expectations and the Perception of Color."

[173] This begs the question of why the actor is confident. Some of the discussion above on the interaction between perceptions and pre-existing beliefs is relevant to this point.

[174] Bruner and Potter, "Interference in Visual Recognition." For further experimental evidence, see Engel, "Binocular Methods in Psychological Research."

[175] "Definition of the Situation as a Determinant of International Action," in Kelman, ed., *International Behavior*, p. 411.

explanation would be inadequate and other variables would have to be considered only if it were found that beliefs that the other had extreme intentions, even when held without extreme confidence, were especially hard to modify.

The third corollary is that a person is less apt to reorganize evidence into a new theory or image if he is deeply committed to the established view. Commitment here means not only the degree to which the person's power and prestige are involved but also—and more importantly—the degree to which this way of seeing the world has proved satisfactory and has become internalized. The "new math" gives less grief to school children than it does to their parents. Twenty-five years' use of a number system with a base of ten makes it hard to imagine any other system. This means that training and experience, the main determinants of commitment, are functional if the environment is stable but have high costs if it is not. Experiments show that success with one method inhibits the development of new ones where needed. For example, subjects were given containers of known volume and asked to measure out a given amount of water. The first several problems could be solved by a formula, which the subjects soon learned. But when they came to problems that looked similar but could not be solved by this formula, they were much slower to find the solution than were other subjects who had not dealt with the earlier examples.[176] This was true even though the former subjects soon realized that the old method would not work. Similarly, it is difficult for people to solve problems that require the novel use of familiar objects.[177] The strength of this effect increases with stress (e.g. time pressures, hostility displayed by the experimenter, social tension, previous failure on a supposedly easy test), with the complexity of the method learned, and, within limits, with the number of problems successfully solved by the method.[178] Merely giving subjects experience with a series of problems that first establishes and then requires the breaking of a set will not help them avoid premature cognitive closure in future problems. More effective are previous exposure combined with an ex-

[176] Luchins and Luchins, *Rigidity of Behavior.*

[177] Robert Adamson, "Functional Fixedness as Related to Problem Solving: A Repetition of Three Experiments," *Journal of Experimental Psychology* 44 (1952), 288-91; K. Duncker, "On Problem Solving," *Psychological Monographs* 58 (1945), no. 270; Herbert Birch and Herbert Rabinowitz, "The Negative Effect of Previous Experience on Productive Thinking," *Journal of Experimental Psychology* 41 (1951), 121-25.

[178] Luchins and Luchins, *Rigidity of Behavior*; Wilbert Ray, "Mild Stress and Problem-Solving," in Ray, ed., *The Experimental Psychology of Original Thinking* (New York: Macmillan Co., 1967), pp. 191-97; Irving Maltzman and Lloyd Morrisett, Jr., "Different Strengths of Set in the Solution of Anagrams," *Journal of Experimental Psychology* 44 (1952), 242-46; R. P. Youtz, "The Relation Between the Number of Confirmations of One Hypothesis and the Speed of Accepting a New and Incompatible Hypothesis," *American Psychology* 3 (1948), 248-49.

planation, warnings that problem-solving often requires the breaking of a set, or a pause between the time the subjects are given a problem and the time they begin working on it.[179]

A similar pattern is evident outside of the laboratory. Scientific breakthroughs are often made by investigators who are either young or trained in another branch of science.[180] These people can more easily free themselves from the established framework, although sometimes they do not realize this. James Watson once became interested in a field that one scientist had dominated by virtue of the "prodigious number of pretty experiments" he had carried out. Watson thought he had a new approach and was particularly pleased by "the possibility that [the dominant scientist] might be so stuck on his classical way of thinking that I would accomplish the unbelievable feat of beating him to the correct interpretation of his own experiments."[181] This feat would not have been so unbelievable as Watson thought.

The same reasons account for the fact that many innovators in industry were not trained in the areas in which they innovated. This is clearly brought out by Morison's fascinating study of the early steel industry. Neither Bessemer nor the less well-known William Kelly "had grown up in the iron trade. Bessemer came to his experiments . . . at forty-two after attending to such matters as the design of machines to make glass, velvet, sugar, and bronze powder. Kelly was in his thirties when he drifted out of dry goods and into the kettle business. . . . [T]hey were possibly freer to discover meaning in accidental deviations from normal results . . . simply because their thoughts and expectations had not been steadily confined within the boundaries of common practice."[182]

Similarly, two of the men who led the industry in the next phase—the transformation of the technological breakthrough into viable, large-scale production—lacked experience in the iron industry. One "was a surveyor with some engineering training . . . ; [the other] had been a journalist, an

[179] Luchins and Luchins, *Rigidity of Behavior*, pp. 377-78, 503, 519-23. Norman Maier, "An Aspect of Human Reasoning," *British Journal of Psychology* 24 (1933), 144-55, found that warning inhibited the establishment of a set. Milton Rokeach, "The Effect of Perception Time upon Rigidity and Concreteness of Thinking," *Journal of Experimental Psychology* 40 (1950), 206-16, provides evidence of the value of a pause before problem-solving, but M. E. Tresselt and D. S. Leeds, "The Einstellung Effect in Immediate and Delayed Problem-Solving," *Journal of General Psychology* 49 (1953), 87-95, found that a delay of a day or more increases the effect.

[180] Kuhn, *The Structure of Scientific Revolutions*, pp. 89-90. Kuhn also notes that, while everyone seems to agree with this position, it is yet to be subject to careful empirical research. Some negative findings are cited in Hagstrom, *The Scientific Community*, p. 243. But some of these data are not relevant because of the confusion between productivity, which involves mainly normal research within an accepted paradigm, and breakthroughs that change the paradigm.

[181] *The Double Helix* (New York: Atheneum, 1968), pp. 142-43.

[182] Elting Morison, *Men, Machines, and Modern Times* (Cambridge, Mass.: M.I.T. Press, 1966), p. 129.

editor, a railroad expert." And the only steel company in the United States that was not staffed by English workers who had experience with the early British Bessemer plants soon "established a commanding lead over all competitors" by adopting the latest techniques. The industry was later reorganized and dominated by another outsider, Andrew Carnegie, who realized that technology and the demand for steel had reached the point where the industry could break out of its limited and protected pattern of production and marketing. Morison notes the contrast he presented to the established leaders: "Shut up in their own enclosure, living off the information of a decade earlier, wedded to their own small concerns, and bemused by their investments of time, money, and pride . . . , they could not discern that the changing times required new solutions; they could not even discern that times had changed."[183]

This generalization is not limited to the steel industry. Two of the three outstanding discoveries in the aluminum industry before 1937 were made by outsiders. A study of innovations in petroleum processing concluded that "The most novel ideas . . . occurred to independent inventors." Students of the history of aircraft argue that "Of all the major inventions made in the past half century, only those of two types of flap can wholly be credited to the employees of aircraft manufacturers."

> [There is a long] list of instances where a fresh and untutored mind has succeeded when the experts have failed, or have not thought it worth while trying. . . . Some of them seem almost fantastic yet there is good authority for them; Gillette, the inventor of the safety razor, was a travelling salesman in crown corks. The joint inventors of Kodachrome were musicians. Eastman, when he revolutionized photography, was a bookkeeper. Carlson, the inventor of xerography, was a patent lawyer. The inventor of the ball-point pen was at various times sculptor, painter and journalist. The automatic telephone dialling system was invented by an undertaker. All the varieties of successful automatic guns have come from individual inventors who were civilians. Two Swedish technical students were responsible for the invention of domestic gas refrigeration; a twenty-year-old Harvard student for success in producing the first practical light-polarising material. The viscose rayon industry was largely the result of the work of a consulting chemist, a former glass blower and a former bank clerk. An American newspaperman is credited with being the father of the parking meter. J. B. Dunlop, one inventor of the pneumatic tyre, was a veterinary surgeon.[184]

[183] *Ibid.*, pp. 161, 40, 204.

[184] John Jewkes, David Sawers and Richard Stillerman, *The Sources of Invention* (2nd ed., New York: Norton, 1969), pp. 131, 204, 97.

This pattern is also apparent in military and political perceptions. Just as "a number of nonscientists . . . saw the light [of the theory of evolution] well before the professionals," so all the professional military experts failed to predict the shape of World War I. In "The fifty years before the First World War the only writers who came anywhere near to seeing how science and industry might change the traditional pattern of warfare were" amateurs—novelists and a Polish banker. Similarly, the "strategic usefulness of railways in war was first realized by civilians." And within the military, those who propose major innovations are often outside the mainstream of the profession.[185]

Innovators' accounts parallel the explanations given by psychologists. The president of the steel company that did not employ experienced workers credited his success largely to this fact. "We thus had willing pupils with no prejudices and no reminiscences of what they had done in the old country." The head of a textile firm that made major innovations explained that when he chose the personnel for the research group in his firm, "provided there was evidence of ability to conduct research, lack of experience was regarded even as an advantage, since such workers would not have got into ruts, and would be more likely to bring a new outlook."[186]

The same kind of accounts are often given by scientists. Pulsars were discovered by a graduate student, Jocelyn Bell, and a famous astronomer, Anthony Hewish. The radio signals that Bell detected made little sense within the framework of contemporary scientific theories, and so, before accepting the implications of their startling findings, all the astronomers searched for alternative explanations of them. But Bell was a bit less skeptical. "My background in astronomy wasn't as good as Hewish's and I didn't appreciate all the risks. He ruled it out as a star— [I] didn't realize why it could not have been a star." Perhaps a more

[185] Ernst Mayr, "The Nature of the Darwinian Revolution," *Science* 176 (June 2, 1972), 982; I. F. Clarke, *Voices Prophesying War, 1763-1984* (London: Oxford University Press, 1966), p. 190; E. L. Woodward, *Peace and War in Europe, 1815-1870* (London: Constable, 1931), p. 21; Morison, *Men, Machines, and Modern Times*, p. 73; Gerald Wheeler, "Mitchell, Moffett, and Air Power," *Airpower Historian* 8 (April 1961), 79-81. It should be noted, however, that military innovations often come from people trained in the area when they are justified not "in terms of any new grand strategy" but rather "in terms of simply a better way to perform [an existing] . . . mission." (Vincent Davis, *The Politics of Innovation* [Denver: University of Denver Monograph Series in World Affairs, 4, No. 3, 1967], pp. 19-20.) Indeed, many weapons are developed and deployed for old tasks for which they are not particularly well suited. Only later is it realized that there are new and important missions that these weapons could perform. See Marshall Wolff, "The Structure of Military Innovation," Harvard Senior Honors Thesis, 1970.

[186] Quoted in Morison, *Men, Machines, and Modern Times*, p. 40; quoted in Jewkes, Sawers, and Stillerman, *Sources of Invention*, p. 122.

knowledgeable investigator, knowing how little sense the signals made, would have failed to explore the original data or would not have noticed them at all. For what Bell did, a scientist in the midst of "normal science" does not do. As another astronomer put it, she showed "a willingness to contemplate as a serious possibility a phenomenon that all past experience suggested was impossible." Similarly, in discussing the scientific breakthroughs that many scientists feel have been made by a self-taught inventor, Stanford Ovshinsky, one physicist conjectured that "Ovshinsky may have been lucky to avoid the conventional crystal-oriented instruction dished out to solid-state physicists in universities, for he was thus presumably better able to appreciate the possibilities of" new kinds of materials. A second scientist, who had worked with Ovshinsky in another area of science, noted that he "brought an attitude toward the work that was a little different. He would raise questions that made you stop and think about things you usually take for granted." This outlook is often supported by a belief in the importance of "abstract science" and "sound principles," to use the words of two innovators. Thus a third innovator remarked that because he lacked experience he had no choice but to start with theory and so question the framework that others took for granted.[187]

We should note two alternative explanations of these findings. First, in some cases the leading firms in an industry, realizing that innovation increases uncertainty, may calculate that they are better off minimizing change. But this cannot account for the fact that inventions are often made not by individuals or small firms who have had experience with the industry but lack a stake in its existing structure, but rather by complete outsiders. Second, innovators may have "creative personalities." Morison argues that for several of the innovators in the steel industry "the particular medium, Bessemer steel, and money were of secondary interest, but the medium gave them opportunities to express themselves in new ways, to make new and exciting arrangements, to create something out of their thoughts and feelings that had not existed before. Once achieved, they were readier to move on into other mediums that gave them renewed opportunities for creation. . . . They did not identify themselves with their creations or find satisfaction so much in continuing the artifacts they created as in the act of creation itself."[188] This suggests the possibility that the correlation between inventiveness and lack of training in the field may be at least partly spurious. The innovator's creativity may lead him

[187] Nicholas Wade, "Discovery of Pulsars," *Science* 189 (August 1, 1975), 362, 358; quoted in Philip Coffey, "Ovshinsky: Promoter or Persecuted Genius?" *Science* 165 (August 15, 1969), 474-75; quoted in Morison, *Men, Machines, and Modern Times*, p. 160; *ibid.*, p. 159.

[188] *Ibid.*, p. 202.

to refuse to undertake long and narrowing training, to reject the accepted framework of analysis, to resist the pressures to do "normal science," and to move from one field to another as different problems appear more interesting. If this is so, the lack of training could then be an intervening variable mediating the relationship between personality and inventiveness and might have limited independent impact.

IMPLICATIONS FOR DECISION-MAKING

If commitment to an image inhibits the development of a new one, those who are most involved in carrying out policies guided by the old image will be the least able to innovate. This, of course, is part of the rationale for a policy planning staff. Not having to solve immediate problems provides both the time and the intellectual flexibility to question established policies and to notice evidence that prevailing images cannot explain. Similarly, individuals newly assigned to a problem or to a foreign country should have perceptual openness.[189]

Another implication of this corollary is that review committees are more apt to see problems in a new light and recommend non-incremental changes if their members have not previously worked on the problem. Such a group may fail to give adequate weight to constraints well known to those more familiar with the area and so may design impractical or unbalanced proposals, but since most policy reviews are not characterized by an excess of imagination, this risk will usually be worth running. For example, a prime reason why the 1961 Ad Hoc Committee on Public Welfare appointed by the secretary of HEW did not consider basic changes in the system was that its membership was drawn from those who were "friends, colleagues, [and] coarchitects of current policy."

> What this meant was that the Ad Hoc Committee could take on faith as matters of agreement the very kinds of questions that most require reexamination and inquiry. The people whose professional lives were dedicated to services as a necessary element of welfare could neither fail to stress services nor be expected to think it necessary to wipe the slate clean and build a new empirical theory of public assistance.[190]

As a result, the committee did not, for example, ask whether the accepted goal of rehabilitation was a feasible objective for many programs. Nor did it try to determine whether the social and political changes that

---

[189] But to the extent that commitment to an image is shared by all members of the elite, direct involvement will not make perceptual reorganization easier.

[190] Gilbert Steiner, "Advisory Councils and National Social Warfare Policy," in Thomas Cronin and Sanford Greenberg, *The Presidential Advisory System* (New York: Harper and Row, 1969), p. 254.

have taken place since 1935 required fundamental alterations of policy. Not only were the committee's recommendations completely within the established framework, but the report would not enable others to judge this framework because the relevant questions were not asked nor the necessary data gathered. Similarly, when a new Japanese cabinet set out to re-examine foreign policy in the fall of 1941, the attempt to proceed with a "clean slate" was inhibited by the fact that "the holdovers from the [last] Cabinet exerted greater influence than the newcomers; they were also more imprisoned in their thinking by what had gone before. Despite their enormous personal responsibility for the welfare of their countrymen, these leaders of Japan, old and new alike, never once asked themselves *why* they were confronted by such a critical choice. They did not look at the record or otherwise seek in past policies an explanation for present difficulties."[191] These considerations can also be applied to the optimum relations between the foreign policy committees of Congress and the policy-makers in the Executive. The best route to influence may not be through extensive involvement in the implementation of policies. Rather, the committees may gain perceptual, as well as political, independence by remaining less involved. Their detailed suggestions may be less valuable, but they will be in a better position to ask basic questions and make wide-ranging criticisms.

[191] Butow, *Tojo and the Coming of the War*, p. 315.

CHAPTER FIVE

The Impact of the Evoked Set

PERCEPTIONS are influenced by immediate concerns ("evoked sets") as well as by more deeply rooted expectations. A person will perceive and interpret stimuli in terms of what is at the front of his mind. To predict the inferences a person will draw from a bit of evidence, we often need to know what problems concern him and what information he has received recently. In the last chapter we pointed out that people are quicker to see familiar objects than unfamiliar ones. But, as the discussion here will show, familiarity with an object is not enough. The person must also expect it to be present. Thus, for example, we are often slow to recognize a person we know well if he appears in an unusual context.

EVOKED SET IN THE ABSENCE OF COMMUNICATION

Actors are often misled by incorrectly assuming that others share their concerns. But even when this belief is absent the evoked set is an important influence on perceptions, as is illustrated by an experiment employing the classic figure that can be seen either as a goblet or as facing profiles. If the person is thinking about faces, he will see the profiles; if he has been looking at glasses, he will see a goblet. The impact of the evoked set in everyday life is no less apparent. Walter Lippmann points out that "Anyone who has stood at the end of a railroad platform waiting for a friend, will recall what queer people he mistook for him."[1] In this case the perception can be understood as a rational guess about an ambiguous stimulus since there is a reasonable chance that any approaching person will be the friend. In other cases, however, this explanation is inadequate. Thinking about a friend increases the probability of "see-

---

[1] Muzafer Sherif and Carolyn Sherif, *Groups in Harmony and Tension* (New York: Harper and Brothers, 1953), p. 140; Walter Lippmann, *Public Opinion* (New York: Harcourt, Brace, 1922), p. 115. A psychologist provides an illustration of "how elusive and incidental such a set can be: Just before I alighted from the tram in front of the City Hall, I heard, without paying any great attention to it, the tones from a horn orchestra somewhere in the distance. I walked in my own thoughts along Vestergade and saw a man coming toward me carrying a horn. When I passed him, I discovered that the horn was a reading lamp and only when I began to speculate over why I first had seen a horn did I remember the orchestra. It is not unreasonable to suppose that the sound of the orchestra had created in me a sort of set with the result that I processed the stimuli from the lamp into the perceived horn." Franz From, *Perception of Other People*, translated by Erik Kvan and Brendan Maher (New York: Columbia University Press, 1971), p. 82.

ing" him even if I know he is not around. Similarly, my perceptions of the dark streets I pass walking home from the movies will be different if the film was a spy story than they would be had I seen a comedy.

In politics, too, the evoked set is influential even in simple situations that lack two-way communications. As in the case of the man awaiting his friend, it is not irrational that the confirmed attack by North Vietnam on an American destroyer in the Tonkin Gulf made it more likely that the decision-makers would quickly see ambiguous evidence as indicating a second attack two nights later.[2] But, like the man thinking about a friend in another city, the evoked set influences perceptions even when there is no reason the phenomenon being thought about is more likely to be present. For example, the spending of a considerable amount of time preparing a contingency plan increases the probability that the decision-makers will see future events as resembling the situation they had contemplated and as calling for the plans they have developed.[3]

Rational or not, people interpret incoming information in terms of what is of concern to them at the time the information arrives. Barber and Fox found that the inferences and research strategies of two scientists who independently stumbled upon the strange side effect of a drug were influenced by their main research interests. As one of the scientists put it: "Since I was primarily interested in research questions having to do with the muscles of the heart, I was thinking in terms of muscle. That blinded me, so that changes in the cartilage didn't occur to me as a possibility. I was looking for muscles in the [cross-section of tissue], and I never dreamed" that changes were taking place in the cartilage.[4] It should be stressed that the scientist's examination of the muscle cells was not based on the belief that the payoff for finding changes there would be high because it would contribute to his main interest. Rather his decision, if it can be called that, was made without calculation or reflection.

The evoked set may be strong enough to lead the person to ignore information that is not relevant to his immediate concerns even if in retrospect it seems clear that the message merited serious attention. When asked why he did not follow up Senator Eagleton's report that he

[2] Chester Cooper, *The Lost Crusade* (New York: Dodd, Mead, 1970), p. 242.

[3] For a similar argument, see Dean Pruitt, "The Definition of the Situation as a Determinant of International Action," in Herbert Kelman, ed., *International Behavior* (New York: Holt, Rinehart and Winston, 1965), p. 401. Contingency planning also introduces rigidities by structuring the kinds of operations the organization is capable of performing. The contingency plans drawn up before Pearl Harbor drew some of their influence from both the factors. See Samuel Morison, *The History of U.S. Naval Operations in World War II*, vol. 1: *The Battle of the Atlantic* (Boston: Little, Brown, 1948), p. 47.

[4] Bernard Barber and Renée Fox, "The Case of the Floppy-Eared Rabbits: An Instance of Serendipity Gained and Serendipity Lost," *American Journal of Sociology* 64 (September 1958), 132.

had been hospitalized for exhaustion, a McGovern assistant replied that this information came as "an answer to the alcoholism charge, that's what we were looking for. No one really thought of it on its own."[5]

COMMUNICATION AND ESTIMATING THE EVOKED SET OF THE OTHER

The propensity for an actor to perceive the messages and behavior of another in terms of his own evoked set is usually reinforced by the belief that the other shares his concerns and information. So if messages are sent from a background that differs from that of the receiver, misunderstanding will result unless either party is alert to this danger and knows the other's perspective.[6] What the sender means to be central may strike the receiver as unimportant or unintelligible. What is obvious to the former may be hopelessly ambiguous to the latter or, worse yet, have a clear meaning that is different from the intended one. When actors send complex and subtle messages, these problems are compounded. And matters are not helped when receivers are attuned to subtleties, because in searching for subtleties the impact of the receiver's expectations is increased.

Furthermore, these are barriers to what I have called the first level of communication—the ability to understand what message the other is trying to convey—and so are present even when the receiver does not have to take account of the possibility that the sender's message is not an accurate reflection of his actual beliefs and intentions.[7] Thus a message from the president of a firm will mean one thing to someone working on increasing sales and quite another to someone in charge of cutting costs—and neither of these interpretations may coincide with what the president had in mind. To take an international example, in late August 1939 Hitler tried to play on British fears by exaggerating his strength in a talk with the Italian foreign minister, who, he assumed, would see that the ominous news reached London. But the Italians cared more about their own weakness and their attention was caught and their reports shaped by one of Hitler's offhand remarks that referred to their position. More direct attempts at deterrence can be similarly deflected. Because the Spanish decision-makers in 1898 believed that the Cuban rebels

---

[5] Quoted in "Eagleton Reports Surprise McGovern," *Boston Globe*, evening edition, November 15, 1972.

[6] For a similar argument see Albert Mehrabian and Henry Reed, "Some Determinants of Communication Accuracy," *Psychological Bulletin* 70 (November 1968), 378-79 and the literature cited there. For experimental evidence, see Matthew Bonham, "Simulating International Disarmament Negotiations," *Journal of Conflict Resolution* 15 (September 1971), 299-316.

[7] For a discussion of this distinction, see Robert Jervis, *The Logic of Images in International Relations* (Princeton: Princeton University Press, 1970), pp. 24-25.

would not accept the sought-for "negotiated settlement as long as they hoped for eventual aid from the United States":

> [the] ministers in Madrid scrutinized McKinley's annual message, not for indications of American intentions toward Spain, but for words that might hearten or discourage the rebels. A translation circulated to the cabinet is in the Spanish archives. It has innumerable marginal marks and underlinings, but none around McKinley's warning of "other and further action" in the "near future." The Spanish government was not yet concerned with anything McKinley said or did, except as it seemed likely to affect rebel morale. Since the message contained passages discouraging recognition and praising the offer of autonomy, the Foreign Minister advised the Spanish ambassador in Paris that the cabinet found it "very satisfactory."[8]

Misunderstandings within a Government:
Differences in Information, Perspectives, and Time Lags

It is not surprising to find differences in evoked sets creating misperception under conditions of hostility and restricted communication.[9] What is more striking is that differences in information, perspectives, and time lags can produce this effect even when there is complete common interest between the actors, when deception is neither intended nor suspected, and when both actors wish to communicate accurately. An important example is the misunderstanding between Washington and Pearl Harbor in the days preceding the Japanese attack. "Washington advised General Short [in Pearl Harbor] on November 27 to expect 'hostile action' at any moment, by which it meant 'attack of American possessions from without,' but General Short understood this phrase to mean 'sabotage.' "[10] A seemingly unambiguous message was read entirely differently than was intended because Washington did not realize that information of slight importance to Washington was highly salient to General Short and that vital facts had not been sent to the field. First, Washington did not understand that previous messages and experiences had made the local authorities highly sensitive to the danger of sabotage. Washington officials therefore never thought to state explicitly that the warning referred to attack from without, nor were they aware of the significance of their additional notices that defensive measures should not "alarm civil

8 Jon Kimche, *The Unfought Battle* (New York: Stein and Day, 1968), pp. 99-100; Ernest May, *Imperial Democracy* (New York: Harcourt, Brace, 1961), p. 161.

9 Robert Blake and Jane Mouton, "Comprehension of Own and of Outgroup Positions under Intergroup Competition," *Journal of Conflict Resolution* 5 (September 1961), 304-10.

10 Roberta Wohlstetter, *Pearl Harbor: Warning and Decision* (Stanford: Stanford University Press, 1962), p. 74.

population" and that "subversive activities may be expected."[11] Second, those who wrote the warning not only had been reading the intercepts of MAGIC—the Japanese diplomatic code—and knew that war was likely, but thought these intercepts had been sent to Pearl Harbor and that General Short would also be aware of the heightened danger. But this assumption was incorrect, and Short's evoked set was not influenced by this vital stream of data. Short could not know that Washington possessed incorrect beliefs about what information he had and ask to be enlightened. The actors did not realize they were not communicating.[12]

The failures of communication leading to the ill-fated charge of the Light Brigade were largely caused by unrecognized differences in evoked sets created by different geographical perspectives, time lags, and contrasting experiences. The scene witnessed by the commander-in-chief, Lord Raglan, differed from that seen by his subordinates because Raglan was stationed on the heights above the battlefield. "Only to the watchers above, looking down, did the plain appear flat and the movements of the enemy clear; the troops engaged in the battle had their view obscured by hillocks, by rises on the ground, and above all by the ridge of the Causeway Heights. Unless Lord Raglan could put himself in the place of his generals 600 feet below and could perpetually bear in mind when issuing orders that what was clear to him would by no means be clear to them, his position high above the battle was dangerous indeed."[13]

One reason why Raglan's order "to advance . . . and try to prevent the enemy carrying away the guns" seemed so ambiguous to Lucan, the commander of the cavalry, was that only Lord Raglan could see the guns being moved. "Lucan from his position could see nothing; . . . no single enemy soldier was in sight; nor had he any picture of the movements of the enemy in his mind's eye, because he had unaccountably neglected to acquaint himself with the Russian dispositions." Although Raglan may have realized that the rise in the ground would obscure Lucan's sight, he probably assumed that Lucan had reconnoitered and so knew enough about the enemy's movements to understand the order.[14]

The courier could have been expected to provide the necessary clari-

---

[11] Quoted in Elting Morison, *Turmoil and Tradition: A Study in the Life and Times of Henry L. Stimson* (Boston: Houghton Mifflin, 1960), p. 528.

[12] As an army board of inquiry noted, officials in Washington should have guessed that their message had been misinterpreted because of General Short's response to the warning: "Report Department alerted to prevent sabotage." (Wohlstetter, *Pearl Harbor*, p. 260; Morison, *Turmoil and Tradition*, pp. 533-34.) Wohlstetter attributes this error to the distraction created by the "press of work," but I suspect that the recipients' certainty that their warning was unambiguous was at least as important.

[13] Cecil Woodham-Smith, *The Charge of the Light Brigade* (New York: Signet, 1968), p. 212.

[14] *Ibid.*, pp. 225-26.

fication. But when Lucan asked him which guns he was to attack, the courier answered incorrectly because his evoked set differed from that of his superiors in two ways. First, he had not seen an earlier order which referred to the guns that Raglan wanted taken. (Lucan had read this order but did not connect it with the later one.) Second, the courier had done much to develop the cavalry and had just witnessed its failure to take advantage of a magnificent opportunity to pursue a large Russian force. So when he read the order "He leapt to the joyful conclusion that at last vengeance was to be taken on those Russians who had been suffered to escape."[15]

The thirty minutes that it took a message to go from Raglan to the battlefield added to the divergence of evoked sets. In a rapidly changing battle, what was salient when the order was written might not be significant when it was received. It was hard for Lucan to think of what would have seemed most important half an hour before; even if he were aware of the problem, Raglan could only guess at what the context would be half an hour later. Thus an earlier order led to troop movements that made little sense in the changed situation. Similarly, one reason for the ineffectiveness of the messages exchanged by the United States and Great Britain designed to avoid the War of 1812 was that they were interpreted in the light of events that had not been foreseen when they were written. And in July 1914 Lord Grey, the British foreign secretary, could not know that his note warning Germany of the disastrous consequences of a war would reach the kaiser immediately after the latter had learned of the Russian mobilization, therefore predisposing him to view Grey's message as part of a plot. When, during the same crisis, the German chancellor told his ambassador to "impress on M. Sazonov [the Russian foreign minister] very seriously that further continuation of Russian mobilization measures would compel us to mobilize and that then European war could scarcely be prevented," he could not know that the message would be delivered soon after Sazonov, who had spent the day trying to soften the Russian position, had been told of the Austrian bombardment of Belgrade.[16]

To return to the Light Brigade example, differences in previous experiences contributed to Lucan's incorrect interpretation of one of the orders:

Raglan's treatment of the cavalry throughout the campaign made it highly improbable that he would order an attack by cavalry alone.

[15] *Ibid.*, p. 227.

[16] For excerpts from Lord Grey's note and the kaiser's marginal comments, see Robert North, "Perception and Action in the 1914 Crisis," *Journal of International Affairs*, 21, No. 1 (1967), 114. For the German message and Sazonov's reaction, see L.C.F. Turner, *Origins of the First World War* (New York: Norton, 1970), pp. 105-106.

Again and again . . . the cavalry had been restrained, recalled, forbidden to take the offensive, prohibited from engaging the enemy. Only an hour or so ago Lord Raglan had withdrawn the cavalry from their position at the entrance to Balaclava, where they were preparing to engage the Russian cavalry, and placed them in an inactive position under the heights. It never crossed Lucan's mind that he was expected to launch an attack by cavalry with the prospect of being supported at some future time by the infantry.

Lucan could not know that Raglan, "with his power to divine the temper of troops, perceived that the whole Russian army had been shaken by the triumphant and audacious charge of the Heavy Brigade and that, threatened again by British cavalry, they would retire." Failing to appreciate that his insight was not shared by Lucan and neglecting the impact of his previous tactics, Raglan wrote an order that did not make sense to its recipient.[17]

Uneven Distribution of Information within Governments

Differences in evoked sets caused by differences in information can lead various parts of a state's bureaucracy to different perceptions of others' actions. Well-known are the consequences of major differences in perspective caused by the division of labor within a government. Worthy of more attention are the unrecognized effects of the uneven distribution of relevant information, usually highly classified information, some of which deals with the state's own behavior. Thus in his famous balance of power memorandum Eyre Crowe sees the Anglo-German convention on the Portuguese colonies as an example of German aggressiveness. "[B]ecause his information was restricted to what was printed, [Crowe] underestimates the pro-German feeling in the Cabinet and as a result views the agreement as one which the Germans extracted from the British." Sanderson, the former permanent undersecretary, knew what the British position had been and was better able to interpret the German behavior. More recently it has been argued that the American intelligence community was handicapped in its efforts to understand Russian military policy because Secretary of State Kissinger withheld important information about the SALT I negotiations and agreements.[18]

Several incidents in the Cold War illustrate this phenomenon. Interpretations of the North Vietnamese attack on the *Maddox* in the Gulf of Tonkin varied depending on whether the person knew that the ship had been close to the shore gathering electronic intelligence and that South

---

[17] Woodham-Smith, *The Charge of the Light Brigade*, pp. 222-23.

[18] Zara Steiner, *The Foreign Office and Foreign Policy, 1898-1914* (Cambridge: Cambridge University Press, 1969), p. 69; Clarence Robinson, "Kissinger Deliberately Concealing SALT Violations, Zumwalt Claims," *Aviation Week and Space Technology*, December 8, 1975, p. 14.

Vietnamese commandoes had raided the nearby coast two days before. Similarly, Roger Hilsman points out: "Those who knew of the peripheral reconnaissance flights that probed Soviet air defenses during the Eisenhower administration and the U-2 flights over the Soviet Union itself . . . were better able to understand some of the things the Soviets were saying and doing than people who did not know of these activities." For the same reason an ambassador who is unaware of messages passed between his home government and the one he is dealing with is apt to misinterpret both nations' behavior. To avoid this, the State Department has a rule that reports of conversations with foreign diplomats in Washington are to be sent to the appropriate American embassy.[19] By contrast, British diplomats in the 1930s were not informed of important conversations between foreign governments and Chamberlain's secret emissaries and therefore found it harder to gauge others' intentions or the impact of their own behavior.

Facts that would make a third party's behavior comprehensible may also be withheld by allies. For example, Britain stood by France in the Moroccan crisis of 1905 partly because she interpreted German demands as indicating unreasonable hostility aimed at establishing German domination of the continent. "If the British government had known that France had surreptitiously made an offer of territorial compensation to Germany, Britain could not have been as enthusiastic as she was in her diplomatic support." Against this background, German behavior would not have seemed so unusual. Britain's interpretation of German motives in the second Moroccan crisis was similarly influenced by a lack of information about past dealings between Germany and France. The British were predisposed "to assume, or at least suspect, that Germany had some far-reaching territorial claims. No other explanation seemed adequate." The idea that Germany would act so belligerently in order to make relatively minor gains appeared implausible without the knowledge that before the crisis broke out Germany had been negotiating for compensation from France in the hinterland of the Congo.[20]

Differences in perception are also produced when information about the adversary is distributed unevenly within a government. Soviet be-

---

[19] *To Move a Nation* (Garden City, N.Y.: Doubleday, 1967), p. 66; Robert Elder, *The Policy Machine* (Syracuse, N.Y.: Syracuse University Press, 1960), p. 32. In the early 1930s relevant communications between Washington and other governments were not passed on to the American ambassador to Japan, who complained that this was "like playing baseball without being able to see the pitcher." Quoted in Christopher Thorne, *The Limits of Foreign Policy* (New York: Putnam, 1973), p. 88.

[20] S. L. Mayer, "Anglo-German Rivalry at the Algeciras Conference," in Prosser Gifford and Wm. Roger Louis, eds., *Britain and Germany in Africa* (New Haven: Yale University Press, 1967), p. 226; E. L. Woodward, *Great Britain and the German Navy* (Oxford: Clarendon Press, 1935), pp. 311-12.

havior would appear one way to those who not only knew of the U-2 flights but also had access to the resulting intelligence estimates and another way to those who lacked this information and overestimated Soviet missile strength. A British convoy in World War I was destroyed in part because those officers who knew that a German force was out did not know the convoy schedule and those who knew where the convoys were did not know of the movements of German ships. More important consequences followed from the fact that the first American officials to read the interceptions of the Japanese message designed to immediately precede the attack on Pearl Harbor were not familiar with diplomatic practice and so did not realize that it was odd that the ambassadors were told to deliver the message at a specified time.[21]

Greater complications arise when vital information is unevenly distributed within the governments of *both* states. Misperception is apt to occur when the part of the government of state A that is sending a message has incorrect beliefs about the information available to the part of the government of state B that is receiving it and when, conversely, the part of B's government interpreting the message has incorrect beliefs concerning the information and evoked set held by the sender. This means not only that the receiver will misinterpret messages that are sent from a background of information that he does not have but also that the receiver can go astray if he knows certain information and incorrectly assumes that the sender does also. To return to Hilsman's example, those Americans who knew of the U-2 flights may have made *less* accurate interpretations of Soviet behavior than those who were less well informed if they assumed that their opposite numbers were concerned with, or even knew of, these flights.

Differences in Evoked Set Caused by Differences in Concerns

Differences in what most concerns an actor are a major cause of misperception. Issues that are very important to a decision-maker take up so much of his time and intellectual resources that he not only sees most events in terms of these issues but cannot realize that others do not share these preoccupations. One psychologist notes that people "become completely 'tuned' to the processing" of matters to which their attention is

---

[21] Arthur Marder, *From the Dreadnought to Scapa Flow*, vol. 4: *1917: Year of Crisis* (London: Oxford University Press, 1969), p. 295. It seems probable that a lack of knowledge of standard operating procedures led a British naval officer to miss the importance of some crucial German signals intercepted during the battle of Jutland. See Marder, *From the Dreadnought to Scapa Flow*, vol. 3: *Jutland and After*, p. 154. For another example, see Douglas Robinson, *The Zeppelin in Combat* (London: G. T. Foulis, 1962), pp. 148-49.

turned; Richard Neustadt argues that "awareness filters through [decision-makers'] self-absorption"; and an historian of the reversal of Belgian foreign policy in 1936–1937 notes that one reason why the Belgian decision-makers did not contemplate possible adverse foreign reactions to their policy was that they "were engrossed in [the] endeavor [of] mobilizing public and party support for their military proposals."[22] A strong concern with a problem can then create a kind of tunnel vision. The decision-maker's perceptions are restricted not in the sense that he examines information on a narrow range of subjects, but in the sense that he assumes that others are focused on that which concerns him. So he not only tries to determine the impact of others' behavior on his problem but also believes that producing these consequences was the others' goal.

This misperception is related to the propensity of actors to see themselves as central to others' behavior.[23] An actor's knowledge of what he wants, what he fears, and what he has done sets the framework for his perceptions. Others are seen as orienting themselves toward his concerns, as helping or hurting him. Thus a strong supporter of Neville Chamberlain reacted to the German persecution of the Jews on "crystal night" by writing in his diary: "I must say Hitler never helps, and always makes Chamberlain's task more difficult." When the Germans took over Czechoslovakia in March 1939 he noted: "Hitler is never helpful." Similarly, before the United States entered the war some American decision-makers thought Hitler timed his moves to overshadow Roosevelt's speeches.[24]

If it is hard for a person to believe that others see him as being on the opposing team, it is even more difficult for him to realize that the other is playing an entirely different game. For example, when black students suffer indignities at the hands of professors and administrators, they tend to attribute this to their race, not their status as students.[25] The same

[22] From, *Perception of Other People*, p. 112; *Alliance Politics* (New York: Columbia University Press, 1970), p. 66; Pierre Henri Laurent, "The Reversal of Belgian Foreign Policy, 1936-37," *Review of Politics* 31 (July 1969), 379-80. For an example of the impact of Churchill's absorption in naval affairs after 1911, see Robert Rhodes James, *Churchill: A Study in Failure 1900-1939* (New York: World, 1970), p. 44.

[23] This phenomenon is discussed from another perspective in Chapter 9.

[24] Robert Rhodes James, ed., *Chips: The Diary of Sir Henry Channon* (Harmondsworth, Middlesex, England: Penguin, 1970), pp. 220, 230; Robert Sherwood, *Roosevelt and Hopkins* (New York: Harper and Brothers, 1948), pp. 228-96, 504. Also see James, ed., *Chips*, p. 305. For an example from Vietnam, see *The Pentagon Papers* (New York: Bantam, 1971), p. 166.

[25] Similarly, an NAACP official noted that he became angry when the traffic cop who had stopped him called him by his first name. "I was raised in the South where I know that a white man never calls a Negro anything except by his first name or 'boy.' You don't do that with a Negro [up here]. Now if he called you 'Jim,' you probably wouldn't think anything about it. But it's different for Negroes." (James Q. Wilson, *Varieties of Police Behavior* [New York: Atheneum, 1970],

cause explains many of the misunderstandings between the West and the Bolsheviks immediately following the revolution:

> the unbalanced preoccupation of the Allied chanceries with the war against Germany interfered with their ability to get a clear and useful view of what was happening in Russia [before the March revolution]. To the extent they took note of the disturbing signs of disintegration in Russia's capacity to make war and of the growing crisis of the dynasty, they tended to attribute these phenomena primarily to German influence.[26]

Another scholar points out that "the March Revolution was conceived at first in Britain as a revolt, not against the war, but against Tsarist inefficiency in conducting it." The same reaction was displayed by the French ambassador when

> walking through the streets amid the kaleidoscopic events of the February Revolution [he] found himself surrounded by a group of celebrating students, half-curious, half suspicious. . . . [T]hey called upon him to accompany them to the Tauride Palace, the home both of the Duma and of the Petrograd Soviet, and to do homage there to the red flag of the Revolution which now waved over the building. His answer was eloquently revealing: "I can render no better homage to Russian liberty," he said, "than by asking you to join me in shouting 'Vive la Guerre.' "[27]

And after the Bolsheviks came to power, Woodrow Wilson believed that the Russian willingness to make a separate peace had been spawned by the Allies' lack of clear and liberal peace aims.[28]

Even those Western observers who were in close touch with the events in Russia and who sympathized with the new regime underestimated the degree to which the Bolsheviks' agenda differed from theirs and that of the Allies. Thus Raymond Robins and Bruce Lockhart failed to see that the Soviets had no interest in fighting Germany and would do everything possible to conclude a truce. A variant of this type of misperception caused the Allied agents who saw their tasks as technical to believe that

---

p. 192.) In fact, traffic policemen make it a standard practice to call by their first names people they have stopped in order to establish their dominance. The NAACP official was being treated as a suspect, not as a Negro. But since the latter identification was more salient to him than the former, he assumed that it was equally important to the policeman.

[26] George Kennan, *Russia and the West under Lenin and Stalin* (New York: Mentor, 1962), pp. 18-19.

[27] F. S. Northedge, "1917-1919: The Implications for Britain," *Journal of Contemporary History* 3, No. 4 (1968), 195; Kennan, *Russia and the West*, p. 22.

[28] Kennan, *Russia Leaves the War* (New York: Atheneum, 1967), p. 94.

the Bolsheviks shared their overriding concern with the problems they were sent to Russia to deal with.[29]

The Allies' preoccupations not only adversely affected their ability to predict and alter Soviet behavior but also distorted their perceptions of the relations between Russia and Germany. Everything the Bolsheviks did that interfered with the war effort was taken to show that the Soviet leaders were either German agents or at least desired to aid the German cause. The Allies could not see that the Russians were not concerned about whether their actions helped or hindered the Allies, but only about whether they helped preserve the Soviet regime. The same process explains how the Americans, concerned with their security in the Caribbean, could believe that the French and Germans might cooperate in 1915 to establish a naval base in Haiti.[30]

Kennan argues that the cause lies in the way democracies respond to pressure:

> There is . . . nothing in nature more egocentrical than the embattled democracy. It soon becomes the victim of its own war propaganda. It then tends to attach to its own cause an absolute value which distorts its own vision of everything else. . . . It will readily be seen that people who have got themselves into this frame of mind have little understanding for the issues of any contest other than the one in which they are involved. The idea of people wasting time and substance on any *other* issue seems to them preposterous.[31]

But Kennan's own account shows that the Bolsheviks were equally victims of "egocentricity." They did not realize that the Allies cared about little but the war and that the varying urgency with which the Allies sought to use Russia against Germany—with or against the desires of the Bolsheviks—was understandable only in light of events on the Western front. Instead, as Kennan notes, what the Soviets "did in 1917 appeared to them then, as it does now, the most important of world happenings. They cannot believe it could have appeared otherwise to anybody else."[32]

Even actors who have a history of communication and cooperation may misperceive each other because of unrecognized differences in evoked sets. Indeed their previous experiences will make each assume more quickly that the other shares its concerns and understands its mes-

[29] Kennan, *Russia Leaves the War*, p. 515; Kennan, *The Decision to Intervene* (New York: Atheneum, 1967), p. 288.

[30] Richard Ullman, *Anglo-Soviet Relations, 1917-1921*, vol. 1: *Intervention and the War* (Princeton: Princeton University Press, 1961), pp. 123-25; Hans Schmidt, *The United States Occupation of Haiti, 1915-1934* (New Brunswick, N.J.: Rutgers University Press, 1971), p. 53.

[31] Kennan, *Russia and the West*, pp. 11-12.

[32] *Ibid.*, pp. 16-17.

sages. This partly explains the Anglo-American misperceptions over Suez. In stressing the value of a Canal Users Association, Dulles "invited Eden to take the initiative, adding that any interference with an association convoy [through the canal] would be a breach of the Convention calling for appropriate action. By this Dulles privately meant the alternative Cape route; to Eden it was an invitation to force a way through the canal if Nasser tried to interfere."[33] While some of the ambiguity may have been intended, the secretary of state did not mean to invite Britain to use force, nor did he realize Eden thought that he had done so. This misunderstanding is less puzzling when it is realized that the two officials were concerned with very different things—one with overthrowing Nasser or at least reducing his influence, and the other with resolving the dispute in any way that would minimize conflict—and so interpreted the exchange in different ways.

CONCLUSIONS

In the last chapter we discussed the influence of pre-existing beliefs on perceptions and the prevalence of premature cognitive closure. But we left open the question of the content of the expectations that exercise such an influence on perceptions. This chapter has supplied some of the answers by discussing several short-term determinants of what the person will be thinking when he receives new information (some of the long-term determinants will be discussed in the next chapter). People perceive incoming information in terms of the problems they are dealing with and what is on their minds when the information is received. To re-orient one's attention is difficult. A dramatic illustration is provided by the discussion in the cockpit of the Libyan airliner that was shot down over Israel in February 1973. The crew was so immersed in their task of finding the Cairo airport that they paid little attention to the fighters that suddenly appeared. Even the firing of warning shots could not jog their minds into realizing that they were facing a very different problem.

Captain: "Now is that Lima Uniform [code for Cairo airport] on your right?"

Captain: "Did you have the I.L.S.?" [I.L.S. stands for instrument landing system.]

Captain: "What's that you have there?"

Co-pilot: "Ah, we have rockets."

Captain: "Eh?"

[33] Terence Robertson, *Crisis* (New York: Atheneum, 1965), p. 111.

Co-pilot: "I have seen some rockets here."

Captain: "Oh, eh?"

(A 15-second beep was heard, signaling that the under-carriage was being lowered as if for landing. Noise of aircraft passing the airliner.)

Engineer: "You have the I.L.S. Is it descending?"

Captain: "No."

Captain: "Check the I.L.S. on yours."

Co-pilot: "What?"

Captain: "The I.L.S. of Cairo."[34]

Furthermore, actors often fail to send appropriate messages or draw accurate inferences because of the incorrect assumption that the other shares their evoked set. The Israeli pilots took for granted that the Libyans knew the nationality of the fighters, understood that they were being told to land, and chose to try to escape rather than comply. The idea that the Libyans were so engrossed in their own task that they completely failed to grasp the situation probably never occurred to the Israelis, and if it had been suggested to them they probably would have dismissed it as unbelievable.

Actors thus overestimate the degree to which each understands what the other is trying to say. This does not mean they overestimate their common interest. They may neither trust the other nor believe that the meanings the other intends to convey are a valid guide to the other's future behavior. But they rarely take into full account the degree to which the other may be concerned with different tasks and problems. This occurs on both a large and a small scale. The Allies were slow to see that defeating the Germans was not the most important issue in Russia after 1917, and Washington did not realize that sabotage was seen as the major danger by Pearl Harbor. The result is that each side overestimates the extent to which the two sides share a common agenda and rarely sees the extent to which its—and others'—perceptions are shaped by an evoked set that is formed by a particular combination of concerns and information.

[34] "Transcript of Cockpit Talk," *New York Times*, February 25, 1973.

CHAPTER SIX

How Decision-Makers Learn from History

INTRODUCTION

HOW DO past events influence current perceptions? Some have argued that they do not. A.J.P. Taylor says that "men use the past to prop up their own prejudices." Stanley Hoffmann agrees with John Fairbank that Americans tend to use history as a "grabbag from which each advocate pulls out a 'lesson' to prove his point." Herbert Butterfield argues that "Those who [in 1919] talked of 'avoiding the mistakes of 1815' were using history to ratify the prejudices they had already."[1] In this view, international experiences do not affect statesmen's perceptions. Instead, analogies are seized upon only to bolster pre-existing beliefs and preferences. This chapter will contend that this argument is wrong. What one learns from key events in international history is an important factor in determining the images that shape the interpretation of incoming information. If history merely reinforced established beliefs, people with different outlooks would not draw the same lessons from events, people would not disproportionately use as analogies events they experienced firsthand, and historical experiences would not alter decision-makers' views.

Where can the statesman find the concepts he needs to interpret others' behavior and guide his own actions? Later we will briefly discuss the influence of the decision-maker's nonpolitical training and the domestic political system with which he is familiar. At least as important is history. Previous international events provide the statesman with a range of imaginable situations and allow him to detect patterns and causal links that can help him understand his world. The problem is that, as Kenneth Thompson has put it, "History is the best teacher but its lessons are not on the surface." Yet it is the surface lessons that are learned most easily, quickly, and thoroughly. We cannot make sense out of our environment without assuming that, in some sense, the future will resemble the past. But a too narrow conception of the past and a failure to appreciate the impact of changed circumstances result in "the tyranny

---

[1] Taylor, *From Napoleon to Lenin* (New York: Harper and Row, 1966), p. 64; quoted in Hoffmann, *Gulliver's Troubles* (New York: McGraw-Hill, 1968), p. 135; Butterfield, *History and Human Relations* (London: Collins, 1951), p. 177. The rest of Butterfield's analysis of learning is more persuasive than the sentence quoted here.

of the past upon the imagination." Some events—like wars—leave such an impression that equally dramatic developments are required to displace them. Because they have overlearned from traumatic events, decision-makers often resemble bullets, to return to Deutsch's simile, in being insensitive to incoming information.[2]

Central are the three related subjects of how decision-makers learn (i.e. what is the process by which people extract lessons from a given event); what events decision-makers learn most from (i.e. what kinds of events have the greatest impact); and what general kinds of lessons commonly result. These questions will be explored in depth in the body of this chapter. Here we will provide a few illustrations of the kinds of phenomena we are seeking to explain.

Learning from history is revealed dramatically when decision-makers use a past event as an analogy for a contemporary one. For example, when President Truman was told about the North Korean invasion of South Korea, he quickly thought in terms of previous cases of aggression that had had far-reaching consequences.

> In my generation, this was not the first occasion when the strong had attacked the weak. I recalled some earlier instances: Manchuria, Ethiopia, Austria. I remembered how each time that the democracies failed to act it had encouraged the aggressors to keep going ahead. Communism was acting in Korea just as Hitler, Mussolini, and the Japanese had acted ten, fifteen, and twenty years earlier. I felt certain that if South Korea was allowed to fall Communist leaders would be emboldened to override nations closer to our own shores. If the Communists were permitted to force their way into the Republic of Korea without opposition from the free world, no small nation would have the courage to resist threats and aggression by stronger Communist neighbors. If this was allowed to go unchallenged it would mean a third world war, just as similar incidents had brought on the second world war.[3]

[2] Thompson, *Political Realism and The Crisis of World Politics* (Princeton: Princeton University Press, 1960), p. 36; C.F.G. Masterman, quoted in Harold and Margaret Sprout, *An Ecological Paradigm for the Study of International Politics* (Princeton: Princeton Center of International Studies, RM. #30, March 1968), p. 48.

[3] *Memoirs*, vol. 2: *Years of Trial and Hope* (Garden City, N.Y.: Doubleday, 1956), pp. 332-33. For other discussions of this example, see Alexander George, "American Policy-Making and the North Korean Aggression," *World Politics* 7 (January 1955), 209-32, and George Kennan, *Memoirs*, vol. 2: *1950-1963* (Boston: Little, Brown, 1972), p. 91. Truman may have been especially quick to seize explicitly on an analogy because he was "a devoted student of history who was confirmed in the belief that the 'lessons of history' offered clear guides to 'right principles' of action to those who knew them." (Glenn Paige, *The Korean Decision* [New York: Free Press, 1968], p. 114.)

The 1930s did more than provide Truman with handy figures of speech which allowed him to summarize his independently developed views. Rather, the analogy preceded his analysis and shaped his later perceptions. Even if the analogy did not establish the image of the communists as hostile, it encouraged the view that the aggression was unprovoked and reinforced the prediction that further attacks would follow if this one was not met by firm resistance.

This learning often is not entirely conscious. Dean Rusk is reported to have said that "he was not the village idiot; he knew that Ho was not Hitler, but, nevertheless, there was an obligation to stand."[4] But the decision-maker need not explicitly identify the current situation with a past one, as President Truman did, in order to learn from it. Rather the past can influence his perceptual predispositions without his being aware of it. Indeed, although many officers in the Royal Navy in the interwar period said that there was little to be learned from World War I because "it's all so different now,"[5] in fact they were deeply influenced by the earlier conflict. Similarly, the history of the 1930s made Rusk more likely to believe that the United States had "an obligation to stand" because it predisposed him to see others as aggressors.

Had the earlier period displayed a different pattern, statesmen would have been sensitive to different perceptions of later events. If the interwar years had provided important cases of tension-hostility spirals, more decision-makers would have considered the possibility that in Korea the Soviets were reacting to what they thought were threatening American measures.[6] If war had broken out in 1938 as a result of what the Allies believed to have been Czech provocations, Truman probably would have carefully examined the possibility that South Korea shared responsibility for the attack. Or if Hitler had behaved erratically, and little connection was seen between his aggression against one country and his later behavior, the consequences of losing Korea might well have been seen as relatively minor. If Germany and the Allies had engaged in limited wars before the outbreak of a general war, American postwar planning would have been more likely to have provided for such conflicts. Alternatively, if the 1930s had witnessed

[4] David Halberstam, *The Best and the Brightest* (Greenwich, Conn.: Fawcett, 1973), p. 770.

[5] Arthur Marder, *From the Dardanelles to Oran* (London: Oxford University Press, 1974), p. 59. Also see below, p. 237.

[6] In response to Kennan's claim that the attack on Korea might have been triggered by the American decision to press for a peace treaty with Japan which permitted American bases in that country (*Memoirs*, vol. 1: *1925-1950* [Boston: Little, Brown, 1967], p. 498), Dean Acheson said: "I must confess that there never entered our minds the idea that unilateral concessions . . . would change, by ameliorating, Soviet policy." (*Present at the Creation* [New York: Norton, 1969], p. 430.)

small attacks serving as diversions, Truman probably would have immediately concluded that he should not waste his scant military resources in the secondary arena of Korea but should save them for the coming war in Europe. And if Nazi Germany had not been initially weak and easy to defeat, Truman might not have thought it so important to nip aggression in the bud. Had Germany lost the battle for France and Hitler fallen without the United States entering the conflict, the entire history of the 1930s would not have exercised such a strong hold on Truman's perceptions.

By making accessible insights derived from previous events, analogies provide a useful shortcut to rationality. But they also obscure aspects of the present case that are different from the past one. For this reason, a dramatic and important experience often hinders later decision-making by providing an analogy that will be applied too quickly, easily, and widely. Often the actor would perceive more accurately had he not undergone the earlier experience. It is thus not true that an increase in knowledge necessarily increases the actor's ability to cope with his environment.

For some purposes the biases in the selection of events from which people learn do not matter. Knowing that an outcome has occurred teaches an important lesson if people previously believed it was impossible or had never thought about it (e.g. the danger, revealed in 1914, that inflexible war plans could rule out desired political options). Experiments have indeed shown that once people realize that they may be presented with new objects (e.g. words composed of reversed letters, playing cards with colors and suits mismatched), they can recognize them relatively quickly.[7] But when decision-makers are dealing with the more common situation where they know the categories into which the evidence could fit but are uncertain as to which of a number of known possibilities is correct—e.g. whether or not the other state is highly aggressive—they will be misled because dramatic events alter their perceptual thresholds too much.[8]

For example, Russia and China are not more likely to be seeking

[7] Mary Henle, "An Experimental Investigation of Past Experience as a Determinant of Visual Form Perception," *Journal of Experimental Psychology* 30 (1942), 1-22; Jerome Bruner and Leo Postman, "On the Perception of Incongruity: A Paradigm," in Jerome Bruner and David Krech, eds., *Perception and Personality* (Durham, N.C.: Duke University Press, 1950), pp. 211-12.

[8] An event can sometimes alter actors' values and beliefs so as to make it more likely that the event will recur. History can change actors' intentions as well as their perceptions of others' intentions. For example, a "Munich" could lead both sides to believe that the outcome of a minor conflict will be seen as a test of strength and will set the pattern of the states' future relations, thus leading them to correctly believe that minor concessions will have major repercussions.

world domination because Nazi Germany did so; Nasser was no more likely to seek control of the Mediterranean because Mussolini did. And the probability of an aggressor's spelling out his plans in advance is not increased (if anything it is decreased) by the fact that Hitler wrote *Mein Kampf*. Yet American, British, and perhaps Russian decision-makers are more sensitive to these possibilities and more apt to perceive ambiguous evidence as indicating that these possibilities apply than they would have been had there been no Nazi Germany. This is acknowledged, and defended, by Dean Rusk when he stresses the history of the 1930s as justifying American intervention in Vietnam: "Once again we hear expressed the views which cost the men of my generation a terrible price in World War II. We are told that Southeast Asia is too far away—but so were Manchuria and Ethiopia." Many of those who disagreed with him did so, Rusk concludes, because they had not lived through the earlier period: "World War II to them is a chapter like the War of the Roses, you can't blame people who have no chance to remember."[9] But the prescriptive element in this argument is much less persuasive than Rusk believes. It did not take the experience of dealing with Hitler to convince decision-makers that it was dangerous to try to appease an aggressor. This has always been known. Rather the crucial question is whether the other side in any particular encounter must be stopped by force. Even if decision-makers were too slow to see that this was true of Hitler, it does not follow that successive generations of leaders should adjust their perceptual thresholds so as to be quicker to see others as aggressive.

The pressures to apply the lessons learned from one salient situation to others that resemble it are so powerful that even those who are aware of the pitfalls of this practice may succumb. Harold Nicolson criticizes Castlereagh for "surrendering to the all too common error of estimating the factors of future stability in terms of those factors which had caused and influenced the recently concluded war" and argues that the history of the Congress of Vienna drawn up to inform the British delegates in 1919 how to avoid the mistakes of the earlier conference was of little use. Yet when, in the middle of the Second World War, Nicolson revised his book about the making of the Treaty of Versailles he added a lengthy section on lessons to guide the drawing of the next peace treaty—e.g. "After a long war it is impossible to make a quick peace, . . . The enemy must be left in no doubt as to the terms on which they surrender, . . . The Conference must not be held in a war area."[10] Whatever the validity of

[9] Quoted in G. G. Gutierrez, "Dean Rusk and Southeast Asia: An Operational Code Analysis," paper presented to the 1973 meetings of the American Political Science Association, pp. 33-34. For a series of similar statements, see pp. 30-32.

[10] *The Congress of Vienna* (New York: Viking, 1946), p. 121; *Peacemaking, 1919* (rev. ed., London: Methuen, 1964), pp. 31-32, pp. xi-xxiv.

these conclusions as criticisms of the Treaty of Versailles, their applicability to a peace treaty to be made under circumstances vastly different from those of 1919 is highly questionable. Nicolson made the same error he criticized in others: he assumed that the world is stable enough so that a policy which would have had a desired effect in one peace conference would have the same result in another. He overgeneralized his conclusions, failed to analyze the reasons why certain policies had had unintended consequences at Versailles, and did not consider whether the states of many important variables were different in the two cases.

Lessons as Predispositions

We will develop two-stage propositions of the form: events ⟶ lessons ⟶ future behavior. Of course both links are probabilistic. (Indeed if this model was complete and determined, we would not need to use the decision-making approach.)[11]

To know what lessons a person will learn from an event we often need to know more than general principles of learning and a description of the event. What a person learns at time t is influenced, sometimes decisively, by his outlook at $t - 1$. In some cases, well-known influences prevent the learning of what seem to be the obvious lessons. Since we know that actors develop a stake in certain tactics and instruments we are not surprised to find members of the cavalry maintaining their belief in the efficacy of that branch even after several wars demonstrated the devastation wrought by increased firepower. Similarly, it is not completely surprising that even though "the colonists [in America] had been close observers of the Indians for years, . . . [they] continued to place too much faith in the old European drill manuals." Fighting in fixed formations was considered the essence of being military. The British navy defined its mission as fighting the enemy's main battle fleet. So memories of World War I and postwar training were dominated by the battle of Jutland—a kind of battle that was almost certain not to recur—and the fight against U-boats was forgotten even though these submarines nearly cost Britain the war. When the Second World War broke out, all the old anti-submarine lessons had to be learned anew, almost as though there had been no relevant experience. Similarly, commitment to an independent air force and to a mission that could justify its being a separate arm at least co-equal with the others made it predictable that the air force would learn little from World War II about the limitations of strategic bombing. The powerful influence of definition of role and identity is not limited to military organizations. As we will see in a later chapter,

---

[11] See the discussion in Chapter 1.

the Forest Service's identity precluded it from learning from a series of what would have seemed to others to have been decisive tests.[12]

In other cases, we will need more detailed knowledge about the person's pre-existing beliefs before we can predict what he thinks an event has demonstrated. This is true, for example, for one of the most-frequently used analogies—Munich. Most scholarly accounts of the 1930s conclude that appeasement was an error because it allowed Hitler to grow stronger, but that deterrence was not possible because Hitler preferred war to being contained. The common lesson American statesmen have drawn, however, is quite different—in President Johnson's words, "surrender in Vietnam [would not] bring peace, because we learned from Hitler at Munich that success only feeds the appetite of aggression."[13] This fits with the belief that a policy of firmness will avoid a major war, but is somewhat removed from the events of the 1930s. And many people will no doubt conclude that the American experience in Vietnam shows that foreign conventional forces cannot defeat native guerrillas. But this lesson cannot be explained entirely by the objective history of the war, since the American troops in fact succeeded in crushing the Viet Cong, and the South Vietnamese army was finally defeated, not by guerrillas, but by the invasion of a conventional army.

To take an earlier case, given only Truman's policy toward Palestine, we could not predict that the British Foreign Office would conclude that the president had sacrificed foreign policy goals to the courting of the Jewish vote. To understand this inference, we have to know about the British beliefs about the Middle East and American politics. And to understand why the British admirals paid little attention to the engagements in the first eighteen months of World War I that tended to show that long-range gunfire was not apt to be decisive, we need to know about the beliefs that made them acutely sensitive to the risks of getting too close to the enemy. At times we will need even more ad hoc explanations to account for the lessons that are drawn or the events that are ignored. Thus it is not easy to see why two British generals who had much in common drew conflicting lessons about the future of the cavalry from the Boer War. And it remains surprising that the unexpected suc-

[12] Brian Bond, "Doctrine and Training in the British Cavalry, 1870-1914," in Michael Howard, ed., *The Theory and Practice of War* (New York: Praeger, 1966), pp. 95-125; Edward Katzenbach, Jr., "The Horse Cavalry in the Twentieth Century," in Carl Friedrich and Seymour Harris, eds., *Public Policy*, vol. 8 (Cambridge, Mass.: Harvard University Graduate School of Public Administration, 1958), pp. 120-50; David Leach, *Flintlock and Tomahawk* (New York: Macmillan Co., 1958), pp. 71 and 91; Marder, *From the Dardanelles to Oran*, pp. 38-48; see Chapter 12.

[13] Quoted in Halberstam, *The Best and the Brightest*, p. 729.

cess of a German U-boat in sinking three British cruisers in the second month of World War I did not play a larger role in setting the still unformed German policy on the mission of submarines.[14]

In the second step of our model—the link between lessons learned and future behavior—our propositions are again only probabilistic. When we know what lessons the person thinks the past teaches, we can better estimate how he will judge later events. But because so many other variables influence later perceptions, we must talk in terms of perceptual predispositions. Because perceptual predispositions involve assertions about the interpretations of evidence that will be made with all other things being equal, not all perceptions will follow the contours of the predispositions. The impact of learning from history can be outweighed by other influences. For example, even though Munich made British decision-makers perceptually sensitive to the dangers of appeasement, their fear of a nuclear confrontation and their desire to play an independent and mediating role in international politics led them to favor a conciliatory policy in the Berlin crises of 1958–1962. Unfortunately, this makes it hard to disconfirm our propositions. We cannot directly measure predispositions and so must rely for our evidence on how people perceive incoming information. But because predispositions do not by themselves determine perceptions, cases in which people do not see what we think they are predisposed to see do not disprove the existence of these predispositions. Many of the arguments in this chapter are designed to cope with this problem.

Sometimes we can see the tendency to follow the lessons of the past being overcome by other influences. Truman initially planned to present the proposal to aid Greece and Turkey in 1947 as limited in scope and concept. "Because of the searing political lessons of the past twenty-eight years . . . the cautious, limited, backdoor approach to involvement in world affairs had become almost a reflex." But when congressmen responded more to a sweeping justification than to the cautious approach, the administration decided on a broad and dramatic appeal.[15] In other cases, it is difficult to determine why the perceptions do not conform to the expected predispositions. The previous event may have been striking, the lessons noted, the current evidence ambiguous, and yet the situation not seen as like the past. For example, one would have expected the experience of Pearl Harbor to sensitize American decision-makers to the danger of surprise attack. Yet, at the start of the Cold War, and indeed

---

[14] Katzenbach, "The Horse Cavalry in the Twentieth Century," pp. 132-35; Arthur Marder, *From the Dreadnought to Scapa Flow*, vol. 2: *The War Years: To the Eve of Jutland, 1914-1916* (London: Oxford University Press, 1965), pp. 55-59.

[15] Joseph Jones, *The Fifteen Weeks* (New York: Harcourt, Brace, 1964), p. 143.

until the mid-1950s, the United States did not carefully guard against a sneak attack on its strategic air bases and nuclear stockpile. Even though all the protection that was needed was an early warning system to provide enough time for the bombs to be dispersed (and even though we would not have been taken by complete surprise at Pearl Harbor had the radar system been operating around the clock), the United States had only four radar stations in operation in 1947, and these were working only part-time.[16]

Alternative Explanations

If our propositions cannot account for cases like these, this does not mean that all instances in which current perceptions coincide with lessons from the past support our position. Interpretations of past events are not "unmoved movers." To disprove the arguments cited at the beginning of this chapter, causality must be shown to flow from the interpretations of the past to the perceptions of the present. We must be able to rule out the alternative possibilities of spuriousness (i.e. that both the interpretations of the past and the current perceptions are caused by a common third factor) and of current preferences influencing memories. These two explanations are often appropriate. For example, it is difficult to say how much America's interpretation of its intervention in World War I influenced interwar foreign policy and how much the isolationism of that era influenced the histories of the war.

That current policy preferences can influence memories of the past is shown most clearly when shifts in the latter follow shifts in the former. For example, the British analyses of the role of the cavalry in the American Civil War changed in conformity with official doctrine. During World War II President Roosevelt's beliefs about the causes of the failure of the League of Nations changed as he received new information about the possible shape of the postwar world. Originally Roosevelt felt that the League's failure demonstrated the "frailty of pledges of great scope but diffused obligation," and "was thus inclined to the idea that [in the new international organization] three (or four, if China were included) great powers should be self-appointed 'policemen' to supervise the conduct of nations and together enforce the peace." But neither Secretary Hull nor the British were enthusiastic about this plan, arguing that the smaller powers would refuse to play such a subordinate role. "Then, as [Roose-

---

[16] George Quester, *Nuclear Diplomacy* (New York: Dunellen, 1970), pp. 33-34. In testifying before a Senate committee in 1950, Secretary of the Air Force Symington was asked about the possibility that a surprise attack could destroy our stored B-29s. At first he misunderstood the question and, when he did respond, he revealed little information and less concern. (*Defense Department Appropriations for 1951*, Hearings before the Senate Appropriations Committee, 81st Congress, 2nd session, 1950, pp. 236-37.)

velt's] own trust in the good faith and reasonableness of the Soviet Union began to wane in 1944, the President became receptive to a quite different interpretation of history," the view that there were no "intrinsic or insuperable faults in the Covenant," but that failure was attributable to factors that could be coped with within a framework that would give "all countries, even the smallest, . . . an adequate chance to influence the decision of the collectivity."[17] But even in cases like this where beliefs about history clearly did not determine policy, they may have provided a number of possible analogies and, conversely, excluded or made less accessible other models that would have been salient had the earlier events been different. (Similarly, when different people draw different lessons from the same event, this does not mean that another experience would not have produced other, although perhaps still conflicting, predispositions.)

When the interpretation of the past is strikingly incorrect, it is likely that it was influenced by current preferences rather than the other way around. Thus French military thinkers who espoused the doctrine of the offensive before World War I said that their defeat in the Franco-Prussian War was caused by their defensive posture. But this was a great distortion of the history of the war.[18] Unless there are some general principles of learning that explain this belief, it is probable that the contemporary preferred strategy was the cause.

In other cases the same factors that cause current perceptions and preferences also explain the memories and analogies that the person draws on. When this is true the correlation between lessons and later perceptions is spurious. Third factors usually explain instances in which people with different policy preferences rooted in different basic values hold different interpretations of the past. Thus when debating the extension of price controls after World War II, liberals and conservatives gave contrasting versions of the health of the American economy during and after the First World War.[19] It is unlikely that differing experiences with the initial inflation led to differing prescriptions for the later one or that memories of the former were altered to conform to current preferences.

---

[17] Jay Luvaas, *The Military Legacy of the Civil War* (Chicago: University of Chicago Press, 1959), pp. 196-97; Herbert Feis, "Some Notes on Historical Record-Keeping, the Role of Historians, and the Influence of Historical Memories During the Era of the Second World War," in Francis Loewenheim, ed., *The Historian and the Diplomat* (New York: Harper and Row, 1967), pp. 7, 119-21.

[18] B. H. Liddell-Hart, "French Military Ideas Before the First World War," in Martin Gilbert, ed., *A Century of Conflict, 1850-1950* (London: Hamish Hamilton, 1966), p. 140.

[19] Ralph Huitt, "The Congressional Committee: A Case Study," reprinted in Ralph Huitt and Robert Peabody, *Congress: Two Decades of Analysis* (New York: Harper and Row, 1969), p. 98.

It is more likely that a liberal or conservative perspective led to both a certain stand on price controls and a matching analysis of past events.

Spuriousness is a plausible explanation for some of the cases of the apparent effects of history that will be discussed below. Because the problems are somewhat different for each category of effects, detailed discussion will be postponed. In general, spuriousness is most likely when the initial and later situations are most similar or when the person has either chosen to place himself in the initial situation or learned a lesson that others did not. In the former case, the same external stimulus that led the person to adopt the policy initially may be responsible for the similar response in the later situation. Conversely, the experience probably had an impact in cases where an early response is repeated in a very different situation (i.e. a situation that is seen to be different by people who did not undergo the earlier experience).

In cases in which the person chose the situation or the resulting lessons, the same factors of belief or personality that explain the initial response are apt to explain later ones. Thus before we can argue that Dean Rusk's stand on Vietnam can be explained by his experiences as assistant secretary of state for Far Eastern affairs during the Korean War, we must remember that shortly before the outbreak of the war he asked to be transferred to that post from a higher-ranking position so that he could assume direct responsibility for the Far East. Conversely, spuriousness is not a plausible explanation when the person did not choose to place himself in the initial situation. If we are looking for experiences that may have influenced Rusk's views of China, we should examine his service in the China-Burma-India theater in World War II—service that first marked him as a man of extraordinary talent—and his role in suggesting the 38th parallel as the administrative dividing line in Korea. Unlike his better-known activities during the Korean War, these were jobs he did not seek. Spuriousness is also unlikely when people with different personalities and beliefs learn the same lesson from an event, or when an experience changes the person's mind. In these cases the person's pre-existing outlook cannot account for the lessons he learns, and so if he applies them later in a different situation the past must be playing an independent role.

THE LEARNING PROCESS

An understanding of why events turned out as they did contributes to better decision-making. Lessons of this type cannot be applied as a unit, but rather constitute the building blocks out of which beliefs and policies are created. Because productive learning "involves the acquisition . . .

of certain broad, non-specific, general notions about the properties of the object or method experienced," it has been found that "the more general and abstract the previous learning, the more help and the less barrier it is likely to prove in future problems." The same thought has been expressed by an historian: the study of the past should make us "Wise for always; not clever for another time."[20] In one sense, decision-makers learn broad, general lessons from history, but this kind of learning hinders rather than aids productive thinking. Decision-makers apply an analogy in its broad outlines to many disparate cases. There is generality —indeed too much generality—both in the kinds of situations that are seen as similar to the earlier one and in the range of aspects of the case that are seen as similar. But because the learning has not involved an understanding of many of the important causal relations, it is not general in the sense of grasping the crucial characteristics of the situation and the patterns that are likely to recur in the future. Decision-makers usually fail to strip away from the past event those facets that depend on the emphemeral context. They often mistake things that are highly specific and situation-bound for more general characteristics because they assume that the most salient aspects of the results were caused by the most salient aspects of the preceding situation. People pay more attention to *what* has happened than to *why* it has happened. Thus learning is superficial, overgeneralized, and based on post hoc ergo propter hoc reasoning. As a result, the lessons learned will be applied to a wide variety of situations without a careful effort to determine whether the cases are similar on crucial dimensions.[21]

An example of scientists' methods of analysis illuminates the contrast between the two kinds of generality we have been discussing. Several years ago a scientist discovered a substance that causes cancer cells but not normal cells to clump together, thereby killing them. Because this substance has certain properties that prevent its use as a cancer treatment, researchers had to seek other chemicals with the cancer-killing power of the original substance but without its drawbacks. The important point here is that the scientists have not searched for materials that appeared similar to the substance, but rather have tried to understand

---

[20] Herbert Birch and Herbert Rabinowitz, "The Negative Effect of Previous Experience on Productive Thinking," *Journal of Experimental Psychology* 41 (1951), 124; Bernard Berelson and Gary Steiner, *Human Behavior* (New York: Harcourt, Brace, 1964), p. 206; Jacob Burckhardt, quoted in Pieter Geyl, *The Use and Abuse of History* (New Haven: Yale University Press, 1955), p. 86. Also see Kenneth Hammond, "Computer Graphics as an Aid to Learning," *Science* 172 (May 28, 1971), 903-907.

[21] In their examination of international crises, Glenn Snyder and Paul Diesing find "no examples . . . of historical analogies producing a correct interpretation of a message." (*Systems, Bargains, Decisions* [Princeton: Princeton University Press, forthcoming], Chapter 4.)

"what it is about the surface proteins of cancer cells that selectively allows the substance to cause them to clump." This knowledge would be general in the sense of penetrating to the lasting characteristics of the cell membrane and the substance. It would increase our understanding not only of the problem under immediate consideration, but also of other aspects of cells. This knowledge would not, however, be carried over in toto to other materials and interactions that bear some resemblance to the context from which it was derived. This approach parallels the basic shift in biological thinking introduced by Darwin: "Instead of finding patterns in nature and deciding that because of their conspicuousness they seem important, we discover the underlying mechanisms that impose order on natural phenomena, whether we see that order or not."[22]

Decision-makers rarely adopt this mode of inquiry. Instead, the search for causes is usually quick and oversimplified. The most salient features of the pre-existing situation and the actors' strategies are seen as causing the most obvious characteristics of the short-run outcome, and no careful examination is made of the links that are supposed to be present. Few attempts are made to make the comparisons that are necessary to render a judgment on the causal efficacy of the variables. Although the quality of the analysis that precedes decisions can often be faulted, it is almost always much better than that involved in the attempt to understand the causes of past events. Neither immediately after an event nor later, when they use the event as an analogy, do decision-makers engage in a thorough reconstruction and a self-conscious effort to examine critically the proposed causes. And when the decision-maker thinks he knows the cause of a previous outcome, he rarely takes the next steps of looking for other cases in which this variable was present to determine its influence in other situations or of trying to locate additional instances of the same outcome to see whether other causes could produce the same result.

Extreme examples of the failure to understand what in the previous behavior led to the outcome have been noted in animal behavior: "a cat that happened to back into the post, which opens the door, may repeat in stereotyped manner what he did when the door opened instead of moving directly to the post." Prescientific peoples sometimes reason similarly. "When confronted by an infirmity, they search for both cause and cure. . . . Often their line of reasoning is both logical and complex." But lacking an appropriate method of developing and testing hypotheses they look for an odd event in the period immediately preceding the sickness. "Thus we find, because someone's great-grandmother, years ago, ate an

[22] Harry Nelson, " 'Submarines' in Sea of Cells May Assist War on Cancer," *Los Angeles Times*, July 15, 1974, part II, p. 1; Michael Ghiselin, *The Triumph of the Darwinian Method* (Berkeley and Los Angeles: University of California Press, 1969), p. 83.

orange in the evening and that night dies of a heart attack, that today no one . . . will touch an orange after sundown."[23]

Decision-makers are rarely misled by small oddities. Rather they tend to see causes that are as dramatic as the results. Thus during the Franco-Prussian War Helmuth von Moltke noted: "We are now living through a very interesting time when the question of which is preferable, a trained army or a militia, will be solved in action. If the French succeed in throwing us out of France, all the Powers will introduce a militia system, and if we remain the victors, then every State will imitate us with universal service in a standing army."[24] Moltke's prediction was correct, and indeed there were grounds for concluding that the result was partly attributable to the different form of the armies. But other, less dramatic variables, such as the meticulous Prussian staff planning, the skillful use of railways, and their superior artillery were at least as important.

Derived from the sloppy search for causes and their location in large events is the tendency to slight the importance of the conditions and circumstances under which the outcome occurred. When a person constructs an account of events that stresses the overriding importance of a few variables and simple connections between them, he will learn a set of rigid rules that will not be a good guide to a changing world. If he has correctly identified a major cause, and if other factors are either unimportant or can be neglected because they are constant in all the cases he will confront, he can indeed use one event as an analogy to many others. But if the previous outcome depended on the interaction of several factors, the application of the lessons without a careful analysis of the two situations will be misleading. The person will see the world as more unchanging than it is[25] and will learn overgeneralized lessons.[26]

Thus one consequence of the analysis of the cause of the Prussian victory over France referred to earlier was that in 1914 Britain and France, discounting the possible use of reserves, were confident that Germany lacked sufficient troops to attempt to envelop Paris. The British and

[23] Abraham Luchins and Edith Luchins, *Rigidity of Behavior* (Eugene: University of Oregon Press, 1959), p. 327; David Werner, "Healing in the Sierra Madre," *Natural History* 79 (November 1970), 66.

[24] Quoted in Michael Howard, *The Franco-Prussian War* (New York: Collier, 1969), p. 299. For another example, see Clark Reynolds, *The Fast Carriers* (New York: McGraw-Hill, 1968), p. 199.

[25] Thus when Butterfield argues that "if men shape their minds too rigidly by a study of the last war, they are to some degree unfitting themselves for the conduct of the next one," he assumes that each war is significantly different from the last. (Butterfield, *History and Human Relations*, p. 180.)

[26] As Mark Twain has put it: "We should be careful to get out of an experience only the wisdom that is in it—and stop there; lest we be like the cat that sits down on a hot stove lid. She will never sit down on a hot stove lid again—and that is well; but also she will never sit down on a cold one." Quoted in Arthur Schlesinger, Jr., *The Bitter Heritage* (Boston: Houghton Mifflin, 1967), p. 92.

French had learned that militias were ineffective, but had failed to understand that this rule was contingent, not absolute, because they did not realize why it had held in 1871. One reason why the British navy in the interwar years paid little attention to the submarine threat was "the thought that unrestricted submarine warfare by the Kaiser's Navy had brought the United States into the First War, and so had lost it for the Kaiser, and nobody would be stupid enough to try *that* again!" Similarly, the shortness of Bismarck's wars deeply impressed European statesmen and led them to expect the same pattern in the future. Had they thought more carefully about both the impact of technology and the political context in which the short wars had taken place—i.e. the need to end the war quickly lest other states join and endanger the fruits of victory—they would have been less confident that a war involving all European powers would have resembled the earlier ones.[27]

Context was also neglected by the British decison-makers who overestimated their influence over Italy on the eve of the Italo-Ethiopian war because they thought that, in the words of their foreign secretary, "Mussolini was on very bad terms with Hitler," as shown by his reaction in putting troops on the Brenner pass after the assassination of Dollfuss the year before. But the British were insensitive to the changes in the world that should have prevented them from simply extrapolating Mussolini's behavior into the future. This kind of insensitivity also contributed to the success of the German surprise attack on Norway in April 1940. Halvdan Koht, the Norwegian foreign minister, has acknowledged that he thought Hitler would follow the pattern he had set in the conflicts with Austria, Czechoslovakia, and Poland, and would issue demands before he struck.[28] But Koht overlooked the fact that the earlier German behavior was the product of a peacetime context in which it was important to develop a justification for the use of coercion. Once the war started, however, the incentives shifted sharply toward attacks without warning. Unfortunately Koht merely detected the previous pattern without understanding how it was molded by a changed context.

A similar overgeneralization caused by learning a noncontingent rule was responsible for Admiral Halsey's mistake in the battle for Leyte Gulf in sending all his forces in pursuit of a Japanese decoy fleet, thereby leaving the American invasion forces open to attack from another Japanese fleet. The decoy fleet looked powerful to Halsey because it contained aircraft carriers; yet all but one of these were small, converted ships of

[27] Geoffrey Blainey, *The Causes of War* (New York: Free Press, 1973), pp. 208-209; Marder, *From the Dardanelles to Oran*, p. 43.

[28] Viscount Templewood, *Nine Troubled Years* (London: Collins, 1954), p. 153; Johan Holst, "Surprise, Signals and Reaction: The Attack on Norway," *Cooperation and Conflict*, 1966, No. 1, p. 39.

"trivial military value." The other Japanese fleet, although without carriers, was built around modern battleships that constituted the greater menace. The problem was that Halsey was guided by "two axioms . . . (a) 'the enemy's main force is where his carriers are' . . . , and (b) 'don't divide the fleet in the presence of the enemy.' " Both axioms had been useful earlier in the war, but were no longer valid once the Japanese carriers were unimportant and the American fleet large enough to deal with two forces simultaneously. Halsey and his staff had not learned why the axioms should be followed; they did not understand the detailed causal linkages; and so, not noticing the importance of changed circumstances, they applied the axioms when they were no longer appropriate.[29]

To take an example from another arena, because the development of railroads was, or was believed to be, instrumental in the economic development of the West, underdeveloped states such as Nigeria quickly concluded that it was better to build railways than to use their resources for a trucking and highway system. The point here is not that the Nigerians made the wrong choice, but that they overlooked many important factors because they did not explore the conditions that had made railroads effective in other countries—e.g. the lack of effective substitutes, ease of transportation to the railheads, absence of extreme ethnic conflicts.[30] They acted as though the superiority of railroads was universal and unconditional and attributed too much generality to what was actually the product of a combination of variables many of which were not operating in the situation they confronted. Had the Nigerians studied previous cases to learn why railroads had been effective they not only would have thought more carefully about their program but also would have gained useful knowledge about the general processes of economic development, knowledge that could have shed light on aspects of many other choices and problems they faced.

Further problems arise as outcomes are often categorized as "success" or "failure." This determination is usually made by applying a simple standard, such as whether the actor was better off at the end of the encounter than it was before. With a successful outcome, relatively little attention is paid to the costs of the policy, the possibility that others might have worked even better, or the possibility that success was largely attributable to luck and that the policy might just as easily have failed.[31] It is especially rare for decision-makers to ask themselves whether the

[29] Bernard Brodie, *War and Politics* (New York: Macmillan Co., 1973), p. 450.

[30] For a different explanation of the Nigerian decision, see Albert Hirschman, *Development Projects Observed* (Washington: Brookings Institution, 1967), pp. 46, 109, 140-48.

[31] For experimental evidence, see Robert Jones and James Welsh, "Ability Attribution and Impression Formation in a Strategic Game," *Journal of Personality and Social Psychology* 20 (1971), 171-73.

favorable outcome might have been produced in spite of, not because of, their choices. The result is that, as we will discuss later in this chapter, policies that were followed by success will be too quickly repeated in the future. The other side of this coin is that in cases of failure it is usually assumed that the rejected alternatives would have produced better results. The possibility that the outcome, although undesired, was better than that which would have been secured by most alternatives is infrequently considered. Furthermore, a more extreme assumption is often made: not only would most alternatives have fared better but the decision-makers should have known this. In other words, the information available at the time should have led statesmen to recognize the situation and take appropriate steps. The lessons drawn thus rarely leave room for the possibility that, although the policy was not as good as alternative ones, it may still have been the best one to choose given the information available. It can be argued, for example, that although appeasing Hitler was a bad policy there was no way to have known this at the time. Not only was German behavior compatible with that of a normal revisionist state, but Hitler was a rare exception—very few decision-makers were willing to try to expand recklessly as he was. If this is true, it might not be wise for later statesmen to adjust their perceptual predispositions so as to be quicker to see aggressors and slower to see others as controllable revisionists.

Exceptions to these generalizations can usually be explained by the same variables that inhibit the formation of the predicted perceptual predispositions. British proponents of the cavalry admitted that "the Boer horsemen had done reasonably well against cavalry, though they carried neither lance nor sabre. . . . [but argued] that the Boers would have done even better had they" fought in the traditional manner. A strong proponent of the view that "infantry armed only with musket and bayonet could not withstand mounted attack" argued that the failure of the French cavalry at Waterloo to break the British infantry squares "did not necessarily mean that cavalry as such was inferior to infantry; Napoleon's cavalry [was] simply . . . inferior cavalry." Similarly, the American success in fighting the air war in Korea with a relatively small number of obsolescent aircraft did not lead air force officials to abandon their claims for a large, modern force; instead they attributed the outcome to factors peculiar to the Korean conflict.[32] By seeing success and failure

[32] Bond, "Doctrine and Training in the British Cavalry," pp. 109-10; Jay Luvaas, *The Education of an Army* (Chicago: University of Chicago Press, 1964), p. 50 (for a similar example from European observations of the American Civil War, see Luvaas, *The Military Legacy of the Civil War*, p. 17); Robert Futrell, with the assistance of Lawson Moseley and Albert Simpson, *The U.S. Air Force in Korea, 1950-1953* (New York: Duell, Sloan, and Pearce, 1961), p. 646. Also

as caused by special factors, observers were able to preserve the beliefs that were most important to them.

Because an actor's actions loom large to him, overgeneralizing often involves the belief that his behavior was a major influence on the outcome. He will therefore think that a wide variety of situations are amenable to the same strategy that worked, or, if the earlier outcome was a failure, would have worked, previously. If he underestimates the importance of variables that were not under his control, he will be predisposed to see very different cases as similar to the earlier one. He will not notice alterations in the context in which the policy is to be applied or, if they are called to his attention, will deny that they should influence his actions.[33] When the aspects of a situation that make it distinctive are not detected, policies that failed previously will be shunned, and policies that succeeded will be applied again even under conditions that are so different that the earlier outcomes tell little about what the results will be if the policies are repeated. So it is not surprising that scholars have felt the need to warn Washington not to assume that the apparent success of the intervention in the Dominican Republic could be repeated in other countries.[34]

A similar process often occurs in the analysis of continuing issues. People sometimes remember that they hold a certain value, but forget why. When conditions change, the policies are discussed in the old terms without considering the ends they will now serve. For example, since all good liberals know that discrimination and segregation are bad, they opposed the demands for preferential treatment for Negroes and the establishment of all-Negro dormitories in colleges. Without arguing the merits of the issues, I think it is fair to say that many liberals were slow to consider that segregation sought by a weak minority group might have very different consequences from segregation imposed by the dominant race or that, while discrimination had served bad ends in the past, the discrimination now being proposed could have major benefits. The lesson that discrimination and segregation were evil had been oversimplified and overgeneralized, and insufficient attention had been paid to the reasons why, and conditions under which, the conclusion held. This reasoning process is also related to the tendency for actors to forget the higher

---

see Forrest Pogue, *George Marshall*: vol. 1: *Education of a General* (New York: Viking, 1963), p. 250.

[33] For a related discussion of the way in which constancies "can cut a system to pieces" and thereby make learning easier, see W. Ross Ashby, *Design for a Brain* (2nd ed., London: Chapman and Hall, 1960), pp. 158-70.

[34] Jerome Slater, *Intervention and Negotiation* (New York: Harper and Row, 1970), pp. 208-13; Abraham Lowenthal, "The Dominican Intervention in Retrospect," *Public Policy* 18 (Fall 1969), 133-48.

ends that their subgoals were designed to serve and to seek the latter as goals in their own right, often to the detriment of the higher ends.[35]

The prevalence of inappropriate learning is explained not by the decision-makers' lack of mental abilities and only partially by their lack of social science training. More important are the complexity of the subject matter, the small and biased sample of cases available for study, the conditions under which learning takes place, and the decision-makers' failure to realize how much they are influenced by their views of the past. The detrimental effect of complexity on scholars' understanding of international relations has been discussed at length, and we will only add that there is no reason to expect decision-makers to do much better.

Further inadequacies in the learning process arise because decision-makers, like many social scientists, start their analysis by directing their attention, or having their attention drawn, to dramatic outcomes. Not desiring explanations in general and lacking explicit theories that would predict what events, minor as well as major, are surprising, people learn little from negative outcomes—aggression that does not occur, crises that are avoided, quiet compromises, and slow, peaceful transformations.[36]

The other side of this coin is that people pay most attention to what happens to them and to those they identify with. As we will discuss below, a person learns most from events that are experienced firsthand, that influence his career, or that have major consequences for his nation. This sample is idiosyncratically biased because of the accidental nature of what the person happens to experience firsthand or the fact that one dramatic event rather than another occurs in his lifetime.

Additional handicaps are created by the fact that the sample is not only biased but small. Psychologists have found that "in the process of learning there is a general progression from the simple to the complex."[37] With only a few cases available, it is difficult to make the numerous comparisons that are necessary to develop the complex and abstract explanations that would help the decision-maker cope with contemporary problems. One might ask how far our understanding of voting behavior would progress if we had data on, say, only five or ten individuals. Because so few events have a major impact, those that do are overworked as analogies and decision-makers are insensitive to changes in variables that were constant in familiar cases. Thus people who tried to gauge naval strength in the interwar period by turning for guidance to past performance had little choice but to rely on the one big battle of the First World War. All

[35] For further discussion of this point, see below, Chapter 12, pp. 419-23.
[36] For experimental evidence, see Jerome Bruner, Jacqueline Goodnow, and George Austin, A Study of Thinking (New York: Wiley, 1962), pp. 168-69.
[37] Donald Campbell and Walter Gruen, "Progression from Simple to Complex as a Molar Law of Learning," Journal of General Psychology 59 (1958), 237-44.

that could be produced from Jutland were extrapolations. They were sure to be misleading, but there was no other experience.

Just as decision-makers learn from a small number of cases, so they have only a few occasions on which to verify the appropriateness of the lessons. By contrast, our perceptual predispositions concerning our physical environment serve us very well because of the frequent and unambiguous opportunities for verifying the relationships between incoming information and the stimulus that produced it. "The cues we use for judging an object 'distant' or a surface 'impenetrable' are checked a thousand times a day in getting about: walking, driving, reaching." The problems are much greater in those areas, like foreign affairs, in which cues cannot be readily checked. A decision-maker will not apply the same analogy often, and after he does apply it he will rarely receive unambiguous information about its validity. If the result was a failure, where did he go wrong? Was the lesson misleading? What were the crucial differences from the earlier event? Was this case a freakish exception? These questions are hard enough with a large sample of instances. And, as *A Study of Thinking* points out,

> Infrequent opportunity for validation may have the effect of increasing the reliance on preferred cues that are considerably less than certain. If in learning to categorize aircraft silhouettes attempted identifications are not frequently checkable against external information, the effect may be to lead the learner to utilize excessively some cues that have permitted him to make a few successful identifications in the past. One may . . . stabilize one's cue utilization too soon and end with a level of performance that is less efficient than warranted by the goodness of cues available.[38]

Conversely, the salutory effects of learning from a large number of cases are important in explaining how humans and animals cope with their everyday environment. Ross Ashby notes that his *Design for a Brain*

> may . . . be regarded as amplifying the view that the nervous system is not only sensitive but "delicate": that its encounters with the environment mark it readily, extensively, and permanently, with traces distributed according to the "accidents" of the encounter. Such a distribution might be expected to produce a merely chaotic alteration in

---

[38] Jerome Bruner, "Social Psychology and Perception," in Eleanor Maccoby, Theodore Newcomb, and Eugene Hartley, eds., *Readings in Social Psychology* (New York: Holt, Rinehart and Winston, 1958), p. 93; Bruner, Goodnow, and Austin, *A Study of Thinking*, p. 68 (for a similar discussion of the pathologies arising from attempts to solve tasks that are too difficult, see Luchins and Luchins, *Rigidity of Behavior*, pp. 326-27).

the nervous system's behaviour, but this is not so: as the encounters multiply there is a fundamental tendency for the system's adaptation to improve, for the traces tend to such a distribution as will make its behavior adaptive in the subsequent encounters.[39]

Furthermore, the conditions under which learning takes place are far from ideal. Events that have most influence usually involve much of the person's time and thought. If he is playing a role in these situations it is extremely important for him to handle them well. But these "high drive" surroundings inhibit the most flexible and useful kind of learning. Starting with "the reasonable assumption . . . that under high drive conditions, the organism seeks to maximize goal attainment . . . [w]e would expect that high drive would have the effect of reducing the operation of any processes not essential to attaining the immediately present goal as rapidly as possible. This would presumably include any processes that go beyond simple response learning. Since speed of goal attainment is in no way increased by recoding the learned pathway to the goal in terms of a principle . . . we may expect that learning under high drive conditions would not be of the 'principle' type."[40] Events that are too overwhelming then produce overgeneralized and oversimplified lessons. This reasoning is supported by the finding that a person who suffers a "near-miss" from a natural disaster may find that "his usual feeling that nothing can happen to him gives way to the sudden terrible apprehension that he is about to suffer a devastating loss." Decision-makers are often too involved in the events that make most impact to derive the most useful information from them.[41]

Finally, being pragmatic men, decision-makers rarely waste much time over what is past. We saw in a previous chapter that decision-makers underestimate the degree to which their interpretations of incoming information are influenced by their pre-existing beliefs and so grow more confident than the evidence warrants. Their lack of awareness of the impact of the past similarly leads statesmen to believe that the study of history is at best an interesting diversion from their work and so discourages them from investing their energies in it. If they understood the impact of lessons they have learned, they would devote greater attention and care to seeing that those lessons were correct and applicable to other situations.

[39] *Design for a Brain* (1st ed., New York: Wiley, 1952), p. v.

[40] Jerome Bruner, J. Mandler, M. O'Dowd, and Michael Wallach, "The Role of Overlearning and Drive Level in Reversal Learning," in Robert Harper et al., eds., *The Cognitive Processes* (Englewood Cliffs, N.J.: Prentice-Hall, 1964), p. 280.

[41] Martha Wolfenstein, *Disaster: A Psychological Essay* (Glencoe, Ill.: Free Press, 1957), p. 65.

Organizational Learning

Although a full-scale treatment of this subject cannot be given here, we should note that when an event affects the perceptual predispositions of many members of an organization we can speak of organizational learning. The lessons can become institutionalized in textbooks, rules, and even language itself—e.g. the development of the pejorative meaning of "appeasement" after 1939. Lessons become working assumptions and form the basis for future planning. In the military they involve not only strategic and tactical thinking but the conduct of maneuvers, formal instruction, and standing orders. In 1934 the Royal Navy Staff College spent three days studying Jutland and totally ignored the U-boat crisis of 1917 and the methods that had been devised to contain it. One British admiral "recalls that in the Tactical School 'as late as 1935 (or later) great effort was given to extracting the utmost guidance from Jutland.' [Another admiral] states that until the late 1930s 'Fleet cruising orders were based on the . . . [cruiser scouting line] principle of the first war and air reconnaissance was not wholly trusted.' "[42]

Past successes and failures are reflected in changes in organizational routines and guidelines. For example, the Allies met much stiffer resistance than expected at Salerno, and the German counterattacks against the overextended beachhead nearly pushed the invaders into the sea. So at the next landing, at Anzio, things were different: the force was given an especially strong defensive component, a commander was chosen who was skilled at defensive operations and was known to take few risks, and the instructions given him were conservative. Supplementary advice passing through informal channels also echoed the organization's memory of the most recent encounter. The commander recalled that "The last thing [General Clark] said to me on D Day was 'Don't stick your neck out, Johnny. I did at Salerno and got into trouble.' "[43] This time, however, the road to Rome was open, and the Allies' cautious tactics caused them to forego an easy victory.

Success is apt to consolidate the power of those who advocated the policy, defeat to undermine it and strengthen the hand of those who had different views. Thus Japan's initial success in World War II reinforced the position of the dominant group in that country, which believed she could win a limited victory, and made it even more difficult for dissenters to ask what Japan would do if the Allies refused to accept the verdict of

[42] Marder, *From the Dardanelles to Oran*, p. 48; Stephen Roskill, *Naval Policy Between the Wars* (London: Collins, 1968), p. 535.

[43] Martin Blumenson, "General Lucas at Anzio," in Kent Roberts Greenfield, ed., *Command Decision* (Washington: Office of the Chief of Military History, Department of the Army, 1960), pp. 331-40. The quote is from p. 340.

a short struggle.[44] An event will exercise an especially powerful influence over an organization's memory if the organization's structure is altered so that part of it (perhaps a newly created part) has a special interest in seeing that the previous event is taken as the model for the future.

EVENTS FROM WHICH PEOPLE LEARN MOST

The four variables that influence the degree to which an event affects later perceptual predispositions are whether or not the person experienced the event firsthand, whether it occurred early in his adult life or career, whether it had important consequences for him or his nation, and whether he is familiar with a range of international events that facilitate alternative perceptions. We can make only two observations about the relative importance of these variables and the way they interact. First, when several of the variables are positive (e.g. firsthand participation in dealing with an important national problem) the event will have especially great salience. But it would be attempting too much precision to say whether the impact of the variables is additive or multiplicative. Second, events that are terribly important for the nation (e.g. wars) can have so great an impact that the perceptual predispositions of those who did not participate in the making of the policy will be affected almost as much as those who did.

Firsthand Experiences

Bismarck once said that fools learn by experience, wise men learn by other people's experience.[45] By this definition, few men are wise. Before the Bay of Pigs, President Kennedy knew that expert advise should not be accepted without scrutiny, but it took his personal involvement with that disaster to drive this lesson home. The main problem, however, is not that so little is learned without direct experience, but that these experiences exercise too great an influence over a person's predispositions. The utility of the lessons that can be extracted from an event is determined only in part and only indirectly by whether the person experiences it firsthand. To the extent that the person has reason to believe that the other's circumstances differ drastically from his, he will be wise to limit what he learns from their experiences. But even when this analysis is not made or this conclusion could not be sustained, the amount of learning

[44] See, for example, the findings of Robert Blake, Herbert Shepard, and Jane Mouton, *Managing Intergroup Conflict in Industry* (Houston, Texas: Gulf Publishing Company, 1964), p. 41; Robert Butow, *Japan's Decision to Surrender* (Stanford: Stanford University Press, 1954), p. 10.

[45] Cited in Kenneth Waltz, *Man, the State, and War* (New York: Columbia University Press, 1959), p. 220. Also see Brodie, *War and Politics*, p. 457.

from an event varies with the degree to which it involved the actor's time, energy, and ego. Participating in the formation of a policy has more impact than witnessing it; being a spectator (e.g. a citizen of a nation involved in the event) has more impact than reading about it in history books. This is not to claim that actors learn nothing from events they hear about only indirectly. Given the range of situations possible and the small number that any one person is ever involved in, most learning must come from such sources. But events seen and participated in leave disproportionate impressions. Furthermore, as our previous discussion has indicated, the lessons drawn from firsthand experiences are overgeneralized. So if people do not learn enough from what happens to others, they learn too much from what happens to themselves.

Thus a person who has been bitten by a snake will be predisposed to see ambiguous figures as snakes. He will be quicker to see snakes when they are present—and will often mistake branches and shadows for them. His behavior also will be changed—he will take detours around snake-infested areas and will add extra weight to his pack in order to carry a snake-bite kit. His unbitten friends will be less affected even though it was only luck that determined that he, and not they, would be bitten and even though they are as likely as he is to get bitten in the future.

Similarly, a diplomat stationed in a country that "goes communist" after the triumph of what appeared to be a reform movement will have different perceptions of peaceful change in other countries than will a diplomat who had observed a successful reformer. This will be true even though each diplomat knows about the events in the other country. Professors are not immune to this form of egocentrism. As some have been surprised to discover, having one's own university or one's own classroom disrupted by protesting students affects one's attitudes more than reading about such activities on other campuses.

A corollary of the importance of personal involvement is that not only the event but also the position the person holds will influence his contemporary perceptions and later predispositions. Someone whose job it was to get troops into South Korea after the attack will remember the Korean War differently from someone who was deciding what messages should be sent to the Chinese. They will share some lessons that those less directly involved did not learn, but each will have some specific perceptual sensitivities that the other lacks.

Several experiments support our proposition. A study of the mental rigidities formed by solving problems by formula found that "experience in which the subject took an active part exerted more influence on subsequent behavior than did the demonstration period in which the subject was a more passive spectator." An exploration of the effects of learning about deception in psychological experiments reached a similar conclusion: "experiencing deception and knowing of deception (without experiencing it) are not functionally equivalent." Subjects who knew they had been deceived altered their responses, but "Merely learning about deception had the same effect as being relatively ignorant about deception."[46]

Evidence from outside the laboratory is highly suggestive. People who experience a natural disaster are much more affected than those who only see the damage, although both may be equally vulnerable to future harm.

A newcomer in a town which previously underwent a severe tornado remarks on this continual apprehension of recurrence, which he, who was not there at the time of the disaster, does not share: "These people are tornado-happy. Every time a dark cloud comes up they go into their caves. A fellow can walk into a beer tavern on Saturday night and say, 'There's a storm coming up,' and empty the place in a minute."[47]

Although our illustrations involving political perceptions are only anecdotal, we have found *no* instances of the reverse of our proposition—cases in which an event made more of an impression on bystanders than on the actor. Many examples can be found in the area of military strategy, tactics, and weapons. "[R]arely if ever does a major power remodel her defenses because of the so-called lessons of a foreign war." Compare, for example, what the United States learned about guerrilla wars from the experiences of France in Indochina and Algeria and Britain in Malaya on the one hand and its own involvement in Vietnam on the other. The nonparticipants similarly learned little from the American Civil War, the Russo-Japanese War, and the Boer War. States also fail to learn from others' specific military operations.[48] Thus in criticizing

---

[46] Luchins and Luchins, *Rigidity of Behavior*, p. 385; Thomas Cook et al., "Demand Characteristics and Three Conceptions of the Frequently Deceived Subject," *Journal of Personality and Social Psychology* 14 (1970), 185, 192.

[47] Wolfenstein, *Disaster*, p. 152. Similarly, a public health study found that "respondents in families where respiratory illness had occurred during the weeks prior to the interview were more likely to believe that an epidemic was in progress than those in families in which there had not been any such illness." (Irving Janis, "Psychological Effects of Warnings," in George Baker and Dwight Chapman, eds., *Man and Society in Disaster* [New York: Basic Books, 1962], p. 84.)

[48] Luvaas, *The Military Legacy of the Civil War*, pp. 44-45. (For examples, see Katzenbach, "The Horse Cavalry in the Twentieth Century"; Jay Luvaas, "European Military Thought and Doctrine, 1870-1914," in Howard, *The Theory and Practice of War*; Theodore Ropp, *War in the Modern World* [New York: Collier, 1962], p. 220. Ropp offers the further explanation that "many of the [European] front-line observers [in these non-European wars] were company or field grade officers, whose ideas take time to percolate into the official manuals.")

the attempt to force the Dardanelles in World War I, a British admiral argues:

> It was not difficult to foresee that the mine would prove the principle obstacle. In the Russo-Japanese War, the Japanese had lost nearly one-third of their battleship strength from one small minefield, whereas in the Dardanelles a mined channel five miles long separated our fleet from its objective. It would be interesting to know if anyone referred to the experience of the Russo-Japanese War available in the Official History by Sir Julian Corbett. For example, did Admiral Carden know that the Japanese Fleet had bombarded the defences of Port Arthur with little or no result? Did he ask himself why our late Ally had not tried to force the entrance by ships alone and why she landed a large army equipped with eleven inch howitzers?[49]

The British, in turn, overgeneralized from their failure at Gallipoli and concluded that amphibious operations were not likely to succeed. The Americans, who were not involved in this assault, saw that new doctrines and technology pointed to possible solutions to the problem and proceeded to develop the tactics that proved so successful against the Japanese.[50]

In choosing weapons systems, nations are also more heavily influenced by their own experiences than by others'. The British development of a breech-loading naval gun in the mid-nineteenth century was retarded by the initial British failure, and little attention was paid to the French and German successes. Similarly, one reason why the Germans and French did not appreciate the value of machine guns in the late nineteenth century was that the French had tried to use an early version of the gun as artillery in the Franco-Prussian War. So both sides learned firsthand that these guns were ineffective. The British, who had not participated in this initial failure, saw that the gun should not be judged by an instance in which it was misused and pushed ahead with its development.[51]

The amount one learns from another's experience is slight even when the incentives for learning are high and the two actors have much in common and face the same situation. Thus in wartime it is one's own battles, rather than those of allies, that produce changes in one's tactics. The British offensive on the Somme in 1916 ignored much of the earlier French experiences. And after one of the first offensives involving Amer-

---

[49] K.G.B. Dewar, *The Navy from Within* (London: Gollancz, 1939), p. 170.

[50] Jeter Isely and Philip Crowl, *The U.S. Marines and Amphibious War* (Princeton: Princeton University Press, 1951), p. 5.

[51] Anthony Preston and John Major, *Send a Gunboat* (London: Longmans, 1967), p. 145; Katzenbach, "The Horse Cavalry in the Twentieth Century," p. 130; G. S. Hutchison, *Machine-Guns* (London: Macmillan and Co., 1938), pp. 35-36.

ican troops, a British historian noted that "American casualties. . . . lay upon the ground in evenly-spaced, regular lines, like fallen bean poles, or corn-stooks [sic] blown over by the wind. Or like the British dead on the Somme." Similarly, the French did not learn about the Germans' new methods of attack in 1918 from German victories over the Italians and British. In the next war, interallied cooperation was higher. But still the Americans were slow to learn from the British experience in combatting the U-boats; and they paid little attention to the intolerable loss rates inflicted on British (and German) bombers engaged in unescorted daylight raids. Not until the Americans experienced these losses themselves did they recognize the need for fighter protection. An even more extreme manifestation of this pattern is that one military service will not pay much attention to the experiences of other services in the same country. Thus even though the German army and navy launched similar zeppelin attacks on London in World War I, neither gleaned much information about central problems such as navigation and vulnerability from the fate of airships in the other service.[52]

SOME CONSEQUENCES

Firsthand experience can be a powerful determinant of images of other actors, images that, as we discussed in a previous chapter, are maintained in the face of large amounts of discrepant information. A person will therefore be slow to detect changes in another actor with whom the person has had previous firsthand contact. Thus Lord Curzon's participation in the efforts to protect Persia from Russian domination before World War I contributed to his being "blinded by what, in 1919, [when he was Foreign Secretary] was an essential factor in the situation. The roles had been reversed. No longer was Russia regarded [by Persia] as the enemy and Great Britain as the well-meaning, if slightly impotent, friend. It was the British of whom the Persians were now frightened. It was to Moscow that, with timid doubt and sly expectancy, they looked for consolation."[53] Similarly, many of the American decision-makers who most strongly supported proposals such as the multilateral force that were based on the premise that tight European integration was possible and desirable had been deeply involved in European affairs in the late 1940s and early 1950s. In this period American influence was at its highest, the need for European unity was seen as great, and unification was favored by the most thoughtful and imaginative of Europe's leaders.

[52] Quoted in Harvey De Weerd, *President Wilson Fights His War* (New York: Macmillan Co., 1968), p. 323 (also see pp. 296-97); *ibid.*, p. 290; Peter Gretton, *Former Naval Person* (London: Cassell, 1968), p. 293; Douglas Robinson, *The Zeppelin in Combat* (London: G. T. Foulis, 1962), pp. 179-89.
[53] Harold Nicolson, *Curzon: The Last Phase, 1919-1925* (Boston: Houghton Mifflin, 1934), pp. 128-29.

The impact of firsthand experience makes the person insensitive not only to changes in circumstances and actors over time but also to variables that change from one situation to another. Thus in explaining why he thought it had been unwise to raise publicly the issue of the presence of Soviet troops in northern Iran, Trygve Lie said that "the Iranian government should have given direct negotiations a longer trial. After all, Norway had had a very positive and satisfactory experience with the withdrawal of Soviet troops. A little more private prodding would probably bring results."[54] This conclusion may have been correct, but the relevance of Russian behavior in Lie's country under very different circumstances is questionable.

The predispositions created by firsthand experience also affect perceptions of actors other than one involved in the initial experience. Playing a large role in one situation will lead the person to see other cases as similar. Dealing with one kind of adversary will increase the chances that other adversaries will be seen as similar. Thus one reason why the British governor of South Africa, newly arrived in the country, saw the settlers' reactions to the abolition of slavery as a greater threat to peace than the border friction that soon led to war was that he had previously served in the West Indies, where the slavery issue was a very troublesome one. In the same way, the policies of later governors can be partly explained by their earlier experiences in India.[55]

A second consequence is that, because differences in firsthand experiences lead to differences in perceptual predispositions, the chance of misperception is increased by events that one actor experiences but that others with whom he interacts know of only indirectly. Furthermore, each actor may be unable to understand how the other is perceiving and why it is behaving as it is. For example, the Soviets made certain demands on Finland in 1939 because incidents in the Russian civil war had given the Russians an incorrect view of what would help protect Leningrad. The Finns, not having experienced the same trauma as the Russians, could not understand how the Russians could believe that the granting of their demands would make them more secure. They therefore concluded that Russia's arguments were disingenuous and that the demands were only the first in a series aimed at destroying Finland's independence.[56] Similarly, the American and British leaders' memories of

[54] Gary Hess, "The Iranian Crisis of 1945-46 and the Cold War," *Political Science Quarterly* 89 (March 1974), 132.

[55] John Galbraith, *Reluctant Empire* (Berkeley and Los Angeles: University of California Press, 1963), pp. 103, 214, 230.

[56] Max Jakobson, *The Diplomacy of the Winter War* (Cambridge, Mass.: Harvard University Press, 1961), pp. 132-40. For another example, see Stan Taylor and Robert Wood, "Image and Generation: A Social-Psychological Analysis of the Sino-Soviet Dispute," *Brigham Young University Studies* 7 (Winter 1966), 143-57.

the disastrous effects of exacting heavy reparations from Germany after World War I contributed to their resistance to the Russian demands for high payments after World War II. But the Russians, not having been deeply involved in the earlier settlement and the resulting financial distress, saw hostility as the only explanation for the Western behavior.

Third, this analysis implies that the common desire to "see for yourself" and to judge a situation by direct observation will often be a mistake if the problem is complex and the visit short. Thus after witnessing an unusually successful antisubmarine exercise, Winston Churchill "came away with too optimistic a picture of the efficiency of [sonar], which coloured his appreciation of warships' immunity to submarine attack." Even more serious consequences flowed from the fact that the officer who made the German decisions that set the stage for the battle of the Marne had been sent out from the General Staff Headquarters and so was getting his initial exposure to actual battle conditions.

Nothing he saw with his inexperienced peacetime eye along the roads behind Bulow's and Kluck's armies awakened optimism. His driver had to manoeuvre the heavy car past convoys of cavalry-division supply echelons "falling back in all haste" towards Fere-en-Tardenois. "Groups of wounded [a novelty to (a General Staff) officer] flowed in the same direction; they were afraid of being cut off." At Neuilly-St. Front, Hentsch was much impressed by an experience that would have been banal to the fighting troops and their comrades on either side.

"Different columns were bottled up in a jam; an air attack had caused a complete panic. I had to get out of my car several times to clear a way by force."[57]

A political example is provided by John Bartlow Martin's report that what he saw on his brief trip back to the Dominican Republic in 1965 played a large role in convincing him that the rebels were communist-dominated. In all these cases the masses of information at the decision-maker's disposal carried less weight than the scattered incidents that, although possessing no claim for special importance or representativeness, were personally witnessed.[58]

In the same way, we would expect a participant in a summit conference to give undue consideration to his firsthand impressions of his opposite numbers. So in his desire to avoid reliance on the judgment of others, a statesman may be led to acquire information which, because it will

[57] Gretton, *Former Naval Person*, p. 248 (we should note, however, that overestimation of the capabilities of sonar was widespread in the British navy); Correlli Barnett, *The Swordbearers* (New York: Morrow, 1964), pp. 89-90.

[58] John Bartlow Martin, *Overtaken by Events* (Garden City, N.Y.: Doubleday, 1966), pp. 661-94.

have impact out of proportion to its validity, will decrease the accuracy of his perceptions. This danger will be compounded if, as is often the case, the decision-maker has excessive confidence in his ability to judge others in face-to-face meetings.

The final implication is that an actor will learn most fruitfully from events that he knows well enough to analyze in some detail, but that are not so close that they dominate his future perceptions. While decision-makers do not learn *most* from reading about history or observing other states' policies, they may learn *best* from these sources. Furthermore, the range of cases in these categories is larger than that provided by the recent history of the decision-maker's own state and this means that, as we will discuss below, he will have to think more about the situation before seizing on an analogy. For example, one reason why Spain was able to maneuver so adroitly in World War II may have been that, not having been deeply affected by the last war she had fewer overriding perceptual predispositions.

ALTERNATIVE EXPLANATIONS

Before closing this section, three alternative explanations for the impact of firsthand experience should be considered. Two argue that more relevant information can be extracted from it and imply that this aspect of learning raises the quality of decision-making. The third explanation affirms the position mentioned at the start of the chapter—the apparent impact of history is spurious because both the lessons and the later policy preferences are caused by the same third variables.

First, it can be argued that at least some of the impact of direct involvement is attributable to the rational factor of the depth of information that this experience provides. Thus a person may know of a social problem, for example bad schools or inadequate insurance coverage, but he will have much more information—although it may not be representative—when his children go to school or he gets into an accident. In diplomacy it is similarly true that dispatches cannot recount everything that has happened. Even if the participant and his listeners had sufficient time (and the latter had sufficient interest), not all the nuances and subtleties could be conveyed. This is one historian's explanation of why two English statesmen favored involvement with Europe after 1815:

> Others . . . had had personal experience of the difficulty of conducting a war against the Napoleonic empire, but this had not made them enthusiasts for the emerging "Congress System." It may be more than a coincidence that only Castlereagh and Wellington, of all leading British personalities, had actually been on the Continent of Europe in the thick of many of the great events of the last few years. They thus had personal knowledge and personal acquaintanceships which

their countrymen could not share; they had seen how easily the Alliance could disintegrate, how deep the rivalries ran, how narrowly disaster had been averted.[59]

Similar reasons may partially explain Roosevelt's observation that although presidents learn little from the experiences of most of their predecessors, he had learned from Wilson's because "he hadn't had to learn about Wilson's methods from reading; he had been close enough to watch."[60]

These causal linkages would explain why people learn more from events they participated in. But they would not lead us to expect that people would use these events as analogies or apply the lessons wholesale. On the contrary, a person who knows the details and complexities of a case should be slow to see other situations as being like it and should draw only careful, limited conclusions. As this chapter shows, these propositions are not correct, and so the explanation of the impact of firsthand experience that produced them is probably wrong.

Second, it can be argued that it is only appropriate that a state learn most from what has happened to it because this history provides the best indicators of what situations the state will face in the future and what strategies it should adopt. But this is not sufficient to explain the magnitude of the differences in learning or the lack of analysis of the similarities and differences in the situations. Thus European soldiers argued that the settings of the American Civil War and the Russo-Japanese War made them "irrelevant to warfare conducted in Europe by highly trained professional forces fighting over limited terrain plentifully provided with roads and railways."[61] But the unique aspects of these wars did not mean that others could afford to neglect the firepower that was displayed and the countermeasures of trenches and earthworks that were developed.

Furthermore, this explanation cannot apply to cases where events involving the actor have no special relevance for the future. For example, each of the Scandinavian countries learned from its own experiences in World War II, not those of its neighbors. Sweden, which succeeded in staying neutral in the war, continued a policy of neutrality in the Cold War. Norway's attempted neutrality was ended by a German invasion, and after the war she joined NATO.[62] Yet because the postwar context

---

[59] C. J. Bartlett, *Castlereagh* (New York: Charles Scribner's Sons, 1966), pp. 159-60.

[60] Rexford Tugwell, *The Brains Trust* (New York: Viking, 1968), p. 444. For a similar argument about the value to the decision-maker of detailed studies of diplomatic complexities, see Butterfield, *History and Human Relations*, pp. 175-76.

[61] Michael Howard, *Studies in War and Peace* (New York: Viking, 1971), p. 187.

[62] Annette Baker Fox, *The Power of Small States* (Chicago: University of Chicago Press, 1959).

was so different from the prewar one, it is hard to argue that one country's experience was a better predictor of its future than was the fate of its neighbor.

The same pattern can be found in lessons about military tactics. Actors rarely examine what happened both to them and to others in light of reasoned conjecture about probable future situations. They are influenced by their own experience even when analysis would not sustain a claim for its greater relevance. For example, many of the West German generals do not employ close air support in maneuvers, preferring to rely on artillery. According to a West German military commentator the reason is that "the failure of Goering's air force to maintain superiority over the battlefields after 1943 caused many army generals to despair forever of adequate air support for ground operations." The other side of this coin is that in the 1972 NATO maneuvers most "Unit leaders were casual, almost complacent, about the possibility of 'enemy' air attack. This is because with a few exceptions Western forces, particularly American, have enjoyed almost complete air superiority in war since 1942. Neither junior officers nor men appeared to conceive of war in any other circumstances."[63] Whatever the relevance of any World War II experiences, it cannot be argued that which side one was on should influence beliefs about future tactics. It is similarly hard to argue that greater relevance explains the fact that during a war countries learn from their own battles, not from those of their allies.

A third alternative explanation cannot be eliminated so easily. The correlation between participation in a situation and later perceptions may be spurious if self-selection or other forms of nonrandom selection are present. For example, it was not entirely accidental that certain people were deeply involved in United States relations with Europe after the war. The values and beliefs that led to an active role in this period could also have led to support for the MLF. The evidence that would most conclusively disprove this kind of explanation would be comparisons that showed differences in the perceptions of two actors who were otherwise similar in all respects except that one had firsthand experience with an event. Although such experimental or quasi-experimental data are not available, spuriousness is unlikely when the actor did not choose to enter the situation and when all those who had the experience learned the same lessons; when variables that could explain later perceptions did not affect the events they experienced or the conclusions they drew; and when the experience changed the views of the participants. Thus, third variables

---

[63] David Binder, "Commander Says West German Army Will Deemphasize Tanks in Major Shift of Strategy," *New York Times*, September 16, 1969; Drew Middleton, "NATO War Games End in 'Victory,' but Norway Defense Problem Stays," *New York Times*, September 23, 1972.

cannot explain the reactions of Sweden and Norway to their World War II histories, the differences in the German and American generals' preferences for artillery and air support, or Curzon's belief that the Persians looked to Britain for protection after World War I.

Since nations have less choice than individuals in the situations they face, spuriousness due to self-selection is rarely a plausible explanation of why states' perceptual predispositions are correlated with their previous experiences. But the other side of this coin is that aspects of the state's environment (e.g. its geographical setting) are more constant than those of individuals, and so repetition of previous perceptions and policies may be caused by common situational variables.

The possibility of spuriousness is hard to eliminate in the many cases where we cannot show that anyone who experienced a given event would have developed the same perceptual predispositions. If different people learned different lessons from the event, both the person's analysis of the event and his later perceptions may have been determined by his pre-existing beliefs. For example, Stimson's biographer argues that his advocacy of an uncompromising policy toward Japan in 1940-1941 "arose from [his] belief that Japan had yielded to a firm policy at Shantung in 1919, at the Washington Conference in 1922 and at London in 1930. He remembered also that from 1931 onwards, where it had been impossible to construct firm consistent policies, the Japanese had not yielded."[64] Because others did not draw the same lessons from the earlier conflicts, we cannot immediately conclude that Stimson's personal participation in them influenced his views. His analysis of Japan's strategic position, a general belief in the efficacy of force, or any number of other variables could account for the evidence. In these cases we could compare the person's views with those of someone who shared his pre-existing beliefs but was not involved in the earlier event. But this can rarely be accomplished satisfactorily, and some doubts must often remain. As we will see in the next two sections, this problem appears in other contexts. By the same token, however, we can be fairly confident that events exert an independent influence when large numbers of people with a range of characteristics and beliefs all learn the same lessons from an event.

Early Experiences and Generational Effects

Among the events experienced firsthand, those that occur early in the person's adult life have an especially great impact on his perceptual predispositions. We can distinguish four kinds of such events that leave somewhat different effects but with the same basic cause: at an early stage in their lives people are open to new ideas and concepts that, once

[64] Elting Morison, *Turmoil and Tradition: A Study of the Life and Times of Henry L. Stimson* (Boston: Houghton Mifflin, 1960), p. 523.

they have taken root, maintain a discernible influence for the rest of the person's life. Later events, although not without impact, are seen within a more established framework and so leave an impression that is not only reduced but also influenced by the earlier events. Thus the influence of an event varies with the period in a person's life at which it occurs, and we can often find traces throughout a person's career of what he heard, said, and did when he was coming of age. Many of the person's most fundamental orientations—e.g. his feelings about his ability to influence his environment, his judgment of whether the world is hostile or benign —are formed in his childhood. But these are not of central concern here because they are too far removed from beliefs about politics, and especially world politics. While they may influence these beliefs, there still is a great deal of room for variation.

One of the four kinds of early experiences affects political beliefs only indirectly through its impact on the person's general outlook on how to order his relations with other people and his work. Experiences that established the person as an autonomous and valued individual influence his general beliefs about how he can best cope with his environment. James Barber argues that a president's style in office "is a reflection of the ways of performing which brought him success at the time, usually in late adolescence or early adulthood, when he emerged as a personality distinctive from his family heritage, in a role involving relatively intensive participation in a socially organized setting." For example, it was through his successful race for Congress that Richard Nixon "emerged from obscurity to wide notice. He did it, very nearly, on his own. . . . The infusion of confidence must have been massive. The *way* Nixon won set his style." The style often is not displayed in much of the future president's career because of the constraints of the role he is filling or the offices he is seeking, but "A new president, scanning (though seldom consciously) his life's repertoire of successful strategies, might well turn to those which had worked so well for him as he became a man."[65] Although Barber calls these experiences the person's "first independent political success," *political* is used extremely broadly and *social* would seem to catch his meaning better. These experiences are thus less apt to provide analogies for international events than to create a general outlook.

Less theoretical accounts also detect similarities between the way a person handles an early problem and his behavior as a political decision-maker. Henry Stimson delayed his marriage for five years until he could

---

[65] James David Barber, "Classifying and Predicting Presidential Styles: Two Weak Presidents," *Journal of Social Issues* 24 (July 1968), 52; Barber, *The Presidential Character* (Englewood Cliffs, N.J.: Prentice-Hall, 1972), p. 415 (italics in the original); Barber, "Classifying and Predicting Presidential Styles," p. 79.

convince his father of the wisdom of his choice. His biographer's comments are to the point:

> Certainly others with a different kind of strength would have resolved the problem in a shorter time, if in a different way. But for the young man the time expended was worth it. By the force of will, patiently and undramatically applied, he sustained his original policy and gained his purpose. And in the end he reached his object without ever having said or done those things that would have broken off the old allegiances or destroyed the familiar environment. . . . He found on this occasion that he could come out from the enclosing decision of others and emerge as his own man ready to survive in more dangerous surroundings even than the wilderness. All his life he was to respect those in authority and to wish for their approval, but here he discovered what he remembered afterwards, that there were ways to hold and support his own opinions without placing in jeopardy the relationship between himself and those in greater authority. He and his father lived from that time forward in mutual respect and constructive amity —just as in later administrations he argued differences and stood his ground while serving with great usefulness and in mutual respect along with the highest authorities.[66]

Similarly, in his childhood George Marshall showed no sign of special abilities. But his final year at the Virginia Military Institute "was a year of blossoming because it was a year of success. The boy who wished all his life to be first in everything was now first in the soldierly ways that to him counted most." "He had also developed an austerity and coolness of manner that characterized him thereafter. . . . [E]xcept for his roommates . . . , he had no intimate friends at the Institute. He wished above all else to command. He found that he had the power to command but that to keep it he could not let himself get too close to those who had to obey." By using "the reflexes of discipline" he met initial challenges to his position of first captain of the cadets and "emerged master of the situation, secure in the admiration and respect of his fellows." After his graduation, Marshall displayed boldness and initiative, as well as a distance from his peers, that had not been apparent before.[67]

A more specific influence is apt to be exerted by the political issues and stands that advanced the person's early career and established him as someone of great talent and potential. These events will provide analogies for future situations and the lessons learned will be applied with relatively little discrimination. A man who first makes his mark by calling an adversary's bluff will later be more prone to stand firm than will one who

[66] Morison, *Turmoil and Tradition*, p. 60. Also see pp. 189, 639.
[67] Pogue, *George Marshall*, vol. 1, pp. 54-55, 64.

was first seen as talented because he averted a crisis by measured concessions. For example, "it is significant that three of the [British] Foreign Secretaries in the 1930s, Sir John Simon (1931-5), Sir Samuel Hoare (1935) and Lord Halifax (1938-40) had *made their reputations* by appeasing the Indian demands for more self-government." Similarly, one reason why Lord Cromer was not able to fully understand politics in Egypt, where he was consul-general, was that he "was too much of an Indian administrator to make a success of Egyptian politics. It was in India that he had gained his early experience."[68] To take a contemporary example, the transcripts of President Nixon's conversations with his aides reveal that the *only* previous event he talks about and tells others they should learn from is the Hiss case, the event that first brought him into the public eye.

The third kind of early experience that is significant is not a dramatic personal success but rather the more diffuse influence of the values, problems, and ways of thinking that dominate a particularly gripping career (i.e. one that involves all the person's time and keeps him in close contact with those who have the same perspective). Thus it has been argued that "some of Churchill's . . . mistakes in the handling of naval operations . . . were caused by his inability to address himself to naval problems other than with a soldier's mind." This is not surprising since Churchill's first careers were as a soldier and a journalist covering land wars. And an historian argues that much of Hitler's "pattern of thought, like that of most of his followers, is better traced to the death-misery-glory of 1914-18 than what had happened before or since. Veterans returned with a 'front socialism,' the ideal of which was an anti-class, egalitarian community. . . . Proper behavior meant obedience and activism."[69]

[68] Neville Thompson, *The Anti-Appeasers* (Oxford: Clarendon Press, 1971), p. 32 (italics added); Ronald Robinson and John Gallagher, *Africa and the Victorians* (London: Macmillan and Co., 1967), p. 274. The perspective gained in India was institutionalized in his administration of Egypt because Cromer not only drew lessons from his earlier experiences, "From India he also had drawn most of the British officials who filled key posts in the government of Egypt." *Ibid.* For another example, see A.J.P. Taylor, *Beaverbrook* (New York: Simon and Schuster, 1972), p. 542.

[69] Gretton, *Former Naval Person*, p. 84; Edward Peterson, *The Limits of Hitler's Power* (Princeton: Princeton University Press, 1969), p. 11. For a discussion of the impact of World War I on other aspects of Hitler's outlook, see Albert Speer, *Inside the Third Reich* (New York: Macmillan Co., 1969), p. 278. Sigmund Neumann, *Permanent Revolution* (New York: Praeger, 1968), pp. 236-44, argues that fighting in the First World War made a crucial impact on a whole generation of young Germans and notes that all Hitler's "important lieutenants belonged to the young war generation . . . [while] all the non-National Socialist Cabinet members belonged to an older generation" (p. 243). But for a thorough analysis of Hitler's belief system that does not invoke these experiences, see Eberhard Jackel, *Hitler's Weltanschauung*, translated by Herbert Arnold (Middletown, Conn.: Wesleyan University Press, 1972).

GENERATIONAL EFFECTS

A fourth manifestation—generational effects—is more important because the claim for a causal role of the early experience is especially strong and because it affects large numbers of people. We have previously discussed early experiences in which the person chose to participate. This both raises the question of spuriousness and means that only those who chose to share this experience will be influenced by it. But people also absorb many of the values and beliefs that dominate the climate of opinion at the time when they first begin to think about politics. Since the concerns and events that are most important in any period of time pervade the society, all those who come of age at the time are affected similarly. Because, as we discussed above, the orientation that is first formed is not easily replaced but instead structures the interpretation of later events, the result is a generational or cohort effect. As Karl Mannheim pointed out, individuals "who share the same year of birth are endowed, to that extent, with a common location in the historical dimension of the social process" which predisposes them to a "certain characteristic mode of thought and experience, and [creates] a characteristic type of historically relevant faction." As a soldier in *All Quiet on the Western Front* explained: "[I]f we go back . . . men will not understand us—for the generation that grew up before us, though it has passed these years with us here, already had a home and a calling; now it will return to its old occupations, and the war will be forgotten."[70]

To find the source of the basic political ideas that a person holds one must often go back to the events that demanded attention in his early life. Sometimes he will explicitly use these events as analogies for specific current events. More often they will support a general outlook. Thus two contending generations of French diplomats offered conflicting policies toward Britain in the late 1870s based on the different climates that had dominated their early adulthood: the older ones who learned about international politics in the period when France was recovering from the defeat of Napoleon favored a policy of conciliation "based upon an acceptance of French weakness," while the younger ones who were "bred in the tradition of Republican opposition to Napoleon III" called for a more assertive and independent course.[71]

Similarly, William Quandt explains many of the divisions within the Algerian political elite by the series of salient events that conditioned the

---

[70] "The Problem of Generations," in Karl Mannheim, *Essays on the Sociology of Knowledge*, edited by Paul Kecskemeti (London: Routledge and Kegan Paul, 1952), pp. 290-91; Erich Maria Remarque, *All Quiet on the Western Front* (Boston: Little, Brown, 1929), p. 290.

[71] Agatha Ramm, "Great Britain and France in Egypt, 1876-1882," in Prosser Gifford and Wm. Roger Louis, eds., *France and Britain in Africa* (New Haven: Yale University Press, 1971), pp. 75-76.

views of successive waves of political activists as they were first entering political awareness. Clear differences are apparent between those who came of age at the time of the failure of the liberal-assimilationist proposals of 1938, the suppression of the uprising of 1945, and the 1954 revolution itself. In a less dramatic arena, Warner Schilling finds that the belief in "technology for its own sweet sake" "is likely to be more characteristic of the scientists who had their graduate training and early professional experience in the years before World War II than of those who have known only war or Cold War conditions. . . . The result is that the senior scientists tend to be especially sensitive to possibilities which hold some promise for restoring the former order" by decreasing secrecy and increasing international scientific exchanges. Similarly, we would expect that American diplomats who started their careers around 1950 were deeply marked by the Korean War and that the war in Vietnam has left a stronger impression on those who came of age in the years 1965–1971 than on those older or younger.[72]

Historians also talk of generational effects. In discussing why American statesmen were so worried about the dangers of thwarting expansionist public opinion after the Spanish-American War, Ernest May notes that "Spaniards were to speak in retrospect of a disillusioned 'generation of ninety-eight.' Perhaps Americans also had a generation of ninety-eight—a generation of public leaders so frightened by the outbursts of mass emotion they had witnessed that their thoughts were dominated by dread of witnessing it again." Richard Hofstadter speculates that individuals' ages influenced their attitudes toward the replacement of the Articles of Confederation by a strong federal system.

> Men who were young enough to have come of age around 1775 when the agitations of a dozen years finally irrupted into open violence found the challenge of organization and power that came with the Revolutionary War practically coincident with their adult political experience; whereas those who came of age during or before the agitations against British tyranny that quickened after 1763 had had their minds fixed at a formative age more upon the dangers of arbitrary governmental power and would be harder to dislodge from the combative and militant anticentralist republicanism that the Revolution called into being.[73]

72 William Quandt, *Revolution and Political Leadership: Algeria 1954-1968* (Cambridge, Mass.: M.I.T. Press, 1969); Warner Schilling, "Scientists, Foreign Policy, and Politics," in Robert Gilpin and Christopher Wright, eds., *Scientists and National Policy-Making* (New York: Columbia University Press, 1964), pp. 160-61.

73 *Imperial Democracy* (New York: Harcourt, Brace, 1961), p. 269; *The Progressive Historians* (New York: Knopf, 1968), pp. 235-36.

Here too academics are not immune. Hofstadter also reveals how an historian's lifelong outlook can be influenced by the political disputes of his early days. And we all know that many of our colleagues—but not, of course, ourselves—are apt to re-fight continually the scholarly battles that raged when they were in graduate school.

More systematic studies of large numbers of individuals in several countries have also found generational differences traceable to the events of early adulthood. Differences in political outlook characterize the generations that came of age before, during, and after the Finnish Civil War. The reasons given by Soviet refugees for leaving their country varied according to whether they had been politically aware before the revolution or had political memories of only the Soviet system. And contemporary West European attitudes on several issues show generational differences. Ingelhart demonstrates not only that age is inversely correlated with support for European integration but that there are two breakpoints in the data—people over 55 were much more hostile to integration than those who were younger, and those who were 16–19 were much more favorable to integration than those who were older. Within the span of 20–50, there was almost no difference of attitude. "The age group which was 55 and older in 1963 [when the polls were taken] was at least 10 years old at the end of World War I. These individuals were exposed to the period of intense nationalism which preceded that war, and to the powerful fears and suspicions the war aroused during a relative[ly] impressionable stage of life." The 16–19 year olds, by contrast, "have gained their first political perceptions in a world where European organization seems natural and right, and nationalism seems archaic and dangerous." Further support for this explanation is that only in Holland is there no break between those under and those over 55. "Alone among these four countries [surveyed], Holland did not participate in World War I—nor was she deeply involved in the preceding great-power rivalries." Furthermore, in England the break-point at 55 but not the one at 20 is found: when the youth of Britain, but not those of the other three countries, came to political awareness their country was not participating in a common European venture. Similarly, Inglehart found a shift from "acquisitive" to "post-bourgeois" values associated with whether the person grew up in an era of economic scarcity or of relative plenty. Several of the more detailed findings show that this effect cannot be entirely explained by third variables such as the spread of higher education.[74]

[74] Marvin Rintala, *Three Generations: The Extreme Right Wing in Finnish Politics* (Bloomington, Ind.: Indiana University Press, 1962, Russian and East European Series, vol. 22); Raymond Bauer, "Some Trends in Sources of Alienation from the Soviet System," *Public Opinion Quarterly* 19 (Fall 1955), 277-91; Ronald Inglehart, "An End to European Integration?," *American Political Science Review* 61 (March 1967), 93-94; Inglehart, "The Silent Revolution in Europe,"

Studies of elites in Europe also reveal generational differences. In both England and Italy, the younger politicians are less hostile to the opposition. "The biggest difference in hostility in the British sample is found within the Conservative Party between those who reached political maturity before the wartime coalition Government and the postwar Labour Government and those whose entrance into politics came later. . . . The implication seems clear. For the older Tories, the Labour Party remains a slightly sinister intruder. Their younger colleagues, by contrast, entered a political world in which Labour was simply 'the other side.' " Similarly, in Italy "Many older politicians formed their basic impressions of their opponents during the Fascist era, when ordinary political interchange was impossible. During our conversations a few of these older and more suspicious respondents themselves acknowledged the impact their life experiences have had on their views." Not only images of the opposition party but also more general beliefs about how much conflict there is in one's society and conceptions of democracy are strongly influenced by the political climate that prevailed when the person was socialized into the political world. And if it is plausible to argue that the connection between years of political activism and partisanship can explain why older politicians are more hostile to the opposition party, neither aging nor selection can account for the sharp break-points in the data, nor can they explain the irregular shape of the other curves.[75]

Survey research of American political attitudes also indicates that different generations are characterized by different distributions of opinion. Indeed this effect, rather than the process of aging, may be responsible for the fact that older people now tend to be conservative and to have stronger party identification than younger citizens.[76] *The American Voter* found that those who "came of age during the 1920's have a lower proportion of Democratic identifiers than do any of the groups that entered the electorate in later years" and that the Depression gave the Democratic party "a hold on [the new] generation which it has never fully relinquished." Similarly, Lipset explains the fact that religion is more highly correlated with political preferences for old people than for

ibid. 65 (December 1971), 991-1017 (for a criticism of this article see Alan Marsh, "The 'Silent Revolution,' Value Priorities, and the Quality of Life in Great Britain," *ibid.* 69 [March 1975], 21-30).

[75] Robert Putnam, *The Beliefs of Politicians* (New Haven: Yale University Press, 1973), pp. 70, 141, 223.

[76] William Klecka, "Applying Political Generations to the Study of Political Behavior: A Cohort Analysis," *Public Opinion Quarterly* 35 (Fall 1971), 358-73; Norval Glenn and Ted Hefner, "Further Evidence on Aging and Party Identification," *ibid.* 36 (Spring 1972), 31-47; Michael Hout and David Knoke, "Change in Voting Turnout, 1952-1972," *ibid.* 39 (Spring 1975), 52-62; Stephen Cutler and Robert Kaufman, "Cohort Changes in Political Attitudes," *ibid.*, 63-81.

younger ones by arguing that the latter formed their loyalties in the pre-Depression era when religious conflicts were more important than class conflicts. Especially striking are the results of a survey of racial attitudes in the South in the mid-1960s. Contrary to the common finding that tolerance varies inversely with age, those in their early twenties were found to be slightly more prejudiced than those ten years older. The probable explanation is that the post-1954 school desegregation controversy increased the salience of anti-Negro attitudes during the period when the younger group was forming their political ideas.[77]

Finally, we must note a difficulty. Early adulthood is only an approximate and sometimes inadequate operationalization of the time at which a person first pays serious attention to political issues. The latter is the period when a person is most influenced by contemporary events, and the exact year it occurs varies among individuals. Thus Truman was only two years younger than Roosevelt, but drew much less on the lessons of the Treaty of Versailles than did Roosevelt. McGovern was only five years younger than John Kennedy but was less concerned with the danger of Munichs. Part of the explanation is that Truman and McGovern became interested in politics later in life than did Roosevelt and Kennedy. When Roosevelt was playing important roles in Washington, Truman was an artilleryman and then a haberdasher. Kennedy was traveling through Europe and writing a book on *Why England Slept* when McGovern was finishing high school.

ALTERNATIVE EXPLANATIONS

The possibility of spuriousness arises once we substitute the time of first political concerns for chronological age. The time when a person first pays close attention to politics is determined not only by objective events, but also by his internal characteristics and beliefs, and these characteristics and beliefs could also explain the predispositions that he later displays. This is especially true when we consider the role of the person's first success. It is difficult to draw inferences of causality from the facts

[77] Angus Campbell et al., *The American Voter* (New York: Wiley, 1960), pp. 154-55. Samuel Lubell makes a similar argument about voting patterns being strongly influenced by when a person entered the middle class [*The Future of American Politics* (2nd ed., Garden City, N.Y.: Doubleday, 1956), pp. 61-64]. Also see Paul Abramson, "Generational Change in American Electoral Behavior," *American Political Science Review* 68 (March 1974), 93-105. Seymour Martin Lipset, *Political Man* (Garden City, N.Y.: Doubleday, 1963), p. 282; Paul Sheatsley, "White Attitudes toward the Negro," *Daedalus* 95 (Winter 1966), 226. Also see Davis Bobrow and Neal Cutler, "Time-Oriented Explanations of National Security Beliefs," *Peace Research Society (International) Papers* 8 (1967), 30-57. For good summaries of this literature see Neal Cutler, "Generational Analysis in Political Science," paper delivered at the 1971 American Political Science Association meeting, and Alan Spitzer, "The Historical Problem of Generations," *American Historical Review* 78 (December 1973), 1353-85.

that soldiers who reach the highest ranks tend to follow career paths that diverge somewhat from the standard pattern; that, as a senator, Joseph Clark repeated the stress on reform that had brought him to power in Philadelphia years earlier; that in his first success General Marshall displayed the aloofness that was to characterize his later career; or from Barber's findings.[78] The way an individual copes with the challenges of early adulthood is not apt to be accidental, and so both this response and the later behavior may be caused by underlying characteristics. Indeed in discussing Stimson's handling of the crisis with his father in his early adulthood, his biographer pointed out that "others with a different kind of strength would have resolved the problem . . . in a different way."[79]

Of course this is not an all-or-none matter. Early success can reinforce pre-existing habits. At the time of the person's first success, his beliefs could have been compatible with a range of strategies, but the nature of the situation or other variables not related to deep personality traits could have led him to adopt the approach that he did. Because of the initial success, the style might be maintained even after the variables that were the immediate cause of its being chosen ceased to operate.

As in the case for firsthand involvement in general, it is hard to establish a causal role for early experiences when the individual learned lessons that others did not. Thus we may not be able to explain what Vansittart learned in his early years without reference to pre-existing beliefs.

His early impressions of Germany were formed at an unfortunate time. During the Boer War he spent a few months in Germany and sampled the Anglophobe hostility of the master race. . . . Of British diplomacy in his early career he retained two impressions: a magisterial memorandum by Sir Eyre Crowe in 1907 had clearly defined the threat of German military power to Europe, but the Cabinet had not been sufficiently impressed by it. In 1911 the Foreign Secretary, Sir Edward Grey, had failed, so Vansittart thought, to bring home to the Commonwealth prime ministers the imminence of the danger in Europe. These lessons Vansittart had laid up in his heart.[80]

[78] Morris Janowitz, *The Professional Soldier* (New York: Free Press, 1964), pp. 168-71; Janowitz, *The Military in the Political Development of New Nations* (Chicago: University of Chicago Press, 1964), pp. 45-49; Edward Kolodziej, "Joe Clark (Reformer, Pa.), Profile of a New Senatorial Style," in Lawrence Pettit and Edward Keynes, eds., *The Legislative Process in the U.S. Senate* (Chicago: Rand McNally, 1969), pp. 29, 38. Indeed it is not clear whether Barber is claiming that the first independence success is only predictive—his book is subtitled "Predicting Performance in the White House"—or whether it is a cause of later behavior.

[79] Morison, *Turmoil and Tradition*, p. 60.

[80] Ian Colvin, *Vansittart in Office* (London: Gollancz, 1965), pp. 19-20.

These incidents do not seem objectively distinguishable from others that Vansittart witnessed, and many people who shared these experiences received impressions that differed from Vansittart's. The general process of learning and the nature of the objective experiences are therefore not sufficient to explain which events had most impact or the impressions that the events left.

The correlation between a decision-maker's early experiences and his later behavior is less likely to be spurious if we take as our independent variable the situations the person faced rather than the strategies he employed. While the latter usually involve a choice, the nature of the experiences the person had, the actors that he dealt with, and the challenges he confronted are more apt to be out of his control. Thus the young diplomat is assigned to a country and given certain tasks. And if the problems and situations that he dealt with are mirrored in later behavior, the explanation cannot lie in self-selection or pre-existing predispositions. Similarly, spuriousness is rarely a plausible explanation for generational effects because the people have not chosen the experiences they will be exposed to and many people with different characteristics have learned the same lessons.

But lacking time-series data, two other kinds of alternative explanations—life cycle and selection effects—must be examined for each case. Some general points can be made, however. The most obvious arguments about life cycles attribute changes to aging—e.g. older people are more conservative than younger ones—but less direct effects are also possible. For example, certain opinions or orientations could appear when a person is at the peak of his career, and thus the views of this group could differ from those who are both older and younger. In the former, more common, life-cycle argument, the curve of opinions plotted against age should be, if not straight, at least of one slope. Even in the less common argument the curve should be relatively smooth. And in both cases, of course, the curve should be the same no matter when the data are collected. In many of the cases we have discussed, however, these claims cannot be sustained. The curve shifts sharply and even reverses direction at points corresponding to earlier events that differentially marked each generation. For example, the differences in the attitude of different cohorts of Cuban workers toward the revolution and the communist party can be explained only by generational effects. Neither the life cycle nor the selection process (i.e. disproportionate migration in certain cohorts) could produce the irregular and complex curves.[81] Furthermore, in many of the cases that bear most directly on foreign policy—e.g. predisposi-

---

[81] Maurice Zeitlin, *Revolutionary Politics and the Cuban Working Class* (Princeton: Princeton University Press, 1967), pp. 211-41.

tions to see conflicts in terms of the spiral or the deterrence models—there is no reason to expect any life cycle effects.

When we examine the views of elites, we must also consider selection effects. Perhaps one generation of leaders displays distinctive beliefs because holding those views made it more likely that a person would become a leader. This explanation implies the existence of many potential leaders who are excluded from the elite because they retain unacceptable views. The lower ranks of the organization will contain many people who do not share the opinions of the top leadership, but the explanation is not that they had different early experiences, but that they have not yet been screened for their views. As they move up the career ladder, only those with opinions suitable to positions of greater power will be promoted. This explanation is often valid. One reason that Winston Churchill was excluded from power in the 1930s was that he did not share the dominant view about Germany. But this explanation applies only to elites, and then is plausible only when the number of people excluded for inappropriate views is large and when the variations in views by the level in the organization fits a coherent pattern that is linked to the criteria for selection to higher positions.

DELAYED IMPACT ON POLICY

Several consequences follow from the impact of early experiences. Most generally, part of the explanation of the perceptions and behavior of a person throughout his life are the events that were important to him years earlier. Even without being psychoanalytic, we can deepen our understanding of a person's views by learning what he saw and did in early adulthood. Since a person rarely gains political power until 20 or 30 years after the early events, the political impact of those events can be long delayed. This is most dramatically true of generational effects, where a whole age-band of people is influenced by the events and opinions that are salient when it first becomes politically aware. Thus the lessons learned from a major war, to take an example that will be discussed at greater length below, may have less impact on policy in the immediate postwar years than they will 20 years later when those people who were most strongly stamped by the war take power.[82]

How strong will these delayed effects be? The answer lies in part in how long the event dominated the political climate and in how wide the ruling age-band is. The two world wars influenced later beliefs not only

[82] For discussions of delayed effects, see Gosta Carlsson and Katarina Karlsson, "Age, Cohorts and the Generation of Generations," *American Sociological Review* 35 (August 1970), 710-18; Michael Roskin, "From Pearl Harbor to Vietnam: Shifting Generational Paradigms," *Political Science Quarterly* 89 (Fall 1974), 587-88; Putnam, *Beliefs of Politicians*, pp. 147-48.

because they were highly salient but because they held attention over many years. The lessons thus became deeply embedded, and successive groups learned the same beliefs. The Cuban missiles crisis, campus unrest, and even the war in Vietnam dominated the scene for shorter periods and so even if their impact on those who first became interested in politics in this period was as great as was that of the world wars, fewer people were affected. The width of the age-band of the elite determines the degree to which generations share power and thus the degree to which the experiences that marked one generation will guide later policy. When people of different cohorts hold power together, the generational effect is diluted. And when the government is dominated by people who shared the same formative experiences, as is often the case in following a revolution, the effect is much stronger.

Although a pure generation model would imply that events would have no immediate effect on the images held by those in power, this is obviously not true. The Munich analogy was applied in the late 1940s as well as in the late 1950s. Three factors explain this. First, important events often change a state's political leadership, bringing to power those whose views were appropriate to the earlier event. Thus those who wanted to stand firm against the Soviets were elected and appointed to office after World War II. Second, these upheavals often bring younger people into the government, people for whom the recent event constituted a formative experience. Third, as we will discuss below, events that are very important, like major wars, can change the cognitive predispositions of those who had other formative experiences.

The combination of both immediate and delayed effects can produce generational cycles in policies. A new policy or general orientation forms in reaction to a traumatic event, usually a war or a dramatic failure of the old views. The new policy and underlying beliefs receive support not only from those in power but also from those younger people who will govern 20 years later. Indeed the latter group has learned the lessons especially well, but because of the flawed nature of the way they will have learned, the lessons will be oversimplified and overgeneralized and therefore will be likely to be applied to inappropriate situations. And because their perceptual predispositions will have been so strongly affected, these people will be very slow to abandon their views. This will insure that, when the lessons are misapplied, the failure of the policy will be important and dramatic and so will set a new generation on its course.[83]

[83] For discussion of cycles, especially in American foreign policy, see Arthur Schlesinger, "Tides in American Politics," *Yale Review* 29 (December 1939), 217-30; Frank Klingberg, "The Historical Alternation of Moods in American Foreign Policy," *World Politics* 4 (January 1952), 239-73; Dexter Perkins, *The*

Events Important to the Person's State or Organization

We argued earlier that firsthand experiences have the most impact. But everyone has countless such experiences. Within this category, the influence of an event varies directly with its importance for the person and the groups to which he is loyal. Since events with major consequences for a nation absorb so much of the citizens' time and attention, they both socialize the previously unconcerned and change the perceptual predispositions of many people with established views. Major events not only affect the perceptual predispositions of large numbers of people, they influence people deeply. Just as people believe that big events must be explained by big underlying causes, so they act as though events with major consequences must contain more information about the way the world works than do less dramatic happenings. Indeed the resulting lessons are apt to be so salient that they will be passed down to those who did not experience the events.

REVOLUTIONS

One such category of events are those by which the state gains its independence or undergoes a revolution. Although the impact will be attenuated for the postrevolutionary generations, it will still be detectable. Those who participated in the events will be even more affected. The way they took power, looming so large for them, will influence the concepts and strategies that they later apply to ruling their country and dealing with the world.

Impressed by the success of their own efforts, actors will be vigilant to the possibility of their opponents' employing similar tactics. Adam Ulam argues that this helps explain several aspects of Soviet behavior. The Bolsheviks' rapid rise to power and the success of their conspiratorial approach fed an almost paranoid fear of domestic opposition. "Stalin and his colleagues were haunted by history. Barely twenty years before, another exile had returned to Russia to lead a handful of supporters, and within six months they were in power." Thus all remnants of Trotskyism had to be destroyed. This fear was reinforced by Stalin's memory of the fact that even though prewar Russia had seemed stable, years of suffering opened the way to revolution. So as the European political scene grew tense with growing German assertiveness, the need for purges increased. If war came, there should be no alternative leaders to capitalize on the discontent.[84]

American Approach to Foreign Policy (rev. ed., New York: Atheneum, 1968), pp. 148-49; Frank Denton and Warren Phillips, "Some Patterns in the History of Violence," *Journal of Conflict Resolution* 12 (June 1968), 182-95.

[84] Adam Ulam, *Expansion and Coexistence* (New York: Praeger, 1968), pp. 246, 240.

The Soviet leaders also saw the internal politics of other countries in light of their own triumph. The tactics that had worked for them would work for others. The authorities would be no more effectual. That the communists were few in numbers and opposed by powerful forces had not prevented the revolution in Russia and so need not prevent it elsewhere. Just as World War I had weakened Russia and left it ripe for revolution, so the postwar dislocation would set the stage for communism in Western Europe.

The Bolsheviks had not seized power by collaborating with other socialist and radical groups or by respecting legal norms and proprieties. They succeeded by showing to the proletariat that they were fighters, by seizing upon every social and political grievance, and by adopting the most radical position on practically every issue. . . . The prize was bound to go to the audacious and uncompromising. As to competing right-wing radicals, again the Soviet experience taught that they could not compete with a militant party of the left. The Kornilov episode had been of the briefest duration. Could German militarism or National Socialism be much more durable? . . . This unsophisticated use of the "lessons" of 1917 weighed heavily on the fortunes of Communism between 1928 and 1933. The Bolsheviks had been defeatists, i.e., they worked openly for the demoralization and disintegration of the Russian army. They had embraced the slogan of national self-determination and independence for the Poles, Finns, and Ukrainians. Now the same tactics were prescribed for parties working under hugely different conditions. The French Communists were made to embrace the postulates of the Alsatian separatists, and their leaders in some cases had to learn German, in which they addressed Party gatherings in Alsace! In Yugoslavia the directives imposed by the Comintern upon the Communist Party required it to demand "self-determination until secession" of every constituent nationality. The Party's leadership until 1928 was condemned for its "Great Serbian chauvinism," and their successors were called upon to endorse the most extreme separatist demands, not only of the Croats, but also of Slovenes, Macedonians, and Albanians.[85]

The strategies and circumstances of their success also shaped the Bolsheviks' beliefs about international relations. Their perceptions of international adversaries mirrored their experiences with those who had opposed them—and those whom they thought should have opposed them—in their struggle to gain power at home. They were aware that they might not have survived after 1906–1907 had it not been for

[85] *Ibid.*, pp. 188-89.

the tolerance extended to them by socialist and liberal circles both in Russia and abroad. Foreign socialists provided shelter and funds for the Bolshevik leaders within Russia. Liberal lawyers sprang to the defense of accused party members. . . . Such practices were bound to give some Bolsheviks, especially Lenin, the impression of essential weakness and lack of self-assurance on the part of liberals and other socialists. Marx's teaching about the tenacity with which the bourgeoisie holds on to power and its ruthlessness in pursuing its aims were thus shown to be no longer fully applicable. . . . The lingering effect of these impressions was to be displayed in the Bolsheviks' foreign policies following November 1917. They were to show but little respect for the sense of realism and tenacity of purpose of social democratic regimes and hardly more for those foreign governments and movements that could be called liberal. In world politics, they were to see images of their former domestic protagonists like the Mensheviks and the Kadets.[86]

Two objections similar to those discussed earlier can be raised. First, it can be argued that these experiences merely add to the decision-makers' store of concepts and information. The revolutionaries learn of new tactics and different kinds of adversaries. But the revolution does more than this—it does not supplement pre-existing beliefs, it overshadows them. The fact that many disparate events are seen as recapitulating the earlier experience indicates that something more than expansion of knowledge is occurring. The second and more important objection is that the correlation between the course of the revolution and later perceptions may be spurious. Both may have been caused by the revolutionaries' pre-existing belief system. Although this variable is important, the Russian revolution does seem to have had an independent impact. It molded perceptual predispositions in areas in which the ideology was silent. Nothing in Marxism required the stress on national self-determination that was adopted by communist parties after the success of this tactic in Russia. Nor were the strictures on relations with other left-wing parties an outgrowth of earlier views. And in other areas, the revolution altered perceptions. The behavior of the Russian bourgeoisie was different from that predicted by Marxism, and later perceptions followed the revolutionary, rather than the Marxist, heritage.

Further evidence against spuriousness is provided by other examples. Dennis Austin and Scott Thompson have noted the impact of the pre-independence conflicts within Ghana on Nkrumah's later perceptions of opponents and choice of strategies. The most obstinate foe with which Nkrumah had had to contend in the fight for independence was not Britain, but the Ashanti tribesmen, who demanded a federal system.

[86] *Ibid.*, p. 21.

It was a power struggle in which, as Austin suggests, the position on the central question of federalism could as easily have been reversed. But Nkrumah thenceforth equated federalism with feudalism, bourgeois reaction, and tribalism. . . . He looked back to the three years of effort . . . which had brought him domestic power and assumed he could repeat this process on that broader map of Africa that had always been his focus. But [when] obstacles appeared . . . he later equated obstinate heads of states, who would not [join a unified African government and] surrender their "petty national sovereignty" (as he called it) with Ashanti chiefs.[87]

That the association between Nkrumah's opponents and federalism was fortuitous lends credence to the conclusion that this experience influenced Nkrumah, rather than merely reflecting already deep-seated views. Although Nkrumah probably would have favored close cooperation among the African states had his earlier experiences been different, it seems unlikely that he otherwise would have opposed proposals that fell short of complete unification. The vehemence with which he held to his position and his refusal to recognize the overwhelming strength of the opposition also can be traced to his earlier triumph over formidable adversaries.

Similarly, the perceptions and strategies of leaders of Communist China have been influenced by the way they achieved success in their own struggle for power. The narrow range of revolutionary tactics supported in other countries is not required by a Marxist or Chinese heritage nor is it clearly the most appropriate for the varied contexts for which it has been prescribed.

There is no *a priori* reason why revolutionary war should be guerrilla or, for that matter, why it should be centered in the countryside. Further, is it not permissible to take part in a united front which the Communist party does not lead? This reluctance has kept local Communist parties out of the mainstream of politics in many developing countries. Finally, is it really necessary to find latter-day actors [in world politics] analogous to the characters present in the Chinese drama [as Lin Piao did in his well-known article in September 1965]? Does this not severely limit the freedom of local revolutionaries to think and act in terms of the local situation, as they must do, if they are to be successful?[88]

[87] Scott Thompson, *Ghana's Foreign Policy* (Princeton: Princeton University Press, 1969), p. 5; Dennis Austin, *Politics in Ghana* (London: Oxford University Press, 1969), pp. 279-81, 323-27.

[88] Thomas Robinson, "Peking's Revolutionary Strategy in the Developing World: The Failures of Success," *Annals of the American Academy of Political and Social Science* 386 (November 1969), 77. Also see Tang Tsou and Morton Halperin, "Mao Tse-tung's Revolutionary Strategy and Peking's International

Almost 200 years after their revolution, American decision-makers are predisposed to see this past as providing the model for diverse circumstances. For example, American support for a united Europe after World War II was partially rooted in the inherited memories of its own regional cooperation. Indeed in explaining their support for European integration, Americans often pointed to their history as showing unification to be both possible and valuable. Of course it can be argued that this was a mere rationalization for more "realistic" motives. But this explanation would be more convincing were it not so hard to show that a united Europe would indeed further "hard-headed" American interests and were it not so easy to point to costs and dangers (e.g. discrimination against American goods, the development of a neutralist foreign policy). Realism cannot explain President Roosevelt's letter to Winston Churchill in 1942 in which he argued that the Articles of Confederation contained a valuable lesson for British India: "Perhaps some such method, with its analogy to the problems and travails of the United States from 1783 to 1789, might cause the people of India to forget past hard feelings, and to become more loyal to the British Empire, and to emphasize the danger of domination by the Japanese, and the advantages of peaceful evolution as contrasted with revolutionary chaos." Not surprisingly, Churchill called this "an act of madness." Even were the British to have tolerated American meddling in the Empire, it is hard to see why a "realistic" Roosevelt would have expected this analogy to be persuasive.[89]

THE LAST WAR

The only thing as important for a nation as its revolution is its last major war. Because of the dramatic and pervasive nature of a war and its consequences, the experiences associated with it—the diplomacy that preceded it, the methods of fighting it, the alliances that were formed, and the way the war was terminated—will deeply influence the perceptual predispositions of most citizens. Major wars so dominate the life of the country that in a real sense all those old enough to remember it will have experienced it firsthand. Thus, members of the British cabinet who were not active in politics before World War II, as well as those who had

---

Behavior," *American Political Science Review* 59 (March 1965), 80-99, and Alexander Dallin and George Breslauer, *Political Terror in Communist Systems* (Stanford: Stanford University Press, 1970), p. 70.

[89] Quoted in Robert Sherwood, *Roosevelt and Hopkins* (New York: Harper and Brothers, 1948), p. 511; quoted in Maxwell Schoenfeld, *The War Ministry of Winston Churchill* (Ames: Iowa State University Press, 1972), p. 180. Also see Lynn Davis, *The Cold War Begins* (Princeton: Princeton University Press, 1974), pp. 385-86. For similar examples in the perception of statesmen of other countries, see David Vital, "Czechoslovakia and the Powers, September 1938," in Hans Gatzke, ed., *European Diplomacy Between the Two Wars, 1919-1939* (Chicago: Quadrangle, 1972), p. 217; Samuel Huntington, *The Soldier and the State* (Cambridge, Mass.: The Belknap Press of Harvard University Press, 1967), p. 47.

served during that period, applied the appeasement model to relations with Nasser. And the diplomacy of this period had important enough consequences for the United States, which was not an active participant, to make the Munich analogy at least as salient for this country as for Britain and France.

What was believed to have caused the last war will be considered likely to cause the next one. The impact of the two world wars on later perceptions shows that as generals are prepared to fight the last war, diplomats are prepared to avoid it. The League of Nations was constructed to deal with the kinds of events that were believed to have been responsible for the preceding conflict. Thus because the First World War had seemed to erupt so suddenly, much attention was paid to mechanisms for enforcing a "cooling off" period. But this did not help keep the peace in the 1930s. "The Italo-Abbyssinian dispute, which ended in war in October 1935, began in December 1934. The cooling-off procedures which occupied the intervening months played into Italy's hands because she had no intention of being 'cooled off' and used those months to hot up her preparations for war. Only when the war itself began was the League's machinery galvanized into real action against the aggressor."[90] More generally, appeasement in the 1930s grew out of the belief that World War I could have been avoided by intelligent and conciliatory diplomacy. Thus statesmen were especially alert to the danger of spirals of hostility and were highly sensitive to the possibility that incompatibility might be illusory. Similarly, beliefs about the origins of the Second World War made the West more apt to see Russia and China as aggressors to whom few concessions could safely be made. Western leaders would have been even quicker to see Russia as aggressive had the period following the end of the First World War been marked by fierce conflict between the former allies instead of a resurgence of the threat from the defeated enemy. The Congress of Vienna had occurred too long before to shape decision-makers' perceptions.

The American perception of the nature of the communist threat has similarly shifted with the most recent armed conflict. The Second World War contributed to a perceptual sensitivity to all-out attack. Perceptual thresholds were altered by the Korean War, which led to the expectation that limited wars would probably recur and would resemble Korea in their causes and their military manifestations. So Dulles and others concluded that the American alliance system had to be expanded to reduce the risk that the communists would misjudge American commitments. And many military officers not only felt that the armies of our Asian allies should be trained to repel conventional attacks but held to this view in the face of mounting guerrilla warfare in South Vietnam. After the

[90] Frank Hardie, *The Abyssinian Crisis* (London: B. T. Batsford, 1974), p. 73.

nature of this latest war became unmistakable, it became the model for the future. And ambiguous cases—e.g. the conflict in Cambodia—were seen as guerrilla warfare and subversion when, if they had occurred in the 1950s, they would have been considered a conventional invasion, resembling Korea.

Specific lessons are also drawn from the most recent war. For example, the 1939 Soviet demand for a naval base on the northern shore of the Gulf of Finland was rooted in the memory of the battles of the Russian Civil War. Stalin told the Finns that the winner of World War II "will sail into the Gulf of Finland. Yudenitch attacked along the Gulf, and later the British did the same." The tsars, he pointed out, had had a base at Porkkala to close the gulf to enemy warships. The Soviet Union had the same need. But Stalin did not examine the reasons why it had been advantageous to have guns on both sides of the gulf to see if changes in circumstances and technology had altered the tactics of attack and defense. Even though the Finns pointed out that the gulf was too narrow to permit a naval assault under modern conditions as long as either shore was defended, the Soviets would not budge. Because the French expected World War I to be short, they sent as many men as possible to the front and left few behind for industrial production. Because they believed in the supremacy of the offensive, they launched ill-prepared attacks. In the interwar years they altered their military doctrine and army structure to correct the earlier deficiencies, and so produced a force that was ill-equipped for the changed circumstances. Similarly, because the American army was all in one place in the First World War, the interwar plans for the relations between Washington and the field "assumed a major effort in a main theatre—a single front—overseas. Significantly, there was no thought of huge forces deployed in a global war waged in many theatres." And because France had not fallen in World War I, until June 1940 "army planners continued to think in terms of such dock facilities as those of Cherbourg and Le Havre for the easy transfer of America's land power onto the European continent." Finally, because Nazi Germany was seen not only as an unprovoked aggressor but as initially weak and easy to have stopped had the Allies acted quickly, soldiers and diplomats learned not only that they must stand firm but that it is possible and advantageous to respond before the offender reaches full strength. Thus the United States air force's postwar plans stressed the need for military force "capable of immediate action to forestall any armed threat to this country before it gains momentum."[91]

---

[91] Jakobson, *The Diplomacy of the Winter War*, p. 117. (Although the war proved the Finns to have been correct, this did not seem to impress the Russians, who in 1945 demanded and obtained Porkkala. At this time they may not have

Only if the next confrontation is likely to resemble the last will this effect aid decision-making. It is reasonable for states to adopt many of the military tactics and forms of organization displayed by the winner in the most recent war, but for many basic questions—e.g. the intentions of other actors, the costs and benefits of alliances, the possibilities of staying neutral—there usually is no reason why the recent past will be a better guide than the remote past or why what happened to one's state will be more informative than what happened to others. Before 1914 statesmen realized that overestimating others' hostility could lead to an unnecessary war. Before 1939 statesmen knew that it was not wise to make concessions to a leader who sought to overthrow the system. And unless one believes that the recent event represents a trend (e.g. that Hitler's behavior not only shows the danger of appeasement but also demonstrates that modern conditions breed aggressive states), the occurrence of another instance of a well-known phenomenon should not call for a large change in the decision-maker's estimate of the probability of such a situation recurring. But it does produce drastic changes, and thereby often decreases the accuracy of later perceptions.

It is usually the last major war, rather than earlier ones, that has most impact because major wars rarely come more than once a generation and most people have firsthand memories of only the most recent one. Earlier wars have only been read about and so will not create such powerful predispositions. When wars occur more frequently and the person remembers not only the lessons of the last one but the contradicting lessons of the conflict that occurred early in his adulthood, the impact of both will be diluted.[92] As we will discuss in the next section, the greater the number of analogies available to the person, the less will be the influence of each individual event. This means that the perceptions of elder statesmen will usually be less influenced by the most recent war than will those of young decision-makers, and the older leaders will therefore be less likely

---

cared about the strategic value of the base, wanting only to be in a good position to influence Finnish internal politics. Or they may still have been thinking in terms of 1918 technology and tactics.) Richard Challener, *The French Theory of the Nation in Arms* (New York: Columbia University Press, 1955), pp. 257-77; Judith Hughes, *To the Maginot Line* (Cambridge, Mass.: Harvard University Press, 1971), pp. 79-81, 109-10; Maurice Matloff, "The American Approach to War, 1919-1945," in Howard, ed., *Theory and Practice of War*, p. 224; Isely and Crowl, *The U.S. Marines and Amphibious War*, p. 3; Perry McCoy Smith, *The Air Force Plans for Peace* (Baltimore: Johns Hopkins Press, 1970), p. 46. For a similar example see Alan Cassels, *Mussolini's Early Diplomacy* (Princeton: Princeton University Press, 1970), pp. 350-53.

[92] For a review of some of the experimental literature on the persistence of painfully learned lessons, see Justin Aronfreed, *Conduct and Conscience* (New York: Academic Press, 1968), pp. 20-21, and Ashby, *Design for a Brain* (2nd ed., Chapman and Hall, 1970), p. 216.

to advocate policies that are based on lessons of the immediate past. Their presence will then often be a moderating influence.

Range of Available Alternative Analogies

The final variable that influences the degree to which an event will shape later perceptions is the presence or absence of alternative analogies (i.e. the extent of knowledge of different kinds of actors and situations). Often without being fully aware of it, scientists and decision-makers have before them a wider or narrower array of alternative models. If narrower, data are more apt to be automatically interpreted in one way. Students of visual perception and of the philosophy of science make similar arguments. Norwood Hanson notes: "Suppose no alternative systems of concepts were available with which to describe and explain a type of phenomenon; the scientist would then have but one way of thinking about the subject-matter." It would then always make sense to adjust the data to the theory because the latter could not be abandoned.[93] A decision-maker whose conceptual framework is dominated by a few categories will fit events into them quickly and on the basis of little information. On the other hand, those who are familiar with multiple possibilities will be less influenced by any single historical case. This means that decision-makers who are amateurs, who have participated in only a few types of situations, or whose nations have experienced a relatively short period of important international politics will be especially influenced by a few dominating analogies. Thus American decision-makers are apt to see situations in terms of the relatively few major international events that have been important for their country and to be slow to appreciate

[93] Norwood Hanson, *Patterns of Discovery* (Cambridge: Cambridge University Press, 1965), p. 103. Also see Jerome Bruner, "On Perceptual Readiness," 136 and Roberta Wohlstetter, *Pearl Harbor: Warning and Decision* (Stanford: Stanford University Press, 1962), p. 302. Robin Horton argues that the awareness of alternative ways of seeing the world distinguishes scientifically oriented or "open" cultures from traditional or "closed" ones. He is thereby able to explain the resistance to change of African traditional thought: An "important consequence of lack of awareness of alternatives is vividly illustrated by the reaction of an Ijo man to a missionary who told him to throw away his old gods. He said: 'Does your God really want us to climb to the top of a tall palm tree, then take off our hands and let ourselves fall?'" For the same reason, the frequent failures of witch doctors or diviners do not induce these people to question their faith. "In these traditional cultures, questioning of the beliefs on which divining is based and weighing up of successes against failures are just not among the paths that thought can take. They are blocked paths because the thinkers involved are victims of the closed predicament. For the established beliefs have an absolute validity, and any threat to such beliefs is a horrific threat of chaos. Who is going to jump from the cosmic palm tree when there is no hope of another perch to swing to?" ("African Traditional Thought and Western Science," Part Two, *Africa* 37 [April 1967], 156, 168.)

the variety of goals and strategies that other actors can pursue.[94] Perhaps their participation in three wars within little more than a generation will increase the variety of perspectives that Americans are likely to bring to bear on future conflicts.

WHAT LESSONS DO PEOPLE LEARN?

Even if we have discovered how people learn and what events people learn most from, we have not discussed what lessons will be drawn. People may learn from personal experience, or from the last war, but what will they learn? To argue that the conclusions drawn from traumatic events will be oversimplified and overgeneralized still leaves open some of the content of these conclusions. Although we cannot fill these gaps completely, we can find several different kinds of lessons that are common.

Impact of Constant Factors

First, people living in a period characterized by a particular kind of actor will tend to see a new and different one as though it fit the familiar pattern. This perceptual readiness helps the decision-maker to reach better decisions if the original conditions continue to be present, but makes it harder for him to recognize and cope with change. Thus John Fairbank notes that China's well-developed tribute system made her "adjustment to the West much more difficult than it might otherwise have been. If the British barbarians had been an entirely unprecedented phenomenon in Chinese life, the Manchu rulers of the day might easily have formed a fresh and realistic view of them." Indeed because the Chinese totally dominated their international environment, they did not know of—and could not conceive of—relations between equal powers. Prior to the Opium War when a British representative in Canton, in the course of trying to negotiate with a Chinese official, spoke of the need "to settle the differences between the 'two nations' peacefully, [the Chinese official] is said to have been puzzled by the term 'two nations,' which he mistook for England and the United States." And one reason why people were slow to recognize the threat posed by Napoleon was that previous events had accustomed statesmen to actors who sought only to modify the existing system, not overthrow it.[95]

[94] See, for example, William W. Kaufmann, "Two American Ambassadors: Bullitt and Kennedy," in Gordon Craig and Felix Gilbert, eds., *The Diplomats* (Princeton: Princeton University Press, 1953), p. 654, and Gaddis Smith, *American Diplomacy During the Second World War* (New York: Wiley, 1965), p. 15.

[95] John Fairbank, *Trade and Diplomacy on the China Coast* (Stanford: Stanford University Press, 1964), p. 7; Immanuel C. Y. Hsu, *China's Entrance into*

In the same way, if an actor's environment consistently presents him with certain problems and opportunities, he will be predisposed to see later situations as fitting the earlier pattern. A major reason why American officials approved the 1972 grain deal with the Soviet Union without considering the possibility of the unfortunate effects that did, in fact, follow, was that for all their lives the problem had been how to control farm production and dispose of surplus crops. Because excess demand had never forced prices higher than they wanted, they were insensitive to this danger. Similarly, the failure of the U.S. Economic Development Administration's program in Oakland is in part explained by the fact that the agency's previous experience was in geographically isolated regions such as Appalachia where any jobs that were created went to the target group. Oakland, however, was surrounded by a mobile, skilled population. So the problem was to see that any new jobs were filled by the "hard core" unemployed. But because EDA officials had always operated in environments like Appalachia, they did not see the difference between the two kinds of regions and so applied an inappropriate strategy. For the same reasons, a state that has often been the object of hostile coalitions can be expected to see even innocent conferences among her neighbors as presaging an attack. An actor who has frequently made gains against divided opponents will perceive ambiguous evidence as indicating that a bold policy will again succeed. Thus Britain's history partially explains her failure to anticipate the German attack on Norway in 1940. Accustomed to taking initiative in opening new fronts—especially those requiring use of the seas—Britain was not ready to see ambiguous evidence as indicating that Germany was preparing such a coup.[96]

The influence of a constant historical context is strikingly revealed by the perceptions of decision-makers of countries whose national security problems have been alleviated by exceptionally propitious conditions. Until recently, her physical separation from strong neighbors gave the United States, and to a lesser extent Great Britain, the luxury of relative invulnerability. These powers were therefore able to maintain small armies, avoid entangling alliances, view foreign policy more in terms of freedom of choice and morality than of compulsion and *raison d'état*, and react to foreign threats only in their later, and more clear, stages of development.[97] But this happy circumstance had several less fortunate

---

the Family of Nations (Cambridge, Mass.: Harvard University Press, 1960), p. 13; Henry Kissinger, *A World Restored* (New York: Grosset and Dunlap, 1964), pp. 2-3.

[96] Jeffrey Pressman and Aaron Wildavsky, *Implementation* (Berkeley and Los Angeles: University of California Press, 1974), pp. 149-58; Holst, "Surprise, Signals and Reaction," p. 35.

[97] Arnold Wolfers, *Discord and Collaboration* (Baltimore: Johns Hopkins Press,

effects on British and American perceptions. First, to the extent that these powers did not realize that their interests and perceptions were shaped by their unusual geographical position, they could not understand why others felt that their security required extreme suspiciousness and quick reaction to distant or uncertain threats. In other words, the United States and Britain did not understand fully the implications of international anarchy and the security dilemma. This may also have contributed to the American tendency to categorize others as completely friendly or completely hostile, since they could not see limited hostility as a natural product of the international system.

Second, and related to this, when these powers saw other states taking actions that threatened them, they were less apt to give full consideration to the possibility that the other was motivated by a desire to safeguard its own security. Furthermore, Britain and the United States seem even less sensitive than other nations to the risk that their own actions will inadvertently endanger others' security. As we noted earlier, Britain did not fully realize that, in reaching an entente with France in 1904 and fulfilling (and more than fulfilling) the resulting obligations, she was harming legitimate German interests. She therefore viewed the resulting German reactions as unprovoked and beyond the pale of normal statecraft.[98]

Finally, when circumstances changed and physical isolation no longer guaranteed security, it took a while for those states to perceive the change. Britain was slow to abandon her "splendid isolation," and America withdrew from much of world politics after World War I and might have done so again after World War II had not Soviet behavior been so precipitous and the Munich analogy so strong.[99]

1962), pp. 233-51. Also see Felix Gross, *Foreign Policy Analysis* (New York: Philosophical Library, 1954), pp. 62-63. These propositions apply less to Britain than to the United States partly because the former sacrificed many of the security advantages of being an insular power when it acquired a colonial empire. For the argument that scholars have exaggerated the degree to which America was free from threats to her national security in the nineteenth century, see William Goetzmann, *When the Eagle Screamed: The Romantic Horizon in American Diplomacy, 1800-1860* (New York: Wiley, 1966).

[98] George Monger, *The End of Isolation* (London: Nelson and Sons, 1963), pp. 132-61. For a further discussion of this case, see Jervis, *The Logic of Images in International Relations* (Princeton: Princeton University Press, 1970), pp. 110-12.

[99] When these countries did become aware of the changed circumstances they felt their insecurity more acutely than states accustomed to living in moderate peril. (See Wolfers, *Discord and Collaboration*, p. 151.) The arguments about American policy since 1945 are well-known, although of course the case is far from proven. Less familiar is the degree to which the British felt menaced by Germany in the early twentieth century and refused to take actions that might offend France. Even though ending the entente does not seem to have been a

Lessons about Specific Actors

An actor's contact with another on an important issue can establish so firm an image of him that it will be very hard to dislodge. The actor will therefore be misled if this piece of the other's behavior constitutes a biased sample or if, even though the inferences were correct at the time they are drawn, the other later changes. This is a manifestation of the problem of premature cognitive closure discussed in Chapter 4. Hypotheses are formed early and influence the interpretation of subsequent information. The problem is compounded when observers overestimate the importance of the other's internal characteristics and predispositions in determining his behavior and concomitantly underestimate the influence of the context in which the other is acting.[100] This means that images become overgeneralized as expectations established from behavior in one set of circumstances are carried over into quite different situations. Thus because Italy had joined the Allied side in World War I, the French in the 1920s underestimated Mussolini's hostility and believed that "sooner or later Italy would have to turn to France for protection against pan-Germanism."[101]

This kind of overgeneralization largely explains the mistrust of Bismarck in the years following the series of wars he initiated to unify Germany. "The astute diplomacy or, depending on the point of view, the trickery, of Bismarck in the sixties . . . left its mark. No one wished to be duped again as Palmerston and Russell had been duped; suspicious caution marked every negotiation with Berlin." On several occasions Europe's statesmen believed Bismarck to be planning aggression when in fact he sought to preserve the status quo. Of course the evidence was ambiguous, especially since Bismarck's tactics changed less than his aims.[102] But that his maneuvering was taken as indicating aggressiveness even though he had an obvious stake in the status quo is largely attributable to the impact of Bismarck's earlier actions. Another way of putting this is to note that the inferences drawn from Bismarck's pre-1870 behavior were superficial. What was one part of Bismarck's pattern of

reasonable option for France, Britain was so worried about that possibility that she carefully avoided any conciliatory gestures toward Germany.

It is difficult, however, to separate the element of perceptual sensitivity (i.e. the degree to which previously protected actors perceive high threat when more experienced actors do not) from the element of toleration of perceived threat (i.e. the extent to which a previously protected actor is willing to pay a higher price than would an experienced one to cope with a perceived threat of a given magnitude).

[100] See, for example, Fritz Heider, "Social Perception and Phenomenal Causality," *Psychological Review* 51 (1944), 361-62; Gustav Ichheiser, *Appearances and Realities* (San Francisco: Jossey-Bass, 1970), pp. 49-59.

[101] Cassels, *Mussolini's Early Diplomacy*, p. 374.

[102] Raymond Sontag, *Germany and England* (New York: Russell and Russell, 1964), p. 94.

behavior (i.e. the willingness to launch aggressive wars) was seen as a permanent characteristic because observers did not realize that the wars were a means to an end—the unification of Germany—and that once this goal was reached the aggressive behavior, being no longer appropriate, would be discontinued.

More generally, states that have been expansionist under one set of circumstances or leaders are likely to be seen as posing a continuing threat. The state's aggressiveness will be seen as rooted in factors such as geography and national character that change slowly, if at all. Sometimes, of course, this conclusion will be correct. But it is rarely the product of considered judgment, and there is usually little effort to ask exactly why the other was aggressive and to determine the degree to which this behavior was caused by short-term conditions that are not likely to be present in later years.

In some cases the state will benefit from the fact that a series of encounters can establish the perceptual predispositions held by others. If images of resolve and of friendship are overgeneralized, the actor who has stood firm or been friendly in one case will gain the advantages of having others expect this kind of behavior from him in other contexts.

Reactions to Failure

A third type of common lesson is to avoid policies that have failed in the immediate past. Though we cannot predict what alternative policies will be followed, what usually happens is that high and even medium-level goals are not altered but tactics that are the opposite of these that failed are tried.[103] At times this is sensible, for example when the modernization of military organization and equipment is spurred by defeat in war. But in most political cases, insufficient attention is paid to whether alternative policies would have worked better in the past and whether the new situation resembles the old one. As a result of this kind of overgeneralized learning Santayana's maxim can be turned on its head: "Those who remember the past are condemned to make the opposite mistakes."

Henry Kissinger has written that

> [the Austrian] Emperor Franz was one of those mediocrities who believed that the lesson of experience resides in mechanical remem-

---

[103] Two problems should be noted. First, we cannot completely specify how a person decides, even after the fact, that a policy has failed. For example, what determined when—and whether—a person decided that America's policy in Vietnam was a failure? Second, sometimes people attribute a policy's failure not to its inherent flaws but to its not having received a fair trial. In this case they will argue that the policy should be repeated, only in a more thoroughgoing manner, when the next occasion arises. This belief will occur when: 1) the original policy is rooted in important values; 2) the policy was implemented half-heartedly or halted soon in the initial application; or 3) there were obstacles in the original case that could be singled out as important and nonrecurring.

brance. . . . [H]is notion of causality was succession in time. Because the centralizing tendencies of his predecessor, Joseph II, had led to civil strife, all reform was to be avoided. Because the attempt to rally the people had not succeeded in achieving victory in 1809, no reliance whatever was to be placed on popular support.[104]

One reason why many decision-makers more skilled than the emperor behave similarly is that the explicit decision to avoid strategies that have failed is coupled with an increased readiness to perceive a wide range of situations as resembling the ones that have previously caused the state the most trouble. Once actors believe that they are in a similar situation, they naturally and often wisely adopt a policy different from the one that recently led to disaster. The error then resides in the perceptual stage of the decision-making process. For example,

> In September, 1701, James II [of England] died, and, in defiance of the Treaty of Ryswick, his son was recognized by Louis [XIV of France] as King of England, Scotland, and Ireland. The reason for this step is not far to seek: French diplomacy had blundered badly in 1660, [when Charles II was restored to the English throne], and Louis did not want to be caught napping by a second Stuart restoration. This time the returned monarch should have cause to be grateful to France.[105]

But the circumstances of 1701 were very different from those of 1660, and there was no support for James II, as Louis probably would have recognized had he not been especially alert to the earlier type of situation.

Similarly, the failures of American peacemaking after World War I influenced perceptions and policies during the next war. Because the Allies had entered into secret agreements during the First World War and the postwar world had proved to be unstable, it was believed that such agreements should be shunned.[106] After the first conflict, the United States withdrew from active maintenance of the peace and President Roosevelt thought this a major cause of the renewal of the fighting; as a result he was preoccupied with building a domestic coalition that

---

[104] Kissinger, *A World Restored*, p. 211.

[105] Charles Petrie, *Earlier Diplomatic History* (London: Hollis and Carter, 1949), pp. 222-23.

[106] Feis, "Some Notes on Historical Record-Keeping," p. 114; Davis, *The Cold War Begins*, pp. 370, 384. But some officials drew the opposite conclusions from the earlier experience. Assistant Secretary of State Berle argued that "if we want to have anything to say about postwar settlement, we had better start now. Otherwise, we shall find, as President Wilson did, that there were all kinds of commitments which we shall be invited to respect; and we shall not be able to break the solid front any more than we were at Versailles." (Quoted in *ibid.*, p. 12.)

would support postwar involvement. The Allies also remembered all too well that they had previously failed to demonstrate to the German people that their army had been smashed, thus allowing the "stab in the back" myth to flourish. This error would not be repeated. As President Roosevelt said in the summer of 1944: "Practically all Germans deny the fact they surrendered in the last war, but this time they are going to know it. And so are the Japs." More generally, it was believed that it had been a mistake to leave the central sources of German power untouched. "The main inspiration behind the [Allied unconditional surrender] policy was the passionate belief that the more completely the enemy was stripped of power at the end of hostilities, the more securely peace would be established." This policy was supported by the desire to do the reverse of another aspect of the policy that had failed before: Germany's grievances had been fed by her belief that she had been cheated by being "tricked into an armistice on the basis of conditions [i.e. Wilson's 14 points] that were then violated." Thus commitments to the Axis were to be avoided so that there would be nothing "that might justify, later on, a revisionist claim on the part of the defeated nation or give another rabble-rouser the opportunity to charge the victors with going back on their word."[107]

Even the details of the plans for dealing with a defeated Germany followed the obvious alternative to the failed policies of 1918:

Then, the Allies had asked that war criminals be punished but had left it to German courts to hear the cases, and the accused parties had all been freed or let off lightly. This time arrangements were made for their trial by the victors. Then, the Allies had stipulated that the general staff be disbanded and the armed forces kept at low levels, and the Germans had circumvented these terms. Now the Allies were to break up the high command and themselves ensure Germany's demilitarization. After World War I the Allies had sought to limit Germany's capacity for war by demanding large reparations payments. The Germans had resisted, defaulted, and eventually rebuilt their armaments industries. This time the Allies were to dismantle factories and themselves determine the character and level of German industrial output.[108]

[107] Quoted in John Gaddis, *The United States and the Origins of the Cold War, 1941-1947* (New York: Columbia University Press, 1972), p. 9; Paul Kecskemeti, *Strategic Surrender* (New York: Atheneum, 1964), p. 237; Smith, *American Diplomacy During the Second World War*, p. 56; Hans Rothsfels, "The German Resistance in Its International Aspects," in A. O. Sarkissian, ed., *Studies in Diplomatic History in Honor of G.P. Gooch* (London: Longmans, 1961), p. 361. Kecskemeti also notes that the opponents of unconditional surrender, as well as its advocates, thought in terms that were too strongly colored by the World War I experience.

[108] Ernest May, *"Lessons" of the Past* (New York: Oxford University Press, 1973), p. 8.

Even if the actors were correct in their beliefs about the causes of the previous failure, they too quickly assumed that the contemporary situation resembled the past one so closely that the same sequence would occur. Was there any reason for the United States to have expected a repetition of the pattern in which the power defeated in the last war would be most apt to start the next one? Only if this were true was it sensible to lean so heavily on the lessons of the World War I settlement. If the danger was a falling out among the former allies, then other events and other lessons were relevant. Even if the decision-makers had grounds for believing that Germany was the main potential enemy, was there any justification for expecting that the details of the new situation would match the earlier one?

Nothing Fails Like Success

A fourth kind of lesson is the reverse of the one just discussed. When a policy has brought notable success, actors are likely to apply it to a range of later situations. Seeing these cases as resembling the past one, the actor will believe that they are amenable to the policy that worked previously. But when insufficient attention is paid to the reasons why the policy worked in the past, the new situation will not be scrutinized to see if it has the attributes that made the earlier success possible. Because the actor is apt to overestimate the degree to which his policy was responsible for the earlier success, as we discussed above, he will be especially insensitive to variation in the situation.

"Nothing fails like success," as one commentator has noted. An instance was recorded by Thucydides, and examples have continued to accumulate. One reason why Japan believed that limited war with the United States was possible in 1941 was that earlier in the century she had seen Russia settle for a limited defeat rather than engage in a long and costly struggle to regain lost territory and influence. Annette Baker Fox has pointed out that "Norway's success in remaining non-belligerent though pro-Allied [in the First World War] gave the Norwegians confidence that their country could . . . stay out of" World War II. If the attempt to use exiles to overthrow Arbenz in Guatemala in 1954 had failed, would the CIA have proposed a similar plan for the Bay of Pigs in 1961? And were the situations similar enough to have warranted this influence? The same pattern can be found outside of politics. A company that is making high profits will be slow to detect changes in the market that call for modifications of its behavior. Thus the success of the Model T delayed Henry Ford's recognition of the trend of consumer preferences toward "comfort, styling and performance," and not until sales fell disastrously did Ford take measures to cope with the new situation. Even technical improvements were long shunned.[109]

The unfortunate effects of this way of learning are magnified because successful policies often alter the environment in ways that make their repetition unwise. Others are apt to change their positions to thwart new attempts by the first state or to be willing to pay high costs to avoid another defeat, especially if the first state's actions provided information that made them see greater dangers in allowing the state to succeed again. But an actor who is preoccupied with his successful strategy will be slow to realize that his success has undermined the conditions that made it possible. The origins of both world wars provide examples of this process. Hitler felt that Britain and France would not fight for Poland; they had not fought before, when Germany was weaker. But he failed to see that his opponents, who he said showed themselves to be "little worms" at Munich, would now behave differently because the series of German triumphs had convinced them that German ambitions were unlimited. And one of the reasons why Austria was willing to stand firm in July 1914 was that Russia had twice retreated in the face of Austrian ultimata, most recently in the Balkan crisis of the previous year. "Vienna concluded it would be safe to repeat the performance."[110] It was not. The Austrian victories had made Russia more anxious to win the next encounter and had led Britain and France to believe that they might lose Russian friendship unless they altered their policy and supported Russia in the Balkans.

ALTERNATIVE EXPLANATIONS

Before we can be confident that an earlier success has been a cause of the later policy, we must examine two alternative explanations. First, the repetition of successes may be part of a wider pattern in which many policies are repeated, not because of the outcomes they are believed to produce, but because of the nature of the decision-making process. The

[109] William Inge, *Outspoken Essays*, First Series (London: Longmans, Green, 1923), p. 88; *The Peloponnesian Wars*, translated by Rex Warner (Baltimore: Penguin, 1954), p. 266; Nobutaka Ike, ed., *Japan's Decision for War* (Stanford: Stanford University Press, 1967), p. xxv; Fox, *The Power of Small States*, p. 81; Philip Selznick, *Leadership in Administration* (Evanston, Ill.: Row, Peterson, 1957), p. 109; John Jewkes, David Sawers, and Richard Stillerman, *The Sources of Invention* (2nd ed., New York: Norton, 1969), pp. 144-45. For an alternative argument stressing the role of bureaucratic politics, see Snyder and Diesing, *Systems, Bargains, Decisions*, Chapter 5.

[110] Raymond Sontag, *European Diplomatic History, 1871-1932* (New York: Appleton-Century-Crofts, 1933), p. 186. While later studies have downgraded Austria's role in the diplomatic maneuvering of July 1914 and placed greater responsibility on Germany's shoulders, the factor mentioned here still should not be ignored.

intellectual and political difficulties of deciding general lines of policy and the influence that reaching a tentative decision exerts on later perceptions of alternatives often explains why similar policies will be applied to a wide range of cases. Having once made the major effort of thinking through the probable consequences of a line of action, actors may later apply the policy without careful re-examination or a study of the new circumstances. This effect is unlikely if the initial policy was a failure, but can occur if the policy's impact was unclear or it was not implemented in the first place. Thus one historian notes the "extraordinary" similarity between the German planning during the Balkan crisis of 1912 and her policy in July 1914, and another points out that in the week before the war the Russian foreign minister "was merely reviving the scheme for partial mobilization already formulated" in the 1912 crisis.[111] These were not cases of repeating successes, nor is all the rigidity to be explained by the limited capacity of bureaucracies to respond to changed circumstances. Rather the decision-makers never saw a need for different plans because the initial decision made it more likely that other situations would be seen as calling for the same response. In general, only the most dramatic and obvious aspects of the case (e.g. a crisis in the Balkans) will be used to determine whether it is like the one for which the policy was originally designed.

Second, instead of the initial success causing the later repetition, both may be caused by the same independent variables—e.g. the objective situation, the decision-makers' operational code, or national style. For example, we should admit a rebuttal to our claim that the Japanese success in the Russo-Japanese War contributed to her willingness to attack the United States and Britain in 1941. "In describing the situation to the throne [in 1904], the Japanese Premier reportedly declared: 'Things have come to such a pass that our Empire cannot avoid fighting for the sake of the peace of the Orient.' Interestingly enough, Hideki Tojo and his colleagues were to use largely the same argument in their reports to the throne prior to the decision for war in 1941."[112] As this formulation implies, the reason may lie in the similarities in the strategic situation and the Japanese conception of the requirements of national survival. Similarly, it can be argued that the variables that explain Norway's decision to choose neutrality in World War I also explain her parallel policy at the start of World War II.

While we cannot disprove this contention in some cases, several points

[111] J.C.G. Röhl, "Von Muller and the Approach of War, 1911-1914," *Historical Journal* 12 (December 1969), 672; L.C.F. Turner, *Origins of the First World War* (New York: Norton, 1970), p. 91.

[112] Robert Butow, *Tojo and the Coming of the War* (Princeton: Princeton University Press, 1961), p. 9.

cast doubt on it as a general explanation. Sometimes the people who made the initial decisions are different from those who made the later ones. In these cases the idiosyncratic characteristics of the decision-makers cannot explain the common behavior. Often the ideological climate and domestic political system of the state change from the initial to the later events, thus eliminating another category of possible causes. Most importantly, the two objective situations usually have little in common. The differences between the United States in 1941 and Russia in 1904 and between the challenge to Scandinavian countries posed by World War I and by World War II seem great enough to render implausible the claim that the similarity of responses can be explained by the similarity of the stimuli. Although the decision-makers of the countries concerned saw the later situations as being like the earlier ones, these perceptions were not shared by those for whom the earlier events loomed less large (like decision-makers in other countries and later scholars). Furthermore, as we discussed above, when states do face similar situations—e.g. Sweden and Norway after World War II—the perceptions and policies will differ if the states' previous experiences have been different. Finally, the experiments discussed earlier show that previous success can alter perceptual thresholds.[113]

SUMMARY

Recent international history is a powerful source of beliefs about international relations and images of other countries. Events that are seen firsthand, that happen early in the person's adult life, and that affect him and his country have great impact on his later perceptual predispositions. While these events do in fact contain valuable information, the learning process is beset with three linked flaws that seriously affect the quality of decision-making. First, there is often little reason why those events that provide analogies should in fact be the best guides to the future. Why should the last war, rather than earlier ones, most closely resemble the contemporary situation? Why should what has happened to the decision-maker and his state be so much more relevant than the fates of others? Second, because outcomes are learned without careful attention to details of causation, lessons are superficial and overgeneralized. Analogies are applied to a wide range of events with little sensitivity to variations in the situation. Furthermore, people employ lessons taken from a major event to explain a general situation rather than trying to see what smaller and often less dramatic aspects of the past case can be used to help understand contemporary events. Third, decision-makers do not examine a

[113] See the experiments cited in chapter 4, footnotes 176-78.

variety of analogies before selecting the one that they believe sheds the most light on their situation. Instead, because of their predispositions, they see the present as like recent and dramatic events without carefully considering alternative models or the implications of this way of perceiving. They thereby fail to apply fully their intelligence to some of the most important questions they face.

APPENDIX: The Impact of Domestic Politics and Training on Perceptual Predispositions

Learning from Domestic Politics

Another important source of the predispositions that shape the images of other states is the decision-maker's own political system. From this he learns many of his most basic ideas about politics, ideas that often color his view of both international relations and others' internal systems. Our treatment of this subject will be much briefer than its importance calls for. The reasons for this are three. First, some of the analysis in the main body of this chapter applies here and need not be repeated. Second, few psychological theories provide much assistance. Third, the best evidence for propositions would involve comparisons of the perceptions of the same situation held by the leaders of different nations. Since these comparisons, like those needed for arguments about national style, are extremely hard to make, good evidence is short in supply. Without desiring to discourage others from exploring this general question, these considerations seem sufficient reason to limit the analysis here to a few broad lines of tentative argument.

George Kennan notes that "It has never occurred to most Americans that the political principles by which they themselves lived might have been historically conditioned and might not enjoy universal validity." William Kaufmann points out that Secretary of State Hull and many of his advisers saw the world as "peopled largely by foreign-speaking Americans."[1] This propensity, though, is not uniquely American. Often without realizing it, most decision-makers draw on their knowledge of their own domestic political systems in their efforts to understand others. Given the range and salience of what a person knows of his country's politics, it could hardly be otherwise. Especially for a statesman who rises to power through the political processes (as opposed to a career diplomat), domestic politics has supplied both his basic political concepts and the more detailed lessons about what strategies and tactics are appropriate to reach desired goals. Predispositions are most influenced by those domestic practices that are so deeply ingrained throughout the society that people do not realize the possibility of alternatives. These are most prevalent in homogeneous or isolated societies.

The framework within which American decision-makers see the world is conditioned by the fact that their country never had a social revolution. As Tocqueville realized, Americans were "born equal"—i.e. never had a feudal aristocracy that had to be overthrown by a bourgeois revo-

---

[1] George Kennan, *Soviet-American Relations, 1917-1920*, vol. 1. *Russia Leaves the War* (New York: Atheneum, 1967), p. 12; Kaufmann, "Two American Ambassadors," p. 654.

lution and thus also never developed a working-class revolutionary movement that in Europe grew out of this struggle. As Hartz puts it, "The absence of the experience of social revolution . . . in a whole series of specific ways . . . enters into our difficulty of communication with the rest of the world. We find it hard to understand Europe's 'social question' and hence tend to interpret even the democratic socialisms of Europe in terms of our own antiradical fetishism. We are not familiar with the deeper struggles of Asia and hence tend to interpret even reactionary regimes as 'democratic.' "[2]

Two related effects can be detected. First, Americans have difficulty understanding the nature and depths of social conflict abroad. This is Kennan's explanation for the failure of the Allied, and especially the American, statesmen "to picture to themselves the passions of the Russian civil war. . . . We represent . . . a society in which the manifestations of evil have been carefully buried and sublimated in the social behavior of people, as in their very consciousness. For this reason, probably, despite our widely traveled and outwardly cosmopolitan lives, the mainsprings of political behavior in such a country as Russia tend to remain concealed from our vision." Kennan similarly argues that one of the main mistakes of American policy during the civil war in China "was to underrate the depth of the inner political differences which racked that country."[3]

This view in turn partially accounts for the American underestimation of the difficulty that other countries have in establishing a democracy. Wilson and others "believed that a little persuasion and pressure could make real democracies out of even the strife torn states of Central America and the Caribbean," and that after three years of revolution, counterrevolution, and civil war, democracy could be established in Mexico by "a cease fire, free election, and a popularly chosen government that would govern constitutionally." One result of these perceptions was an underestimation of the costs and an overestimation of the gains involved in intervening in South America. Similarly, American leaders did not understand the indigenous obstacles to democracy in East Europe after World War II and so were further encouraged to resist Soviet pressures on these countries.[4]

Second, the United States tends to neglect the possibility that internal violence in other countries may further democratic values or be a prerequisite for long-term stability. Of course it can be argued that the

[2] *The Liberal Tradition in America* (New York: Harcourt, Brace, 1955), p. 306.

[3] Kennan, *Russia and the West under Lenin and Stalin* (New York: Mentor, 1962), pp. 142-43, 351. Also see Kennan, *Russia Leaves the War*, p. 148 and Hartz, *The Liberal Tradition in America*, p. 295.

[4] Julius Pratt, *Challenge and Rejection* (New York: Macmillan Co., 1967), pp. 87, 105; Davis, *The Cold War Begins*, pp. 385-87.

American aversion to violence abroad is based on its role as the defender of the international status quo and the calculation that the probable gains for democratic values following from such violence would be outweighed by considerations of national security. But Americans have felt that little good could come out of bloodshed in other countries during periods when national security was not a major concern (e.g. the opposition of Wilson and others to revolutions in Latin America). In contrasting the American view to the much greater French tolerance of revolutions and revolutionary regimes, Alfred Grosser notes that the roots of these outlooks go "back very far: The American Revolution was basically liberal—there was no Convention or French-style Terror. . . . The French have learned that the Terror does not necessarily last forever—and this may lead them to underestimate the horror of violence in the name of progress, but it likewise leads them to understand that change ought not necessarily to be judged according to a violence that might be only passing."[5]

When we move away from the impact of the state's ideology to more narrow aspects of its domestic system, little more than speculation is possible. Do statesmen in countries whose domestic politics are characterized by quiet compromises shun the use of force and extreme demands in international relations? Do leaders of states that are held together by coercion believe in the efficacy of international threats? If a decision-maker lives in a system where pragmatic bargaining is frowned upon, is he apt to follow a more rigid foreign policy? Will a nation that traditionally has had trouble controlling its military be prone to perceive a minor civil-military conflict in another state as a prelude to a military coup? Leites argues that "members of the French political class frequently act in the field of foreign affairs as if their foreign counterparts were so like themselves that the issue at stake could be treated as a domestic one." Kogan claims that Italy's "historic penchant for straddling alignments is not explained solely by Italy's weak position on the international scene. It was also a product of the 'transformist' character of domestic Italian politics, in which a change in position was common in the scramble for honors and perquisites."[6] These propositions are highly plausible. But they are yet to be supported by good evidence and careful comparisons.

One kind of detailed experience with one's domestic system—the role a person has played in domestic politics—does not seem to influence the decision-maker's perceptual predispositions. Do the perceptions of statesmen who have served as senators differ from those who have been

[5] *French Foreign Policy Under De Gaulle* (Boston: Little, Brown, 1967), p. 143.
[6] Nathan Leites, *On the Game of Politics in France* (Stanford: Stanford University Press, 1956), pp. 2, 131, 135; Norman Kogan, *The Politics of Italian Foreign Policy* (New York: Praeger, 1963), pp. 31-32.

governors or those who have not held elective office? Do southern politicians see other countries differently from northern politicians? Do members of the elite who have worked in the judiciary develop a special perspective? The expected differences do not appear in the comparisons we have made. If we had better data, some of these effects might be discovered. But it is also possible that any predispositions created by greater familiarity with one part of the system are overwhelmed by the impact of a broad knowledge of the domestic politics of one's country. In trying to understand the politics of other states, the concepts provided by the shared and generally accepted view of one's own system are apparently more useful than those provided by particular political experiences.

A different kind of effect does appear to be potent, however. When one believes that the other state has a general resemblance to one's own, there is a tendency to overestimate the degree of congruence between the structures, norms, and patterns of behavior of the two states. Statesmen in Britain and the United States realize that legislative-executive relations in the two countries are different because one has a presidential and the other a parliamentary system. But in areas where the differences are less obvious each side generalizes from its own domestic politics. Thus, as Richard Neustadt has shown, American and British decision-makers have tended to assume that the relative power of the departments in the other country is the same as it is in their own (e.g. Americans have underestimated the importance of the Treasury in Britain) and that the same internal rules prevail (e.g. the British defense minister assumed that if McNamara was powerful enough to prevail over the military services and cancel Skybolt, he was also powerful enough to see that his colleagues agreed to providing Britain with a substitute weapon).[7]

Training

A person's perceptual predispositions are influenced by his tasks and training. As Lord Salisbury noted: "If you believe the doctors, nothing is wholesome: if you believe the theologians, nothing is innocent: if you believe the soldiers, nothing is safe." Many of the experiments discussed in Chapter 4 show the impact of short-run training. One effect of more extensive training that teaches the person about the dangers, opportunities, and responsibilities associated with his job is revealed by an ingenious study of an actual job training program. When ambiguous pictures were shown to both beginning and advanced police-administration students, the latter perceived more scenes as violent than did the former. We cannot say which group perceived the pictures more accurately. The point is that training influenced perceptual predispositions. Thus policemen will be quicker to detect actual violence. But the cost is that, more

[7] *Alliance Politics* (New York: Columbia University Press, 1970), pp. 80-114.

often than untrained men, they will make the opposite error and see violence when it is not present and in those cases will act inappropriately.[8]

A striking parallel in foreign policy perceptions is revealed when the backgrounds of the appeasers in Britain are compared to their opponents'. Only one difference stands out: "A substantially higher percentage of the anti-appeasers (irrespective of class origins) had the kind of knowledge which comes from close acquaintance, mainly professional, with foreign affairs." Since members of the diplomatic corps are responsible for meeting threats before they grow to major proportions and are familiar with cases in which aggressive states were not recognized until very late, they may be prone to interpret ambiguous data as showing that others are aggressive. Thus rather than arguing that the professionals of the 1930s were more likely to make accurate judgments, it may be that they were more sensitive to the chance that others were aggressive, and they happened to be correct in this instance. Diplomats may then rarely mistake an aggressor for a status quo power, but may more frequently make the opposite error and see threats where they do not exist. In the years before World War I the permanent officials in the British Foreign Office were in the forefront of those who overestimated German aggressiveness. Similarly, William Kaufmann shows how the perceptions of Ambassador Joseph Kennedy were affected by his past:

> As befitted a former chairman of the Securities Exchange and Maritime Commissions, his primary interest lay in economic matters. . . . The revolutionary character of the Nazi regime was not a phenomenon that he could easily grasp. . . . It was far simpler, and more in accord with his own premises, to explain German aggressiveness in economic terms. The Third Reich was dissatisfied, authoritarian, and expansive largely because her economy was unsound.[9]

[8] Lord Salisbury, quoted in Samuel Huntington, *The Soldier and the State* (Cambridge, Mass.: Belknap Press of the Harvard University Press, 1967), p. 66; Hans Toch and Richard Schulte, "Readiness to Perceive Violence as a Result of Police Training," *British Journal of Psychology* 52 (November 1961), 392 (italics omitted). The authors oversimplify the problem when they claim that the policeman's perceptual sensitivity to violence "is highly functional. It permits the [policeman] to cope with otherwise improbable situations. . . . To the extent to which vocational training affects perception, it helps to accomplish its purpose. It increases the trainee's readiness to act in the sort of world he is likely to face." A balanced judgment requires consideration of the costs of incorrectly perceiving violence when it is not present.

It has also been shown that boys are more likely to perceive violence than are girls and that the propensity to perceive violence increases with age (at least until the age of 18—the oldest subjects used) for both sexes. This may be the result of variations in socialization and exposure to violence. See Marv Moore, "Aggression Themes in a Binocular Rivalry Situation," *Journal of Personality and Social Psychology* 3 (1966), 685-88.

[9] Donald Lammers, *Explaining Munich* (Stanford: Hoover Institution, Stanford University, 1966), p. 15; Kaufmann, "Two American Ambassadors," pp. 658-59.

CHAPTER SEVEN

Attitude Change

Bolivians' reaction to the report that the Gulf Oil Corporation had given a helicopter and large sums of money to General Barrientos, a very popular leader before his death:

"General Barrientos used the helicopter to serve the people."

"If Barrientos took all that money, he probably distributed it to peasants on his trips."

"I am outraged by attacks on the dead."[1]

INTRODUCTION

PREVIOUS chapters have stressed the tendency of people to maintain their images and beliefs in the face of discrepant information. This raises two related questions. First, when such information cannot be ignored, how is it reconciled with the prevailing views? Second, how are beliefs altered in response to new information? Some would argue as does Max Planck that "A new scientific truth does not triumph by convincing its opponents and making them see the light, but rather because its opponents eventually die, and a new generation grows up that is familiar with it." Proponents of an innovation, even one that does not alter the scientific paradigm or the structure of the organization, have found that a successful trial under rigorous conditions does not guarantee acceptance. If tests and new evidence are ineffective, coercion may fare no better. Even though the United States battered Japan's army, cut the flow of vital raw materials, and leveled her cities, "No major figure in Japanese ruling circles changed his mind about the desirability of war with the United States from the beginning of the war to the end. Those who wanted to begin the war remained opposed to surrender."[2]

[1] "Bolivians View Gulf Oil Maligning National Hero," *New York Times,* May 18, 1975.

[2] Planck is quoted in Warren Hagstrom, *The Scientific Community* (New York: Basic Books, 1965), p. 283 (also see Norman Storer, *The Social System of Science* [New York: Holt, Rinehart and Winston, 1966], pp. 120-22); for an example of resistance to technological innovation, see Harold Bowen on the opposition to the introduction of high-pressure, high-temperature boilers in the navy in the 1930s in

Although this extreme position serves the purpose of reminding us how much information people can reject or assimilate, it cannot be accepted. People do change their minds, even on questions that matter a great deal to them. While some scientists never accept a new paradigm, others are converted. Many innovations are adopted only after the opponents leave their positions of power, and some are never put into practice. But other skeptics are convinced, even at the cost of pride, face, and influence. The punishment of Japan referred to earlier changed the intensity of people's beliefs even if it did not make converts. If we consider views on waging war as forming a continuum from strongly in favor to strongly against, the presence of uniform movement in one direction is as significant as the absence of shifts over the midpoint. In other cases of war–peace decisions, statesmen have changed their minds, sometimes more than proportionately to alterations in the environment. This was the case when the German generals called for an armistice after the successful Allied attacks in the fall of 1918. In Japan the dissenters may have maintained their doubts even after the war began, but this was not true in Europe in World War I. In other cases that involve men's deepest interests and emotions we can even find changes that are best explained by the much-slighted process of persuasion, as Richard Hofstadter reminds us in his discussion of the debate over the ratification of the American Constitution.[3]

We need not ignore evidence from introspection—most readers have changed their opinions about the war in Vietnam. Indeed, in many cases changes have taken place in views about a wide range of matters not obviously connected with the war—e.g. the role of the president, United States' foreign policy toward Europe, United States' domestic priorities, and even Soviet foreign policy. We might also ask those people who argue that minds do not change how they reached that conclusion. If they once held a different view, what changed their opinion?

Since the extreme position cannot be sustained, the interesting questions remain. How do people treat discrepant information? When do they change their beliefs? How do they change? What do they change? What beliefs are especially resistant to discrepant information? To answer these questions we will start by drawing on attitude change literature,

---

Ships, Machinery, and Mossbacks (Princeton: Princeton University Press, 1954), pp. 70-73; Graham Allison and Morton Halperin, "Bureaucratic Politics," *World Politics* 24 (Supplement, Spring 1972), 66.

[3] See, for example, the discussion of the British decision to enter World War I in Cameron Hazlehurst, *Politicians at War* (London: Jonathan Cape, 1971), pp. 25-117; Richard Hofstadter, *The Progressive Historians* (New York: Knopf, 1968), p. 279. For examples of persuasion in international negotiations, see Paul Schroeder, *Metternich's Diplomacy at its Zenith* (New York: Greenwood, 1969), pp. 45-46, 55, 65, 71, 83.

which has found that people employ a variety of mechanisms to cope with information that contradicts their beliefs. It is only a first step to list these mechanisms, but unfortunately, but not surprisingly, research is less advanced on "the major unresolved question in balance theory: the question of what determines the particular mechanism that a person chooses, out of a range of possibilities available to him in a given situation, in order to restore balance or reduce dissonance."[4] Here we will present the mechanisms in the order in which they are apt to be used as discrepant information mounts. Four caveats are in order, however. First, the evidence is scanty.[5] Few good political studies are available, and the psychology experiments usually deal with opinions on questions of little importance to the person. Second, several mechanisms can operate simultaneously. Early ones may be retained when later ones are brought into play. Third, personality variables can cause individual differences in modes of handling discrepant information.[6] Finally, some conditions favor the use of particular mechanisms—e.g. if information comes from an unreliable source, the source is apt to be discredited; if the information deals with a special aspect of an object, the person is likely to divide the object into two and maintain different attitudes toward each of the parts. In these cases other mechanisms will not even be tried.

[4] Herbert Kelman and Alice Eagly, "Attitude toward the Communicator, Perception of Communication Content, and Attitude Change," *Journal of Personality and Social Psychology* 1 (1965), 64. Also see Daniel Katz, "Consistency for What? The Functional Approach," in Robert Abelson et al., eds., *Theories of Cognitive Consistency* (Chicago: Rand McNally, 1968), pp. 188-90 and the articles in section IV C. The argument in Herbert Kelman and Reuben Baron, "Determinants of Modes of Resolving Inconsistency Dilemmas: A Functional Analysis" (*ibid.*, pp. 670-83) is especially interesting, but may not apply to the kinds of situations with which we are concerned. One kind of consistency theory, Osgood and Tannenbaum's, does give precise predictions and avoids the question of which of a variety of mechanisms will be invoked to cope with discrepant information. (Charles Osgood and Percy Tannenbaum, "The Principle of Congruity in the Prediction of Attitude Change," *Psychological Review* 62 [1955], 42-55.) But while experiments have confirmed the general outlines of the model (which are similar to other kinds of consistency theories), the specific predictions have not been borne out. These experiments are summarized in Roger Brown, "Models of Attitude Change," in Brown et al., *New Directions in Psychology* (New York: Holt, Rinehart and Winston, 1962), pp. 30-34.

[5] There have been very few studies of how decision-makers change their minds. For an exception, see Paul Diesing and Glenn Snyder, *Systems, Bargains, Decisions* (Princeton: Princeton University Press, forthcoming), Chapter 4.

[6] Ivan Steiner, "Sex Differences in the Resolution of A-B-X Conflicts," *Journal of Personality* 28 (1960), 118-28; Ivan Steiner and Evan Rogers, "Alternative Responses to Dissonance," *Journal of Abnormal and Social Psychology* 66 (1963), 128-36. For a review of this literature see Norman Feather, "A Structural Balance Approach to the Analysis of Communication Effects," in Leonard Berkowitz, *Advances in Experimental Social Psychology*, vol. 3 (New York: Academic Press, 1967), pp. 150-54.

Even though the latter cases violate a simple ordering of the methods of coping with discrepant information, they can be explained by the general principle that underlies the ordering: people change as little of their attitude structure as possible. If they must change something, they will first alter those beliefs that are least important, that are supported by the least information, and that are tied to fewest other beliefs.[7] If the discrepant information is ambiguous, slight, or unimportant it will be dismissed, assimilated, or put to one side. Thus the first mechanisms to be invoked preserve all of the person's original attitudes. If the amount and quality of the discrepant information renders these mechanisms inadequate, processes that involve minor or peripheral changes will have to be invoked. If these cannot cope with the contradictions, mechanisms that necessitate more far-reaching changes will be called into play. Because many beliefs are interconnected, large-scale changes can be avoided only if the person treats new information in a way that limits the implications of his initial response. These interconnections partly explain both the prevalence of incremental decision-making and the far-reaching changes that occur when central beliefs are finally altered.

Mechanisms of Attitude Preservation and Change

A person's failure to see that new information might contradict his beliefs is the first mechanism to be invoked. This requires no changes in attitudes and no conscious strain of reconciling discrepant information with old beliefs. This may mean that the information is immediately and automatically dismissed or that it is not noticed at all. Or the person may, in the words of a pioneering study of how prejudiced people respond to anti-prejudice propaganda, "evade the issue psychologically by simply not understanding the message."[8] Active defense mechanisms, an inability to conceive of an alternative view, or incompatible frames of reference may obviate the necessity for dealing with the information. In other cases the person may understand the information and take it as valid, but not see it as discrepant with his views. In 1917 British generals reacted to the news that few Germans were surrendering during a major British offensive by saying: "We are killing the enemy, not capturing him."[9] As

---

[7] See, for example, Charles Osgood, "Cognitive Dynamics in the Conduct of Human Affairs," *Public Opinion Quarterly* 24 (Summer 1960), 357. For a slightly different formulation see Milton Rosenberg and Robert Abelson, "An Analysis of Cognitive Balancing," in Milton Rosenberg, et al., *Attitude Organization and Change* (New Haven: Yale University Press, 1960), pp. 112-63.

[8] Eunice Cooper and Marie Jahoda, "The Evasion of Propaganda: How Prejudiced People Respond to Anti-Propaganda Propaganda," *Journal of Psychology* 23 (1947), 16 (italics omitted).

[9] Leon Wolff, *In Flanders Fields* (New York: Viking, 1958), p. 182.

we noted in Chapter 4, two people with different beliefs can each see an event as consistent with his views, and we cannot specify a general rule to determine who is right. Thus it is not surprising that even when an alternative interpretation of the evidence is called to the person's attention, he may claim that not only is his belief correct, but that this evidence supports it. Because of the ambiguity of most evidence available to statesmen and the complexity of their beliefs, this is a potent force for the maintenance of images of others.

Second, the information may be seen as discrepant but its validity explicitly rejected. This is frequently the fate of scientific findings that clash with an accepted theory. In politics, too, people often conclude that, because their general beliefs are certainly correct, specific events that would contradict them must not have occurred. The British defeat before the Taku forts in 1857 made so little sense that many observers argued that the guns must have been manned by Russians, not Chinese. In 1914 because the French knew that Germany did not have sufficient troops to hold the line with their left wing while launching a major sweep with their right they concluded that the attack through Belgium must be a feint. Indeed deductive logic may be employed to "prove" that the discrepant information is not correct. Thus a Nazi leader gave the following answer to criticism of his permitting the performance of an operetta written by a Jew: "A Jew could not have written something so beautiful; he must have stolen it from a Christian."[10] This method of resolving the conflict is especially useful because it is the easier to invoke the greater the inconsistency between the established opinion and the bit of information.

Rejection of the validity of discrepant information is made easier if accompanied by the operation of the third mechanism—the discrediting of the source. The person can believe that the source is an unreliable reporter or an untrustworthy analyst, doubting either his motives or his skill.

The likelihood that the source will be discredited is influenced by several variables. First, because "Credibility and like terms do not represent attributes of communicators; they represent judgments by the listeners," a source that advocates a position too discrepant from the one held by the listener is likely to be disregarded.[11] Second, information varies in the

[10] Stuart Miller, *The Unwelcome Immigrant* (Berkeley and Los Angeles: University of California Press, 1969), p. 130; Edward Peterson, *The Limits of Hitler's Power* (Princeton: Princeton University Press, 1969), p. 227.

[11] Carolyn Sherif, Muzafer Sherif, and Roger Nebergall, *Attitude and Attitude Change* (Philadelphia: Saunders, 1965); Carolyn Sherif and Norman Jackman, "Judgements of Truth by Participants in Collective Controversy," *Public Opinion Quarterly* 30 (Summer 1966), 173-86. The quote is from Sherif, Sherif, and Nebergall, *Attitude and Attitude Change*, p. 201.

degree to which judgments about its validity are necessarily bound up with judgments about the source. As we pointed out in Chapter 4, while some arguments can be examined completely on their merits, subjective observations of other actors must be seen in light of values and skills of the person making them. We would therefore expect that discrediting of the source would be more common in the latter than in the former context. Third, the more the source is thought to be deficient in skill and objectivity, the more likely it is to be discredited. Thus discrepant information from trusted advisers is least likely to be handled by this mechanism and such information when received from opponents (e.g. Senator Keating's warning to Kennedy that the Russians were installing offensive missiles in Cuba, Ambassador Pannikkar's message to Truman that the Chinese would intervene in the Korean War if U.N. troops continued toward the Yalu) is most likely to be met by discrediting the source.

Fourth, if the person cannot avoid dealing with the information, he may preserve his old beliefs by admitting his puzzlement with what he has heard. He can acknowledge that the information is both correct and embarrassing to his view and argue that, for the time being at least, it simply cannot be explained. The information will then have no immediate impact on anything else the person believes. It will not, if he is a scientist, alter his research program or his interpretation of other data, or, if he is a decision-maker, change his policies or views of other actors. But it will remain available as relatively raw data for use in support of a new interpretation should the person's beliefs later undergo significant changes. Thus in science it is not uncommon for an experiment that yields results that can neither be reconciled with prevailing theories nor explained away to be put aside in the expectation that future research will find the cause of the deviation without disturbing anything of importance. In this way some European military experts limited the inferences they drew from their observations of the cavalry's ineffectiveness in the American Civil War. Although they provided some explanations for this unexpected fact, they usually admitted that they could not fully understand why neither side employed the tactics that accepted doctrine indicated would be most successful. More recently, Ambassador Maxwell Taylor admitted his inability to understand how the Viet Cong could maintain its strength.

> The ability of the Viet-Cong continuously to rebuild their units and to make good their losses is one of the mysteries of this guerrilla war. We are aware of the recruiting methods by which local boys are induced or compelled to join the Viet-Cong ranks and have some general appreciation of the amount of infiltration personnel from the outside. Yet taking both of these sources into account, we still find no

plausible explanation of the continued strength of the Viet-Cong if our data on Viet-Cong losses are even approximately correct. Not only do the Viet-Cong units have the recuperative powers of the phoenix, but they have an amazing ability to maintain morale. Only in rare cases have we found evidences of bad morale among Viet-Cong prisoners or recorded in captured Viet-Cong documents.[12]

He did not deny the validity of the evidence, but neither did he modify the view that led him to expect the contrary. In another case, two days before the Arab attack of October 1973 Israeli intelligence officers learned that the Russians were rushing the families of their advisers out of Egypt and Syria. They could not explain this to their satisfaction but neither did they conclude that they should solve the puzzle by adopting an explanation that would have necessitated the alteration of many of their beliefs about Arab behavior.[13]

When the person acknowledges that a bit of evidence contradicts his beliefs and is not satisfied merely to put it to one side, he may engage in bolstering—seeking new information and considerations that support his views. "This is a mechanism not for eliminating imbalance entirely but only for drowning it out, so to speak."[14] Bolstering usually refers to the development of new arguments and data, but it can also be applied to the rearranging of attitudes in order to decrease the impact of the discrepant information. Thus a person can admit that, while one aspect of a valued object is associated with something negatively valued, other aspects of it are more important than he had thought previously. This is one explanation for the tendency for shifting rationales to be used to support the same program, a subject to which we will return later in this chapter. For example, strategic bombing in the Korean War initially was justified largely in terms of interdiction. As the disappointing results became clear, greater stress was laid on increasing the war's cost to the enemy. In the 1930s decision-makers in the United States and Britain defended their policy toward Japan with the argument that it would help maintain

[12] Michael Polanyi, "Commentary," in A. C. Crombie, ed., *Scientific Change* (New York: Basic Books, 1963), p. 376; Jay Luvaas, *The Military Legacy of the Civil War* (Chicago: University of Chicago Press, 1959), p. 21; *The Pentagon Papers* (New York: Bantam Books, 1971), p. 372. For another example, see Dwight Eisenhower, *The White House Years*, vol. 2, *Waging Peace, 1956-1961* (Garden City, N.Y.: Doubleday, 1965), p. 268.

[13] Ephraim Kam, "The Why of Surprise Attack" (unpublished MS, 1974), p. 46. For other examples, see Vladimir Dedijer, *The Battle Stalin Lost* (New York: Viking, 1970), pp. 3-104 and Roderick Macleod and Denis Kelly, *Time Unguarded: The Ironside Diaries, 1937-1940* (New York: McKay, 1962), p. 377.

[14] Robert Abelson, "Modes of Resolution of Conflict," *Journal of Conflict Resolution* 3 (December 1959), 345. The existence of more cognitive consistency than can be explained by a rational analysis of the situation can be considered a form of bolstering.

the "open door" in Manchuria. But "When it became clear that the door was rapidly being shut . . . , the matter was accorded a lower priority, by what seems to have been almost an unconscious process."[15] Similarly, a person could acknowledge that Russia's willingness to sign a nonproliferation treaty is evidence of her desire to preserve peace and lower tensions but not alter his image of Russia as aggressive by elevating the significance of other Soviet behavior, such as her buildup of intercontinental missiles.

Bolstering can more than counteract the influence of the upsetting stimulus because this process has a momentum of its own and may not stop when the person is as confident as he was initially. If the attack is strong enough to mobilize the person's defenses without being so strong as to overwhelm them, it can set off a "backlash" effect, making the belief stronger than it was before the attack.

Undermining, the sixth mechanism, is the opposite side of the coin of bolstering. Additional elements can be adduced to weaken the information that creates the inconsistency. Thus a person who smokes and knows of reports linking cigarettes with cancer can point to the studies of these reports that fault their methodology and analysis. He can seek evidence that the reports contradict well-established findings and that the people who wrote them are not good scientists. Discrediting the source contributes to undermining, as this example illustrates.

All of the mechanisms discussed so far cope with the discrepant information without resorting to attitude change. Either the information has not been recognized as discrepant or its impact has been neutralized. But when the evidence is too significant to be disposed of in these ways, some of the pre-existing views must be sacrificed. In this case the route to the least possible change often lies through the seventh mechanism, differentiation, by which the person splits the object by sloughing off the parts that are causing attitudinal conflict. When the Brooklyn Dodgers (for whom I rooted fervently) moved to Los Angeles (which I disliked), I was able to disassociate the players from their owner, who had made the decision to move, and was able to continue liking the former while developing a dislike for the latter.

One of the more common forms of differentiation, which indeed may occur prior to some of the mechanisms mentioned previously, is to separate the evaluation of an individual's personal qualities from judgments of the policies he is implementing or the views he is advocating. In this way one can remain friends with a person of a different political per-

---

[15] Robert Frank Futrell, with the assistance of Lawson S. Moseley and Albert F. Simpson, *The United States Air Force in Korea, 1950-1953* (New York: Duell, Sloan, and Pearce, 1961); Christopher Thorne, *The Limits of Foreign Policy* (New York: Putnam, 1973), p. 362.

suasion. This mechanism will not be adequate, however, when the opinion deals with matters that the person believes to be very important or an index of negatively valued personal characteristics. Alternatively, one may separate what the person is doing from what he normally does or what he would do if he had more freedom. As we mentioned in Chapter 2, because Germany understood that Italy depended on France for coal, she interpreted Italy's support for the French occupation of the Ruhr "not as voluntary action, but the product of unavoidable circumstances" and did not react with hostility.[16] In the same way, if a friend does something I don't like I will be quick to believe or even seek out evidence that he acted as he did for special reasons (e.g. he was forced to do it, he was sick at the time, he wasn't paying attention). By differentiating a single object (my friend) into two (my friend as he normally is and my friend when he is not really himself), I can positively value one and negatively value the other.

As the last example shows, creating exceptions to a generalization is a form of differentiation. By treating some aspects of the other's behavior as special, the person can contain the impact of discrepant information. Thus I can resolve the inconsistency of believing that the U.S.S.R. is a status quo power but thinking that her recent actions in the Middle East are destabilizing and aggressive by separating her underlying characteristics from her Mid-East policy and believing that the latter is for some reason unique. I could hold that from the time of the tsars Russia had tried to increase her influence in that area, or that commitments had been given that carried Russia further than she wanted to go, or that a particular group in the Kremlin was responsible for Middle Eastern policy. The result would be that I could condemn Russia's policy in this area without having to revise my general evaluation of her.[17]

In extreme cases of differentiation, the person will redefine whole categories of objects, thereby permitting himself to hold different attitudes toward things that are no longer seen as alike. Southerners were able to support both the American creed of equality and the institution of slavery by placing slaves in the category of nonhumans. If they had seen them as men and women, they could not have maintained their ideology without seeing themselves as oppressors.

Eighth, and less frequently, transcendence, the opposite mechanism from differentiation, can be invoked. "Elements, instead of being split down, are built up and combined into large units organized on a super-

---

[16] Alan Cassels, *Mussolini's Early Diplomacy* (Princeton: Princeton University Press, 1970), p. 146.

[17] Logical and psychological problems are raised by the needs to judge how unlikely to recur the discrepant behavior is and to decide how many deviations can be tolerated before the generalization has to be discarded.

ordinate level."[18] For example, smoking can be joined with several safer habits to form a unit of modes of relaxation that help the person lead a more enjoyable, productive life. Or a person who dislikes both Russia and China but realizes that the two are in conflict can resolve the incongruity by grouping them together as powers that hold abhorrent values. The reconciliation of disparate scientific findings under a new paradigm can be considered to be an especially creative example of this mechanism.

CENTRALITY

Only if all these ways of coping with the information are found to be insufficient will the person be forced to change his views on some of the main questions. But what parts of the opinion will be altered? Just as in science "when certain consequences of a theory are upset by experimental contradiction, we learn that this theory should be modified, but we are not told by the experiment what must be changed,"[19] so there usually are many parts of an image or attitude that could have been responsible for the prediction's being incorrect and several modifications that could accommodate the discrepant information. We hypothesize that those parts of the image that are least central—i.e. the fewest other cognitions depend on them—and least important will change first.[20] The same rule of minimal change that explains the order of the invoking of the mechanisms discussed above applies here.[21] This generalization also describes the common and approved reaction of scientists to unexpected findings: to make the smallest possible alterations of the prevailing hypotheses. Important hypotheses are challenged only when there is no other way to

[18] Abelson, "Modes of Resolution of Conflict," p. 346.

[19] Pierre Duhem, "Physical Theory and Experiment," in Herbert Feigl and May Brodbeck, eds., *Readings in the Philosophy of Science* (New York: Appleton-Century-Crofts, 1953), p. 250.

[20] O. J. Harvey and Harold M. Schroder, "Cognitive Aspects of Self and Motivation," in Harvey, ed., *Motivation and Social Interaction* (New York: Ronald Press, 1963), p. 110. Robert Abelson is certainly correct to point out that the explanation for many attitude change phenomena lies not in the centrality of the beliefs under attack but rather in the strength or weakness of the stimuli that are brought to bear on the belief system. ("A Summary of Hypotheses on Modes of Resolution," in Abelson et al., eds., *Theories of Cognitive Consistency*, pp. 719-20.) The discussion in the last two sections of this chapter touches on this subject. Abelson is also correct in noting several other ambiguities and inadequacies in the explanation of the importance of centrality. (*Ibid.*, pp. 716-17.)

[21] Central beliefs may be slow to change partly because they are learned early (Edward Bruner, "Cultural Transmission and Cultural Change," in Neil J. Smelser and William T. Smelser, eds., *Personality and Social Systems* [2nd ed., New York: Wiley, 1970], pp. 563-69). To test this explanation against the one offered here, one could compare the resistance of early, peripheral beliefs with that of central ones learned later.

account for large amounts of intractable data. Theories are altered only as a last resort. Thus the tendency to avoid changing the basic aspects of an image need not be seen as a pathological attempt to protect a psychologically satisfying view of the world.

Experiments demonstrate that change is held to a minimum. In one case, subjects were asked to give their impressions of a person on the basis of a list of adjectives, one of which clashed with a stereotype that could be formed by the others. Those who did not cope with the discrepancy by the mechanisms that kept their images completely intact made their changes "as innocuous as possible, preserving the main dimensions of the original" image.[22] Similarly, Rosenberg found that subjects adjusted to discrepant information by making as few opinion changes as possible. His data generally supported the predictions

> that the communication which would make possible the balancing of a particular structure through only one sign change [i.e. changing the attitude toward one object from positive to negative or vice versa] would be the most acceptable of the three communications [offered to the subject and that]. . . . of the two other communications, the one implying two sign changes to reach balance would be better received than the one implying three sign changes.[23]

Even when one attitude was more stressed and firmly established by the instructions than the others it would be changed in preference to changing two others.[24] In this experiment all the elements were equally central. Where this is not the case we would expect not that in the short run the fewest elements would be changed but rather that several peripheral elements would be altered instead of a smaller number of more central ones, thereby minimizing the magnitude of the eventual change.

Of course, if we are not careful, this proposition can become circular since the change of one part of an image could be used to show that it was less central. What is needed is to establish in advance which parts of the image have more or fewer ramifications. Often this can be done. For example, evaluations of significant objects are apt to be tied to more elements of the belief system than are instrumental beliefs. Thus Rosenberg found that, when subjects were placed in a position where they would have to change either their evaluation of American business or their beliefs about the effect of foreign aid, the subjects altered the latter. This change could be contained with relative ease, whereas a change in

---

[22] Mason Haire and Willa Freeman Grunes, "Perceptual Defenses: Processes Protecting an Organized Perception of Another Personality," *Human Relations*, 3, no. 4 (1950), 403-12 (the quote is from page 409).

[23] Rosenberg and Abelson, "An Analysis of Cognitive Balancing," p. 130.

[24] *Ibid.*, pp. 138-39.

evaluation of business would have created many other inconsistencies.[25] In other cases, even a cursory knowledge of the person's belief system will reveal which areas of substantive belief underpin much of his view of the world and so will be especially resistant to change. For example, many of the opponents of the theory of evolution held orthodox religious beliefs, so it is not surprising that they reacted to unimpeachable evidence that some species had died out and new ones had appeared by developing the theory of "special serial creations" that held that God had periodically destroyed existing creatures and established new ones. Although this abandoned important beliefs, it preserved the central role of the Creator. And since the belief in a harmony of interests between the U.S.S.R. and the good of world socialism was the starting point for many Yugoslav values and beliefs, it was predictable that many other views would be sacrificed before the Yugoslavs recognized Stalin's true character.[26]

To take a general category of political beliefs, when one country thinks that another is its enemy, the perception of hostility is usually more central than other aspects of the image; it is used to explain much of the other's behavior and is in turn often linked to prior variables such as the other's domestic system or geographical position. To decide that the other is no longer hostile, or perhaps never has been hostile, requires that many other beliefs must also be changed. So when the other acts with restraint, our hypothesis would predict that the actor would be more likely to change his view of the other's strength than of its intentions. Thus in the late 1950s and early 1960s most Americans felt that Russian weakness, not Russian friendship, was the reason Russia built fewer missiles than the United States had predicted. Similarly, during the conflict between Bolivia and Paraguay over the Chaco, "Bolivia . . . called attention to her reduction of armaments as a sincere gesture to bring an end to the threat of armed conflict. The Paraguayan Chargé replied that if Bolivia had reduced her armaments, it was due to poor finances and not to her pacifistic intentions."[27]

A person's view of himself is usually highly central and will be maintained at the cost of altering several other elements. People usually believe that they are just and fair. If evil has been done, they cannot have done it. And if they did it, it cannot be evil. As Lieutenant Calley explained his feelings about charges of a massacre at My Lai: "I had

[25] Milton Rosenberg, "An Analysis of Affective-Cognitive Consistency," in Rosenberg, et al., *Attitude Organization and Change*, p. 62. But instrumental beliefs that are used in many contexts cannot be changed with so few consequences.

[26] Ernst Mayr, "The Nature of the Darwinian Revolution," *Science* 176 (June 2, 1972), 982-86; Dedijer, *The Battle Stalin Lost*, pp. 92-94.

[27] William Garner, *The Chaco Dispute* (Washington: Public Affairs Press, 1966), p. 62.

found, I had closed with, I had destroyed the VC: the mission that day. I thought, *It couldn't be wrong or I'd have remorse about it.*"[28] Theodore Roosevelt similarly argued that the result of governmental policy must be good because he was in charge of it. Those whose self-images are involved with succeeding will strongly resist accepting blame for failures. Thus MacArthur's reaction to the Chinese intervention in Korea: "The one salient fact was that MacArthur had been taken by surprise and badly defeated in the moment of victory. And to MacArthur this was intolerable. . . . Since the disaster could not be attributed to MacArthur it had to be the fault of the Truman administration." Similarly, the French generals explained the mutinies of 1917 by the defeatism of politicians instead of the disastrous offensives they had ordered, and in World War II Admiral Doenitz attributed the Allied success in locating his submarines to spies rather than to his excessive demands for radio transmissions from the U-boats.[29] For a citizen who strongly identifies with his state and for the statesmen who act in its name, national self-images are similarly central. Not many people are willing to see their own states as aggressive, or even as inadvertently threatening, thus increasing the danger of spirals of hostility discussed in Chapter 3.

The tendency to preserve central beliefs helps explain why people often fail to see the basic causes of undesired events and instead focus on the supposedly idiosyncratic acts of a few individuals. As Tang Tsou notes in his analysis of the most common reaction to the communist takeover of China, "It was difficult to see that for fifty years a nation had pursued a policy which was doomed to eventual failure by its inherent contradictions. But it was easy to attribute the responsibility for failure to individual officials." Even Ambassador Hurley, who had much more information, did not change his basic assumptions about China but instead blamed "the failure of his policy on the opposition or sabotage of the career officials who, according to him, 'sided with the Chinese Communist armed party.' "[30] And when De Gaulle began his campaign to limit American influence in Europe, many Americans who objected to that policy argued that the general was speaking mostly for himself. Americans who were more critical of their country's policy, by contrast, had few beliefs that could not accommodate the view that De Gaulle

[28] Quoted in John Sack, *Lieutenant Calley* (New York: Viking, 1971), p. 8. Italics in the original.

[29] Walter Millis, *Arms and Men* (New York: Capricorn, 1967), p. 332; Richard Watt, *Dare Call It Treason* (New York: Simon and Schuster, 1963), p. 198; Ladislas Farago, *The Tenth Fleet* (New York: Ivan Obolensky, 1962), p. 161. The tendency for people to see themselves as responsible for successes and others as responsible for failure will be discussed in Chapter 9.

[30] Tang Tsou, *America's Failure in China, 1941-50* (Chicago: University of Chicago Press, 1963), pp. 494, 343-44.

represented widespread European opinion and so did not see the general as an isolated individual.

This hypothesis helps account for the prevalence of conspiracy theories. Unexpected and undesired events need not alter many important attitudes if they can be attributed to the machinations of a small, evil group. For example, historians argue that the widespread American labor strikes of 1877 had many causes, including "cruel economic distress, employer arrogance or lack of understanding, the birth pangs of a new age, [and] the precipitant of idle men and boys. . . . Yet to many, especially among the gentry of letters and trade, such an explanation seemed both too complex and too unflattering to their world. They preferred to blame the trouble on a conspiracy."[31] To do otherwise would have required them to alter many of their beliefs about the workers' motivations and values, the nature of industrial society, and the role of the employers.

This analysis implies that the more important the subject and the greater the number of beliefs that would have to be changed if the causes of an event were seen as deep-seated, the greater the acceptance of conspiracy theories. Thus many Germans attributed their defeat in the First World War to a "stab in the back," and Indians who favored close ties with China said that "It is difficult to understand the aggressive moves of the People's Republic of China on India's border, except that the leaders of that seemingly great country have become insane."[32] Similarly, one factor common to most authorities' interpretations of anticolonial and campus protests was the tendency to underestimate the degree of indigenous support for the movement and to overestimate the influence of "outside agitators." White southerners' perceptions of Negro protests also fit this pattern. To have accepted the belief that the demonstrations had widespread and voluntary support would have undermined the southerners' central belief that the Negroes valued the system. Many commentators on the black riots in the 1960s similarly saved most of their important and interrelated beliefs by arguing that only the "riff raff" had participated.

When conspiracy theories are clearly inappropriate, others will be sought that also leave unchanged the person's central beliefs. Thus failure is often attributed not only to external sources, but, more specifically, to temporary obstacles that can be removed. For example, the lack of success of the efforts to spread Christianity and trade in China was traced to "unreasonable restrictions" that could be lifted by treaties. Making use

[31] Robert Bruce, *1877: Year of Violence* (Chicago: Quadrangle, 1970), pp. 223-24.
[32] G. Eric Hansen, "Indian Perceptions of the Chinese Communist Regime and Revolution," *Orbis* 12 (Spring 1968), 288.

of a related mechanism, many European observers attributed the ineffectiveness of cavalry in the American Civil War to the unusual terrain and the soldiers' lack of training, numbers, and leadership. In this way the Europeans were able to avoid recognizing the importance of the new factor that would appear in their own future wars—the growth of firepower. Similarly, when Prussia defeated Austria in 1866, France "adopted with enthusiasm" the explanation that Prussia won because of her superior breech-loading rifle. If this were the case, all France had to do to retain her military pre-eminence was to copy this innovation. More far-reaching reforms were not needed.[33]

Central beliefs can also be shielded from the effects of failure if causation, although internal, is attributed to a factor that need not operate in future cases—e.g. the person's not having worked up to his capacity. With a bit more effort, things will turn out as they should. Thus for the first year after America's entry into World War II, naval officers explained the large number of ships sunk by U-boats not by the inherent defects of their antisubmarine strategies, but rather by the lack of planes and ships. Only after the material constraints became less stringent without diminishing the losses did the navy seek to supplement the convoy system. Indeed perceptions of special obstacles or lack of effort can save so much of a person's belief system that they may be adopted even when they cast doubt on the person's own courage or ability.[34]

When claims for conspiracies or special conditions are not relevant and connections among beliefs are tight, men will find themselves led to strange and ramifying conclusions by the interaction between important discrepant information and their central beliefs. Although observers will be puzzled or astounded, the person is not being illogical. Quite the con-

---

[33] Miller, *The Unwelcome Immigrant*, p. 203; Luvaas, *The Military Legacy of the Civil War*, pp. 17, 27, 73, 197; Michael Howard, *The Franco-Prussian War* (New York: Collier, 1969), p. 29. The French did adopt an excellent rifle, one that was much better than that used by the Prussians, and this gave them significant military advantages.

A price of blood as well as opinion was paid by the French nobility for the lessons they learned from their defeats at the hands of the English archers in the fourteenth and fifteenth centuries. To have concluded that archers rather than knights were dominant would have undermined the nobility's role within France and threatened widespread changes in both beliefs about the proper ordering of society and the distribution of values. To avoid this, more limited conclusions were drawn from the battles. These saved deeply rooted beliefs but could not reverse the English advantage. (C.W.C. Oman, *The Art of War in the Middle Ages*, revised and edited by John Beeler [Ithaca, N.Y.: Cornell University Press, 1953], pp. 129, 137.)

[34] Elting Morison, *Turmoil and Tradition: A Study of the Life and Times of Henry L. Stimson* (Boston: Houghton Mifflin, 1960), pp. 571-72; Harry Holbert Turney-High, *Primitive War* (2nd ed., Columbia: University of South Carolina Press, 1971), p. 35.

trary. He is using deductive reasoning to find the only explanation that will reconcile undeniable fact and immovable premises. For example, Governor Rockefeller could not easily cope with the fact that the inmates of Attica did not carry out their threat to kill their hostages when the police, on Rockefeller's orders, stormed the prison. Rather than admit that the prisoners were not totally bloodthirsty—which would imply that they might have freed the guards had he adopted a different policy— Rockefeller had to draw what others would see as a most unconvincing conclusion. As he explained at a press conference:

> I want to tell you I just was absolutely overwhelmed. I just didn't see how it was possible, with 1,200 men in there armed, with electrified barricades, with trenches, with a pledge which they said that they would all go right down fighting to the last man, how it was going to be possible [to save any of the guards].
> Q. What does this tell you about the prisoners, Governor, the fact that so many men did emerge unharmed?
> A. I think what it tells is that the use of this [tear] gas is a fantastic instrument in a situation of this kind.[35]

Even more strikingly, if discrepant information is not allowed to disturb central beliefs, the reaction may have a far-reaching effect on many less important beliefs. Thus the introduction of the Marshall Plan caused great and frightening alterations in the Soviet analysis of U.S. intentions. "The Program's apparent altruism, its 'unsordid' character, now enhanced Soviet suspicions to a nightmarish extent. Since when do capitalists divest themselves of billions of dollars just to save another country's economy?" So the Russians had to conclude

> that the ultimate meaning of the ERP went beyond an attempt to save Western Europe from Communism or to seduce the Russian satellites by the example of a higher standard of living. The eventual aims were clearly military. While unwilling to expand her own armies, and still deliberating whether to pull her forces out of Europe, the United States was clearly bent upon recreating the military potential of Western Europe, with the view to eventually employing it to restore the balance of power and wrest from the U.S.S.R. her wartime gains. The real purpose of the Marshall Plan was to create large standing armies that could threaten Russia while the Americans would back them up, if necessary, with their naval strength and their atomic-armed Strategic Air Command.[36]

[35] Joseph Lelyveld et al., "The Attica Revolt: Hour by Hour," *New York Times*, October 4, 1971.
[36] Adam Ulam, *Expansion and Coexistence* (New York: Praeger, 1968), p. 447.

Although these conclusions were neither desired nor simple nor closely limited, they made all the pieces fall into place within the framework established by the central Soviet beliefs.

Three implications follow. First, a tightly connected belief system will only sometimes change in an incremental fashion. As long as the discrepant information can be handled by the mechanisms discussed in the first section of this chapter, the incrementalism model applies quite well. But when this is not true, the pattern is different. Either the maintenance of central beliefs will require far-reaching changes in peripheral ones, as in the cases just discussed, or the central beliefs themselves will change, setting off a series of further changes. Sometimes the alteration of a central belief merely removes the obstacle to subsidiary changes. For example, early astronomers applied incredible efforts to reducing the paths of the planets to combinations of circular motion because they believed in the existence of hard crystal spheres along which the planets traveled. But when it was demonstrated (as we will discuss below) that these spheres did not exist, "the circular motion ceased to be the thing that really mattered" and men no longer found it impossible to conceive of planets traveling in ellipses.[37] More often, a change in a central belief requires other changes if the person is not to suffer a high degree of inconsistency.

Second, the processes discussed in the previous paragraphs are driven by tight connections between central and peripheral beliefs. When these links are weak, the person will be quicker to change individual beliefs— because his views on one question will not be strongly reinforced by his views on others—but for the same reason an alteration in relatively central beliefs will not bring in its train a series of derived changes. Thus it has been found that people with more centralized belief systems change fewer opinions in the face of low pressure to change than do people with less centralized beliefs but that they change more than the latter under high pressure.[38]

Third, compromises involving central beliefs are likely to be unstable. A person may breach a principle without realizing it at the time and then

[37] Herbert Butterfield, *The Origins of Modern Science* (rev. ed., New York: Collier Books, 1962), pp. 76-77.

[38] David Sears, "Social Anxiety, Opinion Structure, and Opinion Change," *Journal of Personality and Social Psychology* 7 (1967), 142-51; Walter Crockett and Paul Meisel, "Construct Connectedness, Strength of Disconfirmation, and Impression Change," *Journal of Personality* 42 (1974), 290-99. For mixed findings, see Howard Leventhal, "The Effects of Set and Discrepancy on Impression Change," *ibid.* 30 (1962), 1-15; William Watts, "Logical Relationships Among Beliefs and Timing as Factors in Persuasion," *Journal of Personality and Social Psychology* 16 (1970), 571-82; Ronald Dillehay, Chester Insko, and M. Brewster Smith, "Logical Consistency and Attitude Change," *ibid.* 3 (1966), 646-54.

later bring other attitudes into line with his new position.[39] George Bernard Shaw's remark to his dinner partner about having agreed on the principle and the rest being merely haggling over the price is not without its validity. At times drastic changes are not foreseen or desired, but occur as the person develops the implications of what seemed to be, when it was accepted, a minor and limited innovation. If the person realized at the start that his new idea required the overthrow of much that he believed in, he might well have rejected it. But lacking such foresight he sees only that the idea is a reasonable response to the problem and information at hand. Later, as the implications of the idea are explored, the person comes to see that further changes are required. To take an example from science, "The development of electrical theory continued for a long time within the Newtonian system . . . until Faraday and Maxwell, without themselves realizing the impact their innovations would have, introduced the idea of the field which came to be viewed as a disturbance in the aether. This notion proved in time to be the thin end of the wedge that split the entire system by making a mechanistic account of the aether continually more and more difficult as the implications of field phenomena came progressively to light."[40]

Although at this point the new idea is highly disruptive, it has sufficient support and promise that the person will be loath to abandon it. And once he realizes that the idea he has accepted contradicts many other things he believes, the same dynamics that protected the old concept will spread the implications of the new one by altering subsidiary beliefs. Thus Gladstone's decision to intervene unilaterally in Egypt in 1882 against many of his deep principles was made easier by his earlier acceptance of the idea of a joint European intervention. Similarly, much of the British opposition to entry into World War I was broken once the dissenters agreed not to allow German ships to attack the French coast— "a course that carried with it the possibility of having to go to war at the side of the French." According to Bernard Bailyn, this process accounts for some of the development of the radically new ideas in pre-revolutionary America. Ideas which did not seem great breaks with the past

[39] For interesting experiments along these lines, see Jonathan Freedman and Scott Fraser, "Compliance without Pressure: The Foot-In-The-Door Technique," *Journal of Personality and Social Psychology* 4 (1966), 195-202 and Patricia Pliner, Heather Hart, Joanne Kohl, and Dory Saari, "Compliance Without Pressure: Some Further Data on the Foot-in-the-Door Technique," *Journal of Experimental Social Psychology* 10 (1974), 17-22. For the opposite argument, see Robert Cialdini et al., "Reciprocal Concessions Procedure for Inducing Compliance: The Door-in-the-Face Technique," *Journal of Personality and Social Psychology* 31 (1975), 206-15. Also see the discussion on pp. 391-92, Chapter 11, below.

[40] Errol Harris, *Hypothesis and Perception* (London: Allen and Unwin, 1970), p. 212.

when they were adopted ramified in drastic ways as men followed out the implications of what they had come to accept.[41]

We can see this process at work when one person tries to persuade another that the other's premises lead to a different position than the one the other presently holds. Thus when the World Council of Churches protested the fate of the Palestinian refugees but refused to enter more directly into the political issues of the Middle East an Arab Christian leader pointed out: "We keep saying we do not want as Churches to take a political position. But when you say that injustice has been suffered by the Palestinians, you already have taken a political position, so why not take the next logical step and say what justice means in this respect?" Similarly, after the New York legislature passed a law prohibiting women from working after 10 p.m. Governor Alfred Smith called for a 48-hour work week and a minimum wage for women. "Is there any difference in principle," he asked, "between such laws designed to preserve the health and vigor of women in industry and a law to fix a minimum salary to enable her to live in decency and health?"[42] Because they can often anticipate these arguments, people who desire to take one step down a slippery slope will be careful to justify their behavior—to themselves as well as to others—by arguments and principles that cannot be applied to a wide range of other cases.[43]

In closing this section, the question of whether the pattern of minimum attitude change is rational should be raised if not fully answered. This pattern is rational if the central and important elements not only support a wide range of beliefs but also are substantiated by a solid base of theories and data. For if there is less evidence for the validity of the peripheral elements as compared to the central ones, the person should alter the former first and tamper with the latter only if he has to. This is the case in most scientific investigations. But the tendency toward minimum change is irrational if the central elements do not have this kind of backing but rather receive their power of resistance from the fact that to change them would require changing many other perceptions, beliefs, and plans that rest only on them. For in that case, in preserving the

[41] C. J. Lowe, *The Reluctant Imperialists* (New York: Macmillan Co., 1969), p. 48; Hazlehurst, *Politicians at War*, p. 48; Bernard Bailyn, *The Ideological Origins of the American Revolution* (Cambridge, Mass.: The Belknap Press of the Harvard University Press, 1967).

[42] Quoted in Judith Elizur, "The Image of Israel in Protestant Eyes: A Study of the World Council of Churches" (Harvard Ph.D. thesis, 1974), p. 219; quoted in David Colburn, "Governor Alfred E. Smith and the Red Scare, 1919-20," *Political Science Quarterly* 88 (September 1973), 439-40.

[43] For a discussion from a different perspective, see Robert Jervis, *The Logic of Images in International Relations* (Princeton: Princeton University Press, 1970), pp. 190-216.

central elements of his belief system the person is preserving his psychological well-being, but this is no reason why the beliefs should be right. To take a hypothetical example, if a state has planned for years on the assumption that its neighbor would aid it in war, and if this belief is based on careful analysis of the neighbor's history, commitments, and interests, then it is rational for decision-makers to find limited explanations for discrepant information—e.g. contrary reports are unreliable, unfavorable trends in the neighbor's country are only temporary, a small group is spreading unfriendly propaganda. But if the assumption of support does not rest on strong evidence, then minimal change would be irrational. This example also shows how difficult and subjective is this judgment of rationality.

One rule of thumb is available, however: cases in which policy remains constant while circumstances change drastically are apt to involve irrational resistance to change. For example, after World War II the air force insisted that a fleet of 70 air groups "should be achieved and thereafter firmly maintained through a future in which every factor which one might suppose would affect air policy promised to shift with the utmost fluidity and unpredictability." And a former science adviser to the president explained why he thought that the proposed Safeguard ABM System was not likely to achieve its goal of protecting Minuteman sites by noting that "although Presidents may change, Secretaries of Defense may come and go, the philosophies enunciated by political leaders may change, the design of our ABM system hardly changes at all. It includes the same radars, the same rockets, and largely the same deployment which was contemplated for" a defense of cities. Similarly, in 1917 the French chief of staff, General Nivelle, meticulously planned an attack on an exposed German salient. When the Germans withdrew to shorten their lines, many thought it obvious that the offensive would have to be canceled. But the planners of the attack made only slight changes even though what had been thought to be essential pre-conditions were no longer met.[44] To take an example on the strategic level, German policy remained relatively constant from the end of the nineteenth century to the start of World War I although the international environment and Germany's problems were greatly altered. Of course the same policy may be appropriate for many different situations, but this is rare. And in cases like those mentioned above no analysis was made to determine whether the old policy would work in the new circumstances. Indeed there was rarely an explicit consideration of the relevant changes. When this is the

[44] Millis, *Arms and Men*, p. 309; quoted in Herbert York, *Race to Oblivion* (New York: Simon and Schuster, 1970), pp. 213-14; Watt, *Dare Call It Treason*, pp. 159-61. Also see the discussion in Chapter 4, pp. 137-38 above.

case it seems likely that the psychological difficulty in altering a policy upon which so much rests is apt to account for this stability.[45]

THE RATE AT WHICH DISCREPANT INFORMATION IS RECEIVED

We have previously discussed the discrepant information with which the person has to cope as though only its total amount mattered. But this is not true. Greater change will result when discrepant information arrives in a large batch than when it is considered bit by bit. In the former case, the contradictions between it and the prevailing view will be relatively obvious. But when discrepant information arrives gradually, the conflict between each bit and what the person believes will be small enough to go unnoticed, be dismissed as unimportant, or necessitate at most slight modifications (e.g. addition of exceptions to the rule). By these mechanisms each piece of evidence will be considered to have been adequately accounted for, and the actor will not perceive that discrepant information is accumulating. If his explanation for any single event is questioned, a defender of the image can reply, and believe, that while this one explanation is not completely satisfactory, the image still is surely correct because it accounts for such a wide range of data. In this way one questionable interpretation will be used to support an image that in turn can be used to justify other dubious explanations. This is an especially great danger in judging other states' intentions since interpretations of past events often quickly become enshrined.

This hypothesis is supported by an experiment in which subjects are led to believe that half the cards in a deck are orange and half are white. In fact, two-thirds of them are white. Half of the subjects looked at the cards one at a time, while the other half viewed them in sets of threes. By the end of the experiment nine of the ten latter subjects realized that the deck contained a preponderance of white cards, while only three of the ten subjects who saw the cards one at a time came to this conclusion.[46] This hypothesis also accords with experiences of everyday life. It is easier to detect both physical and psychological changes in another person if one sees him again after a period of separation. In politics, sudden events influence images more than do slow developments. The Czech coup of 1948 had a greater impact on the United States than did the gradual consolidation of Russian control in the other East European countries. Neville Chamberlain eventually accepted the German demands on Czechoslovakia, which had increased steadily over a period of months.

---

[45] Several examples are discussed in Alexander George and Richard Smoke, *Deterrence in American Foreign Policy* (New York: Columbia University Press, 1974).

[46] I am indebted to Edwin Murphy for conducting this experiment.

If he had been confronted with the final demands immediately, Chamberlain's reaction probably would have been different. Arthur Link makes the parallel argument that the American opposition to the British blockade during World War I would have been greater had the British instituted their restrictions all at once. Indeed, one can look at a slowly changing object and detect no movement even though the cumulative shift is great. For example, Roland Evans and Robert Novak argue that, as majority leader, Lyndon Johnson produced great changes in Senate procedures, drawing power away from the floor and increasing the number and scope of negotiated agreements made behind the scenes. But these changes "evolv[ed] so slowly that they were ignored by the public and scarcely recognized in the Senate itself."[47]

Actors who want to disguise behavior that is contrary to their images can take advantage of this phenomenon. Perhaps the British and Germans in the examples mentioned above raised their demands gradually in order to disturb others' images of them as little as possible. During World War II the Germans employed a similar device to delay the detection of *Scharnhorst, Gneisenau,* and *Prinz Eugen* when they dashed up the English Channel from Brest back to Germany. The ships could escape only if they had both surprise and air cover, but if the British noted large numbers of German fighters circling an area moving up the French coast, surprise would be lost. A sudden jamming of British radar would also reveal unusual German activity. The German solution to this set of problems was ingenious. "At dawn each day during January English radar stations had a few minutes of jamming, deliberately made to appear like atmospherics. Every day the length of the jamming increased slightly. By February British radar operators were wearily accustomed to this interference. They reported it as 'caused by atmospheric conditions.' "[48]

This hypothesis leads to the expectation that a diplomat who returns to a country after a long assignment elsewhere will be more apt to detect changes than will a person who had been living there all along. Similarly, the hypothesis explains why American officials derived so little information from reading intercepts of the communications between Tokyo and the Japanese Embassy in Washington. Security was so tight that intercepts were sent out one at a time and returned to the intelligence office as soon as they were read. No one was allowed to keep a complete file,

[47] Arthur Link, *Wilson the Diplomatist* (Chicago: Quadrangle, 1965), p. 41; Roland Evans and Robert Novak, "The Johnson System," in Lawrence Pettit and Edward Keynes, *The Legislative Process in the U.S. Senate* (Chicago: Rand McNally, 1959), p. 196.

[48] John Deane Potter, *Fiasco: The Break-out of the German Battleships* (New York: Stein and Day, 1970), p. 30.

and so no one ever reviewed the entire series of messages. Had they done so, a pattern might have been detected, and the dominant image of the Japanese plans altered. As it was, no single intercept was striking enough to change anyone's views.[49]

The demands on statesmen's time require that most matters be brought to their attention only when decisions are needed. The costs that accrue when decision-makers fail to become involved in problems until they have been well defined are familiar.[50] By this stage, commitments have been made, options foreclosed, and alternatives structured. On the other hand, the lack of early involvement also means that top decision-makers will receive information in large packets rather than in a steady stream and therefore will be in a better position to detect inadequacies in the prevailing assumptions and formulations. President Johnson's lack of day-to-day involvement made it easier, for example, for him to see the disadvantages of the proposed multilateral force and to reverse U.S. policy at the last moment.[51]

Decision-makers can capitalize on this phenomenon by increasing the degree to which information comes to them in sizable chunks, which will make them more sensitive to discrepant evidence. To some degree, this is an automatic by-product of normal decision-making in any large organization, but additional mechanisms, to be discussed in the concluding chapter, can be developed to enhance this effect.

BELIEFS ESPECIALLY RESISTANT TO DISCREPANT INFORMATION

The amount and kind of information necessary to alter a belief depends in part on its substance. Some beliefs are especially resistant to change, particularly those that do not imply observable, relatively short-run consequences. The most important type of political image of this kind is the "inherent bad faith model," which can provide an explanation for almost any possible behavior the other may engage in. Hostility needs no special explanation, and conciliatory actions can be seen as an attempt to lull the perceiver into lowering his guard, or, as the kaiser interpreted British overtures to end the naval race before World War I, as evidence that the other responds only to power and that pressure should therefore be continued.[52]

---

[49] The fact that information accumulated gradually may help explain why some statesmen failed to predict the international financial crisis of 1931. See Morison, *Turmoil and Tradition*, p. 345.

[50] Richard Neustadt, *Presidential Power* (New York: Wiley, 1960).

[51] Philip Geyelin, *Lyndon B. Johnson and The World* (New York: Praeger, 1966), pp. 167-74.

[52] Henry Kissinger, *The Necessity for Choice* (New York: Harper and Row, 1961), pp. 191-98. Also see Ole Holsti, "Cognitive Dynamics and Images of the

Inherent good faith models are also possible, although they are rare and, if incorrect, will eventually be altered. Chamberlain's report to the cabinet of the impressions he gained from his trip to Italy in January 1939 shows the flavor of this kind of image.

I am convinced that Signor Mussolini and Herr Hitler cannot be very sympathetic to each other, and that although they have some interests in common their interests are not identical. . . . Accordingly I, on several occasions, gave Mussolini a chance to express his real feelings of Herr Hitler. He never took the opportunity offered to him, but remained throughout absolutely loyal to Herr Hitler. At the time I was somewhat disappointed at this attitude, but on reflection I think that it reflects credit on Signor Mussolini's character.[53]

The belief that the other is trying to help the perceiver but must contend with powerful opposition is also highly resistant to change because it can account for both the other's friendly and unfriendly behavior. Thus one historian notes that in the years before he was foreign minister, Ribbentrop's "feuding with the German foreign ministry automatically endeared him to Hitler: failures could be attributed to foreign ministry sabotage, while success showed his superior abilities in overcoming all obstacles."[54] Similarly, the image of a friendly Stalin held by some Western observers was not disturbed by hostile Soviet acts because they believed there was a powerful militant faction in the Russian leadership.

Moving away from these extreme cases, images vary in the amount of discrepant information they can absorb because they vary in the degree to which they provide deductions that can be checked against the available evidence.[55] Thus it is not surprising that, while John Foster Dulles

---

Enemy: Dulles and Russia," in David Finlay, Ole Holsti, and Richard Fagen, *Enemies in Politics* (Chicago: Rand McNally, 1967), pp. 26-27. The kaiser's perceptions are presented in Raymond Sontag, *European Diplomatic History, 1871-1932* (New York: Appleton-Century-Crofts, 1933), p. 143. Similar cases are discussed above, pp. 84-86.

These models are still empirical propositions—i.e. evidence could refute them. The image would be disconfirmed if the supposedly hostile state totally disarmed or did not take advantage of a situation in which the perceiver was completely at its mercy. The other side of this coin is also interesting: if you think that the other has an "inherent bad faith model" of you, you will feel there is nothing you can do to reassure him that you are not aggressive. You may then be forced to accept his definition of your behavior and work within a system of high illusory conflict.

[53] Quoted in Roger Parkinson, *Peace for Our Time* (London: Rupert Hart-Davis, 1971), pp. 91-92.

[54] Gerhard Weinberg, *The Foreign Policy of Hitler's Germany* (Chicago: University of Chicago Press, 1970), p. 175.

[55] The degree to which measurements are thought to be accurate is relevant here. Butterfield notes that "Those who attacked astrology often took the line that the observation of the paths of the heavenly bodies was not sufficiently accurate

eventually decided that the Soviet economy was in fact not failing, "he never rejected his longstanding theory that the Soviet regime was wholly without support from the Russian people."[56] There were concrete indications that the Soviet economy was healthy, but it was always possible to interpret the behavior of Soviet citizens in terms of forced compliance or opportunistic acquiescence. Related beliefs underlay the British attempt to force the Straits in 1915, the Suez invasion of 1956, and the landing at the Bay of Pigs. The attacker thought that internal opposition would topple the other's government as soon as the invaders appeared. Since reliable indicators of a regime's strength are rare (most observers were surprised when no one rose to defend Ben Bella or Nkrumah), it is relatively easy for decision-makers to maintain their beliefs on this subject.

The other side of this coin is that sharply defined propositions that observations can contradict are vulnerable, even if they are central elements of the belief system. Thus in 1577 when a comet "cut a path straight through what were supposed to be the impenetrable crystal spheres that formed the skies, it encouraged the view that the spheres did not actually exist as part of the machinery of the heavens; Tycho Brahe, conservative though he was in other respects, henceforward declared his disbelief in the reality of these orbs."[57]

Some beliefs are vulnerable only to specific events that cannot occur until it is too late. The claim that the other side is standing firm only because of an impending election cannot be shown to be wrong until the campaign is over, by which time positions on both sides may have hardened. Even more dangerously, the conclusion that the other side is bluffing can be disconfirmed only when war starts. All threats, leaks of plans for an attack, and military preparations can be accounted for within this image because the aim of a bluffer is to behave as it thinks a country willing to go to war would behave. Beliefs that the other side will give in only after a long struggle during which it will not display its weakness also cannot quickly be disconfirmed. In 1806 the view that Britain's economy depended on trade with the United States could be disproven only after America had paid a high price.[58] And a person who thought that North Vietnam's willingness to continue fighting would suddenly collapse when

---

as yet to allow detailed predictions. Astrologers themselves, when their prophecies were found to be inaccurate, would blame the faultiness of astronomical observation rather than the defects of their own supposed science." *The Origins of Modern Science*, p. 35.

[56] Holsti, "Cognitive Dynamics and Images of the Enemy," p. 86.

[57] Butterfield, *The Origins of Modern Science*, pp. 72-73.

[58] Bradford Perkins, *Prologue to War* (Berkeley and Los Angeles: University of California Press, 1961), p. 120.

the United States inflicted great enough pain on her would not have been disturbed by the absence of evidence that her will was being eroded. Only when North Vietnam was ready to make peace would there be visible indications that the bombing had worked. Similarly, during World War I the heavy losses of life and minor gains of territory could not influence the proponents of the strategy of attrition. The other side would surrender when its strength was drained, but clear evidence of the coming victory would not appear until the final stages.

Other beliefs can be disconfirmed only slowly not because of their content but because of the way they have been established. If in the past a belief has been confirmed by information that arrived infrequently and irregularly, long periods of time without further evidence are not likely to disturb it because the person will believe that the expected event will eventually occur, as it always has. If, on the other hand, confirming information has been arriving on a precise schedule, its non-appearance will have more impact.[59]

Other beliefs are highly resistant to particular categories of discrepant information, often those that are most readily available. Frequently those attacking a position produce information they consider crucial only to be told by the defenders that the information is irrelevant because, as anyone who understood their view would see, it does not bear on the claims they are actually making. This pattern is common in scholarly debates, and so we should not be surprised to learn that in the early twentieth century the proponents of the cavalry argued that "statistics showing the proportionate losses caused by bullet and saber in battle are worthless because it is the latter's moral effect that counts." Even more difficulties are created when the person does not realize that the evidence he is seeking cannot disconfirm his hypothesis. At best, his effort will be wasted; at worst he will gain unwarranted confidence in his belief. Thus some people looked out their windows to try to determine whether Martians had invaded, as reported in Orson Welles' broadcast, without being aware that nothing they saw could reassure them:

> "I looked out of the window and everything looked the same as usual so I thought it hadn't reached our section yet."
>
> "Wyoming Avenue was black with cars. People were rushing away, I figured."

[59] Thus, it is not surprising that experiments have shown that "The stability [of behavior] can be bolstered by the use of training schedules in which the original positive reinforcement occurs as a highly intermittent and sometimes unpredictable outcome of the appropriate behavior." Justin Aronfreed, *Conduct and Conscience* (New York: Academic Press, 1968), pp. 20-21. Also see J. McV. Hunt, "Motivation Inherent in Information Processing and Action," in Harvey, ed., *Motivation and Social Interaction*, pp. 92-93.

"No cars came down my street. 'Traffic is jammed on account of the roads being destroyed,' I thought."[60]

More important in politics is the belief that the other's signals (i.e. statements and actions whose meanings are established by understandings, usually tacit) have no value in predicting his later behavior. His signals then cannot change his image. Thus shortly before the Boer War British decision-makers became convinced that any pledges the Boers might give would be violated as soon as Britain relaxed her pressure. As a result, no agreement could be satisfactory. Since the consequences of living up to his signals are only one of several considerations that determine an actor's behavior, he is apt to feel least bound by his word when other payoffs are very high (e.g. in crises). Perceivers know this, and are therefore less influenced by the actor's claims in these cases.[61]

Even if the actor has an adequate signaling reputation, others will not pay close heed to his words if they believe that they understand the actor and the objective situation well enough to predict how he will behave. Indeed, as we discussed in Chapter 2, the perceiver may think, sometimes correctly, that he can predict the actor's reactions better than can the actor himself. In these cases the perceiver need not suspect deception to discount the actor's messages. Harold Macmillan explains his incorrect prediction of American behavior in the Suez crisis by saying: "I believed the Americans would issue a protest, even a violent protest in public; but that they would in their hearts be glad to see the matter brought to a conclusion." He had not misread Eisenhower's warnings—instead, conclusions derived from his longstanding knowledge of America and its president outweighed the evidence derived from the contemporary messages. Adversaries—especially those who are guided by deeply embedded theories—may also feel that they know each other so well that there is little point paying much attention to the other's notes. Thus in August 1939 Ribbentrop told Ciano that "his information, but above all his psychological understanding of England, made him certain that any British intervention was out of the question." Again, at several points during the Berlin crisis neither Dulles, who "prided himself on his knowledge of the Soviet Union," nor Khrushchev could be much influenced by the other's signals.[62]

[60] Brian Bond, "Doctrine and Training in the British Cavalry, 1817-1914," in Michael Howard, ed., *The Theory and Practice of War* (New York: Praeger, 1966), p. 116; Hadley Cantril, *The Invasion From Mars* (Princeton: Princeton University Press, 1947), p. 93.

[61] J.A.S. Grenville, *Lord Salisbury and Foreign Policy* (London: Athlone Press, 1964), pp. 251-57. For a further discussion of this phenomenon, see Jervis, *The Logic of Images in International Relations*, pp. 90-96.

[62] Harold Macmillan, *Riding the Storm* (London: Macmillan and Co., 1971), p. 157; Gordon Craig, *From Bismarck to Adenauer: Aspects of German Statecraft*

Two factors make images of other states especially resistant to discrepant information. First, because deception is common, many of the other's behaviors that do not fit his image can be dismissed as attempts to mislead. Second, students of visual illusions have found that "The most effective way of accomplishing perceptual reorganization is through action by the perceiver."[63] If a person tries to touch things in a room that appears normal but really is greatly distorted, he will not succeed, and soon he will perceive the room as it actually is. But other actors are neither unchangeable nor passive. The behavior the other displays and the intentions he develops are partly a function of the actor's behavior toward him. Some prophecies are self-fulfilling; others can be self-denying. Even when these effects do not occur, the ambiguity of information means that it is rarely possible to establish "tests" of others' intentions. The clearest evidence that an image is inadequate is provided by policies that are disasters. By this time it may be too late to make effective alterations.

(Baltimore: Johns Hopkins Press, 1958), pp. 118-19; Jack Schick, *The Berlin Crisis, 1958-1962* (Philadelphia: University of Pennsylvania Press, 1971), pp. 40-45. I am indebted to Robert Bowie for discussion on this point.

[63] Franklin Kilpatrick, "Perception in Critical Situations," in Kilpatrick, ed., *Explorations in Transactional Psychology* (New York: New York University Press, 1961), p. 319.

Part III

Common Misperceptions

CHAPTER EIGHT

Perceptions of Centralization

Unity and Planning

A common misperception is to see the behavior of others as more centralized, planned, and coordinated than it is. This is a manifestation of the drive to squeeze complex and unrelated events into a coherent pattern. As Francis Bacon put it: "the human understanding, from its peculiar nature, easily supposes a greater degree of order and equality in things than it really finds." And a recent study found that "People seem to be unable to accept the idea of a random situation. Instead, they try to read order into random data."[1] People want to be able to explain as much as possible of what goes on around them. To admit that a phenomenon cannot be explained, or at least cannot be explained without adding numerous and complex exceptions to our beliefs, is both psychologically uncomfortable and intellectually unsatisfying.

We even resist explanations that involve several independent elements. This can be shown in three different areas. First, disjunctive concepts (i.e. those whose members exhibit one of several possible defining characteristics) are hard to learn. Second, in explaining others' behavior we minimize the number of causes that are operating by, for example, overestimating the degree to which this behavior can be explained by consistent and powerful personality factors. Third, as Abelson has noted in his summary of an ingenious set of experiments, "individuals seeking an account of their own behavior seem to prefer unitary explanations to conjunctive explanations." Thus if a man is told—wrongly—that his heart-beat rate increased when he saw a picture of a particular woman, he will rate her as more attractive than will someone who did not have this information. "The photograph viewers do not act as though they believe, 'This girl is really ordinary looking and my heart rate increase is due to something else.' It is mentally much more economical to suppose

---

[1] Quoted in Donald Campbell, "Systematic Error on the Part of Human Links in Communication Systems," *Information and Control* 1 (1958), 363; Earl Hunt, Janet Marin, Philip Stone, *Experiments in Induction* (New York: Academic Press, 1966), p. 140 (similarly, Raymond Bauer notes that "the notion of 'accident' is alien to the enterprise of understanding. We feel impelled to give cognitive structure to all the data available to us." "Problems of Perception and the Relations Between the United States and the Soviet Union," *Journal of Conflict Resolution* 5 [September 1961], 225).

that physiological and affective reactions are covariant."[2] In these diverse contexts, as many events as possible are seen as linked to a minimum number of causes. As a result, most people are slow to perceive accidents, unintended consequences, coincidences, and small causes leading to large effects. Instead coordinated actions, plans, and conspiracies are seen.

This is a product not only of a psychological need but also of the law of Occam's Razor—the preference for the most parsimonious explanation of the data at hand. But while it is not naive or unreasonable to try to encompass most of another's behavior under a very few rules, the more complete information available later usually shows that the behavior was the product of more numerous and complex forces than contemporary observers believed. And, more important from our standpoint, the predictions that the highly oversimplified model yields are often misleading.

The context of international politics shapes the content of the perceptions of unity and planning. An awareness of the implications of anarchy leads decision-makers to be alert for dangerous plots. If another's behavior seems innocuous, they will look for a hidden and menacing significance. They see not only plans, but sinister ones. Within society this perspective characterizes the paranoid. But since threats and plots are common in international relations, the perception that others are Machiavellian cannot be easily labeled pathological. It may have been extreme of Metternich, when he heard that the Russian ambassador had died, to ask "I wonder why he did that," but the search for the devious plan believed to lurk behind even the most seemingly spontaneous behavior is neither uncommon nor totally unwarranted.

I am not arguing that actors never carefully and skillfully orchestrate moves over a long period of time and a wide geographical area or claiming that there is a simple way for a contemporary observer to determine whether a given case fits this model. Secretary of State Dulles believed that "The Russians are great chess players and their moves in the world situation are . . . attempted to be calculated as closely and carefully as though they were making moves in a chess game."[3] Dulles may have been right; similar claims are correct in other cases. But these beliefs are

---

[2] Jerome Bruner, Jacqueline Goodnow, George Austin, *A Study of Thinking* (New York: Wiley, 1962), pp. 156-81; see footnote 9 below for several findings of the overestimation of the importance of personality; Robert Abelson, "Social Psychology's Rational Man," in G. W. Mortimore and S. I. Benn, eds., *The Concept of Rationality in the Social Sciences* (London: Routledge & Kegan Paul, forthcoming).

[3] Ole Holsti, "Perceptions of Time, Perceptions of Alternatives, and Patterns of Communication as Factors in Crisis Diplomacy" (Stanford: Stanford Studies in Conflict and Integration, October 1964), p. 74.

much more common than the reality they seek to describe. Nor can they be entirely explained by a conscious desire to "play it safe." Decision-makers often spontaneously perceive an evil plan rather than make a calculated decision to act on the assumption that it lies behind the disparate events. Furthermore, they tend to be uncomfortable with explanations that point to the importance of chance or blunders.

Plans, Not Accidents and Confusion

Accidents, chance, and lack of coordination are rarely given their due by contemporary observers. Instead, they suspect that well-laid plans give events a coherence they would otherwise lack. Many would echo Einstein's refusal to accept the uncertainty principle: "God is subtle, but He is not malicious." Political examples are countless, but one example will remind us of many more. In the spring of 1918 England witnessed a bitter debate when General Maurice accused Lloyd George of providing Parliament with false information about British troop strength. The prime minister responded by claiming that, if the figures were misleading, the blame lay with his accuser, who had given them to him in the first place. Neither thought of the possibility, later shown to be the case, that the prime minister might have been sent the most recent correct figures but had never opened and read them.[4]

Men are also hesitant to believe that actions affecting them and occurring in rapid sequence could have occurred by coincidence. For primitive peoples, the idea that important outcomes can "come about through the accidental convergence of two independent chains of events is inconceivable because it is psychologically intolerable." Although modern men know of coincidences, psychologists have noted that it is nevertheless true that "when two events are appropriately coincidental in time, space, and sequence, an unavoidable and indivisible experience of causality occurs." Most of us have probably had the experience of, say, slamming a door just as a light in the room burns out. It is hard to avoid the immediate perception that the former caused the latter even though we know this is nonsense.[5]

It should not be surprising, therefore, that it is much less common for a decision-maker to see as coincidental a set of events that are planned than for him to see as part of a plan actions that are in fact coincidental. If two actors simultaneously increase their hostility toward a third, the

[4] Roy Jenkins, *Asquith* (London: Collins, 1964), pp. 467-74.

[5] Robin Horton, "African Traditional Thought and Western Science," Part 2, *Africa* 37 (April 1967), 174; Donald Campbell, "Social Attitudes and Other Acquired Behavioral Dispositions," in Sigmund Koch, ed., *Psychology: A Study of a Science*, Vol. 6 (New York: McGraw-Hill, 1963), p. 122. For a political example, see John Gaddis, *The United States and the Origins of the Cold War, 1941-1947* (New York: Columbia University Press, 1972), p. 305.

latter will believe they are acting in concert even if there is evidence that such cooperation is unlikely. If important events coincide with the arrival or departure of a powerful individual, observers will almost always believe he played a major role in them. Of special interest is that the movements of military forces are almost always seen as supporting foreign policies. Thus the Russians and Germans attributed particular significance to the fact that soon after the meeting between the tsar and the kaiser at Bjorko the British staged naval maneuvers in the Baltic without giving advance notice to other powers. They did not believe the British explanation, which was true, that the maneuvers had been long planned and the lack of notification was a mere oversight. Thirty years later when, shortly before the Italian attack on Ethiopia, the British foreign secretary's affirmation of Britain's commitment to her League obligations was immediately followed by fleet maneuvers in the Mediterranean, other states assumed the action was designed to give weight to the verbal message. In fact "The two acts were not . . . part of a single or coordinated policy and were causally unrelated." A more recent, and more dangerous, example of the tendency for a coincidence to be perceived as part of a plan was the difficulty Kennedy had in persuading Khrushchev that the U-2 reconnaissance plane that flew over Russia during the Cuban missile crisis was not conveying a threat, but really was lost. And so it is not surprising that when the American bombing raids on Hanoi and Haiphong practically ceased in late 1966 because of inclement weather, some North Vietnamese leaders thought that the United States was signaling its support for the "Marigold" peace initiative.[6] The other side of this coin is that, because decision-makers know that others are not apt to believe in coincidences, they may delay or change their behavior in order to avoid the appearance of being influenced by other events that are happening at the time.

Because chaos and confusion are not intellectually and psychologically satisfying explanations, actors must often seek hidden manipulations. For example, many observers believed the German fifth column was largely responsible for the Allies' mobilization difficulties and the swift German victories in World War II. Even those who were puzzled by the lack of direct proof of espionage and traitors could not rid themselves of this perception. Thus the British general in charge of home defense noted in his diary in July 1940: "It is extraordinary how we get circumstantial reports of 5th Column and yet we have never been able to get anything worth having. One is persuaded that it hardly exists. And yet

[6] Eugene Anderson, *The First Moroccan Crisis, 1904-1906* (Hamden, Conn.: Archon Books, 1966), pp. 292-93; George Baer, *The Coming of the Italian-Ethiopian War* (Cambridge, Mass.: Harvard University Press, 1967), p. 351; Chester Cooper, *The Lost Crusade* (New York: Dodd, Mead, 1970), p. 338.

there is signalling going on all over the place and we cannot get any evidence." Later investigation showed that fifth columnists had done very little and that the incidents attributed to them were caused by Allied disorganization and natural disorder.[7]

Like confusion, stupidity is rarely given its due. Instead, otherwise inexplicable behavior is seen as part of a devious plan, usually a hostile one. For example, in the late nineteenth century the American military attaché in France bought the plans of French fortifications. There was no reason for him to do this; as the American ambassador noted, it was "perfectly useless for us to possess plans of seaboard fortresses in France." As a consequence, however, French decision-makers concluded that the American must have been in league with the Germans or Italians. At the start of World War I the German chancellor was reinforced in his belief that England would look for a political end to the conflict by the escape of the *Goeben* from a superior British force. "To attribute this *coup* to a blunder on the part of the British admiral in command seemed so unlikely that Bethmann-Hollweg and the German Chief of the Admiralty were inclined to conclude that Britain was unwilling to strike any 'heavy blows' against Germany."[8]

One Actor, Not Several

Coherence and consistency are further imposed on the world by the propensity of actors to see others as trying to maximize the same set of values in different situations and in different periods of time. As we will discuss at the end of this chapter, this parsimonious assumption often leads to powerful explanations, but it can be misleading when the other's decisions are the outcome of shifting interactions among conflicting forces and interests. Although the bulk of this section will discuss the underestimation of the degree to which the other's behavior is produced by independent actions of separate parts of the other's government, we should also note that the behavior of individuals is often similarly mis-

[7] Louis De Jong, *The German Fifth Column in the Second World War*, translated by C. M. Geyle (Chicago: University of Chicago Press, 1961), passim; Roderick Macleod and Denis Kelly, eds., *Time Unguarded: The Ironside Diaries, 1937-1940* (New York: McKay, 1962), p. 377, also pp. 341, 347, and 360.

[8] Alfred Vagts, *The Military Attaché* (Princeton: Princeton University Press, 1967), pp. 222-23; Egmont Zechlin, "Cabinet versus Economic Warfare in Germany: Policy and Strategy during the Early Months of the First World War," in H. W. Koch, ed., *The Origins of the First World War* (London: Macmillan and Co., 1972), p. 187. A variant of this is the propensity to see sophisticated bargaining tactics in behavior that is actually the result of the other's inexperience. Edward Peters, a professional labor conciliator, has observed many cases in which one side is not experienced in bargaining and the other side, not realizing this, makes over-sophisticated interpretations of the first side's behavior. *Strategy and Tactics in Labor Negotiations* (New London, Conn.: National Foremen's Institute, 1955), p. 137.

perceived. Because each person seeks a variety of goals in a complex environment, his behavior may be self-contradictory. As we showed in Chapter 4, people pursue multiple goals without recognizing the trade-offs among them and act to further one value in one context and another value in a different situation. In other words, the view of the individual as a billiard ball is often as invalid as the analogous view of the state. We can see the person, just as we see the state, as governed by differing and often incompatible values that sometimes produce strange compromises and sometimes act independently in their own spheres. But because of the drive "to complete the incomplete, to unify, to achieve closure," people tend to "overestimate the unity of personality." Furthermore, observers usually overestimate the influence of the other's internal characteristics and underestimate the influence of the situation the other is in. As a result, greater constancy is expected, and observers are surprised when the person behaves differently under changed circumstances. As Heider puts it:

> Often the momentary situation which, at least in part, determines the behavior of a person is disregarded and the behavior is taken as a manifestation of personal characteristics. . . . In *She Stoops to Conquer* Goldsmith presents a young man whose behavior varies extremely with the momentary situation. The other characters attribute the temporary behavior to the permanent personality and this error produces many of the comic situations in this play.[9]

But what is of most importance for international relations is that decision-makers generally overestimate the degree to which their opposite numbers have the information and power to impose their desires on all parts of their own governments. The state's behavior is usually seen as centrally controlled rather than as the independent actions of actors trying to further their own interests and their partial and biased conceptions of the national interest. For example, because most U.S. decision-makers analyze Soviet defense policy as though it were the embodiment of a coherent plan, they use weapons procurement as an index of Soviet

---

[9] H. C. Smith, "Sensitivity to People," in Hans Toch and Henry Smith, eds., *Social Perception* (Princeton: D. Van Nostrand, 1968), pp. 15-17; Gustav Ichheiser, *Appearances and Realities* (San Francisco: Jossey-Bass, 1970), pp. 49-59; Fritz Heider, "Social Perception and Phenomenal Causality," *Psychological Review* 51 (1944), 361-62. Also see Edward Jones and Victor Harris, "The Attribution of Attitudes," *Journal of Experimental Social Psychology* 3 (1967), 1-24. As has been widely noted, this tendency has strong moral implications when it leads people "to see the cause of [individuals'] successes and failures in their personal characteristics and not in other conditions." (Heider, "Social Perception and Phenomenal Causality," p. 361.) This is also consistent with the experimental findings discussed in Harold Kelley, *Attribution in Social Interaction* (Morristown, N.J.: General Learning Press, 1971), p. 19.

strategy. The development of an inefficient system useful only in a first strike and the deployment of very large missiles thus were taken as showing that the Soviets must be contemplating aggression. Senator Ervin did not think much of the claim that it was difficult to draw inferences from the Russian build-up:

> I don't see anything wrong with a man using a bit of commonsense. If I saw a man going to the woodpile with an axe, I would think he was going to cut some wood, and if he was going to work on a still, I would figure he was going to make a little liquor.
>
> You tell me you don't infer that when the Russians build SS-9's with a 25-megaton yield, that they had the idea of knocking out our missiles, our Minuteman?[10]

But if the Russian military budget reflects the outcome of parochial interservice conflicts, then procurement tells us little about Soviet foreign policy intentions. The latter will be determined under a different power distribution, or by different people, or by the same people acting on different values.

A misperception of this kind was partly responsible for the Chinese decision to enter the war in Korea. "Peking ignored the pluralistic political process in the West and failed to differentiate between the true locus of power in Washington and the confusion of voices on both sides of the Pacific Ocean. Utterances by 'authoritative spokesmen' in Tokyo were given equal weight (if not greater) with statements from Secretary Acheson and President Truman." The Chinese found it hard to believe that officials of the United States' government could be advocating a policy which did not represent the views of the highest circles. Similarly, in 1913 when California prohibited Japanese from owning or leasing land in that state, the Japanese government was "unable to believe that the federal government was powerless to abrogate a state law, and [was] convinced that the action was a deliberate insult."[11]

Decision-makers tend to overestimate the centralization of the other's policies even if they are familiar with the other's domestic politics and elite divisions. Richard Neustadt has demonstrated that the dispute between the United States and Britain about the cancellation of Skybolt was exacerbated because each side failed to understand the other's internal bargaining processes even though the two countries had experi-

---

[10] *Military Implications of the Treaty on the Limitations of Anti-Ballistic Missile Systems and the Interim Agreement on Limitation of Strategic Offensive Arms*, Hearings before the Committee on Armed Services, United States Senate, 92nd Congress, 2nd Session, p. 387.

[11] Allen Whiting, *China Crosses the Yalu* (Stanford: Stanford University Press, 1968), p. 169; Barbara Tuchman, *The Zimmermann Telegram* (New York: Viking, 1958), pp. 40-41.

enced years of intimate and complex cooperation, knowledge about how the other's government worked was widely diffused throughout both countries, and personal contacts between the governments were extensive. These distortions can only be more pronounced between states that are less familiar with each other.[12]

Two important cases do not fit our generalization. Before World War II many people, while underestimating the confusion and bargaining on small disputes within the Reich, overestimated the pluralism on the vital foreign policy issues that concerned Hitler most. Similarly, during the war many Allied statesmen were puzzled by rapid alterations of Soviet attitude, and "the most usual explanation . . . was that when Stalin got really tough he was expressing the attitude of the mysterious Politburo rather than his own personal appraisal of the main issue."[13] Even in these cases, however, what was perceived involved a minimum of confusion—two factions vying for control of a centralized policy.

SPECIAL CASES

The tendency for an actor to believe that others are highly unified can be observed in two other contexts. First, alliances usually appear more durable and binding from the outside than from the inside. For example, "During the tense years preceding the outbreak of the Second World War, many people believed that an alliance had existed between Germany and Italy ever since 1936 and that they had conducted a concerted policy in which every move was carefully planned and agreed upon." The fact that coordination was hard to discern and its existence denied by these countries led to the conclusion that they "pretended to act independently . . . in order to obtain greater concessions from the Western Powers."[14] In fact, Germany and Italy not only failed to develop joint plans, but each was often unsure of the other's intentions and took important actions without informing the other.

More important consequences followed from the fact that the Axis powers also overestimated the degree to which their opponents were united. Even though the Japanese ambassador to the United States correctly told his government that American leaders thought that the Axis alliance was tighter than it was, he overestimated the extent of Anglo-

[12] *Alliance Politics* (New York: Columbia University Press, 1970). That Neustadt underestimates the degree of real incompatibility between the United States and Britain in these cases should not obscure his well-documented argument that neither side adequately understood the ways in which the other's internal conflicts affected its policies.

[13] Robert Sherwood, *Roosevelt and Hopkins* (New York: Harper and Brothers, 1948), p. 621. For another exception, see Raymond Esthus, *Theodore Roosevelt and Japan* (Seattle: University of Washington Press, 1966), p. 66.

[14] Felix Gilbert, "Ciano and His Ambassadors," in Gordon Craig and Felix Gilbert, eds., *The Diplomats* (Princeton: Princeton University Press, 1953), p. 529.

American cooperation.[15] This view led Japan to believe that America, even if not directly attacked, would enter the war if Japan moved against the British and Dutch resource-rich Asian territories. This meant that Japan had either to forego access to these resources, thus giving up her aim of dominating China, or else attack the United States. In fact, if Japan had moved south without such an attack, Roosevelt would have been placed in a terrible dilemma, as he well realized. Similarly, in the postwar world the United States overestimated the Russian control over Tito and was slow to recognize the Sino-Soviet split.

Second, domestic groups in conflict see the other side as more unified than it is. In local labor-management disputes each side is apt to believe incorrectly that the other is controlled from above (i.e. from the international union office or from the company's central headquarters). Pressure groups believe that the opposition is better organized than it is. Both Democrats and Republicans in the House of Representatives see the other party as the one that is the more organized and disciplined. Similarly, Lewis Anthony Dexter reports that "in shifting from Democratic campaigning to Republican campaigning [one finds that] each side has a picture of the other as well organized, purposive, intense, which is quite incompatible with what one sees and feels when one is actually over there."[16]

Variables Encouraging the Perception of Unity and Planning

While the tendency to see the other side as centralized and Machiavellian is widespread, it is especially strong in some actors. The Soviets, whose operational code indicates "nothing is accidental," believe all the moves of their bourgeois enemies to be carefully planned.[17] Many com-

[15] T. B. Kittredge, "United States Defense Policy and Strategy; 1941," *U.S. News & World Report*, December 3, 1954, pp. 123-24. For other examples see David Walder, *The Chanak Affair* (New York: Macmillan Co., 1969), p. 123, Saul Friedlander, *Prelude to Downfall* (New York: Knopf, 1967), p. 192 (for an exception, see p. 224), and Allen Whiting, *The Chinese Calculus of Deterrence* (Ann Arbor: University of Michigan Press, 1975), pp. 62-72.

[16] Robert Blake, Herbert Shepard, and Jane Mouton, *Managing Intergroup Conflict in Industry* (Houston, Texas: Gulf Publishing Co., 1964), p. 182; Raymond Bauer, Ithiel de Sola Pool, and Lewis Anthony Dexter, *American Business and Public Policy* (New York: Atherton, 1963), p. 399; Charles Clapp, *The Congressman* (Washington: Brookings Institution, 1963), pp. 17-19; Dexter, *The Sociology and Politics of Congress* (Chicago: Rand McNally, 1969), pp. 132-33. Similar perceptions of the other side's unity have been found in the conflict between two groups favoring different kinds of treatment for the mentally ill. See Anselm Strauss et al., *Psychiatric Ideologies and Institutions* (New York: Free Press, 1964), pp. 130-31.

[17] Early in the life of the U.S.S.R. Louis Fischer noted that the "Bolsheviks often thought too primitively." (*The Soviets in World Affairs* [New York: Vintage, 1960], p. 544.) It was observed of Molotov twenty years later: "He is innately suspicious. He seeks for hidden meanings and tricks where there are none. He

mentators argue that French leaders make decisions with the aid of long-range plans and orderly calculations and so often see others as operating in this way. Stanley Hoffmann notes that France sees "American moves . . . not as improvisations but as the unfolding of a design," and Dorothy Pickles argues that

> one of the most important factors in Franco-British misunderstanding is the British preference for cautious empiricism, and dislike of specific commitments in fields of general principles . . . . [as compared to the French] Cartesian preferences for precision, and for progression from the general to the particular, and for commitments and guarantees. . . . Unfortunately [this] tends to make the French suspect the British more often of duplicity than of simplicity. . . . [O]ne British aircraft executive involved [in conversations with the French over the Concorde] was reported as having complained that: "The French always think we're being Machiavellian, when in fact we're just muddling through."[18]

Some individuals are prone to see others as centralized and Machiavellian. This was true of Friedrich von Holstein, who played a large part in the formation of German foreign policy after Bismarck's retirement. Without fail, he saw ambiguous events as evidence that England was engaging in elaborate plots to harm Germany. The fear "that Germany might be made a cat's-paw 'to pull English chestnuts out of the fire' became an obsession with him." While others in Germany shared some of these beliefs[19] (and some people in England had similar views about Germany), the consistency with which Holstein perceived that British

---

takes it for granted that his opponents are trying to trick him and put over something nefarious." (In Gordon Craig, "Totalitarian Approaches to Diplomatic Negotiations," in A. O. Sarkissian, ed., *Studies in Diplomatic History in Honor of G.P. Gooch* [London: Longmans, 1961], p. 120.) Also see Nathan Leites, *A Study of Bolshevism* (Glencoe: Ill.: Free Press, 1953), pp. 67-73. Although this position is generally accepted, it should be noted that a content analysis of Soviet elite publications found that the Russians tend to think that U.S. foreign policy is formed haphazardly, "merely responding to events" rather than following a carefully developed plan. (J. David Singer, "Soviet and American Foreign Policy Attitudes: Content Analysis of Elite Articulations," *Journal of Conflict Resolution* 8 [December 1964], 442.) But it is difficult to be sure that these publications accurately mirror the views of the Soviet elite.

[18] "Perceptions, Reality, and the Franco-American Conflict," *Journal of International Affairs* 21, No. 1 (1967), 67; *The Uneasy Entente* (London: Oxford University Press, 1966), pp. 5-7. The cause of these misperceptions is not ideology, as in the case of the Soviets, but national style.

[19] Raymond Sontag, *European Diplomatic History, 1871-1932* (New York: Appleton-Century-Crofts, 1933), p. 71. One scholar notes that "over-profundity [was] characteristic of official German reasoning" on foreign policy around the turn of the century. (J.A.S. Grenville, *Lord Salisbury and Foreign Policy* [London: Athlone Press, 1964], p. 39.)

behavior was not only hostile but involved a careful plan to trap Germany, is unusual and seems at least partially related to his own propensity to engage in plots. Similarly, it has been noted that Lloyd George, "himself a master of the art of political intrigue, attributed to [Generals] Haig and Robertson a similar subtlety, and assumed that they based their calculations on the same kind of considerations that actuated him."[20] For different reasons, it is probable that people with low tolerance for ambiguity and low cognitive complexity are also especially likely to perceive more centralization than is present. People with these psychological characteristics find it difficult and disturbing to cope with confusion.

Finally, perceptions of overcentralization and over-Machiavellianism are more apt to occur if the two sides are in conflict. Part of the explanation is that actors who are cooperating usually have detailed information about each other, and the greater the information, the greater the differentiation and diversity that will be perceived. Thus before the Opium War the Chinese emperor and his agents in Canton were equally hostile to the British. But the latter had more information about the British and realized that the emperor was incorrect in considering the British traders and government officials to be united.[21] Furthermore, there are usually more numerous and complex lines of communication between allies than between enemies. Decision-makers receive information from several parts of an ally's government, units of the two bureaucracies communicate directly with each other, and each side learns about the other's internal conflicts. Adversaries not only lack such diverse information but are also especially apt to see each other as highly centralized because behavior that might seem incompatible with a careful plan can be explained as attempted deception.[22] This perception is often supported by the desire to act on the conservative assumption that the other's hostility will be implemented with great skill and efficiency.

BEING MISINFORMED ABOUT ONE'S OWN BEHAVIOR

The previous discussion leads to the proposition that actors will tend to perceive the behavior of subordinates and agents of the other side (e.g. ambassadors, low-level officials) as carrying out the other's official policy. Actors underestimate the degree and frequency of violations of the spirit and letter of instructions. They are slow to see that the agents

[20] Robert Blake, "Great Britain," in Michael Howard, ed., *Soldiers and Governments* (London: Eyre and Spottiswoode, 1957), p. 47.

[21] Immanuel C. Y. Hsu, *China's Entrance into the Family of Nations* (Cambridge, Mass.: Harvard University Press, 1960), pp. 99-108.

[22] See, for example, Elting Morison, *Turmoil and Tradition: The Life and Times of Henry L. Stimson* (Boston: Houghton Mifflin, 1960), p. 431.

may not be truly representing their masters. Thus after the liberation of France in 1944 "General Gerow, the highest-ranking American in [Paris] conducted his French relations with remarkable insensitivity. . . . De Gaulle, hypersensitive about American motivations, was persuaded that Gerow could not have been so consistently insulting without orders from a higher authority." Similarly, in 1918 the initial landings of a small number of British soldiers in Murmansk and Vladivostok were ordered by the local military authorities on their own for reasons unconnected with general Anglo-Russian relations. But the Soviets assumed they indicated that London had decided on large-scale intervention.[23]

These misperceptions resemble those discussed earlier. But further complexity, and often illusory incompatibility, is created when the agent's home government, as well as the government he is dealing with, does not realize that he failed to convey the desired impressions. Although decision-makers know that their own state is not monolithic, that policy is often the result of bargaining, and that different parts of the government often follow different policies, they overestimate the degree of centralization in their own state's implementation of policy. Unless they have evidence to the contrary, decision-makers assume that their agents act as instructed. When this belief is incorrect, leaders will be misled about the actions taken in the name of their state.[24]

We are dealing not with the familiar limits on the decision-maker's ability to enforce his will on his government, but with the defects in his

[23] Milton Viorst, *Hostile Allies* (New York: Macmillan Co., 1965), p. 216; Richard Ullman, *Anglo-Soviet Relations, 1917-1921*, vol. 1: *Intervention and the War* (Princeton: Princeton University Press, 1961), pp. 109-19, 146-50; James Crowley, *Japan's Quest for Autonomy* (Princeton: Princeton University Press, 1966), p. 166. A few exceptions can be found. The Germans incorrectly blamed the breaking off of colonial negotiations with England in 1890 on the English agent involved; C. J. Lowe, *The Reluctant Imperialists* (New York: Macmillan Co., 1969), p. 144. In 1926 Mussolini "attributed Anglo-Italian difficulties to the 'excessive zeal of local British agents'"; Alan Cassels, *Mussolini's Early Diplomacy* (Princeton: Princeton University Press, 1970), p. 304. In 1932 Secretary of State Stimson exaggerated the degree to which the British foreign secretary could act on his own without cabinet approval; Robert Ferrell, *American Diplomacy in the Great Depression* (New York: Norton, 1970), p. 182.

[24] This is not to deny that even if the actor delivers the message himself he may not understand its impact and may thus misunderstand the other's later behavior. For example, in 1939 the Finnish foreign minister went to Moscow to try to ease tensions and protect Finnish independence by balancing his country's ties to Germany with links to Russia. He thought his mission had failed to convince Russia that Finland wanted better relations. In fact, he had "succeeded far too well. He had created in Moscow the impression that Finland was prepared to entrust her security to the Soviet Union"; Max Jakobson, *The Diplomacy of the Winter War* (Cambridge, Mass.: Harvard University Press, 1961), p. 28. Had the foreign minister known of the impression he had made, he might have been able to design his later behavior in a way to reduce the unnecessary aspects of the conflict.

knowledge of what his government is doing. This is important here because the other state's behavior is partly a function of what the decision-maker's state does. So if the decision-maker is misinformed about the actions taken in the name of his state, he will believe that the other is responding to a different set of events than that which the other has seen, and so he will not be able to understand why the other is acting as it is. To explore this topic we must consider the reasons why decision-makers are incorrectly informed about their own state's behavior and, more specifically, the ways in which behavior can diverge from the decision-maker's instructions without his awareness.

Misinformation about Physical Effects

Even if subordinates faithfully implement their instructions, the decision-maker's beliefs about what has been done may be inaccurate because the actions were based on false premises or did not produce the reported effects. For example, in late July 1965 the United States attacked some anti-aircraft sites in North Vietnam. Washington believed that by doing this and killing Russian technicians the United States had demonstrated its determination and need not take other actions that were being considered (e.g. declaring a national emergency and calling up the National Guard). It was later discovered, however, that the missile sites were dummies and the attack had killed no one.[25] Similarly, had the Israelis sought to demonstrate their resolve by destroying anti-aircraft missile sites that they thought were deployed in violations of the 1970 cease fire, the impression conveyed would not be the desired one if the missiles had been installed legally or if the Egyptian decision-makers thought this was the case.

Second, even if his information about the physical environment is correct, the actor's behavior will not yield the expected or reported results if his instruments and techniques are less precise than he believes. For example, George Quester shows that one reason why the restraints on bombing civilians in World War II broke down was that neither side realized that it was not able to bomb accurately enough to hit military targets without doing collateral damage. Each side believed that it and the other were bombing accurately. Each therefore thought it was not killing the other's civilians and that the bombs that fell on its civilians reflected the other's policy. Inevitably, then, restraints could not be maintained.[26]

[25] Peter Lisagor, "Missile Site Raid Called a Failure," *San Francisco Chronicle*, August 7, 1965. A related problem is reported in James Feron, "Israelis Report Seven MIG's Downed in Syrian Clash," *New York Times*, July 9, 1969.

[26] George Quester, *Deterrence Before Hiroshima* (New York: Wiley, 1966), pp. 105-22. Similarly, in World War I the British attributed the accidental bombing of a royal palace to official German policy. See Douglas Robinson, *The Zeppelin in Combat* (London: G. T. Foulis, 1962), p. 174.

Disobedience by Agents

Failures of tools are a less important cause of a decision-maker's incorrect view of what his state has done than is the human element. In the previous discussion we assumed that the decision-maker's subordinates faithfully carried out their instructions. When this is not true, two problems are created. First, and most obviously, the decision-maker does not fully control foreign policy. Undesired impressions and commitments will be given. For example, unauthorized actions by agents on the spot contributed to colonial expansion in the nineteenth century.[27] A second and less well-known set of problems arises when the agent does not report his actions accurately. The decision-maker will then be misinformed about what information the other side has about his state and so will not be able to understand the image the other holds or the policy that it follows.

CAUSES OF DISOBEDIENCE

Agents may disobey instructions when their values, payoffs, and tactical judgments differ from those of the decision-makers at home. Their selection and self-selection are important here. The kind of person who had the skills, knowledge, and desire to serve in Africa and Asia in the nineteenth century usually wanted to see his country expand its control. In addition, serving as an agent can alter the person's values and create divergences where there were none initially. Ambassadors are often "captured" by the state they deal with. And an agent engaged in negotiations will often develop political and psychological incentives to reach an agreement that are not shared by the decision-makers at home.[28] The agent may then not only try to convince his government to accept a settlement it finds unacceptable, but may also break his instructions, for example by withholding some demands or by indicating to the other side that if it stands firm the agent's side will retreat.

The agent's beliefs about what tactics are appropriate may also differ from the views of those at home. The man on the spot almost always feels he knows more about the local situation than his superior and believes many of his instructions to be hopelessly out of touch with the reality he sees. His superiors, he is apt to conclude, do not understand what is happening or what can be achieved. In labor-management nego-

[27] W. David McIntyre, *The Imperial Frontier in the Tropics, 1865-75* (London: Macmillan and Co., and New York: St. Martin's, 1967) (also see John Galbraith, "The Turbulent Frontier," in Robert Art and Robert Jervis, eds., *International Politics* [Boston: Little, Brown, 1973]); Richard W. Van Alstyne, *The Rising American Empire* (Chicago: Quadrangle, 1965), pp. 158-59.

[28] Fred Iklé, *How Nations Negotiate* (New York: Harper and Row, 1964), pp. 143-50.

tiations, as Walton and McKersie have shown, agents of both sides often form an alliance to convince their "home governments" to scale down their expectations. In these cases the agent has to convince his own side that he is following his instructions to stand firm and yet indicate to the agent from the other side that he will make concessions if need be.[29]

TYPES OF DISOBEDIENCE

An agent's disobedience can take various forms. In some cases an agent may refuse to deliver a message or may substitute one of his own for that of his government. In negotiations with Portugal in 1943 George Kennan gave the Portuguese government an assurance that was "in direct violation of the written orders I had in my safe." Before Pearl Harbor, Japan's ambassador to the United States sometimes withheld his government's proposals and on other occasions altered them. In 1809 the British minister to the United States broke his instructions and signed a treaty with America that did not meet major British demands. More often than breaking his instructions an agent will twist them by transmitting his message in a manner that alters its impact, most commonly by expressing a "private opinion" that contradicts the official message. Thus when the English ambassador to Germany, Nevile Henderson, was instructed to protest the take-over of Austria he did so but added that he thought that the Austrians "had acted with precipitate folly." He expressed similar opinions during the negotiations over Czechoslovakia when

> he went very far in accepting the German point of view on Central European questions. . . . [and] was wholly uninhibited in expressing views which could only encourage the Nazi leaders in their plans. . . . [W]hen he was arguing in his reports to London that a special warning to Hitler was unnecessary since the German government must be fully aware of Britain's determination to stand with France and Czechoslovakia, he told a German S.S. leader that "he personally had no sympathy at all with the Czechs and moreover considered the placing of the Sudeten Germans under Czech domination to be a grave mistake."[30]

Similarly, Joseph Kennedy, the American ambassador to Britain, told

[29] Richard Walton and Robert McKersie, *A Behavioral Theory of Labor Negotiations* (New York: McGraw-Hill, 1965), pp. 316-47.

[30] George Kennan, *Memoirs*, vol. 1: *1925-1950* (Boston: Little, Brown, 1967), p. 155; Robert Butow, *The John Doe Associates* (Stanford: Stanford University Press, 1974), pp. 236, 255; Bradford Perkins, *Prologue to War* (Philadelphia: University of Pennsylvania Press, 1955), pp. 211-19; Felix Gilbert, "Two British Ambassadors: Perth and Henderson," in Craig and Gilbert, eds., *The Diplomats*, pp. 538, 540-41.

"the counselor of the German embassy in London that he intended to use all his influence to keep the U.S. out of war."[31]

Such unofficial remarks can affect the perceiving state's image in three ways. First, the comments may be seen as signals. That is, the perceiver may believe that the state told its representative to make the "private" statements. Because such statements can be disavowed if necessary, they are often used for probes and feelers.[32] Second, the perceiving state may take the agent's views as representing strong trends within the other state which, while not yet official policy, will become so. For example, in 1939 German and Italians were warranted in paying more attention to the unofficial comments of Japanese ambassadors than to the messages these agents were instructed to deliver. The ambassadors' private statements reflected the views of the army, and the army strongly influenced the most important foreign policy decisions. Third, and least likely, the perceiver may believe that the agent's private views are likely to influence his government's policy either because of their persuasiveness or because the agent has an independent political base at home.

CONSEQUENCES OF LACK OF AWARENESS OF AGENTS' BEHAVIOR

To focus not on the simple effects that follow from agents' independent actions but on the more complex consequences of a decision-maker's being misinformed about his agents' behavior and thus holding incorrect views about the evidence confronting the other side, we should re-examine two of the examples cited above. Immediately after George Kennan gave the Portuguese government a forbidden assurance, he explained his actions to Washington.[33] As a result, the U.S. government knew what the Portuguese believed the U.S. position to be and adjusted its policy accordingly. On the other hand, Nevile Henderson did not report home many of the "private opinions" he expressed to the Germans. Although the British decision-makers realized that Henderson made comments that were more pro-appeasement than the official position, they did not know the extent or vehemence of his remarks. They were

[31] William Kaufmann, "Two American Ambassadors: Bullitt and Kennedy," in *ibid.*, p. 663. This is not to imply that if the agent follows his instructions the desired message will always be conveyed throughout the other state's hierarchy. Lewis Namier notes the tendency of each participant in a discussion to file reports that sharpen his own remarks and weaken those of his opposite number; *Diplomatic Prelude* (London: Macmillan and Co., 1948), p. 240. This conclusion has been confirmed by Glen Stassen's research on the differences between the reports written by Henderson and the German officials.

[32] For an unusual example of an agent's being instructed to "express a personal opinion" and the perceiver taking the message only at face value, see Anderson, *The First Moroccan Crisis*, pp. 241-44.

[33] Kennan, *Memoirs*, vol. 1, p. 155.

thus denied access to an important input into the German image of Britain, were handicapped in their efforts to determine German perceptions, and therefore found it more difficult to design a policy that would convince Germany that Britain would resist further demands. They thought their resolve was clear. Had they known what Henderson was saying, they might have sent additional, stronger messages.

Being misinformed about the activities of one's agent will often increase conflict since it will increase the chances that the state will behave in ways that appear erratic and deceptive. Because each side is proceeding on different beliefs about what has been done in the name of the state, the potential for misunderstanding is enormous. Thus when in the spring of 1941 the Japanese ambassador to the United States failed to report that Secretary of State Hull had said only that a draft proposal merited further discussion, and instead reported that Hull had sponsored it, he inflated his government's expectations and thereby diminished the chances that the negotiations could succeed. When the less conciliatory official note arrived two months later, the Japanese believed

> that the American mood was stiffening. . . . The initial Japanese hope of being able to retain the essence by compromising on the form . . . gradually waned and, as it did so, Japan's own bearing in the negotiations stiffened. Those who had been suspicious of Washington's motives from the outset, or who were opposed to even the slightest diplomatic concession, began finding it easier to interfere. A typical method was to attack the sincerity of the United States by pointing to the marked differences between the "American" offer of mid-April . . . and [the] "second" proposal.[34]

The American reaction was similar, if less extreme. Hull was deeply disappointed by an authentic Japanese message of September 1941 because he "had been 'conditioned' by the earlier statements [that misrepresented the official position] . . . to expect much more than Japan was currently offering. He now felt that the Japanese were presenting a far narrower program of settlement than before."[35]

A classic example of this effect is supplied by the activities of Paul von Hatzfeldt and Hermann von Eckardstein, respectively the German ambassador to England and the first secretary of the embassy around the turn of the twentieth century. These agents believed that the interests of both Germany and England would be served by an alliance but that "the technicalities of diplomatic procedure" prevented either side from taking

[34] Robert Butow, *Tojo and the Coming of the War* (Princeton: Princeton University Press, 1961), p. 241. The draft understanding presented by the priests was actually written by a Japanese colonel.

[35] Butow, *The John Doe Associates*, p. 270.

the initiative.[36] Over a period of years each of them attempted to bring the two states together by developing a tentative offer of his own design, telling the British that this was a German feeler, and reporting to Berlin that the British had authored the proposal. The difficulty with this procedure became apparent when the two states entered into direct talks. Because each side had been given different information, divergent expectations had developed. Each thought that the other had shown itself to be very interested in an agreement, and each therefore expected the other to take the initiative and make further concessions. Even if the initial proposal had been acceptable to both sides, the negotiations might have broken down because each side could have thought it a wise strategy to hold out for an even more favorable settlement.[37] But the agents had underestimated the magnitude of the obstacles to an alliance, and the consequences were even worse. Thus in 1895 Hatzfeldt told his government that Lord Salisbury had proposed that the great powers divide the Ottoman Empire. Expecting to find a cooperative partner, the kaiser raised this subject when he visited England. But Hatzfeldt's fictional report backfired when Salisbury would not consider such a plan and replied in a manner quite out of keeping with his supposed initiative. As a result, the kaiser grew angry and felt that "The British policy of trying to reach agreement with all the Powers . . . was just another attempt to sow distrust among the continental countries."[38]

Several years later the British and Germans again considered an agreement, and the agents repeated their distortions. When the negotiations broke down, the British were "not sure what to think," and the Germans less charitably felt that the "British" action of first originating a proposal and then displaying no interest in it constituted "a gratuitous insult." A minor incident reinforced this impression. Germany sent an agent, Stuebel, to England to settle a dispute with England over Chinese customs rates. The British were told by Eckardstein that

> Stuebel did not represent the Kaiser's views and so refused to yield an inch. In fact, . . . the opposite was true. It was Stuebel, and not Eckardstein, who represented the views of Berlin, and he returned to Germany full of complaint at the brusque treatment he had suffered. It was this episode which led the Kaiser into his famous denunciation of the British government as "unmitigated noodles" and into angry complaints that they were not treating him with confidence.[39]

[36] Grenville, *Lord Salisbury and Foreign Policy*, p. 64.
[37] For an example of such a German perception, see *ibid.*, p. 355.
[38] *Ibid.*, p. 43.
[39] *Ibid.*, pp. 355, 363; George Monger, *The End of Isolation* (London: Nelson and Sons, 1963), p. 32. The British ambassador to Germany similarly once made

Another German agent failed to report an unauthorized promise, with a different but equally striking result. At the start of the 1905 Moroccan crisis the German chancellor instructed his ambassador to the United States, Sternburg, to try to win President Roosevelt's support by telling him that if the negotiations with France ran into difficulties Sternburg would be willing to urge on the kaiser any practical and fair solution that the president might suggest. But by accident or design the ambassador told the president that the kaiser had promised to *adopt* any such proposal that the president would make. When the conference at Algeciras deadlocked, the president decided to invoke the "promise."

Roosevelt's message caused consternation in Berlin. [The chancellor] realized for the first time the sweeping nature of Sternburg's letter to Roosevelt. . . . [and] knew that Sternburg's inexplicable blunder had placed Germany in an almost hopeless position. If it were impossible to disavow the letter, [the chancellor] telegraphed Sternburg, "his Majesty will probably hardly be able to avoid accepting the present proposal."[40]

When a nation has interests throughout the world, other states will draw important inferences from the behavior of its agents in a third area. If both sides' agents break their instructions and deceive their home governments, misunderstandings will be compounded because each state will overestimate the degree to which both sides are centralized. This partially explains the hostility between France and Britain preceding the Seven Years' War, between France and Britain over Greece and Tahiti in the early 1840s, and between the United States and Germany over Samoa in the late 1880s.[41] In these situations the home governments adopted a policy of cooperation, but the agents on the spot sought to expand their nation's influence. This not only increased the local conflict but led to increased suspicion and tension between the home governments. Each assumed that both sides' agents were obeying instructions. Thus both thought that their agents were trying to cooperate, as they had been told to do, and that the antagonistic behavior of the other state's agents represented official policy. As a result, the other state was seen as

---

a proposal to the kaiser and in his report home implied that it had originated with the Germans. (Grenville, *Lord Salisbury and Foreign Policy*, p. 175.)

[40] Raymond Esthus, *Theodore Roosevelt and the International Rivalries* (Waltham, Mass.: Ginn-Blaisdell, 1970), pp. 81-82, 99. In fact, the situation was even worse than the Germans knew. Roosevelt had communicated to the French ambassador both the German "promise" and his own decision to invoke it.

[41] Patrice Higonnet, "The Origins of the Seven Years' War," *Journal of Modern History* 40 (March 1968), 57-90; Robert William Seton-Watson, *Britain in Europe, 1789-1914* (New York: Macmillan Co., 1937), p. 233.

responding with hostility to a policy of friendship. The other's protestations that it was the aggrieved party, that it was willing to settle the local conflict but was being taken advantage of, were rejected as deceitful hypocrisy.

Finally, it is not always the agent who deserves the blame if the home government does not know what he has done. Those at home sometimes fail to give clear instructions or to pay careful attention to the agents' reports. Knowing what messages he wants to convey, even the most experienced statesman may assume too quickly that both his agent and the other state understand his position. For example, in 1884–1885 Bismarck reversed his earlier policy and sought African colonies. Believing that this new stance had been adequately communicated to the British, he interpreted their intransigence as hostility and decided that only a more anti-British policy could coerce England into cooperating. In fact, Britain—and the German ambassador as well—had not understood what Bismarck wanted. While this may be partly traceable to British "slow-wittedness," Bismarck himself never carefully considered the information he was transmitting to England. He forgot how strongly his earlier notes had disclaimed any interest in the area he now wanted and "was obviously taken aback when [the German ambassador] later quoted to him the relevant passages of [a] dispatch by way of explaining his own failure to detect the change in German policy." Furthermore, Bismarck neglected to dispatch a message he had drafted that clearly explained his new policy. And, what is more important here than the source of the misunderstanding between the chancellor and his ambassador, even though an analysis of England's interests would have indicated that Britain was unlikely to defy Germany on a marginal issue, Bismarck never seriously considered the possibility that his agent might not have acted as he thought he had told him to.[42]

CONSEQUENCES OF PERCEPTIONS OF UNITY AND PLANNING

The perception of greater coherence than is present leads the actor astray in three ways. First, taking the other side's behavior as the product of a centralized actor with integrated values, inferring the plan that generated this behavior, and projecting this pattern into the future will be misleading if the behavior was the result of shifting internal bargaining, ad hoc decisions, and uncoordinated actions. A momentary or transient phenomenon will be endowed with enduring qualities that are expected to determine policy at later times and on other issues. Thus states make

---

[42] Henry Ashby Turner, Jr., "Bismarck's Imperialist Venture: Anti-British in Origin?" in Prosser Gifford and William Roger Louis, eds., *Britain and Germany in Africa* (New Haven: Yale University Press, 1967), pp. 63-64.

sophisticated, and often alarming, inferences from the policy that the other pursues in one issue-area without giving sufficient consideration to the possibility that the coalition that decides the policy in that area may not be the one that establishes other policies, or that, even if the same people have power in both arenas, the values served in one are different from those that will be given priority in the other. Similarly, when the behavior of scattered agents is seen as part of a centrally directed plan, observers will draw far-reaching inferences from isolated actions. For example, when at the turn of the nineteenth century negotiations between the United States and Britain over the disposition of pre-Revolution debts broke down just as the Americans were dispatching a mission to France to try to improve relations, the British saw the two events as linked to a coherent anti-British position that would continue for several years. A decade later when there was trouble with the Indians on the western frontier, most Americans assumed this was connected with British efforts to put pressure on the United States. More recently, China's entry into the Korean War was caused in part by her interpretation of "*ad hoc* American decisions on Korea and Taiwan . . . as the outcome of carefully designed schemes for 'aggression' in Asia."[43] There is no doubt that the American policy was against the interests of China, but to China it appeared even more hostile and dangerous because it was seen as the initial stages of a plan whose later phases would strike directly at her homeland.

An even more extreme case occurred when the British severed relations with Russia in 1927. The Bolsheviks did not think that Britain had acted "merely as a demonstration or to rid London of a Soviet Embassy." While they did not expect a direct military attack (Stalin noted that "England always has preferred wars fought with the hands of others"), they did think that "the Baldwin Cabinet would avail itself of the services of Marshal Pilsudski and Marshal Chang So-lin." More recently, when a U-2 was shot down over Cuba during the missile crisis, American leaders quickly concluded that the "Soviet action . . . seemed to mean that they had decided on a showdown." This alarming inference assumed a higher degree of centralization, planning, and foresight than was probably present.[44]

Second, the effectiveness of attempts to influence the other's policy will be reduced because the importance of internal conflict will be under-

[43] Perkins, *The First Rapprochement*, p. 221; Perkins, *Prologue to War* (Berkeley and Los Angeles: University of California Press, 1961), pp. 282-85 (for another example from this period see Samuel Bemis, *Jay's Treaty* [2nd ed., New Haven: Yale University Press, 1962], p. 239); Whiting, *China Crosses the Yalu*, p. 169.

[44] Fischer, *The Soviets in World Affairs*, pp. 544-45; Roger Hilsman, *To Move a Nation* (Garden City, N.Y.: Doubleday, 1967), p. 220, also see p. 222.

estimated. The state will therefore devote insufficient resources to trying to learn about the factions, bureaucratic structures, and domestic preoccupations in the other side. As we discussed in a previous chapter, when these variables are noticed at all, the actor will rely heavily on his knowledge of his own domestic system for their interpretation. Even when the two systems have a great deal in common, this method will lead the actor astray on vital details.[45]

Third, illusory incompatibility is created because duplicity rather than confusion is perceived when the other's policy is inconsistent. Since no simple, straightforward design can explain the other's diverse actions if they are believed to be coherently serving a set of integrated values, it is inevitable that the perceiver will "look for intricate, machiavellian explanations."[46] It is possible that such explanations would not imply that the other is hostile, but this is unlikely, especially in an environment of anarchy. The more friendly segments of a policy that is erratic or vacillating will be seen as deceptive, and the entire policy will be judged, as the United States judged the uncoordinated Russian policy in the Far East in the early twentieth century, to be "two-faced and treacherous."[47] When the other's agent is more hostile than the direct voice or final position of the other's government, the perceiver is apt to believe that the agent represents the other's hostile intentions, which have been only temporarily thwarted. When the agent takes a more conciliatory position and is overruled, the perceiver will think that the other side was never serious about trying to settle the dispute. Thus in 1810 when the British government rejected the agreement that its agent had signed in violation of his instructions, many Americans believed that the whole episode "had probably been a trick." Similarly, before the outbreak of the Italo-Ethiopian War the British ambassador told the Italians that "the British were taking a new approach to the problem and what Britain had to offer would satisfy, in his opinion, half of the Italian demands and create conditions which could be developed further in Italy's favor." On this basis the Italians welcomed a visit by the British foreign secretary. But when his proposal did not meet their expectations, the Italians concluded, in the words of one of their diplomats, that the offer was a "trap" and the visit a "most maladroit gesture."[48]

[45] For several examples, see Neustadt, *Alliance Politics*.

[46] This was the common inference that observers drew from German behavior in the late nineteenth and early twentieth centuries. Jonathan Steinberg, *Yesterday's Deterrent* (New York: Macmillan Co., 1965), p. 56. For further discussion, see Steinberg, "Germany and the Russo-Japanese War," *American Historical Review* 75 (December 1970), 1965-86.

[47] William Braisted, *The United States in the Pacific, 1897-1909* (Austin: University of Texas Press, 1958), p. 145.

[48] Baer, *The Coming of the Italian-Ethiopian War*, pp. 193, 197. For another example, see John Wills, Jr., "Ch'ing Relations With the Dutch, 1662-1690," in

The impact of these incidents can go a step further. When state A reacts with anger and suspicion to what it incorrectly believes to have been a double cross by state B, state B will not be able to understand A's reaction. B knows that its own behavior was unexceptionable. So A's outburst must be an unpleasant bargaining tactic, a smokescreen for its own devious plans, or a refusal to observe the standard rules of diplomacy. These were among the British interpretations of the seemingly inexplicable German displays of temper that followed the breakdown of negotiations discussed above.[49] Such inferences contributed to the developing British image of Germany as not only hostile but also unreasonable.

Three considerations prevent us from flatly concluding that decision-makers should avoid explanations based on images of unity and planning. First, this belief, although inaccurate, may be a useful assumption that leads to relatively accurate predictions. If the interests and power of the contending elements in the other's government are fairly stable, the belief that the other acts as though it were centralized may be fruitful, just as the assumptions of "economic man" have been invaluable in economics. Second, even if predictions based on this assumption are not very accurate, they still may be the best that can be made under most circumstances. It is one thing to know that the other's policy is a product of conflicts and bargains; it is quite another to have detailed information about the values, beliefs, and power positions of the other's factions. Even if predictions made with the benefit of complete knowledge of these variables would be more accurate than those possible with the assumption of centralization, it does not follow that those based on only incomplete and unreliable information will be more accurate than the alternative. Third, if in, say, one-third of the cases predictions based on the available evidence about the other's internal divisions are better than those following from the assumption of unity, and if decision-makers are not able to determine which method is best applied to each individual case, then they may always act as though the other is centralized since they will be better off two-thirds of the time. The strategy of probability matching (distributing one's guesses or bets in proportion to the distribution of outcomes in the sample), although common, is not rational. In the absence of additional information, it is best always to utilize the method of prediction that works in the largest number of cases.

So only weaker advice can be given. Decision-makers should not jump to the conclusion that the other is a centralized actor implementing a well-developed plan. When Eyre Crowe examined England's interna-

---

John Fairbank, ed., *The Chinese World Order* (Cambridge, Mass.: Harvard University Press, 1968), pp. 248-50.
 [49] Grenville, *Lord Salisbury and Foreign Policy*, p. 360.

tional position before World War I he admitted that the consistent hostility he attributed to Wilhelmine Germany might be "no more than the expression of a vague, confused, and unpractical statesmanship, not fully realizing its own drift." But, he went on, "It is, of course, necessary to except the period of Bismarck's Chancellorship. To assume that so great a statesman was not quite sure as to the objects of his policy would be the *reductio ad absurdum* of any hypothesis."[50] Perhaps, but it is important for decision-makers to be sensitive to alternative explanations involving internal conflict and lack of coordination. When it seems that only hostility and duplicity could account for the other's behavior, observers should not immediately assume that *any* coherent policy lies behind the activities.

[50] "Memorandum on the Present State of British Relations with France and Germany," January 1, 1907, in G. P. Gooch and Harold Temperley, eds., *British Documents on the Origins of the War, 1898-1914*, vol. 3 (London: His Majesty's Stationery Office, 1928), p. 415.

CHAPTER NINE

Overestimating One's Importance
as Influence or Target

INTRODUCTION

ACTORS exaggerate the degree to which they play a central role in others' policies. Content of the resulting perception, however, varies with the effect of the other's behavior on the actor. When the other behaves in accord with the actor's desires, he will overestimate the degree to which his policies are responsible for the outcome. When the situation is fluid, there is a less pronounced tendency for the actor to overestimate his potential influence. When the other's behavior is undesired, the actor is likely to see it as derived from internal sources rather than as being a response to his own actions. In this case the actor believes that the other is trying to harm him rather than that the effect was an unintended consequence or a side-effect.

The first and third propositions are often conjoined. For example, the replacement of the Liberal government by a coalition in England in 1915 was preceded by two events, the resignation of the First Sea Lord in protest against the government's conduct of the Dardanelles operation and the revelation of a shortage of artillery shells. First Lord of the Admiralty Winston Churchill had been the chief advocate of the attempt to force the Straits and a strong supporter of the government. General John French, the British commander on the Western Front, tried to undermine the government because he held it responsible for the lack of ammunition. Both men incorrectly attributed the government's fall to the shell shortage. French exaggerated his role in bringing about an outcome he desired; Churchill underestimated his responsibility for an outcome he had not sought. Similarly, most successful candidates for Congress believe their own behavior strongly contributed to their victory; most of those who lose blame their defeat on factors beyond their control.[1]

In many cases the same individual will display both parts of this effect. "We are prone to alter our perception of causality so as to protect or

---

[1] Roy Jenkins, *Asquith* (London: Collins, 1964), pp. 355-58; John Kingdon, *Candidates for Office: Beliefs and Strategies* (New York: Random House, 1968), pp. 22-34. Also see Chong Lim Kim and Donald Racheter, "Candidates' Perceptions of Voter Competence: A Comparison of Winning and Losing Candidates," *American Political Science Review* 67 (September 1973), 906-13.

enhance our self-esteem." If a prisoner responds favorably to trust and leniency, the authorities are apt to credit their policy; if he does not they are apt to conclude that he was incorrigible. And while parents often trace any good traits their children display to the way they raised them, they usually do not give a similar explanation for undesired behavior. What one scholar said of Charles of Burgundy could be said of many people: "Whatever he accomplished, in council or on the field, he attributed to his own genius. Such failures as had to be recognized he laid to the ineptitude or cowardice of his subordinates and the machination of his enemies." Experiments have borne this out. Subjects are more apt to see their own actions as an important cause of their successes than of their failures. When workers or students do badly, the supervisors or teachers perceive the former as responsible. But when they do well, the latter claim the credit.[2] In international politics, while American officials did not believe that United States policy inadvertently encouraged Russia to put up the Berlin Wall, they did see the United States stand as largely responsible for the subsequent Soviet relaxation of pressure on Berlin.

Overestimating One's Effectiveness

Examples of the propensity to overestimate one's effectiveness abound. In the Opium War, China interpreted every favorable British move as a response to Chinese policy when in fact the British acted as they did for other reasons. The United States overestimated the degree to which the French withdrawal from Mexico in the 1860s was caused by American pressure. The British Conservatives believed that their letter of August 2, 1914, promising support for entry into the war tipped the balance in the cabinet. The United States and Britain each claimed that its pressure caused the Japanese to end hostilities in Shanghai in 1932. American interventionists believed that their opposition to Ambassador

---

[2] Albert Hastorf, David Schneider, and Judith Polefka, *Person Perception* (Reading, Mass.: Addison-Wesley, 1970), p. 73 (also see Fritz Heider, "Social Perception and Phenomenal Causality," *Psychological Review* 51 [1944], 368, and Harold Kelley, *Attribution in Social Interaction* [Morristown, N.J.: General Learning Corporation, 1971], pp. 19-21); Paul Murray Kendal, *Louis XI* (New York: Norton, 1971), p. 265. In addition to the experiments summarized in Hastorf et al., *Person Perception*, p. 73, and Kelley, *Attribution in Social Interaction*, pp. 19-20, see William Davis and D. Elaine Davis, "Internal-External Control and Attribution of Responsibility for Success and Failure," *Journal of Personality* 40 (1972), 123-35; Thomas Ruble, "Effects of Actor and Observer Roles on Attributions of Causality in Situations of Success and Failure," *Journal of Social Psychology* 90 (1973), 41-44. For a conflicting finding see Lee Ross, Günter Bierbrauer, and Susan Polly, "Attribution of Educational Outcomes by Professional and Nonprofessional Instructors," *Journal of Personality and Social Psychology* 29 (1974), 609-18.

Kennedy was instrumental in securing his resignation. The Germans attributed the fact that the British were not bombing German cities early in World War II to their desire to reciprocate the German restraint rather than to a shortage of planes.[3] (The last example is striking because one expects wartime opponents to attribute the least charitable motives to each other and not to believe that the other will observe limits.) In contemporary cases we cannot be sure that perceptions of effectiveness are incorrect. But the generalization is clear—actors almost always feel responsible for exerting influence when the other acts as they wish. This belief is often incorrect. We have found almost no cases in which an actor underestimated his influence in producing a desired outcome.[4]

In some cases the person will perceive that the other is responding not only to the state he serves, but to himself personally. Experiments and several international incidents support this conclusion. In a whole series of events, Allied agents in post-revolutionary Russia greatly overestimated their influence. Raymond Robins protested the actions of an official; the official was removed, and Robins incorrectly believed this was cause and effect. Similarly, Robins told the Russian leaders that he would regard their response to the anarchist challenge as a test of their ability to rule; the Soviets moved against the anarchists, and Robins "was elated at what he took to be a new demonstration of his own influence with the Soviet leaders." Later research indicates that Robins's urgings had little to do with the Soviet actions. When John Reed was appointed Soviet consul to the United States, three of the American agents made independent efforts to have the appointment revoked. When it was revoked, "All three Americans were . . . convinced that it was the result of their own individual representations." To take a less impressionable person, Secretary of State Stimson believed he was largely responsible for preventing a Russo-Japanese war over Manchuria in 1929, and in 1931 he attributed Japanese concessions to "the stiff tone which I have taken." Although these examples show that it is often difficult to separate perceptions of personal efficacy from perceptions of national efficacy, the presence of the former is indicated by the fact that in the 1929 crisis the

---

[3] Arthur Waley, *The Opium War Through Chinese Eyes* (New York: Macmillan Co., 1958), pp. 22, 186; Richard Van Alstyne, *The Rising American Empire* (Chicago: Quadrangle, 1965), p. 161; Cameron Hazlehurst, *Politicians at War* (London: Jonathan Cape, 1971), p. 41; James Cable, *Gunboat Diplomacy* (London: Chatto and Windus, 1971), p. 191; Mark Chadwin, *The Warhawks* (New York: Norton, 1970), p. 127; George Quester, *Deterrence before Hiroshima* (New York: Wiley, 1966), p. 120.

[4] For an exception to this generalization see Douglas Robinson, *The Zeppelin in Combat* (London: G. T. Foulis, 1962), p. 192.

undersecretary, who was not deeply involved in the crisis, did not believe that Stimson's actions mattered.[5]

A common type of exaggeration of one's influence is the belief that one has thwarted the adversary's evil intentions when in fact the latter was not actually planning any action. When generals take vigorous actions and the enemy does not attack, they are quick to perceive that they succeeded in disrupting an offensive. For example, "American and South Vietnamese officials who predicted a major Communist offensive . . . during President Nixon's visit to Peking are now saying that it was prevented by timely allied bombing."[6] More important in their political implications are the frequent cases in which an actor believes that his threats have affected the other's intentions rather than capabilities. For example, the United States claimed that by moving ships into the Bay of Bengal during the India-Pakistan War of 1971 it made the Indians reverse their plan to smash West Pakistan. Although for reasons of bargaining American decision-makers could want others to think they believed this even if they did not,[7] it seems probable that the claim represented actual beliefs. While we cannot be certain that this belief was incorrect, it is significant that it was not shared by those not responsible for the action.

This kind of perception of course enhances faith in deterrence. Not having the historian's knowledge of the other side's intentions, the decision-maker is relatively free to select a pleasing interpretation of why the adversary has not harmed him. He is more apt to believe that deterrence worked than that it was not necessary. And if, in spite of the actor's threats, the other does take hostile action, the actor can believe that the other would have taken even more damaging steps had it not been for his stance.

Of course an actor will try to deter the other only if he believes there is a significant chance that, if he does not, the other will take undesired

[5] For the Russian examples see George Kennan, *Russia Leaves the War* (New York: Atheneum, 1967), p. 404, also see p. 500; Kennan, *The Decision to Intervene* (New York: Atheneum, 1967), p. 178, also see pp. 108-109; *Russia Leaves the War*, p. 408. For the 1929 Manchurian incident see Robert Ferrell, *American Diplomacy in the Great Depression* (New York: Norton, 1970), pp. 61-62. For the 1931 incident see James Crowley, *Japan's Quest for Autonomy* (Princeton: Princeton University Press, 1966), p. 143.

[6] Craig Whitney, "U.S. Bombing Raids Said to Bar Drive Timed to Nixon's Journey," *New York Times*, February 22, 1972. For other examples, see Alan Clark, *The Donkeys* (New York: Morrow, 1962), p. 83; Robert Frank Futrell, with the assistance of Lawson Moseley and Albert Simpson, *The United States Air Force in Korea, 1950-1953* (New York: Duell, Sloan, and Pearce, 1961), p. 381. For another example, see Allen Whiting, *The Chinese Calculus of Deterrence* (Ann Arbor: University of Michigan Press, 1975), p. 70.

[7] Jervis, *The Logic of Images in International Relations* (Princeton: Princeton University Press, 1970), pp. 201-204.

actions. Third parties who believe that the other was not contemplating a move will feel that the actor's policy did little good. But the correlation between acting and perceiving credit for success will be spurious since both variables are explained by the original perceptions of the other's intentions. To surmount this problem, we would like to compare beliefs about the causes of restraint, holding perceptions of the adversary constant. Our hypothesis predicts that those responsible for the deterrence policy would see it as more efficacious than would observers, but we do not have many matched cases.

The tendency for actors to attribute valued outcomes to their own efforts provides an exception to the generalization that observers see others as autonomous causes of their own behavior. Fritz Heider notes the "tendency to perceive persons as origins" and "to ascribe . . . changes [in behavior] entirely to persons," ignoring external influences. But if A has tried to influence B and B has acted as A desired, A will not see B as an origin of behavior, but rather as reacting to him. This sheds a different light on William Gamson's argument that when A distrusts B, he will attribute friendly actions of B not to B's autonomous good will —which could later be withdrawn—but to A's power. Although a high level of distrust would reinforce this phenomenon, it is not necessary.[8]

One result is that tension-reducing initiatives will be less effective since the perceiver is likely to believe that they show, not that the other actor is friendly, but that the perceiver's policy of firmness is working. Thus the kaiser interpreted any sign that Britain was slackening in the naval race as proof that Germany's pressure was effective and should be increased. Indeed whether the actor has used rewards or threats, the tendency to attribute a desired outcome to his own efforts will hinder cooperation. Rewards are costly when effective because the actor must pay for the other's compliance. He will therefore want to offer the smallest reward possible. If initial success leads him to believe he has a great deal of influence, he will decrease his future offers. And if he has overestimated his influence, these rewards will be insufficient and an agreement will not be reached, thus limiting the experience of cooperation. Furthermore, the actor will be surprised by this turn of events and, as we will discuss further below, will probably attribute it to the other's unfriendly

[8] Heider, "Social Perception and Phenomenal Causality," p. 361; William Gamson, *Power and Discontent* (Homewood, Ill.: Dorsey, 1968), pp. 172-76. Once we understand the meaning of trust in international politics, Gamson's argument— but not the one proposed here—follows almost by definition (see chapter 4, p. 120 and Robert Jervis, "Notes on the Concept of Trust," unpublished paper prepared for the Society for the Psychological Study of Social Issues workshop on trust, September 1972). For an example, see Constantine Melnik and Nathan Leites, *House Without Windows* (Evanston, Ill.: Row, Peterson, 1958), pp. 200-201.

intentions. He may also reevaluate the earlier interactions in light of his new belief and decide he had been deceived. On the other hand, because threats have relatively low cost when they do not have to be carried out, an actor who attributes success to their use will not be tempted to decrease their magnitude. Instead, his belief that the other is hostile will be reinforced and he will rely still more on negative sanctions. Furthermore, the overestimation of his power may lead him to overreach himself, thus further increasing the chances of war.

Two factors explain the overestimation of successful influence. First, such a perception gratifies the ego. The person has mattered; he has been efficacious; he is able to shape his environment. If, to return to an example cited above, the British were limiting their bombing of Germany in response to the German policy, the Germans would have had greater influence over the future conduct of the war and the degree to which their civilians would be attacked.

Second, and more important, the actor is familiar with his own efforts to influence the other but knows much less about other factors that might have been at work. He may not know what actions third parties have taken. His knowledge of the other's domestic processes is apt to be slight, and, as we saw in the previous chapter, his understanding of the role of internal conflicts in the making of foreign policy is likely to be inadequate. In the absence of strong evidence to the contrary, the most obvious and parsimonious explanation is that he was influential. Thus it is not surprising that the Cleveland administration assumed that Spain's reforms in Cuba "had resulted from American importunities, [but] the fact was that the Spanish government had been moved almost entirely by domestic considerations." Similarly, Stimson's overestimation of his role in resolving the 1929 Manchurian dispute is partly explained by the fact that "It is doubtful if . . . [he] realized the complexities of the rivalries in China and Manchuria, much less the practice of Soviet revolutionary strategy."[9]

Perceptions of Influence and Turning Points

The exaggeration of one's own importance also leads actors to overestimate their potential influence when the other is poised between taking actions which can greatly help or greatly harm the actor. Thus just as Robins and others believed they were responsible for many Bolshevik favors, so they also incorrectly felt that Allied promises of aid might have persuaded the Soviets not to ratify the Brest-Litovsk treaty. Three cases during the Second World War also illustrate this phenomenon. During the early years of the war, Britain and America bitterly debated what

[9] Ernest May, *Imperial Democracy* (New York: Harcourt, Brace, 1961), p. 107; Ferrell, *American Diplomacy in the Great Depression*, p. 64.

policy would best keep Spain from joining the Axis. Although the British held that aid would provide Franco with an alternative to ties to Hitler, and the United States argued that threats and sanctions would be more effective, each country felt that the policy adopted would have great impact on Spain. In fact Franco's decisions were mostly guided by his fear of becoming dominated by Germany and his beliefs about who would win the war. Allied policies toward his country were a decidedly secondary concern. Similarly, the American agents in French North Africa overestimated the impact of aid on the loyalties and behavior of important groups and underestimated the role of factors beyond American control. Third, after comparing the debate over the Allied policy of unconditional surrender with the actual influences on the Axis powers' decisions, Paul Kecskemeti argued that

> Addicted to a naive stimulus-response philosophy, we tend to take it for granted that people's actions depend on nothing but the momentary stimuli they receive, stimuli that we, the manipulators, can control at will. Where this philosophy holds sway, the possibility that conduct might also have other sources is not even taken into consideration. . . . Accordingly, during the war, the enemy's own permanent and deep-rooted loyalties, his own spontaneous assessment of his interests, and similar autonomous factors were not taken into account when we tried to foresee and influence his conduct in the terminal situation. Nothing seemed to matter except what we did to him and what we told him then and there.[10]

Injury and Perceptions of the Other's Autonomy

The third part of our hypothesis is that when others' actions hurt or threaten the perceiver, he is apt to overestimate the degree to which the behavior was a product of internal forces and was aimed at harming him. This inference is fed by the phenomenon just discussed. If an actor overestimates his potential influence, he will conclude from the other's undesired behavior that the other must have had strong motives for his actions. It in turn feeds the tendency for actors to attribute other's desired behavior to their efforts, since the discontinuing of undesired behavior will not be seen as showing that the other was not seeking to harm the state in the first place. Here, as in the cases where the other's be-

---

[10] Richard Ullman, *Britain and the Russian Civil War*, vol. 1: *Intervention and the War* (Princeton: Princeton University Press, 1961), p. 128; Herbert Feis, *The Spanish Story* (New York: Norton, 1966), p. 108; William Langer, *Our Vichy Gamble* (New York: Norton, 1966), pp. 133, 241; *Strategic Surrender* (New York: Atheneum, 1964), p. 233. Kecskemeti implies that this is a peculiarly American failing. But if this tendency is especially pronounced among American decision-makers, it is also found in other nations.

havior is desired, actors overestimate the degree to which they are the focus of other's policy. This indicates a general propensity for actors to exaggerate their own importance.

The two types of this misperception correspond to the two ways in which an actor analyzes another's reasons for behaving as he did. He tries to infer, first, what goals the other was seeking, and, second, what forces led him to act as he did. In the first kind of inference, if the other's behavior has the *effect* of injuring the actor, he is apt to believe that this was the other's *purpose*. Research on how we form impressions of others has found "a tendency [for perceivers] to assume that people always intend to do what they do and intend it to have the effect it has." In international relations this is especially pronounced when the other's behavior is undesired. Rather than seeing any injuries as a by-product of a policy that was pursued with little regard for him, the actor puts himself at the center of the other's attentions. In coalition wars, each actor tends to overestimate the fraction of the enemy's resources that are devoted to fighting him. Small moves by the actor are seen as important enough to lead the other to take drastic counteractions. Thus because "On the night when Roosevelt gave his Fireside Chat [in December 1940], the Germans subjected London to one of the heaviest bombings of the war," Robert Sherwood concluded that the Germans "timed the creation of some major disturbances in the hope that it would blanket the speech in the morning's news and mitigate the effect that Roosevelt's words might produce on American and British morale." And a staunch supporter of Neville Chamberlain recorded in his diary the opinion that, in launching his attack in May 1940, Hitler "seized on the psychological moment when England is politically divided, and the ruling caste riddled with dissension and anger" as a result of domestic criticisms of Chamberlain. Chamberlain himself shared this view, writing to a friend: "as I expected Hitler has seized the occasion of our divisions to strike the great blow."[11]

When relations between the states are not completely hostile, conflict will be increased. The aggrieved side will not only note the injury done but will assume that this was the main goal the other side was seeking and, projecting this motivation into the future, will foresee greater harm unless it reacts strongly. Thus not only is consistency expected, but consistency based on the belief that the impact on the perceiver was the central cause of the other's previous behavior. For example, when Russia prosecuted several German engineers in 1928 Germany believed that this

[11] Mark Cook, *Interpersonal Perception* (Baltimore: Penguin, 1971), p. 53; Sherwood, *Roosevelt and Hopkins* (New York: Harper and Brothers, 1948), p. 228, also see pp. 296, 504; Robert Rhodes James, *Chips: The Diaries of Sir Henry Channon* (Harmondsworth, Middlesex, England: Penguin, 1970), p. 305; quoted in A.J.P. Taylor, *Beaverbrook* (New York: Simon and Schuster, 1972), p. 410.

was part of a policy designed to weaken her. In fact the trial "was tailored for Russia's internal needs." Several of the United States' actions in occupied Germany were aimed at France, but Russia assumed that the motive was to harm her. Similarly, because Russia did not understand the degree to which Allied intervention in Russia in 1918 was aimed at defeating Germany, she expected the West to follow a more extreme and consistent anti-Soviet policy than it did. And while Stalin's bellicose speech in February 1946 may have been mainly intended to rally domestic support and Khrushchev's promise of support for "wars of national liberation" in January 1961 may have been designed as part of a propaganda battle with the Chinese, many Western observers shared William O. Douglas's view that the former was "the Declaration of World War III," and President Kennedy felt the latter was such "an authoritative exposition of Soviet intentions [that he] discussed it with his staff and read excerpts from it aloud to the National Security Council."[12]

Part of the explanation for these perceptions is grounded in the second type of analysis—beliefs about the sources of the other's conduct. Actor A usually overestimates the degree to which B's undesired behavior is a product of B's autonomous desires and underestimates the degree to which it is a response to an action of A's—usually an action that A and B interpret differently. Thus A sees himself as the object of B's unprovoked and inner-directed hostility. As we discussed in the previous chapter, actors are slow to see the causes of other's behavior as located in blunders, intragovernmental conflict, and domestic politics. They are also slow to see that their own actions may explain the other's undesired behavior. An anecdote from outside of politics illustrates this phenomenon:

> One early morning a convoy of armored personnel carriers of the 11th Armored Cavalry Regiment rolled through a rubber plantation a few miles inside Cambodia. There assembled were several score

[12] Harvey Dyck, *Weimar Germany and Soviet Russia* (New York: Columbia University Press, 1966), p. 135; John Gimbel, *The American Occupation of Germany* (Stanford: Stanford University Press, 1968), pp. 26-27, 60-61; Walter Millis, ed., *The Forrestal Diaries* (New York: Viking, 1951), p. 134; Arthur Schlesinger, Jr., *A Thousand Days* (Boston: Houghton Mifflin, 1965), p. 302. For other examples, see John Wills, Jr., "Ch'ing Relations with the Dutch, 1662-1690," in John Fairbank, ed., *The Chinese World Order* (Cambridge, Mass.: Harvard University Press, 1968), pp. 248-50; J.A.S. Grenville, *Lord Salisbury and Foreign Policy* (London: Athlone, 1964), pp. 206-207; Henry Ashby Turner, Jr., "Bismarck's Imperialist Venture: Anti-British in Origin?" in Prosser Gifford and Wm. Roger Louis, eds., *Britain and Germany in Africa* (New Haven: Yale University Press, 1967), pp. 64-67. A rare exception was Lloyd George's reaction to Wilson's peace proposal in 1916: "I know the American politician. He has not international conscience. He thinks of nothing but the ticket, and he has not given the least thought to the effect of his action upon European affairs." Sterling Kernek, "The British Government's Reactions to President Wilson's 'Peace' Note of December 1916," *Historical Journal* 13 (December 1970), 759-60.

Cambodian civilians who stared in wonderment, but no apparent fear, at the hulking APCs [Armored Personnel Carriers] and at the white-skinned giants atop them. The Cambodians are hungry, most of them have had no food for two days. But not a palm goes out in supplication. "Cambodians seem like nice people. They ain't spoiled like the gooks in Nam who always got their Goddamned hands out," says a gunner on an APC.

That said, he rummages around inside the APC and emerges triumphant with a carton of Chicklets which he begins tossing, pack by pack, from the track top to the Cambodians assembled down below. All the children, and a fair share of the adults, begin grappling in the dust for their first American goodies. The gum carton is soon exhausted. The Cambodian crowd moves on to the next APC, this time with open hands outstretched.[13]

In international affairs, the appeasers did not realize the extent to which Hitler's behavior was caused by his belief that England had shown that she would not fight for East and Central Europe. Similarly, in 1925 the Italians did not consider that their maladroit diplomatic initiative might have been responsible for the stiffening of the French position in colonial negotiations. More common than an actor's failure to realize that the other's undesired acts may flow from the actor's unintended invitation is the failure to appreciate that the other side's hostility may be a product of his fear of the actor. An experiment has shown that when a person with a competitive orientation plays the Prisoner's Dilemma game with a more cooperative adversary, and the latter reacts by adopting a competitive style of play, the former will infer not that the latter's behavior was a response to his moves, but that the latter is always competitive. Similarly, in the winter of 1949-1950 George Kennan made no impression when he argued that the American decision to establish military bases in Japan might lead to an undesired Russian reaction. So the outbreak of war reinforced "the tendency . . . to view Soviet intentions as something existing quite independently of our own behavior." "[T]he idea that in doing things disagreeable to our own interests the Russians might be reacting to features of our own behavior . . . was one to which the mind of official Washington would always be strangely resistant." Similarly, few American decision-makers have traced Chinese hostility to the American attempts to undermine the Chinese regime.[14]

[13] Peter Kahn, "In Cambodia: Impressions of the War," *Wall Street Journal*, May 26, 1970.
[14] Alan Cassels, *Mussolini's Early Diplomacy* (Princeton: Princeton University Press, 1970), p. 358; Harold Kelley and Anthony Stakelski, "Social Interaction Basis of Cooperators' and Competitors' Beliefs About Others," *Journal of Personality and Social Psychology* 16 (1970), 66-91 (it should be noted, however, that

But this is not a uniquely American failing. Before World War I, both England and Germany failed to appreciate the extent to which the other's unfriendly acts grew out of the belief that the hostility it was receiving was unprovoked. Instead, each believed the other's "motives were fixed and independent of our behaviour, whereas our motives were a response to their behaviour and were varied accordingly." And before World War II, Japan was similarly unable to see that her expansion in China could have been a major cause of American hostility.[15]

The result, of course, is a neglect of the possibilities of favorably affecting the other's behavior by moderating one's own actions and an increase in illusory incompatibility. If the other's hostility is seen as rooted in autonomous drives, there is no reason to examine one's own policies to see if they may be self-defeating. There is no need to make special efforts to demonstrate your willingness to reach reasonable settlements. Further concessions would not alter the other's behavior. As Colonel House reported Woodrow Wilson's reasoning about the peace negotiations with Germany in the fall of 1918: "He fell back time and again on the theory offered when the last note was written: that was, if Germany was beaten, she would accept any terms. If she was not beaten, he did not wish to make any terms with her." Similar is the belief that the other state's decision to go to war is highly autonomous. The other will attack when, and only when, it is ready to. It can neither be appeased nor provoked. As Robert Kennedy put it during the Cuban missile crisis: "We all agreed in the end that if the Russians were ready to go to nuclear war over Cuba, they were ready to go to nuclear war and that was that. So we might as well have the showdown then as six months later."[16]

---

observers also drew the same inference); Kennan, *Memoirs*, vol. 1: *1925-1950* (Boston: Little, Brown, 1967), pp. 395, 497-98; Allen Whiting, "What Nixon Must Do to Make Friends With Peking," *New York Review of Books*, October 7, 1971, pp. 10-14. Gabriel Kolko similarly argues that the United States misinterpreted Soviet behavior in Iran after the war because it ignored previous American actions in that country that contributed to Soviet policy. *The Politics of War* (New York: Random House, 1968), p. 311.

[15] Lewis Richardson, "Mathematics of War and Foreign Politics," in James Newman, ed., *The World of Mathematics*, vol. 2 (New York: Simon and Schuster, 1956), p. 1244; Robert Butow, *Tojo and the Coming of the War* (Princeton: Princeton University Press), passim. See also Crowley, *Japan's Quest for Autonomy*. For an example of this phenomenon at the level of the individual rather than the state, see the discussion of Churchill's surprise at the Conservatives' strong reaction to his opposition to the party position on India in the mid-1930s. Robert Rhodes James, *Churchill: A Study in Failure* (New York and Cleveland: World, 1970), p. 236.

[16] Charles Seymour, *The Intimate Papers of Colonel House*, vol. 4 (Boston: Houghton Mifflin, 1928), p. 83; quoted in Stewart Alsop and Charles Bartlett, "In Time of Crisis," *Saturday Evening Post*, December 8, 1962, p. 16 (the American decision-makers fortunately did not act in accord with this analysis). For other examples, see John Gaddis, *The United States and the Origins of the Cold*

Belief that the Other Understands that You Are Not a Threat

The other side of this proposition is that, as we noted in Chapter 3, actors injure others more than they mean to because they do not see the degree to which their policies conflict with the other's interests. The problem is compounded because the actor usually does not understand the process just discussed which leads the perceiver to conclude that if the actor's behavior has harmed him, this must have been the actor's intention. The actor thus believes that even if he has inadvertently damaged the other's interest, the other will realize that this was not the actor's goal. The actor then fails to realize that the other will perceive more hostility than would a disinterested observer.

There are several reasons for this failing: lack of understanding of the context in which the other sees the actor's behavior; the familiarity that the actor has with his own intentions, which makes it harder for him to believe others might not see them as he does; and the self-righteousness that inhibits the conclusion that the other's undesired behavior was provoked. Such a conclusion may imply an unfavorable self-image. Raymond Sontag argues that Anglo-German relations before World War I deteriorated partly because "The British did not like to think themselves selfish, or unwilling to tolerate 'legitimate' German expansion. The Germans did not like to think themselves aggressive, or unwilling to recognize 'legitimate' British vested interests."[17]

It takes great insight to realize that actions that one believes to be only the natural consequence of defending one's vital interests can appear to others as directed against them. In rebutting the famous Crowe "balance of power" memorandum which justified a policy of "containing" Germany, Thomas Sanderson, a former permanent undersecretary in the Foreign Office, wrote: "It has sometimes seemed to me that to a foreigner reading our press the British Empire must appear in the light of some huge giant sprawling over the globe, with gouty fingers and toes stretching in every direction, which cannot be approached without eliciting a scream."[18] But few other Englishmen could be convinced that others might see them this way.

The result is that when an actor believes he is not a threat to another,

---

War, 1941-1947 (New York: Columbia University Press, 1972), p. 90; Charles Neu, *An Uncertain Friendship* (Cambridge, Mass.: Harvard University Press, 1967), p. 213.

[17] *European Diplomatic History, 1871-1932* (New York: Appleton-Century-Crofts, 1933), p. 125.

[18] "Memorandum," in G. P. Gooch and Harold Temperley, eds., *British Documents on the Origins of the War*, vol. 3 (London: His Majesty's Stationery Office, 1928), p. 430.

he usually assumes that the other knows he is not hostile. Earlier we noted that people usually identify other's intentions with the effects of their actions. Actors reverse this procedure with their own behavior; although they are aware of the difficulty of making threats and warnings credible, they usually believe that others are not likely to misinterpret behavior that is meant to be compatible with the other's interest. An actor's failure to understand that he may not have communicated his non-hostile intentions feeds spirals of misperception. For if the actor believes that the other is not only hostile, but perceives the actor as peaceful, he will feel it is clear that the other is aggressive and must be met with strength and firmness.

CHAPTER TEN

The Influence of Desires
and Fears on Perception

THE INFLUENCE of affect on perception is the subject of much attention and debate in psychology.[1] One of the first assertions was Aristotle's: "Under the influence of strong feeling we are easily deceived regarding our sensations, different persons in different ways, as e.g., the coward under the influence of fear and the lover under that of love have such illusions that the former owing to a trifling resemblance thinks he sees his enemy and the latter his beloved." Both halves of this argument have been applied to international relations and indeed raise the most important issues in this area—the impact of desires and fears. Clausewitz said that during a battle "The timidity of men gives fresh force to lies and untruths. As a general rule, everyone is more inclined to believe the bad than the good."[2] More common, however, is the claim that men generally perceive what they want to perceive—that they engage in "wishful thinking."[3] (These two claims are not contradictory if one specifies the circumstances under which each of these divergent effects will occur.)

WISHFUL THINKING

The complexity of this subject and the difficulties in gathering data from international relations make it best to start with a critical examination of the experimental findings. The best evidence that desires influence beliefs would be provided by manipulating desires and showing that altera-

[1] Few psychologists are satisfied with the theories and data in this area. The key variables often are imprecise, the effect of the experimental manipulations unclear, the correlations relatively low, and the explanation for the correlations ad hoc and unconvincing. For good reviews of this literature see William Dember, *The Psychology of Perception* (New York: Holt, Rinehart and Winston, 1961), ch. 9; William Epstein, *Varieties of Perceptual Learning* (New York: McGraw-Hill, 1967), pp. 143-64; Noel Jenkin, "Affective Processes in Perception," *Psychological Bulletin* 54 (March 1957), 100-123; M. D. Vernon, *The Psychology of Perception* (Baltimore: Penguin, 1962), ch. 11; and Matthew Erdelyi, "A New Look at the New Look," *Psychological Review* 81 (1974), 1-25.

[2] In David Krech, Richard Crutchfield, Egerton Ballachey, *Individual in Society* (New York: McGraw-Hill, 1962), p. 23; Bertram Gross, *The Managing of Organizations* (New York: Free Press, 1964), p. 798.

[3] See for example, Otto Klineberg, *The Human Dimension in International Relations* (New York: Holt, Rinehart and Winston, 1965), p. 91; Charles Osgood, *An Alternative to War or Surrender* (Urbana: University of Illinois Press, 1962), pp. 22-23.

tions of perceptions and cognitions follow. One such ingenious experiment exists but, as we shall see, it is not without difficulties. The second best evidence would be experiments and non-laboratory cases where we could examine groups of people who were similar on all dimensions except their desires and determine whether their perceptions and beliefs also differed. A few experiments fit in this category, but usually the best we can get are correlations between desires and perceptions that lack good controls and from which the possibility of spuriousness cannot be eliminated. When we look at these experiments we will see that while many of them seem at first to provide solid evidence for wishful thinking, closer examination reveals the results to be highly ambiguous.

Experiments: Lack of Incentives for Accuracy

Before looking at this evidence in detail, we should point out that most experiments omit a major consideration that is present in international politics and that several kinds of puzzles that have received much attention from psychologists are not relevant to decision-making.

First, almost no experiments provide the incentives for accuracy that operate in "real life."[4] Because the subjects' perceptions do not lead to behavior, they gain nothing by correctly perceiving the stimuli and lose nothing by mistakenly seeing desired objects. In most situations outside the laboratory, on the other hand, the accuracy of the person's perceptions strongly influences his welfare. A statesman would like his enemies to be weak—or, better yet, for them not to be his enemies at all—but if he believes this and it is not true, he will pay a high price. It may well be the absence of this constraint that permits the wish fulfillment effects found in many experiments. Indeed, in reviewing the relevant literature, one scholar notes that a necessary condition for food deprivation to lead subjects to perceive ambiguous stimuli as food related is that "the material must be presented to [subjects] in a task which allows [them] freedom to react to the material without being obliged to describe it in an ac-

---

[4] Only a few experiments in one subarea of this field give even small incentives for accuracy. Henry Morlock, "The Effect of Outcome Desirability on Information Required for Decisions," *Behavioral Science* 12 (1967), 296-300, found that incentives made no difference, but his experiment did not involve the making of predictions. Vaughn Crandall, Dan Solomon, and Richard Kellaway, "Expectancy Statements and Decision Times as Functions of Objective Probabilities and Reinforcement Values," *Journal of Personality* 24 (1955), 192-203, stressed accuracy in their directions, but gave no concrete incentives for it. Francis Irwin and Joan Snodgrass, "Effects of Independent and Dependent Outcome Values upon Bets," *Journal of Experimental Psychology* 71 (1966), 282-85, and Dean Pruitt and Robert Hoge, "Strength of the Relationship between the Value of an Event and Its Subjective Probability as a Function of Method of Measurement," *ibid.* 69 (1965), 483-89, found that incentives decreased, but did not remove, the tendency to overguess the occurrence of desired outcomes. All these incentives were small, however.

curate way." The other side of the coin is that incentives to be accurate produce more accurate responses.[5]

In politics and everyday life, rewards and punishments are often such that it is in the actor's interest to have biased perceptions. If the costs of mistaking A for B are slight, but those that follow from mistaking B for A are great, the actor will be well advised to perceive and respond to an ambiguous stimulus as B. That people do in fact respond to incentives in this rational way is illustrated by an experiment in which dots were flashed briefly on a screen and subjects asked to report whether a specific number of them (e.g. 25) appeared or not. One group was instructed only to report accurately while the other was told that it was more important to detect the 25s than to avoid calling a non-25 a 25. The latter group reported many more 25s than did the former. Furthermore, this seems to have been a difference in perception, not in conscious calculations to "play it safe."[6] Thus striving for accurate perceptions can be considered a special case of the influence of incentives on perceptions— a consideration neglected in most experiments.

A second problem is that much of the research on the impact of affect has dealt with such questions as whether people perceive valued objects (e.g. coins) as larger than they are, whether depriving a person of food or water makes him more apt to perceive ambiguous stimuli as food- or water-related, and whether rewarding the subject when a figure is shown will make him quicker to recognize it later.[7] Even if we leave aside the many problems that make it hard to interpret the results within their own frames of reference, these experiments have little relevance for decision-making. Although the results may show the impact of affect on perceptions, they do not demonstrate wishful thinking. These perceptions do not fulfill the person's wishes. What good would it do the person if the coin were as large as he thinks it is? Seeing ambiguous stimuli as food- or water-related does not make the subject less hungry or thirsty. And seeing the previously rewarded profile does not provide payment. Indeed in these experiments no implications for action and no external consequences follow from any perceptions.

[5] Per Saugstad, "Effects of Food Deprivation on Perception-Cognition," *Psychological Bulletin* 65 (1966), 89; Jerome Bruner, Jacqueline Goodnow, and George Austin, *A Study of Thinking* (New York: Wiley, 1956), p. 220.

[6] *Ibid.*, pp. 216-19. Also see Kendon Smith, Gardiner Parker, and G. Allen Robinson, Jr., "An Exploratory Investigation of Autistic Perception," *Journal of Abnormal and Social Psychology* 46 (1951), 324-26, Richard Cyert and James March, *A Behavioral Theory of the Firm* (Englewood Cliffs, N.J.: Prentice-Hall, 1963), pp. 75-76, and Ewart Thomas and David Legge, "Probability Matching as a Basis for Detection and Recognition Decisions," *Psychological Review* 77 (1970), 65-72.

[7] The literature on these subjects is immense. See, for example, Saugstad, "Effects of Food Deprivation on Perception-Cognition"; George Klein, "Need and Regulation," in Marshall R. Jones, ed., *Nebraska Symposium on Motivation, 1954* (Lincoln: University of Nebraska Press, 1954), pp. 224-74.

Desires or Expectations?

A further objection to these experiments raises a more general problem. Expectations rather than affect may explain many of the findings. For example, it is likely that the reason why subjects are slower to recognize taboo (i.e. dirty) words than normal words lies not in affect but in the subjects' greater familiarity with normal words. When subjects are fore-warned that taboo words may be shown, much of the effect disappears.[8] Similarly, giving a reward when a particular profile is shown may lead the subject to pay more attention to it, thus making him more familiar with it than with another figure that has been displayed just as often. Indeed for this reason punishment also can make a stimulus quickly recognizable.[9] In food deprivation experiments, the argument is somewhat different. Both the experimental and the control groups were equally familiar with pictures and words involving food and water. But the experiment probably changed the subjects' evoked set (see Chapter 5) because hunger is likely to bring thoughts of food to the person's mind.

Much of the influence of expectations can be understood as unconscious rationality. The different perceptual thresholds for different words are based on a projection into the future of the relative frequency with which a person has seen the words in the past. The subject would have no grounds for rejecting this as an explicit strategy. A similar explanation applies to the profile recognition test if the subject believes that anything the experimenter rewards must be important and therefore likely to appear in the post-training sessions. But this argument cannot be made in cases like the food recognition experiments unless the subject has reason to believe that the stimulus to be shown will conform to his evoked set.[10]

---

[8] Emory Cown and Ernst Beier, "The Influence of 'Threat-Expectancy' on Perception," *Journal of Personality* 19 (1950), 85-94; Donald Dorfman, "Recognition of Taboo Words as a Function of A Priori Probability," *Journal of Personality and Social Psychology* 7 (1967), 1-10. For a finding that forewarning had no effect, see Justin Aronfreed, Samuel Messick, and James Diggory, "Re-examining Emotionality and Perceptual Defense," *Journal of Personality* 21 (1953), 517-28. For a critical review of the claims for the importance of expectancy, see Erdelyi, "A New Look at the New Look," 4-7.

[9] Michael Reece, "The Effect of Shock on Recognition Threshold," *Journal of Abnormal and Social Psychology* 49 (1954), 165-72. Also see Leo Postman, "The Experimental Analysis of Motivational Factors in Perception," in Judson Brown, ed., *Current Theory and Research in Motivation* (Lincoln: University of Nebraska Press, 1953), p. 84; and Donald Campbell, "Systematic Error on the Part of Human Links in Communication Systems," *Information and Control* 1 (1958), 350-51.

[10] Leo Postman and Richard Crutchfield have demonstrated that the manipulation of the subjects' set in food-deprivation experiments influences perceptions of ambiguous words and that the effects of set "are of a much larger order of magnitude than are the differential effects of hunger." "The Interaction of Need, Set, and Stimulus-Structure in a Cognitive Task," *American Journal of Psychology* 65 (1952), 205-16.

So in this case even if affect exercises influence only indirectly, it will still reduce the accuracy of perception.

Expectations rather than wishful thinking may account for one of the best known findings of misperception in American politics. A study of the 1948 presidential election found that people who disagreed with the stand of the candidate they supported tended to misperceive the candidate's views. "In almost every instance respondents perceive their candidate's stand on . . . [the major issues of the campaign] as similar to their own and the opponent's stand as dissimilar—whatever their own position. For example, [70 percent of] those Republicans who favor price control perceive Dewey as favoring price controls." Only a little over half the Republicans who were against the Taft-Hartley law knew that Dewey was in favor of it while almost all the Republicans who favored the law knew Dewey's position. Democrats who favored the Taft-Hartley bill were four times as likely to believe Truman took this position than were Democrats who opposed the law.[11]

But from these data we cannot conclude that wishes determine perceptions. First, other studies indicate that party loyalty influences a person's policy preferences.[12] Since voters often follow the perceived lead of their party's standard-bearer, some Democrats may have come to favor the Taft-Hartley act because they incorrectly thought Truman supported the bill. Second, and more important in his context, the candidate's supporters may have misperceived his position because they expected him to agree with them. If a person finds that he and a candidate agree on many issues, he will overestimate the degree to which he and the candidate see the world in the same way and have similar positions on all other issues. Those who feel strongly about their choice of candidates will be more apt to expect that their candidate agrees with them, thus accounting for the finding that "when objectively they are *not* in agreement with their own party, *strong* Republicans and Democrats perceive their candidate's stand on the issues as more in harmony with their own stand than do weak Republicans and Democrats in the same situation."[13]

When desires and expectations coincide, analysis should not stop with the conclusion that expectations are adequate to explain the subsequent perceptions. One can ask what influenced expectations, and specifically whether desires did. This, unfortunately, is a difficult question. In one interesting experiment it seems that affect, while perhaps not directly in-

[11] Bernard Berelson, Paul Lazarsfeld, and William McPhee, *Voting* (Chicago: University of Chicago Press, 1954), pp. 220-21. For a replication, see Drury Sherrod, "Selective Perception of Political Candidates," *Public Opinion Quarterly* 35 (Winter 1971-72), 554-62.

[12] Warren Miller, "Party Preference and Attitudes on Political Issues: 1948-1951," *American Political Science Review* 47 (March 1953), 45-60.

[13] Berelson, Lazarsfeld, and McPhee, *Voting*, p. 223.

fluencing perceptions, had an indirect influence through expectations. In viewing films of a penalty-filled football game between Princeton and Dartmouth, Princeton students "saw the Dartmouth team make over twice as many infractions as were seen by the Dartmouth students." It seems likely that the students at each college expected to see the other side as guilty, but that their ties to their college helped establish that expectation.[14] Further evidence is supplied by an experiment that separated cognitive set from motivational factors and found that the latter influenced pre-recognition guesses, but, with expectations held constant, did not directly influence perceptions.[15] More experiments along these lines are needed, however, before we can draw conclusions with any confidence.

It can be argued that it does not matter whether desires influence perceptions directly or act through intervening variables. Whatever the details of the linkages, the results will be the same, i.e. the frequent occurrence of wishful thinking. But it does matter, for if desires act only through expectations their impact will be diluted by their further remove from the outcome. There are many nonaffective influences on expectations, and variables other than expectations influence perceptions, which further reduces the impact of desires.

Direct Impact of Affect

EXPERIMENTAL MANIPULATION OF AFFECT

Some studies indicate that affect influences cognitions and perceptions directly, without working through the intervening variables of expectations. One ingenious experiment even surmounted the major obstacle of determining whether affect or cognitions changed first. Milton Rosenberg first explored subjects' affect toward certain objects (e.g. foreign aid, Negroes moving in next door) and their beliefs about how these objects influenced their values (e.g. does foreign aid lead to stability? does the presence of Negroes lower property values?). Not surprisingly he found a high degree of consistency between affect and cognitions. He then hypnotized the subjects and told them to change their affect toward the object. If the person's belief system was to regain balance, other changes would have to follow. Thus if he now dislikes foreign aid, the subject might reverse his previous belief that aid furthered other values (e.g. aided American business). Or balance could be restored without changing the instrumentality of the object if the value of what it contrib-

[14] Albert Hastorf and Hadley Cantril, "They Saw a Game," *Journal of Abnormal and Social Psychology* 49 (1954), 129-34.

[15] Ruth Wylie, "Cognitive Set and Motivational Factors in the Perception of Neutral and Threat-Related Stimuli," *Journal of Abnormal and Social Psychology* 55 (1957), 227-31.

utes to was altered. Thus the subject could still believe that foreign aid helps American business, but whereas he previously valued this end, after hypnosis he might dislike it.[16]

The results showed that hypnotically induced changes in affect did lead to changes in beliefs about instrumentality and, to a lesser extent, to changes in evaluations of goals. Although this is not exactly the same kind of wishful thinking displayed by bringing predictions into line with desires, it does indicate the influence of affect on beliefs. But the relevance of the findings is limited by the artificial nature of the experimental manipulations. Although most objects and policies are valued as both means and ends, those manipulated by Rosenberg are predominantly instrumental and have little independence. Whether a person values them is largely determined by his beliefs about how they serve other goals. This is especially true of foreign aid, as is revealed by Rosenberg's hypnotic instructions—"The mere idea of the United States giving economic aid to foreign nations will make you feel very displeased and disgusted."[17] Decision-makers who oppose aid are not "disgusted" by it; rather they believe it conflicts with their interests (e.g. is wasteful, incurs dangerous commitments). Indeed in the absence of hypnosis it is hard to see how their affect toward aid could change in the absence of previous alterations in instrumental beliefs or higher values. That these changes followed the manipulation of affect in the experiment does not provide strong evidence for the operation of such a sequence in other settings. But this experiment does point in an interesting direction and, as we will discuss in a later section, we can look for natural situations in which alterations in circumstances lead, in ways that cannot be explained by rational processes, to changes in evaluations and beliefs that maintain affective-cognitive consistency.

JUDGMENTS OF DESIRABILITY AND PROBABILITY

Although they lack the advantages of dealing with complex opinions, other experiments are more directly relevant because they have found that subjects overguess the frequency of desired outcomes and underguess the frequency of undesired ones. For example, after drawing several cards from a deck that portrayed either happy or angry faces, subjects greatly underestimated the percentage that displayed pictures of angry faces. In another experiment subjects received points if they

[16] Milton Rosenberg, "An Analysis of Affective-Cognitive Consistency," in Milton Rosenberg et al., Attitude Organization and Change (New Haven: Yale University Press, 1960). (Also see Milton Rosenberg, "A Structural Theory of Attitude Dynamics," Public Opinion Quarterly 24 [Summer 1960], 319-40.) Milton Rosenberg, "Cognitive Reorganization as Response to Hypnotic Reversal of Attitudinal Affect," Journal of Personality 28 (1960), 39-63.

[17] Rosenberg, "An Analysis of Affective-Cognitive Consistency," p. 38.

drew a marked card and lost them if they drew an unmarked one. When they were asked to guess which kind of card they would draw next (thus revealing expectations rather than perceptions), they overguessed the probability of drawing a valued card. And, to a less pronounced extent, they had greater confidence in their guesses that the desired outcome would occur.[18]

An experiment utilizing a more realistic setting produced similar results. High school boys were told that a three-man board could award them a ticket to a college basketball game on the basis of an interview. Unbeknownst to the boys, "The behavior and attitudes of the board members were prescribed by a script designed to express in each board member different intensities of Power and Approval. Three such scripts or stimulus conditions were employed and these varied along a dimension of restraint expressed toward the boy."[19] "Facilitative distortion" was found. Most boys perceived the board member who was friendly and approved his answers as powerful and influential in the board's decision. The boys were divided into two groups before they saw the board; half were experimentally induced to be highly motivated to win a ticket, and in the other half less motivation was induced. It was expected that the highly motivated group would show greater facilitative distortion, and while this was true under some conditions, under other conditions motivation led to more accurate perceptions. These experiments, however, would be more significant if they had included incentives for accuracy. But in most cases the subject's payoffs were independent of his perceptions and predictions.

OTHER EXPERIMENTS

Wishful thinking seems to appear in several experiments that are not as open to the previous criticisms. It has been shown that subjects are more tolerant of inconsistency when "the attitudinal cognition in question conveys a hedonistic assertion or promise of gain" than when the cogni-

[18] David Rosenhan and Samuel Messick, "Affect and Expectation," *Journal of Personality and Social Psychology* 3 (1966), 38-44; Francis Irwin, "Stated Expectations As Functions of Probability and Desirability of Outcomes," *Journal of Personality* 21 (1953), 329-53; Francis Irwin and Marsha Metzger, "Effects of Independent Outcome-Values of Past Events Upon Subsequent Choices," *Psychonomic Science* 9 (1967), 613-14; Richard Jessor and Joel Readio, "The Influence of the Value of an Event Upon the Expectancy of its Occurrence," *Journal of General Psychology* 56 (1957), 219-28. For a contrary finding, see Philip Brickman, "Rational and Nonrational Elements in Reactions to Disconfirmation of Performance Expectancies," *Journal of Experimental Social Psychology* 8 (1972), 112-23. Also see the experiments cited in footnote 4, above.

[19] Albert Pepitone, "Motivational Effects in Social Perception," *Human Relations* 3 (1950), 75. Also see Richard Bootzin and Mark Stephens, "Individual Differences and Perceptual Defense in the Absence of Response Bias," *Journal of Personality and Social Psychology* 6 (1967), 408-12.

tion "conveys an anti-hedonistic assertion or promise of loss."[20] In a more complex experiment, Rosenberg and Abelson asked subjects to imagine that they were the manager of a department store who held certain beliefs about the head of a department, the head's past sales record, his current plans, and the probable effects of implementing those plans. When the subjects read a number of statements that contradicted earlier information they altered "their beliefs and evaluations in ways that . . . maximize[d] expected gain and minimize[d] expected loss" in sales even when this meant that balance was either not achieved or was reached by making more than the minimum number of changes necessary.[21]

While these findings seem to show the impact of desires on beliefs, two reservations about the latter experiment should be entered. First, the subjects may have drawn on their general knowledge of business behavior. If managers do not retain subordinates with bad sales records or allow them to carry out programs that will lose money, then it is rational for the subjects to rearrange their beliefs so that gains rather than losses are expected even if doing so entails imbalance or extra changes. Second, if the subjects heeded only what they were told, they had no guidelines for treating the discrepant information. They had little evidence, and all of it was to be taken as equally valid. Under the greater constraints common outside the laboratory, desires are apt to have less impact.

Wishful thinking is also revealed by the high correlation between subjects' ratings of the desirability and of the truth value of a series of statements. Furthermore, the statements formed hidden syllogisms, and desires seemed to influence the degree to which the responses were logically consistent. (Since the subjects were giving opinions, the lack of incentives for accuracy that marred other experiments was not a problem.) But the subjects were the quicker to accept information if it increased logical consistency at the expense of wishful thinking than if it was in accord with desires but not logic. Furthermore, taking the test seemed to

[20] Milton Rosenberg, "Some Content Determinants of Intolerance for Attitude Inconsistency," in Silvin Tomkins and Carroll Izard, eds., *Affect, Cognition, and Personality* (New York: Springer, 1965), p. 134. Also see Milton Rosenberg, "Hedonism, Inauthenticity, and Other Goads toward Expansion of a Consistency Theory," in Robert Abelson et al., eds., *Theories of Cognitive Consistency* (Chicago: Rand McNally, 1968), pp. 89-96. O. J. Harvey, "Concluding Comments on the Current Status of the Incongruity Hypothesis," in Harvey, ed., *Motivation and Social Interaction* (New York: Ronald Press, 1963), pp. 295-96, discusses a similar experiment. However, wishfulness was not found by Robert Wyler, Jr., and Lee Goldberg, "A Probabilistic Analysis of the Relationships among Beliefs and Attitudes," *Psychological Review* 77 (1970), 114.

[21] Milton Rosenberg and Robert Abelson, "An Analysis of Cognitive Balancing," in Rosenberg et al., *Attitude Organization and Change*, p. 145. For a different finding on a related subject see Eugene Burnstein, "Sources of Cognitive Bias in the Representation of Simple Social Structures," *Journal of Personality and Social Psychology* 7 (1967), 36-48.

call the subjects' attention to their biases, for in re-tests the impact of wishful thinking was less.[22]

The implications of these experiments are not entirely clear. Syllogisms, even when not openly presented, are less congenial to wishful thinking than is the ambiguous evidence that surrounds most political decisions. But since these decisions usually permit time for reflection, we should remember that the experiment indicates that wishfulness decreased (although it did not disappear) when the questions were made salient and the subjects induced to think about their answers.

In summary, the experimental evidence for the existence of wishful thinking is not as strong as is usually believed. Psychologists have argued fiercely about the inferences that can be drawn from the diverse experiments we have discussed. Controlling for third factors has been extremely difficult. Nevertheless, some findings (e.g. the boys' estimates of the relative power of panel members to award them a desired ticket) seem to demonstrate the direct impact of desires upon perceptions. Others are consistent with wishful thinking, although alternative explanations are not always excluded and intervening variables such as expectations must be considered. It must be remembered, too, that in even these experiments there were no incentives for accuracy.

Wishful Thinking in International Relations

Commenting on a critical analysis of these experiments, one scholar argued that we should "give full consideration to the observational data taken from real-life situations. Shipwrecked sailors and lost explorers report perceptual motivation which is apparently far more persuasive than has been demonstrated by the controlled experiments."[23] But when we look at "real life" situations in international relations, the results are not so clear, partly because of two related problems with forming propositions in this area. First, wishfulness often predicts the same behavior that is predicted by the more general hypotheses discussed in Chapter 4. The strong tendency for people to see what they expect to be present explains many apparent cases of wishful thinking.

The second and even greater problem is that it is hard to draw specific propositions about what decision-makers will think and do from the general concept of wishful thinking. In a broad sense, wishfulness implies

---

[22] William McGuire, "A Syllogistic Analysis of Cognitive Relationships," in Rosenberg et al., *Attitude Organization and Change*, pp. 77-95. But for a report of somewhat contradictory results with subjects of higher academic accomplishments, see Ronald Dillehay, Chester Insko, and M. Brewster Smith, "Logical Consistency and Attitude Change," *Journal of Personality and Social Psychology* 3 (June 1966), 646-54.

[23] Harry Harlow, "Comments," in Brown, ed., *Current Theory and Research in Motivation*, p. 108.

the minimization of costs and value trade-offs that we discussed in Chapter 4. But this gives no clue to the content of the beliefs. At first glance, wishfulness would seem to imply that people are likely to continue their policies because they will see them as succeeding. But if they are carried away by their desires they will cease their efforts since they will believe their goal has been reached. Thus wishful thinking might lead the United States to conclude that it could withdraw its troops from Europe since the Europeans are strong enough to defend themselves, or, more broadly, that containment has succeeded so well that deterrence is no longer needed. Again, at first glance wishfulness would seem to lead to over-extension, to an actor's trying to accomplish more than is possible. But the actor might try very little in the belief that the world is benign enough so that his values will be protected even if he remains passive. Did American policy in Vietnam display wishful thinking because the chances of victory were overestimated? Or did it show "unwishful thinking" because the consequences of not fighting were seen as so costly? It is even harder to link wishfulness with the means that are selected to reach a given goal. Would wishfulness predispose one to see force or conciliation as more productive? To believe that alliance or isolation is best? Wishfulness may lead decision-makers to overestimate the chances of success of the policy they have adopted, but it does not tell us which policy they will select.

If we cannot generalize about the content of perceptions, we must look for evidence of covariance. Most conclusive would be cases where a shift in desires was followed by a shift in perceptions. For example, Otto Klineberg argues that in the 1860s Californians changed their stereotype of Chinese from hard-working, peaceful, law-abiding citizens to an unassimilable, filthy, criminal rabble. "The only acceptable explanation is that the change in economic conditions [in California] made it advantageous for the whites to try to eliminate the Chinese from economic competition, and the stereotype was altered in a direction that would help in justifying such action."[24] Similarly, U.S. opinions about the Soviet domestic system changed after the United States became allied with Russia in World War II and changed again after the onset of the Cold War.[25] To take a hypothetical example, if a state increases its power, do others think it more likely that the state will support them? If a statesman comes to believe that unrest within other countries would help him, will he see it as more likely? Unfortunately, we have little data on

[24] Klineberg, *The Human Dimension in International Relations*, pp. 40-41. For a different view, see Stuart Miller, *The Unwelcome Immigrant* (Berkeley and Los Angeles: University of California Press, 1969).

[25] Since some people may have consciously believed, following Woodrow Wilson, that only states with evil domestic systems are aggressive, this change may not meet the requirement that logical links be absent.

questions such as these. Even when we can find cases in which changes in desires have occurred and been followed by changes in perceptions, we must deal with the possibility of spuriousness. Since changes in desires are often caused by factors that could rationally lead to altered estimates of probable outcomes, it is hard to find many cases that, like the changed images of the Chinese, unambiguously show the impact of affect.

We can also try to detect rationalization—cases where shifts in desires follow rather than precede shifts in estimates of what will happen. Do grim outcomes appear less menacing when they are sure to occur? If a state moves from one alliance to another, do states in the alliance that it left lower their estimate of that state's power, and do the states in the alliance which it joins raise their estimates? (Professors might ask themselves if their evaluation of the work of one of their colleagues is changed by that colleague's joining or leaving their university.) Have the American beliefs about the value of a British presence east of Suez been altered by the British withdrawal from this area?

But one must not conclude that all such shifts are rationalizations. Shifts can occur because the actor has been forced to examine the situation more carefully and has learned how he can make the best of it. For example, American decision-makers may believe that their values have not been harmed by the withdrawal of British troops because they now realize that the previous British stance was ineffective or because they have developed new policies to fill the gap left by the British. When an outcome is highly desired and not improbable, decision-makers may not explore what they will do if it does not occur. But when the need arises and they turn their attention and resources to designing a new policy, they often find they are able to do better than they previously had thought possible.[26]

The second best kind of evidence is correlations between desires and perceptions with as many other factors as possible held constant.[27] Thus a re-analysis of European public opinion toward the Common Market reveals that nearly 70 percent of those who thought that the EEC would "increase United States influence in European affairs" and a slightly

[26] See Albert Hirschman's discussion of the "hiding hand" in *Development Projects Observed* (Washington: Brookings Institution, 1967), pp. 9-34. For a related argument from psychology, see Richard Lazarus, "Emotions and Adaptation: Conceptual and Empirical Relations," in William Arnold, ed., *Nebraska Symposium on Motivation, 1968* (Lincoln: University of Nebraska Press, 1968), pp. 228-29.

[27] Such correlations could be caused by rationalization. But this is not a plausible explanation where we can identify long-standing hopes that pre-date expectations—e.g. the desire for peace or for winning a war.

smaller percentage of those who thought the EEC would have the opposite effect believed that the expected result was "a good thing."[28] Such comparisons are hard to construct for statesmen, however, because desires are usually linked to many other important variables, making the independent impact of each variable difficult to determine. And when many other variables are the same—e.g. when the decision-makers come from the same, well-integrated political system—desires are apt to be also similar.

Third, we can ask an even cruder question: are statesmen usually over-optimistic? Do they think that what will occur is good and what is good will occur? This raises problems, however, because it is hard to establish a baseline of the correlation between desires and beliefs that would exist in the absence of wishful thinking. This correlation would not be zero if people are optimistic for reasons unrelated to the influence of affect. A belief in a certain kind of God, for example, would lead to the view that whatever occurred will be good. Similarly, psychological theories are not needed to explain the optimism of the classical analysis of a free market. More generally, to say that wishful thinking is common implies a comparison between what people believe and the true state of the world. If desired outcomes actually occurred most of the time, statesmen could be optimistic without engaging in wishfulness. Furthermore, since decision-makers choose a policy because they think it will have some measure of success, some correlation between beliefs and desires should be expected. Thus it is hard to determine when we have found something that requires further explanation.

To see whether decision-makers are not only optimistic, but over-optimistic we could compare their views with those of disinterested scholars. We would undoubtedly find many instances where decision-makers overestimated the probabilities of desired events. But in an uncertain world, this does not demonstrate wishfulness. For even if incorrect estimates occurred at random, or occurred for reasons unrelated to affect, estimates would often coincide with desires. It is not certain that errors in the direction of desires actually outnumber those in the opposite direction. As we have seen, statesmen often overestimate others' hostility. History is replete with examples of decision-makers who were too cautious, who underestimated the probability that a decisive stand could lead to a highly desired goal. Furthermore, cases of wishful thinking are more likely to be recorded than are the opposite errors. The former lead to policies that clearly, and often dramatically, fail, while the latter often generate self-justifying reactions or result in inactivity, which does not

---

[28] Recalculated from USIA survey data presented in Donald Puchala, "The Common Market and Political Federation in West European Public Opinion," *International Studies Quarterly* 14 (March 1970), 47.

attract the notice of contemporary observers or later scholars. Proposals are rejected every day because decision-makers feel their probability of success is too low, and there is no easy way to tell how many are cases of "unwishful thinking."[29]

Many of the cases in which beliefs and perceptions correspond with desires can be accounted for by the more general explanation of the influence of the expectations generated by the actor's beliefs about the world and images of the other states. For example, the United States and U.S.S.R. both think that the trend of world history is in their direction, but it would not be credible to ascribe this difference to the difference in desires, omitting the wider differences in values and belief systems. Similarly, Chamberlain's belief that Hitler could be appeased, Kennedy's belief that an emigré landing in Cuba would spark a revolt against Castro, and the State Department's view that French policy would be more tractable after De Gaulle may not have been the products of desires. Behind all these beliefs are hypotheses and theories that, as we have shown, do and must influence perceptions of incoming information. In such cases one has to demonstrate that the consideration of affective variables makes the explanation significantly more complete or satisfactory.

The primacy of expectations is shown by the fact that when they conflict with desires they usually prevail. Thus when the captain of the cruiser shadowing the *Bismarck* reported that the ship had altered course and was now headed back toward the pursuing British force, the admiral in charge did not believe him. He devoutly wished this message to be correct, but the German behavior reported made no sense. So he immediately concluded that the captain, although an experienced observer, had simply made an error.[30]

Unfortunately there is little experimental evidence concerning the relative impact of expectations and desires, although one study found that interviewers' reports were biased more by the responses they expected to hear than by their personal opinions. But the sample was small and

[29] Similar problems arise with Ralph White's claim that decision-makers tend to overestimate the chances of military success (*Nobody Wanted War* [Garden City, N.Y.: Doubleday, 1970, rev. ed.], pp. 27-30, 122-30, 222-28). There may be many instances where decision-makers did not go to war because they underestimated the chances of victory. These cases are much less dramatic and harder to sample than are cases of wars. It is therefore hard to compare the frequency of this error with that of the opposite one. Furthermore, decision-makers may feel that the costs of avoiding war are high enough to justify a conflict even though there is only a slight chance of success. Thus the fact that a state loses the war does not mean that the decision-makers were overoptimistic in entering it. Geoffrey Blainey's *The Causes of War* (New York: Free Press, 1973)—a much better book—makes a similar error.

[30] Ludovic Kennedy, *Pursuit: The Chase and Sinking of the Battleship Bismarck* (New York: Viking, 1974), p. 173.

the results not statistically significant.[31] We would like to compare perceptions under conditions where expectations were held constant and desires varied and where desires were the same but expectations differed. Few cases provide such clear comparisons, but it is easy to find instances in international relations where perceptions mirror expectations rather than desires. For example, statesmen would like to believe that the international environment is benign, but in fact they often overestimate others' aggressiveness. Most Western leaders would like to believe that the underdeveloped areas can quickly be transformed into modern democracies, but almost none holds this view. Indeed at least as common as overoptimism have been mistaken predictions that these countries would quickly "go communist."

More specific perceptions also show the dominance of expectations. In order to avoid breaking off negotiations with the Americans aimed at ending the War of 1812, the British made a major concession. But the American negotiators, who expected the British to be unresponsive, failed to perceive the new British position correctly. Theodore Roosevelt hoped for war with Spain in 1898, but his image of McKinley led him to complain "only two weeks before the war declaration that the President was determined to have peace at any price." Similarly, in 1931 the Germans ignored intelligence reports indicating that President Hoover would propose a desired debt moratorium because this information "did not fit in with the prevailing line of thought." And although the Allies hoped for as quick a victory as possible, the bitter experience with their foes' strength led them to underestimate the extent of the military collapse of Germany at the end of World War I and of Germany and Japan at the end of World War II. More recently, many American liberals incorrectly predicted that the intervention in the Dominican Republic would lead to the drastic growth of anti-Americanism in that country and the rest of Latin America and thought that the withdrawal of American troops from Vietnam would be immediately followed by the establishment of a communist government not because they desired these results, but because of expectations created by their theories about how people react to foreign interference. Finally, to take an example from mass opinion, the evaluations made by both "hawks" and "doves" of President Nixon's Vietnam policy in the first two years he was in office shifted away from their desires, probably in part because of the influence of their expectations.[32]

[31] Dale Wyatt and Donald Campbell, "A Study of Interviewer Bias as Related to Interviewer's Expectations and Own Opinions," *International Journal of Opinion and Attitude Research* 4 (Spring 1950), 77-83.

[32] Frank Freidel, "Dissent in the Spanish-American War and the Philippine Insurrection," in Samuel Eliot Morison, Frederick Merk, and Frank Freidel, *Dissent in Three American Wars* (Cambridge, Mass.: Harvard University Press, 1970), p. 72; Bradford Perkins, *Castlereagh and Adams* (Berkeley and Los Ange-

Differing perceptions of other states can rarely be explained by differing desires. Chamberlain and Churchill, the proponents of deterrence and of conciliation in the Cold War, those Finns who wanted to make concessions to Russia in 1939 and those who wanted to stand firm, all wanted peace and security. The Americans who urged a "hard line" against Spain and Portugal during the Second World War and the British who favored a "soft line" agreed on their goals and the events they wished to occur. Indeed a person who accuses another of wishful thinking usually shares the other's wishes, but not his perceptions.

One might argue that this analysis does not contradict the hypothesis that desires influence perception. First, it can be claimed that people do not want their expectations to be proven wrong or to have to change their images and policies.[33] If an American decision-maker came to believe that Russia was not a menace, he would have to admit previous errors and devote a great deal of energy and ingenuity to designing new policies. Furthermore, unless most people had undergone a similar change of opinion, he would have to convert others, a costly task that would open the prospect of losing political power. But if this argument is valid and decision-makers want to perceive minimum change, expectations and desires will always coincide and propositions about wishful thinking will add nothing to those purely cognitive ones advanced in Chapters 4 and 7.

Second, it can be argued that desires act "in an indirect and devious fashion."[34] While this may be true, it raises the question of how to specify

---

les: University of California Press, 1964), pp. 84-87; Edward Bennett, *Germany and the Diplomacy of the Financial Crisis, 1931* (Cambridge, Mass.: Harvard University Press, 1962), p. 156; the data, but not the interpretation, are taken from Arthur Miller, "Political Issues and Trust in Government, 1960-1970," *American Political Science Review* 68 (September 1974), 969. Mixed support for our proposition was found by Paul Diesing and Glenn Snyder (*Systems, Bargains, Decisions*, [Princeton: Princeton University Press, forthcoming], chapter 4) in their study of crises. Misperceptions that were consistent with desires but not expectations were slightly less frequent than misperceptions that were consistent with expectations but not desires (15 versus 23).

[33] Some students of cognitive dissonance have argued that the disconfirming of expectations, even unpleasant expectations, will create discomfort. (J. Merrill Carlsmith and Elliot Aronson, "Some Hedonic Consequences of the Confirmation and Disconfirmation of Expectancies," *Journal of Abnormal and Social Psychology* 66 [1963], 151-56.) Indeed people may even lower their accomplishments to bring them into line with low expectations (Aronson and Carlsmith, "Performance Expectancy as a Determinant of Actual Performance," *ibid.* 65 [1962], 178-82) or choose an unpleasant but expected task over a more pleasant but unexpected one (Aronson, Carlsmith, and John Darley, "The Effects of Expectancy on Volunteering for an Unpleasant Experience," *ibid.* 66 [1963], 220-24). For a criticism of this position and contrary findings see Kenneth Mace and Russell Enzie, "Dissonance Versus Contrast in an Ego-Involved Situation with Disconfirmed Expectancies," *Journal of Psychology* 75 (1970), 107-21.

[34] Klineberg, *The Human Dimension in International Relations*, p. 91.

this influence in any given case without resorting to ad hoc and post hoc explanations. Most attempts to deal with the non-obvious influences of desires have been in the realm of psychoanalytic theories, which is beyond the scope of this study. It can merely be noted that propositions in this area are extremely difficult to test.

Third, and most importantly, even if there were no more cases of correspondence between desires and perceptions than would be predicted by chance—or indeed if there were no such cases at all—this would not show that wishes have no influence. It would only prove that any influence they might have is outweighed by other factors. That expectations are more powerful than desires does not mean that the latter have no influence. The net effect of two variables working in opposite directions will disguise the existence of the weaker one. Fear and vigilance—the product of the decision-makers' knowledge of the anarchic nature of the international system—lead to perceptions of hostility and conflict. But, it can be argued, were it not for the impact of desires, perceptions would be even more pessimistic. Or the combination of hopes and fears could lead to offsetting errors in a more complex fashion. The existence of anarchy and the psychological processes discussed earlier may lead decision-makers to perceive the others as more hostile than they are; wishfulness may lead them to overestimate their ability to cope with the perceived menace. If the perceptions of threat were accurate, the policies would by their failure be shown to be influenced by desires. But since the threat is overestimated wishfulness is not revealed so clearly.

These arguments may be correct, but, until they can be tested, the best conclusion is still the one reached by Walter Lippmann more than 45 years ago: "Our stereotyped world is not necessarily the world we should like it to be. It is simply the kind of world we expect it to be."[35]

PERCEPTIONS OF DANGER: VIGILANCE OR DEFENSE?

Related to wishful thinking are questions about perceptions of harm. Are people highly sensitive to evidence that an undesired outcome is likely (perceptual vigilance)? Or do they avoid such evidence and underestimate the chances of harm (perceptual defense)? Psychological treatments of international relations often make the latter claim.[36] But we

[35] *Public Opinion* (New York: Harcourt, Brace, 1922), p. 104. We must, however, acknowledge that Solley and Murphy's point applies to foreign policy contexts as well as to experiments: "in order to relate perceptual expectancy before the perceptual stimulus' occurrence to perception itself we must obtain independent measures of both perceptual expectancy and perceptual reports. . . . In most studies on expectancy and perception, expectancy is *assumed* and it is impossible to test the correlation of the two." (Charles Solley and Gardner Murphy, *Development of the Perceptual World* [New York: Basic Books, 1960], p. 163.)

[36] Klineberg, *The Human Dimension in International Relations*, p. 91; Osgood, *An Alternative to War or Surrender*, pp. 22-23.

know that decision-makers often see imaginary dangers. They are sensitive to threats to their security that critical observers regard as minuscule.

A large number of diverse experimental studies have explored these questions. At first glance the results seem as contradictory as the claims made in the previous paragraph. Sometimes people are highly alert to noxious stimuli, and sometimes they are insensitive to them. Sometimes a fear-arousing message induces more attitude change than a reassuring one, and sometimes the reverse is true. Outside the laboratory, people sometimes believe any slight indication of an impending disaster, and sometimes they refuse to accept overwhelming evidence. But most of these findings can be accounted for by a twofold proposition that accords with common sense and is directly relevant to foreign policy perceptions: if there is nothing a person can do to avoid the pain that accompanies a stimulus, his perceptual threshold for the stimulus will be raised (defense). If, on the other hand, he can avoid the pain by recognizing the stimulus and taking corrective action, his threshold will be lowered (vigilance).[37]

In the latter cases, however, it is difficult to tell whether perceptions, or only responses, have been affected. Even if he is uncertain, the person has an incentive to act as though he sees the noxious stimulus, provided only that the costs of doing so are low. Some experiments have dealt with this ambiguity and shown that avoidable punishments can alter subjects' perceptions without their being aware of it.

> At the beginning of each . . . trial [in one experiment], either a short or a tall rectangle is presented. The subject adjusts the figure to appear square. There is, of course, some variability in his final setting from trial to trial. When the subject adjusts the rectangle *below* a certain height and reports the figure as square, he is immediately [given an electric shock]. However, the subject does not "know" he has made a constant error. By setting the rectangle above this height, he can avoid the shock. [Preliminary results indicated that the subjects made] the rectangle taller and taller during the series of trials, yet always perceive[d] a square at the end of each trial.[38]

In another experiment subjects were given a shock whenever they mentioned certain words. They not only learned to avoid these words but did

[37] See Alexander Rosen, "Change in Perceptual Threshold as a Protective Function of the Organism," in M. D. Vernon, ed., *Experiments in Visual Perception* (Baltimore: Penguin, 1966), pp. 395-407. Also see the discussion in Jerome Bruner, "On Perceptual Readiness," *Psychological Review* 64 (1957), 123-52, Solley and Murphy, *Development of the Perceptual World*, p. 286, and Richard Lazarus, "Emotions and Adaptation: Conceptual and Empirical Relations," p. 198.

[38] Charles Snyder quoted in Solley and Murphy, *Development of the Perceptual World*, p. 246.

not realize that uttering these words had brought on the shock or that they had altered their pattern of responses.[39]

For our purposes, more important than whether the adjustment is conscious or unconscious is the argument that the predisposition to perceive a threat varies with the person's beliefs about his ability to take effective counteraction if he perceives the danger. Evidence from three fields supports our position although many anomalies, confusions, and contradictions remain. The area with most evidence—and most contradictions— is that of the impact of fear on attitude (and occasionally behavior) change. At first scholars tried to determine whether high fear would induce more attitude change than low fear or whether it would be less effective because it arouses mechanisms of defense, denial, or aggression. It soon became clear that this question had no invariant answer but depended on the state of other variables. Although they do not explain all the results, the presence or absence of instructions on how to cope with the danger and discussions of the effectiveness of countermeasures greatly affect the influence of fear. When the subjects are told how to meet the threat, high levels of fear produce more attitude change than low levels. But when the subjects think that there are few effective steps that they can take, high fear produces less change than low fear. As Irving Janis and Seymour Freshbach put it, "When fear is strongly aroused but is not fully relieved by the reassurances contained in a . . . communication, the audience will become motivated to ignore or to minimize the importance of the threat."[40]

[39] Charles Eriksen and James Kuethe, "Avoidance Conditioning of Verbal Behavior without Awareness: A Paradigm of Repression," *Journal of Abnormal and Social Psychology* 53 (1956), 203-209. Also see Rosen, "Change in Perceptual Threshold as a Protective Function of the Organism."

[40] Irving Janis and Seymour Freshbach, "Effects of Fear-Arousing Communications," *Journal of Abnormal and Social Psychology* 48 (1953), 92. Five excellent reviews of the literature on different aspects of the impact of fear on attitude change present analyses consistent with this general argument. See Irving Janis, "Effects of Fear Arousal on Attitude Change: Recent Developments in Theory and Experimental Research," in Leonard Berkowitz, ed., *Advances in Experimental Social Psychology*, vol. 3 (New York: Academic Press, 1967); Howard Leventhal, "Findings and Theory in the Study of Fear Communications," *ibid.* 5 (1970); Kenneth Higbee, "Fifteen Years of Fear Arousal," *Psychological Bulletin* 72 (1969), 426-44; Chester Insko, *Theories of Attitude Change* (New York: Appleton-Century-Crofts, 1967), pp. 34-43; and, from a different perspective, Richard Lazarus, *Psychological Stress and the Coping Process* (New York: McGraw-Hill, 1966). For additional supporting experiments see Godwin Chu, "Fear Arousal, Efficacy, and Imminency," *Journal of Personality and Social Psychology* 4 (1966), 517-24; James Dabbs, Jr., and Howard Leventhal, "Effects of Varying the Recommendations in a Fear-Arousing Communication," *ibid.*, pp. 525-31; Howard Leventhal, Jean Watts, and Francia Pagano, "Effects of Fear and Instruction on How To Cope with Danger," *ibid.* 6 (1967), 313-21; and Ronald Rogers and Donald Thistlethwaite, "Effects of Fear Arousal and Reassurance on Attitude Change," *ibid.* 15 (1970), 227-33.

People react to warnings of natural disasters in the same way. Whether they are vigilant or defensive depends in large part on whether they think they can act effectively on the undesired information. "Vigilance increases when the person is exposed to signs indicating that adequate protection for himself and his family will require self-initiated action." When people feel they lack the ability or the need to protect themselves, they react very differently. "People feeling more ineffective should be less sensitive to incoming information. People feeling overconfident should be equally indifferent, but not as a defense—just because they feel they do not need the information." From a more psychoanalytic perspective, Martha Wolfenstein notes that "the feeling of immunity . . . may be . . . especially strong when there is nothing one can do to ward off an impending danger." Thus a woman who had "doubted the tornado warnings, saying that she didn't think anyone was smart enough to know [when the storm was coming], went on to acknowledge: 'We didn't have any place to go and didn't know which direction to run. . . . I couldn't have gone anywhere for protection.' " Similarly, one survey found that people who did not think nuclear weapons would ever be used tended to believe that civil defense preparations would do no good.[41]

Reactions to near-disasters also cluster around the opposite poles of vigilance or defense. Much of the explanation for which response occurs is to found in how the near-miss "is interpreted by the individual. If it tells the person he is hopelessly vulnerable, extreme or defense reactions will occur in the next situation of warning or danger. If it tells him that he is not vulnerable, especially if he takes certain reasonable precautions of which he is capable, the reactions to any future warnings will not be characterized by extreme emotions and will be more realistically attuned to the incoming evidence."[42]

Similarly, it has been found that wild rumors flourish only when they do not affect decisions. "Where action is impossible or not seriously contemplated, accuracy . . . is not decisive, and people may say things that please them." But when people are prepared to act on what they learn, they do not shun undesired news. This conclusion is supported by experiments in the serial transmission of information that have found that

[41] Irving Janis, "Psychological Effects of Warnings," in George Baker and Dwight Chapman, eds., *Man and Society in Disaster* (New York: Basic Books, 1962), p. 75; Stephen Withey, "Reaction to Uncertain Threats," in *ibid.*, p. 114; Martha Wolfenstein, *Disaster: A Psychological Essay* (Glencoe, Ill.: Free Press, 1957), pp. 20, 5-6. Wolfenstein also argues that beliefs about one's ability to influence the outcome were one of the determinants of whether people in earlier times reacted to threats such as plagues by asceticism or by abandoning restraints; *ibid.*, pp. 37-38.

[42] Lazarus, *Psychological Stress and the Coping Process*, p. 110 (italics omitted).

involvement with the material decreases distortion and that more important items are transmitted more accurately than less important ones.[43]

These findings and explanations are also consistent with studies that have shown that a sense of efficacy and the belief that one can control his environment are associated with effort and striving.[44] They also fit with the finding that people tend to prefer material that opposes their position to material that supports it when the former will be useful (e.g. preparing to debate, serving on a mock jury, deciding whether to resist the draft).[45]

Our proposition about vigilance and defense parallels the earlier discussion of wishful thinking. The shutting out of undesired information is most apt to occur when there are no incentives for accuracy.[46] If the person can do nothing to avert a danger, there is no payoff, from either a psychological or a rational perspective, in detecting it. When there is no price to be paid for being ignorant, when reality-testing can serve no useful purpose, the person might as well gain the passing satisfaction of avoiding unpleasant thoughts. To take an analogy from national security policy, there is no point in constructing an early warning system if the state cannot act on the information received.

The best evidence that this proposition holds true in international relations would be cases where changes in an actor's beliefs about his ability to cope with a danger were followed by shifts in his perception that he was indeed facing the danger. Such evidence is very scarce, partly for the reasons discussed in connection with similar tests of wishful thinking. Changes in the independent variable are hard to isolate. The actor may not think enough about a problem to grow more confident of being able to solve it unless he sees it as significant in the first place. And since the international environment does not remain constant, it is very hard to eliminate the possibility that changes in the perception of danger are externally induced. Thus the American estimate of the threat from the Soviet Union has decreased as has her ability to respond to Soviet aggression. But the reason may be that the danger has indeed decreased.

Inter-nation and inter-individual comparisons are also useful, although again not easy to make. There is some evidence that weaker states perceive a given country as less a menace than do stronger ones. Throughout the postwar era the United States has seen Russia as more aggressive

---

[43] Tamotsu Shibutani, *Improvised News* (Indianapolis, Ind.: Bobbs-Merrill, 1966), pp. 91-94, and the experiments cited there.

[44] See Sumati Dubey, "Powerlessness and Mobility Orientations among Disadvantaged Blacks," *Public Opinion Quarterly* 35 (Summer 1971), 183-86, and the literature cited there.

[45] For citations, see footnote 14 in Chapter 11.

[46] It should be noted, however, that we are assuming that the person's belief that he cannot act on threatening information is correct. This may not be so, and we have not discussed the determinants of beliefs about the possibility of effective counteractions.

than has its smaller allies even though the latter are more directly threatened by any danger that may exist. In the 1950s French political leaders, who could do little to deter the outbreak of nuclear war, tended to seek less information about costs and effects of a future war than did American and British leaders.[47] Similarly, a number of small states were victims of surprise attacks in World War II (e.g. Norway, Denmark, Finland). But several large states also failed to predict the attacks on the small states or even the attacks against themselves.[48]

On the individual level too, estimates of the likelihood that a threat will materialize will vary with the expected efficacy of potential countermeasures. For example, American isolationists such as Charles Lindbergh who believed that Nazi Germany could not be defeated did not think that German ambitions clashed with American security. Interventionists saw Germany not only as a menace but one that could be coped with by the proper policy. Although in both of these cases it is hard to say which belief came first, each of the pair supports and facilitates its partner. We would similarly expect that a statesman who thought that he was powerless to bring about changes in his state's policy if he detected a threat would perceive such threats less readily than a person who believed that his views would matter.

Our propositions are also supported by a number of international perceptions, although they do not involve explicit comparisons and are susceptible to alternative explanations. During 1918 the Allies were extremely sensitive to the possibility that the leaders of the new Soviet regime were German agents or would fall under German influence, and they worried about the outlandish possibility that the Bolsheviks would rearm the Central Powers' prisoners in Siberia "and use them to ship the war stores at Vladivostok to the Central Powers."[49] While our earlier analysis helps explain why the Allies overestimated the degree of cooperation between Russia and the Central Powers, a factor contributing to the Allies' unrealistic fears may have been their belief that these dangers could be avoided by vigorous actions. Similarly, the view that grave international and domestic consequences would follow if the Dominican Republic developed into "another Cuba" coupled with the belief that this outcome could be prevented may have contributed to the overestimation of the communist danger. On a more general question, the American perception of the threat posed by Russia at the end of World War II may

[47] Wolfenstein, *Disaster*, pp. 20-21.

[48] Furthermore, even if it were found that small or vulnerable states failed to detect threats as frequently as large states, we would have to determine whether the former, because of their relative lack of resources, had generally less effective intelligence systems than the latter.

[49] Richard Ullman, *Anglo-Soviet Relations, 1917-1921*, vol. 1: *Intervention and the War* (Princeton: Princeton University Press, 1961), p. 87.

have been facilitated, or even permitted, by the belief that this menace would be contained by the appropriate policies.

The other half of this hypothesis is that actors will be slow to recognize dangers when even a policy based on accurate perceptions would not be adequate. Tang Tsou points out that American policy toward China for the past half-century has been characterized by a variety of "unfounded hopes."[50] A major reason may have been that, in the absence of the willingness to spend the resources necessary for an effective policy, there was little the United States could do even if it had correctly diagnosed the problem.

Avoidance of Perceptions of Extreme Probabilities

A final, highly tentative, hypothesis can be proposed. Under the conditions described below, if the advantages of an outcome are great and the probability of success is slight, decision-makers will tend to overestimate this probability, although not for reasons of simple wishfulness. This hypothesis rests first of all on research indicating that people are conservative and "unable to extract from the information all the certainty that [is] in it."[51] Experiments have shown that subjects avoid judgments of extreme probabilities. Even when the evidence is overwhelming and subjects should give probability estimates of above .95 or below .05, they keep their estimates much closer to .50. Thus they underestimate the probability of extremely likely events and overestimate the likelihood of very unlikely ones. This means that once decision-makers consider the possible occurrence of danger or the possible success of a policy, they are not likely to assign it a terribly low or a terribly high probability. Of course in most cases a danger will be considered only if its chance of occurring is above some minimum, and a policy will be examined only if it seems to have some promise of success. But when the payoffs are

[50] Tang Tsou, *America's Failure in China, 1941-50* (Chicago: University of Chicago Press, 1963), p. 550.

[51] This quote is from a summary of the literature by Ward Edwards, *Nonconservative Probabilistic Information Processing Systems*, Technical Documentary Report No. ESD-TR-66-404, December 1966, Institute of Science and Technology, University of Michigan. For experiments on this subject see Lawrence Philips and Ward Edwards, "Conservatism in a Simple Probability Inference Task," *Journal of Experimental Psychology* 72 (1966), 346-54; and Ward Edwards, "Utility, Subjective Probability, Their Interaction, and Variance Preferences," *Journal of Conflict Resolution* 6 (1962), 42-51. This argument implies that people will acquire more information than they need. For such a finding, see Amos Tversky and Ward Edwards, "Information versus Reward in Binary Choices," *Journal of Experimental Psychology* 71 (1966), 680-83. For a similar conclusion reached by a different route, see Amos Tversky and Daniel Kahneman, "Judgment Under Uncertainty: Heuristics and Biases," *Science* 185 (September 27, 1974), 1129.

very high, plans and outcomes that normally would be immediately dismissed will be examined. The high affect then does not operate directly on perceptions, but rather puts proposals in a position where other cognitive mechanisms will lead to exaggerated estimates of the probability of success. This proposition of course does not predict the content of the policies considered or adopted. The outcomes will still be seen as quite unlikely, but because the payoffs are so high, the marginal distortion of the probabilities can influence policies.

The Allied evaluations of the plans to re-open the eastern front in 1918 can be accounted for by this hypothesis. The urgency of the military situation and the belief in the great value of a new front kept proposals for reaching this goal constantly before the decision-makers. And, as our proposition predicts, while the Allies were pessimistic about most of these plans—including the ones they eventually implemented—they were not pessimistic enough. At first, officials were slow to recognize that there was no chance that the Soviets would continue fighting. Then "London and Paris conjured up the mirage of a new Eastern Front manned by the Japanese. Viewed in any way but through the myopia of a wasteful war, the idea that a large army could have been transported, by poor and inefficient railroads, over the 7,000 miles from the Pacific to the Carpathians, would have been dismissed as madness. Yet, spurred by Russia's collapse, negotiations for such an expedition took place."[52] Even though the Japanese clearly indicated that they would not go far enough west to engage the Germans, the British and French still favored the expedition. They refused to see that the chances of re-opening the eastern front were not just slight—they were infinitesimal. Similarly, although the British realized that the chances that the White forces in south Russia would be able to hinder the Germans were small, they seemed to have overestimated them.[53] This explanation may also apply to American decision-makers in Vietnam. Official documents reveal both pessimism and a high valuation of the outcome. Had the goal been less important, many of the plans would not have been seriously debated. But once the plans for saving Vietnam drew the decision-makers' attention, they were not viewed pessimistically enough.

We cannot be sure that this analysis is correct because the decision-makers may realize that the chances of success are slight yet calculate that the policy is still worth pursuing because the potential gains are so large. The American representative to the Allied Supreme War Council

---

[52] Ullman, *Intervention and the War*, pp. 85-86. For a more charitable view of the British policy, see V. H. Rothwell, *British War Aims and Peace Diplomacy, 1914-1918* (Oxford: Clarendon Press, 1971), p. 186.

[53] Ullman, *Intervention and the War*, pp. 45-57, 93. The United States also made this error. See George Kennan, *Russia Leaves the War* (New York: Atheneum, 1967), p. 177.

said of the British and French mood in the winter of 1918: "I found the general conviction that the situation was desperate and warranted taking a desperate chance." Secretary of State Hull favored exploring a feeler from Japan in 1941 even though he thought that "there was not one chance of success in twenty or one in fifty or even one in a hundred." Before the start of World War II Sir Henry Tizard recommended that Britain acquire all the uranium it could, although he put the odds of developing a bomb at 100,000 to 1.[54] When the payoffs are very high, small differences in estimates of success can tip the balance between favoring and opposing a policy. Even in the absence of systematic biases, it may be impossible for most actors to make the fine distinctions that are necessary for effective decision-making in these cases.

SUMMARY

The conventional wisdom that wishful thinking pervades political decision-making is not supported by the evidence from either experimental or natural settings. Statesmen sometimes see what they want to see, but whether this error is more common than the opposite one or more frequent than would be expected by chance and nonaffective variables has yet to be demonstrated. Expectations are usually crucial and a re-analysis of studies from several fields leads to the conclusion that desires and fears have most impact when perceptions matter least—when the person has no incentives to perceive accurately because he cannot act on what he believes will happen.

More experiments and continued analysis of historical materials may enable us to move further away from crude statements about the existence of wishful thinking and perceptual defense toward more detailed and productive consideration of the kinds of influence that affect has under various conditions. Perhaps as we control for more variables, no correlation between affect and perception will be found. But it is also possible that the gross correlations between affect and perception are weak because we have not isolated other variables. Affect may influence perceptions in different directions depending on the situation or the individual's personality, thus producing low overall correlations.[55] When we

[54] Ullman, *Intervention and the War*, p. 103 (also see p. 57); Cordell Hull, *Memoirs*, vol. 2 (New York: Macmillan Co., 1948), p. 985; Margaret Gowing, *Britain and Atomic Energy, 1939-1945* (London: Macmillan and Co., 1964), p. 35. Psychological experiments on perceptual vigilance and perceptual defense also have been plagued by the difficulties of separating perceptual effects from response effects. For a good discussion, see Thomas Natsoulas, "Converging Operations for Perceptual Defense," *Psychological Bulletin* 64 (1965), 393-401.

[55] Scholars have presented evidence for the "represser-sensitizer" dimension to personality. There is "a consistency in defensive reaction within individuals that extends across learning, perceptual and interpersonal situations." People who are

are able to control for these mediating variables, more impressive correlations may appear. At this point, however, there are few important and verified conclusions about the impact of affect on perception.

"repressers" on personality tests will tend to show "perceptual defense"; Charles Eriksen, "Perception and Personality," in Joseph Wepman and Ralph Heine, eds., *Concepts of Personality* (Chicago: Aldine, 1963), p. 49; R. Lazarus, C. Eriksen, and C. Fonda, "Personality Dynamics and Auditory Perceptual Recognition," *Journal of Personality* 19 (1951), 471-82. Partial support for the relevance of this personality dimension for the topics covered in this chapter is provided by June Andrew, "Recovery from Surgery, with and without Preparatory Instruction, for Three Coping Styles," *Journal of Personality and Social Psychology* 15 (1970), 223-26.

CHAPTER ELEVEN

Cognitive Dissonance and International Relations

COGNITIVE DISSONANCE THEORY

THE theory of cognitive dissonance can explain a number of puzzling misperceptions. The basic outlines of the theory are not startling, but some of its implications are contrary to common sense and other theories of cognitive consistency. The definition of dissonance is relatively straightforward: "two elements are in a dissonant relation if, considering these two alone, the obverse of one element would follow from the other." For example, the information that a Ford is a better car than a Chevrolet is dissonant with the knowledge that I have bought a Chevy. Information that the MLF is not favored by most Europeans is dissonant with the decision-maker's knowledge that he adopted this policy believing it would reduce strains within the alliance. The basic hypotheses are: "1. The existence of dissonance, being psychologically uncomfortable, will motivate the person to try to reduce dissonance and achieve consonance. 2. When dissonance is present, in addition to trying to reduce it, the person will actively avoid situations and information which would likely increase the dissonance."[1]

The basis of dissonance theory lies in the postulate that people seek strong justification for their behavior.[2] They are not content to believe merely that they behaved well and chose wisely—if this were the case they would only have to maintain the beliefs that produced their decisions. Instead, people want to minimize their internal conflict. This leads them to seek to believe that the reasons for acting or deciding as they did were overwhelming. The person will then rearrange his beliefs so that they provide increased support for his actions. Knowledge of the advantages of rejected courses of action and costs of the chosen one will be a source of uncomfortable dissonance that he will try to reduce. To do this he will alter his earlier opinions, seeing more drawbacks and fewer ad-

---

[1] Leon Festinger, *A Theory of Cognitive Dissonance* (Stanford: Stanford University Press, 1957), pp. 13, 31: also see Jack Brehm and Arthur Cohen, *Explorations in Cognitive Dissonance* (New York: Wiley, 1962), p. 16.

[2] This indicates that dissonance theory, unlike theories of cognitive balance and congruity, implies the existence of ego-defensive motivations. Indeed some scholars have argued that "postdecision dissonance occurs only under conditions which stimulate self-defensiveness about one's decision." Morton Deutsch, Robert Krauss, and Norah Rosenau, "Dissonance or Defensiveness?," *Journal of Personality* 30 (1962), 27. Also see p. 386 below.

vantages in the policies he rejected and more good points and fewer bad ones in the policy he adopted. He may, for example, come to believe that the rejected policy would not satisfy certain criteria that he originally thought it would, or that those criteria are less important than he originally believed, or that the chosen policy will not cost as much as he first thought. The person may also search out additional information supporting his decision and find new reasons for acting as he did and will avoid, distort, or derogate new dissonant information. If doubts nevertheless creep in, he will redouble his efforts to justify his decision. As a result, "Following a decision there is an increase in the confidence in the decision or an increase in the discrepancy in attractiveness between the alternatives involved in the choice, or both."[3] This is known as the "spreading apart of the alternatives" because of the perceived increase in the gap between the net advantages of the chosen policy and those of the rejected ones.

As the last quote implies, the theory has been developed only for postdecision situations.[4] Two further conditions are necessary. First, there must be a "definite commitment resulting from the decision. . . . It seems that a decision carries commitment with it if the decision unequivocally affects subsequent behavior."[5] Second, the person must feel that his deci-

[3] *Ibid.*, p. 83. Little research has been done on the question of whether dissonance will be reduced by increasing the valuation of the chosen alternative or by downgrading the rejected one. One experiment reached the plausible conclusion that the process "which is unlikely to come under reality attack in the future" will be invoked; Elaine Walster, Ellen Berscheid, and Andrew Barclay, "A Determinant of Preference Among Modes of Dissonance Reduction," *Journal of Personality and Social Psychology* 7 (1967), 211-16. Also see Elliot Aronson, "The Theory of Cognitive Dissonance," in Leonard Berkowitz, ed., *Advances in Experimental Social Psychology*, vol. 4 (New York: Academic Press, 1969), pp. 15-17 and the study reported in Charles Kiesler and Paul Munson, "Attitudes and Opinions," in Mark Rosenzweig and Lyman Porter, eds., *Annual Review of Psychology*, vol. 26 (Palo Alto: Annual Reviews, 1975), pp. 424-25. Since in most political cases the decision-maker has more unambiguous evidence about the consequences of the chosen alternative than he has about the hypothetical effects of the rejected policies, dissonance reduction is likely to be accomplished by denigrating the latter.

[4] For discussion and evidence, see Irving Janis and Leon Mann, "A Conflict-Theory Approach to Attitude Change and Decision Making," in Anthony Greenwald et al., eds., *Psychological Foundations of Attitudes* (New York: Academic Press, 1968), pp. 351-52; Jon Davidson and Sara Kiesler, "Cognitive Behavior Before and After Decisions," in Leon Festinger, ed., *Conflict, Decision, and Dissonance* [Stanford: Stanford University Press, 1964], pp. 10, 21; and the articles in section IV A in Robert Abelson et al., eds., *Theories of Cognitive Consistency* (Chicago: Rand McNally, 1968). Because of the difficulty of locating the precise moment of decision that is discussed below, we can usually ignore the subtle arguments and distinctions in this area.

[5] Festinger, ed., *Conflict, Decision, and Dissonance*, pp. 155-56. For a variant of this position that stresses the importance of commitment, see Charles Kiesler, *The Psychology of Commitment* (New York: Academic Press, 1971), and the articles in Abelson et al., eds., *Theories of Cognitive Consistency*, section III D.

sion was a free one, i.e. that he could have chosen otherwise. If he had no real choice, then the disadvantages of the policy will not create dissonance because his lack of freedom provides sufficient justification for his action.

Making such a decision will, according to dissonance theory, greatly alter the way a person thinks. Before reaching his decision the individual will seek conflicting information and make "some compromise judgment between the information and his existing cognitions or between bits of information inconsistent with each other and with his existing cognitions." But once the person has reached a decision, he is committed and "cannot process information and make some compromise judgment."[6] Quite the contrary, the person must minimize the extent to which the evidence pointed in opposite directions.

An ingenious demonstration, an anecdote, and an international example illustrate the meaning of this phenomenon and show that it occurs outside the laboratory. Immediately after they place their bets, race track bettors become more confident that their horse will win. A few hours after deciding to accept a job offer that he had agonizingly considered for several months, a professor said, "I don't understand how I could have seriously thought about not taking the job." And the doubts of British Liberals about whether to go to war in 1914 were almost totally dissolved after the decision was reached.[7]

We should note that contrary to first impressions, dissonance reduction does not always imply wishful thinking. First, reducing dissonance can involve changing evaluations of alternatives, thus altering desires themselves. Second, selecting and interpreting evidence so as to confirm that one's decision was wise may not conform to one's desires. For example, the decision to take costly precautions against the possibility that a negatively valued event will occur can generate dissonance reduction that will lead to unwishful thinking. Thus if I decide to build a bomb shelter, I may reduce dissonance by not listening to people who argue that the peace is secure. But I will still hope for peace.

Three conceptual problems[8] are apparent from the start. First, one

[6] Brehm and Cohen, *Explorations in Cognitive Dissonance*, p. 106.

[7] Robert Knox and James Inkster, "Postdecision Dissonance at Post Time," *Journal of Personality and Social Psychology* 8 (1968), 319-23; Cameron Hazlehurst, *Politicians at War* (London: Jonathan Cape, 1971), pp. 46-48, 92-117.

[8] In addition, criticism has been directed against the experimental evidence supporting dissonance theory. It has been argued, for example, that some of the results are caused by the subjects' guesses about what behavior is expected of them and that the experimental manipulations may not actually have aroused dissonance. For discussion of these issues see Milton Rosenberg, "When Dissonance Fails: On Eliminating Evaluation Apprehension from Attitude Measurement," *Journal of Personality and Social Psychology* 1 (1965), 28-42; Homer Johnson and Ivan Steiner, "Effort and Subjective Probability," *ibid.*, 365-68; Natalia

must be able to draw a line between pre- and post-decision situations. This is easy to do in most laboratory experiments. At a given time, subjects are made to choose a toy, an appliance, or a side of an argument. But in most political cases there is no such clear moment of decision. Even if one can determine when orders were given or papers signed, this may not coincide with the time of commitment. It is even harder to pinpoint the time when an actor decides what the other's intentions are. This does not mean, however, that no distinctions are possible. Even if we cannot tell exactly when the actor decided, we can contrast the early stages when he was obviously undecided with later ones when he is carrying out a course of action. Similarly, as images become firmly established and policies are based upon them, we can consider the actor to be committed to this image and can analyze his behavior in terms of dissonance theory.

Second, and more important, when we deal with complex questions and subtle reasoning it is not clear what beliefs and bits of information are consonant or dissonant with each other. Is the information that Russia seeks a disarmament agreement dissonant with the belief that Russia is hostile? Is the perception that relations between China and the United States have improved dissonant with the belief that the previous American "hard line" policy was appropriate? Dissonance research has usually avoided these questions by constructing experiments in which it seems obvious that certain elements are dissonant.[9] But the theoretical question of how one determines if an element follows from the obverse of the other has not been answered. Perhaps the best we can say is that a dissonant cognition is one that the person would have counted as a reason against following the course of action that he later chose, and the exact specification of what is dissonant will therefore vary with the person's beliefs.[10]

This problem is further complicated by the fact that evidence that the policy is incurring high costs or proving to be a failure is dissonant with the person's knowledge that he chose that policy only if he feels that he could have predicted this outcome on the basis of the information he

---

Chapanis and Alphonse Chapanis, "Cognitive Dissonance: Five Years Later," *Psychological Bulletin* 61 (1964), 1-22; and, for a general discussion of the problems of verifying one important set of dissonance propositions, Ramon Rhine, "Some Problems in Dissonance Theory Research on Information Selectivity," *ibid.*, 68 (1967), 21-28. For a rebuttal see Irwin Silverman, "In Defense of Dissonance Theory: Reply to Chapanis and Chapanis," *ibid.*, 62 (1964), 205-209.

[9] For discussion, see Festinger, *A Theory of Cognitive Dissonance*, pp. 2-3, 9-15, and Aronson, "The Theory of Cognitive Dissonance," pp. 5-8, 25-26.

[10] This formulation is consistent with the definition of dissonance in Douglas Lawrence and Leon Festinger, *Deterrents and Reinforcements* (Stanford: Stanford University Press, 1962), p. 34.

had, or should have had, when he made his decision. Dissonance reduction is employed to ward off the perception that the decision was unwise or inappropriate, not to inhibit the conclusion that in an unpredictable world the policy had undesired consequences. So the person can recognize, with hindsight, that the decision was wrong without believing that, given the evidence available when he chose, he made a bad decision.[11] This makes it important for us to know how much the decision-maker thinks he should be able to foresee future events. On the one hand, most statesmen see the world as highly contingent and uncertain. But they also have great confidence in their own abilities. Unfortunately, we do not know the relative strengths of these conflicting pressures and have little evidence about the degree to which and conditions under which decision-makers will consider evidence that their policy is failing to be dissonant with their knowledge that they initially favored the policy.

Although we cannot treat this topic at length here, we should note that the counterargument has been made, and supported by a good deal of evidence, that "When a person gets himself into a situation, and therefore feels responsible for its consequences, inconsistent information should, no matter how it comes about, arouse dissonance." Thus even if the person could not have foreseen an undesired consequence of his decision, its occurrence will be dissonant with the cognition that he made the decision and so was, in some sense, responsible for the consequence. At the heart of this debate are differing conceptions of the driving forces of dissonance. The view we have endorsed sees dissonance arising out of an inconsistency between what a person has done and his image of himself. The alternative view sees the sources of dissonance as inconsistencies between the person's values and the undesired effects of his behavior. The former position has better theoretical support, but the experimental evidence is mixed.[12]

Third, little is known about the magnitude of dissonance effects. Pressures that appear in carefully controlled laboratory situations may be

[11] J. Merrill Carlsmith and Jonathan Freedman, "Bad Decisions and Dissonance: Nobody's Perfect," in Abelson et al., eds., *Theories of Cognitive Consistency*, pp. 497-503. Also see the other articles in *ibid.*, section III E.

[12] The quote is from Brehm and Cohen, *Explorations in Cognitive Dissonance*, p. 202. In addition to the studies cited in footnote 41 below, see Michael Pallak, Suzanne Sogin, and Arvin Van Zante, "Bad Decisions," *Journal of Personality and Social Psychology* 30 (1974), 217-27; Joel Cooper, "Personal Responsibility and Dissonance," *ibid.*, 18 (1971), 354-63; Steven Sherman, "Attitudinal Effects of Unforeseen Consequences," *ibid.*, 16 (1970), 510-20; William Watts, "Commitment Under Conditions of Risk," *ibid.*, 3 (1966), 507-15; Joel Cooper and Jack Brehm, "Prechoice Awareness of Relative Deprivation as a Determinant of Cognitive Dissonance," *Journal of Experimental Social Psychology* 7 (1971), 571-81; Jack Brehm and Russell Jones, "The Effect on Dissonance of Surprise Consequences," *ibid.*, 6 (1970), 420-31. This debate is also linked to the one discussed on pp. 403-404 below.

slight compared to those produced by forces active in decision-making in the outside world. Such influences as institutional interests, political incentives, and feelings of duty may dwarf the impact of dissonance. Indeed even in the laboratory, this effect is far from overwhelming, producing changes ranging from 4 percent to 8 percent in the relative attractiveness of the alternatives.[13]

Cognitive Dissonance and Inertia

If this theory dealt only with the ways people increased their comfort with decisions already reached we would not be concerned with it since it could not explain how people decide. In reducing dissonance, however, people alter their beliefs and evaluations, thereby changing the premises of later deliberations, and so the theory has implications for the person's future decisions, actions, and perceptions. One of the most important is the added force that dissonance provides to the well-known power of inertia. Many reasons why tentative decisions become final ones and why policies are maintained in the face of discrepant information do not require the use of complex psychological theories to be understood. The domestic or bureaucratic costs of policy change are usually high. The realization of the costs of change makes subordinates hesitant to call attention to the failure of current practices or to the potential of alternatives. There are external costs as well since international policies often involve commitments that cannot be broken without damaging the state's reputation for living up to its word. Decision-makers may calculate that the value of this reputation outweighs the loss entailed by continuing an unwise policy.

Other psychological theories that stress consistency also predict that discrepant information will not be given its due and imply that policies will be maintained longer than political calculations can explain. Dissonance theory elaborates upon this point in two ways, neither of which, however, is easy to verify in the political realm. First, dissonance theory asserts that, after making a decision, the person not only will downgrade or misinterpret discrepant information but will also avoid it and seek consonant information. This phenomenon, known as "selective exposure," has been the subject of numerous experiments that have not resolved all the controversies.[14] But even the founder of dissonance

[13] Richard Harris, "Dissonance or Sour Grapes?" *Journal of Personality and Social Psychology* 11 (1969), 338.

[14] David Sears and Jonathan Freedman ("Selective Exposure to Information: A Critical Review," *Public Opinion Quarterly* 31 [Summer 1967], 194-213; Freedman and Sears, "Selective Exposure," in Leonard Berkowitz, ed., *Advances in Experimental Social Psychology*, vol. 2 [New York: Academic Press, 1965], pp. 57-97), have re-examined the evidence for the preference for supportive information and find it tenuous. More recent studies support this position. See William

theory now admits that this effect "is small and is easily overcome by other factors" including "the potential usefulness of dissonant material," curiosity, and the person's confidence that he can cope with discrepant information. Thus "avoidance would be observed only under circumstances where other reasons for exposure . . . were absent."[15] Such a weak effect is hard enough to detect in the laboratory; it is harder to find and less relevant in the arena of political decision-making.

A second hypothesis that may explain why policies are continued too long is more fruitful: the aim and effect of dissonance reduction is to produce post-decision spreading apart of the alternatives. There are important political analogues to experiments that show that if a person is asked to rate the attractiveness of two objects (e.g. toys or appliances), is allowed to choose one to keep, and then is asked to rate them again, his ratings will shift to increase the relative desirability of the chosen object. After they have made a choice, decision-makers too often feel certain that they decided correctly even though during the pre-decision period that policy did not seem obviously and overwhelmingly the best. The extent and speed of this shift and the fact that contemporary participants and later scholars rarely attribute it entirely to political considerations imply that dissonance reduction is taking place.

Before we discuss the evidence from and implications for political decision-making, two objections should be noted. First, modifications of dissonance theory consider the possibility of the opposite of the spreading of the alternatives—"post-decision regret." But the slight theory and data on this subject do not show that the phenomenon is of major importance. Second, some scholars have argued that, especially when the decision-maker does not expect to receive further information and the choice is a hard one, the spreading apart of the alternatives precedes and facilitates the decision. But the bulk of the evidence supports the dissonance position.[16]

McGuire, "Selective Exposure: A Summing Up," in Abelson et al., eds., *Theories of Cognitive Consistency*, the other essays in section IV E of that volume, and Irving Janis and Curt Rausch, "Selective Interest in Communications that Could Arouse Decisional Conflict," *Journal of Personality and Social Psychology* 14 (1970), 46-54. For modifications of the arguments on selective exposure, see Timothy Brock and Joe Balloun, "Behavioral Receptivity to Dissonant Information," *ibid.* 6 (1967), 413-28; Michael Ray, "Biases in Selection of Messages Designed to Induce Resistance to Persuasion," *ibid.* 9 (1968), 335-39; and Timothy Brock, Stuart Albert, and Lee Becker, "Familiarity, Utility, and Supportiveness as Determinants of Information Receptivity," *ibid.* 14 (1970), 292-301.

[15] Festinger, ed., *Conflict, Decision, and Dissonance*, pp. 155, 96.

[16] For discussions of the first objection, see Leon Festinger and Elaine Walster, "Post-Decision Regret and Decisional Reversal," in Festinger, ed., *Conflict, Decision, and Dissonance*; Walster, "The Temporal Sequence of Post-Decision Process," *ibid.*; Jack Brehm and Robert Wicklund, "Regret and Dissonance Reduction as a Function of Postdecision Salience of Dissonant Information," *Journal of Per-*

We should also remember that this whole argument is irrelevant if a decision changes the state's environment and destroys the availability of alternative policies. Some decisions to go to war do this. For example, once Japan bombed Pearl Harbor, she could make little use of new information that the United States was not willing to suffer a limited defeat but would prefer to fight the war through to complete victory. Even had dissonance not made it more difficult for the Japanese to think about ways of ending the war, it is not certain that viable alternatives existed.

Many decision-makers speak of their doubts vanishing after they embarked on a course of action, or they say that a situation seemed much clearer after they reached a decision. Evidence that would have been carefully examined before the decision is rejected at later stages. These effects are illustrated by President Madison's behavior in 1811 after he accepted an ambiguous French offer to lift her decrees hindering American trade in return for Madison's agreement to allow trade with France while maintaining the ban on trade with England. When he took this step, "Madison well understood the equivocal nature" of the French offer and realized that Napoleon might be deceiving him. But even as evidence mounted that this was in fact the case, Madison firmly stood by his earlier decision and did not recognize even privately that the French were not living up to their bargain. The British, who had the same information about the French actions as the Americans had, soon realized that Napoleon was engaging in deception.[17]

Similarly, only slowly and painfully did Woodrow Wilson decide to ask for a declaration of war against Germany. His awareness of the costs of entering the war was acute. But after the decision was made, he became certain that his policy was the only wise and proper one. He

sonality and Social Psychology 14 (1970), 1-7; Wicklund, "Prechoice Preference Reversal as a Result of Threat to Decision Freedom," ibid., pp. 8-17. On the second point, see Chapanis and Chapanis, "Cognitive Dissonance: Five Years Later"; Janis and Mann, "A Conflict-Theory Approach to Attitude Change and Decision Making"; Mann, Janis, and Chaplin, "Effects of Anticipation of Forthcoming Information on Predecisional Processes," Journal of Personality and Social Psychology 11 (1969), 10-16; and Brehm and Cohen, Explorations in Cognitive Dissonance, pp. 236-44. For a related argument, see Jack Brehm, Responses to Loss of Freedom: A Theory of Psychological Reactance (Morristown, N.J.: General Learning Press, 1972).

[17] Bradford Perkins, Prologue to War (Berkeley and Los Angeles: University of California Press, 1961), pp. 250-59. These differing perceptions contributed to the outbreak of the War of 1812. Assuming that Napoleon's deception would be as obvious to the Americans as it was to them, the British believed that the United States would "either reverse their policy or insist upon effective French repeal." (Ibid., p. 275.) Whichever alternative America pursued, there would be little conflict between the United States and Britain, and so Britain saw no need to speed her plans to withdraw the Orders in Council that the Americans opposed. The Americans, because they did not understand the British perceptions, interpreted this British decision as unprovoked hostility.

had no second thoughts. In the same way, his attempt to reduce the dissonance that had been aroused by the knowledge that he had had to make painful compromises during the negotiations on the peace treaty can explain Wilson's negative reaction to the last-minute British effort to alter the treaty and bring it more in line with Wilsonian principles: "The time to consider all these questions was when we were writing the treaty, and it makes me a little tired for people to come and say now that they are afraid that the Germans won't sign, and their fear is based upon things that they insisted upon at the time of the writing of the treaty; that makes me very sick." There were political reasons for not reopening negotiations, but the vehemence with which Wilson rejected a position that was in harmony with his ideals suggests the presence of unacknowledged psychological motivation. Wilson's self-defeating refusal to perceive the strength of the Senate opposition to the League may be similarly explained by the fact that the belief that alterations in the Covenant were necessary would have been dissonant with the knowledge that he had given away a great deal to get the Europeans to accept the League. Once the bargains had been completed, dissonance reduction made them seem more desirable.[18]

More recently, the American decision not to intervene in Vietnam in 1954 was followed by a spreading apart of the alternatives. When they were considering the use of force to prevent a communist victory, Dulles and, to a lesser extent, Eisenhower believed that a failure to act would expose the neighboring countries to grave peril. When the lack of Allied and domestic support made intervention prohibitively expensive, American decision-makers altered their perceptions of the consequences of not intervening. Although they still thought that the immediate result would be the fall of some of Indochina, they came to believe that the further spread of communism—fear of which motivated them to consider entering the war—would not necessarily follow. They altered their views to reject the domino theory, at least in its most deterministic formulation, and held that alternative means could save the rest of Southeast Asia. It was argued—and apparently believed—that collective action, which had initially been sought in order to hold Vietnam, could stabilize the region even though part of Vietnam was lost.[19] By judging that military victory was not necessary, the decision-makers could see the chosen policy of not intervening as greatly preferable to the rejected alternative of uni-

[18] Quoted in Richard Watt, *The Kings Depart* (New York: Simon and Schuster, 1968), p. 450. For another psychological explanation that is linked to other episodes in Wilson's life, see Alexander George and Juliette George, *Woodrow Wilson and Colonel House* (New York: Dover, 1964).

[19] Melvin Gurtov, *The First Vietnam Crisis* (New York: Columbia University Press, 1967), pp. 119-22.

lateral action, thereby reducing the dissonance aroused by the choice of a policy previously believed to entail extremely high costs.[20]

This spreading apart of the alternatives increases inertia. By altering their views to make it seem as though their decision was obviously correct, decision-makers increase the amount of discrepant information necessary to reverse the policy. Furthermore, continuing efforts to reduce dissonance will lead decision-makers to fail to seek or appreciate information that would call their policy into question if they believe that they should have foreseen the negative consequences of their decision.

The reduction of dissonance does more than help maintain policies once they are set in motion. By altering instrumental judgments and evaluations of outcomes, it indirectly affects other decisions.[21] Most of us have at times found that we were determining our values and standards by reference to our past behavior. For example, no one can do a complete cost-benefit study of all his expenditures. So we tend to decide how much we can spend for an object by how much we have spent for other things. "If the book I bought last week was worth $10.00 to me, then this record I'm now considering buying is certainly worth $1.98."

Acting on a value or a principle in one case can increase its potency and influence over future cases. The value is not depleted in being used, but rather replenished and reinforced because of the effects of dissonance reduction aimed at easing the person's doubts about acting on that value. Thus if a person refuses a tempting bribe he is more likely to display integrity in the future because dissonance reduction will lead him to place greater value on this quality, to place less value on the money he might receive, and/or to come to believe that he is likely to get caught if he commits an illegal act. Similarly, if a professor turns down a tempting offer from another university, his resistance to future offers will increase if he reduces dissonance by evaluating his own institution more favorably or by raising his estimate of the costs of leaving. Statesmen's post-decision re-evaluations of their goals and beliefs can have more far-

[20] It can be argued that only after it became clear that multilateral military action was impossible was attention focused on alternative means of preventing other countries from following Indochina into communism and that the study of these previously unexplored policies convinced the decision-makers that their previous beliefs about falling dominos were incorrect. For a further discussion of this point, see Chapter 10, p. 367. But the amount of new information received by the decision-makers in this period does not seem great enough to explain the magnitude of change of their beliefs.

[21] For experimental evidence, see David Marlowe, Robert Frager, and Ronald Nuttall, "Commitment to Action Taking as a Consequence of Cognitive Dissonance," *Journal of Personality and Social Psychology* 2 (1965), 864-68, and Donald Penner, Gordon Fitch, and Karl Weick, "Dissonance and the Revision of Choice Criteria," *ibid.* 3 (1966), 701-705. I am indebted to Paul Diesing for discussion on this point.

reaching consequences. If in reducing the dissonance created by the decision to intervene to prevent revolution in one country, the statesman inflates his estimate of the bad consequences of internal unrest, he will be more likely to try to quell disturbances in other contexts. Or if he reduces dissonance by increasing his faith in the instrument he chose to use, he will be more likely to employ that instrument in later cases. Similarly, downgrading a rejected goal means that it will not be pursued even if altered circumstances permit its attainment. This may be one reason why once an actor has decided that a value will be sacrificed if this becomes necessary—i.e. once he has developed a fall-back position—he usually fights less hard to maintain his stand. But because these effects, although important, are hard to verify and because other theories predict that policy-making will be characterized by high inertia, we must turn to other hypotheses, some of which run counter to common sense, in order to further demonstrate the utility of cognitive dissonance theory.

The Magnitude of Dissonance

Dissonance is not an all-or-none phenomenon, but occurs to a greater or lesser extent. The degree of dissonance, and therefore the strength of the efforts to reduce dissonance, is hypothesized to be proportional to: "1) the attractiveness of the rejected alternative; 2) . . . the qualitative dissimilarity of the choice alternatives; and 3) . . . the importance of the choice." This means that "the greater the conflict before the decision, the greater the dissonance afterwards. Hence the more difficulty the person had in making the decision, the greater would be his tendency to justify that decision (reducing the dissonance) afterward." A report by James Reston can be seen in this light. In discussing the decision to initiate bombing of North Vietnam he says: "We had a big argument in the government and the press [about whether to bomb the North] . . . and in the process the decision . . . became such an important thing in Washington that at least some officials thought it would bring the Communists to the conference table."[22]

But it is especially disadvantageous to the state, if not to the individual decision-maker whose psychological needs are being met, to have hard decisions considered as closed. If the policy chosen was only slightly better than the alternative the chances are relatively good that new information will show that modifications are called for. If the policy concerns vital interests it is especially important that decision-makers be open to new information since the costs of carrying out inadequate policies in these areas are so high. On the other hand, because these choices are so close or so important, efforts to reduce dissonance will be especially

[22] Brehm and Cohen, *Explorations in Cognitive Dissonance*, p. 308; Festinger, ed., *Conflict, Decision, and Dissonance*, p. 5; *San Francisco Chronicle*, June 20, 1965.

great. Thus the same factors that make new evidence of most value to the decision-maker also generate greatest psychological pressures against openness.

This does not mean, however, that a hard decision is less likely to be re-opened than an easy one. The amount of dissonance reduction is only one of several factors that determine the total amount of information that is seen as discrepant, and this in turn is only one of the factors that determines whether a decision will be re-examined. Although the spreading apart of the alternatives will be greater after a hard decision than an easy one, the alternatives will be further apart to start with in the latter case. Unless the spreading is extreme, even after the decision is made the alternatives will seem closer in the hard case than in the easy one. So if the decision was hard, less information *perceived* as discrepant will usually be needed to bring it into question. Even if strong dissonance screens out much of this information, the chances of enough penetrating to change the decision-maker's mind may be sufficiently great that hard decisions are more likely to be reversed than are easy ones.

Support for this argument is provided by the finding that although voters who make up their minds late in the campaign perceive their choice as more difficult than do early-deciders and therefore should experience greater dissonance, after the vote the late-deciders show less rather than more disparity in their rating of the candidates than do the early-deciders. While the latter had less dissonance to reduce and thus less reason to increase the disparity in their ratings after the vote, their ratings were widely separated for the same reason that they made up their minds early—they saw one candidate as clearly superior.[23]

THE IMPACT OF SPENDING RESOURCES

A major deduction from dissonance theory is that expending resources increases dissonance and thus increases the pressures to believe that the policy is succeeding. The argument here is the reverse of the obvious one that people will pay a high price for things they value highly: sacrifices increase the value placed on the goals that are sought and achieved.[24] If a person is to see his own decisions as wise and his behavior as consistent, he will have to believe that his gains are proportionate to the resources expended. We must, however, note a problem derived from our earlier discussion of the fact that the person may believe that although his decision did not lead to a desired outcome, it was appropriate given the information available at the time. For the same reasons, dissonance

[23] Leon Mann and Ronald Abeles, "Evaluation of Presidential Candidates as a Function of Time and Stage of Voting Decision," *Journal of Psychology* 74 (1970), 167-73.

[24] For related explanation of this and other dissonance effects, see Daryl Bem, "Self-Perception Theory," in Leonard Berkowitz, ed., *Advances in Experimental Social Psychology*, vol. 6 (New York: Academic Press, 1972), pp. 1-62.

theory does not deny that the person can believe that although his strenuous efforts produced only meager results, the chance of a large success explains and justifies his actions. Even though this escape from dissonance is possible, the main effect seems to be the dominant one. This conclusion is supported by the results of experiments in which subjects undergo a test or initiation rite to join a group or to hear a tape-recorded discussion. The preliminary was made simple and painless for half the subjects and quite embarrassing for the other half. All were later questioned on their attitudes toward the group or discussion, and those who had undergone the embarrassing experience as the price for gaining admission were more favorable than those who had reached this goal easily. So it is not surprising that a prospective scientist-astronaut who originally had doubts about the program reported that the long and painful medical examination "had a strong effect on me; I had invested a great amount of energy into this competition and I was damned if I wouldn't give it a strong try."[25]

There are a number of implications of this aspect of dissonance theory for foreign policy decision-making. When a policy has high costs, decision-makers are likely to believe they have accomplished something worthy of their sacrifice. Two related manifestations of this effect are the propensities to overvalue what has been achieved and to perceive failures as successes. Both evaluations of outcomes and estimates of the factual situation may be altered. Of course on this point, as on several of others, firm evidence is difficult to come by because we cannot easily measure changes in the person's valuations and estimates of the outcome of a policy over time. We could try simply to correlate the resources a person spent on a policy with the value he places on it, but the obvious problem is that the relationship is likely to be spurious—i.e. both factors could be explained by the opinions the person held before he embarked on the course of action. Thus the best evidence would be supplied by comparisons between people who initially held the same views but who had expended different amounts of resources to see their position adopted and carried out. We expect that the person who had made greater sacrifices would later evaluate the decision more favorably than would the less involved person.

Although we have no evidence as good as this, we can look at cases where the costs of a policy are borne unequally in ways that cannot be

[25] Elliot Aronson and Judson Mills, "The Effect of Severity of Initiation on Liking for a Group," *Journal of Abnormal and Social Psychology* 59 (1959), 177-81; Harold Gerard and Grover Mathewson, "The Effects of Severity of Initiation on Liking for a Group: A Replication," *Journal of Experimental Social Psychology* 2 (1966), 278-87; Brehm and Cohen, *Explorations in Cognitive Dissonance*, p. 29. The latter two citations present rebuttals to criticisms of the initial experiment. Brian O'Leary, *The Making of an Ex-Astronaut* (Boston: Houghton Mifflin, 1970), p. 42.

explained by self-selection. In such cases dissonance theory provides another reason why the people most involved with a policy will be the most deeply committed to its continuance. For example, in explaining the anger with which Ambassador Nolting received the news that his deputy had come to believe that the Viet Cong could not be beaten while Diem remained in power, Roger Hilsman points out that "Nolting had staked his whole career and future on getting along with Diem and building up credit with him that could be drawn upon during difficult periods. His tour of Vietnam cost him and his family much personal sacrifice, financially and in terms of the well-being of his children, two of whom he had had to leave back in the United States at a crucial time in their lives." Those who had given up less in order to support and work with Diem found it easier to change their minds. This analysis also helps explain why negotiators tend to value agreements they make more highly than do the less involved members of the home governments.[26]

We can also look at several types of situations in which actors have made a great effort and determine whether, as the theory predicts, these actors perceive that they have reached a highly valued goal. In some of these cases, decision-makers express their reaction in terms highly compatible with dissonance reduction. The American ambassador to Britain said to Woodrow Wilson in the fall of 1914: if this war does not prove to be the last one, then "life's not worth living and civilization is a delusion." Similarly, when Neville Chamberlain learned that his cousin had been killed in the First World War he wrote a friend that "Nothing but immeasurable improvements will ever justify all the waste and unfairness of this war—I only hope that those who are left will *never, never* forget at what sacrifice those improvements have been won." Note also the great feeling and strange logic in Woodrow Wilson's words when, in speaking at an American cemetery on the first anniversary of the end of the war, he explained his allegiance to the Treaty of Versailles:

> If I may speak a personal word, I beg you to realize the compulsion that I myself feel that I am under. By the Constitution of our great country I was the commander-in-chief of these men. I advised the Congress to declare that a state of war existed. I sent these lads over here to die. Shall I—can I—ever speak a word of counsel which is inconsistent with the assurances I gave them when they came over? It is inconceivable.[27]

[26] Roger Hilsman, *To Move a Nation* (Garden City, N.Y.: Doubleday, 1967), p. 479; Fred Iklé, *How Nations Negotiate* (New York: Harper and Row, 1964), p. 171.

[27] Quoted in Arno Mayer, *Wilson vs. Lenin: Political Origins of the New Diplomacy, 1917-1918* (Cleveland and New York: World, 1964), p. 30; Chamberlain is quoted in Martin Gilbert, *Roots of Appeasement* (New York: New American Library), p. 21; Wilson is quoted in Seth Tillman, *Anglo-American Relations at*

The costs of war can lead to an increased valuation of winning and/or an overestimation of the probability of success. What was accomplished will be highly valued, and valued objectives will be seen as attained. If a war ends in a negotiated settlement, both sides will value their gains more highly than they would have had the war been less costly. Perhaps one reason why some people saw U.S. policy in Vietnam as successful (either in terms of the progress of the war in the South, lessons taught to would-be aggressors, or the buying of time for the rest of Asia) was an acute awareness of the domestic and foreign costs of the war. If a state that thought it would win finds itself losing, it will justify its original decision by making more negative its evaluation of what would have happened if it had chosen to make concessions rather than fight. This in turn may lead it to revise upwards its estimate of the costs of a settlement negotiated from a position of weakness, thereby increasing the state's willingness to continue fighting as long as it believes there is even a slight chance that it can eventually win the war. And the winners of costly wars will develop inflated estimates of the fruits of their victory even if they do not inflate their demands. They will perceive the same specific outcomes as being associated with more desirable consequences. This is one reason why modern wars, which tend to be very costly, are apt to be seen by their participants as bringing about a much better, safer world. This perception did not occur in the eras of limited wars. And Wilson came to this view only after April 1917.[28]

Dissonance reduction will also increase the value placed on specific objectives and possessions gained by war. Thus shortly after World War I the Turks, who were fighting the Greeks near the Dardanelles, broke through and advanced toward the Straits and the town of Chanak, which was under British control. Speaking for his government, Churchill told the Dominions that Britain had to defend "the Freedom of the Straits for which such immense sacrifices were made in the war." Because the Brit-

---

the Paris Peace Conference of 1919 (Princeton: Princeton University Press, 1961), p. 355. Of course this does not tell us the content of the policy the person will support, but only that he will hold with special fervor to whatever policy preference he does adopt.

[28] Wilson's view was extreme, but the general vision was not uniquely his or uniquely American. "By 1918 many of the junior staff of the Foreign Office hoped that the peace conference . . . would solve all international problems and not those raised by the war only"; V. H. Rothwell, *British War Aims and Peace Diplomacy, 1914-1918* (Oxford: Clarendon Press, 1971), p. 209. A general point made earlier needs to be applied here: a state will enter a war that it expects to be costly only if the perceived gains of doing so (and/or the perceived costs of refraining from fighting) are extremely high. Furthermore, if the war is costly because it is fought to a decisive finish, the victorious state can impose its will on the loser and so is likely to expect far-reaching gains. But these considerations cannot entirely account for the expectations that are not only high, but that grow as money and lives are spent.

ish had fought so hard for this goal, it was hard for them to take a fresh look at its importance in the postwar world, which in fact was slight. Instead it was assumed, in the words of Lloyd George, that Gallipoli was still "the most important strategic position in the world."[29]

Peacetime policies involving heavy expenditure of resources also constitute pressures on the decision-maker to believe that he has reached his goal. This helps explain why many Germans thought that England would remain neutral in July 1914. Their knowledge that they had spent so much money and diplomatic good will to build a fleet to deter Britain from entering a continental war was dissonant with the belief that England would nevertheless do so. Thus Gottlieb von Jagow, the German foreign secretary, argued that England would not fight; after all, he said, "we have not built our navy for nothing."[30]

In other cases the effort expended on means transforms them into ends. For example, George Kennan argues that, in the face of the Berlin blockade,

> The three Allied powers were busy working out a new occupation statute, to come into effect when the West German government was established. These procedures were elaborate; the attendant negotiations were difficult and full of anguish. As the process went forward, it gained steadily in momentum and in the aura of legitimacy. People's *amour propre* as well as their enthusiasms became engaged. There was growing personal commitment to what was being accomplished. Increasingly . . . the idea of suspending or jeopardizing it for the sake of wider international agreement became . . . less and less acceptable.[31]

The increase in the value placed on achieving the goal that results from the expenditure of resources acts as positive feedback. As Albert Hirschman points out, a "situation of dissonance may produce not only alterations of beliefs, attitudes, and cognitions, but could lead to *actions* designed to change the real world when that is an alternative way (and particularly when it is the only way) of overcoming or reducing dissonance." Thus making a decision provides additional impetus for carrying it through to success. Spending resources on a policy generates pressures to put in additional effort to make the policy work and thereby

[29] Churchill is quoted in Gilbert, *Roots of Appeasement*, p. 90; Lloyd George is quoted in David Walder, *The Chanak Affair* (New York: Macmillan Co., 1969), p. 179 (also see p. 189). For another example, see Lynn Davis, *The Cold War Begins* (Princeton: Princeton University Press, 1974), p. 284.

[30] Quoted in Ludwig Reiners, *The Lamps Went Out in Europe* (Cleveland: Meridian, 1966), p. 129. For the argument that the German government did not count on British neutrality, see Wolfgang Mommsen, "Domestic Factors in German Foreign Policy Before 1914," *Central European History* 6 (March 1973), 38-41.

[31] *Memoirs*, vol. 1: *1925-1950* (Boston: Little, Brown, 1967), pp. 427-28.

justify the earlier behavior. Furthermore, the increased valuation of the goal will provide the actor with even greater incentives to redouble his efforts. This leads us to expect that sunk costs, ignored by a rational man, will influence behavior. Thus it is not surprising that by 1918 there had developed "a conviction [in England] that the war and all the sacrifices so far made would be futile unless it was continued to a point where Germany realized that for her it had been a failure." Similarly, a student of the Prussian conspiracy to rebel against Napoleon argues that one reason why the plans continued even after the "original goals had been achieved by other means . . . . was that, once significant energies were invested in the scheme, the leaders felt the need to justify that investment by success—and the more so, the more they put into just keeping their scheme alive." More recently, in explaining his opposition to an American proposal shortly before Pearl Harbor, Prime Minister Tojo said that the demand that Japan withdraw its troops from China was unacceptable: "We sent a large force of one million men [to China], and it has cost us well over 100,000 dead and wounded, [the grief of] their bereaved families, hardship for four years, and a national expenditure of several tens of billions of yen. We must by all means get satisfactory results from this."[32]

Positive feedback can occur in a more extreme fashion when the person not only increases his valuation of the goal and puts in more effort but actually expands his objectives. This is likely to occur when the price he has paid is so high that it could not justify his original goal even if the person exaggerates the value of this outcome. This, of course, is thought to be a common response to unexpected wartime costs although recent studies of war aims in World War I have not found the predicted progression.[33]

When will the person reduce dissonance by trying harder and when will he do so by perceiving success and perhaps cease his efforts? Although dissonance theory says little about this kind of question, it seems likely that if one method is blocked, the other will operate.[34] Thus if the

[32] *Exit, Voice, and Loyalty* (Cambridge, Mass.: Harvard University Press, 1970), p. 94; Rothwell, *British War Aims and Peace Diplomacy*, p. 206; R. C. Raack, "When Plans Fail: Small Group Behavior and Decision-Making in the Conspiracy of 1808 in Germany," *Journal of Conflict Resolution* 14 (March 1970), 15; Tojo is quoted in Nobutaka Ike, *Japan's Decision for War* (Stanford: Stanford University Press, 1967), pp. 229-30. For experimental evidence consistent with this proposition, see Elliot Aronson and David Mettee, "Dishonest Behavior as a Function of Differential Levels of Induced Self-Esteem," *Journal of Personality and Social Psychology* 9 (1968), 212-27.

[33] See Fritz Fischer, *Germany's Aims in the First World War* (New York: Norton, 1967); Rothwell, *British War Aims and Peace Diplomacy*; and Z.A.B. Zeman, *The Gentlemen Negotiators* (New York: Macmillan Co., 1971).

[34] For experimental support for this position, see Jane Hardyck, "Predicting Response to a Negative Evaluation," *Journal of Personality and Social Psychology* 9 (1968), 128-32.

person can do no more, he is apt to inflate his judgment of his accomplishments. If failure is unambiguous but the situation is not hopeless, he is more likely to increase his efforts (see the discussion of the boomerang effect at the end of this chapter). In circumstances falling between these extremes, both methods may be employed so that they complement each other. The person may think that his chances for reaching a valued outcome are great if, and only if, further efforts are made. There may be little to show for the resources expended, but perseverance is necessary; success is just around the corner.

INCENTIVES AND COMPULSION

Perhaps the most startling implication of dissonance theory is the "psychology of insufficient reward," which asserts that the relationship between the incentives given for behavior that the person would not otherwise engage in and the amount of dissonance reduction that follows the behavior is inverse. Although this conclusion follows from the basic dissonance postulate that people seek more than adequate justification for their behavior, it runs counter to common sense. Common sense indicates that if a person is persuaded to behave contrary to his beliefs (e.g. make a speech advocating a position he disagrees with) the greater the incentives that were offered, the greater the attitude change following the counterattitudinal behavior. Dissonance theory makes the opposite prediction: the *fewer* the cognitions that support the discrepant behavior or the exposure to dissonant information, the *greater* the attitude change. The reason is that large incentives are sufficient to allow the person to justify his action to himself. He can think, for example: "I gave the speech because I was paid $10. This is ample payment for a little hypocrisy." If he complies for only $.50, on the other hand, this explanation is not convincing, and dissonance will have to be reduced in the only other way possible—by bringing attitudes more in line with behavior. A wide range of incentives has been investigated—money, the attractiveness of the experimenter, the cohesiveness of the group, the nutritional value of evil-tasting foods to be eaten. The effects are the same—under many conditions the fewer the incentives, the greater the attitude change.[35]

[35] The debate on this subject is too extensive to permit the citation of individual experiments. For good summaries and analyses, see Milton Rosenberg, "Some Limits of Dissonance: Toward a Differentiated View of Counterattitudinal Performance," in Shel A. Feldman, ed., *Cognitive Consistency* (New York: Academic Press, 1966); William McGuire, "The Nature of Attitudes and Attitude Change," in Gardner Lindzey and Elliot Aronson, eds., *The Handbook of Social Psychology*, vol. 3 (2nd ed., Reading, Mass.: Addison-Wesley, 1969), pp. 237-40; the articles in section IV F in Abelson et al., eds., *Theories of Cognitive Consistency*, and especially the summary, Milton Rosenberg, "Discussion: On Reducing the Inconsistency between Consistency Theories," *ibid.*, pp. 827-33, and Milton Rosenberg, "Hedonism, Inauthenticity, and Other Goads toward Expansion of a Consistency

As in other aspects of dissonance theory, it is crucial that the person choose to comply. This raises a problem and an opportunity. The problem is that those who comply are a self-selected sample. Those who comply for low rewards or low punishments are especially unusual. They may, for example, be highly susceptible to influence attempts. The opportunity is that we can compare the attitude change of subjects who volunteered to listen to a persuasive communication with that of subjects who were "accidentally" exposed to the same message. Dissonance theory predicts that in the former group there would be more change when the speaker had unattractive personal characteristics (low incentives) than when the speaker was attractive (high incentives). But if the exposure was "accidental"—i.e. the subjects had not made a decision to listen—the attractive speaker should produce more change. These predictions were borne out.[36]

Negative sanctions as well as positive incentives can make it unnecessary for the person to reduce dissonance following a decision or counterattitudinal behavior. A person who is told he will be shot if he does not do something he would otherwise not do will not experience dissonance, since he will not need extra reasons to justify his behavior. Again this is not an either/or matter. The less the decision is felt to be voluntary— i.e. the greater the negative sanctions—the less the dissonance. Paradoxically, then, the politician who voluntarily leaves office or the professor who chooses to leave his university will feel more pressure to reduce dissonance, and will therefore engage in more dissonance-based derogation of their previous positions, than the politician who was defeated for re-election or the professor who was fired.[37]

The political implications are clear—if a decision-maker feels he had no choice but to make a given decision, he will be less prone to avoid or distort information than he would if he had acted freely. If, for example,

---

Theory," *ibid.*, pp. 109-11; Harold Gerard, Edward Conolley, and Roland Wilhelmy, "Compliance, Justification, and Cognitive Change," in Leonard Berkowitz, ed., *Advances in Experimental Social Psychology*, vol. 7 (New York: Academic Press, 1974), pp. 217-47. Also see the citations in footnotes 41 and 42 below.

[36] Russell Jones and Jack Brehm, "Attitudinal Effects of Communicator Attractiveness When One Chooses to Listen," *Journal of Personality and Social Psychology* 6 (1967), 64-70. Similarly, greater incentives should yield greater attitude change when the subject has no choice but to adopt counterattitudinal behavior. See Steven Sherman, "Effects of Choice and Incentive on Attitude Change in a Discrepant Behavior Situation," *Journal of Personality and Social Psychology* 15 (1970), 245-52.

[37] Other theories such as those based on the propensity for people to reciprocate sentiments (e.g. to like those who like them) and those based on the need to protect one's ego predict greater derogation when the person's departure from the institution is involuntary. Dissonance theory does not deny the validity of these theories, and since none of them specifies the magnitude of the effects to be expected, we cannot say which effect will be stronger.

President Johnson believed that domestic politics required him to build an ABM system, he would have been under little psychological pressure to believe in the system and would not have felt a need to reject information indicating that it would not work, would cost too much, or would have bad international consequences. Similarly, if a legislator is to take a bribe to vote against his conscience, it will distort his opinions less, as well as enrich him more, if he receives a large rather than a small payment.

Applying this analysis to subordinates' attitudes and behavior, we see that the greater the positive and negative incentives for implementing or endorsing a policy (e.g. material rewards, praise, loyalty, and the belief that public servants should preserve a facade of unity), the less the pressure on the officials' private attitudes and therefore the greater the diversity of views and perceptual sensitivities that will be maintained within the organization. By contrast, the belief that one has had an opportunity to influence a decision increases feeling of choice and so increases dissonance. Thus we expect that an unintended consequence of the fact that the governmental deliberations during the Cuban missile crisis were unusually open was to make the participants strongly committed to the decisions and resistant to new information. Similarly, Eisenhower's alteration of the ground rules for decisions of the Joint Chiefs of Staff increased cognitive dissonance. Under Truman, the Chiefs were given budget ceilings. Eisenhower, on the other hand, told them to take economic factors into account in their budget requests.[38] Since under Truman the Chiefs were compelled to accept the ceiling as a given, they would not have felt psychological pressure to alter their private views on the proper size of the military budget. More attitude change could be expected from Eisenhower Chiefs because they had greater responsibility for setting the limits on military spending.

Three considerations complicate the impact of feelings of compulsion on later perceptions, however. First, we noted above that while easy decisions involve less dissonance than hard ones, the same forces that made the former easy are apt to sustain them. A similar argument applies here. If the strong incentives continue the person will maintain his counter-attitudinal behavior even though his private opinions will not be changed. Only if the compulsion ends will the person be able to take advantage of the fact that the low dissonance has allowed him to preserve his views.

Second, the sense of compulsion is not objective. In the same situation one person will feel he has great freedom of choice whereas another will

[38] Glenn Snyder, "The 'New Look' of 1953," in Warner Schilling, Paul Hammond, and Glenn Snyder, *Strategy, Politics and Defense Budgets* (New York: Columbia University Press, 1962), p. 504.

feel he has little. In addition to idiosyncratic factors, two systematic biases will often be at work. On the one hand, perceptions of compulsion from domestic politics or orders from superiors may be inhibited because they themselves are dissonant with other values. So a person who is merely following orders or who hopes his actions will bring him bureaucratic advancement or political advantage may go to special lengths to convince himself that he is acting freely and believes in the policy he has adopted. By contrast, members of organizations like the military that stress the necessity and legitimacy of following orders will accept compulsion and so will not change their private opinions to conform to their behavior. On the other hand, the feeling of compulsion, eliminating as it does the source of dissonance, can itself be a form of dissonance avoidance or reduction. Experimental evidence indicates that when a person's decision leads to undesired consequences that he could have avoided, he will feel that he had little choice in the matter. Thus decision-makers may believe that they had no freedom of action in order to relieve themselves of a psychological burden. This may explain why it is that "In tense . . . situations [involving decisions to begin or end wars], the decision-maker is likely to feel that he is acting from necessity rather than from deliberate choice." Ole Holsti argues that the decision-makers' perceptions that they had no choice but to go to war in 1914 may have been rooted in the desire to avoid the dissonance aroused by the knowledge that the war would entail enormous costs.[39] Of course it is hard to determine when the desire to avoid dissonance rather than a straight-forward analysis of the alternatives is responsible for the actor's belief that he has no real choice, but the latter explanation is less plausible if those who are less involved, even if they favor the policy that was selected, see a wider range of options or if continued thought by the decision-maker usually decreases rather than increases the number of alternatives seen as viable.

Third, the dissonance created by counterattitudinal behavior is only one of many variables that influence attitude change. The degree to which the original view is anchored in the person's belief system and sustained by social pressures is probably more important. We would therefore expect that members of the bureaucracy who have strong ties to each other and to their organization usually will be able to withstand the pressures of dissonance aroused by counterattitudinal behavior.[40] By

[39] Festinger, *A Theory of Cognitive Dissonance*, pp. 43-44; Ben Harris and John Harvey, "Self-Attributed Choice as a Function of the Consequences of a Decision," *Journal of Personality and Social Psychology* 31 (1975), 1013-19; Paul Kecskemeti, *Strategic Surrender* (New York: Atheneum, 1964), pp. 19-20; Ole Holsti, *Crisis, Escalation, War* (Montreal and London: McGill-Queen's University Press, 1972), pp. 17-18.

[40] Indeed in most democracies the problem raised here is usually far less than the problem of seeing that subordinates actually carry out the policies favored by

contrast, even though presidential aides will experience less dissonance because their loyalty to their chief and lack of job security will generate greater compulsion in carrying out the president's wishes, the lack of organizational and social support for their views makes them more apt to reduce what dissonance they do feel by bringing their opinions into line with their behavior. We can therefore conclude that while there is little chance that dissonance will lead to homogeneity of views throughout the government as a whole, this danger will be greater in the decision-maker's personal staff.

Further research has led to the argument that counterattitudinal behavior with insufficient justification will produce attitude change only if the person believes that his actions had significant consequences for which he feels responsible.[41] If what he did had no impact, the person will have no reason to seek justification. Attitude change will not occur, for example, if the counterattitudinal essay the person writes is not going to be read by an audience that might be influenced by it. Although we have no good evidence from the political realm, the implications of this line of reasoning are clear. Political actors will not feel the need to bring their private attitudes into line with their public behavior unless the latter influences others. For example, even when the Joint Chiefs of Staff operated under President Eisenhower's guidelines, they would have felt no dissonance if the Congress and public rejected their pleas to hold down the defense budget. The subordinate who urges on his superior a course of action that he actually opposes will not feel pressure to adopt this position unless his superior is persuaded by his arguments. In most actual cases, however, this hypothesis is not easy to apply because it is not easy for the person to determine what consequences, if any, followed from his action. There may be no immediate, detectable impact and yet there could be important long-run or indirect consequences. Alternatively, others may have adopted the person's position, yet his actions may not have been the cause. Although earlier we developed an argument about the conditions under which the person will attribute causation to his own efforts as contrasted with the other's internal motivation, this is not sufficient to tell us how the person will estimate what the consequences of his behavior have been. A further objection, although one that has been subject to vigorous rebuttal, is that the claim that the per-

---

the top decision-makers. Dissonance theorists acknowledge that they do not deal with the question of the conditions under which people comply.

[41] See Barry Collins and Michael Hoyt, "Personal Responsibility-for-Consequences," *Journal of Experimental Social Psychology* 8 (1972), 558-93; Bobby Calder, Michael Ross, and Chester Insko, "Attitude Change and Attitude Attribution," *Journal of Personality and Social Psychology* 25 (1973), 84-99; Gerard, Conolley, and Wilhelmy, "Compliance, Justification, and Cognitive Change."

son will experience dissonance only if he thinks his counterattitudinal behavior has influenced others implies that the person's knowledge that he has behaved contrary to a belief of his is not, by itself, dissonant with his knowledge that he holds that belief.[42] The validity of this implication depends on the person's self-image. It will hold for a person who thinks that only consequences matter; but it will not for someone who holds to the principle that he should not espouse a view unless he believes it.

Boomerang Effects

The final aspect of dissonance theory with important implications for political decisions holds that the introduction of discrepant information can start a process that will reduce dissonance to a level lower than it was to begin with. If contradictory evidence arouses sufficient discomfort to trigger dissonance reduction but is not convincing enough to change the person's mind, he may end up holding his views even more strongly than before.[43] This leads to behavior that is the opposite of that predicted by learning theories. Instead of modifying one's actions to conform to the "obvious" conclusions of new evidence and experience, the actor may intensify his previous attitudes and behavior.

This "boomerang dissonance reduction" is apt to occur if the individual is "relatively resistant to changing his own position. At the same time, the dissonance arousing information to which he is exposed must also be resistant to change. With both sets of dissonance elements resistant to change, the individual can do little else to reduce dissonance except to add further consistent elements to one of the two sets of dissonance elements."[44]

The classic example is the behavior of the millennarian sect that prophesied that the world would be destroyed on a particular night. When this date passed uneventfully, some members left the sect. But those who stayed[45] had to reduce the dissonance. Most of them did so by

---

[42] In addition to those articles cited in the previous footnote and the experiments summarized in Kiesler and Munson, "Attitudes and Opinions," pp. 421-24, see Aronson, "The Theory of Cognitive Dissonance"; Elizabeth Nel, Robert Helmreich, and Elliot Aronson, "Opinion Change in the Advocate as a Function of the Persuasibility of His Audience," *Journal of Personality and Social Psychology* 12 (1969), 117-24; Joel Cooper and Stephen Worchel, "Role of Undesired Consequences in Arousing Cognitive Dissonance," *ibid.*, 16 (1970), 199-206.

[43] Festinger, *A Theory of Cognitive Dissonance*, pp. 231-32; Kiesler, *The Psychology of Commitment*, pp. 74-89.

[44] Brehm and Cohen, *Explorations in Cognitive Dissonance*, p. 59.

[45] The existence or absence of social support was a main determinant of whether a person left the sect or stayed in. Those who were isolated from other members at the time when the prophecy was disconfirmed lost their faith, while those who were with fellow-believers retained theirs. See Leon Festinger, Henry Riecken, and Stanley Schachter, *When Prophecy Fails* (Minneapolis: University of Minnesota Press, 1956). The expected effect was not found in Jane Hardyck and Marcia

seeking publicity and converts, activities that had been shunned in the past when the members faced less discrepant information.

Although no political cases are as striking as this, there are examples of "anti-learning"—cases in which failure leads the actor to hold more strongly to his policy. This partially explains Woodrow Wilson's initially friendly attitude toward the Russian revolution. Kennan argues that:

> [Wilson's] image of himself as a statesman was built around his role as the defender of the helpless, the simple, the innocent, against the economic and social mighty of this world. The most serious problem of foreign policy he had had to face before the World War was the troublesome Mexican situation of 1912-1915. Here he had labored to appear as the unselfish friend of the Mexican people. . . . The fact that this approach had not worked in Mexico had been for him a great disappointment; but the dream was not shattered. On the contrary, *the frustration in Mexico seems to have made him all the more eager to vindicate the concept* in some other framework of circumstances.[46]

Wilson may have been especially prone to react to discrepant information by redoubling his faith in the correctness of his behavior, but he is not alone in this characteristic. Even after the disastrous results of forcing the Chinese Communist party to incorporate itself into Kuomintang,

> [Stalin] was still reluctant to give up his belief that the Kuomintang could be employed as a useful instrument of Soviet policy. He insisted, therefore, that the Chinese Communists now adopt the same sort of semi-subservience to the more liberal wing of the Kuomintang . . . that they had previously been required to adopt toward Chiang. This, too, ended in a woeful setback.[47]

This evidence is hardly conclusive because the same underlying predispositions could have been responsible for the repeated behavior. Better would be cases in which failure was followed by intensified activities that could not be explained by a pre-existing analysis of the situation. The observation that Wilson sought vindication[48] supports the psycho-

---

Braden, "Prophecy Fails Again: A Report of a Failure to Replicate," *Journal of Abnormal and Social Psychology* 65 (1962), 136-41, but the explanation may lie in the absence of some of the necessary conditions.

[46] George Kennan, *Russia and the West under Lenin and Stalin* (New York: Mentor, 1962), p. 118 (emphasis added).

[47] *Ibid.*, p. 257.

[48] It has been noted in a different context that "Opposition to a course upon which he had reached a firm decision only irritated Wilson without causing him to change his mind"; Seward Livermore, *Woodrow Wilson and the War Congress, 1916-18* (Seattle: University of Washington Press, 1968), p. 222. Another scholar

logical explanation, but the "boomerang effect" remains to be more fully investigated both in and out of laboratory.

SUMMARY

The central contribution of the theory of cognitive dissonance is the argument that people seek to justify their own behavior—to reassure themselves that they have made the best possible use of all the information they had or should have had, to believe that they have not used their resources foolishly, to see that their actions are commendable and consistent. If men could reach these goals by merely thinking well of themselves the theory would not be of concern here. But in constructing defensible postures to support their self-images, people must often rearrange their perceptions, evaluations, and opinions. To see that their decisions were correct may involve increasing the value they place on what they have achieved and devaluing what they sacrificed. By spreading apart the earlier alternatives and heavily weighing sunk costs, inertia and incrementalism are encouraged. Each step in the process of developing a policy adds psychological pressures to take further steps.

The consequences of dissonance reduction extend to other decisions as the person tries to maintain consistency between his past and future behavior. If in justifying what he has done, the person alters his values or beliefs, later decisions will follow the new path. Without knowing how dissonance is reduced in the first case we cannot say exactly how the later behavior will be altered, but the process will introduce an unintended and unfortunate continuity into policy. Ironically, then, the drive to see one's self as a better, more rational decision-maker will reduce the person's rationality by impairing his ability to utilize information and examine his own values. The person will take positions that, while consistent with his earlier ones, do not take full advantage of the circumstances he is currently facing.

---

argues that "many men . . . apparently damaged rather than advanced [their causes] by trying to change Woodrow Wilson's mind"; Gaddis Smith, *Britain's Clandestine Submarines, 1914-1915* (New Haven: Yale University Press, 1964), p. 48. This argument is also compatible with the more general psychological explanation of Wilson's behavior in George and George, *Woodrow Wilson and Colonel House.*

Part IV
In Lieu of Conclusions

CHAPTER TWELVE

Minimizing Misperception

ALTHOUGH prescription is not the purpose of this book, our analysis suggests a number of measures that would decrease misperception. If decision-makers become aware of common perceptual errors, they may be able to avoid or compensate for them. And they can adopt safeguards to decrease their unwarranted confidence in prevailing beliefs, make them more sensitive to alternative explanations and images, and thus decrease the amount of discrepant information needed to make them reexamine their views. But while the amount and quality of self-conscious judgment employed in decision-making can be increased, no formula will eliminate misperception or reveal what image is correct. Faced with ambiguous and confusing evidence, decision-makers must draw inferences that will often prove to be incorrect. Indeed, as we pointed out in Chapter 4, the interpretation of the other side that best fits with the available evidence may be wrong. There are, however, ways to increase the likelihood that the decision-maker will apply the full measure of his intelligence to the tasks before him. All too often this is not the case. Decision-makers assimilate evidence to their pre-existing beliefs without being aware of alternative interpretations. Conclusions are reached without careful thought. As Secretary of State Kissinger said recently when he was asked if he regretted the decision to deploy multiple warheads on American missiles: "I would say in retrospect that I wish I had thought through the implications of a MIRVed world more thoughtfully in 1969 and 1970 than I did. What conclusions I would then have come to I don't know."[1] Helping decision-makers be more thoughtful will not solve all our problems, but neither is it a trivial goal.

Both to interpret others' behavior and to design one's own behavior so that others will draw the desired conclusions from it, the actor must try to see the world the way the other sees it. Or, rather, on those frequent occasions when the actor cannot be sure what the other's perspective is, he must examine the world through a variety of possible perspectives. Of course the actor will often fail in his attempt to see the world and himself as the other does, but at least he can avoid the common error of assuming that the way he sees the world is the only possible one. He can also avoid the trap of believing that the other sees his actions as he sees them. Actors frequently assume that their intentions, especially

[1] Press briefing, December 3, 1974, pp. C2-C3.

peaceful ones, are clear to others. Failing to realize that others may see the actor as a threat to their security, the actor concludes that others' arms increases can only indicate unprovoked aggressiveness.

Actors must remember that both they and others are influenced by their expectations and fit incoming information into pre-existing images. The danger that the actor's lack of knowledge of this influence will lead him to prematurely exclude alternative perceptions and grow too confident of his views was discussed earlier. Here we should note that because people underestimate the impact of established beliefs and predispositions, they are slower to change their minds than they think they are. As a consequence the actors are likely to overestimate both the degree to which they are sensitive to variations in others' behavior and the ease with which they can influence others' images of them. Because pre-existing beliefs so strongly color perceptions, the success of an actor's efforts to convince others to accept a desired image of him and his behavior will be in direct proportion to the degree to which this image is compatible with what others already believe. So to the extent possible, the actor should design his behavior to work with, rather than against, the other's expectations. And when he has to try to alter the other's beliefs (e.g. when he has to convince the other that he is not aggressive) he should be aware that this will require prolonged and/or dramatic behavior that for a long time may be misperceived.

MAKING ASSUMPTIONS AND PREDICTIONS EXPLICIT

Decision-makers will usually benefit from making their beliefs and values more explicit. As we have seen in the discussion of spiral and deterrence theorists, people often misunderstand the issues that divide them. They 'know that they disagree on many specific points without understanding how these disputes are related to broader questions. As we noted in Chapter 4, it is often more fruitful to debate the merits of two opposed images or theories as a whole rather than to argue over the interpretation of each individual incident.

People often not only have a limited understanding of the workings of others' arguments, they also do not know the structure of their own belief systems—what values are most important, how some beliefs are derived from others, and what evidence would contradict their views. Particularly dangerous is the tendency to take the most important questions for granted. Analysis of policies that failed indicates that many crucial errors occur not because decision-makers arrive at the wrong answers, but because they ask the wrong questions. This often involves taking too many things for granted and failing to scrutinize basic assumptions. For example, much of British foreign policy in the late nineteenth century was based on the fear that a hostile power controlling the upper Nile could dam the river, ruin the Egyptian economy, drive England out of that country, and thereby cut the route to India.[2] A parallel fear was that, if Russia advanced in central Asia, her armies would menace India's northern frontier. But the key assumptions that the Nile could be blocked and that large numbers of troops could be transported from central Russia to the Indian border were never examined. A more careful scrutiny of the terrain could have spared England many burdens. And Britain "nearly lost [World War I] by assuming that because of Grand Fleet needs there could not possibly be enough destroyers to guard mercantile convoys." The limited number of destroyers was a key bottleneck even before the demands of the convoys—ships of the Grand Fleet had been left in port because of an inadequate destroyer screen. But the navy never closely examined the effectiveness of these ships or explored ways to make do with fewer of them. During the next war, the British over-estimated the danger that the Germans would seize and utilize the French navy after France surrendered because, while they analyzed how Germany could take the ships, they paid little attention to the equally crucial question of whether Germany could repair and man them. Had the British carried out this analysis, they might have decided against the costly and dangerous step of attacking the French fleet to prevent it from coming within reach of the enemy.[3]

More frequently, the beliefs that need to be made explicit concern the relations among objects at the higher end of the actor's means-ends chain. Because the most important goals (e.g. security, high influence) are too general to provide guidelines for actions, actors must establish subgoals (e.g. strong alliances, military preponderance) that are believed to contribute to the higher ones. Partly because of the difficulties inherent in the problems they face, decision-makers often fail to analyze the reasons why their subgoals, if reached, would have the desired effect.

---

[2] For the contrary argument that prestige was as important a motive to the British as security, see G. N. Sanderson, "The Origins and Significance of the Anglo-French Confrontation at Fashoda, 1898," in Prosser Gifford and Wm. Roger Louis, eds., *France and Britain in Africa* (New Haven: Yale University Press, 1971), pp. 286-93.

[3] Arthur Marder, *From the Dreadnought to Scapa Flow*, vol. 5, *Victory and Aftermath, 1918-1919* (London: Oxford University Press, 1970), p. 302; Arthur Marder, *From the Dardanelles to Oran* (London: Oxford University Press, 1974), pp. 285-87. For other examples, see Richard Ullman, *Anglo-Soviet Relations, 1917-1921*, vol. 3, *The Anglo-Soviet Accord* (Princeton: Princeton University Press, 1972), p. 19; Walter Anselm, *Hitler Confronts England* (Durham, N.C.: Duke University Press, 1960), p. 133; and Lynn Davis, *The Cold War Begins* (Princeton: Princeton University Press, 1974), p. 385.

Thus when the British decided to force the Dardanelles in World War I few questioned the prediction that the Turkish government would fall if British ships appeared before Constantinople.[4] Similarly, the British and French invasion of Egypt in 1956 was predicated on the assumption that once Cairo was taken Nasser would be overthrown and a more reasonable leader would take his place. Both of these predictions were probably wrong and, what is of more importance here, they were not scrutinized by the decision-makers.

The failure to examine the plausibility of crucial beliefs, especially those relating ends and means, is evident when the environment changes in a way that should, but does not, lead to changes in beliefs and policies. For example, one reason why the United States was taken by surprise at Pearl Harbor was that the initial American analysis of Japan's alternatives had led to the reasonable conclusion that Japan would not attack American territory. But as the situation changed, American decision-makers realized that Japan might strike at the Philippines. Since such an attack meant war with the United States, Americans should have noted that one of the major reasons why the Japanese would not attack Pearl Harbor was now removed and should have looked at the dangers again. But they did not, and the policy deriving from the old beliefs remained even though the beliefs themselves had been changed.

Examination of the beliefs that underlie policies is inhibited by the transformation of means or subgoals into ends, a process whose organizational components will be discussed later. Here we should note that subgoals often come to be valued for their own sakes, especially when their attainment requires a great deal of time, effort, and attention.[5] The original rationale for the subgoal—its contribution to a higher end—is lost sight of. Thus as circumstances change and new obstacles and possibilities arise, policies do not shift in an optimum manner. Instead of trying to see whether these changes mean that the desired end might be better reached through new subgoals, decision-makers continue to strive for the old ones that may now be wasteful or self-defeating. While this is partly explained by the emotional attachments that people form to goals that consume much of their time and energy, purely cognitive factors are also at work. As we saw in Chapter 4, once a person has conceived of a problem in a given way, it is very hard to break out of his pattern of thought. New information, rather than calling the established subgoal into question, will be interpreted within the old framework. New answers will be sought to the old questions, but the questions themselves will be

---

[4] Arthur Marder, *From the Dreadnought to Scapa Flow*, vol. 2, *The War Years: To the Eve of Jutland* (London: Oxford University Press, 1965), p. 217; Marder, *From the Dardanelles to Oran*, pp. 20, 29-31.

[5] For an example, see George Kennan, *Memoirs*, vol. 1, *1925-1950* (Boston: Little, Brown, 1967), p. 443.

taken as givens.[6] Thus a person who has not worked on the problem before, or one who has been away from it for a while, will often be able to see that the old subgoal no longer needs to be attained.[7]

Of course if the initial specification of the means-ends chain was appropriate and if the environment does not change, this problem will not arise. But the latter requirement is rarely met. And so it is common to find that policies are maintained after the situation that gave rise to them is passed. For example, the German navy was developed to reach the subgoal of threatening to weaken the British navy in battle, thus leaving it prey to third parties. This subgoal depended on British fear of other naval powers, but when the ententes with France and Russia removed this fear, the Germans continued their policy without realizing that the original rationale no longer applied.

Earlier we argued that irrational cognitive consistency increases the probability that policy will remain constant in the face of drastic shifts in the environment. Because this consistency is not in the interest of the decision-maker when it is not covering a weakness or problem that is too painful and difficult to face,[8] it can be at least partly diminished by a re-examination of the reasons why the policy was first adopted. In terms of the kind of policies being discussed here, this examination will involve making explicit the structure of the means-ends chains and looking carefully at the question of why a favored policy is supposed to lead to a desired goal.

To make their important beliefs and assumptions explicit, decision-makers should not only try to discover the crucial elements that underlie their policy preferences but should also consider what evidence would tend to confirm, or, more importantly, disconfirm, their views. If they are aware of what they expect, or rather what their images and beliefs should lead them to expect, actors will be more apt to heed unsettling incidents. By contrast, when the implications of a theory or image have not been carefully considered, a wide variety of events can take place without disturbing one's faith in it. Discrepant information will not be noticed, will be seen as consistent with the prevailing view, or at most will be thought to require minor adjustments in beliefs. But when the actor—scientist as well as statesman—has thought about what events are excluded

[6] For experimental evidence, see Abraham Luchins and Edith Luchins, *Rigidity of Behavior* (Eugene: University of Oregon Press, 1959), p. 312, and Tolman's study cited there.

[7] For an argument about the role of memory in this process, see Herbert Simon, "Scientific Discovery and the Psychology of Problem Solving," in Robert Colodny, ed., *Mind and Cosmos* (Pittsburgh: University of Pittsburgh Press, 1966), pp. 32-34.

[8] In some cases, the motivations underlying the irrational consistency are so strong that it would be too painful to face and so the argument made in the text does not apply. For a further discussion of this point, see footnote 64, Chapter 4.

by his hypotheses, he is more apt to notice and react to such events if they occur.

Although deciding ahead of time what would be surprising cannot tell the decision-maker when his image is wrong, let alone tell him what image is right, it will sensitize him to discrepant evidence and facilitate the re-examination and eventual alteration of his beliefs. This is one reason why opponents of a policy often ask the proponents to spell out exactly what they expect to happen if the policy is adopted. Thus those who doubted the wisdom of the Flanders offensive of 1917 repeatedly asked General Haig for his objectives "so that they might be able to judge whether the operation had, up to that stage, succeeded or not."⁹ If in the spring of 1938, Chamberlain had thought about the sort of German demands and behavior that he would consider as indicating that Germany's aims outran limited revisionism, he might have reacted more strongly to the terms that emerged at Munich. As this example illustrates, the designation of events that would be surprising will make it more likely that discrepant evidence arriving in small bits will call the image into question rather than being automatically assimilated to it.

In some cases, trying to specify what evidence would count against his hypothesis will help the actor to realize that his image is in fact invulnerable to most events. For example, decision-makers are often unaware that they hold an "inherent bad faith model" of another and believe instead that the other has had manifold opportunities to reveal that he is friendly. Furthermore, people will then see events as confirming their image even when they would have perceived the opposite of these events as supporting the same conclusion. Thus in 1967 President Johnson said that the American bombing "has . . . created very serious problems for [North Vietnam]. The best indication of how substantial is the fact that they are working so hard, every day, with their friends throughout the world, to try to get us to stop."¹⁰ But the lack of such a reaction probably would have been interpreted as showing that the North was trying to disguise her pain.

Three problems with relying on explicit predictions should be noted. First, and most fundamentally, the study of science has shown that the role of critical experiments has been exaggerated.¹¹ As we discussed in Chapter 4, individual facts are susceptible to multiple interpretations. A scientific theory should not be discarded because it cannot explain a par-

---

⁹ The British Official History cited in Leon Wolff, *In Flanders Fields* (New York: Viking, 1958), p. 123.

¹⁰ "Text of President Johnson's Nashville Address," *New York Times*, March 16, 1967, p. 8.

¹¹ Imre Lakatos, "Falsification and the Methodology of Scientific Research Programmes," in Imre Lakatos and Alan Musgrave, eds., *Criticism and the Growth of Knowledge* (Cambridge: Cambridge University Press, 1970), pp. 154-77.

ticular fact. Nor should an image automatically be changed because it meets with an embarrassment. Furthermore, because international politics is very complex, even good theories will yield predictions only when a large number of facts are given, and even then the predictions will be only probabilistic. So there are severe limits to the degree of assistance that greater explicitness can provide even under the best of conditions.

Second, the conditions that prevail in foreign policy analysis are far from the best. A high degree of knowledge is needed before expectations, even negative expectations, can be stated precisely,[12] and this requirement is rarely met in foreign policy analysis because theories of international relations are poor. Most of us are not sure what events present either "puzzles" to be explored within the paradigm or "anomalies" that cast doubt on our basic theories.

Finally, people may not be affected by witnessing events that they had previously said would count against their hypotheses. For example, in the debate within Finland in 1939, the foreign minister argued that important support for his belief that Russia would not fight if Finland stood firm was furnished by the fact that Russia had refrained from making her demands public. But when Molotov brought the conflict into the open in a major address, the foreign minister did not re-examine his position.[13]

DEVIL'S ADVOCATES

To expose implicit assumptions and give themselves more freedom of choice, decision-makers should encourage the formulation and application of alternative images. As we noted in a previous chapter, psychologists have shown that "where one and only one hypothesis is operative with no competing alternatives, it tends to be more readily confirmable." Actors can be less closed to discrepant information by acting on the implications of Roberta Wohlstetter's argument that "A willingness to play with material from different angles and in the context of unpopular as well as popular hypotheses is an essential ingredient of a good detective, whether the end is the solution of a crime or an intelligence estimate."[14]

It is often difficult, psychologically and politically, for any one person to examine many alternatives. Thus, just as a decision-maker should en-

[12] Thomas Kuhn, *The Structure of Scientific Revolutions* (Chicago: University of Chicago Press, 1962), p. 65.

[13] Max Jakobson, *The Diplomacy of the Winter War* (Cambridge, Mass.: Harvard University Press, 1961), pp. 132-34.

[14] Jerome Bruner, "On Perceptual Readiness," *Psychological Review* 64 (1957), 136; Wohlstetter, *Pearl Harbor: Warning and Decision* (Stanford: Stanford University Press, 1962), p. 302. See W.I.B. Beveridge, *The Art of Scientific Investigation* (3rd ed., New York: Norton, 1957), p. 93, for a discussion of the idea that a scientist should keep many hypotheses in mind when conducting and analyzing experiments.

sure that his subordinates have conflicting policy preferences so that they do not foreclose important decisions by agreeing with one another,[15] so should he ensure that a variety of analysts, with a variety of perceptual predispositions, confront the evidence. Rather than seeking "unbiased" treatments of the data, decision-makers should seek to structure conflicting cognitive biases into the decision-making process to help themselves maintain their intellectual freedom. To make it more likely that they will consider alternative explanations of specific bits of data and think more carefully about the beliefs and images that underlie their policies, they should employ devil's—or rather devils'—advocates.[16]

If the differences are basic enough, one person will be unable to represent the opinions of someone else or try to see the evidence as an opponent would see it. Scientists usually do a bad job of testing theories with which they disagree, and we should not expect political advisers to do much better. The reason for this is not so much the conscious weight of the stake one has in one's own position, but rather the difficulty of seeing how the world looks from a different framework. It takes time, energy and commitment—at least temporary commitment—to understand an image well enough to apply it. Thus there are limits to the utility of a "devil's advocate" who is not a true devil.

Of course the correct image will not necessarily emerge from this adversary process. But—and this is important enough—the decision-maker can be given a wider range of choice in two related ways. First, because he is exposed to conflicting interpretations of events and shown how alternative images make the world appear differently, he will have to exercise explicit judgment to select his explanations and images rather than immediately seeing one view as the only possible one. Second, debates will help to bring out the implicit assumptions discussed above. An individual rarely has the ability or the incentive to expose the structure of his beliefs, and interaction with someone who holds a different position usually is the best, if not the only, way for those he is advising, and indeed for the person himself, to see where his arguments are most vulnerable. It is unlikely that any participant will be converted. But those who listen to the arguments are in a good position to learn what perspectives they are rejecting, what evidence they should examine more closely, and what assumptions need further thought. As a result, fewer important questions will be overlooked because everyone agrees on the answer.

To some extent this kind of examination will be provided by the di-

---

[15] Richard Neustadt, *Presidential Power* (New York: Wiley, 1960).

[16] For similar suggestions, see James Schlesinger, *Organizational Structures and Planning*, RAND P-3316, February 25, 1966; Joseph De Rivera, *The Psychological Dimension of Foreign Policy* (Columbus, Ohio: Merrill, 1968), pp. 61-64, 209-11; Stanley Hoffmann, *Gulliver's Troubles* (New York: McGraw-Hill, 1968), p. 270; and Alexander George, "The Case for Multiple Advocacy in Making Foreign Policy," *American Political Science Review* 66 (September 1972), 751-85.

vergence of interests, goals, training, and information that exists naturally within any large organization. But this normal diversity often will be insufficient. First, underlying assumptions may be so widely shared that anyone who admits to doubting them will be considered "unsound" and lose influence. Without special efforts to encourage and reward devil's advocates, there are few incentives for questioning what most people believe. Second, decision-makers are not likely to solicit conflicting views when an issue has a long history, when everyone's position is known, and when all the considerations are believed to be understood. In the absence of special efforts, even information that is logically independent of the main issue will not be studied it if comes from an opponent.[17] Third, the pressures toward homogeneity are especially strong among the president's personal assistants. They have no institutional ties and biases and are quick to pick up the president's perspectives and preferences. Fourth, as secrecy and urgency increase, the number of participants in the decision decreases. Although it may be liberating to get away from predictable and self-interested departmental views, small high-level groups also get away from expertise and built-in conflict. In these cases the need to develop compensating diversity is especially great.

There are problems with this proposal. First, it is not easy to determine which perceptual predispositions should be represented. The variety of specific intentions that other states may have is infinite. Just as the government cannot prepare for all eventualities, so there cannot be devil's advocates for all positions. Second, organizations and individuals develop defense mechanisms against differing perspectives. As Daniel Ellsberg notes, the fact that people who oppose the prevailing policy are usually labeled devil's advocates indicates resistance to sincere opposition. A minority view is especially easy to dismiss when it is believed that those who are propounding it are doing so only to provide a public service. So it is not surprising that Dean Rusk has said that George Ball opposed the war in Vietnam only when he was "assigned" the role of devil's advocate.[18] Even when the opposition is genuine, decision-makers may expose themselves to it in order to be able to tell others, and themselves, that they have considered all views. They may then gain renewed confidence in their policy from the incorrect belief that they have been especially open-minded.

[17] Aaron Wildavsky, *Dixon-Yates* (New Haven: Yale University Press, 1962), pp. 308-309.

[18] Ellsberg's comments are in Richard Pfeffer, ed., *No More Vietnams?* (New York: Harper and Row, 1968), p. 110. Rusk is quoted in Henry Graff, *The Tuesday Cabinet* (Englewood Cliffs, N.J.: Prentice-Hall, 1970), p. 136. For arguments that for this reason the institutionalization of devil's advocates will be useless or counter-productive, see George Reedy, *The Twilight of the Presidency* (New York: Mentor, 1970), p. 24, and James Thomson, Jr., "How Could Vietnam Happen?," *Atlantic Monthly* (April 1968), 47-53.

Conversions

In a safeguard related to the use of devil's advocates, a decision-maker should pay special heed when many of his subordinates who had previously held differing views reach the same conclusion—especially one that differs from his. Thus one reason why President Johnson altered his Vietnam policy was that several of his advisers, even those like Dean Acheson who not only had agreed with the president on Vietnam but who generally took a "hard line" on foreign policy, became convinced that the old policy was failing. And Kaiser Wilhelm paid heavily for maintaining his confidence that the growing German navy was not a cause of British hostility in the face of a kind of opposition that should have disturbed him. As one historian notes, "nothing is more remarkable in the whole history of Anglo-German relations than the uniform testimony of the last four Ambassadors [to Britain] before the war" that naval rivalry and not British encirclement was the main source of conflict between the two countries. Even an ambassador "who came [to England] after nearly two decades of Anglophobe activities, found himself converted to similar views." German ambassadors reached these conclusions in spite of strong sanctions. One ambassador was fired because he took issue with his government's image of England. His replacement had written an article defending Germany's naval policy that had caught the kaiser's eye. "Yet within a few months this new Ambassador was convinced that Great Britain had no aggressive intentions."[19] Decision-makers are wise to take such conversions with a grain of salt if they can be caused by the role the subordinates are placed in, but this does not seem to be the explanation for this case.

IDENTITIES AND MISSIONS

It is clearly dangerous to allow those with an interest in the maintenance of a policy to judge its effectiveness. Thus when the Germans gave the British false specifications for the *Bismarck* to disguise the fact that the ship violated the Anglo-German naval agreement of 1935, the office of the British navy that had negotiated the treaty accepted the German figures, saying that they showed the Germans to be "looking toward the Baltic with its shallow approaches more than in the past."[20] And to give the same individual who shares the primary responsibility for negotiating the SALT I treaty the job of monitoring Soviet compliance is to invite a one-sided interpretation of the evidence.

[19] Robert William Seton-Watson, *Britain in Europe, 1789-1914* (New York: Macmillan Co., 1937), pp. 630-31; E. L. Woodward, *Great Britain and the German Navy* (Oxford: Clarendon Press, 1935), p. 366.
[20] Donald McLachlan, *Room 39* (New York: Atheneum, 1968), p. 136.

But the problem is not only with self-interest. Individuals and organizations should not allow their tasks, prospects for the future, and identities to become tied to specific theories and images of other actors.[21] If this occurs it is highly probable that subgoals will take on value of their own and information about alternative routes to the higher goals will not be considered. An example of the harmful effects of an organization's permitting its identity to become bound up with the answers to questions that should have been left open is provided by the resistance of the United States Forest Service to the idea that controlled burning in forests could benefit valuable species of trees. An original goal of the organization was to combat forest fires, many of which were started in order to clear land. It was difficult to work at this job without coming to see "the necessity for absolute protection; fire, man's universal enemy, would be attacked with equal vigor on all fronts." Furthermore, the service had from the beginning been a crusading organization, seeing its job more as a mission than as the carrying out of technical tasks. In this atmosphere "the Service could hardly accept the argument that fire might prove a blessing in disguise. The question as to whether good might issue from evil was a discussion fit only for sophists."[22] While part of the service's reluctance even to study controlled burning can be traced to the rational calculation that this would hinder the fight against uncontrolled burning, much of the resistance must be credited to the fact that the service's distinctive competence was not in promoting the best use of lands but in preventing fires. And so the linkage between this, which was once considered a subgoal, and the higher goals could not be questioned and reformulated.

The founders of the Forest Service had anticipated that the action arm of the service must become committed to incorrect ideas. "Still, they confidently expected that research, acting in a critical capacity, could supply the stimulus needed to keep the organization flexible both in purpose and procedure. Indeed, Pinchot, [the service's founder] had held research's greatest contribution to administration to be the inquisitive spirit it introduced into the conduct of Service affairs." But the great hopes for the research division were not fulfilled. Its autonomy was un-

[21] As Philip Selznick puts it, "Commitments [are] enforced by institutionalization. Because organizations are social systems, goals or procedures tend to achieve an established, value-impregnated status"; "A Theory of Organizational Commitment," in Robert Merton et al., *Reader in Bureaucracy* (Glencoe, Ill.: Free Press, 1952), p. 200. Also see Selznick, *Leadership in Administration* (Evanston, Ill.: Row, Peterson, 1957), and Selznick, *TVA and the Grass Roots* (Harper and Row, 1966).

[22] Ashley Schiff, *Fire and Water: Scientific Heresy in the Forest Service* (Cambridge, Mass.: Harvard University Press, 1962), p. 23. This book is a fascinating and valuable study with important implications for the behavior of many kinds of organizations.

dermined by its internalization of the substantive beliefs and crusading zeal that characterized the larger organization as well as by its dependence on the service for financial support. As a result, most of its research on this matter was conducted to "prove a theory instead of to find out the facts."[23] Controlled experiments, not difficult to carry out, were avoided for years, and, when they were finally tried, the results unfavorable to the prevailing ideology were ignored. As outside sources produced evidence showing the value of controlled burning, the research division saw its standing in the scientific community jeopardized and made some compromises. The Forest Service as a whole, however, questioned its position only after private landowners and other branches of the government adopted new policies, thus isolating the service. Even so, policy was not altered until a series of disastrous forest fires were fed by the accumulation of undergrowth and debris that controlled burning would have eliminated.[24] Thus the eventual change in policy was justified not in terms of general land management principles, but in terms of fire-fighting, which remained the center of the organization's identity.

Similarly, before World War II the British Bomber Command's faith in the possibility of effective bombing—and an air force leader later indeed described this as "an act of faith"—made it next to impossible for the organization to carefully study how such a campaign might be carried out. As a new and embattled organization staffed by professionals who passionately believed that wars would be longer and bloodier if the other services could dictate the uses of air power, the Royal Air Force not only shunned analysis of the assumptions behind their proposed policy but also avoided realistic preparations and practices of the operations that were planned.

> The best method of bomber evaluation, although many could be employed, was photographic reconnaissance; yet there was a startling reluctance on the part of the RAF Bomber Command to seek out the critical evaluation of the doctrine upon which its very existence rested.

[23] *Ibid.*, pp. 169, 173. Similarly it has been argued that the AEC's "regulatory staff never achieved full independence" from the more powerful parts of the organization that were in charge whose mission was to develop atomic power. As a result, considerations of safety often have been slighted. Robert Gillette, "Nuclear Safety (part 3): Critics Charge Conflicts of Interest," *Science* 177 (September 15, 1972), 970-75. This was one motive for the recent splitting of the AEC and the establishment of a separate regulatory agency. For evidence that researchers within an organization are usually more likely to favor dissemination of the results of research if the findings support rather than undermine established policy, see Joseph Eaton, "Symbolic and Substantive Evaluative Research," *Administrative Science Quarterly* 6 (March 1962), 421-42.

[24] The Forest Service in the western United States still resists controlled burning. See Mark Oberle, "Forest Fires: Suppression Policy Has Its Ecological Drawbacks," *Science* 165 (August 8, 1969), 568-71.

When World War II began, there was no developed military organization for carrying out photographic reconnaissance and evaluation. Only a private firm in Britain had developed the technology to measure with considerable accuracy the evidence supplied by photographs, and the Air Ministry showed no particular interest in acquiring its services.[25]

Michael Howard calls this absence of planning and studies "one of the most remarkable facts in the whole history of British defence policy." But this is less surprising when it is realized that if analysis had shown that strategic bombing would not produce the desired consequences at an acceptable cost a new mission for the bombers might have had to have been found, probably involving supporting ground troops rather than carrying out an independent role. Alternatively, if the leaders of the RAF had maintained their plans in the face of research indicating their difficulties and costs, they would have had "to think dispassionately about the responsibility of chucking a lot of green young men in badly armed aircraft against a country which had for years been preparing to fight." The American air force similarly failed to recognize the problems of navigation and target location that would sharply limit the effectiveness of strategic bombing. The results of the few realistic tests were ignored and no one stressed "the central contradiction [of the planned bombing program]: that there would not be enough clear days to execute the massive campaign, that weather forecasts would be fallible, and that bombing through clouds and industrial haze would be necessary."[26]

In the same way, the American air force's commitment to an independent role of strategic bombing explains the neglect of fighter development during the interwar years and the slow and fumbling efforts to develop means of protecting the bombers against enemy fighters during the war. Even though bombers in World War I had needed escorts, interwar planners drastically underestimated the bombers' vulnerability because it was believed that heavily armed and armored bombers that flew in tight formations were more than a match for interceptors. Complementing this view was an overestimation of the difficulties entailed in developing a long-range fighter escort and an unwillingness to examine carefully ways of surmounting the problems, which, although exaggerated at the time, were indeed formidable. Even the Battle of Britain

---

[25] Sir John Slessor, *The Central Blue* (London: Cassell, 1956), p. 204; Maxwell Schoenfeld, *The War Ministry of Winston Churchill* (Ames: Iowa State University Press, 1972), p. 92.

[26] Michael Howard, *The Continental Commitment* (Harmondsworth, Middlesex, England: Penguin, 1974), p. 113; Anthony Verrier, *The Bomber Offensive* (New York: Macmillan Co., 1968), pp. 68-69; Monte Wright, *Most Probable Position* (Lawrence: University of Kansas Press, 1972), pp. 194-201 (the quote is from p. 201).

and the failure of early British raids on Germany did not produce the necessary re-direction of effort. The degree to which the dominance of the bomber inhibited intelligent consideration of the problem of strategic bombing is also revealed by the fact that for the first 18 months of the war most of the work on escorts went into modifying a number of bombers by replacing bomb-carrying capability with added guns and armor so that these "fighter destroyers" could protect the bombing fleet. These planes were favored by the air force because they did not disturb the dominant position of bombers, but they were not able to carry out their mission. Indeed, only a little disinterested analysis would have been necessary to demonstrate that success was most unlikely. The long-range fighter escorts equipped with droppable wing-tanks that finally proved so effective were developed for other missions and were seized on as the answer to bomber vulnerability only after all else had failed.[27]

After the war, the power of organizational identity was revealed by the air force's resistance to guided missiles, which it maintained into the 1960s. The members of the organization had come to see its distinctive mission not as carrying out strategic bombardment, but as carrying out strategic bombardment by means of manned bombers. Furthermore, the organization was hostile to pilotless drones and to the concept of a slow, long-endurance, unglamorous bomber that would attack targets by employing stand-off missiles that would be launched from a distance well beyond the enemy's reach. Instead it favored a high-speed, technologically advanced plane that would have to penetrate increasingly dense and sophisticated defenses. And the air force did not rush to embrace the doctrine of counterforce, even though this would have meant an increase in the size of its arsenal, because this doctrine involved a shift away from the idea on which the organization was founded—the idea that war would be won not by defeating the enemy's army but by devastating his homeland.[28]

---

[27] Bernard Boylan, *Development of the Long-range Escort Fighter* (Maxwell Air Force Base, Montgomery, Alabama: USAF Historical Study No. 36, 1955). The fact that the air force's leaders who stressed the central role of strategic bombing had been fighter, not bomber, pilots earlier in their careers shows the extent to which the ideology of bomber-dominance characterized the entire organization, rather than being isolated in the group that actually was in charge of bombing; Perry McCoy Smith, *The Air Force Plans for Peace* (Johns Hopkins Press, 1970), p. 33.

[28] The behavior of the air force can also be seen in terms of the process by which subgoals take on a life of their own independent of their contribution to higher goals (see pp. 411-13, above). First, the subgoal of strategic bombardment became a surrogate for victory and made it impossible for the organization to examine whether alternative uses of air power might make a greater contribution to this goal. Then the further subgoal of developing and deploying bombers hindered the most effective methods of bombing by limiting consideration of ways of protecting the bombers against hostile aircraft. Then, after the war, this sub-

Organizations may not realize the extent to which their identity has become linked to certain beliefs. Thus Allen Dulles saw the dangers too narrowly when he said, "I grant that we are all creatures of prejudice, including CIA officials, but by entrusting intelligence coordination to our central intelligence service, which is excluded from policy-making and is married to no particular military hardware, we can avoid, to the greatest possible extent, the bending of facts obtained through intelligence to suit a particular occupational viewpoint."[29] This argument overlooks the possibility that the CIA has developed a view of international relations and the Cold War that maximizes the importance of covert information-gathering, espionage, and subversion. Since the CIA would lose its unique place in the government if it were decided that the "back alleys" of world politics were no longer vital to United States' security, it is to be expected that the organization will interpret information in a way that implies the continued need for its distinctive competence.

AWARENESS OF COMMON MISPERCEPTIONS

The final, and most obvious, safeguard is for decision-makers to take account of the ways in which the processes of perception lead to common errors. If they know, for example, that their belief systems are apt to display irrational consistency, they will be more likely to examine the evidence supporting their beliefs to see if there are hard choices that should be made explicitly. An awareness of the dangers of forming an image too quickly could lead decision-makers to suspend judgment for longer periods or to consult people who have been less involved with the issue. The knowledge that evidence that is consistent with one's pre-existing beliefs is likely to be taken as disconfirming other views even when this is not justified would lead decision-makers to proceed more carefully and would restrain them from developing unwarranted confidence out of the incorrect belief that events are showing that their images must be correct. The realization that people seize on certain past events as analogies because of characteristics of those events that are, from a rational standpoint, irrelevant (e.g. the person or his nation participated in them, the event occurred at a time when the person was first forming his political ideas, the event had important consequences) would lead the person to search the past more widely for possible guidelines to action. And an appreciation of the superficial nature of most learning from history would lead decision-makers to think more about the causes of previous

---

goal hindered the reaching of the higher subgoal of strategic bombardment by delaying the development of missiles and inhibiting the consideration of bombers that did not utilize all the latest technology.
[29] *The Craft of Intelligence* (New York: Signet, 1963), p. 53.

outcomes and so to be in a better position to determine what past cases are relevant to his current situation.

Decision-makers should not only try to correct for these limitations in the processes of perception, but should also note the distortions that commonly result—e.g. the belief that the other side is highly centralized and carefully plans its moves, the belief that favorable actions by the other are a response to the actor's behavior but that unfriendly acts spring from unprovoked hostility. Awareness that these beliefs are frequently wrong should cause the decision-makers to hesitate before affirming them in any particular case. This is especially important because, as we have noted at several points in this book, many of these misperceptions lead to an overestimation of the other side's hostility.

But we must note that the finding that a certain misperception is more common than its opposite does not necessarily mean that this distribution of errors is less than optimum. Before we can say more than "This kind of misperception is common—why don't you look at the evidence again," we have to know about the costs of the misperception and the costs of the opposite error.[30] If it is disastrous to mistake an enemy for a friend but not so costly to take a friend for an enemy, then decision-makers are well-advised to suffer the latter misperception rather than run a high risk of the former. Perhaps decision-makers believe this. History is filled with calls for vigilance. Although this book has not compared the costs of various misperceptions, my impression is that the cost of overestimating the other's hostility is itself often underestimated. Too often decision-makers believe that if the other is not aggressive it will see that their state is seeking only peace and security. And they overestimate the ease with which a suspicious but nonaggressive state can show that it does not seek expansion. I strongly suspect that decision-makers have not accurately assessed the costs of various kinds of misperceptions and would be wise to correct for the tendency to be excessively vigilant.

[30] This point is missed by Jerome Bruner when he argues that "the most appropriate pattern of [perceptual] readiness . . . would be that one which would lead on the average to the most 'veridical' guess about the nature of the world." ("On Perceptual Readiness," 130.)

Bibliography

This bibliography lists only the most general books and articles in each of three categories: treatments of international relations from a psychological perspective; discussions of the relevant psychological theories; and works in the philosophy of science. None of the historical materials or psychological experiments that provided the bulk of the evidence is mentioned here.

I. Discussions of International Politics
   from the Psychological Perspective

Axelrod, Robert, "Psycho-Algebra: A Mathematical Theory of Cognition and Choice with an Application to the British Eastern Committee in 1918," *Peace Research Society International Papers* 18 (1972).

———, ed., *The Structure of Decision* (Princeton: Princeton University Press, forthcoming).

Bauer, Raymond, "Problems of Perception and the Relations between the United States and the Soviet Union," *Journal of Conflict Resolution* 5 (Sept. 1961).

Bonham, G. Matthew, and Michael Shapiro, "Explanation of the Unexpected: Computer Simulation of a Foreign Policy Advisor," in Robert Axelrod, ed., *The Structure of Decision* (Princeton: Princeton University Press, forthcoming).

———, eds., *Thought and Action in Foreign Policy* (Basel: Birkhauser Verlag, 1976).

Boulding, Kenneth, "National Images and International Systems," *Journal of Conflict Resolution* 3 (June 1959).

Deutsch, Karl, and Richard Merritt, "Effects of Events on National and International Images," in Herbert Kelman, ed., *International Behavior* (New York: Holt, Rinehart and Winston, 1965).

De Rivera, Joseph, *The Psychological Dimension of Foreign Policy* (Columbus, Ohio: Merrill, 1968).

George, Alexander, "American Policy-Making and the North Korean Aggression," *World Politics* 7 (Jan. 1955).

George, Alexander, "The 'Operational Code': A Neglected Approach to the Study of Political Leaders and Decision-Making," *International Studies Quarterly* 13 (June 1969).

———, "The Case for Multiple Advocacy in Making Foreign Policy," *American Political Science Review* 66 (Sept. 1972).

George, Alexander, and Juliette George, *Woodrow Wilson and Colonel House* (New York: Dover, 1964).

Greenstein, Fred, "The Impact of Personality on Politics: An Attempt to Clear Away Underbrush," *American Political Science Review* 61 (Sept. 1967).

Holst, Johan, "Surprise, Signals, and Reaction: The Attack on Norway," *Cooperation and Conflict* No. 1 (1966).

Holsti, Ole, "The 1914 Case," *The American Political Science Review* 59 (June 1965).

———, "Cognitive Dynamics and Images of the Enemy: Dulles and Russia," in David Finlay, Ole Holsti, and Richard Fagen, *Enemies in Politics* (Chicago: Rand McNally, 1967).

———, "Individual Differences in 'Definition of the Situation,' " *Journal of Conflict Resolution* 14 (Sept. 1970).

———, *Crisis Escalation War* (Montreal and London: McGill-Queen's University Press, 1972).

Holsti, Ole, Robert North, and Richard Brody, "Perception and Action in the 1914 Crisis," in J. David Singer, ed., *Quantitative International Politics* (New York: Free Press, 1968).

Knorr, Klaus, "Failures in National Intelligence Estimates: The Case of the Cuban Missiles," *World Politics* 16 (April 1967).

Klineberg, Otto, *The Human Dimension in International Relations* (New York: Holt, Rinehart and Winston, 1965).

Osgood, Charles, *An Alternative to War or Surrender* (Urbana: University of Illinois Press, 1962).

Pruitt, Dean, "Definition of the Situation as a Determinant of International Action," in Herbert Kelman, ed., *International Behavior* (New York: Holt, Rinehart and Winston, 1965).

Shapiro, Michael, and G. Matthew Bonham, "Cognitive Process and Foreign Policy Decision-Making," *International Studies Quarterly* 17 (June 1973).

Sprout, Harold, and Margaret Sprout, *Man-Milieu Relationship Hypotheses in the Context of International Politics* (Princeton: Center of International Studies, 1956).

———, *The Ecological Perspective on Human Affairs* (Princeton: Princeton University Press, 1965).

———, *An Ecological Paradigm for the Study of International Politics* (Princeton: Center of International Studies, Princeton University, Research Monograph No. 30, March 1968).

Stagner, Ross, *Psychological Aspects of International Conflict* (Belmont, California: Brooks/Cole, 1967).

Steinbruner, John, *Some Effects of Decision Procedures on Policy Outcomes* (Cambridge, Mass.: M.I.T. Center for International Studies, February 1970).

———, *The Cybernetic Theory of Decision* (Princeton: Princeton University Press, 1974).

Whaley, Barton, *Codeword BARBAROSSA* (Cambridge, Mass.: M.I.T. Press, 1973).

Wohlstetter, Roberta, *Pearl Harbor: Warning and Decision* (Stanford: Stanford University Press, 1962).

———, "Cuba and Pearl Harbor: Hindsight and Foresight," *Foreign Affairs* (July 1965).

Zinnes, Dina, "The Expression and Perception of Hostility in Prewar Crisis: 1914," in J. David Singer, ed., *Quantitative International Politics* (New York: Free Press, 1968).

———, "Some Evidence Relevant to the Man-Milieu Hypothesis," in James Rosenau, Vincent Davis, and Maurice East, eds., *The Analysis of International Politics* (New York: Free Press, 1972).

II. THEORIES FROM PSYCHOLOGY

Abelson, Robert, "Modes of Resolution of Conflict," *Journal of Conflict Resolution* 3 (December 1959).

Abelson, Robert, and Milton Rosenberg, "Symbolic Psycho-logic," *Behavioral Science* 3 (Jan. 1958).

Abelson, Robert, et al., eds., *Theories of Cognitive Consistency* (Chicago: Rand McNally, 1968).

Brehm, Jack, *A Theory of Psychological Reactance* (New York: Academic Press, 1966).

———, *Responses to Loss of Freedom: A Theory of Psychological Reactance* (Morristown, N.J.: General Learning Press, 1972).

Brehm, Jack, and Arthur Cohen, *Explorations in Cognitive Dissonance* (New York: Wiley, 1962).

Bruner, Jerome, "On Perceptual Readiness," *Psychological Review* 64 (1957).

Bruner, Jerome, Jacqueline Goodnow, and George Austin, *A Study of Thinking* (New York: Wiley, 1956).

Bruner, Jerome, and A. Leigh Minturn, "Perceptual Identification and Perceptual Organization," *Journal of General Psychology*, 53 (1955).

Bruner, Jerome, and Leo Postman, "On the Perception of Incongruity: A Paradigm," in Jerome Bruner and David Krech, eds., *Perception and Personality* (Durham, N.C.: Duke University Press, 1950).

Campbell, Donald, "Systematic Error on the Part of Human Links in Communication Systems," *Information and Control* 1 (1958).

————, "Social Attitudes and Other Acquired Behavioral Dispositions," in Sigmund Koch, ed., *Psychology: A Study of a Science* 6 (New York: McGraw-Hill, 1963).

Cook, Mark, *Interpersonal Perception* (Baltimore: Penguin, 1971).

Cooper, Eunice, and Marie Jahoda, "The Evasion of Propaganda: How Prejudiced People Respond to Anti-Propaganda Propaganda," *Journal of Psychology* 23 (1947).

Dember, William, *The Psychology of Perception* (New York: Holt, Rinehart and Winston, 1961).

De Soto, Clinton, "Learning a Social Structure," *Journal of Abnormal and Social Psychology* 60 (1960).

De Soto, Clinton, Nancy Henley, and Marvin London, "Balance and the Grouping Schema," *Journal of Personality and Social Psychology* 8 (1968).

Duncker, K., "On Problem Solving," *Psychological Monographs* 58 No. 270 (1945).

Epstein, William, *Varieties of Perceptual Learning* (New York: McGraw-Hill, 1967).

Erdelyi, Matthew, "A New Look at the New Look," *Psychological Review* 81 (1974).

Feather, Norman, "A Structural Balance Approach to the Analysis of Communication Effects," in Leonard Berkowitz, ed., *Advances in Experimental Social Psychology* 3 (New York: Academic Press, 1967).

Feldman, Shel, ed., *Cognitive Consistency* (New York: Academic Press, 1966).

Festinger, Leon, *A Theory of Cognitive Dissonance* (Stanford: Stanford University Press, 1957).

Fishbein, Martin, ed., *Readings in Attitude Theory and Measurement* (New York: Wiley, 1967).

Freedman, Jonathan, and David Sears, "Selective Exposure," in Leonard Berkowitz, ed., *Advances in Experimental Social Psychology* 2 (New York: Academic Press, 1965).

From, Franz, *Perception of Other People*, translated by Erik Kvan and Brendan Maher (New York: Columbia University Press, 1971).

Greenwald, Anthony, et al., eds., *Psychological Foundations of Attitudes* (New York: Academic Press, 1968).

Hastorf, Albert, David Schneider, and Judith Polefka, *Person Perception* (Reading, Mass.: Addison-Wesley, 1970).

Heider, Fritz, "Social Perception and Phenomenal Causality," *Psychological Review* 51 (Nov. 1944).

————, *The Psychology of Interpersonal Relations* (New York: Wiley, 1958).

Ichheiser, Gustav, *Appearances and Realities* (San Francisco: Jossey-Bass, 1970).

Insko, Chester, *Theories of Attitude Change* (New York: Appleton-Century-Crofts, 1967).

Jones, Edward, and Keith Davis, "From Acts to Dispositions: The Attribution Process in Person Perception," in Leonard Berkowitz, ed., *Advances in Experimental Social Psychology* 2 (New York: Academic Press, 1965).

Jones, Edward, and Richard Nisbett, *The Actor and the Observer: Divergent Perceptions of the Causes of Behavior* (New York: General Learning Press, 1971).

Kelley, Harold, *Causal Schemata and the Attribution Process* (Morristown, N.J.: General Learning Press, 1972).

————, "Attribution Theory in Social Psychology," in David Levine, ed., *Nebraska Symposium on Motivation*, 1967 (Lincoln: University of Nebraska Press, 1967).

————, *Attribution in Social Interaction* (Morristown, N.J.: General Learning Press, 1971).

Kiesler, Charles, *The Psychology of Commitment* (New York: Academic Press, 1971).

Kilpatrick, Franklin, ed., *Explorations in Transactional Psychology* (New York: New York University Press, 1961).

Luchins, Abraham, and Edith Luchins, *The Rigidity of Behavior* (Eugene: University of Oregon, 1959).

McGuire, William, "The Nature of Attitudes and Attitude Change," in Gardner Lindzey and Elliot Aronson, eds., *The Handbook of Social Psychology* 3 (2nd ed., Reading, Mass.: Addison-Wesley, 1968).

Mischel, Walter, *Personality and Assessment* (New York: Wiley, 1968).

Osgood, Charles, "Behavior Theory and the Social Sciences," in Roland Young, ed., *Approaches to the Study of Politics* (Evanston, Ill.: Northwestern University Press, 1958).

————, "Cognitive Dynamics in the Conduct of Human Affairs," *Public Opinion Quarterly* 24 (Summer 1960).

Postman, Leo, "Perception and Learning," in Sigmund Koch, ed., *Psychology: A Study of a Science* 5 (New York: McGraw Hill, 1963).

Rosenberg, Milton, "A Structural Theory of Attitude Dynamics," *Public Opinion Quarterly* 24 (Summer 1960).

———— ,"Cognitive Structure and Attitudinal Affect," *Journal of Abnormal and Social Psychology* 53 (1956), pp. 367-72.

————, et al., *Attitude Organization and Change* (New Haven: Yale University Press, 1960).

Sears, David, and Jonathan Freedman, "Selective Exposure to Information: A Critical Review," *Public Opinion Quarterly* 31 (Summer 1967).

Segall, Marshall, Donald Campbell, and Melville Herskovits, *The Influence of Culture on Visual Perception* (Indianapolis: Bobbs-Merrill, 1966).

Swingle, Paul, ed., *The Structure of Conflict* (New York: Academic Press, 1970).

Tversky, Amos, and Daniel Kahneman, "Judgment under Uncertainty: Heuristics and Biases," *Science* 185 (Sept. 27, 1974).

Vernon, M. D., *The Psychology of Perception* (Baltimore: Penguin, 1962).

Warr, Peter, and Christopher Knapper, *The Perception of People and Events* (London: Wiley, 1968).

Wyatt, Dale, and Donald Campbell, "On the Liability of Stereotype or Hypothesis," *Journal of Abnormal and Social Psychology* 44 (Oct. 1950).

Zajonc, Robert, "Cognitive Theories in Social Psychology," in Gardner Lindzey and Elliot Aronson, eds., *The Handbook of Social Psychology* 1 (2nd ed., Reading, Mass.: Addison-Wesley, 1968).

III. Relevant Literature from the Philosophy of Science

Butterfield, Herbert, *The Origins of Modern Science* (New York: Collier, 1962).

Crombie, A. C., ed., *Scientific Change* (New York: Basic Books, 1963).

Hanson, Norwood, *Patterns of Discovery* (Cambridge: Cambridge University Press, 1965).

Harris, Errol, *Hypothesis and Perception* (George Allen and Unwin, 1970).

Kuhn, Thomas, *The Structure of Scientific Revolutions* (Chicago: University of Chicago Press, 1962; 2nd ed. 1970).

Lakatos, Imre, and Alan Musgrave, *Criticism and the Growth of Knowledge* (Cambridge: Cambridge University Press, 1970).

Polanyi, Michael, *Science, Faith, and Society* (Chicago: University of Chicago Press, 1964).

———, "The Unaccountable Element in Science," in Marjorie Grene, ed., *Knowing and Being, Essays by Michael Polanyi* (London: Routledge and Kegan Paul, 1969).

Scheffler, Israel, *Science and Subjectivity* (Indianapolis: Bobbs-Merrill, 1967).

Shapere, Dudley, "Meaning and Scientific Change," in Robert Colodny, ed., *Mind and Cosmos* (Pittsburgh: University of Pittsburgh Press, 1966).

Suppe, Frederick, ed., *The Structure of Scientific Theories* (Urbana: University of Illinois Press, 1974).

Toulmin, Stephen, *Foresight and Understanding* (New York: Harper and Row, 1961).

Index

Publications Written under the Auspices of the Center for International Affairs, Harvard University

Created in 1958, the Center for International Affairs fosters advanced study of basic world problems by scholars from various disciplines and senior officials from many countries. The research of the Center focuses on economic, social, and political development, the management of force in the modern world, and the evolving roles of Western Europe and the Communist nations, and the conditions of international order.

The Soviet Bloc, Zbigniew K. Brzezinski (sponsored jointly with the Russian Research Center), 1960. Harvard University Press. Revised edition, 1967.

The Necessity for Choice, by Henry A. Kissinger, 1961. Harper & Bros.

Rift and Revolt in Hungary, by Ferenc A. Váli, 1961. Harvard University Press.

Strategy and Arms Control, by Thomas C. Schelling and Morton H. Halperin, 1961. Twentieth Century Fund.

United States Manufacturing Investment in Brazil, by Lincoln Gordon and Engelbert L. Grommers, 1962. Harvard Business School.

The Economy of Cyprus, by A. J. Meyer, with Simos Vassiliou (sponsored jointly with the Center for Middle Eastern Studies), 1962. Harvard University Press.

Entrepreneurs of Lebanon, by Yusif A. Sayigh (sponsored jointly with the Center for Middle Eastern Studies), 1962. Harvard University Press.

Communist China 1955-1959: Policy Documents with Analysis, with a foreword by Robert R. Bowie and John K. Fairbank (sponsored jointly with the East Asian Research Center), 1962. Harvard University Press.

Somali Nationalism, by Saadia Touval, 1963. Harvard University Press.

The Dilemma of Mexico's Development, by Raymond Vernon, 1963. Harvard University Press.

Limited War in the Nuclear Age, by Morton H. Halperin, 1963. John Wiley & Sons.

In Search of France, by Stanley Hoffmann et al., 1963. Harvard University Press.

The Arms Debate, by Robert A. Levine, 1963. Harvard University Press.

Africans on the Land, by Montague Yudelman, 1964. Harvard University Press.

Counterinsurgency Warfare, by David Galula, 1964. Frederick A. Praeger, Inc.

People and Policy in the Middle East, by Max Weston Thornburg, 1964. W. W. Norton & Co.

Shaping the Future, by Robert R. Bowie, 1964. Columbia University Press.

Foreign Aid and Foreign Policy, by Edward S. Mason (sponsored jointly with the Council on Foreign Relations), 1964. Harper & Row.

How Nations Negotiate, by Fred Charles Iklé, 1964. Harper & Row.

Public Policy and Private Enterprise in Mexico, edited by Raymond Vernon, 1964. Harvard University Press.

China and the Bomb, by Morton H. Halperin (sponsored jointly with the East Asian Research Center), 1965. Frederick A. Praeger, Inc.

Democracy in Germany, by Fritz Erler (Jodidi Lectures), 1965. Harvard University Press.

The Troubled Partnership, by Henry A. Kissinger (sponsored jointly with the Council on Foreign Relations), 1965. McGraw-Hill Book Co.

The Rise of Nationalism in Central Africa, by Robert I. Rotberg, 1965. Harvard University Press.

Pan-Africanism and East African Integration, by Joseph S. Nye, Jr., 1965. Harvard University Press.

Communist China and Arms Control, by Morton H. Halperin and Dwight H. Perkins (sponsored jointly with the East Asian Research Center), 1965. Frederick A. Praeger, Inc.

Problems of National Strategy, ed. Henry Kissinger, 1965. Frederick A. Praeger, Inc.

Deterrence before Hiroshima: The Airpower Background of Modern Strategy, by George H. Quester, 1966. John Wiley & Sons.

Containing the Arms Race, by Jeremy J. Stone, 1966. M.I.T. Press.

Germany and the Atlantic Alliance: The Interaction of Strategy and Politics, by James L. Richardson, 1966. Harvard University Press.

Arms and Influence, by Thomas C. Schelling, 1966. Yale University Press.

Political Change in a West African State, by Martin Kilson, 1966. Harvard University Press.

Planning without Facts: Lessons in Resource Allocation from Nigeria's Development, by Wolfgang F. Stolper, 1966. Harvard University Press.

Export Instability and Economic Development, by Alasdair I. MacBean, 1966. Harvard University Press.

Foreign Policy and Democratic Politics, by Kenneth N. Waltz (sponsored jointly with the Institute of War and Peace Studies, Columbia University), 1967. Little, Brown & Co.

Contemporary Military Strategy, by Morton H. Halperin, 1967. Little, Brown & Co.

Sino-Soviet Relations and Arms Control, ed. Morton H. Halperin (sponsored jointly with the East Asian Research Center), 1967. M.I.T. Press.

Africa and United States Policy, by Rupert Emerson, 1967. Prentice-Hall.

Elites in Latin America, edited by Seymour M. Lipset and Aldo Solari, 1967. Oxford University Press.

Europe's Postwar Growth, by Charles P. Kindleberger, 1967. Harvard University Press.

The Rise and Decline of the Cold War, by Paul Seabury, 1967. Basic Books.

Student Politics, ed. S. M. Lipset, 1967. Basic Books.

Pakistan's Development: Social Goals and Private Incentives, by Gustav F. Papanek, 1967. Harvard University Press.

Strike a Blow and Die: A Narrative of Race Relations in Colonial Africa, by George Simeon Mwase, ed. Robert I. Rotberg, 1967. Harvard University Press.

Party Systems and Voter Alignments, edited by Seymour M. Lipset and Stein Rokkan, 1967. Free Press.

Agrarian Socialism, by Seymour M. Lipset, revised edition, 1968. Doubleday Anchor.

Aid, Influence, and Foreign Policy, by Joan M. Nelson, 1968. The Macmillan Company.

Development Policy: Theory and Practice, edited by Gustav F. Papanek, 1968. Harvard University Press.

International Regionalism, by Joseph S. Nye, 1968. Little, Brown & Co.

Revolution and Counterrevolution, by Seymour M. Lipset, 1968. Basic Books.

Political Order in Changing Societies, by Samuel P. Huntington, 1968. Yale University Press.

The TFX Decision: McNamara and the Military, by Robert J. Art, 1968. Little, Brown & Co.

Korea: The Politics of the Vortex, by Gregory Henderson, 1968. Harvard University Press.

Political Development in Latin America, by Martin Needler, 1968. Random House.

The Precarious Republic, by Michael Hudson, 1968. Random House.

The Brazilian Capital Goods Industry, 1929-1964 (sponsored jointly with the Center for Studies in Education and Development), by Nathaniel H. Leff, 1968. Harvard University Press.

Economic Policy-Making and Development in Brazil, 1947-1964, by Nathaniel H. Leff, 1968. John Wiley & Sons.

Turmoil and Transition: Higher Education and Student Politics in India, edited by Philip G. Altbach, 1968. Lalvani Publishing House (Bombay).

German Foreign Policy in Transition, by Karl Kaiser, 1968. Oxford University Press.

Protest and Power in Black Africa, edited by Robert I. Rotberg, 1969. Oxford University Press.

Peace in Europe, by Karl E. Birnbaum, 1969. Oxford University Press.

The Process of Modernization: An Annotated Bibliography on the Sociocultural Aspects of Development, by John Brode, 1969. Harvard University Press.

Students in Revolt, edited by Seymour M. Lipset and Philip G. Altbach, 1969. Houghton Mifflin.

Agricultural Development in India's Districts: The Intensive Agricultural Districts Programme, by Dorris D. Brown, 1970. Harvard University Press.

Authoritarian Politics in Modern Society: The Dynamics of Established One-Party Systems, edited by Samuel P. Huntington and Clement H. Moore, 1970. Basic Books.

Nuclear Diplomacy, by George H. Quester, 1970. Dunellen.

The Logic of Images in International Relations, by Robert Jervis, 1970. Princeton University Press.

Europe's Would-Be Polity, by Leon Lindberg and Stuart A. Scheingold, 1970. Prentice-Hall.

Taxation and Development: Lessons from Colombian Experience, by Richard M. Bird, 1970. Harvard University Press.

Lord and Peasant in Peru: A Paradigm of Political and Social Change, by F. LaMond Tullis, 1970. Harvard University Press.

The Kennedy Round in American Trade Policy: The Twilight of the GATT? by John W. Evans, 1971. Harvard University Press.

Korean Development: The Interplay of Politics and Economics, by David C. Cole and Princeton N. Lyman, 1971. Harvard University Press.

Development Policy II—The Pakistan Experience, edited by Walter P. Falcon and Gustav F. Papanek, 1971. Harvard University Press.

Higher Education in a Transitional Society, by Philip G. Altbach, 1971. Sindhu Publications (Bombay).

Studies in Development Planning, edited by Hollis B. Chenery, 1971. Harvard University Press.

Passion and Politics, by Seymour M. Lipset with Gerald Schaflander, 1971. Little, Brown & Co.

Political Mobilization of the Venezuelan Peasant, by John D. Powell, 1971. Harvard University Press.

Higher Education in India, edited by Amrik Singh and Philip Altbach, 1971. Oxford University Press (Delhi).

The Myth of the Guerrilla, by J. Bowyer Bell, 1971. Blond (London) and Knopf (New York).

International Norms and War between States: Three Studies in International Politics, by Kjell Goldmann, 1971. Published jointly by Läromedelsförlagen (Sweden) and the Swedish Institute of International Affairs.

Peace in Parts: Integration and Conflict in Regional Organization, by Joseph S. Nye, Jr., 1971. Little, Brown & Co.

Sovereignty at Bay: The Multinational Spread of U.S. Enterprise, by Raymond Vernon, 1971. Basic Books.

Defense Strategy for the Seventies (revision of *Contemporary Military Strategy*), by Morton H. Halperin, 1971. Little, Brown & Co.

Peasants Against Politics: Rural Organization in Brittany, 1911-1967, by Suzanne Berger, 1972. Harvard University Press.

Transnational Relations and World Politics, edited by Robert O. Keohane and Joseph S. Nye, Jr., 1972. Harvard University Press.

Latin American University Students: A Six Nation Study, by Arthur Liebman, Kenneth N. Walker, and Myron Glazer, 1972. Harvard University Press.

The Politics of Land Reform in Chile, 1950-1970: Public Policy, Political Institutions, and Social Change, by Robert R. Kaufman, 1972. Harvard University Press.

The Boundary Politics of Independent Africa, by Saadia Touval, 1972. Harvard University Press.

The Politics of Nonviolent Action, by Gene E. Sharp, 1973. Porter Sargent.

System 37 Viggen: Arms, Technology, and the Domestication of Glory, by Ingemar Dorfer, 1973. Universitetsforlaget (Oslo).

University Students and African Politics, by William John Hanna, 1974. Africana Publishing Company.

Organizing the Transnational: The Experience with Transnational Enterprise in Advanced Technology, by M. S. Hochmuth, 1974. Sijthoff (Leiden).

Becoming Modern, by Alex Inkeles and David H. Smith, 1974. Harvard University Press.

Multinational Corporations and the Politics of Dependence: Copper in Chile, 1945-1973, by Theodore Moran, 1974. Princeton University Press.

The Andean Group: A Case Study in Economic Integration among Developing Countries, by David Morawetz, 1974. M.I.T. Press.

Kenya: The Politics of Participation and Control, by Henry Bienen, 1974. Princeton University Press.

Land Reform and Politics: A Comparative Analysis, by Hung-chao Tai, 1974. University of California Press.

Big Business and the State: Changing Relations in Western Europe, edited by Raymond Vernon, 1974. Harvard University Press.

Economic Policymaking in a Conflict Society: The Argentine Case, by Richard D. Mallon and Juan V. Sourrouille, 1975. Harvard University Press.

New States in the Modern World, edited by Martin Kilson, 1975. Harvard University Press.

No Easy Choice: Political Participation in Developing Countries, by Samuel P. Huntington and Joan M. Nelson, 1976. Harvard University Press.

Natural Resources and the Changing Economic Order, by Zuhayr Mikdashi, 1976. Cornell University Press.

HARVARD STUDIES IN INTERNATIONAL AFFAIRS*

[formerly Occasional Papers in International Affairs]

† 1. *A Plan for Planning: The Need for a Better Method of Assisting Underdeveloped Countries on Their Economic Policies*, by Gustav F. Papanek, 1961.

† 2. *The Flow of Resources from Rich to Poor*, by Alan D. Neale, 1961.

† 3. *Limited War: An Essay on the Development of the Theory and an Annotated Bibliography*, by Morton H. Halperin, 1962.

† 4. *Reflections on the Failure of the First West Indian Federation*, by Hugh W. Springer, 1962.

5. *On the Interaction of Opposing Forces under Possible Arms Agreements*, by Glenn A. Kent, 1963. 36 pp. $1.25.

† 6. *Europe's Northern Cap and the Soviet Union*, by Nils Orvik, 1963.

7. *Civil Administration in the Punjab: An Analysis of a State Government in India*, by E. N. Mangat Rai, 1963. 82 pp. $1.75.

8. *On the Appropriate Size of a Development Program*, by Edward S. Mason, 1964. 24 pp. $1.00.

9. *Self-Determination Revisited in the Era of Decolonization*, by Rupert Emerson, 1964. 64 pp. $1.75.

*Available from Harvard University Center for International Affairs, 6 Divinity Avenue, Cambridge, Massachusetts 02138.

†Out of print. May be ordered from AMS Press, Inc., 56 East 13th Street, New York, N.Y. 10003.

10. *The Planning and Execution of Economic Development in Southeast Asia*, by Clair Wilcox, 1965. 37 pp. $1.25.
11. *Pan-Africanism in Action*, by Albert Tevoedjre, 1965. 88 pp. $2.50.
12. *Is China Turning In?*, by Morton Halperin, 1965. 34 pp. $1.25.
†13. *Economic Development in India and Pakistan*, by Edward S. Mason, 1966.
14. *The Role of the Military in Recent Turkish Politics*, by Ergun Özbudun, 1966. 54 pp. $1.75.
†15. *Economic Development and Individual Change: A Social-Psychological Study of the Comilla Experiment in Pakistan*, by Howard Schuman, 1967.
16. *A Select Bibliography on Students, Politics, and Higher Education*, by Philip G. Altbach, UMHE Revised Edition, 1970. 65 pp. $2.75.
17. *Europe's Political Puzzle: A Study of the Fouchet Negotiations and the 1963 Veto*, by Alessandro Silj, 1967. 178 pp. $3.50.
18. *The Cap and the Straits: Problems of Nordic Security*, by Jan Klenberg, 1968. 19 pp. $1.25.
19. *Cyprus: The Law and Politics of Civil Strife*, by Linda B. Miller, 1968. 97 pp. $3.00.
†20. *East and West Pakistan: A Problem in the Political Economy of Regional Planning*, by Md. Anisur Rahman, 1968.
†21. *Internal War and International Systems: Perspectives on Method*, by George A. Kelley and Linda B. Miller, 1969.
†22. *Migrants, Urban Poverty, and Instability in Developing Nations*, by Joan M. Nelson, 1969. 81 pp.
23. *Growth and Development in Pakistan, 1955-1969*, by Joseph J. Stern and Walter P. Falcon, 1970. 94 pp. $3.00.
24. *Higher Education in Developing Countries: A Select Bibliography*, by Philip G. Altbach, 1970. 118 pp. $4.00.
25. *Anatomy of Political Institutionalization: The Case of Israel and Some Comparative Analyses*, by Amos Perlmutter, 1970. 60 pp. $2.50.
26. *The German Democratic Republic from the Sixties to the Seventies*, by Peter Christian Ludz, 1970. 100 pp.
27. *The Law in Political Integration: The Evolution and Integrative Implications of Regional Legal Processes in the European Community*, by Stuart A. Scheingold, 1971. 63 pp. $2.50.
28. *Psychological Dimensions of U.S.-Japanese Relations*, by Hiroshi Kitamura, 1971. 46 pp. $2.00.
29. *Conflict Regulation in Divided Societies*, by Eric A. Nordlinger, 1972. 137 pp. $4.25.
30. *Israel's Political-Military Doctrine*, by Michael I. Handel, 1973. 101 pp. $3.25.
31. *Italy, NATO, and the European Community: The Interplay of Foreign Policy and Domestic Politics*, by Primo Vannicelli, 1974. 67 + x pp. $3.25.
32. *The Choice of Technology in Developing Countries: Some Cautionary Tales*, by C. Peter Timmer, John W. Thomas, Louis T. Wells, Jr., and David Morawetz, 1975. 114 pp. $3.45.
33. *The International Role of the Communist Parties of Italy and France*, by Donald L. M. Blackmer and Annie Kriegel, 1975. 67 + x pp. $2.75.
34. *The Hazards of Peace: A European View of Detente*, by Juan Cassiers, 1976. $6.95, cloth; $2.95, paper.
35. *Europe in the Energy Crisis*, by Robert J. Lieber, 1976.